MASTERPLOTS II

SHORT STORY SERIES
REVISED EDITION

MASTERPLOTS II

SHORT STORY SERIES
REVISED EDITION

Volume 5
Loo–Ope

Editor, Revised Edition
CHARLES MAY
California State University, Long Beach

Editor, First Edition
FRANK N. MAGILL

SALEM PRESS
Pasadena, California   Hackensack, New Jersey

Editor in Chief: Dawn P. Dawson

Editorial Director: Christina J. Moose	*Assistant Editor:* Andrea E. Miller
Project Editor: R. Kent Rasmussen	*Research Supervisor:* Jeffry Jensen
Production Editor: Cynthia Beres	*Acquisitions Editor:* Mark Rehn
Copy Editor: Rowena Wildin	*Layout:* Eddie Murillo

Some of the essays in this work originally appeared in *Masterplots II, Short Story Series*, edited by Frank N. Magill (Pasadena, Calif.: Salem Press, Inc., 1986), and in *Masterplots II, Short Story Series Supplement*, edited by Frank N. Magill and Charles E. May (Pasadena, Calif.: Salem Press, Inc., 1996).

∞ The paper used in these volumes conforms to the American National Standard for Permanence of Paper for Printed Library Materials, Z39.48-1992 (R1997).

Library of Congress Cataloging-in-Publication Data

Masterplots II : Short story series / editor Charles May. — Rev. ed.
    p. cm.
    Includes bibliographical references and index.
    ISBN 1-58765-140-8 (set : alk. paper) — ISBN 1-58765-145-9 (vol. 5 : alk. paper) —
    1. Fiction—19th century—Stories, plots, etc. 2. Fiction—19th century—History and criticism. 3. Fiction—20th century—Stories, plots, etc. 4. Fiction—20th century—History and criticism. 5. Short story. I. Title: Masterplots 2. II. Title: Masterplots two. III. May, Charles E. (Charles Edward), 1941-
PN3326 .M27 2004
809.3′1—dc22

                           2003018256

First Printing

TABLE OF CONTENTS

TABLE OF CONTENTS

TABLE OF CONTENTS

MASTERPLOTS II

SHORT STORY SERIES
REVISED EDITION

LOOKING FOR MR. GREEN

Author: Saul Bellow (1915-   )
Type of plot: Realism
Time of plot: The Depression
Locale: Chicago
First published: 1951

> *Principal characters:*
> GEORGE GREBE, a relief worker
> MR. RAYNOR, his supervisor
> MRS. STAIKA, a welfare recipient
> WINSTON FIELD, another welfare recipient and one of George
>   Grebe's cases

The Story

"Looking for Mr. Green" recounts the efforts of George Grebe to deliver relief checks to handicapped residents of the South Side of Chicago. Grebe, thirty-five and an instructor of classical languages, has been reduced by the hard times of the Depression to taking a series of trivial, part-time jobs until an old schoolmate secures for him a position at the relief office. Grebe's desire to do well at his new job is hampered by its peculiar difficulty: "He could find the streets and numbers, but the clients were not where they were supposed to be." Grebe is particularly frustrated by his inability to find Mr. Tulliver Green but persists in his search long after quitting time. As the story develops, Grebe's quest to find Mr. Green becomes a symbolic quest to find his own identity.

Grebe systematically questions a local grocer, the janitor, and several tenants of Mr. Green's building. Their responses are hostile and evasive. Grebe is viewed "as an emissary from hostile appearances" because he is not yet a familiar face in the territory and because he is white. Although Grebe himself has known hardship, he is out of place in this rundown district of the city, where he is shocked by the distrust of the people and the blighted physical setting.

Before Grebe continues his hunt, he recalls his first meeting with his supervisor, Mr. Raynor. Their conversation establishes somewhat of a kinship between them. Both are well educated and speak foreign languages, and they exchange a few Latin phrases. Their views on the nature of reality, however, establish that they are indeed from different worlds. Although Grebe treats the problem of appearance and reality philosophically, Raynor's reality comes down to money, "even though nothing looks to be real, and everything stands for something else, and that thing for another thing, and that thing for still a further one—there ain't any comparison between twenty-five and thirty-seven dollars a week, regardless of the last reality." Grebe's and Raynor's perceptions of Mrs. Staika further illustrate their differences.

Staika is called the "Blood Mother of Federal Street" because she is a professional donor of blood, dragging her children around with her as she defies the world. After notifying the press, Staika sets up her ironing board at the agency office to protest their failure to pay her electric bill. Raynor believes that Staika will "get what she wants. . . . She's got [the commissioner] submerged; she'll submerge everybody in time, and that includes nations and governments." Grebe, however, disagrees completely; he does not believe that Staika's yelling will bring about change, because her protests are so outrageous. Staika reminds Grebe of "the war of flesh and blood, perhaps turned a little crazy and certainly ugly." Grebe temporarily gives up his search for Mr. Green and looks for Winston Field.

Field's insistence on identifying himself with a Social Security card, his relief certification, and other credentials suggests the problem of the identity of the individual in modern society. For Field, like Raynor, identity is related to money, and he tells Grebe his scheme for making black millionaires who would employ black workers in their businesses. Field's idealism rekindles Grebe's, and after a long review of the philosophical problem that he has been facing, Grebe continues his search for Mr. Green.

In the end, Grebe finds Mr. Green's bungalow, inhabited by a heavy woman, naked and drunk, who screams furiously at him and knocks into him with her huge breasts. Grebe is shocked and embarrassed at "what he had tracked down, in his hunting game." Although he believes Mr. Green to be upstairs, Grebe does not go up, afraid that Mr. Green will be similarly naked and drunk. Recalling Field's insistence that Grebe obtain proper identification before handing over relief checks, Grebe nevertheless gives the check to the woman, who might or might not be Mrs. Green, for "whoever she was, the woman stood for Green, whom he was not to see this time." The story ends with Grebe elated that Mr. Green has been found. By handing over the check, Grebe does what the epigraph of the story suggests he do: "Whatsoever thy hand findeth to do, do it with thy might."

Themes and Meanings

Grebe's search for Mr. Green becomes a search for the nature of reality and, ultimately, a search for his own identity. Grebe's trek through the streets and tenements of Chicago prompts him to think about appearance and reality. "Rebuilt after the Great Fire, this part of the city was, not fifty years later, in ruins again." Grebe comes to find that people create their own reality by consent. The El, for example, built by the financier Charles T. Yerkes, existed because people consented to its existence. They agreed to pay their ten cents to ride in its crash-box cars, so it was a success. If people created their own reality by consent, why, Grebe asks himself, should they consent to cities of misery and painful ugliness? "Because there is something that is dismal and permanently ugly?" Unable to reach any conclusions about the reality people create for themselves, Grebe returns to his own predicament—finding Mr. Green and delivering his check.

It having been established by Raynor and Field that identity in modern society is determined by money, Mr. Green essentially does not exist until Grebe delivers his check. Grebe's own identity is linked to Mr. Green's. The similarity in their names parallels a similarity of condition: Both suffer or have suffered hardships. If Mr. Green exists and Grebe is able to deliver his check, then Grebe's life is meaningful. Because the woman to whom Grebe gives the check clearly stands for Mr. Green, Grebe has proved, through delivery of the check, that the ordinary individual's life is important. "Looking for Mr. Green" embodies the major theme of Saul Bellow's fiction: People need not be passive victims of their situations but in humanity can somehow transcend alienating environments.

Style and Technique

Structurally, "Looking for Mr. Green" consists of two scenes set on the streets and in the tenements of Chicago, separated by a scene at the relief agency in which a philosophical discussion between Grebe and Raynor is interrupted by a welfare mother's tirade. Within this basic structure, a number of ironies and contrasts occur. It is, for example, oddly ironic that Grebe would have trouble delivering relief checks to people who have desperate need of them.

The realistic, richly detailed characters and setting also are in contrast to the symbolic intentions of the work. The conversation in Grebe's office makes apparent that the story exists on two planes, the concrete and the symbolic. The drunken, naked woman whom Grebe meets in Mr. Green's bungalow is, for example, not only a living character but also a symbolic figure: She, like Staika, represents the misdirected human spirit. Several allusions and metaphors during the course of the work also place the story in a larger context. The walls of the tenement, with their writings and scribblings, are like "the sealed rooms of pyramids" and "the caves of human dawn." When Grebe enters one of the apartments, he finds ten or a dozen people "sitting on benches like a parliament." Field is described "like one of the underground kings of mythology, old judge Minos himself." The ghetto and its inhabitants become metaphors for man and the dark, incomprehensible world in which he moves.

The most interesting technique that Bellow utilizes, however, is the absence of the title character, Mr. Green. Because Grebe never actually meets Mr. Green, there have been diverse assertions concerning Grebe's "success" in delivering Mr. Green's check. Some critics thinks that Grebe has put himself in the position of deliberate self-deception, although others think that Grebe's giving the check to "Mr. Green" should not be interpreted as an act of failure or defeat but as a symbolic gesture connected with all he has experienced and learned that day. In this reading, the story does not end with self-deception but rather with hope, with Grebe's awareness of his own identity and function in society.

Patricia A. Posluszny

THE LOONS

Author: Margaret Laurence (1926-1987)
Type of plot: Sketch
Time of plot: The 1930's
Locale: Manawaka, a small prairie town in Canada
First published: 1963

> *Principal characters:*
> VANESSA MACLEOD, a doctor's daughter and the narrator
> PIQUETTE TONNERRE, a Meti girl, two years older than Vanessa
> DR. MACLEOD, Vanessa's father
> MRS. MACLEOD, Vanessa's mother

The Story

Jules Tonnerre, half French, half Indian, settled in Manawaka after the Meti Indian uprising of 1885. Three generations of his family now live in a collection of shacks, surrounded by junk, in the river valley outside Manawaka. The town is Scots-Irish and Ukrainian, and the Tonnerres are not part of it in any sense. They work irregularly, they are sometimes involved in drunken brawls, and their domestic lives are as chaotic as their housing.

Because Piquette Tonnerre, Jules's granddaughter, has a tubercular leg, Dr. Mac-Leod wants to take her with his own family to their summer cabin at Diamond Lake, for she will have little chance to recuperate at home. Grandmother MacLeod refuses to join them if a half-breed is included in the household. Preferring Piquette to her mother-in-law, the doctor's wife agrees to have the girl come along. Vanessa, age eleven at this time, loves the unspoiled beauty of Diamond Lake and hopes Piquette will share this love, for Vanessa romanticizes the Indian heritage, its warlike past, and its bond with the wilderness.

Piquette, however, rejects all overtures. She silently helps Mrs. MacLeod with the housework, but she will not play and cannot walk or swim far. Most significantly, she will not go to the lake at night to listen to the loons calling mysteriously across the dark water. Vanessa and her father sit by the lake while Piquette remains indoors. The following winter, the doctor dies of pneumonia and Vanessa does not even notice Piquette's disappearance from school.

Four years later, the girls meet again. Vanessa is going away to college; Piquette, gaudily dressed and garishly made up, has been drifting from town to town. Repelled and embarrassed, Vanessa can find nothing to say, but when Piquette recalls Dr. MacLeod's kindness to her and confides that she is going to marry a blond Englishman, Vanessa bursts into congratulations; she suddenly realizes how desperately Piquette must want to belong somewhere if she will marry into the culture that she so firmly rejected when she was younger.

Another two years pass. Vanessa returns from college for the summer. Piquette, says Mrs. MacLeod, is dead. When her marriage failed, she returned—fat, slovenly, and drunken—to Manawaka and lived in one of the family shacks with her two very young children. One evening, after Piquette had been drinking all day, it caught fire and she and the children burned to death.

Although her summer home has been sold, Vanessa visits Diamond Lake again and goes to the shore. A tourist resort has been built there, the smell of junk food fills the air, and the place is noisy. At night, though, the lake is dark and silent—quite silent, for the loons have departed or died. Vanessa wonders whether, even as a child, Piquette did not need to hear their song because it was her own.

Themes and Meanings

One of Margaret Laurence's constant themes in her Canadian work (there are four major novels and a collection of short stories about Manawaka and its people) is the pain and conflict out of which a multicultural community is born. The limitations of contact and understanding in such a settlement, its tendency to stratify socially along ethnic lines, are always evident in her portrayal of Manawaka and are part of the point of this story. In "The Loons," the respectable Scots and the far-from-respectable Tonnerres convey the message. Laurence often stresses the need for an immigrant tradition to come to terms with the genius of its new place. Here, however, she concentrates more on the disastrous effect of the dominant society on the prior inhabitants of the land. They wish merely to exist undisturbed, but in the eyes of the new majority, they are peripheral and dispensable.

However, the invading culture is not monolithic. The MacLeods are genteel and superior (Grandmother will not tolerate a part-Indian girl in the house), but the doctor and his wife are genuinely compassionate, and Vanessa gains a belated understanding of Piquette. Rapprochement, Laurence suggests, is a slow process: Acceptance takes generations.

As always in this author's work, the narrator is preoccupied with making sense of the past. If it is to be nourishing, not stultifying, it has to be comprehended and shaped into coherence. The content of the past is thus not static because its meaning changes as a character's understanding of her experience grows. In this story, the violation of Diamond Lake and the disappearance of the loons illuminate, for Vanessa, Piquette's refusal to accompany her to the lake in their childhood. With Vanessa, the reader finally comprehends the likeness between the Metis and the loons.

Style and Technique

Laurence's style evokes by specifying. She evokes the color and sound of the river, the shape of Jules Tonnerre's shack and its building materials. Such description, packed with factual detail, modulates easily into a narrative that appears equally matter-of-fact. The reader learns how the Tonnerres speak neither Cree, French, nor English adequately; they are half-breeds; they do not live with the Indians at Galloping Mountain or with the Europeans in Manawaka. Slowly the significance of these items strikes the reader. Just as they are the biological product of the meeting of Europeans and Indians and yet are neither, so the Tonnerres are located in spirit, as in fact, on the edge of the community. Thus, the facts build into a symbol of not belonging. The failure of Piquette's marriage has the same dual quality.

Similarly matter-of-fact is the introduction of the Tonnerres' housing in the first paragraph and their drunkenness in the second. Grandfather Jules and his son Lazarus are routinely picked up by the Mounties, sobered up overnight, and released; yet the shacks and the drinking, both familiar and unstressed, create Piquette's appalling death.

The structure is a seeming recital of facts; they are pieced together into meaning by the grown-up Vanessa and by the reader as new experiences and insights are added to the old. Laurence has a fine ear, and she can produce sentences that are almost incantatory: "He came back from Batoche with a bullet in his thigh, the year that Riel was hung and the voices of the Metis entered their long silence." More usually, this skill is evident in dialogue, for no character utters speech that could come from another mouth. Not only are Piquette's brief, slovenly, ungrammatical speeches quite distinctive, but also Grandmother MacLeod, Vanessa, her mother, and her father are clearly distinguishable by variation in tone and formality. Moreover, speech alters with mood. Dr. MacLeod, irritated at the breakfast table, sounds different from Dr. MacLeod, the father who sits with Vanessa at the lake.

Vanessa's attitudes toward Piquette are not only honestly stated but also evident in the embarrassment of their conversation. There is no common ground; there is nothing to say, even though things ought to be said. The dialogue relentlessly displays the chasm between the girls and the inability of even the well-meaning to cross social and racial boundaries.

"The Loons" depends considerably on other contrasts, too. The great names of Indian history—Big Bear, Poundmaker, Tecumseh—have no more connection with Piquette than the romantic fantasies of Henry Wadsworth Longfellow or Pauline Johnson. The dark quiet lake and the neat well-lit houses, the vulgarity of the new resort and Diamond Lake as it once was, are all significantly contrasted.

The most significant contrast is that between the two girls: one loved, loving, hopeful; the other uncared for, indifferent, despairing. Their homes, their education, and their futures are different. Piquette has no future.

However, there are also some similarities between them. Piquette's mother has disappeared; Vanessa's father dies. The MacLeods' summer home is sold and Vanessa's childhood "Kingdom," Diamond Lake, is despoiled by the tourist industry. It is the loss of both the place she loved and the father with whom she shared it, symbolized in the fact that the loons have gone, which finally gives Vanessa some understanding of Piquette's sullen despair.

The identification of Piquette with the loons is implied in the last lines, for the narrator suggests that the mournful indecipherable cry of the birds and the silence of the Meti girl are both signals from the doomed and the dispossessed.

Jocelyn Creigh Cass

THE LOST BOY

Author: Thomas Wolfe (1900-1938)
Type of plot: Autobiographical, realism, impressionistic
Time of plot: 1904-1935
Locale: Altamont, North Carolina, and St. Louis, Missouri
First published: 1937

> *Principal characters:*
> GROVER GANT, a twelve-year-old boy
> ELIZA GANT, his mother
> HELEN GANT, his older sister
> EUGENE GANT, his younger brother

The Story

"The Lost Boy" offers another glimpse of the Gants, the fictionalized version of Thomas Wolfe's own family that is featured in his first novel, *Look Homeward, Angel* (1929). This story focuses on Grover Gant, the lost boy and older brother of Eugene Gant (Wolfe). It is told in four sections, viewed through the perceptions of Grover himself, his mother, his sister, and Eugene.

In April of 1904, the twelve-year-old newsboy Grover waits in the courthouse square of Altamont (actually Wolfe's hometown of Asheville, North Carolina), for the newspapers he will sell. Grover, who is alive only in this section, is identified by his olive skin, his black hair and eyes, and the brown berry birthmark on his neck. He notes small details of the streets and shops he passes and takes comfort in the thought that in the square nothing ever changes.

Attracted by the smell of fresh, warm chocolate from the candy shop, Grover decides to buy fifteen cents' worth of fudge with some stamps he has received from the pharmacist as payment for running errands. He mistakenly pays with eighteen cents in stamps, but the shopkeeper accuses Grover of stealing the extra stamps and refuses to return them. In tears, the boy goes to his father, who is able to set things right, and the world regains its balance and safety for Grover.

The second section of the story is told in a monologue that takes place years later as Eliza Gant, the mother, addresses the adult Eugene. Her distinctive voice is chatty and colloquial, with a country accent. She recalls the family's journey through Indiana in 1904 when they traveled by train to the World's Fair in St. Louis, Missouri, as well as a recent interview with a reporter who sought to learn more about Eugene, who is now a writer. Eliza takes great pleasure in pointing out that Grover was by far the shrewdest, most intelligent, and best of all her children; he has become her most loved child. She praises him while at the same time undercutting her famous son Eugene, whom she calls lazy because he has an easy job as a writer. Although she asserts that she has never bragged about any of her children, she speaks constantly of Grover.

The hearty voice of Helen, the older sister, is punctuated by slang, but underneath her enthusiasm lies a surprising melancholy. A family photo taken before Eugene's birth has reminded her of their past, and the aging of their siblings now makes her uncomfortable. She describes for the adult Eugene that summer in St. Louis when she was fourteen, when their mother ran a boardinghouse while Grover worked and took the younger children to the fair. Eugene retains no memory of his brother, who died of typhoid when Eugene was only three, but Helen relates how, when she would bathe Eugene, he used to cry for Grover instead. Finally she confesses to sneaking off one afternoon with Grover and eating pork and beans in a downtown diner. Afterward he became immediately and fatally ill. As Helen recalls her childhood dream of becoming a famous musician, she cannot understand how everything has turned out to be different from what she had imagined.

In the final section, Eugene recovers memories of his childhood and his brother Grover, whom he alone has forgotten. In 1935, he returns to the same St. Louis house where his family spent the summer of 1904, to search for any recollection of his dead brother. As he looks around, he begins to remember long-ago odors and sensations. He feels the silence of the family's absence in the house. Even the quality of the summer heat has changed. These memories emerge not from what he has been told but through the confirmation of his physical senses. When he finally speaks with the woman who lives there now, he is able to give her details about the house that even she does not know. He asks to visit the front room where Grover died, too ill to be moved. As he is ready to leave, a sudden vivid image of Grover floods over him—the dark eyes and hair, the berry birthmark, even Eugene's own childish voice struggling to pronounce his brother's name. Then the lost boy is gone forever.

Themes and Meanings

One of Wolfe's great themes is loss. Grover himself is lost, first in the candy store in a situation he cannot handle, then lost in time and to his family in a deeper, irrevocable sense, through his death. His mother, too, in a way, is lost in the past, perhaps the only way she can still be with the son she loves so much, although possibly to the detriment of her living children. Helen is lost in confusion, desperately seeking an explanation for an unanswerable situation, the loss of something precious—a past that she remembers as happy. Sick with guilt, she still blames herself for Grover's death. Only Eugene, who lost his brother so long ago, briefly finds him again and is left with a fuller awareness of transience, mutability, and the loss of illusions.

In addition, Wolfe's world seems to overflow with the paradox of time. Time is arrested; time passes, yet remains always. The past and present coexist, as they do in the St. Louis house and in the lives of all the characters. Nothing, yet everything, changes.

Consequently, each character is deeply affected by time and change. Grover wants to believe that time remains in stasis in the courthouse square but is forced to recognize that it does not, and as a result, his perception of the world is subtly and disturbingly altered. To his mother, nothing is the same now, so she chooses to live in the familiar past rather than in the present. In Helen's voice, there is always a note of deep regret. Life has not brought her what she expected, and she does not understand why. Bewildered and struggling to express herself, she begs college-educated Eugene to explain to her why their lives have turned out as they have. Finally, through his visit to the St. Louis house, Eugene is briefly able to recapture the memory of his forgotten brother and accept the changes that time has brought.

Style and Technique

The story's use of four separate viewpoints offers the advantage of a fully rounded, lifelike rendering of Grover, observed both in the present and in memory, and of his family. In section one, he is seen through a third-person omniscient point of view that allows a reader to share an external view as well as the boy's internal thoughts. In contrast, the mother's first-person monologue is as limited as she is; she is unable to move beyond her loss. Sister Helen's perceptions, also limited, are nevertheless far more thoughtful, for she is aware of questions that she cannot answer. Like Grover, Eugene is revealed through an omniscient, external point of view, but with full knowledge of his thoughts and memories.

At the same time, a tightly knit underlying structure can be found in the phrase or visual image that links each section of "The Lost Boy" with the next. For example, at the end of the first section, a buggy laden with a World's Fair poster passes down the street and flows immediately into the image of the train journey to St. Louis that begins section two. A repeated word links sections two and three, and the final sections are connected by two intense images of the St. Louis house.

Wolfe's characteristic style, impressionistic realism, is heavy with a wealth of sensory imagery, as when Eugene's memory of St. Louis returns and he can recall the heat of the sun on his mattress, the coolness of the cellar, and the scent and texture of the grass by the streetcar tracks. Typically unrestrained, his language is often lyrical, and descriptive passages can pulse forth like the spray from the fountain in the courthouse square. Wolfe is a poet of excess; his legendary wordiness is stunning and beautiful, and often truer than truth itself.

Joanne McCarthy

LOST IN THE FUNHOUSE

Author: John Barth (1930-   )
Type of plot: Metafiction
Time of plot: Independence Day during World War II
Locale: Ocean City, Maryland
First published: 1967

> *Principal characters:*
> AMBROSE, a thirteen-year-old boy trying to live through "that
>   awkward age"
> PETER, his brother, age fifteen
> MAGDA, age fourteen, who is the focus of most of Ambrose's
>   attention
> THE NARRATOR, who may or may not be Ambrose

The Story

In "Lost in the Funhouse," the author, John Barth, writes a story about someone, a narrator, who is himself writing a story about Ambrose, a boy of thirteen. In writing the story about Ambrose, the narrator also comments on the techniques of fiction and the problems and concerns that confront a writer of fiction who is trying to write a story. To complicate the matter further, the narrator may or may not be Ambrose. If the narrator is Ambrose, then Ambrose is writing a story about Ambrose writing a story about Ambrose.

"Lost in the Funhouse" is from a 1967 collection of related stories (also titled *Lost in the Funhouse*) that constitute a short-story cycle. As frontispiece to the collection, Barth provides the printed makings of a Möbius strip and directions for readers for cutting and assembling it. Should readers follow the directions to fashion the Mobius strip, the strip itself would read in an eternal cycle: "Once upon a time there was a story that began" once upon a time there was a story that began, and so on. This continuing cycle or pattern of infinite regression is similar to a series of mirrors reflecting one another or to the kinds of reflecting mirrors one finds in funhouses. The funhouse is where the narrator/Ambrose is, and, in reading the story, readers, too, are lost in the funhouse that Barth creates.

Though all of this sounds very complicated, and may be on a first reading, Barth provides for the uninitiated a more or less traditional narrative about Ambrose that has all the conventional elements of fiction, including setting, characters, conflict, foreshadowing, suspense, symbols, and plot. Clearly, the protagonist in his story, Ambrose, is a precocious thirteen-year-old, who, along with his family, is making an annual trip to Ocean City to celebrate Independence Day.

His family consists of his mother and father, his Uncle Karl, and Peter, his fifteen-year-old brother. Accompanying the family is Magda, a fourteen-year-old-girl, who is the object of most of Ambrose's attention and the source of most of his conflict. The family is making the trip in an automobile with the front seat being occupied by the father, who is driving, the mother, who sits in the middle, and Uncle Karl, who is next to the window on the right. In the backseat, the arrangement is duplicated (or mirrored) with Magda between Peter and Ambrose.

Though the children are really too old for it, the mother insists that they play the game of sighting the Towers that they have always played to while away the time, as they make their way to the ocean shore. This time Magda wins and is rewarded with a banana, a piece of fruit difficult to obtain in wartime America. The second half of the trip is consumed by the game of cowpoker played between Peter and Magda on one side and, on the other, mother and Uncle Karl.

When they reach the amusement area on the Boardwalk, Mother jokingly distributes money to the "children" so they may partake of the various foods and games. Some time is spent at the pool because the ocean surf is spoiled by oil, said to have spilled from tankers recently torpedoed offshore. During all these activities, Ambrose is introspective and jealous of his brother Peter, who is able to behave naturally with Magda, while Ambrose is virtually dumbstruck by his love for Magda and his inability to behave as be believes a "normal" boy would. Ambrose is unable to get out of his mind an event that took place the year before, when he and Magda were alone in the woodshed, and he is unable to tell Magda how he feels about her.

When Ambrose, Peter, and Magda enter the funhouse, Peter and Magda laughingly go off together, leaving Ambrose behind to find his own way through, and he experiences the panic of feeling lost and alone in a mirror-maze of thrills and terrors, false starts and betrayals, digressions and hesitations, and erotic fantasies and expectations.

Themes and Meanings

Throughout the story, Ambrose tries to comfort himself by thinking of a future time when he will have conquered his adolescent fears and solved his sexual conflicts through marriage and a "normal" family life. At the same time, however, he fears that he really is different from other people. In his precociousness he knows that he thinks more easily than he acts; that he articulates his perceptions within his own mind more lucidly than he converses with others; that he is intellectual, analytical, and introverted; that he is more of an observer than an actor; and that it is quite possible that he will not marry and live what he perceives to be a normal life.

The question that Ambrose must answer is clear to him. It is expressed in the first sentence of the story: "For whom is the funhouse fun?" The answer he gives is also clear: "Perhaps for lovers." For Ambrose, though, the funhouse is a place of "fear and confusion," as he tries to make his way through it. He knows that he could make funhouses, could create them for other people to enjoy, and he thinks that his future is already manifest: "Therefore he will construct funhouses for others and be their secret operator—though he would rather be among the lovers for whom funhouses are designed."

Style and Technique

Problems facing the narrator as storyteller are complex and everywhere expressed. The narrator questions whether thirteen-year-old Ambrose is capable of thinking the thoughts being attributed to him. The narrator discusses plot structure and wonders how in the world the story he is telling can be graphed along Freitag's Triangle, representing exposition, complication, rising action, climax, and denouement or resolution. The narrator talks about literary symbols and mentions that, for example, diving into a pool would make a suitable symbol. He questions the relevance of the war to the story and inquires of himself whether there should be fireworks. He discusses the use of italics, inverted tags, and first-order and second-order metaphors. He worries over whether he is providing sufficient sensory detail to render the texture of the experience.

At the same time that the narrator discusses these elements of fiction, he puts them to work. For example, in the paragraph in which he discusses the use of italics, he italicizes five passages. When he analyzes the appropriate use of point of view, he points out that the closer authors are to a character, the more they need to distance themselves from that character. Consequently, if the narrator is Ambrose, he would appropriately use the third-person point of view that he does.

Though a description of the contents of "Lost in the Funhouse" suggests a tone of high seriousness, such is not the case at all. The story is based in a series of comic juxtapositions appropriate to the controlling metaphor of the funhouse. In a funhouse, one can get lost in secret mazes and experience fear and panic. Still, the overriding reason one enters a funhouse is to have fun; and a reader knows, if Ambrose does not, that whether the boy grows up to create funhouses or to go through them, he will certainly survive the awkwardness of adolescence.

Mary Rohrberger

THE LOST PHOEBE

Author: Theodore Dreiser (1871-1945)
Type of plot: Domestic realism
Time of plot: The late 1800's or early 1900's
Locale: A farm in the American Midwest
First published: 1916

Principal characters:
HENRY REIFSNEIDER, a poor farmer
PHOEBE REIFSNEIDER, his wife

The Story

Henry Reifsneider was born on a rural farm in the American Midwest where the population is steadily decreasing. His family lived on it for generations, but his children either have moved away or have died. Henry's farm, which he and his wife, Phoebe, now maintain, is in decline. The buildings and even the furniture inside the house are in decay. The fields produce poorly; the animals decrease in number each year; and the apple orchard, full of gnarled old trees, is decomposing.

The story opens with this dismal setting, but the characters' relationship exhibits hope, love, and contentment, expressed in the first three words of the story: "They lived together." Phoebe and Henry have been married forty-eight years, during all of which they have lived on this farm. They spent the first ten years of their married life with Henry's parents, in what would have been a typical extended farming family. Henry and Phoebe are a simple, loving couple whose relationship matures and ripens as their farm decomposes. They take pleasure in the simple daily farm chores. Even their trivial arguments over Henry's misplaced belongings reveal caring. When Phoebe says that she will desert Henry if he blames her for his lost pipe or knife, Henry knows that Phoebe would never abandon him, except in death.

At the age of sixty-four, Phoebe develops a fever and finally does leave Henry. After her death, Henry refuses to move to the house of a relative, insisting that he can supply his simple needs. He is lonely, however, and finds no joy in the daily chores that brought him happiness when he performed them for Phoebe. He longs for her return, and one night the moonlight creates shadows in the kitchen that resemble her. Another night in the garden, an apparition, a pale light or mist that looks like Phoebe, treads the garden. Henry's third encounter with the vision crosses the line from an illusion to a hallucination. Grief transforms the lonely old man into a mentally ill man. When Phoebe appears for this third visit, she speaks to him. In his delusional state, Henry ceases to believe that Phoebe died and begins to imagine that she has left him, as she occasionally threatened. When asking neighbors if they have seen Phoebe, Henry explains that she deserted him when he accused her of losing his pipe.

Each morning, Henry searches for Phoebe. At first, he merely asks neighbors if they have seen her, returning to the farm and hoping that Phoebe will be there. As time passes, Henry widens his search, neglecting the farm and eventually not even returning home. In warm weather, he sleeps in the open; in the winter, he seeks shelter in barns beside animals or under outcroppings of rock. Concerned that Phoebe might not see him, Henry begins calling her name. He becomes known by the locals as an old fanatic, yet he has dignity, and his seven-year search takes on the attributes of a religious pilgrimage.

Occasionally Henry awakens in the night believing that the moonlight and shadows among the brush and trees are Phoebe. He collects his few belongings and follows the apparition. On such a night, while camping in a forest near a precipice known as Red Cliff, Henry awakens at two in the morning with the moon illuminating the forest. As he stares at the brush, he thinks he sees Phoebe, not Phoebe as he knew her in old age but a young Phoebe, the beautiful young woman he married. He leaves his belongings and follows this vision by moonlight through the forest. At the edge of Red Cliff, seeing Phoebe in a moonlit apple orchard below, Henry happily leaps to his death, believing that he will finally join her.

Themes and Meanings

Despite the fact that Theodore Dreiser was the respected author of successful novels at the time he wrote "The Lost Phoebe," this story was rejected nineteen times before it was published. The difficulty of finding a publisher may have been due in part to the story's theme. "The Lost Phoebe" is nostalgic and deals with a happy farm couple. Dreiser's fiction usually examined humans in cities who are mismatched, one partner being more conventional than the other. However, the rural farm life and the depiction of a happily married couple was an American ideal for which Dreiser occasionally longed and that he associated with his first wife, who was raised on a Midwest farm. At the time of writing and publishing "The Lost Phoebe," Dreiser was separating from this wife. In *Twelve Men* (1919), a collection of biographical sketches, Dreiser describes several men, including his first wife's father, who resemble Henry Reifsneider. Although Dreiser was drawn to this American agrarian ideal and tried to capture it in his personal life and occasionally in fiction, he saw it as a passing archetype, one that progress and the city were quickly replacing.

On one level, "The Lost Phoebe" is a simple character sketch that explores the grief that one can experience when a loved one dies, grief that can lead to hallucinations, insanity, and even suicide. On this level, the tale is a realistic representation that enters the unfamiliar world of a simple farming couple. The detailed description of the farm and the dialogues among Henry, his wife, and his neighbors contribute to the realistic portrayal of Henry as a complex character with integrity.

On another level, the story mourns the passing of a way of life, which the deaths of Phoebe and Henry symbolize. As a symbol of this passing life, Phoebe is appropriately named. Although Dreiser as a realist is never overtly symbolic, the name Phoebe has numerous mythological associations. In Greek mythology, Phoebe was another name for Artemis, the twin sister of Phoebus Apollo. The names Phoebus and Phoebe both mean light: Apollo was the sun god and Artemis was the moon goddess. Insofar as Phoebe symbolizes light, the loss of Phoebe is the loss of light. This loss of light parallels the loss of an agrarian way of life; thus, Henry's search for Phoebe becomes an allegory through which one searches and grieves for a lost love and a lost way of life. What appears to be a simple character sketch of a poor midwestern farmer can be read on several levels, ultimately taking on the proportions of a myth. The connection of Phoebe's name to the goddess Artemis reveals a subtle symbolism that is corroborated by the numerous references to light, particularly moonlight, by which Henry ultimately finds Phoebe. Phoebe symbolizes the inconsistent light of the moon and the vanishing family farm.

Style and Technique

Just as the story's simple, realistic plot conveys several levels of meaning, so Dreiser's narrative style conceals complexity and contradiction. Dreiser's writing has often been criticized, and his fiction, although praised as realistic, is occasionally dismissed as lacking consistency. One might claim that Dreiser employs pretentious diction in "The Lost Phoebe," such as the words "immedicable" "perambulations," "albeit," "aberrated" or "peregrinations," which is inappropriate in a simple tale. Dreiser might also be criticized for employing a grand style in a simple story, for example, when he compares the peace of the night to the systolic and diastolic rhythms of the human heart. Dreiser claimed to cultivate this inconsistent style, and there is a connection between the shifting style and the complexity of themes presented. Just as Dreiser thematically juxtaposes the desolation of the rural areas of the United States with the togetherness of the couple, so he employs conflicting methods to communicate these themes. Opposed to the genteel, pretentious words above is the following simple dialogue written in a local dialect: "I kin make a shift for myself."

This apparently simple story is constructed more carefully than it might appear at first. The early argument over Henry's misplaced corn knife foreshadows Henry's later hallucination that Phoebe abandoned him because he accused her of losing his pipe. Phoebe's threat to leave Henry if he accuses her of hiding his belongings foreshadows her eventual death. There is also a crescendo structure. Henry's visions of Phoebe begin as illusions that anyone might have but build into actual hallucinations. His search over seven years climaxes in his most fantastic vision, Phoebe as a beautiful young woman for whom he will leap from a cliff.

Roark Mulligan

THE LOTTERY

Author: Shirley Jackson (1919-1965)
Type of plot: Gothic
First published: 1948
Locale: A small town in New England
Time of plot: The early twentieth century

> *Principal characters:*
> TESSIE HUTCHINSON, a housewife
> BILL HUTCHINSON, her husband
> MR. SUMMERS, a citizen who runs the lottery
> MR. GRAVES, the postmaster who assists in running the lottery
> OLD MAN WARNER, the oldest townsman, who remembers how
> the lottery was conducted many years ago

The Story

On a late summer morning, the villagers of a small New England town gather to conduct their annual lottery. There is an air of festivity among them, especially the children. Only a few in the crowd reveal slight hints of tension or unease.

The lottery has a long history in this and surrounding towns. The people who run it—in this town, Mr. Summers and Mr. Graves—work hard to preserve the rituals that have been passed down from year to year. Changes have crept in, and some old-timers such as Old Man Warner regret what they perceive as a loss of a heritage that has preserved the happiness and prosperity of the town over time.

All the villagers finally arrive, Tessie Hutchinson being one of the last. Mr. Summers conducts the preliminaries, ensuring that each family is represented and that those who are absent have someone on hand to draw for them. Finally the lottery begins: Heads of families step forward and draw small paper slips from the black box that Mr. Summers keeps for the occasion. As this goes on, townspeople engage in small talk, and the air of festivity gives way to a pervasive aura of nervousness.

When all the slips are drawn, Bill Hutchinson discovers that he has picked the one marked with a black spot. Immediately Tessie begins complaining that the drawing was not conducted properly. Others encourage her to be a good sport, however, and her protests fall on deaf ears. She and the other members of her immediate family now come forward and draw slips, as various townspeople whisper apprehensively. Tessie draws the slip with the black spot. Mr. Summers commands, "Let's finish quickly."

The townspeople now move off to a cleared spot outside the town, Tessie in the center of the group. A desperate woman now, Tessie entreats the crowd to go through the ritual again, doing things fairly. Ignoring her protests, the men, women, and children of the town begin stoning her.

Themes and Meanings

The events of "The Lottery" border on the absurd. Nevertheless, the story cries out for interpretation on several levels. Shirley Jackson has skillfully used the elements of several ancient rituals to create a tale that touches on the character of ritual itself and the devastating effects of mob psychology.

At the heart of the story is one of the oldest concepts of humankind: the notion of the scapegoat. Ancient civilizations often conducted a ceremony in which the evils of an entire society were symbolically transferred to one member of the group, either human or animal, and that member was killed or banished. This death or banishment suggested that the evils of the past had been expurgated, allowing for a better future for the group. The Jewish people in Old Testament times conducted the ritual by designating a goat as the recipient of all sins and evil, then turning the goat out into the desert; hence, in Western literature, the term "scapegoat" has been widely adopted to designate this sacrificial victim.

Tessie Hutchinson is the scapegoat in her town in the year in which "The Lottery" takes place; the implication in the story is that the lottery is an annual event. In this town, the scapegoat is used to banish the evils of the society so that the crops will flourish. Thus, two ancient rituals are combined: the notion of banishing evils via a sacrificial victim, and the idea of appeasing higher powers in some way to ensure fertility for the land. Fertility rituals, too, usually involved some kind of sacrifice.

The people of the town are caught up in the ritual to such an extent that they have given up any sense of logic. Mob psychology rules their actions. Though they appear to be sane, sensible individuals, when the time of the lottery comes, they abandon their rational nature and revert to the instincts of the herd. This psychological phenomenon is characteristic of humans throughout history. Although Jackson portrays it in its extreme form in this story, the idea that men and women in groups are willing to forgo personal responsibility and act with great cruelty toward others is evidenced in actions such as lynch mobs, racial confrontations, and similar incidents. The willingness of people to act irrationally as members of the herd displays aspects that, while unpleasant, are still integral parts of their nature that they must recognize if they are to keep them in check.

Style and Technique

A first-time reader of "The Lottery" often finds the ending a surprise. The festive nature of the gathering and the camaraderie of the townspeople as the lottery is conducted belie the horror that occurs at the conclusion of the tale. That is one of the tale's strongest points. Another strength, however, is the skillful way in which Jackson prepares the careful reader for the denouement by including key details so that, on a second reading, one is assured that there is no trick being played on the reader.

Jackson is able to keep the reader off guard by making use of an objective, third-person narrative style in which details are presented but no judgments are made. It is almost as if one is seeing a film or observing events by looking over the shoulders of the participants, without being able to see into the minds of the people. Any hints of inner turmoil are merely suggested by the actions of the characters: a nervous lilt of the voice, a shuffling of feet, a whisper when normal speech would be appropriate. On the other hand, the description of outward actions and physical setting is direct and, when viewed in retrospect, contributes directly to the macabre climax toward which the story moves. The story opens with a scene of small children gathering stones. Townspeople remark about the absence of certain people. These are chilling foreshadowings of what is to come.

Jackson also makes use of symbolic names to give her story universal significance. "Summers" suggests the association with fertility rites. "Graves" signifies the notion of death that runs through the tale. "Warner" characterizes the voice of the past, warning the citizens of the town that breaking with tradition will have dire consequences. The roll call of townspeople goes through the alphabet—Adams to Zanini. Finally, the choice of New England as a setting will suggest to those familiar with history the notion of witchcraft, for which almost two dozen people were put to death in 1692. These and other details help raise "The Lottery" from a simple tale of terror to a study of a universal human problem that persists in all times in one form or another.

Laurence W. Mazzeno

THE LOTTERY IN BABYLON

Author: Jorge Luis Borges (1899-1986)
Type of plot: Fantasy
Time of plot: Unspecified
Locale: Babylon
First published: "La lotería en Babilonia," 1941 (English translation, 1956)

Principal character:
THE UNNAMED NARRATOR

The Story

The narrator, who is about to sail away, recalls his life in Babylon, where everything is ruled by chance. There is a lottery in Babylon that began as most lotteries do, offering relatively modest prizes that did not inspire many to participate. Later the possibility of drawing fines was added to the lottery: For every thirty winning numbers there was to be one requiring payment of a fine. People who did not participate in the lottery came to be scorned as mean-spirited. When some people refused to pay the fines (from which winners were paid), nonpecuniary awards and penalties were added, such as jail sentences. When the stakes were raised, excluding the poor, there were riots. This led to reforms that removed the necessity of even having to buy tickets: Everyone had to participate. Similarly, cash prizes were eliminated; instead, winners could be elevated to the highest reaches of the Company that ran Babylon, while losers could be sentenced to death.

The ship is now ready to sail, but the narrator explains that the Company—arcane and shrouded in mystery as it is and holding Babylon together as it does—may not even exist, that it may never have existed. He concludes that there is a "conjecture no less vile [that] argues that it is inconsequential to affirm or deny the reality of the shadowy corporation, because Babylon is nothing but an infinite game of chance."

Themes and Meanings

It is often said that Jorge Luis Borges deals in metaphysical games and paradoxes, in particular with those having to do with death and time and identity. In "The Lottery in Babylon" he seems to focus mainly on human beings' interest in systematically organizing their surroundings—as do all people in one mythic way or another; either through religion, or literature, sociology, history, or something else. In Babylon it is done by chance.

The use of chance as the basis for running anything is an oxymoronic way of doing things, a way of making sense out of nonsense. It seems significant that Borges wrote this story during the unsettling era of the dictatorial regimes of the Nazis, Fascists, and Soviets. Borges's narrator questions how the lottery is run—if indeed it is being run— and to what end, if any. Amid such uncertainty, one can be, as the narrator says in his opening line, like "all men in Babylon . . . a proconsul . . . a slave," and one can know "omnipotence, opprobrium, jail."

Such uncertainties are, however, possibilities—and not merely metaphysical ones—in all ages, not only those dominated by totalitarianisms or by technologies that offer totalitarian possibilities. This touches on one of the great fears of all people: the idea that life—represented in this story by the Company—makes no sense at all, that it is not ordered even by chance. What guides the Company may be wisdom; it may be astrology, or magic, or arcane information. It may be that the Company is located in a particular place that is hard to find, or it may be that the Company does not even exist. It is that sort of possibility, of course, that leads people to prefer a lottery, to prefer "ordering by chance," to having no perceptible order at all.

This tale is a story-within-a-story, in which the lottery may be a fiction of a particular society within which there may be another society, "the Company." That thereby some doubt is cast on the reasonableness of larger society is of course one purpose of the story of "The Lottery in Babylon."

Borges's narrator asks "if the lottery is an intensification of chance, a periodic infusion of chaos into the cosmos, would it not be desirable for chance to intervene at all stages of the lottery and not merely in the drawing?" Such must be the case; otherwise even chance would be predictable. It is interesting to note that in Greek, both *chaos* and *cosmos* mean "world." Which word is appropriate at any moment seems to be an existential choice. In "The Lottery in Babylon" ordinary people are caught up and whipped about by a system—as sensible as any Platonist, Hegelian, Marxist, or other system proponent—that ultimately makes no more sense than a lottery in which one participates repeatedly. All people try to make sense of life one way or another, although the hell that is raised by some systems seems worse than chaos. Thus it seems reasonable that some people would prefer to find order through chaos.

Style and Technique

Borges's narrators tend to be highly rational and emotionally detached; this is made necessary by the intensity of the intellectual riddles and paradoxes that Borges presents. No other sort of narrator is possible; the idea of an unreliable narrator performing in such a situation, for example, is unthinkable, because the other complexities are nearly overwhelming by themselves. The contrast between the apparent honesty of the narrator and the heavy specific gravity of his complex environment leaves little room to develop passion or feeling for the narrator himself. One of the things that distinguishes Borges's fiction is this detachment. His narrator is not completely flat and one can feel his presence; however, any change in him is apt to be in the reader's mind and not in his persona. This is a markedly different situation from that which one finds in two-dimensional genre literature—such as science fiction, horror, or mystery fiction—in which a certain predictable game is to be played. In such writing the people are not important; only the game is.

With Borges it is a game, but one of people caught in a paradox. For this reason there cannot be rounded people who play off against each other and come to some awareness of themselves. However many characters are needed to develop the paradox, it is the paradox that remains supreme. Thus it is the reader who comes to an awareness. The intensity of intellectual riddles requires that the stories be kept brief; if any of Borges's stories lasted much longer, one might quit reading or go mad. Instead, the pieces are short, though much more work is required in reading them.

Because style and content do not separate in art, Borges's stories, though clearer than any philosophical tract, must be read line by line because of the weight of the paradoxes with which they play. The information necessary to handle each riddle is presented chronologically, as if in recollection—the narrator is hurried, so he says his bit and exits.

J. H. Bowden

THE LOUDEST VOICE

Author: Grace Paley (1922-   )
Type of plot: Domestic realism
Time of plot: A December during the 1930's
Locale: New York City
First published: 1959

> *Principal characters:*
> SHIRLEY ABRAMOWITZ, a young Jewish girl
> MRS. ABRAMOWITZ, her mother
> MR. ABRAMOWITZ, her father

The Story

Shirley Abramowitz lives in a predominantly Jewish community where everyone slams doors and mothers yell out of windows. Shirley has such a loud voice that the neighborhood grocer accuses her of shouting the labels off his cans. Shirley's papa defends her. He says that all will be quiet in the grave.

A happy child, Shirley goes to school in an old red-brick building where the children must stand in straight lines. Because her last name begins with an "A," she is always first in line. One day, the monitor tells her to go quickly upstairs to the sixth-grade room. When she gets there, the teacher, Mr. Hilton, offers her a major part in the Christmas play because she has such a strong voice. He makes her promise that she will work harder than she has ever worked before, and that she will never be tardy or disobedient, because absolutely everything will depend on her.

That afternoon, teachers have the children take down Thanksgiving decorations and put up the Christmas decorations before learning carols. When Shirley's mother hears this, she complains to Mr. Abramowitz, who reminds her that she wanted to come to the United States. After listing all the things that have happened to Jews in other countries, he tells her that the problem they face here is Christmas. He makes it sound like a joke, but his wife does not see the humor in it. She is afraid that Shirley will lose her Jewish faith.

The neighbors are all proud of the good parts that their children have been given in the play. Only one mother will not let her son participate. The rabbi's wife thinks that the whole thing is disgusting, but no one pays any attention to her because she herself wears a strawberry-blond wig.

The days of rehearsal are noisy ones, full of new experiences for Shirley. She is so helpful that Mr. Hilton calls her his right-hand man, says that he could not get along without her, and tells her that her parents should get down on their knees and thank God for a child such as she.

Shirley's father wonders why she stays so late at school that she cannot even set the table for dinner. Her mother answers with one word: Christmas. Mr. Abramowitz says that Christmas and the Jewish festival of lights, Hanukkah, are both descendants of pagan winter celebrations, which makes them historical. Because history belongs to everyone, Shirley will not be pulled away from her religion by the play. Being in it will help her learn to speak up and, perhaps, to have a better life than they.

A Christmas tree decorated by the city for their neighborhood offends most of the adults, but Shirley throws it a kiss with both hands every day, because it is like a stranger in Egypt. The night before the play, Shirley's father kisses her and comments that tomorrow is her big day. Her mother closes all the windows to prevent tonsillitis.

Shirley and everyone else at school work frantically on last-minute preparations for the performance, to which parents, including Shirley's mother, come early. At last, the children are ready. A first-grader parts the curtain and says a poem that tells the audience that the play will be narrated by one person and illustrated by others using pantomime. Shirley begins the long story in a loud voice. As Jesus, she recounts her life from birth to crucifixion, while Jesus is pantomimed by two boys. The twelve friends of Jesus are fourth-grade boys, one of whom, Abie Stock, causes Jesus to be crucified. At the end of the play, everyone gets everlasting life.

Later that evening, Mrs. Kornbluh visits the Abramowitz kitchen for a glass of tea. Shirley's father asks her about the Virgin, whom Mrs. Kornbluh's daughter played in the play's stable scene. She tells him that he has a fresh mouth, so he offers her some lemon to sweeten her disposition. They talk in Yiddish before falling into Russian and Polish. They finally say it was a beautiful affair that taught the children about a different culture. Mrs. Kornbluh says that it is in bad taste that some of the Christian children did not get parts when it was their religion. Shirley's mother tells her that they had small voices and should not be expected to holler. She says that they own the whole thing—the language and the religion. They even look like angels.

Shirley is in bed. She listens to the talk, gets up, kneels, makes a church with her hands, and says "Hear, O Israel. . . . " She prays for the lonesome Christians, her family, cousins, and passersby, and then she calls out in Yiddish to her father. Shirley is sure that God has heard her prayer, because her voice is the loudest.

Themes and Meanings

Grace Paley's little sketch is about ordinary people who belong to her own Jewish religion. Its central theme is how even in the United States, the land of religious freedom, teachers in a New York school can be insensitive to their Jewish pupils by choosing many of them to be characters in a Christmas play based on the biblical story of Jesus. Shirley plays Jesus because she has the strongest voice. She narrates the play, but as she describes what the characters pantomime, it is hilariously funny. Jesus has twelve "friends" instead of disciples, there are some women whom no one likes, and Arab "sheiks" instead of Roman soldiers crucify him.

When Shirley's mother worries that being in the play and celebrating Christmas will cause Shirley to lose her faith, her husband compares Christianity to shaving with a secondhand razor. He tells his wife that Shirley will not be fooled. She will use the play to improve herself and, at the same time, she will learn some history because

Christianity is part of history. In Jewish thought, all history has meaning and significance because it works toward fulfilling the purpose of God.

A distinctive voice makes Shirley different from the Christian children in her school. Her religion makes her different, too. She feels sorry for the city's Christmas tree on the corner, because it is a stranger in Egypt: as out of place in a Jewish neighborhood as the Jews were out of place in Egypt long ago. Shirley may feel that she and her friends are strangers in New York. Many of the Jewish children have trouble with the English language, and even Shirley must speak the words carefully while she is narrating the play.

Her loud voice comes out of the exuberance of her spirit. She is a winner and will go far. The title is symbolic of the piece's theme. Those who use negative experiences as positive opportunities will always be loud voices in the land.

At the end, Shirley has picked up a Christian practice of kneeling in prayer, but she still calls out the Jewish Shema, "Hear, O Israel."

Style and Technique

Irony provides wry humor in this story. Not only is it ironic that Jewish children are chosen as actors in a Christmas play, but the life of Jesus with its orange crates, prayer shawls, and Arab sheiks is a mockery of the New Testament story. It is ironic that a Jewish girl's voice is thought best to portray the voice of Jesus. Shirley's father is being sarcastic when he asks Mrs. Kornbluh, "How is the Virgin?" When he then tells her to have some lemon to sweeten her disposition, he is using ironic statement.

Shirley's mother talks about the Christian children's small voices and says that they are blond like angels. She is insulting them while seeming to give them a compliment—an example of satire, the most sophisticated form of humor.

Christians are described as lonesome. That statement and Shirley's forming of her hands into a church for prayer seem absurd.

Told skillfully through dialogue between the lively, upbeat characters, the story appears to be happening in the present, even though it is a remembered incident from long ago. The dialect of the Bronx has been captured perfectly in short sentences and terse commentary.

First-person point of view puts the reader's concentration totally on the protagonist and suggests autobiographical truth. There is no hint of insecurity in this child. She is so self-assured and confident that she would seem too good to be true if she did not report on the grocer for telling her to be quiet and on the student teacher calling her a show-off. These negative comments make her more believable.

Josephine Raburn

LOVE
Three Pages from a Sportsman's Notebook

Author: Guy de Maupassant (1850-1893)
Type of plot: Adventure
Time of plot: The 1870's
Locale: Normandy, France
First published: "Amour, trois pages du livre d'un chasseur," 1887 (English translation, 1903)

> *Principal characters:*
> THE NARRATOR, a Parisian
> KARL DE RAUVILLE, his Norman cousin

The Story

In a brief introduction, the narrator reacts to a newspaper account of a double killing—a male lover kills his beloved and then himself. He observes that the sexes of the murderer and his victim are irrelevant; it is their love that matters. This news release does not affect the no-longer-young narrator for its sentimentality, shock value, romantic longing, or intrigue but merely reminds him of a hunting expedition in which he took part when he was younger. The narrator introduces himself as someone who was born with primitive instincts, although they have been tempered by civilized responses. Hunting, like a great love or a panoramic vista, fills him with a sense of passion and fulfillment. He recalls that he was summoned by an older cousin, Karl de Rauville, to participate in an early morning hunt in the duck marshes of Normandy. He remembers that he left Paris during an unusually premature, cold, savage winter.

His cousin exemplifies the Norman hunting tradition: a tough, spirited country gentleman, a lovable half-brute. The countryside has a hypnotic effect on the narrator. He finds himself transported into a world that he had known only through the imagination. The colors of the country, the sounds of the underbrush, and the mysterious disorder of the universe induce in him a bewildering, powerful, and magical aspect. As the narrator looks over the marshes, this sense of the unknown is reinforced, and he is tortured by the exotic landscape of fog and enchantment.

On arriving at his cousin's château, the narrator notices the taxidermist environment: Birds of every plumage are mounted on the walls. As a hailstorm engulfs the region, he hears the plans for the coming day. At 3:30 A.M. they will depart for the marshes, dressed in animal skins and accompanied by two dogs and a forester. From the moment they set out, the frozen atmosphere numbs and transforms them into the same dead objects of early winter that surround them. Even the moon seems frightened by the lurid vastness of the incessant cold.

The hunters and the dogs, breathing with the smoldering, intoxicating anticipation of the kill, march through the almost impenetrable forest until they come on an ice shelter designed to protect the hunters from the ravages of the frozen morning. Karl notices that the narrator is coughing, and he orders the forester to build a fire in the ice hut. The flames shoot up suddenly into the frozen air like a monstrous diamond. The silhouettes of the dogs around the fire assume fantastic shapes.

In this state of heightened consciousness, the narrator is called to the hunt as wild birds fly from their nocturnal hideouts. Nothing in his life has prepared the young protagonist for the tumult of emotions that accompanies the arrival of the birds, flying through crevices in the sky of the glacial dawn. When day breaks, the hunters kill several creatures. Once the dawn is fully established, two ducks appear overhead and the narrator shoots one down. Overhead, he hears the plaintive cries of its mate—the drake lamenting the loss of the female. Karl shoots it because it would never leave on its own. The dogs are happy. The narrator deposits the cold carcass into the bag where its dead partner awaits. Later that day, he returns to Paris.

Themes and Meanings

Nineteenth century writers tended to depict city life as decadent and deceptive. The countryside offered renewal and restitution. Among naturalist writers, such as Gustave Flaubert, Émile Zola, and Ivan Turgenev, the portrayal of provincial life was less flattering. Rustic manners and mores often seemed petty and sordid.

Guy de Maupassant was aware of Turgenev's *Zapiski okhotnika* (1852; *Russian Life in the Interior*, 1855; better known as *A Sportsman's Sketches*, 1932), a collection of tales from rural Russia. In "Love: Three Pages from a Sportsman's Notebook," the narrator looks back to an experience that brought him out of the city into the uncanny surroundings of the Normandy marshlands. This sentimental, overwrought Parisian enjoys the primitive exhilaration of the hunt, but when the hunt is successfully concluded, his civilized side produces guilt and sorrow regarding the fate of his animal victims. Maupassant indirectly leads the reader to see the connection between the conquests and tragedies associated with love and those related to the hunt. The narrator is aware that Karl's invitation excites in him an uncontrollable urge to participate in the chase, but the description of his cousin as a "loveable half-brute whose Gallic humour compensates for his mediocrity" reminds the reader that he is also a professional hunter determined to kill.

In sumptuous detail, the narrator conveys the mesmerizing effect of the frozen wetlands, pushing him toward a frenzy that his cousin cannot possibly understand. It is ironic that this transplanted urbanite kills the female duck, whose mate can never relinquish it. After Karl kills the forlorn drake, the hunt ends; passion dissolves into mechanical bestiality. Purged of desire, the narrator quickly returns to the city.

This story reflects some of the themes treated in Maupassant's writings of the 1880's: a profound pessimism regarding the human condition and the perverse satisfactions that regulate human motivation. The once-legendary appeal of the glorified hunter has become commonplace. In this predetermined Darwinian landscape, suffering and self-destruction seem inescapable. The narrator's comparison of this hunting vignette to the vision of the Christian cross is a reminder that he is describing a revealed truth.

As the narrator enters the marshlands, he is immersed in the primeval wonder of creation. This world of awe and mystery, ironically, becomes the scene of death. For his cousin from the country, the hunting trip is one like so many others. Human ingenuity has dominated the natural world, from which there is nothing left to learn. The city dweller, however, is branded by this experience; for him the natural world, although perhaps remote, continues to unravel its secrets.

Style and Technique

Maupassant is recognized as a consummate stylist who strove to render an exact image of life. In "Love: Three Pages from a Sportsman's Notebook," with supple yet powerful prose, he quickly establishes the frame of reference and then sets about to create the atmosphere by means of carefully selected, impressionistic details.

In order for the story to be convincing, a series of acute psychological states must evolve, each attached to a specific characteristic of the natural setting. First, the narrator takes note of the vastness of the river valley and forest. The thought of the unusual creatures who inhabit these lands leaves him with a sense of alienation and dread. As the river basin gives way to marshland, the narrator observes that this watershed region is a world unto itself. He admits he enjoys, with an excessive passion, being around rivers, lakes, and streams, but the rushing sound of gurgling water in the distance troubles him deeply.

The paralyzing cold eventually overwhelms the narrator, and the compelling drama of the night sky in the bog almost deprives him of human sensation. Later, the fire in the hut illuminates the marsh with surreal images, and the eerie distant sound of birds as they move with the first light of dawn is like the sighing of the earth. Finally, the heartbreaking cry of the duck lamenting its fallen mate casts a spell over the narrator that will not soon be broken. Through masterful control over these aggravated mental states, Maupassant conveys the full intensity of the narrator's disorder.

Maupassant uses complex language patterns, in which graphic images fuse with abstract ruminations. The marsh is "peopled" with bulrushes and weeds; the lifeless water is "swollen and turbulent"; strange mists engulf the willows like "shrouds"; seeds of life "vibrate" in the stagnant, murky waters; the frigid air is "firm and palpable"; the winter moon is "disfigured."

The most descriptive passages derive their vigor from the pulsation of repeated nouns or adjectives in succession. Karl is very strong and very bearded; the reeds are lively, brisk, and surging; the ocean is too large and restless; the frigid wind cuts the flesh, tears it, stabs it, twists it, and burns it; there is a strange, lost, wandering scream, a low, wailing, relentless sound; and the coldness of the swamp, ice hut, and sky.

Despite the effortless flow of Maupassant's language, his style is neither pretentious nor melodramatic. In "Love: Three Pages from a Sportman's Notebook," the reader cannot help but think that these are the only pages in the notebook. Economy of space and density of observation strive for a single effect and intention.

Robert J. Frail

THE LOVE DECOY

Author: S. J. Perelman (1904-1979)
Type of plot: Satire
Time of plot: The 1920's
Locale: A college campus
First published: 1930

> *Principal characters:*
> RUSSELL GIPF, previously Donald Fenstermacher, an instructor at Tunafish College for Women
> DOLORES HORNBOSTEL, a student at the same college
> DEAN FOTHERGILL, previously Jim the Penman, an administrator at Tunafish College

The Story

"The Love Decoy" begins in a packed classroom at the Tunafish College for Women. Dolores Hornbostel has just heard from Ivy Nudnick that Professor Gompers, the regular instructor, is ill and that Russell Gipf will be substituting for him. This news sends Dolores into a nostalgic reverie. She recalls going, on a previous autumn afternoon, to Professor Gipf's office to discuss an essay that she had written. Mr. Gipf, it seems, although confiding in her, provocatively, that he was studying dirty limericks for his doctoral thesis, failed to make the "usual indecent proposal." The meeting was not a success, and Dolores left with her vanity considerably piqued.

Dolores's daydream is interrupted when the real Professor Gipf, as handsome as her remembrance, asks her to answer a question that he has just posed to the class. She has not been listening and cannot answer the question, so Professor Gipf, with considerable sarcasm, proceeds to humiliate her in front of her peers. She seethes ineffectually, until a plan for revenge begins to form in her mind. Approaching Professor Gipf after class, she asks him to come to her dorm room, after lights out, to help her get the cap off her toothpaste tube. It is a thinly veiled proposition, which Mr. Gipf is unable to resist.

Late that evening, Dolores awaits her visitor/victim in a seductive negligee. With low lights and incense, she has turned her dormitory room into a love nest. Professor Gipf hurries up four flights of stairs, panting conspicuously, and enters the room with suspicion. He goes into the bathroom to look at the toothpaste tube. When he comes out, he realizes that he has been tricked. Dolores snarls at Professor Gipf that she has barred all avenues of escape, and picks up the telephone. It is clear that she intends to turn him over to the faculty, who have apparently already suspended him once before for a similar indiscretion.

At this point, what little plot there is in "The Love Decoy" breaks down completely. Dolores never gets to complete her call, because Dean Fothergill, mad with desire, crashes into her room and lunges at her. Russell Gipf, to the reader's surprise, defends Dolores's honor, and a nasty fight ensues, during which Dolores, unmoved by the spectacle, studies for her law exam.

The denouement is a hasty barrage of comic epiphanies, in which the understandably confused reader discovers that Dean Fothergill is really Jim the Penman, whose forgeries have sent Dolores's father, Harry Trefusis, to jail. (Why the unmarried Dolores does not bear her father's surname is only one of the story's many unresolved complications.) Professor Gipf turns out to be Donald Fenstermacher, the Splendid Wayfarer, and he takes his position at the end of the story as the tender, romantic hero. "The Love Decoy" fades out, presumably to everyone's relief, to the sweet strains of a strumming guitar.

Themes and Meanings

S. J. Perelman was cynical about Hollywood and screenwriting as only a successful Hollywood screenwriter could be, and it is not surprising that he frequently burlesqued the cinema in his many sketches and stories.

Burlesque is a somewhat schizophrenic technique that lends itself nicely to a double view of things. On one hand, it represents a blatant travesty of the artistic form, or genre, that it mimics. On the other hand, it is a rather flattering tribute to its original. Just as Miguel de Cervantes's *El ingenioso hidalgo don Quixote de la Mancha* (1605, 1615; *The History of the Valorous and Wittie Knight-Errant, Don Quixote of the Mancha*, 1612-1620; better known as *Don Quixote de la Mancha*) shows both the Spaniard's extreme exasperation with and his lingering love for the medieval romance, so Perelman's "The Love Decoy" shows his ambivalence toward the zany, formless, slapstick Hollywood screen comedies of his day.

"The Love Decoy" is as farcical as anything that has been shown on the silver screen, yet it has a linguistic sophistication that argues persuasively against the militant simplicity of the Hollywood comedies of the 1920's and the 1930's. In his unfinished memoirs, *The Hindsight Saga*, published in *The Last Laugh* (1981), Perelman comments, much to the point, on his differences of opinion with Groucho Marx over the scripting of the enormously popular film *Monkey Business* (1931): Groucho "felt that some of the dialogue I wrote for him was 'too literary.' He feared that many of my allusions would be incomprehensible to the ordinary moviegoer, whom he regarded as a wholly cretinous specimen."

Whatever literary frustrations Perelman may have felt with his work as a scriptwriter in Hollywood, he more than compensated for them in his sketches and short stories, whose lusty love for language and convoluted style remind one forcibly of James Joyce, Perelman's favorite "comic writer."

Style and Technique

"The Love Decoy" may be thin on plot, weak in characterization, and even lacking in socially redeeming value, but it is, without question, a virtuoso performance on the level of style and technique. Few writers wield the pen with such brio, such wild abandon, or such precision. From argot to arcana, Perelman is a match for panderers, pick-pockets, and professors. Perelman's prose can, in fact, be confidently approached only with a stack of unabridged dictionaries, several books of quotations, a companion to world literature, and a complete encyclopedia of films. Even the well-equipped reader will stumble across conundrums enough to keep a quizzical look on his or her face. When it comes to language, Perelman frequently "out-Herods Herod."

"The Love Decoy" is a prime example of Perelman's baroque linguistic sensibility. Mrs. Malaprop, Richard Brinsley Sheridan's classic abuser of words, would certainly appreciate Professor Gipf, who tells Dolores Hornbostel in no uncertain terms that she "had better stop galvanizing around nights and pay attention!" W. A. Spooner, the namesake of the spoonerism (in which the initial sounds of words are unintentionally confused or reversed), could hardly improve on Perelman's description of Professor Gompers, with his "grizzled chin and chiseled grin," and could William Shakespeare have made a lowlier pun than the one that sings in Dolores Hornbostel's mind as she is finally being wooed by Professor Gipf? "I tried to resist his overtures, but he plied me with symphonies, quartets, chamber music and cantatas."

Perelman is a great and comic trickster of the English language. He loves fanciful names (for example, the coed "Ivy Nudnick" and the "Absconders' and Defaulters' National Bank"). He thrives on wildly mixed levels of diction ("A cold fury welled up in me and I longed to hang one on his lug for his insolence"). He coins words that are as charming as they are confusing ("bewhiskered, beflanneled, bejasused and bejabered undergraduates strolled under the hoary elms"). He is full of inspired nonsense ("There had been a heavy fall of talcum several hours before and as far as the ground could see the eye was white").

To Perelman, mangled clichés, Tom Swifties, cinematic allusions, oxymorons, obsolete and obscure words, Yiddish slang, hyperbolic gangster jargon, and non sequiturs are all threads in the multicolored tapestry he weaves. For those who are content with a brilliantly textured surface, Perelman's prose will be more than satisfying.

Cynthia Lee Katona

THE LOVE OF A GOOD WOMAN

Author: Alice Munro (1931-   )
Type of plot: Domestic realism
Time of plot: 1951
Locale: Walley, Ontario, Canada
First published: 1996

Principal characters:
D. M. WILLENS, the town optometrist
THREE TEENAGE BOYS
MRS. QUINN, a young woman who is dying
RUPERT, her husband
ENID, her home nurse

The Story

The multilayered plot of "The Love of a Good Woman," a complex treatment of secrets in a small Canadian town, begins when three teenage boys go swimming in the river and find the body of the town optometrist, Mr. D. M. Willens, in his submerged car. They do not report their discovery to the police immediately but instead wait until after dinner to tell the local constable, who is too deaf to hear them. Later, one of the boys tells his mother, and the police find the body.

The second section of the story shifts to a period some time after the death of Mr. Willens. The young Mrs. Quinn, who is dying of kidney failure, is cared for by a home nurse named Enid. Mrs. Quinn is portrayed as a cranky young woman, and Enid is portrayed as a middle-aged spinster tormented by erotic dreams.

The third section links the first two sections by recounting the story of Mr. Willens's death, as Mrs. Quinn tells it to Enid. Mrs. Quinn is having her eyes examined in her home by Mr. Willens, who has a reputation as a lecherous old man. When Mrs. Quinn's husband, Rupert, comes back to the house and sees his wife with her skirt up her thighs and Mr. Willens's hands on her leg, he knocks the older man down and beats his head on the floor until he dies. Mrs. Quinn, who comes up with the idea to put Mr. Willens and his car in the river, helps her husband carry out her plan.

In the fourth section, after Mrs. Quinn dies, Enid, who has feelings for Rupert, believes he should go to the police and confess to killing Mr. Willens. Convinced that he cannot live in the world with such a secret, she tells herself that she will go to the trial every day and then wait for him while he is in prison. Not sure that the story Mrs. Quinn told her is true, Enid devises a scheme to test Rupert. She plans to have him row her out in the middle of the river, tell him she cannot swim, and then tell him what she knows. This will give him the opportunity to kill her if the story is true. "The Love of a Good Woman" ends with Rupert getting the oars while Enid waits for him on the riverbank. The reader never knows whether Rupert killed Mr. Willens or whether he will kill Enid.

Themes and Meanings

The central, overlapping themes of "The Love of a Good Woman" are secrets, lies, and flesh. The basic human reality that pervades the story is that there are hidden realities about which people lie. The ultimate human secret is the flesh, which, by its very nature, is driven by physical desire and inevitably ends in death. The most predominant manifestation of this theme of the connection between flesh and death is the fact that Mr. Willens's lust causes his death and indirectly leads to the death of Mrs. Quinn.

The basic human secret of lust and the corruption of the flesh is suggested by both Mrs. Quinn and Enid. Mrs. Quinn's failing kidneys result in a smell coming from her that is acrid and ominous, an outer manifestation of an inner corruption. In spite of this smell of death, Mrs. Quinn is not self-conscious about her body and is without shame when Enid must bath her. Enid cannot conquer her dislike of the doomed woman, repulsed by the misshapen body she has to wash and powder. She particularly dislikes the physical manifestations of the disease—the smell and discoloration, and the pathetic ferretlike teeth. Enid sees all of this as a sign of willful corruption.

Enid is troubled by ugly dreams in which she is copulating with forbidden and unthinkable partners. "Slick with lust," she accepts these partners, saying they will have to do until something better comes along; this matter-of-fact depravity increases her lust even more until she wakes up with disgust and humiliation. The repulsive, fleshly nature of sex and its relation to death is also suggested by Mrs. Quinn's reaction to the attentions of Mr. Willens, grabbing at her and sucking away at her with "his dribbly old mouth." As she helps Rupert put his body in the car, one of his legs kicks her and she thinks that even in death he is a lusty old devil. She even believes that the horrible smell that resulted from burning the bloodstained blouse she had on when she dragged Mr. Willens's body to the car brought on her illness.

The final connection between the themes of desire and death occurs at the end of the story when Enid's desire for Rupert is such that she is willing to risk her own life to test whether the story Mrs. Quinn told her was true.

Style and Technique

Alice Munro's narrative technique is typical of the modern short story since Anton Chekhov introduced a new kind of thematic realism at the turn of the twentieth century. "The Love of a Good Woman" is not structured around a chronological series of cause-and-effect events. Instead, it is structured in multiple layers of thematic motifs. The story's themes of secrets, lies, and flesh are echoed in seemingly trivial, irrelevant details throughout the story. For example, the father of one of the boys who finds Mr. Willens's body is a heavy smoker who is taken to the hospital with pneumonia. When the nurses wrap him in wet sheets to bring his fever down, the sheets turn brown as he sweats out the tar and nicotine. This is just one minor echo of the story's pervasive theme of an inner reality or secret being externally manifested. Another boy passes his mother dressing a dummy in a store window and can smell in his mind his mother's stockings and underwear, thinking that even clean female underwear has a faint private smell both appealing and disgusting.

By describing numerous details that seem irrelevant to the plot of the story but echo its themes, Munro gives her fiction a thematic complexity through repetition that holds the story together. The story does not have the cause-and-effect structure of many novels. In fact, as in most of Munro's short stories, the nature of cause and effect or motivation—what makes people do what they do—is often left quite mysterious.

"The Love of a Good Woman" is a long story that begins like a novel, but instead of continuing to broaden out, as it introduces new characters and seemingly new stories, it tightens up, slowly connecting what at first seemed disparate and unrelated. It is a classic example of Munro's most characteristic technique of creating a world that has all the illusion of external reality, while all the time pulling the reader deeper and deeper into what becomes a hallucinatory inner world of mystery, secrecy, and deception. Unlike the novel, which would be bound to develop some sort of satisfying closure, Munro's story reaches a moral impasse, an ambiguous open end in which the reader suddenly realizes that instead of living in the world of apparent reality, he or she has been whirled to an almost unbearable central point of intensity.

Although there is always something mysterious and unspeakable in Munro's stories, there is never the cryptic compression of much late twentieth century short fiction. In an almost novelistic fashion, as if she had all the time in the world, Munro lovingly lingers on her characters and seldom misses the opportunity to register an arresting image. However, a Munro story like "The Love of a Good Woman" is deceptive; it lulls the reader into a false sense of security in which time seems to comfortably stretch out like everyday reality, only to suddenly turn and tighten so intensely that the reader is left breathless.

Charles E. May

THE LOVER OF HORSES

Author: Tess Gallagher (1943-   )
Type of plot: Sketch
Time of plot: The mid- to the late twentieth century
Locale: A ranch overlooking an ocean
First published: 1982

> *Principal characters:*
> THE NARRATOR, a young woman adjusting to her father's death
> HER FATHER, a professional card player and drinker
> HER MOTHER, the caretaker of the family
> HER GREAT-GRANDFATHER, a wanderer, drinker, and horse lover

The Story

The narrator reflects on her great-grandfather and the stories about him she heard from her paternal grandmother, his ninth child, who was conceived in a stall. According to her grandmother, the narrator's great-grandfather was obsessed with drinking, drifting, and horses. He was such a lover of horses that he owned twenty-nine of them when he left his wife and eleven children in order to run off with a circus that was passing through town. The narrator concludes that he was stolen by a horse, a dappled gray stallion trained to dance a variation of the mazurka. Seven years later, probably after the death of the circus stallion, the great-grandfather returned home to die, burned out by his obsession. He spent his last years being cared for, and he sometimes went into an open field and danced the circus horse's dance.

The narrator's father, obsessed with drifting, drinking, and card playing, and the narrator's mother, a practical woman, manage to stay together, although the mother never learns to deal with the drinking and gambling. When the narrator's father seems on the brink of self-destruction, her mother calls her home.

When she arrives home, she learns that her father is on a gambling and drinking spree in the local tavern. She prepares a broth that she takes to him and finds him in the middle of a record winning streak. Apparently excited by his run of good luck, she ministers to him by bringing him broth and beer but does not stay too long for fear she may interfere with his luck.

During the next two days and nights of gambling, the father continues to win but becomes deeply exhausted and oblivious to winning. Despite the mother's pleading, the local doctor refuses to order the father home. At the end of the third day, the game folds because the other players are unwilling to challenge his winning streak. In disgust and disappointment, the father gets drunk and is escorted home, with his winnings, by two friends.

Like his grandfather, the narrator's father returns home to die. He withdraws further from the world, engaging in ritualistic acts to evade death. His wife caters to him, even relenting and allowing whiskey in the house. Meanwhile, the narrator begins her grieving. She drifts away from the house, haunts her father's favorite places, and takes up smoking. She finishes her ritual path on a stone bench under a cedar tree overlooking the ocean, her father's favorite place to sit. She tears branches from the cedar tree to make herself a bed under the tree, where she sleeps under the stars, with the hiss of the ocean in her ears. Speaking to herself and to her absent father, she vows to enter the world of dancers and drunkards, gamblers, and lovers of horses to which she now believes she must belong. She vows to plunge into the heart of this new life and be ruthlessly lost forever.

Themes and Meanings

Tess Gallagher's "The Lover of Horses" was first published in the same year that her father died in her arms after a bout with lung cancer. In the sixteen-page story, the narrator reflects on the history of men in her family, particularly her great-grandfather and her father. The exploration of the father-daughter relationship is at the heart of the sketch. The narrator needs to know how she feels about her father and her great-grandfather and to choose her course accordingly. Her final choice is between the course of her deadly practical mother and that of the lover of horses—the person who answers obsessions, plunges into life, and suffers the consequences. She chooses to be a lover of horses.

Related to this choice is the theme of those who can be stolen by things—by drinking, by gambling, by a circus traveling through town, and by a dancing horse. An irony tied to this theme is the role of those abandoned by those who are stolen by things. The great-grandfather returns home after the death of the dancing horse, and his wife agrees to take him in and care for him. The father steals his wife's belongings and wagers them on his card games. After his final immersion in gambling and drink, he returns to her; she takes him in and cares for him. Recognizing obsessions and luck for what they are, the men return home, cast off by the things that have stolen them. They have no deep moment of recognition, no remorse, only the childlike fear of punishment. In the instance of the narrator's father, this punishment comes in his sense of being stalked by death.

To the last, the narrator's father is engaged in rituals to fend off death. He changes his diet to deceive death and avoids his bed, so death cannot find him there. He asks his wife to sweep the doorway as guests come and go, perhaps so that death will not trail in on their heels. The daughter, no more eager than her father to be around when death comes, sleeps outdoors under the cedar tree, one of her father's favorite places. In her ritual acts of grieving, she embraces his rituals of life but will have no part in his rituals of death. The mother concludes what the narrator has realized, that she and her father are too much alike. Unlike her mother, however, the narrator finds solace in her vow to live like her father and great-grandfather, as a lover of horses.

Gallagher also explores the meanings of silence and sound. The narrator's mother desperately tries to deliver her daughter "into the world where people shouted and railed at one another and talked in an audible fashion about things both common and sacred." Juxtaposed against the commotion of the circus, the dancing horse, the bar-room, and the play of children are the unvoiced motives for the actions. The great-grandfather, who was rumored to be a whisperer—someone who could whisper to horses and make them understand—does not explain his leaving or his return. The narrator goes through a time when she will not speak to anyone under the age of eleven. The father is given to muttering to himself, a habit embraced by the narrator as she rests on the cedar branches under the stars and the tree. Her grandmother and mother alone have audible voices, with which they try to make sense of the great-grandfather's and father's lives. They speculate, and through their speculation readers get clues but not firm answers. The play between sound and silence leaves a clear sense that understanding the whispering and muttering, and even the hiss of the ocean, is reserved for those who, as Gallagher's narrator concludes, plunge into the heart of life and are lost forever. As she tears branches from the tree to make her bed, she feels a "painful permission, as when two silences, tired of holding back, give over to each other some shared regret."

Style and Technique

"The Lover of Horses" is told entirely through the interior monologue of the narra-tor, who sketches the great-grandfather and father precisely. These sketches give the story its life and suspense. Reading Gallagher's story is like moving through an art gallery in which the paintings are endowed with sound and movement. Among these sketches are the dancing horse, the great-grandfather's return, the father at the gam-bling table, the stripping away of the furniture in the room where the father dies, and the narrator at rest on the cedar branches near the stone bench, with the hiss of the ocean in her ears. An artful sketcher and a masterful teller of stories, Gallagher uses these skills to reveal the complexities of the father-daughter relationship in "The Lover of Horses."

Carol Franks

THE LUCK OF ROARING CAMP

Author: Bret Harte (1836-1902)
Type of plot: Regional
Time of plot: 1850
Locale: A California mining camp during the gold rush
First published: 1868

> *Principal characters:*
> TOMMY "THE LUCK" LUCK, an orphan born to Cherokee Sal, a
> sinful woman, in Roaring Camp
> KENTUCK, a miner sentimentally attached to "the Luck"
> STUMPY, a miner and the caretaker of the baby
> OAKHURST, a gambler

The Story

In an isolated California mining camp during the gold-rush days, the whole camp is astounded and intrigued at the birth of a baby to a sinful woman named Cherokee Sal, who died at the child's birth. Only such a novel event could involve so completely all the fugitive residents of Roaring Camp, men with questionable pasts and common gold fever. Their tenderness and solicitude for the child is extraordinary and quite out of character for them. These roughs come to pay homage to the babe and to bestow such gifts as they have on this miracle—a silver tobacco box, a navy revolver, a gold specimen, a lady's handerchief, a diamond breastpin, a diamond ring, a Bible (contributor undetected), and money, among other gifts. As a miner named Kentuck bends over the baby, "the little cuss" by chance grasps his finger, an act that causes the man to be overwhelmed by emotion. From then on, the rugged Kentuck is especially attached to the newcomer.

Full of new responsibility, the members of the camp debate what shall be done with the baby. They do not want to part with him by sending him to Red Dog, a camp where there are decent women to care for a child. Nor do they believe it possible to import a decent woman to take charge, and "they didn't want any more of the other kind" of woman. This last consideration is the first spasm of propriety that the camp has known. They vote en masse to adopt and rear the child themselves. Stumpy, because he has two wives (the reason for his flight to Roaring Camp), is chosen to be caretaker of the baby. They send for the best of things that the child will need; they feed the baby on ass's milk; they lavish interest on their charge. Because of their care, or perhaps in spite of it, the child thrives—the nature of the Sierra foothills probably making up for the clumsiness of the men.

At one month the child is given the name Tommy Luck, for it is believed that he has brought luck to the camp. Indeed, "the Luck" has brought rehabilitation, for Stumpy's cabin has been cleaned and tidied, and the men have gathered there about the child rather than at Tuttle's Grocery, where they had been accustomed to gambling and fighting. Even all the shouting that gave the camp its name has been stilled within a distance of the Luck's residence. In short, the miners become pacified and dignified in respect to their Luck. On fair days, the boy is taken out to the digging gulch to lie nearby under the painted blossoms of "Las Mariposas" beneath the beneficial breezes, the center of all attention. To the men, Luck assumes a mystical air of seeming to commune with nature and talk to the birds.

The summer following Luck's birth is golden to the men of Roaring Camp. Flush times of generous gold yield give them not only trust in the Luck but also a protective air, so that they discourage any newcomers from immigration and preempt lands to both sides of the camp as their domain. According to the expressman's glowing report, the camp is trim and bedecked with flowers, and the men wash themselves twice a day. It is also reported that they worship "an Ingin baby." Indeed, with its prosperity Roaring Camp proposes to erect a hotel the next spring and to invite one or two decent families to move into town, for the sake of the Luck.

However, in the winter of 1851, the floods come disastrously to Roaring Camp. Suddenly the river at North Fork leaps its banks and inundates the triangular area of the camp, washing away Stumpy's cabin. The Luck is missing. A relief boat from down the river brings in Kentuck, however, badly bruised and crushed. In his arms is the Luck, dead. Kentuck dies too, declaring the Luck is taking him with him: "Tell the boys I've got The Luck with me now."

Themes and Meanings

The story depends on the local color of the mining camps of the California gold rush for its plot and theme. Not only is the setting in place and time vital to the story but also vital is the formation of the characters by that place, time, and situation. What happens happens because of the gold rush, because of the topography and weather of the place, and because of the sort of men who sought the gold for the reasons they had in the middle of the nineteenth century. The meaning of events is bestowed because of the way the miners thought and felt. Locale is not merely background, then, but is a major determiner in the story. The Luck's name, the way he is treated, and the reformation of the camp and its inhabitants are all attributable to the nature of the dreamers who rear him. His coming is a miracle because his unlikely foster fathers have hope in miracles out of nature.

If the story seems improbable because the effect of the baby is so sudden and so far-reaching, one needs to realize that this is a tale, a yarn, and not a realistic story, despite its use of realistic locale, speech, and mannerisms. Mostly the tale is narrated by a third-person narrator, who may have been one of the Roaring Camp miners or who might have gotten the tale from one of them. The narrator treats the tale with both humor and reverence. The tale is a tall one, to be smiled at; yet it is also offered as the story of a miracle in reformation, and that is supposed to inspire awe. Thematically the mood of the story spans the humorously shady past of the miners to the reverent mood of their hopes.

The allegorical intent is obvious, though it is slight and only to a small degree significantly symbolic. Out of the camp's sinful past (personified by Cherokee Sal), nature bestows luck on the residents (the orphan), and trust in the luck (their devotion to the boy) reforms the community until nature (the flood) takes the luck away—but carries their representative, Kentuck, along with the Luck. Some readers may find a Christian allegory in the events, but it should be noted that it is the characters who bring up the suggestion of allegory and not the narrator, for the miners name the baby.

Style and Technique

The tone is important in this tale. Although this is a story of sentiment, even perhaps of sentimentality, the feeling of perhaps excessive emotion is tempered by humor and the author's distance from the events and from the miners. Much of the narrative deals with Roaring Camp matter-of-factly, with opinion to the side, often put in parenthetical comment: "a silver spoon (the initials, I regret to say, were not the giver's)." Only at the end does the narrator soar to sentimental philosophy that might be taken as sincere. The narrative of events before the flood reflects a teller who views the regeneration of Roaring Camp with detached irony. His language is much elevated above that of the miners, and his background is obviously more refined. His attitude is one of amusement at the miners' roughness but of sympathy for their innocent reaction to the child's coming among them. With the rehabilitation of the miners, the narrator's attitude changes to reverence.

The most effective and lasting achievement of the story is the creation of the society of Roaring Camp. In combining the romance and realism of a time and place about which his readers know—and which in fact did exist and did experience the real dream of a gold rush—Bret Harte was able to cast that romantic air of mystery across realistic events to cause in readers both belief and wish fulfillment. In effect Harte created for the reading public a description of how forty-niners talked and thought in the camps. This sort of realistic romance is unique in being rooted so deeply in the locale of its setting that it could not be placed anywhere else.

The story is very short—ten pages in almost all editions—and has only essential or exemplary quotation of character speech. The pace is not at all breathless, yet the reader is quite conscious that events are being summarized with economy. Most of the attention is placed on what the place and the people are like as events occur around them. However, there are no extended descriptions. Harte draws swiftly: "that air pungent with balsamic odors," "a fire of withered pine boughs added sociability to the gathering." Through small, quick pictures around the events, the reader remains aware of the forests, the rough camp, the stark diggings. This is all significant, for it is the natural world of the wild country that will carry off the Luck and Kentuck. Nature is a character in the story, not a mere piece of scenery. Thus it is constantly worked into Harte's paragraphs, with a touch here and there. At its best this story gives its readers the presence of the mining camp.

William E. Morris

LULLABY

Author: Leslie Marmon Silko (1948-   )
Type of plot: Lyric
Time of plot: The 1970's
Locale: Near Cebolleta, New Mexico, on the Navajo reservation
First published: 1974

> *Principal characters:*
> AYAH, an old Navajo woman
> CHATO, her husband
> THE BARTENDER AND PATRONS, who can be found in Azzie's Bar

The Story

Ayah sits under a cottonwood watching snow fall and recalling events in her past. The sound of the wind reminds her of the songs of the holy people, the Yeibechei, and the snow is like the tufts of wool that her mother and grandmother wove when she was a little girl. Sitting under an army blanket, a gift from her eldest son, Jimmie, she remembers his birth in a stone hogan. Her mind moves to the day a representative from the government came to the ranch where she and Chato, her husband, were living to tell them about Jimmie's death in combat. The messenger had not understood their wish not to have the body returned. She had not cried at the time but had mourned later, when Chato's horse fell on him, breaking his leg, and the rancher for whom they worked refused to pay Chato again until he could work. She remembers grieving, too, for this eldest son after the two youngest surviving children, Danny and Ella, were taken away from her, evidently because the Bureau of Indian Affairs (BIA) authorities feared that the children might contract tuberculosis. She had tried to foil the agents, hiding all day with the children until the government car left. However, more officials and BIA police had arrived the next day and taken the children: Ayah had unwittingly signed her permission. She remembers resenting Chato for many years, punishing him by keeping her distance, because he had taught her the skill that lost her the children. She realizes that she and Chato are really strangers to each other.

Ayah begins walking toward Azzie's Bar, where Chato usually spends most of their monthly welfare check. She plods slowly through the snow, thinking of him as a stranger. As she enters the bar, she feels the stares of the men inside. She remembers brief visits from Danny and Ella, and how the children gradually became estranged from her, until they saw her with the eyes of strangers and could no longer speak to her in Navajo.

Chato is not in the bar, and Ayah continues her search outside. She intends to take him to the adobe barn where they sleep when they come to the village of Cebolleta; afterward they will return to the old hogan. They will tend the few sheep left and their drought-dried garden. After being displaced by the rancher when Chato was no longer able to ride, and after five years of drought, they have finally been reduced to depending on monthly welfare checks.

Ayah catches up with Chato walking along the pavement, and together they start walking out of town. She thinks about how he is becoming forgetful, calling her by her sister's name and trying to go back to the ranch to work. She suggests that they rest in the shelter of some boulders, and she pulls the blanket around both of them. As they sit there, the storm passes and the sky clears. Ayah feels the crystal air begin to freeze. She resolves to let Chato sleep and tucks the blanket around him. Sitting with him, she feels again intense love for her children. She begins to sing a lullaby that begins by telling the baby that "the earth is your mother, she holds you. The sky is your father, he protects you."

Themes and Meanings

Like elegiac poems, "Lullaby" depicts the process of coming to terms with death and loss. Ayah has much to grieve: the death of her eldest son in an incomprehensible and distant war; the deaths in infancy of other children; the forced removal and then deliberate alienation of her two remaining children; the long estrangement from her husband, Chato.

Intertwined with these human deaths is the great loss of heritage, culture, and way of life. There will be no children and grandchildren to teach and nurture as Ayah had been educated and cared for by her mother and grandmother. Art, religion, language, natural history—all is being lost. Even the sacred compact with the earth seems broken in the persistent drought. Where once the land had produced all that the people needed—wool and bright dyes for strong, waterproof blankets, leather for leggings and shoes, meat hung on the rafters to dry—Ayah and Chato now find themselves reduced to the dull army blanket, boots with holes in them, and a meager welfare check that buys only dead flour and tinned peaches.

The harshness and emptiness of present life is reflected in the human society of strangers surrounding the Navajos. After Jimmy dies, the government can offer nothing for her grief but his corpse. Clinical efficiency rather than feeling or tradition rules in the white world into which Danny and Ella disappear. Fear and hostility similarly characterize the bartender and his patrons, who tolerate Chato only insofar as he is like them—speaking their language. His former employer tolerates Chato only so long as the man can be exploited; when Chato can no longer work, he is discarded like a broken machine.

Ayah makes her peace with loss by removing herself, as far as possible, from this world of hostile strangers and returning to the old life. Living in the house of her mother and grandmother with her husband to tend her flocks, she carries on the matrilineal tradition, though she will be the last of her line to do so. More than a physical return, however, is her spiritual return in thought, as on this snowy journey she relives her losses.

The story depicts her realizing those stages of grief recognized by psychologists: denial, of Jimmie's death ("It wasn't like Jimmie died. He just never came back"); anger, at herself and at Chato for being duped into betraying herself and her children; despair, in the long years of numbing depression and estrangement from Chato and the lost children; and finally, reconciliation and peace.

Reconciliation is bound up with memories of the past as well, and these recollections unite her spiritually with the natural world. The snow recalls the weaving and dyeing that she watched as a child, and she is then drawn to remembrances of childbirth. By the end of the story, those recollections come together in the aching love for her children, and in the words of the lullaby, which tell the child that all the universe is her family and she is related as child and sister to the entire natural world.

Style and Technique

The mode of the story is lyrical. There is only one sentence of direct discourse, and the story's movement follows Ayah's consciousness through association of images as she moves forward in her journey to find Chato while drifting back in thought to earlier days.

The story's imagery relates directly to Navajo traditions and culture. The Yeibechei are spiritual beings, called "holy people." They are powerful individuals who inhabit sacred mountains, springs, and other holy sites, and who are called on in ceremonies, especially rituals for healing the sick or injured. A Yeibechei song is a sacred song, a part of such a healing ritual, and when Ayah hears the wind singing such a song, it signifies that her story may be understood as a healing ritual. The lullaby at the end of the story echoes the form of many healing songs in its structure of verse and repetition as well as in imagery of earth mother and sky father, rainbow sister and wind brother. Ayah's elegy concludes with a return to the healing song and a reconciliation on many levels.

Concepts of return and circularity also recur in Navajo thought and iconography. The hogan is a roughly circular dwelling, constructed as a microcosm of the round earth. Pathways and motion are also important. The ideal life is conceived as a journey along the correct, fruitful, beautiful road, often pictured as a rainbow, which will take the individual back to the original—that is, the perfect—harmonious balance with the universe.

As she follows her path in search of Chato, to bring the two of them back to their earliest and final home, Ayah twice makes inward observations about her and Chato's boots, first comparing her worn rubbers to the beautiful elk and buckskin leggings and moccasins that the people formerly had, then chuckling inwardly at Chato's worn and sock-stuffed boots "like little animals." Animals also figure significantly in Navajo thought and iconography. The comparison of Ayah to a spider is ironic, for while the men at the bar feel contempt for the creature, the spider, often portrayed as Grandmother Spider, is a revered figure of wisdom for the peoples of the Southwest. Life with animals—sheep, goats, horses, and cattle—had sustained the traditional way of life, yet the natural world can be as harsh as the human one: The hawk circling over Ayah and her children as they hide parallels the government authorities who will return inexorably to take the children away. Animals, like the Yeibechei, are neither good nor evil but are terrible in their power: At the end of the story, Ayah sees the clouds as horses in the sky, figures of tremendous beauty and power, bringing strength and death at once.

Helen Jaskoski

LUST

Author: Susan Minot (1956-   )
Type of plot: Social realism
Time of plot: The late 1960's or early 1970's
Locale: New England
First published: 1984

Principal character:
THE NARRATOR, an unnamed adolescent girl who attends an
exclusive private school

The Story

At the age of seventeen or eighteen, the narrator attends Casey Academy, a coed school somewhere in New England. She is a child of privilege who vacations at ski resorts, at summer houses on sunny islands, or on camping trips in Colorado. She is also an active participant in the sexual revolution of the 1960's. She does not fear pregnancy because she has been taking birth control pills since she was fifteen years old. The psychological consequences for this young woman, however, become the important focus of her narration.

She begins by listing and briefly describing sexual encounters with fifteen different boys, starting with Leo in the bottom of an empty swimming pool. With Tim it was in the woods off campus; with Willie it was while she tried to do the dishes; with Eben it was at night on the beach; with Mack it was during the hottest summer ever on an island; with Paul it was in Colorado with their sleeping bags zipped together; with Simon it was in the balcony of the school chapel. She concludes her itemization with Wendel Blair, an experienced lover who knew many expert angles.

During these encounters, the narrator usually is emotionally removed from the experience. For example, when Tim returns to her after closing the door, he finds merely a body waiting on the rug. The boy to whom she is attracted, Philip, does not notice her, and she observes that the less a boy notices her, the more she thinks about him.

The narrator's parents are unaware of her promiscuity and of the unsupervised weekends that she and her friends arrange at their parents' beach houses and unused New York apartments. She is alienated from her parents and teachers, holding them in contempt for their naïveté about who she is and what she does. The school doctor gives out birth control pills like aspirin, with no concern about instructions that should accompany his prescriptions.

The narrator admits that she can do certain things well. As a child, she could play whiffle ball just as well as the boys next door, but the boys still would tie up her ankles until she showed them her underpants. Now she is good at math, painting, even sports, but sex interferes with all these skills and dampens her ambition until, she remarks, "it became like sinking into a muck."

She realizes that casual sex is different for a girl but seems helpless in response to male desire. If she does not look when boys yell at her from cars, they call her a bitch and leave her feeling like she has done something wrong. The worst thing, she believes, is to be called a tease, so she feels compelled to comply. She wants to believe that sleeping with someone is perfectly normal, but she discovers problems. She observes that boys who are quite sexually experienced look brighter and have more stories to tell, but for a girl, "it's like a petal gets plucked each time."

She finds that most boys are completely unself-conscious about the act of sex itself, but she cannot get them to answer her when she asks who they are and what they are thinking. As her narrative comes to a close, she admits to feeling like a piece of veal, overwhelmed by sadness and worry. She continues to do everything that the boys want, but afterward she always feels nameless and unknown. The boys just stare at the ceiling as if the girl were not there anymore, and all she can do is "curl up like a shrimp" with something deep inside "ruined, slammed in a place that sickens at slamming."

Themes and Meanings

Susan Minot's theme explains the painful ambivalence a young woman faces as she becomes part of the sexually active world of the early 1970's. The narrator is unprepared to face the pressure of male desire, and although the birth control pill has liberated her to be able to comply with the sexual lust of her boyfriends, she has no idea of her own sexual needs or how connected they are to emotional intimacy. Minot demonstrates the great divide between male and female desire, and the story's title, "Lust," becomes a key word for exploring the psychological complexities of sexual desire. The sexual roles that a young woman might have played ten years earlier have been dramatically altered with the advent of birth control pills and the loosening of strict supervision. The young people in this story drink often, smoke pot, and have sex with a casualness that would astound their parents. Minot wants to show the psychological dangers of such liberation by giving a detailed look at the emotional harm that ensues when a young woman does not have a clear idea of what she can expect, ask for, or demand before she has sexual intercourse.

Although Minot titles her story "Lust," she is also exploring what it might mean to open the heart. This is what the narrator cannot do; she writes, "You open your legs but can't, or don't dare anymore, to open your heart." Not one of her sexual partners ever says "I love you"; it would undoubtedly sound false if one did—nothing more than a sexual come-on. Nevertheless, the narrator does experience physical lust; she luxuriates in the sensual pleasures the experienced Wendel Blair can provide, "his hands never fumbling, . . . giving an extra hip shove, as if to say *There*." She also is afraid of him and feels ashamed, unable to look him in the eye. For her, intercourse involves becoming completely detached from her body; only in foreplay does she find a hint of tenderness. "After the briskness of loving, loving stops," and she says, "you roll over with death stretched out alongside you." She represses her emotional vulnerability and her need for the secure mesh of emotional intimacy that accompanies female sexual desire, but her repression can be maintained only for so long. She knows she is different from the boys she tries to please. Minot provides little sense of what the future might be for this young woman on the threshold of maturity. Some find the story ominous, deadly; some see it as an example of a young woman's growing self-awareness that will finally lead to integrity and self-control.

Ironically, female students in the 1990's sometimes respond with hostility rather than sympathy to the narrator's plight, even though they might be expected to have the greatest rapport. The story is valuable in that it allows both male and female readers the opportunity to inhabit the consciousness of someone whom they might at first condemn but on reflection can come to see as a lost soul in search of love, not sex. In so doing, readers can explore the differences between male and female desire and the necessity to accept responsibility for the consequences of gratifying those desires.

Style and Technique

The first-person narrator begins by explicitly detailing her sexual encounters. She recounts each rendezvous more like a grocery list than an emotionally charged account of an erotic past. The bland delivery is demonstrative of the narrator's attempt to emotionally distance herself from what has occurred. She wants these fifteen encounters to be "no big deal"; she is mimicking, it appears, a male voice, trying for the nonchalance and bravado that a young man would have as he recounted his sexual conquests. The style is revealing but not introspective.

Despite intentions to remain emotionally removed from her story, the narrator subtly moves into self-reflection. She is searching and, at the same time, languishing in sorrow. This more honest tone takes over the story as her mood becomes confessional, revealing pain and loneliness rather than a flat recounting. Minot wants readers to see that for this unhappy narrator, self-awareness follows and is a consequence of impetuous, self-damaging actions.

The plot follows conventional methods. The characters are skillfully delineated in the exposition; the central conflict lies within the narrator herself as she uses her body to gain intimacy and only later realizes that this supposed sexual freedom is, in fact, exacting a heavy price. The reader is taken steadily toward a moment of truthfulness, when the narrator finally reveals just how lonely, used, and tired she feels. The story ends abruptly, and not with a denouement that satisfies and leaves one believing she will get better. Readers are left wondering if she has learned enough from what she has revealed to understand that her actions are self-destructive and there is a need for change.

Janet M. Ellerby

LYUBKA THE COSSACK

Author: Isaac Babel (1894-1940)
Type of plot: Symbolist
Time of plot: About 1914
Locale: Odessa, Russia
First published: "Lyubka Kazak," 1924 (English translation, 1955)

> *Principal characters:*
> LYUBKA SHNEIVEIS (THE COSSACK), a proprietess of an inn
> TSUDECHKIS, a broker, and later the manager of Lyubka's inn
> LITTLE DAVE, Lyubka's infant son
> MR. TROTTYBURN, the chief engineer on the *Plutarch*
> THE UNNAMED NARRATOR

The Story

"Lyubka the Cossack" is set in Moldavanka, the thieves' district of Odessa, the city where Isaac Babel lived after 1905. Although the narrator could be equated with the author, he plays no role in the action. His manner of storytelling, however, is highly colorful, so that the reader is continually reminded of his presence. The narrator becomes a separate, quaintly jocular persona who in fact acts as a substitute for the author. This special persona is to be found in all the stories, of which "Lyubka the Cossack" is one, making up the collection *Odesskie rasskazy* (1931; *Tales of Odessa*, 1955). The narrator informs the reader that his point in telling the story is to reveal how old Tsudechkis got the job of manager of the inn owned by Lyubka, who is nicknamed the Cossack. It is clear, however, that the author has the additional intent of portraying the colorful Moldavanka Jews and the exotic seaport itself.

The tale begins with the information that Tsudechkis has negotiated a sale to a landowner and then brought him to Lyubka's inn. The landowner enjoyed a meal and a girl—and skipped at dawn without paying. Tsudechkis is therefore asked to pay the six rubles. He refuses, however, and is locked up in Lyubka's room by the watchman Yevzel. Tsudechkis declares that God will free him as He led the Jews out of Egypt and out of the wilderness. Later he laments that he is in the "hands of Pharaoh."

From a window, Tsudechkis sees the procuress, Pesya-Mindl, minding Lyubka's baby, Little Dave, and reading a book about the Hasidic Jews. The baby is squalling. Tsudechkis learns that Lyubka has gone for the day and that the baby—already "as big as a Rooski-boy"—will take milk only from his mother's breast.

When Lyubka finally returns in the afternoon, Tsudechkis screams at her from his prison to have pity on the child and feed it. Lyubka pulls out her monstrous breast; the baby sucks at the nipple but finds no milk. Lyubka has been running all over town in the broiling heat. How could there be any milk? Essentially indifferent to the child, Lyubka leaves—but not before asking Tsudechkis one more time for the six rubles. Again he refuses, so Lyubka locks the door behind her.

Awaiting her in the yard is Mr. Trottyburn, the chief engineer on the *Plutarch*. He has brought with him two sailors, one an Englishman and the other a Malay. They have dragged into the yard a heavy box of contraband from Port Said: "cigars and fine silks, cocaine and files, unbonded tobacco from the State of Virginia, and dark wine from the Island of Chios." They make a deal on the goods and then get drunk. Late at night, the three visitors return to their ship, as an "orange star which has slid to the very brim of the horizon gazed wide-eyed at them."

Lyubka returns to her room, where Tsudechkis is rocking Dave's cradle with his bare toes. When Lyubka lies down to sleep, Tsudechkis places the infant beside her and a fine-toothed comb against her breast. When the baby tries to get milk he pricks himself and begins to cry. Tsudechkis quickly gives it a bottle. Within a few minutes the baby is feeding from the bottle on its own. When the sleepy Lyubka realizes that Dave has been weaned, she frees Tsudechkis. The next day she not only gives him a pound of tobacco and some tea but also makes him the manager of her inn.

Themes and Meanings

One of the more obvious themes of the story concerns role reversal. Tsudechkis is a frail little man, perhaps classifiable as a schlemiel—a loser. He plays a woman's role in his weakness, his manipulativeness, and his knowledge of how to soothe a baby to sleep, how to wean it—while the giantess Lyubka is masculine in her size, her business dealings, her indifference toward her child, and her complete sexual dominance. Interestingly, she still remains somehow sexy. The strong, big-busted woman is a type to which the author Babel seems attracted; at the same time he may see himself as Tsudechkis—the weak intellectual who must use trickery to survive.

At a deeper level, these characters carry more interesting meanings. Because of his remarks on being held in captivity ("in the hands of the Pharaoh"), Tsudechkis represents the traditional Jew who places hope in God to free him from bondage. Pesya-Mindl's interest in the heretical Jewish sect of Hasidism, founded by the messianic Baal Shem Tov in the eighteenth century, speaks to a yearning for the immediate appearance of a Messiah who will save the Jews. Lyubka's Yiddish surname, Shneiveis (which ironically means "Snowwhite"), testifies that she is Jewish but at the same time she is half-Russian (or Christian). For example, her sobriquet, "Cossack," is obviously Russian, and her first name is also Russian: Lyubka is the diminutive of "Lyubov," which means "love."

Lyubka's son Dave, whose father is not named (or known), bears the name of royal Jewish lineage (the narrator once refers to him as "a child like a little star"—alluding to the Star of David), but he is also said to be as "big as a Rooski-boy." This child who is both Jewish and Russian (so to speak) has a mother who is not only both Jewish and Russian but also both prostitute and virgin (so to speak, keeping in mind her surname implying purity). She is a strongly mythic and symbolic figure.

On retracing this story "about Tsudechkis," one can note that the action takes place in an inn. To that inn come three exotic men from far away bearing "gifts" of silk, tobacco, wine, and cocaine. Should there be any doubt that these sailors stand, however ironically or blasphemously, for the Three Magi, the author erases it with his description of the single orange star that has slid to the horizon—recalling the star of Bethlehem. In this context, Tsudechkis becomes Joseph (he cares for the child without being its actual father) and Pesya-Mindl stands for Salome, Mary's midwife.

Thus, while Lyubka is a whore and a dealer in contraband, she is also a symbolic madonna who has given birth to a new Messiah, badly needed by the Jews. The baby David is not meant to repeat the role of Jesus but to symbolize the hope that the new generation of Jews (born after the Russian Revolution) will be truly emancipated.

This entire symbolic story is couched in such comic and irreverent language that it cannot be taken fully seriously. Nevertheless, it is a remarkable artistic accomplishment—that such an allegory could be so cleverly concealed beneath the commonplace cover story of "how Tsudechkis got the job as manager of Lyubka's inn." Babel's accomplishment was not achieved casually: He revised this story twenty-two times before publishing it.

Style and Technique

"Lyubka the Cossack," like the other stories in *Odessa Tales*, is written in a highly ornamental and hyperbolic style. It is lyrical, jocular, comic, occasionally even epic in its tone. Most of the characters, Lyubka especially, are painted in mythic proportions. This, together with the exaggerated locutions of the narrator, facilitates the weaving of an allegory between the lines of the main story. However, Babel's ornamental prose also exists for its own sake. Much of his imagery seems simply to celebrate the ecstasy of the poet who sees clearly (by transforming reality) what the ordinary person is not even aware of. For example, there are the images of the sun, the heat of the day, and the moon: The sun "climbed to the middle of the sky and hung there quivering like a fly overcome by the heat." The world is "filled with golden flies and the blue lightning-flashes of July." "The sun lolled from the sky like the pink tongue of a thirsty dog." "Day sat in a gaily-painted coracle, day sailed on toward evening," and there is "a moon that skipped through black clouds like a stray calf."

Such striking images as these seem to make no special contribution to meaning or symbolism, nor does the following remarkable description of the drunken Malay sailor: "His tender yellow eyes hung suspended above the table like paper lamps in a Chinese alley." Nor does that of Mr. Trottyburn, who is described as "a man like a pillar of russet meat."

However, such images contribute to the overall ironic tone of the story, with its continual juxtaposition of opposites and its merry blasphemy in treating religion. Most memorable is the portrait of Lyubka as whore and madonna—a perception of the human sexual condition that first crept into Russian literature through Dmitry and Grushenka in Fyodor Dostoevski's *Bratya Karamazovy* (1879-1880; *The Brothers Karamazov*, 1912).

Donald M. Fiene

MADAME CÉLESTIN'S DIVORCE

Author: Kate Chopin (1850-1904)
Type of plot: Regional, sketch
Time of plot: The 1890's
Locale: Natchitoches Parish, Louisiana
First published: 1894

Principal characters:
MADAME CÉLESTIN, a Creole housewife and mother of two
    children
MR. PAXTON, a lawyer

The Story

"Madame Célestin's Divorce" relates several brief encounters between the title character and a lawyer, Mr. Paxton, through an omniscient narrator. The plot revolves around Paxton's growing infatuation with the very attractive Madame Célestin, while he counsels her to divorce Célestin, her abusive husband. As is typical in most of Kate Chopin's writing, the characters' emotional situations, as well as their regional idiosyncrasies, direct the outcome of the plot.

The story begins with a description of Madame Célestin, a young Creole housewife, busy with her daily morning task, which is sweeping her front steps and patio. She is prettily attired in a calico wrapper with a pink bow at her throat. Mr. Paxton passes her house on the way to his law office and stops to chat with Madame, whose charm and beauty do not escape his notice.

Madame Célestin is an open, talkative, woman who is not afraid to express her opinion or discuss her personal problems. The whole town is aware of how much she suffers at the hands of her husband, who drinks and has been absent for nearly six months. To support herself and her two children, she takes in sewing and gives music lessons. Paxton, appalled by this neglect and aware that Célestin has also beaten her, advises her to seek a divorce. She agrees that her husband's treatment of her is shameful and seriously entertains the idea of ending her marriage.

After a few days, Paxton asks Madame Célestin if she has thought more carefully about divorce. She tells him she does want one but faces serious opposition from her family, which is firmly against a divorce for religious reasons. Her mother tells her that she will bring shame on the family and sends her to seek advice from the priest. Paxton worries that she will lose her resolve in the face of these powerful persuasive forces, but she assures him that, indeed, their protests make her even more determined. Even a tearful visit with the bishop, who remonstrates that she is obligated to practice self-denial, does not dissuade her. She assures Paxton that because no one can understand what she has endured, no one can force her to stay married to her neglectful husband.

Encouraged by her resolve, Paxton allows his feelings for the pretty and vivacious Madame to surface. He spends the next few days improving his appearance, while contemplating what life will be like when they are married. He realizes that the Creole community would not condone her divorce and remarriage but believes they could be happy elsewhere. Paxton's hopes are dashed one morning, when, stopping for his usual chat, he finds Madame more reserved and less self-assured than on previous meetings. He notices, however, that her complexion seems rosier than ever. She tells Paxton that she has changed her mind about the divorce. Célestin, its seems, returned the night before and has promised, once again, to reform and be a good husband.

Themes and Meanings

In "Madame Célestin's Divorce," Chopin explores one of her perennial themes: a woman's struggle between the constraints a closed society places on her versus her quest for self-identity. As in most of Chopin's work, that struggle is situated in Louisiana's Creole community, which differs greatly from nineteenth century mainstream Anglo-American society. The barriers between these two cultures often produce conflicts for the characters, who are at odds with themselves and one another.

Madame Célestin's vivaciousness, mild flirtatiousness, honesty, and self-sufficient attitude reflect the more relaxed gender roles among the French Creoles, which allowed a certain frankness between men and women about personal matters. The general openness among Creoles is best expressed by Madame's daily public appearance dressed in what amounts to a robe or housecoat. The close-knit Creole community supported Madame and her children by giving her work when her husband all but deserted her. In addition, it remained nonjudgmental about her marital problems or her friendship with Paxton. Nevertheless, Madame is restricted from following her natural instincts to free herself from Célestin because of her strong ties to that same community. Her family and her religion forbid divorce; more important, she retains certain emotional and conjugal attachments to her husband, despite the fact he is a reprobate. Madame must also consider her maternal obligations to her two children.

As a divorced woman, Madame would most likely lose custody of those children. She would be forced to flee from her home and her friends to live among strangers, most likely married this time to Paxton. In addition, whether she realizes it or not, Paxton sees Madame as a trophy, something he can claim as a pretty prize, not as an individual with her own identity. In fact, he knows next to nothing about her as a woman or a person. His inability to understand her position as a Creole wife and mother leads him to misunderstand both her firm resolve to divorce Célestin and her overnight change of heart.

Ultimately, as in Chopin's masterpiece *The Awakening* (1899), Madame would be exchanging roles if she divorced her husband and married Paxton, not necessarily achieving independence or self-identity. Although her counterpart in the novel, Edna Pontellier, chooses suicide as a means of escape, Madame makes the less dramatic choice to accept her place within her community.

The end remains ambiguous. Madame has once again submitted to her husband's authority by accepting his promise to reform. The even rosier color that Paxton notices in her cheek may indicate a deep blush of embarrassment because she has given up the idea of divorce, disappointing both the lawyer and herself. However, her color may also express a deep contentment, no doubt sexual in nature, that her husband has returned home and life might now offer all she can hope for. Either way, Chopin's overarching theme remains a woman's lack of autonomy in the face of cultural and social obligations.

Style and Technique

"Madame Célestin's Divorce" is a very short story tightly packed with descriptions and dialogue that reveal a variety of details about the main characters. Chopin is considered a regional writer, and her setting often plays as important a role in the story as do her characters. In "The Storm" (1898), for example, the onset of a hurricane propels two former lovers to rekindle their affair in an isolated cabin, while the woman's husband and son are stranded in town. Although no such atmospheric disturbance occurs in "Madame Célestin's Divorce," its setting in north central Louisiana, where Chopin once lived with her husband and six children, introduces characters that are unique to a specific place and time in American history.

As a resident of Natchitoches Parish, Chopin developed a fine ear for the local dialect and a keen insight into the characteristics of the Creole community. Madame Célestin's conversation sparkles with idiosyncratic diction and French sayings that charm Paxton, whose speech is noticeably more monotonous and didactic. Madame Célestin's language is expressive, dynamic, and forthright, revealing an honest, passionate woman unafraid to possess or express her opinion. Charmed by her wit and wisdom, Paxton, an outsider to the Creole community, does not realize that Madame's honest outbursts are as subject to change as the very nature that produces them. This misunderstanding reveals the cultural barriers that separate the impetuous Creole woman from the more conventional, reserved Paxton. Her abrupt decision to stay with her husband, accompanied by a rosy blush on her cheeks, baffles the lawyer, but remains consistent with Madame's ability to adapt to whatever situation is at hand.

The story's physical setting, Madame's yard planted with rose bushes, does not change. Madame never strays beyond her front gate, which represents both her literal and figurative separation from Paxton and the outside world. A fence always stands between the anxious lawyer and his would-be client. Madame wields her broom expertly, as she complains about the household duties that keep her so busy. Nevertheless, her domestic ties are undeniable. The rose bushes that adorn her garden symbolize Madame's delicate beauty as well as her thorny exterior. The roses also serve as another barrier between Paxton and Madame, specifically when it is a rosy blush in her cheek that indicates her husband has again regained his place within the home. While Paxton dreams of their life together in the wide, wide world, Madame remains contained, if not exactly content, within her fenced-in yard. Thus, Chopin's setting underscores the story's main theme of a woman who is trapped by her environment, willing to contemplate, but ultimately unable, to face the unknown.

Rebecca Dunn Jaroff

MADAME TELLIER'S ESTABLISHMENT

Author: Guy de Maupassant (1850-1893)
Type of plot: Psychological
Time of plot: 1881
Locale: Fecamp and Virville (Normandy)
First published: "La Maison Tellier," 1881 (English translation, 1903)

> *Principal characters:*
> MADAME TELLIER, patroness of the establishment
> FERNANDE,
> RAPHAELLE,
> ROSA THE JADE,
> LOUISE, and
> FLORA, her employees
> MONSIEUR RIVET, her brother

The Story

The events of this story unfold in four easily distinguishable scenes. The first scene describes the location and decor of the establishment and introduces the principal characters. The brothel, a small old house, is located in the town of Fecamp; it is situated behind a church, and from its windows the old chapel dedicated to the Virgin is readily visible. The interior consists of two levels, each with its own separate entrance. The downstairs contains a café of sorts in one corner, with old marble tables on which drinks are placed; it is restricted to those frequenters of lower rank who are quite boisterous and crude. The upper level, or salon of Jupiter, is all blue and boasts a large drawing of Leda stretched out under the swan. Above the entrance, a small lamp burns all night, similar to those that keep vigil over the sanctuary in a church. This level is reserved for the gentlemen who are engaged in trading, government work, or other forms of "respectable" employment. Madame Tellier is the patroness of this brothel. She is cheerful, well liked, and virtuous, in spite of her profession. Of her permanent staff, Fernande, Raphaelle, and Rosa the Jade work on the upper level; Louise and Flora work on the ground floor. Each is supposed to represent the incarnation of a particular feminine type, so that every customer may realize the vision of his ideal. This scene concludes as some of the regular patrons find the house closed because Madame Tellier and her employees are journeying to the country town of Virville to attend the confirmation of Madame Tellier's niece Constance.

The second scene recounts the train journey from Fecamp to Virville and the variety of people Madame Tellier and her entourage encounter along the way. First they share their carriage with a peasant couple who bear a strong resemblance to the three ducks they carry with them; they are awed by the sight of the women dressed in their colorful costumes. Then, a commercial traveler who is well aware of their occupation joins them. He offers free garters to any of the women who will try them on; all of them oblige immediately. They finally arrive in Virville, where they are met by Madame Tellier's brother, Monsieur Rivet, and escorted to his home.

The events of the third segment unfold in Monsieur Rivet's home and in the church. When Madame Tellier and her group arrive at her brother's home, preparations for the confirmation are well under way, and all the women eagerly participate. The next day, dressed in all of their finery, they attend the confirmation ceremony. The religious ambience and the ceremony itself provoke an unexpected display of emotion from the women of Madame Tellier's establishment. They weep uncontrollably and unashamedly as they are overcome by recollections of their youth, when they, too, participated in this ceremony all dressed in white. After the service, they proceed to Monsieur Rivet's home for a dinner celebration. He behaves in a most ungentlemanly manner toward some of his sister's employees, for which he is severely chastised. The events of this segment draw to a close as Monsieur Rivet escorts his guests to the train station for their departure.

The fourth scene unfolds with the return journey to Fecamp. News of their arrival spreads rapidly, and soon the house resounds with activity. It is an unusually festive evening, the highlight of which occurs when Madame Tellier and Monsieur Vassi, her platonic courtier, come to a new understanding. The merriment continues until the early morning hours and concludes as Madame Tellier generously assumes the costs for most of the evening's entertainment.

Themes and Meanings

The most salient theme of this story is that of the power of religion. The brief description of the confirmation ceremony is a most poignant one, especially as it relates to the women of Madame Tellier's establishment and to women in general.

The religious ambience, provided by the confirmation ceremony itself and its symbolic associations, causes the women of Madame Tellier's establishment to become emotionally overpowered by recollections of their own childhoods. Rosa begins to weep silently as she remembers when she herself participated in this ceremony wearing a white dress. She begins to think of her own mother and the feelings of love, security, and comfort that emanate from mother to child during this most innocent stage of life. She also reminisces about her own village church, surrounded by familiar faces of loved ones. As more and more memories of the past sweep before her eyes, her sobs become uncontrollable. Her other companions, including Madame Tellier, succumb to the force of similar remembrances and share her anguish. The first members of the congregation to be touched by this genuine display of emotion and to share their sympathy are women—wives, mothers, and sisters—creating a momentary bond of solidarity among them. In an instant, the whole congregation, including the priest, is reduced to tears.

Style and Technique

The most effective stylistic tool used in this story is that of contrast. The story abounds with comic episodes, so that by contrast the one solemn and emotional scene during the confirmation ceremony becomes even more stirring and significant. There are also frequent juxtapositions of religion and prostitution throughout the story. The brothel is located behind a church with a view of the chapel dedicated to the Virgin; the night lamp that burns outside the brothel is compared to a sanctuary lamp in a church. The journey motif, which allows the plot to unfold in two locales, provides further examples of contrast. The fragrant air and religious silence of the countryside are in direct opposition to the damp and noisy atmosphere of the town.

Dramatic irony is also very much present. The first situation involves the innocent villagers, who are unable to recognize prostitutes when they see them and thus treat the far-from-innocent visitors with solemn deference. The second instance takes place during the scene between Constance and Rosa. The child, unaccustomed to sleeping alone, begins to cry. Rosa comforts her and brings the innocent child to her bed, where she showers her with great displays of affection, until the child falls asleep on her bosom. During the religious ceremony itself, the assembly of God, led by the priest, and the assembly of prostitution, led by Madame Tellier, are momentarily united during an emotional moment, which gives these women a human dimension and provides psychological insight into their feelings and emotions. Their fond recollections are in direct contrast to their present lives. The effect produced by counterposing religion and prostitution is that each loses its negative stereotype and the two unite in a moment of psychological and emotional affinity.

Anne Laura Mattrella

MADAME ZILENSKY AND THE KING OF FINLAND

Author: Carson McCullers (1917-1967)
Type of plot: Psychological
Time of plot: The 1940's
Locale: Ryder College, in upstate New York
First published: 1941

> *Principal characters:*
> MR. BROOK, the quietly competent head of the music department
>   at Ryder College
> MADAME ZILENSKY, an eccentric music composer and college
>   teacher
> BORIS,
> SAMMY, and
> SIGMUND ZILENSKY, her sons by previous husbands

The Story

Mr. Brook, the head of the music department at Ryder College in upstate New York, has hired a woman who will be, he is sure, a very valuable acquisition for his department: Madame Zilensky, whose European credentials are most impressive. Not only does she have a solid reputation as a composer of symphonies but also she is well-known as a fine music teacher. As her immediate superior, Mr. Brook kindly takes it on himself to find for her a house near the college—and, by chance, next door to his apartment.

When he meets her for the first time, he sees a tall, tired woman, shabbily dressed, who is accompanied by her three young sons (Boris, Sammy, and Sigmund) and a Finnish servant. From the beginning, once she starts her teaching tasks, Mr. Brook is uneasy about Madame Zilensky and her children. The boys speak a polyglot language (made up of fragments of Russian, French, German, and other languages), and they will not walk on rugs, simply refusing to go inside rooms that are fully carpeted.

More particularly, weeks after the Zilensky family has supposedly moved in, there is no evidence that the house—whose front door is always open—is inhabited. In fact, Mr. Brook thinks that it looks much like a house that has been abandoned for years.

With regard to Madame Zilensky's professional work, Mr. Brook is very satisfied. She teaches with unbounded energy and verve, giving over considerable time to her students. Somehow she has acquired four pianos for her college studio and has made great strides in teaching piano technique. At night, every night (and, it seems, at any hour of the night), Mr. Brook sees the light on in her home studio. She is diligently composing her twelfth symphony. It occurs to him that she does not seem to sleep.

Carson McCullers is careful in "Madame Zilensky and the King of Finland" to make the reader aware of some very real differences between Mr. Brook and his new colleague. He is self-assured, carrying out both his administrative and his teaching tasks in a competent and quiet manner, though he detests the bureaucracy of college life. There is no genuine excitement in Mr. Brook's life; it is an existence that is highly organized, one in which routine is paramount. His music, his college duties, and an occasional summer trip are his whole life. (One summer, years earlier, quite uncharacteristically, he went off to Peru for a vacation by himself, although the entire department had made plans to band together in Salzburg for the summer.) His one concession to eccentricity is that he is tolerant of the offbeat behavior of others. Indeed, in those situations in which he is confronted with absurdity, he is secretly titillated. On balance, however, Mr. Brook is order and restraint personified. McCullers describes him in a single phrase: "a somewhat pastel person." In a painter's terms, Mr. Brook is a man of soft hues.

Having been careful to describe Mr. Brook as a man of system and propriety, McCullers, on the other hand, depicts Madame Zilensky as a woman who is driven by her work, a woman whose life is in a sense volatile and chaotic. What she shares with Mr. Brook, however, is solitude. He is at his mellowest when he is alone in his study at home by the fire, sipping brandy and reading poetry. He has no family, no female companion, no close friends. She has her sons—and her work. Apparently there is nothing more in life for her. The crisis in this tale arises over Mr. Brook's painfully profound discovery of how Madame Zilensky compensates for such a one-dimensional life.

The crisis is initiated several months into her tenure at the college. When Mr. Brook and she converse from time to time, she relates events and episodes in such a way that he finds himself puzzled at first, and then uneasy. What is unsettling about her conversation is that he has difficulty understanding what she is relating to him. For example, she tells him of having taken Sammy to the barbershop the afternoon before, a mundane event, surely, yet her narrative makes the trip an afternoon's adventure in Baghdad or some other exotic location. At first he thinks that the confusion is on his part: that she has, in fact, been retelling an episode that took place in Europe some years ago. That is not true, he soon discovers; she has indeed been detailing the circumstances of Sammy's haircut.

Mystified by this, Mr. Brook begins to recall the various stories she has told him recently, and he becomes more mystified. Late one night after his brandy, in a moment of Joycean epiphany, he comes to a full understanding, he thinks, of what she has been doing: Madame Zilensky is a compulsive liar. This revelation is prompted by his recollection of a preposterous story she had told him the day before, about once having seen the king of Finland going by her in a sled. Finland, he recalls, is a democracy; it does not have a king. His immediate reaction is one of irritation and exasperation. Calming down, however, he begins in a scholarly way to analyze her behavior. Her lies have no guile in them, he thinks; she does not intend to deceive; and there is no advantage to her in advancing such foolish stories. What is most troubling is, why does she do this?

Two hours later he knows why. His estimate of the whole situation is a simple and plausible one. Her life is given over to work—unendingly. There is no time for anything else: "Through the lies, she lived vicariously. The lies doubled the little of her existence that was left over from work and augmented the little rag end of her personal life."

Early the next morning, he confronts her with the facts of her habitual mendacity. She steadfastly stands by her story: She saw the king herself. She insists on the truthfulness of her eyewitness account; he persists in calling it an absolute lie. When he sees a peculiar pain on her face, he thinks of himself as a murderer, that he is killing part of her. Mr. Brook relents and chats amiably with her about the nonexistent king of Finland.

Themes and Meanings

Two of McCullers's characteristic themes are to be found in "Madame Zilensky and the King of Finland": that solitude is inescapable and, more often than not, is the cause of unhappiness; and that a life without illusions (whether one calls them dreams or lies) is unbearable. Both these themes are illustrated in the life of Madame Zilensky. Her capacity for work and her energy for work are admirable traits in very substantive ways, but they are also traits that make for the kind of wretched and lonely life in which she is caught up. As McCullers says in so many ways in her fiction, in, for example, *The Heart Is a Lonely Hunter* (1940), *Reflections in a Golden Eye* (1941), "The Ballad of the Sad Café"—indeed, in almost every story she wrote: Love is the very core of a human's being; without it, a person is nothing. Without it, one must fall back on one's illusions, dreams, or (in the case of Madame Zilensky) lies.

In other words, Madame Zilensky's parochial existence has not allowed any love into her life, beyond that which she feels for her music and her sons. McCullers would argue that that is not enough. Her solitude is of the worst kind. It is the solitude of loneliness. Rather than disintegrating, as some of McCullers's characters do, Madame Zilensky resorts to a form of childish behavior—lying. She renders her solitude more bearable through the medium of her untruths. From McCullers's description of her lies, it would seem that for the most part they are unimportant—and they do not advance her or any cause of hers in any way. Perhaps she deems them to have some special significance for her, but for her auditors, such as Mr. Brook, the fabrications are merely outrageous. The absurdity of the continual lying is compounded by the fact that her lies are so transparent—so easily recognized for what they are. In the end, McCullers is making a statement about an obsession of hers. A life of illusions may be unpardonable for some, but for the Madame Zilenskys of the world, a life without those sustaining lies is unbearable. That is why Mr. Brook's righteousness changes instantaneously to compassion: He has read that message on Madame Zilensky's fearful face.

Style and Technique

Like many of McCullers's stories, "Madame Zilensky and the King of Finland" is narrated almost exclusively from the point of view of one particular character—in this story, Mr. Brook. Thus, what the reader knows of Madame Zilensky is filtered through

Mr. Brook's consciousness; the reader can know only what Mr. Brook knows or surmises about Madame Zilensky. The reader is thus forced, in a sense, to accept Mr. Brook's interpretation of Madame Zilensky's motive for dissembling. Actually, however, Mr. Brook arrives at the reason he does (that she lies in order to render the vacant expanses of her soul more habitable) because in her he sees his own life—carried to an extreme. In his view, she is a woman who is so obsessed with her work that there are no free hours in the day. Mr. Brook does have his quiet hours at night, with his brandy and his poetry book; he envisions none of that in her life: "All her life long Madame Zilensky had worked—at the piano, teaching, and writing those beautiful and immense twelve symphonies. Day and night she had drudged and struggled and thrown her soul into her work, and there was not much of her left over for anything else."

However, as different as Mr. Brook and Madame Zilensky are, they are in an unlikely way bound together in their respective solitude, in their unshared desolation. He has recognized in her a soul mate of sorts: a lonely human being. This is brought forcibly home to the reader when McCullers writes that, at the moment Mr. Brook sees the pain on Madame Zilensky's face (when he accuses her of lying boldly and without shame): "A great commotion of feelings—understanding, remorse, and unreasonable love—made him cover his face with his hands." That "unreasonable love" is what Mr. Brook feels for a woman who must resort to lying in order to bear the burden of living. Recognizing that a life without those lies is unbearable for her, he will not be the agent of her undoing. After all, her falsehoods are harmless to others and essential to her, performing a valuable function as she goes from day to day: They nourish an otherwise emotionally arid existence; they provide a kind of grace for an otherwise graceless life. She has her music, her boys—and nothing else, except the lies. Mr. Brook becomes quite sure that the truth can kill.

Gerald R. Griffin

MA'DEAR

Author: Terry McMillan (1951-   )
Type of plot: Impressionistic
Time of plot: The 1980's
Locale: The southeastern United States
First published: 1990

> *Principal characters:*
> Ma'Dear, a seventy-two-year-old African American widow
> Jessie, her deceased husband
> The caseworker
> Clarabelle, her neighbor who works in the caseworker's office
> Gunther, her friend who lives in a nursing home
> Thelma, Jessie's niece

The Story

In a grammatically incorrect narrative that ambles through the past and the present, Ma'Dear, the principal character who is not otherwise identified by name, justifies renting rooms in her house to supplement her income and explains that her present single state is not intentional. She introduces herself as a widow of thirty-two years whose husband Jessie was and is without peer. She tried to find a replacement for Jessie but was unsuccessful. Whimpy Davis was crazy, Chester Rutledge was boring, and Bill Ronsonville was a rough lover. She has reconciled herself to being alone and amuses herself by sitting in the park, where she ponders death, eavesdrops on conversations, adds up numbers on license plates, and goes to the matinee if the lines are not slowed by senior citizens.

Although she thinks about death, she insists that she does not dwell on it. A more pressing concern is an imminent visit from the caseworker from whom Ma'Dear hides evidence of revenue beyond her Social Security income. Ma'Dear is convinced that the caseworker's visit has been prompted by Clarabelle, a neighbor whom Ma'Dear considers nosy and envious. Ma'Dear believes that Clarabelle, who works in the caseworker's office, had noticed delivery trucks at Ma'Dear's house and sent the caseworker to spy. The trucks were delivering replacements for a couch and a boiler. Willamae, Jessie's sister, had borrowed the money for the boiler for Ma'Dear, whose own bank would not give her a loan. The bank, however, frequently sends letters offering to refinance her house at a higher rate of interest. Ma'Dear blames the bank's incessant letters, with questions about the effect of her death on family finances, for her preoccupation with death.

Her financial situation does not permit many extravagances—some potato chips, ice cream, and pork chops. She relies on Social Security and the roomers' rent for income. Medicaid pays her medical expenses. She attempted to apply for food stamps but became frustrated and gave up after repeated efforts. She is, however, conscientious about her diet. She remembers that when she was young she worried about eating too many sweets for fear of gaining weight and developing cellulite. The young Ma'Dear's teeth were bright, straight, and white; she looked healthy and attracted the attention of many men. Connie Curtis would curl her hair for a dollar and a beer. The aging Ma'Dear has no teeth, and her skin sags.

She contends that she does not miss being young, having done everything she wanted to do as a girl. She does not understand the choices that today's young people, especially the girls, make. For example, Jessie's niece Thelma did not finish high school, has three children, has never been married, and is on welfare. Ma'Dear never had any children. She believes that Jessie was at fault, but she does not really care because she did not want to share him with anyone. Although she does not regret being childless, she does regret her lack of education. With an education and her sense of style, she would have become an interior decorator.

Although she still misses and often thinks of Jessie—who was her companion, friend, and lover—after thirty-two years, Ma'Dear has other friends. Some are dead. Others are chronically ill or living in nursing homes, an unpleasant prospect for her. She does not like being around sick people, but she visits her friends who are in nursing homes. She repeats, as she has throughout her narrative, that she does not mind growing older. She does mind the solitude; it depresses her. Thelma is the only person who remembers her birthday.

Her thoughts turn to the caseworker's visit for which she must hide evidence of her roomers. She decides first to take a bubble bath, make a cup of tea, and paint her nails. She will postpone preparation for the caseworker, and weather permitting, after the caseworker leaves, she will go to a museum and look at new pictures. For the caseworker, she will pretend to be a lonely widow who is awaiting death.

Themes and Meanings

Ma'Dear's solitude permeates the story. Although the solitude is unwanted, Ma'Dear has chosen it for the thirty-two years following the death of her husband, Jessie. Her efforts to find a man exactly like her deceased husband were doomed from the outset, and the men with whom she had engaged in relationships were patently unsuitable. Her friends—with the possible exception of Gunther, whose relationship to her is unexplained—are those of her childhood. They live in nursing homes and are not free to visit her. Although she mentions saving money for her church's cross-country bus trip, there is no indication that she is involved with members of her church. She rents rooms to three people who are at home so seldom that Ma'Dear can convince the caseworker that she lives alone.

Even in the midst of other people, Ma'Dear remains wrapped in her cocoon of solitude. She participates in confidential conversations by eavesdropping. Her knowledge of out-of-town visitors is gleaned from observing license plates. She goes to matinees if the lines are not slowed by too many senior citizens. She learns about the habits of young people from conversations she overhears at the beauty shop.

Paradoxically, her most intimate relationship appears to be with the unnamed caseworker whom Ma'Dear believes is interested in learning about the roomers in order to reduce her Social Security income. Ma'Dear expends a lot of thought and energy on the caseworker—deceiving her, imagining her affluence, and assuming that the caseworker resents Ma'Dear's low mortgage.

As the story ends, Ma'Dear seems to be beginning to emerge from the unwanted solitude to which she attributes her melancholia. At the same time, she is becoming comfortable with some aspects of the solitude, deciding to treat herself to a bubble bath, a cup of hot tea, and a manicure, despite the impending visit of the caseworker, the nameless character with whom Ma'Dear is becoming less preoccupied.

Style and Technique

Terry McMillan uses style and technique to reinforce the theme of Ma'Dear's solitude, sometimes taking literary license to do so. The term "Ma'Dear" is a truncated endearment for "Mother Dear." In African American families, the appellation typically is applied to mothers, grandmothers, great-grandmothers, and other beloved females who display maternal characteristics. Not only does Ma'Dear in this story have no children, there is no indication that she is maternal. She lavishes her love on a man who has been dead for thirty-two years. The only children mentioned in the story are those of Thelma, Jessie's niece, who is not comfortable with leaving the children in Ma'Dear's care for long periods of time.

Ma'Dear's isolation is emphasized further by McMillan's failure to assign the principal character a first or last name. The only other character with no first or last name is the caseworker toward whom Ma'Dear directs much of her time and energy.

The sparseness and context of dialogue also are telling. There are only eight lines of quoted text. Two are contained in Ma'Dear's fantasy about having pursued a career as an interior decorator. Five are part of a conversation with Gunther, a nursing home resident, and concern his grandson. Two of the quoted lines are with the caseworker.

Perhaps to underscore Ma'Dear's solitude and her intense relationship with the unnamed caseworker, McMillan confers stereotypical characteristics on the caseworker. She further stresses Ma'Dear's isolation in describing the character's ability to overhear conversations while under the hair dryer in the beauty salon. McMillan would have the reader believe that Ma'Dear is so removed figuratively from other people that she has honed her auditory sense so sharply that she can overhear conversations under a commercial bonnet hair dryer.

Ma'Dear's emergence from the self-imposed isolation that depresses her is forecast in the final paragraph of the story. After the caseworker leaves, Ma'Dear plans to go to a museum and look at new paintings. The reader is left to wonder whether during this visit the caseworker will find a lonely old widow who is merely waiting to die.

Ann Marie Depas

MADEMOISELLE FIFI

Author: Guy de Maupassant (1850-1893)
Type of plot: Social realism
Time of plot: 1871
Locale: Urville, a fictional Normandy town
First published: 1882 (English translation, 1922)

> *Principal characters:*
> MAJOR COUNT VON FARLSBERG, commander of the Prussian
>   occupying forces in Urville
> CAPTAIN BARON VON KELWEINGSTEIN, his second in command
> LIEUTENANT OTTO VON GROSSLING
> SECOND LIEUTENANT FRITZ SCHEUNAUBOURG
> SECOND LIEUTENANT WILHELM VON EYRICK, a brutal officer
>   nicknamed "Mademoiselle Fifi"
> FATHER CHANTAVOINE, the local Catholic priest
> PAMELA,
> BLONDINE,
> AMANDA,
> EVA ("THE TOMATO"), and
> RACHEL ("THE JEWESS"), French prostitutes assigned to the
>   Prussian officers

The Story

During the months after the Prussian defeat of the French in 1871, Prussian troops occupy many areas of France. Five bored Prussian officers are among the leaders of the force occupying the small Normandy town of Urville, where they live in a castle. Major von Farlsberg is an older bearded officer; Captain von Kelweingstein is an obese man who lost two teeth on his wedding night, although he could not remember how this accident had happened. The major and captain are both married, but both complain that they have not had sex for several months and do not want this situation to continue. The three lower-ranking officers are also bored. Second Lieutenant Wilhelm von Eyrick has shown himself to be brutal and especially harsh toward French people. His fellow soldiers call him "Mademoiselle Fifi" because of his dandified appearance and the fact that he often adds the French words *"fi, fi donc"* to his German sentences.

After the major again complains about their tedious life in Urville, the captain proposes to organize a feast and orders a corporal to go to nearby Rouen to collect five prostitutes. As the officers await the women's arrival, they pass their time by blowing up pieces of china and complaining about Father Chantavoine, a local Catholic priest who has refused to ring his church's bells since the Prussians occupied his town. Mademoiselle Fifi wants to punish the priest, but his superiors argue that it would not look good for the Prussians to kill a priest.

After the prostitutes arrive at the castle of Urville, the major distributes them among the officers. He chooses Pamela for himself and assigns Blondine to the captain, Amanda to Lieutenant von Grossling, Eva "the Tomato" to Lieutenant Fritz Scheunaubourg, and Rachel "the Jewess" to Mademoiselle Fifi. The officers decide to dine with the prostitutes before making love. As they begin drinking, they deride French soldiers for their alleged lack of heroism and toast Prussia's victory over France.

When Mademoiselle Fifi kisses Rachel so hard that he bites her lip, she warns him that he must pay for this act of violence. Fifi does not realize that she is not referring merely to his paying her extra money. As everyone grows drunk, the Prussians declare that all of France and all Frenchwomen belong to them. No longer able to restrain herself, Rachel says that the Prussians invaded France only in order to gain easy access to prostitutes. When Mademoiselle Fifi slaps her face, she reacts by cutting his throat with a knife and then jumps out of a window. The Prussian soldiers cannot discover Rachel's hiding place and they accidentally kill two of their own soldiers as they search for her.

Looking for an excuse to punish the villagers, the major orders Father Chantavoine to ring the church bells during Mademoiselle Fifi's funeral. The villagers are amazed to see his order obeyed. The bells continue to ring intermittently until the end of the Prussian occupation. Father Chantavoine has hidden Rachel in the church tower, where he takes food to her. After the Prussians leave Urville, the priest takes her back to Rouen, where she gives up prostitution and eventually marries an unprejudiced French patriot and becomes a lady who is worth more than many others.

Themes and Meanings

Like many French citizens of his generation, Guy de Maupassant was traumatized by the Prussian occupation of France after the Franco-Prussian War (1870-1871). As with most of his stories dealing with the horrors of this military occupation, "Mademoiselle Fifi" takes place in his native province of Normandy. The story examines the complete lack of understanding between the Prussian occupation forces and the French. The Franco-Prussian War was begun by the thoroughly discredited French emperor Napoleon III in a vain effort to reestablish his political power in France. After the defeat of his French soldiers in this totally avoidable war, he fled to England with his family, and average French citizens had to pay for his extraordinarily bad political and military decisions.

For the residents of the fictional town of Urville, the boorish behavior of these five Prussian officers illustrates all the suffering that inevitably occurs during a military occupation. It should have been clear to all involved that the military occupation of regions of northern France was designed to force the new French democratic government, which replaced the dictatorship of Napoleon III, to accept Prussian terms for ending this war. Once the French government in Paris agreed to give up the provinces of Alsace and Lorraine to Prussia, the occupation would end, and this is, in fact, what happened. The Prussian officers should have realized that it was not in their self-interest to antagonize French citizens any more than necessary. French people were not happy about their loss of real freedom, but if they were pushed too far, real violence against the occupying forces would take place. The five Prussian officers in "Mademoiselle Fifi" are oblivious to this danger, and they bring unnecessary suffering on themselves and their soldiers through their irresponsible actions. Their failure to respect the dignity of those under their military control transforms a common prostitute and a country priest into patriotic heroes. If the Prussians simply ignored Father Chantavoine's silent act of resistance, Urville's people would quietly tolerate their presence. When even silent resistance provokes strong and potentially violent reactions from the occupying forces, the villagers gradually feel that they also should imitate the courage of their parish priest.

As a prostitute, Rachel sells sexual favors to any man who pays her good money, but she is also a Frenchwoman who does not appreciate hearing derogatory comments about her fellow citizens. When Mademoiselle Fifi physically abuses her and claims that the Prussians have a right to sleep with any Frenchwoman they choose, he goes too far, thereby provoking Rachel's unpremeditated act of violence.

Maupassant's justly famous short story reveals how ordinary people who are normally indifferent to politics can become actively involved in resisting evil if they are pushed too far. As a priest, Father Chantavoine wants no one to tell him when he should ring his church's bells. This intrusion into church matters by Mademoiselle Fifi causes him to become a true patriot.

Style and Technique

Although Maupassant died young and had a brief literary career, he nevertheless ranks as the classic French short-story writer. His literary mentor was Gustave Flaubert, from whom he learned the importance of creating well-crafted and well-organized prose works with multiple levels of meaning. One can, of course, read "Mademoiselle Fifi" at its surface level and interpret it as little more than the description of what happens to an unsympathetic military officer who brings about his own death; however, the story also displays Maupassant's mastery of irony and understatement. It is, for example, marvelously ironic that a calm parish priest and a prostitute come to realize that they have so much in common. Both respect the dignity of ordinary people. Father Chantavoine wants to be left alone so that he can serve the spiritual needs of his parishioners, while Rachel wants only to practice her profession without hearing provocative remarks from her clients. Father Chantavoine does not approve of Rachel's profession but wants to save her from a certain death at the hands of the Prussians, who have not shown sufficient respect for basic religious freedoms. Rachel's decision to stop being a prostitute can be attributed to the heroism of a country priest who saves her life, bringing about her religious and personal transformation.

Edmund J. Campion

THE MADNESS OF DOCTOR MONTARCO

Author: Miguel de Unamuno y Jugo (1864-1936)
Type of plot: Antistory
Time of plot: About 1900
Locale: Spain
First published: "La locura del doctor Montarco," 1904 (English translation, 1955)

> *Principal characters:*
> DR. MONTARCO, a physician who writes fiction
> DON SERVANDO FERNÁNDEZ GÓMEZ, one of his patients
> THE NARRATOR, his close friend
> DR. ATIENZA, director of the asylum

The Story

The narrator introduces Dr. Montarco as a competent physician who is admired and trusted by his patients. The trust begins to waver when it is observed that the doctor is a writer who eschews the composition of medical treatises in favor of writing strange and fanciful fiction. He ignores the objections of his clientele and rejects dissuasion by the narrator. His patients begin to desert him. This happened once before; the doctor, with his wife and two pre-teenage daughters, had to leave his native town when his practice dwindled because of his professional dualism.

Montarco insists that he practices medicine to cure people and to gain his livelihood, and that he does on his own time what he wants to do and not what others want him to do. His personal contempt for patients to whom he is professionally solicitous may be justified, but it signals the instability that will be instrumental in his being institutionalized. Don Servando expresses the sentiment of the patients when he tells the narrator that Montarco is a good doctor but appears to need treatment for a mental ailment. Characteristically overreacting, Montarco calls Don Servando a fool.

As the doctor's practice disintegrates, his verbal aggression becomes excessive and his mental acuity shows signs of diminishing. One sign is his erroneous ascription of the phrase "appetite for divinity." Another sign is his denial that he disdains the people whose opinions he clearly scorns.

The narrator's presentation of his partial responsibility for having Montarco committed to an asylum as an act of friendship is another element of characterization that may be missed by readers who unquestioningly accept the act as such. It is clear that the narrator, who had at first remonstrated with Don Servando in defense of Montarco, now accedes to the will of the townspeople and, instead of continuing the defense of his friend, joins those who insist on closeting Montarco's nonconformity. The effect of the act is further to aggravate the doctor's instability.

In the asylum, Dr. Atienza recognizes that Montarco's madness is not organic but has been induced by pressures to conform. As an inmate, Montarco spends his time reading Miguel de Cervantes's *El ingenioso hidalgo don Quixote de la Mancha*

(1605, 1615; *The History of the Valorous and Wittie Knight-Errant, Don Quixote of the Mancha*, 1612-1620; better known as *Don Quixote de la Mancha*), especially the part in which Don Quixote answers the churchman who has found fault with his mad whims and calls him Mr. Fool. Visited by the narrator, Montarco angrily expatiates on the prohibition in Matthew 5:22 against calling one's brother a fool.

Leaving Montarco, the narrator engages in a long conversation with Atienza and concludes that Atienza has benefited from Montarco's company. Thereafter Montarco's illness becomes physical as well as mental. He passes through pathological depression to death; his last utterances, punctuating his obstinate silence, are repetitions of his refrain of "All or nothing." He leaves behind him a thick manuscript, entitled *All or Nothing*, with instructions that it be burned on his death. The narrator claims not to know whether Atienza has carried out "the last wish of the madman"; his ostensibly sympathetic concern is accordingly marred by his using the judgmental label "madman" instead of the phrase "my friend."

Themes and Meanings

Miguel de Unamuno y Jugo, like the existentialist writers Søren Kierkegaard and Pär Lagerkvist, believed that the fulfillment of an individual human life consisted of a constant struggle to attain the unattainable condition of divinity. Kierkegaard based his struggle on his ineradicable need of God and his assumption that one cannot need what does not exist. Lagerkvist based his own struggle toward holiness on longing, which enriches the individual in proportion to its intensity. Unamuno's struggle was a matter of will, a refusal to accept, as reason dictated, the reality of his own mortality; he wanted nothing short of immortality: all or nothing, as Dr. Montarco demands.

Dr. Montarco's madness amounts to his flouting of reason, which is represented in the story by the townspeople and their ethos. Reason is requisite to livelihood, which in turns depends on conformity. The imagination is, however, for both Unamuno and his character Dr. Montarco, the stuff of life; and reason, as the author insists in one of his essays, cannot predispose itself to the revelation of life. Dr. Montarco, like Unamuno, reveres Don Quixote as the greatest madman who ever lived. By Dr. Montarco's berating the churchman in *Don Quixote de la Mancha* for calling this madman a fool, Unamuno distinguishes the madness that characterizes genius and discloses true life from the foolishness of those who mistake livelihood for life. The irony is that Cervantes's churchman, who should exceed reason in pursuit of faith, upholds rationalist materialism and ridicules the madman whose imagination is consonant with faith as the substance of things hoped for.

Unamuno extends this irony with Montarco's invocation of Matthew 5:22, in which Christ says that whoever calls his brother a fool shall be liable to the eternal fire. Montarco complains that this inhibits him in his conviction that society is made up chiefly of fools; it is impossible, he says, to prove to humans that they are fools. After thus calling his brothers fools, he curiously takes satisfaction in the churchman's being relegated to the inferno for calling Don Quixote a fool. The narrator, either humoring Montarco, or forgetting for the moment that the churchman is a fictional character, or both, suggests that God in his infinite mercy may have consigned the churchman only to purgatory. At this point, the reader does well to recall that the narrator and Montarco are also fictional characters and that their creator, a professor of Greek, would be familiar with the original of Matthew 5:22, in which the person calling his brother a fool in Aramaic (*rhaká*) is said to be subject only to the censure of the Sanhedrin, while the one calling his brother a fool in Greek (*moré*) is said to be liable to the fire of Gehenna. That Unamuno has Montarco mention only the more severe penalty invites the inference that the greater harm attaches to the language in which the rationalist tradition was conceived and nurtured and by which the covenant of faith was expropriated.

Style and Technique

Known for his unorthodox approach to fiction, particularly in his construction of the antinovel, Unamuno y Jugo may be considered to have written an antistory in "The Madness of Doctor Montarco." Anthony Kerrigan, who translated the work, questions whether it is a story at all, and some scholars have called it a "story-essay." It appears, indeed, to be a dialogue, first between the narrator and Montarco, and then between the narrator and Atienza. It has a well-plotted progression of Montarco's demise, however, and a development of contrasting characterizations.

The dialogic and essayistic progression of "The Madness of Doctor Montarco" is marked by the technique of antithesis, which is found in all of Unamuno's writing: science and art in *Abel Sánchez* (1917; English translation, 1956); faith and unbelief in "San Manuel Bueno, Mártir" (1933; "Saint Emmanuel the Good, Martyr," 1956); madness and sanity in his many essays on *Don Quixote de la Mancha* and in "The Madness of Doctor Montarco." Forms of antithesis provide rhetorical configuration for Unamuno's stress on the objective and subjective modes, for example, the opposition of intellect and will and, ultimately, of mortality and immortality. Montarco's struggle is, in the main, against mortality toward immortality, and the struggle is perpetuated by his will in opposition to his intellect in antithetical commitment to all or nothing. If, as most critics claim, this story is analogous to Unamuno's own resistance to demands that he conform to social customs, it must also indicate the author's recognition of his own deleterious impatience.

Antithesis is underscored by various rhetorical figures of opposition, such as antonymy (for example, sanity and madness), oxymoron (for example, practical delusion), and chiasmus, which is the reversal of a sequence. The conclusion of the story is an excellent example of chiastic technique. Montarco's dying wish is that his manuscript be burned without being read; the narrator does not know whether Atienza has resisted the temptation to read it or actually burned it. The chiastic opposition (burned—read—read—burned) is followed by another, the narrator's wish that Montarco rest in peace because Montarco deserves peace and rest. This second chiasmus (rest—peace—peace—rest) dramatizes the narrator's wanting for Montarco the antithesis of what Montarco himself wanted—struggle and activity.

Roy Arthur Swanson

THE MAGIC BARREL

Author: Bernard Malamud (1914-1986)
Type of plot: Psychological
Time of plot: The twentieth century
Locale: New York City
First published: 1954

> *Principal characters:*
> LEO FINKLE, a rabbinic student at Yeshiva University
> PINYE SALZMAN, a marriage broker

The Story

"The Magic Barrel" begins with the introduction of Leo Finkle, who is twenty-seven and in search of a suitable wife, to Pinye Salzman, who has advertised his services as a matchmaker in a local Jewish newspaper. Leo has spent six years in study, with no time for developing a social life. Inexperienced with women, he finds the traditional route of obtaining a bride appealing, an honorable arrangement from which his own parents benefited.

At their initial meeting, Salzman brings names from which to choose a proper wife for a respectable rabbi. The cards on which they appear, which he has selected from a barrel in his apartment, include significant statistical information: dowry, age, occupation, health, and family. When Leo learns who some of his prospects are (a widow, a thirty-two-year-old schoolteacher, a nineteen-year-old student with a lame foot), he dismisses Salzman. The experience leaves Leo in a state of depression and anxiety. Salzman, however, appears the next evening with good news: He has been assured that the schoolteacher, Lily Hirschorn, is no older than twenty-nine.

Leo agrees to meet Lily, whom he finds (as Salzman has claimed) intelligent and honest. However, in addition to being "past thirty-five and aging rapidly" Lily appears overly in awe of Leo's profession—a result, the young man concludes, of Salzman's misrepresentation. Additionally, Lily's questions concerning Leo's love of God are threatening; in a moment of self-revelation, Leo harshly confesses that he desired to become a rabbi not because he loved God but because he did not.

Their meeting results in Lily's disenchantment and Leo's despair. Angry at first with Salzman, Leo comes to realize that it is his lack of self-knowledge and fear of finding himself incapable of affairs with women that have led him to Salzman in the first place. With brutal clarity, Leo sees that he has set limits in his relationships with both God and women, limits that have left him feeling empty and unloved. These insights, although terrifying and painful, serve as turning points in Leo's life as self-realization propels him toward understanding and possible change.

After a week of inner conflict—during which he abandons himself to an all-consuming loneliness—Leo recommits himself to his rabbinic goals and dedicates himself to obtaining love and perhaps even a bride.

Once at peace, Leo is visited again by Salzman. Leo confronts the matchmaker with his unfair misrepresentations, terminates their business agreement, and declares that it is now love he seeks. In a final attempt to make a sale, Salzman gives Leo a packet of photographs with which to find love. After many days, Leo opens the package and examines the pictures. He sees many attractive women, but they all lack a certain quality that he desires. As the photos are returned to the packet, a small snapshot of a woman falls out; although not especially attractive, she seems to possess the soul, the depth, the suffering, the potential—and even a certain lack of goodness—that Leo feels he himself must attain.

Hit hard by this recognition of a bond between them, Leo hurries across town in search of Salzman. Salzman reacts to Leo's choice in inexplicable horror and pain. Claming that the photo fell mistakenly into the packet, he rushes out the door, pursued by Leo, whose only chance for love and happiness is now threatened. Salzman tries to convince Leo that this woman is not a suitable match for a rabbi and eventually reveals the source of his anguish: The snapshot portrays a wild woman who disdains poverty, who Salzman now considers dead—his daughter, Stella.

Tormented by this discovery, Leo finally concludes a plan: He will dedicate himself to God, and Stella to morality and goodness. Encountering Salzman one day in a cafeteria, Leo reveals that he at last has love in his heart and implies that perhaps he can now be the one to provide a valuable service. A meeting is arranged for Leo and Stella one spring evening on a street corner.

Leo approaches Stella, who, although smoking a cigarette under a street lamp, is nevertheless shy and not without innocence. While Leo exuberantly rushes forth, Salzman stands around the corner chanting the traditional Hebrew mourning prayers.

Themes and Meanings

"The Magic Barrel" explores many aspects of the theme of self-discovery: the awakening of passion and desire; the definition of identity; the search for love. As the story begins, Leo is emerging from years of study to embrace life's dilemmas. He experiences the awakening of passion and desire with resistance and confusion; his search for a wife begins not out of desire for love or devotion but, rather, to improve his chances of securing a congregation. Through his experiences with the matchmaker, Leo discovers what kind of bride he does not want—someone who sees him not for who he is but for his position in society.

As he attempts to define his priorities, Leo is caught in a web of contradictions: "apart from his parents, he had never loved anyone. Or perhaps it went the other way, that he did not love God so well as he might, because he had not loved man." Leo's relationship with God constitutes a major part of his struggle for identity. When he accepts the shortcomings of his studies (his books have not taught him to love either God or women) and himself, Leo is able to redefine his goals and begin advancement toward them. His major goal is to achieve love: not only love for God but also love for a woman.

In his efforts to meet and woo Stella, Leo is no longer content merely to take what Salzman has to offer—especially in a situation that causes the matchmaker much pain. Leo can now offer internal peace to both Salzman and himself through his involvement with Stella. Having come to terms with his own limits and with God, Leo is capable of fulfilling his need for love and of allowing himself to influence another's life. He has finally achieved the attributes of passion and compassion that allow him to open his heart and reach for someone else. During their final encounter in the cafeteria, Salzman barely recognizes Leo, who "had grown a pointed beard" and whose eyes were "weighted with wisdom." Clearly, the reference is to a man who looks like and is a rabbi, not to a man studying to become one.

Style and Technique

As Salzman is employed by Leo to procure a bride, so is he employed by the author as the vehicle through which Leo's self-discovery is attained. A man of much depth and sorrow, Salzman conceals a pain so great that he rejects even the attentions of a religious man. However, it is only through Leo that he can hope to find peace of mind and a reunited family.

Salzman is an unsuccessful man whose office, his wife tells Leo, is "in the air." In immigrant English, Salzman explains his lack of success: "When I have two fine people that they would be wonderful to be married, I am so happy that I talk too much. . . . This is why Salzman is a poor man." The compassion lacking in Leo is discovered in Salzman, whose greatest desire is to provide happiness.

References to Salzman's ethereal and somewhat mystical qualities recur throughout the story. He appears and disappears in direct, yet unspoken, response to Leo's needs; he is described as a "skeleton with haunted eyes," his appearance often "haggard, and transparent to the point of vanishing," whose magic barrel, Leo concludes, is probably "a figment of the imagination." In this fusion of the down-to-earth and the otherworldly, the literal and the symbolic, the characterization of Salzman is representative of Bernard Malamud's distinctive style.

Shelly Usen

MAIDEN IN A TOWER

Author: Wallace Stegner (1909-1993)
Type of plot: Psychological
Time of plot: The mid-1950's
Locale: Salt Lake City, Utah
First published: 1954

> *Principal characters:*
>> KIMBALL HARRIS, the protagonist, a middle-aged businessperson
>> McBRIDE, a young mortuary attendant
>> HOLLY, a beautiful young bohemian coed during Harris's college
>> days

The Story

Kimball Harris returns to Salt Lake City, where he attended college, to make funeral arrangements for his last near relative, his Aunt Margaret. Tired from his long drive across Nevada from San Francisco, he checks into a hotel, awash in nostalgia for his "giddy and forgotten youth." When he visits the Merrill funeral parlor, where his aunt has been taken, he is surprised to discover that he knows the building well. Holly, a beautiful young woman who is at the center of many of Harris's recollections of his college days, once lived in an apartment in this old mansion.

Viewing his aunt's body does not excite a particularly sentimental response in him. He recalls her as never very lovable, "only a duty and an expense." However, because of its potent associations with Holly, the house itself resurrects memories of the Jazz Age of his youth with great force. He asks McBride, the parlor attendant, if he can see Holly's apartment, a room with a turret tower on the third floor. Although another deceased woman is laid out in this room, McBride permits Harris to look around.

The staircase, hallways, and other rooms all propel Harris deeper into his nostalgic recollections. He remembers the people he knew in college as a collection of pose-strikers and late adolescent romantics whom he thinks of as "provincial cognoscenti." All these people orbited around Holly. He particularly recalls the rumors of a nude portrait for which Holly supposedly modeled and is surprised to realize that he is still disturbed by this thought.

When he enters Holly's former apartment, he sees the body of a deceased woman. Though disturbed by her chill and silence, he is intrigued by the Navajo squash-blossom necklace on the dead woman, thinking it almost jaunty, an indicator of her former personality. His lively memories are juxtaposed against the quiet of the dead woman in this room.

He recalls an episode, which he cannot fix precisely in time, when he found himself alone with Holly, as he rarely ever was. She was crying; in an effort to comfort her, Harris took her into his arms in a way that was partly a "game" that he had played out before—a burlesquing gesture of consolation. He was nevertheless excited by Holly's proximity and was surprised when she did not push his hands away from her gown's low-cut back. His fingers continued moving, until they reached her breast, which startled him because of its rigid nipple. At that moment, the "maiden in the tower" suddenly became material and attainable, but rather than satisfying his desires, Harris retreated. He recalls this moment as one of the saddest failures of his life. After a final, compassionate view of the dead woman with the Navajo necklace, Harris retreats from both the room and his recollections—"almost with panic."

Themes and Meanings

Two themes thread through "Maiden in a Tower," which derives much of its power through the dissonance between the two themes. The first thread is developed in the opening pages, which describe Kimball Harris's return to Salt Lake City with great clarity, noting details of the city that he remembers—such as parking regulations and the small size of the Salt Lake City phone book. Nothing can be more down-to-earth than his quest—making the final earthly dispositions for his dead aunt. However, this concentration also sets up the problem of the story, as Harris begins a re-examination of his youth. The past is resurrected by its connections to the tangible present, such as the hotel in which Harris caroused during Prohibition and the funeral home, with its direct connection to Holly. Harris then begins noticing the changes that have occurred over the past twenty-five years—such as a miniature golfing course that has been replaced by a car wash and the warped parquet floors of the house that are now covered by a deep-plush carpet. Inevitably, he directs his examination back to his own youth, and to what he himself has become since he last visited this apartment. He finds his life to be safe, clean, and regular, but not spontaneous, perhaps even moribund.

The title "Maiden in a Tower" highlights the story's second thematic thread. Harris first describes Holly in almost mythic tones, as a "Circe or Proserpine," and he compares her to one of the goddesses from "The Judgement of Paris." Despite her bohemian trappings, her false sophistication, and the fact that she was the object of many men's desires, Holly is described as an "innocent." In truth, Holly is a "maiden," who seemingly yearned to be rescued from the falseness of her life. Despite the story's Jazz Age setting, its central theme developed is that of a romantic hero's quest, in which a knight-errant attempts to save a fair young maiden from a tower prison.

In quoting Johann Wolfgang von Goethe's remark that "the essence of a woman draws us on," Wallace Stegner strikes the keynote of Holly's vitality and allure. In his recollections, Harris sees himself as a failed knight-errant, unable to "save" the maiden. He had "played it safe" when the spirit of the times demanded that he "live it dangerously . . . go boom, take chances." Harris never took the romantic chance. In confronting the dead woman in the apartment, he finds himself in recollection a "gargler of whiskey," as much a fake and phony as the others whom he remembers from his college days. Harris recalls a line from William Blake's *The Marriage of Heaven and Hell* (1790), stating that "Prudence is a rich ugly old maid courted by incapacity." Although his recollections of Holly have rekindled his lost romantic dreams, he does not begrudge the choices that he has made in his life. Nevertheless, he feels "the past . . . held him like pain." The thematic conflict between the vibrant past and the sterile present robs Harris of the happy nostalgia that possesses him until he enters Holly's old apartment. The story concludes with a kind of symbolic pun: Harris retreats from the house and from his recollections of the "maiden" who lived there, while McBride, the "Mortuary Max Factor," is left in possession of the house and its dead occupants.

Style and Technique

Throughout the first third of this story, Stegner employs a precise, realistic style to describe Harris's return. The evocation of physical details provides a natural springboard for the problem of the story, for once Harris visits the funeral home, the dissonance between his nostalgic recollections and the present is brought into bold relief. Stegner's writing style changes noticeably as Harris begins to recall his past with Holly. Up to this time, the writing is admirably concrete; it now begins to take on an impressionistic quality, with events no longer precisely fixed in time or space. Further, the writing shows increasing attention to color, revealing Harris's impressionability: "He remembered her in her gold gown, a Proserpine or a Circe . . . how her hair was smooth black and her eyes very dark blue and how she wore massive gold hoops in her ears."

The image that arises in the reader's mind might suggest a portrait by Gustav Klimt—who would be consistent with the names of artists and writers who were revered by Holly's circle of Jazz Age iconoclasts. This vivid image is in stark contrast with the silver Navajo necklace lying on the dead woman's black muslin burial gown.

The conflicts of this story are developed through the use of counterpoint. The past is vividly shown as a little shabby, mock-heroic, and phony, while the present is real, clean, and fresh-painted; it is as sweet-smelling as the flowers and body of the dead woman in the parlor, and it is equally sterile. In many ways the writing style is reminiscent of the work of F. Scott Fitzgerald, but where Fitzgerald might have found the bittersweet moment of reminiscence, Stegner's ending is a bitter recognition by Kimball Harris of his own falseness. Harris remembers himself as an "extraordinary young man, and very little of what had been extraordinary about himself pleased him."

James Barbour

MAMMON AND THE ARCHER

Author: O. Henry (William Sydney Porter, 1862-1910)
Type of plot: Sketch
Time of plot: The early 1900's
Locale: New York City
First published: 1906

> *Principal characters:*
> ANTHONY ROCKWALL, a self-made millionaire
> RICHARD ROCKWALL, his well-educated son
> AUNT ELLEN, his sister

The Story

Anthony Rockwall, a retired soap manufacturer and self-made millionaire, believes that money can accomplish anything; he declares, "I'll bet my money on money every time." He thinks the power of his money can carry his son Richard into the exclusive New York social world. Because he is rough, crude, and down-to-earth, Anthony Rockwall has never been welcome in this elite world of wealth and privilege. By contrast, young Richard, a gentleman in appearance and manners, has recently graduated from college and returned home to find his place in New York's elite society. He has, however, unhappily discovered that money cannot accomplish everything that his father believes it can. In the upper-class circle of his friends, he has met and fallen in love with the beautiful Miss Lantry, whose high social position and wealth make her unattainable to him. Not only can he find no opportunity to propose to her; he can barely find time in her busy social schedule to talk to her. He will see this beautiful woman for only a few minutes the following day; then she leaves New York for a two-year trip to Europe.

While father and son discuss the power and limitations of Rockwall money to make dreams come true, the father forms a plan using the power of wealth. He advises his son that if he wants to succeed, he should make a token offering at the altar of Mammon, the money god. Later Aunt Ellen, having heard about this conversation from her nephew, reproaches her brother, insisting that wealth means nothing in regard to true affection—only love is all-powerful. She gives her nephew a treasured love token, his mother's quaint old gold ring. She counsels him to wear it to bring him luck in love when he meets Miss Lantry.

When young Richard meets his love at the train station, he takes her to her next engagement, a destination several minutes away. Unexpectedly, he drops the gold ring during the cab ride. Stopping briefly, he retrieves the token and plans to speed toward their destination. The journey does not continue smoothly, however. Without warning, dozens of cabs, wagons, carriages, loaded teams, motorized vehicles, and crosstown cars crowd around them, creating an impassable traffic jam.

Two hours later, the young lovers emerge from the traffic jam engaged to be married. When Aunt Ellen shares the happy news with her wealthy brother, she comments that the gold ring, a symbol of the power of love, allowed Richard to win his beloved. Unknown to her, Anthony had his part to play in the engagement too. He meets with an old trusted employee to make the final payment to the many drivers hired to create the enormous traffic jam around his son's cab. Having bought the time his son needed to make Miss Lantry his own, Anthony Rockwall has confirmed to himself the omnipotence of money. The tycoon doubts that Cupid, the bow-and-arrow-carrying god of love, offered any assistance at all.

Themes and Meanings

O. Henry's story of life in turn-of-the-century New York highlights a favorite romantic theme: the contest between love and money. In "Mammon and the Archer," this rivalry manifests itself in a wily old millionaire and his gentle, sentimental sister. Each believes that Richard can fulfill his dream only by relying exclusively on his or her principles: Mammon, the god of wealth, in the father's view; or Cupid, the god of love, in the aunt's view. The author cleverly designed a story making both of them winners, by using both principles to bring about a happy ending. Without the power of the gold ring, which distracted Richard for a minute and delayed his journey, he would have driven across town too soon, missing the huge traffic jam and losing the opportunity to spend time with Miss Lantry and win her love. Without the power of the Rockwall money to orchestrate the traffic jam, Richard's journey would have taken only a few minutes and denied him his chance to make her his own.

The story also effectively captures the stereotypes of masculine and feminine character. In a stereotypically masculine way, Anthony Rockwall formulates a dynamic plan to buy time for Richard to win his love. In a stereotypically feminine way, Aunt Ellen remembers an old promise made to her sister-in-law about a ring and trusts the magic of a love token. The father's strategy to create a blockade of hired vehicles is practical, well planned, well managed in the capable hands of his employees, and well financed. Before setting his scheme into action, he collects the necessary information about its timing and location to ensure its success. On the other hand, Aunt Ellen has only a curious old ring in its moth-eaten case to offer her nephew. Although a precious family heirloom, the ring is much too small for him to wear as a love charm. Not certain what to do with it, he crams it in his pocket and later absentmindedly drops it during the carriage ride. No special planning seems evident in Aunt Ellen's gift, for she does not realize that Richard cannot wear the ring when he needs it. Richard's dropping the ring delays the cab only a minute, hardly enough time to give him the opportunity he needs, but that precious minute makes all the difference to the successful outcome of the story.

An analysis of the story's action shows that both the father's and the aunt's help lead to Richard's happiness, and that neither effort by itself would have worked. Both gods, Mammon and Cupid, act together to bring happiness to the young couple.

Style and Technique

The success of this short story rests on its fast-moving, dramatic plot and the strong characterization of Anthony Rockwall and Aunt Ellen, who represent the respective powers of money and love to bring human happiness. Early in the story, old Rockwall appears to be a rough, harsh businessman totally obsessed with money. Using money as a measurement, he calculates his son to be a gentleman by the price of his clothes and even his soap. He bluntly challenges his son to buy the time he needs with Miss Lantry: "Do you mean to tell me that with all the money I've got you can't get an hour or two of a girl's time for yourself?" He later roughly ends a conversation with his sister to continue reading an adventure story about a pirate on a sinking ship, commenting, "He's too good a judge of the value of money to let drown." This image of the father may be a facade hiding a generous and perceptive man. When he creates a way to help Richard, he shows sensitivity to his sister's and son's feelings by concealing his efforts. As a result of his careful planning, the young couple believe that destiny has brought them together. Thus, Anthony Rockwall is not entirely the heartless tycoon he seems to be.

Aunt Ellen appears to be a sentimental old woman, but she also gives her nephew the means to become engaged. She is described as "a gray-haired angel that had been left on earth by mistake," and as oppressed by her brother's wealth. She wisely reminds her brother that all his gold cannot bring his son happiness. Her remark later proves to be correct, for she gives Richard the quaint old love charm that allows his father's elaborate plan to succeed. Her seemingly minor contribution is as essential to Richard's happiness as old Rockwall's millions.

This story fits the style of the southern tall tale, familiar in folklore and legend. O. Henry absorbed this storytelling tradition growing up in North Carolina after the Civil War. Working at his uncle's store, he spent hours listening to the fantastic yarns of old-timers. Exaggeration and humor, key elements of the tall tale, show strongly in this story. For example, to help his son win a wife, old Rockwall creates a historic public event: "The oldest New Yorker among the thousands of spectators that lined the sidewalks had not witnessed a street blockade of the proportions of this one." An eyewitness comments afterward, "It was two hours before a snake could get below Greeley's statue." Old Rockwall's final comment on the event humorously makes his point, "'You didn't notice,' said he, 'anywhere in the tie-up, a kind of a fat boy without any clothes on shooting arrows around with a bow, did you?'" Surely Cupid usually inspires a more respectful attitude than the old tycoon's.

Patricia H. Fulbright

THE MAN FROM MARS

Author: Margaret Atwood (1939-   )
Type of plot: Social realism
Time of plot: The 1950's and 1960's
Locale: Toronto
First published: 1977

> *Principal characters:*
> CHRISTINE, the protagonist
> A YOUNG ASIAN MAN, most likely Vietnamese

The Story

While walking through a park in Toronto, Christine is stopped by an Asian man asking for directions. She kindly draws him a map, expecting to be done with him; however, the man insists on exchanging names. Christine observes that if this was a person from her own culture, she would think he was trying to pick her up but that does not happen to her because she is big, or "statuesque" as her mother says. Suddenly, however, the young man grabs her arm and insists on accompanying her home. Frightened, Christine escapes by jumping on a streetcar.

When the school year comes to an end, the mysterious man calls her house, and her mother, trying to do her best for Christine, invites him to tea. Christine goes along with her mother but is pleased by her mother's dismay when she answers the door and sees he is not the foreign potentate she had imagined. Christine serves him tea but is outraged when he sets the timer on his camera, abruptly puts his arm around her, and jams his cheek up against her as the shutter clicks.

While teaching sailing at a summer camp, she leaves several letters from him unanswered. When she returns home, he locates her on campus and begins to follow her relentlessly. When she asks him what he wants, he answers that he wants to talk to her, but given the opportunity to do so, he smiles apologetically and says nothing. She is both frightened and embarrassed. This mysterious, emaciated, chain-smoking man with badly bitten fingernails and threadbare clothing who pursues Christine everywhere makes her interesting to other men; they begin to ask her out, when they never had before. Christine begins to feel different, more like Marilyn Monroe, she thinks, than a dolphin.

She becomes truly afraid when the man begins to telephone her, sometimes just breathing into the phone; he follows her down her own street, dodging behind trees when she looks back. One night he terrifies Elvira, the housekeeper, when she finds him peering through the French doors. The police are called, and Christine is relieved that she is not the one who told, although she realizes that had he been a Canadian, she would have called the police long before this. The police decide they must pick him up, so when Christine comes out of a lecture the next day and the man is waiting for her, the police take him into custody and send him back to Montreal. Christine is disappointed when she learns that she is not the first woman he has followed. When he is caught again following a sixty-year-old Mother Superior, he is deported.

Christine's life goes back to its nondescript routine; she graduates, finds employment, and puts on weight. When the Vietnam War begins to be reported in the newspaper, Christine cannot stop thinking of the mysterious man—the only man who ever found her irresistible. She studies magazines searching for his face but, haunted by nightmares of him coming through her mother's French doors, blood streaking his face, she gives away her television and takes to reading nineteenth century novels. When she does think of him, she cannot picture him in the army; instead, he would be "something nondescript, something in the background, like herself."

Themes and Meanings

Margaret Atwood has written this story not only to examine what it is to be the "other" in a foreign culture but also to explore what it is to be "other" in one's own social milieu. The title refers to the enigmatic, unnamed man who is so alien from Christine and her contemporaries that he might as well be from Mars. At their first encounter, Christine is polite, putting on her official welcoming smile, but his differences are so drastic that he is grossly unattractive to her. She concludes their conversation with a terminal smile, but such nuances are lost on him.

A contact zone, a place where two different cultures confront each other, is established between Christine and the man, but it is such unfamiliar territory for both of them that they cannot navigate it in ways beneficial to either of them. The young man's passion seems to be to maintain the contact zone no matter what, but he has no idea how to get to know Christine in the context of Canadian society.

Christine knows people from other cultures and thinks of herself as a liberal. Atwood wants to show that Christine is limited by Western ideology, even though Christine herself believes that she is tolerant and progressive. She has an uneasy relationship with Elvira, her mother's West Indian housekeeper. Puzzled by Elvira's surliness, Christine has no idea how to overcome the barriers between them. Even though Christine's intentions are good, she is constrained by a dominant ideology that necessarily limits her perspective and compassion.

The Asian man is not the only outsider; Christine is an outsider in her own family. Her mother is petite and graceful, and Christine has two beautiful sisters, one already married, the other soon to be. Christine, large and athletic, does not fit her culture's definition of beautiful. She has compensated for her outsider status by becoming involved in politics and athletics. Her male friends feel comfortable with her as a fellow athlete and hard worker, but to them she is neither attractive nor interesting.

It is the "man from Mars" who sees Christine as an alluring woman and, in so doing, brings about a change in her status. She becomes attractive because another man finds her so. It is as if her value as a commodity increases because there suddenly is a demand when there was not one before. While she is living in the contact zone and interacting daily with this unstoppable man, her life becomes exciting, full of the unknown. She looks forward to the daily chases as she and her follower jog-trot between her classes.

The man oversteps the boundaries of what is permissible in the contact zone. He does not realize that his actions are going to be read by Canadian culture as dangerously out of bounds. Although he never does anything physically to harm Christine, the pervasive reality of violence toward women, of stalkers and Peeping Toms, feeds her imagination; she begins to fear he will have a weapon; when called, the police quickly label him as a psychotic.

When he is sent back to Montreal and finally to his home country, Christine's collateral quickly falls, and she returns to her old, dull roles within the social strata of her cultural context. Atwood wants readers to recognize that not only the man but also Christine have missed some kind of chance. Sensitive readers are not so quick to condemn him as a psychotic; they share Christine's sad curiosity and disappointment that they never get to negotiate the contact zone and know who he is and what drives him to pursue Christine with such intensity.

Style and Technique

Atwood invests her story with mystery. Although readers may assume that the man is from Vietnam, they are never told this, nor are they given his name, age, profession, or life story. By keeping him a cipher, he remains as cryptic, and thus unnerving, for the reader as he does for Christine. Atwood puts readers in the contact zone along with Christine, only letting them find out what she finds out—no more. The technique hides the man's identity, while revealing how quickly people judge the "other," basing deduction on details that, in fact, reveal next to nothing. The Asian man remains an alien because Atwood wants readers to see the consequences of their limited but powerful first impressions.

Although the story is plot-driven, it is primarily a study of character, particularly Christine's. Readers witness how there are gradations to being an outsider. Christine is on the margins of her school community until she meets someone even more marginalized. For a while, his presence pulls her into a social context where she is noticed and even appreciated. When he is no longer there to call attention to her, Christine quickly moves back into the position of the outsider.

The exposition is adept in revealing Christine and her social and family contexts well, but the rising action increases the tension between Christine's safe world and that of the unknown man as he gains access to her world. The conflicts are multilayered between Christine and her mother, between Christine and the "man from Mars," and between two cultures that clash rather than combine. The climax occurs when the police are called in and capture the man outside Christine's classroom building. He seems both ominous and pitiful, both an antagonist and a sympathetic character. The denouement is Christine's slow but sure decline after what can be read as her betrayal of the man. Atwood suggests that this will be the most exciting thing that will happen to Christine in her lifetime, and that she is left to retreat into anonymity as does "the man from Mars."

Janet M. Ellerby

THE MAN IN A CASE

Author: Anton Chekhov (1860-1904)
Type of plot: Character study
Time of plot: The 1890's
Locale: A provincial Russian town
First published: "Chelovek v futlyare," 1898 (English translation, 1914)

> *Principal characters:*
> IVAN IVANYCH CHIMSHA-HIMALALSKY, a veterinarian
> BURKIN, a teacher who narrates the story of Belikov
> BELIKOV, a teacher
> MIKHAIL KOVALENKO, a teacher
> VARENKA KOVALENKO, Mikhail's sister

The Story

"The Man in a Case" chronicles the story of a narrow-minded schoolteacher named Belikov. Narrated by Burkin, a fellow teacher, to his friend Ivan Ivanych Chimsha-Himalaisky, after a long day spent hunting in the countryside, this tale provides a sobering view of pettiness and paranoia in a provincial Russian milieu. In Burkin's description, Belikov—a teacher of Greek—emerges as a highly insecure individual obsessed with following official rules and fearful of any suspicion of permissiveness in his environment. From the very way he dresses (in a pair of galoshes and a heavy coat even in the warmest weather), it is clear that Belikov seeks to isolate himself and protect himself from the outside. Unfortunately for his colleagues, Belikov constantly strives to impose his own paranoia on everyone else. Not only does he cling to whatever official regulations he encounters, but he insists that others do so as well. Moreover, even if an activity is not expressly forbidden by some regulation, Belikov is wary of it, because one can never tell what harm might come from it. Because of his incessant criticism and intimidation, he almost always succeeds in getting his way. As Burkin recounts, not only are all of his fellow teachers afraid of Belikov, but the whole town lives in fear of him, too.

However, Belikov's life of unswerving routine and eternal vigilance eventually receives an unforeseen modification. A new teacher named Mikhail Kovalenko is assigned to Belikov's school, and he brings with him his lively and cheerful sister Varenka. Within a short time, the townspeople conceive of arranging a match between Belikov and Varenka, assuming perhaps that marriage would make the dour man's life more complete. Thus, Belikov begins to pay visits to Varenka, and she appears to welcome his attentions; he even begins to speak of marriage. Belikov's courtship, however, does not make him more sociable or relaxed; on the contrary, he becomes even more rigid and retiring.

Burkin believes that Belikov would have gone through with the marriage if it were not for a sudden, unexpected turn of events. Someone in the town draws a caricature of Belikov in his galoshes and umbrella with Varenka on his arm. This caricature is sent to all the teachers and town officials. Humiliated and angry, Belikov soon afterward catches sight of Varenka and her brother riding bicycles on the way to a school outing. For some reason, this strikes him as a shocking deviation from propriety, and he decides to stop in at the Kovalenkos that evening to convey his disapproval. Varenka is not at home, so Belikov begins to reproach Mikhail for his unseemly behavior. Mikhail, however, reacts indignantly to this interference in his personal affairs, and he rebukes Belikov in return. Horrified at Mikhail's evident lack of respect, Belikov declares that he will inform the school principal of his insubordination. Thoroughly aroused, Mikhail shoves Belikov toward the staircase leading down to the apartment house entrance, and Belikov tumbles headlong down the stairs. At that moment, Varenka returns. Seeing Belikov in such a ridiculous position and not knowing the cause of his fall, she bursts into innocent laughter. Although physically unhurt, Belikov is devastated by this final humiliation. He returns home, takes to his bed, and dies a few days later.

Burkin concludes his tale with an account of the consequences of Belikov's death. At first, everyone in the town feels an exhilarating sensation of freedom. Sadly, this atmosphere of freedom quickly evaporates, and before a week has passed, life has resumed its former routine: stern, tiresome, and senseless. As Burkin notes, although Belikov is buried, there remain many more such "men in cases." Burkin's friend Ivan Ivanych reacts to this story with dismay, and he delivers a disconsolate denunciation of the way people lie, endure humiliation, and abuse themselves all for the sake of a secure position or income. "No," he declares, "one cannot live like this any more." While Burkin himself retires for the night, Ivan Ivanych cannot sleep, and the story ends with him going outside to smoke his pipe.

Themes and Meanings

"The Man in a Case" provides a vivid illustration of one of Anton Chekhov's major concerns: humanity's essential need to be free from tyranny and coercion. He once wrote that his "holy of holies" included "the human body, health, intelligence . . . and the most absolute freedom imaginable, freedom from violence and lies, no matter what form the latter two take." In the character of Belikov, he created a memorable portrait of a social tyrant, a mean-spirited individual who not only maintains rigid control over himself but also suppresses impulses toward liberation in others. To oppose this shabby tyrant, Chekhov created the characters of Mikhail and Varenka Kovalenko, two strong, healthy youths whose determination to live life to the fullest cannot be thwarted by the threats and imprecations of the oppressor. Unfortunately, as Burkin's narrative indicates, such free spirits as the Kovalenkos are relatively rare in Russia. The Belikovs of the world are much more numerous, and they have proved frighteningly successful: Burkin's entire town is enslaved to public opinion and to an ineradicable anxiety over social or professional success. Aside from the salutary effect of Kovalenko's defiance and Varenka's laughter, Chekhov's story provides no clear-cut program to break the pernicious pattern set by Belikov and his meek follow-ers. Instead, his tale serves as a kind of sober warning to his readers of a profound yet insidious threat to human freedom and fulfillment.

Style and Technique

This story appeared as the first of three works published by Chekhov in 1898 and linked through a number of structural and thematic elements. One such element is the use of the "frame tale" narrative technique, in which one character relates a personal anecdote to another character. This technique enabled Chekhov to provide the reader with some commentary on the narrated event through the reactions of the person who listens to the tale. Here, Ivan Ivanych's indignation works to underscore the serious-ness of the negative portrait of Belikov sketched by Burkin. Also evident in the frame of the narrative are deftly nuanced descriptions of nature.

After Burkin concludes his story, Chekhov focuses on the nocturnal landscape, cre-ating a palpable aura of peace and calm that contrasts with the grim vision of human weakness and vice evoked earlier. As it does so often in Chekhov's work, the world of nature offers a mute commentary on human life. The freedom and spaciousness found in the natural world expose by contrast the constriction and pettiness of everyday life.

Throughout this tale, one notes Chekhov's characteristic reliance on symbolic or telling detail. It is ironic that Belikov is a teacher of Greek—a dead language—and that his favorite Greek word is *anthropos* (man); he himself is completely cut off from the world of humanity. It is also telling that Belikov shows a predilection for wrapping himself and his possessions in cases and boxes. Not only does this indicate his essen-tial insularity, but it also foreshadows his ultimate resting place: a coffin. Chekhov's entire narrative is constructed from such meaningful details as these.

Julian W. Connolly

THE MAN IN THE BLACK SUIT

Author: Stephen King (1947-   )
Type of plot: Horror, frame story
Time of plot: Summer, 1914
Locale: Motton, Maine, and environs
First published: 1994

Principal characters:
GARY, the narrator
DAN, his brother
THE DEVIL

The Story

The action proper of "The Man in the Black Suit" begins with nine-year-old Gary performing some Saturday chores in the summer of 1914 on his parents' farm, chores that his older brother Dan would have helped with had he not died from a bee sting a year earlier. After his chores, Gary is allowed to go fishing in Castle Stream provided he promises not to go too far in the woods and certainly not beyond where the stream forks. Solemnly promising to go no farther than the fork, he sets out by himself; his dog Candy Bill stays behind for the first time.

Gary soon catches a huge brook trout and then a fine rainbow trout. Leaning back against the riverbank, he dozes off, suddenly to be awakened by a tug on his pole and with the horrible realization that a bee is sitting on the tip of his nose. Terrified that the bee will sting him and that he will die as his brother did, Gary is on the verge of panic when he hears the sharp report of a hand clap and the bee falls dead into his lap.

Gary looks over his shoulder and sees the source of the clap. At the edge of the trees at the top of the riverbank stands a tall man with a pale and long face, black hair plastered tight against his skull. He is dressed in a three-piece black suit, and Gary realizes immediately that the man is not human because his eyes lack irises and his pupils are an orange-red and burning like fire. Frightened beyond measure, Gary wets his pants as the man smiles at him from above and greets him in a pleasant and mellow voice: "Are we well-met, fisherboy?"

Walking down the steep bank without leaving an imprint on the ground, the man squats beside the terrified Gary, who notices the man's hideously elongated fingers with long yellow claws instead of fingernails. Gary knows the man is the devil, but he is too paralyzed by fear to run. The devil sniffs Gary's wet pants and laughs wildly like a lunatic. He then tells the boy that his mother is dead, describing at length in gory detail her agonizing death by a bee sting.

Then abruptly the man in the black suit, his eyes blazing and his sharp little teeth showing between his thin pale lips, tells Gary that he is going to kill him, rip him to pieces, and eat his guts. Too terrified to utter a sound, Gary instinctively holds out the huge brook trout, and the devil opens his mouth wider than any human mouth ever could be, his gullet a fiery red, and swallows the fish. The sight of the devil's eyes emitting tears of blood galvanizes Gary to move, and he scrambles up the riverbank and runs as he has never run before, for his very life, with the devil in deadly pursuit. At long last, his heart pounding and with a painful stitch in his side, Gary realizes the devil has gone. He encounters his father on the road and screams hysterically that "Ma's dead!" After finally being reassured that his mother is alive and well, Gary is not able to share his terrible ordeal with his father, knowing that it is too incredible to be believed. Later in the day the two go back to the fishing spot to retrieve Gary's rod and creel, and his father notices the dead vegetation where the devil has been, smells the burnt-match odor of the grass, throws away the reeking creel, and tells his son "Let's get the hell out of here." The mother is never told about any of this.

"The Man in the Black Suit" concludes with Gary, now ninety years old in his nursing home room, remembering the vivid horror of the devil's visit so long ago and musing about his helpless vulnerability should the devil come again and still be hungry.

Themes and Meanings

The grandfather of a friend of Stephen King's truly believed that he had been visited by the devil in the Maine woods around the turn of the twentieth century. "The Man in the Black Suit" grew out of the friend's account of his grandfather's misadventure, and it was written in tribute to Nathaniel Hawthorne's "Young Goodman Brown," King's favorite story by that author. It is first and foremost a horror story designed to inspire fear in the reader, and in this it succeeds. It would be difficult to imagine a situation more terrifying than that of an innocent child alone in the woods being visited by a hideous monster that torments him with the lie that his mother is dead and then seeks to tear him to shreds and devour him. As with Jakob and Wilhelm Grimm's "Hansel and Gretel," this is the very stuff of primeval terror.

"The Man in the Black Suit" is so enriched by existential themes and questions about the human condition that it is more than a mere horror story. The mystery of evil, the absolute uncertainty of the future, and the sad debilities of old age are major concerns of this story. Why bad things happen to good people is one of life's enduring puzzles. Why was Dan struck down in his youth by the sting of a bee in the summer of 1913? What did this good, God-fearing family do to deserve losing their child? Why was the innocent Gary set on by an unspeakable evil? He was a good boy "and yet the Devil came." Is sick old age the ultimate end for everyone who does not die young? Is Gary's long life a blessing or a curse? Burdened by memories of his vigorous youth and trapped in a body so infirm that he cannot get to the bathroom and back to his bed without his walker, is Gary any more fortunate than his long-dead brother? Of course, these questions must go unanswered, but that they are raised at all places "The Man in the Black Suit" in a category beyond stories whose sole aim is to frighten.

Style and Technique

"The Man in the Black Suit" is a frame story. The frame consists of a decrepit old man resolving to erase his haunting memory of meeting the devil when he was nine years old. Writing it down, he believes, will give him release; and writing it in a book marked Diary and placing it by his bedside will ensure that someday someone will read his story after he is gone. Although this short story is not formally divided into parts, it is as skillfully constructed as a well-made play, the action inside the frame unfolding organically in five stages. First, the milieu of the town of Motton in the early years of the twentieth century is re-created. The world was different then. There were no neighborhoods; farms were separated by long distances and the land was largely forests and swamp. "In those days there were ghosts everywhere." Next, Gary's close relationship with his parents is provided along with a vivid word picture of his mother kneading bread in her kitchen. The third stage consists of Gary's journey through the woods, catching two fine trout, meeting the devil, and narrowly escaping with his life. Stage four is his joyous reunion with his father, and the last stage is their going back to Castle Stream to retrieve Gary's fishing gear and the father instinctively sensing that something is terribly wrong.

This is a retrospective story, the action occurring more than eighty years in the past, and yet King is able to create such convincing characters and clearly realized settings as to make the story as immediate as the present. Verisimilitude is essential to all literature, but it is especially vital to literature of the supernatural. King achieves this quality of believability by creating a narrator of unimpeachable integrity; by references to familiar places, institutions, and products such as the University of Maine in Orono, Ovaltine, and Dr. Grabow pipes; and, perhaps most important, by a kind of matter-of-fact style of narration. "The Man in the Black Suit" is filled with striking images and metaphors, one of the most memorable being the narrator's comparison of his body to a child's sand castle soon to be washed away by the incoming tide.

Robert G. Blake

THE MAN OF THE WORLD

Author: Frank O'Connor (Michael Francis O'Donovan, 1903-1966)
Type of plot: Domestic realism
Time of plot: The early twentieth century
Locale: Ireland
First published: 1957

> *Principal characters:*
> LARRY, the young protagonist
> JIMMY LEARY, the young but experienced man who befriends and
> instructs Larry

The Story

The protagonist, Larry, is a naïve, very young person who knows nothing of the world. Unable to see beyond the appearances of things, he takes everything and everyone at face value. He is first seen in a comic light taking his possessions to spend a few days at his friend's house. He calls this ordinary experience a holiday, and the neighbors laugh at his pretension and innocence. His friend, Jimmy Leary, considers himself to be a man of the world and looks down on nearly everyone in the neighborhood; however, he is willing, even proud, to teach Larry the knowledge of the world he has precociously acquired. He is authoritative about the true nature of women and the neighbors' economic condition; this knowledge is defined, in Larry's words, as sophisticated.

Larry ardently anticipates the promised change that will move him from the world of appearances to understanding the true reality represented by Jimmy's sophistication. He does have doubts about what this initiation will involve; however, when he sees his parents at home in the world, he is troubled by what he is about to learn. He goes to his friend's house to spy on a young couple in the next house. They have recently moved in, and the frugal landlady has not provided the place with shades. Jimmy has promised to show Larry a few things, and Larry agrees because he wishes to become like Jimmy.

The hidden reality that is to be revealed is apparently a sexual one. This is clearly suggested by the repeated use of the word "sophisticated" and the proposed spying on a young married couple. Jimmy is described as being a collector of such illegitimate probing into people's lives; however, when they spy on the couple, the boys discover them praying rather than making love. Larry suddenly feels he is intruding on something intimate and personal. He feels the presence of eternity watching him.

Themes and Meanings

Frank O'Connor's "The Man of the World" is an initiation story, in which Larry is led to the moment in which he will be introduced into the world. His guide, however, is only a year older than he is, and has a premature and jaded view of the world. What Larry is initiated into is merely a loss of innocence, rather than the expected gain of maturity. He passes beyond the anticipated maturity to adult shame and guilt.

Another theme is the reversal of the observer and the observed. In spying on the young couple, Larry thinks that he is a privileged observer. With Jimmy's guidance, he is acquiring knowledge by looking down on people who are living what they think is a private life. He, however, becomes aware of being watched by some higher power, a god who sees and truly knows all, in contrast to the limited and weary false sophistication of Jimmy Leary. A recognition of the reduced role he will now play in the world follows this perception, and there is a permanent diminishment of his sense of self.

The story is also about the consequences of knowledge. Larry loses his innocence forever at the end of the story. He attempts to refuse the inappropriate sophistication that is represented by Jimmy, but he cannot recover his innocence. He has tasted of the tree of knowledge and can never return to his innocent childhood. There thus seems to be a use of the Eden myth to define and describe Larry's change in the story. He has been cast out of his innocent and blessed world of appearances, and he can never return to that state.

A related theme is religious. The presence of an omniscient power is revealed as observing what Larry has been doing. As a result of his awareness of the presence of this deity, Larry can never escape the guilt and shame that he feels. Even if he determines that he will never be as sophisticated as Jimmy, he cannot purge the feeling of someone looking down on him and judging all his actions. He has entered a world of sin and shame that he must live with; the initiation robs him of an innocence he can never recover.

Style and Technique

"The Man of the World" creates much of its effect from its naïve, innocent view of the world. Even though the first-person narrator is looking back with some amusement and no little exasperation at his earlier self, he maintains something of the confusion and wonder of childhood and never intrudes with an adult's perception. O'Connor perfectly renders Larry's sense of wonder in the way he sees his world: "The least thing could excite or depress me: the trees in the morning when I went to early Mass, the stained-glass windows in the church, the blue hilly streets at evening with the green flare of the gas lamps, the smells of cooking and perfume." In contrast, Jimmy's world has no wonder or excitement. Everything is already known and all issues are settled. He cannot change his nature or the way he sees the world.

There are two distinct styles in the story: the naïveté of Larry and the sophistication of Jimmy. Larry is obsessively curious about everything, but he feels that he cannot discover the true nature of things. He sees and describes only appearances, but those appearances make up the world of O'Connor's fiction. Jimmy thinks he possesses knowledge about the secrets of the neighbors or the nature of a young woman, but he is blind to the world that goes on around him as he ignores the concrete world of the story and intrudes on the lives of others. Jimmy has only opinions about his world; he never sees it as truly or fully as Larry does. Jimmy's style is minimalist. It consists of the few judgmental remarks and pronouncements he makes about the people in his world. It has none of the detail of Larry's lovingly observed world.

At the end of the story, Larry attempts to renounce Jimmy's style and view. He will never be sophisticated and view people as objects to be observed or known. There is an intrusion into other people's lives that he cannot accept and will not allow. This is curious, because to intrude on people's lives and innermost secrets is the job of a fiction writer. However, O'Connor—and the representation of his earlier self, Larry—has a reverence for the characters he creates and allows them to retain their secrets and hidden life.

There is a sweetness in the style of the story and a geniality that is one of the most endearing qualities of O'Connor's fiction. He has described his stories as dealing with a submerged population instead of the famous of the world. There are no heroes in O'Connor's stories, only ordinary people who discover something about themselves. He is especially good at portraying the uncertainties and discoveries of adolescence in the tightly knit Irish society.

The plot of the story works by employing multiple reversals and a central recognition by the main character. Larry's expectations are completely altered and so is his character. O'Connor uses some of the most traditional devices of plot—reversal and recognition—to structure the story but manages to make them convincing. The story concerns an ordinary incident that many readers have experienced, but it completely alters the main character; Larry can never be the same or see the world in the same way again. O'Connor is a master of domestic realism as he translates the ordinary events of adolescence into patterns that shape destinies.

O'Connor's methods of characterization and his use of dialogue are important in creating the effect of the story. Most of the story takes place within Larry's mind; it is an internal monologue about himself and his world. In contrast, Jimmy speaks in elliptical and revealing phrases; he is given no internal life at all in the story. We see this at the end of the story after Larry has had his recognition. Jimmy thinks that Larry is still a follower and promises a deeper initiation, never recognizing or realizing the true nature of his intrusion on other people's lives.

James Sullivan

THE MAN THAT CORRUPTED HADLEYBURG

Author: Mark Twain (Samuel Langhorne Clemens, 1835-1910)
Type of plot: Satire
Time of plot: The mid-1800's
Locale: Hadleyburg, a small midwestern American town
First published: 1899

Principal characters:
THE STRANGER, "HOWARD L. STEPHENSON," a gambler who
takes revenge on Hadleyburg for an insult
EDWARD and MARY RICHARDS, the protagonists, a poor elderly
couple who live on Edward's salary as a bank teller
THE NINETEEN, the nineteen top families of Hadleyburg,
including the Richardses
THE REVEREND MR. BURGESS, a disgraced minister
BARCLAY GOODSON, the town cynic, who is deceased

The Story

The story is divided into four parts: first, the introduction of Hadleyburg, the Richardses, and the stranger's plot to corrupt and disgrace the town; then the description of the Nineteeners' vanities and greed as they fall for the plot; third, the exposure of the town's artificial honesty; and finally, the effects of the plot on the Richardses. There are, however, really two stories woven together.

The first is the corruption of Hadleyburg. The town's motto is "Lead us not into temptation." Hadleyburg is famed for, and vain about, its reputation for honesty. However, the narrator, presumably Twain, makes it clear that appearances are all that the town really cares about. It is "a mean town, a hard, stingy town." Eventually Hadleyburg offends a passing stranger, a gambler, who resolves to revenge himself on the town by exposing its artificial virtue. He leaves a sack supposedly containing forty thousand dollars in gold with Mary and Edward Richards, asking them to find an unknown benefactor. This person had given the gambler twenty dollars and advice. Whoever correctly repeats that advice can claim the money.

Edward publishes the stranger's instructions, the story is picked up by the Associated Press, and the town awakes famous and even more conceited. Everyone believes that the only person in town who would have actually given money to a stranger is Barclay Goodson, the "best hated man among us"—the only person willing publicly to call the town narrow, self-righteous, and stingy. Goodson is dead, however, so the money could be claimed by anyone who could figure out the remark made to the gambler. Each Nineteener tries. Soon, each receives a letter from a Howard L. Stephenson, who says that he heard Goodson give the advice, "You are far from being a bad man: go and reform." Each Nineteener immediately leaves a letter with that remark, claiming the sack, with the Reverend Mr. Burgess. Burgess will run "The Test": the reading of the "real" remark sealed in the bag.

In part 3, the first part of the stranger's trap is sprung as the sealed remark is revealed: "You are far from being a bad man. Go and reform—or, mark my words—some day, for your sins, you will die and go to hell or Hadleyburg—TRY AND MAKE IT THE FORMER." Burgess then reads the claims of eighteen of the Nineteen, showing each to be a liar and cheat, but holds on to the Richardses' letter. Edward Richards once saved Burgess from a mob, after "that one thing" (never detailed) which had disgraced Burgess and lost him his congregation. As the rest of the bag's instructions are read, the whole joke is revealed: There is no gold, only painted lead, and no pauper gambler, no twenty dollars, no advice. The town, having thoroughly enjoyed the Eighteen's disgrace, auctions off the bag and gives the money to the Richardses. The stranger also gives them money, as an apology.

The second story focuses on the effect of the joke on Mary and Edward Richards. They are introduced as a sweet, loving old couple, struggling to get by on Edward's tiny salary. They are good people but, as Mary later says, their honesty is as artificial as the rest of the town's. Edward had known that Burgess was innocent of "that thing," but he was too afraid of the town's disapproval to tell the truth and save the minister. Instead, he soothed his conscience by only telling Burgess when to leave town.

In spite of that admission, the Richardses are the sympathetic focus of the story. The reader observes them as they have second thoughts about advertising for the "benefactor" and through two wonderful scenes as they try to rationalize falsely claiming the money. Edward does try to confess during the reading of the names at the test, but he is misunderstood as asking for charity for others, cheered, and forced to sit down.

The last section of the story shows what can happen to good, but weak, people. The Richardses learn how "a sin takes on new and real terrors when there seems a chance that it is going to be found out." Edward and Mary sink into guilty despair and paranoia, eventually burning the money that they have been given and deciding that Burgess saved them only to expose them later. They become ill and delirious, and their participation in claiming the sack is soon known. Just before he dies, Edward tries to do the "right" thing. He calls Burgess to him in front of witnesses, admits his guilt in claiming the money, and clears Burgess of "that thing" that had disgraced him years ago, but then forgives him for doing the "natural and justifiable thing" in exposing the Richardses' envelope too. "Burgess's impassioned protestations fell upon deaf ears; the dying man passed away without knowing that once more he had done Burgess a wrong." Mary dies soon after. The town, mourning for a variety of reasons, changes its name and changes its motto to "Lead us into temptation."

Themes and Meanings

Three of Twain's favorite themes are central to "The Man That Corrupted Hadleyburg": appearance versus reality, the importance of training or habit, and—overlying those two—the evils caused by human vanity. Twain and the stranger both enjoy exposing the town's lies: Mary and Edward Richards read the *Missionary Herald* but are too weak to practice charity at home and save Burgess. Hadleyburg prides itself on its honesty, but everyone, including the Richardses, is willing to lie for the gold. There is no real virtue in Hadleyburg, only show.

Real virtue, as the stranger says, requires testing: People must train to resist temptation. Training can be either bad or good: In Hadleyburg, training is for cowardice, rationalization, and vanity. Edward tries to stand against that norm at the end of the story, but by then it is too late, and he only hurts Burgess again.

The reason that it is so difficult to act well is because doing so requires admitting to faults. In his essay "What Is Man?" Twain says that there is no real altruism—man is motivated only by self-interest. That hurts people's vanity, however, so most people lie to themselves about their motives and morals. It takes a shock such as the Richardses' guilt or Hadleyburg's disgrace to break that pattern. After that, people can perhaps learn to enjoy overcoming their weaknesses rather than ignoring them: "Lead us into temptation."

Style and Technique

Twain's use of two stories is what makes "The Man That Corrupted Hadleyburg" more than merely a joke. Mary and Edward Richards are real, sympathetic people— childish, occasionally, but no more so than are most people. Their destruction shows why vanity, lies, and selfish revenge are not funny. In real life, real people are hurt.

Twain uses two other favorite devices, a mysterious stranger and ironic humor, to force the story's characters to face reality. His stranger in "The Chronicle of Young Satan" says, "For your race, in its poverty, has unquestionably one really effective weapon—laughter. . . . Against the assault of Laughter nothing can stand." Hadleyburg's stranger forces the townspeople to admit to, laugh at, and then change their egotistical illusions. Humor also keeps the audience reading and, one hopes, thinking.

Janice B. Cope

THE MAN TO SEND RAIN CLOUDS

Author: Leslie Marmon Silko (1948-   )
Type of plot: Social realism
Time of plot: The 1960's
Locale: A Pueblo Indian reservation in the Southwest
First published: 1969

> *Principal characters:*
> TEOFILO, an old sheepherder
> LOUISE, his granddaughter
> KEN, her husband
> LEON, Ken's brother-in-law
> FATHER PAUL, a Franciscan missionary

The Story

The old man Teofilo has died peacefully while tending sheep out at the sheep camp, away from the village. Leon and Ken find him under a cottonwood tree, but because his sheep have wandered away, the two brothers-in-law first collect them and put them in the corral. Then they prepare Teofilo for burial by painting his face, tying a gray feather in his hair, and wrapping him in a red blanket. On their way back in the truck, they meet Father Paul, who asks about Teofilo. Leon turns the question aside, avoiding the imposition of a Roman Catholic funeral. After the medicine men have performed the traditional funeral, Louise—Teofilo's granddaughter and Ken's wife—tells Leon that she thinks the priest should sprinkle holy water so that Teofilo will not be thirsty. Leon invites Father Paul to bring his holy water to the grave. In spite of the irregularity—Father Paul tells Leon that last rites and a mass should be said before a proper Catholic burial—he accepts the invitation to be part of the ceremony and sprinkles the water. He cannot understand how and why the water disappears almost before it hits the sand, prompting a moment of crisis and climax in the story, as the puzzled priest returns to the mission unaware of his own effectiveness in the ceremony.

Themes and Meanings

The title "The Man to Send Rain Clouds" demarcates the cultural divide between its Native American protagonists and Father Paul; in the priest's Christian world, only God can send rain clouds, but in the Pueblo world, it is every man's task hereafter to speak to the cloud people and ask them to make rain for the living. From their positions on either side of this cultural divide, the characters enact an episode in the power struggle between the Pueblo and the white world. The struggle has evolved into a ritual not of confrontation, but of assertion of dominance met by strategies of subversion, evasion, and adaptation that not only maintain the Pueblo way but also warrant analogous subversion and adaptation of form by the writer, in order to make the short story accommodate her cultural stance.

In this brief tale of Teofilo's burial and transformation to the man to send rain clouds, Leslie Marmon Silko has rewritten one of the dominant narratives of the Encounter—the conversion of native people to Christianity—to demonstrate the means by which Native American religions (and the cultures from which they are inseparable) have survived. Silko has made the story a parable of cultural endurance, not by rendering belief and ritual in ethnographic or archival detail but by tracing the growth and renewal of the traditional ceremony by incorporating new and useful elements from the Roman Catholic ritual. The story anticipates the principle in Silko's novel *Ceremony* (1977), where the ceremony that leads to the cure for the main character is a hybrid of an ancient Scalp Ceremony that incorporates new elements.

Ironically, Father Paul is the agent of innovation in the Pueblo ceremony, in spite of his unwillingness and his failure to understand the success and significance of his own actions. The cultural distance between the priest and the Pueblo is skillfully defined and manipulated in the first conversation between Father Paul and Leon, who turns aside his inquiry about Teofilo (and his pastoral care) with the assurance that everything is all right. Believing Teofilo to be alive, the priest tries to manage Leon and his supposed authority over Teofilo by telling him that an old man like Teofilo should not be left at the sheep camp alone. He misconstrues the status of the elder among his clan members and misunderstands their attitude toward death, which the Pueblo characters find (as their response to Teofilo's death implies) welcome, natural, and not to be feared or avoided.

Leon replies, in truth, that he will not do that any more. The priest does not pick up the strong suggestion that Teofilo is dead, much less appreciate the humor in being deceived by the truth. Father Paul assumes that Leon can assume an authority over Teofilo that he does not have, warranted in part by the authority that Father Paul assumes he has over Leon. Father Paul, assuming he has made himself clear, congratulates Leon and encourages him to come to Mass on Sunday and to bring Teofilo. The ironies continue to build; Leon understands not what Father Paul wants him to, but what Father Paul does not understand, that Teofilo is dead, that Father Paul is not wanted for the funeral, and that inviting Teofilo to Mass the following week is a serious mistake.

The story's climax places Father Paul, however momentarily, between the Christian and Pueblo cultures. His action has permitted the Roman Catholic element to serve in the Pueblo ceremony, contrary to his church's doctrines, and could result in the priest's own conversion, as it were, to a position from which he might better understand the people to whom he ministers. At the climax of Father Paul's presence in the story, the water he sprinkles disappears "almost before it touched the dim, cold sand," a phenomenon that "reminded him of something—he tried to remember what it was, because he thought if he could remember he might understand this." He might have remembered that, among the Pueblo, the living feed the dead, putting pinches of food in a bowl for them to feast on; and so might he have understood the disappearance of the water, and the subsequent swirling away of the corn meal and pollen from the blanket, as a successful offering.

Father Paul seems on the verge of understanding the water's almost supernatural vanishing. It is inconceivable to him that his Christian ceremony would have an altogether different effect from that of bestowing grace and purification, in a ceremony he would regard as pagan and demoniac. He does not consider the import of Leon's invitation, that the people acknowledge that his holy water has power to serve vital, pragmatic ends, and that they regard him as custodian of that power. He does not recognize that his medicine has succeeded.

Style and Technique

As Leon manipulates Father Paul's ministry to serve the Pueblos' purpose, Silko alters the short story's conventions to accommodate the process of cultural assertion and adaptation. The simplicity of her style seems a strange, unconventional way of storytelling. Silko does not describe her characters physically or psychologically, or develop much sense of individual personality. Characters say little to each other and almost nothing about themselves. Ken and Leon say nothing when they find Teofilo dead, in spite of the momentousness of the event. The first spoken words are not attributed to either man, but whoever says "Send us rain clouds, Grandfather" speaks for both. Among the Pueblo characters, there is only one short exchange, in which Louise tells Ken that she had been thinking about having the priest sprinkle holy water for her grandpa so he will not be thirsty. Moments later, Leon says he will see where he is. They do not consider the implications of asking for the priest's participation in their burial ceremony, which has already concluded. The Indians' interactions are determined not by negotiations of the individual, conflicting will or by self-expression, but by a ritual that is set in motion by the discovery of Teofilo and that is quietly under way at all times.

The story declines to represent the ritual, as if to avoid any anthropological or ethnographic interest. The mourning period and funeral ceremony are conducted outside the narrative and, after Louise's casual remark to Leon, the story centers increasingly and climactically on Father Paul, as he becomes instrumental in making Teofilo the man to send rain clouds. Nearly all dialogue and narration are conducted across the white/Indian cultural divide, where negotiation is necessary to assert and assure identity. The sole moment of interior speech belongs to the priest, who as he sprinkles holy water wonders if the Indians are tricking him by having him bury a blanket, not a man, and by the way the water disappears. Father Paul's uncertainty is fruitless; he enjoys no epiphany or enlargement of his understanding. The moment of epiphany in the modern short story is frustrated, for even though the people accord the priest power in their ceremony and that power has the effect that the people desired, it brings the priest no closer to his parishioners or to an understanding of the cultural processes in which he participates. Father Paul's moment is a false climax and an anti-epiphany, and he returns to the mission unenlightened.

The Pueblo perspective is quietly reasserted at the end of the story, with the success of the ceremony and Leon's pleasure in having added the sprinkling, for now he was sure the old man could send them big thunderclouds.

Robert Bensen

THE MAN WHO BECAME A WOMAN

Author: Sherwood Anderson (1876-1941)
Type of plot: Psychological
Time of plot: The early twentieth century
Locale: Western Pennsylvania
First published: 1923

> *Principal characters:*
> HERMAN DUDLEY, a white man recording a troubling early
> experience
> TOM MEANS, his friend, a horse groomer
> BURT, a black man who works with the narrator as a groomer
> after Tom leaves

The Story

Herman Dudley reflects on his early life, beginning with his childhood in a small Nebraska town and leading up to the event that caused him to leave the racehorse and tramp life forever. He begins his reminiscence in his own home, recalling his home town, a nondescript place. He fills in his family history, which leads him to the western Pennsylvania racehorse circuit, traveling from county fair to county fair, working as a groomer for a horse named Pick-it-boy, during fall until winter sets in.

In late fall, after the departure of Herman's friend Tom Means, Herman is joined by Burt, an African American groomer. Through his relationship with Burt, Herman explores racial issues. He decides that they cannot be friends because too much talk about such issues has put an unnatural strain on relationships between black people and white people. Still, Burt and Herman obviously are friends. Burt covers for Herman's lethargy, and Herman walks both horses to help Burt out.

During the final week of the circuit, circumstances lead to Herman's being left alone, tending to all the horses. Loneliness causes him to leave his post, and he ends up in a miners' bar. As he drinks whiskey at the bar and the miners play cards in the background, he looks into an old, cracked looking glass behind the bar and sees the frightened face of a young girl in his own reflection.

Furthering his transition from male to female, a huge man with red hair forces him to care for his child during a bar fight. As the child begins to howl, the redheaded man stops fighting, reclaims his child, and leaves the bar. The narrator then slinks out and returns, soaked with rain and drink, to Pick-it-boy's stall. He strips himself of his wet clothing and falls asleep under a saddle blanket in the loft above the horse's stall.

When two of the black groomers return drunk from town, they mistakenly stagger into Herman's loft. In the dim light of their lantern, they pull off his saddle blanket and mistake him for a woman. In their surprise, they drop the lantern, which goes out. They lunge for Herman, who is too terrified to scream, and both of them miss him. He runs into the night, trying futilely to scream, unable to see the dark-skinned men and aware that his white skin must be visible even in the darkness. He continues to run long after they have stopped chasing him.

Herman's flight takes him past the racetrack and to the abandoned slaughterhouse, where he stumbles over the bleached white bones of a horse and lands inside the horse's ribs. The terror of being in the horse's skeleton burns all his thoughts about being a girl out of him. He can finally scream. He emerges from the bones a man, but because he is blubbering and crying, he is ashamed to return to the stables. He sleeps that night with several sheep that have gnawed a cave into a straw stack.

In the morning, he must return naked back to the stalls to retrieve his clothing. He knows that he will be taunted and that he will probably blubber in shame, and in fact he does. He is surprised that Burt comes to his defense, brandishing a pitchfork at Herman's tormentors and swearing. Herman is deeply touched by Burt's swearing and blubbers as he puts on his wet clothes, kisses Pick-it-boy good-bye, and leaves. Burt does not notice Herman's departure.

Themes and Meanings

The major themes in "The Man Who Became a Woman" are relationships—between species, between races, and between genders. Sherwood Anderson, known for exploring sexuality and the unconscious, lets this exploration have free play in Herman Dudley, the narrator, who holds fast to a belief that other species are superior because of their simplicity. As his disgust with humanity deepens, his belief in the superiority of other animals, particularly horses, heightens. As he leaves his early life behind him, it is Pick-it-boy that he kisses good-bye on the cheek.

The theme of racial relationships is more complex, influenced by views prevalent in the early twentieth century United States, when the story was published. Although the narrator believes black men and white men cannot be friends in such times, he likes Burt and ponders the differences in races. His observations seem unenlightened but well-meaning. Burt's defense of the guileless Herman seems to be a hopeful note, a possibility even for that time and place in U.S. history. Anderson, through his narrator, clearly shows an unwillingness to ignore this area of human relationships.

As the title suggests, gender relationships are the focus of "The Man Who Became a Woman." Setting the scene for the night Herman becomes a woman, Herman discusses Tom Means, whom he admits he loves. "Americans are shy and timid about saying things like that," Herman adds. "A man here don't dare own up he loves another man, I've found out, and they are afraid to admit such feelings to themselves even." Anderson's narrator feels comfortable in his love for Tom, but he feels uncomfortable about discussing that love. Herman notes that Tom generally speaks poorly of women, but he still married one.

The primary exploration of gender relationships, however, occurs within Herman—the name itself probably chosen as a pun ("her-man"). He watches himself transformed into a girl-woman: not a strong woman, but a pale, fearful woman, too terrified to scream, shameful and cowardly. Herman's shyness with real women leads him to dream and fantasize about women. The dreams intensify in his loneliness after Tom leaves. He contrasts the women of his fantasies with those women who claim they are equal to men, women of whom Herman disapproves. All we know of his Jessie is that she is someone with whom he feels comfortable and that, as he writes his story, she is in the kitchen, making a pie or some such thing.

Although Anderson's story leaves his narrator vulnerable to criticism regarding the exploration of racial and gender relationships, the story is a document of its times, and Anderson, by creating Herman Dudley, with his innocent candor, shows courage in exploring such complex issues.

Style and Technique

"The Man Who Became a Woman" was originally published in Anderson's collection *Horses and Men* (1923), in which the racetrack provides the general setting. The tragicomic style of reminiscence resonates through Anderson's works, earning him the nickname "The Ohio Pagan," taken from the title of one of the stories in the 1923 collection. Critics of Anderson's short stories believe he conceals the seriousness of his stories behind the style of high-spirited recollections, turning dramatic monologue into a story.

Virginia Woolf said that in Anderson's stories the "senses flourish," that the stories are "dominated by instincts rather than by ideas," and that Anderson leaves his characters "exposed, defenseless, naked to scorn and laughter." Her observations are supported by Herman Dudley's experiences in "The Man Who Became a Woman," first, when he sees in his own reflection the face of a terrified girl and hears the scornful laughter of the miners in the bar, suspecting wrongly that the laughter is directed at him; and later, when he is forced to flee from the stables and return naked for his clothing. In the final scenes, Herman is literally exposed, defenseless, naked to scorn and laughter.

Anderson's style appeals to the senses, with sketches of the racetracks and stables, a sketch of the narrator's father exchanging greetings with a beautiful woman at a railroad station, a depiction of the deserted slaughterhouse with its stench and skeletons, and the vivid images of the suspenseful flight at the climax of the story. His story is bound together more by this increasing emotional tension than by the plot. Anderson leaves readers with the final intense image of Burt, swinging his pitchfork at men and trees, swearing, and defending Herman's innocence, as Herman slinks away from the scene of his shame.

"The Man Who Became a Woman" goes beyond sketching to expose the psychology of Anderson's narrator, the mature man examining the psychology of his younger self. The suspenseful final scene blends sketching and psychological realism.

Carol Franks

THE MAN WHO COULD WORK MIRACLES
A Pantoum in Prose

Author: H. G. Wells (1866-1946)
Type of plot: Fantasy
Time of plot: 1896
Locale: England
First published: 1898

> Principal characters:
> GEORGE MCWHIRTER FOTHERINGAY, an unprepossessing, thirty-
> year-old countinghouse clerk
> MR. MAYDIG, a Congregational minister

The Story

An unprepossessing clerk, George McWhirter Fotheringay, is involved in an argument in the Long Dragon bar concerning whether miracles actually exist. Fotheringay does not believe in miracles; he is a skeptic and a rationalist. He states, "Let us clearly understand what a miracle is. It's something contrariwise to the course of nature done by power or Will, something what couldn't happen without being specially willed." By way of example, Fotheringay explains that the gas lamp lighting the bar could not burn upside down. If it were to do so, that would be a miracle. He continues in his charade by telling the lamp to turn upside down without breaking but to go on burning steadily.

The incredible happens: The lamp does just that. Fotheringay is accused of creating a silly trick and asked to leave. Later, alone in his little bedroom, he begins to grapple with what has just happened and realizes that at the exact moment he gave the command for the lamp to turn upside down, his mind had inadvertently willed it to do so. Fotheringay tests his theory with several simple experiments; then recalling that he must rise early in the morning for work, he commands a comfortable night's sleep for himself.

The next day, Fotheringay begins to think about the materialistic means to which he can turn his power. He calls into existence a pair of very splendid diamond studs but hastily annihilates them in fear that his countinghouse boss, the young Mr. Gomshott, might become suspicious about their acquisition. On the way home from work, Fotheringay recalls the story of "Tannhauser" and pokes his walking stick into the turf along the footpath and commands the dry wood to blossom. It does so, and the air is filled with the scent of roses. He hears footsteps and hastily commands the stick to go back—meaning, of course, to the form of a walking stick. The bush literally propels through the air and into the shin of Constable Winch. Fotheringay bungles an explanation to the constable, and chafing under Winch's anger, he wills Winch to Hades. He soon regrets what he has done and transfers Winch from Hades to San Francisco.

This incident brings home to Fotheringay the incredible power he possesses, and on Sunday evening he goes to chapel thinking that perhaps the answer lies in religion. Mr. Maydig, the Congregational minister, preaches about things that are not lawful. Following this quite relevant sermon, Fotheringay requests a private conversation with the vicar, during which he exhibits proof of his power to work miracles.

In the vicar's study on a Sunday evening, the clerk and the vicar begin to hasten the world's progress. They change the vicar's careless housekeeper into a model servant, reform drunkards, change beer to water, drain a swamp, improve railway service, and even cure the Reverend Maydig's wart. Under the influence of Mr. Maydig, Fotheringay attempts to duplicate Joshua's feat of making the sun stand still, but in his naïveté requests the earth to stop moving—whereupon every object on the surface of the earth flies off into space, Fotheringay included. At last, Fotheringay collects himself sufficiently to wish that he be restored, minus his magical powers, to that point in time at which he found he possessed them. The world returns to normalcy, and the story returns full circle to the Long Dragon and the beginning of the discussion about the existence of miracles.

Themes and Meanings

As a work of farcical fantasy, the story is representative of a vast literature about ordinary people who are endowed unexpectedly with miraculous powers, for example, Aladdin of *Alf layla wa-laya* (fifteenth century; English translation, 1706-1708). H. G. Wells himself stated, "It is always about life being altered that I write, or about people developing schemes for altering life." In "The Man Who Could Work Miracles," this idea is presented in a mischievous manner: Wells combines seemingly occult elements with comedy to reflect his perceptive criticism of human limitations and possibilities. In commenting about this approach, Wells stated, "I have never once 'presented' life. My apparently most objective books are criticisms and incitements to change."

Wells foresaw some of the real problems of the twentieth century, such as the congestion of cities and the humane or inhumane use of science. He questioned progress and stated that all of his books asserted "the insecurity of progress and the possibility of human degeneration and extinction." This idea is nowhere more apparent than in the failed efforts of Fotheringay and the vicar to speed up progress and aid the world, and it is clearly a repetition of the theme of *The Island of Dr. Moreau* (1896), wherein the benevolent efforts of Dr. Moreau end in disaster. In like manner, when Fotheringay and the vicar attempt to alter nature, Fotheringay's lack of a sense of human limitations creates a catastrophe. This theme of the necessity of changing the world and the necessity of changing human nature is given a comic twist. Underneath the humor, however, Wells's certainty in the steady progression of humankind through scientific innovation and evolution is clear. The imaginative fantasy of "The Man Who Could Work Miracles" epitomizes Wells's socialist belief that the innovative ideas of liberated individuals must intrude on the conventions of society, and the pessimistic ending of the story clearly reveals Wells's feelings about the infinite plasticity of things.

His treatment of Fotheringay's inadvertent destruction of the universe is speculative and analytical, and the message is clear: The greatest stumbling block to the achievement of improving the world is human nature itself. Thus, "The Man Who Could Work Miracles" is a telling indication of human limitations, even though the theme of global dissolution is treated comically. This combination was to recur in several later works. "The Man Who Could Work Miracles" has been considered by readers in the late twentieth century as a cautionary fable for the nuclear age.

Style and Technique

Wells appears to have an almost innate ability for writing in the genre of fantasy fiction. He explained that in writing these stories, he would take almost anything as a starting point and let his thoughts play about that idea. Presently, some absurd little nucleus would provide the germ for a story, much as Samuel Taylor Coleridge dreamed "Kubla Khan." In some of his stories, the bizarre, the weird, and the apocalyptic create the motif. In others, remote, mysterious worlds ruled by logical order, but not the order of common sanity, form the background and shape the events.

Wells is respected as an admirable storyteller as well as a sociological spectator. "The Man Who Could Work Miracles" is a wonderful example of both of his traits. In it, he artfully uses the apparently trivial items of fact and commonplace touches of formal style to create an incredibly humorous story with a serious underlying message. A binding of the commonplace to a fantastical event succeeds in convincing the reader of the possibility that such an event could occur. In returning full circle to its opening conversation, the story follows the form of its subtitle "A Pantoum in Prose," which reinforces the possibility of the plot.

Wells develops the premise of the story without the interference of rational skepticism. Its appeal lies in the introduction of the fantastic into the mundane events of ordinary life and its focus on incident, not character.

The outstanding characteristic of Wells's fantasies is that they are crammed full of ideas. They represent to an amazing degree the free and open play of imagination. His works provide easy and delightful reading, although they often have been labeled journalistic rather than disciplined. His style is not distinctive in a technical sense, and his ideas were often incompatible and self-contradictory; nevertheless, "The Man Who Could Work Miracles" is a genuine classic of fantasy.

Lela Phillips

THE MAN WHO FOUND A PISTOL

Author: Rudolfo A. Anaya (1937-   )
Type of plot: Psychological
Time of plot: The late twentieth century
Locale: New Mexico
First published: 1992

> *Principal characters:*
> THE NARRATOR, an unnamed middle-aged man
> PROCOPIO, the village bartender
> THE MAN WHO FOUND A PISTOL, an unnamed man who has just
> died

The Story

Procopio, the bartender of a small, isolated mountain town, well known among his clientele for keeping up with the community's daily gossip, re-creates the incidents that led to a man's death. Because the details in the newspaper are skimpy, the bartender's story explains how the dead man's luck changed for the worse the day he found a mysterious pistol. From that moment, the man, who had been a reserved outcast from the community, was known as the man who found a pistol.

The narrator feels a mysterious interest in Procopio's story, because he also has found an enigmatic object. He remembers an incident that took place in an isolated area in the Jemez Mountains. During a car trip with his wife, he stopped to eat lunch by a stream, where he found a double-bladed ax submerged in the water. Wondering about the ownership of the worn-out tool, far from a camp or logging area, he took the ax out of the water. At that moment, he felt the uncomfortable sensation of being observed. Afraid, he put the ax back into the stream and left the place at once.

Meanwhile, the narrator learns from Procopio about the man who found a pistol. The man moved to Corrales, wishing to find peace away from the busy university town in which he worked as a teacher. His daily routine took him to Procopio's bar after his afternoon walk along an irrigation ditch, located in a remote part of town. In the ditch he found a pistol, and after futile attempts to find its owner, he decided to keep it.

The narrator attempts to fill in gaps in Procopio's story by inquiries among acquaintances of the man who found a pistol, but he finds little information. The man was from Texas, and during his childhood there had been a shooting incident that involved one of his brothers. Nobody, including the man's wife, seemed to know the end of that episode. In his quest for information, the narrator experiences a mysterious frenzy that leads him to visit all the places known to the man who found a pistol, and to search in vain for the place where he himself had once found the double-bladed ax.

One afternoon the man who found a pistol got drunk and, in an attack of panic, tried to give his pistol to another patron of the bar, who refused it. That was his last day at the bar. Immediately thereafter he drew away from human contact, even that of his wife, who, tired of doing all the house chores, abandoned him. The man gave up all responsibilities and developed an inexplicable fear of being alone. The town's delivery boy moved in with the man to keep him company, and was present the night of the man's death. The boy swore that, after many nights of hearing mysterious door knocks that the man who found a pistol attributed to a ghost, the man decided to face his visitor. To the boy's terror, he saw the man's double on the other side of the door. The latter coldly fired the pistol at his double, then fell mysteriously dead by his own shot. In desperation, the boy took the pistol from the corpse and threw it away in the fields.

Themes and Meanings

Rudolfo A. Anaya's interest in the close relationship between New Mexico's geography and local Chicano folk stories, or *cuentos*, is in evidence in "The Man Who Found a Pistol." A native of Santa Rosa, a rural town on the New Mexican llano, Anaya has expressed his literary debt to that region's geography: "It's harsh environment. I remember most that sense of landscape which is bleak, empty, desolate, across which the wind blows and makes music." That locale takes on the surrealist tone of a land forgotten by the gods, which reserves for itself numerous supernatural secrets. Nature will reveal its enigmata only to the truly observant character, attuned to his own primal universe.

The metaphysical quest for the true self takes place in the geopolitical concept of Aztlán, the southwestern region United States, presented by Anaya and by other Chicano authors as a place of prophesy. Thus Aztlán's myths, represented in the local folklore of the Native American, the Spanish, the Mexican, or the Chicano, take on a cosmological dimension or, as defined by Anaya, the mirror by which people know themselves. Anaya states that as a Chicano writer his purpose is "to remind our people about their history and their traditions and their culture and their language, things that are under threat, and liable to disappear if we don't look closely at ourselves in a historical process."

"The Man Who Found a Pistol" sets two characters in close contact with the mythical nature of Aztlán. The unnamed narrator recognizes his debt to nature as a means of coming to understand his inner self. The man who found a pistol succumbs to the overpowering danger of nature and loses track of the delicate balance between reality and the inner self. When the narrator recognizes that loss in the man who found a pistol, he enters into a middle-aged crisis, from which he finds an escape in his passage through the Aztlán nature, following the path of the man who found a pistol.

The experiential knowledge gained by the narrator, as he traces the incidents surrounding the death of the man who found a pistol, also serves to bring forward the main philosophical motif: "This is the way of life: remembering one incident kindles another, and one doesn't know where the stampede of thoughts may lead." The narrator is determined to explore a metaphysical concept that, in his opinion, explains the behavior of the man who found a pistol: destiny as forger of the human existence. The narrator realizes at the end of his fruitless quest that destiny's tricks and twists are impossible to account for because life's secrets are not easily understood by rational means: "The past haunts us, and only the person who carries the sack knows how much it weighs."

Style and Technique

A striking stylistic element in "The Man Who Found a Pistol" is the use of the fantastic to describe the eerie relationship between the man who found a pistol and nature. Anaya has defined the Aztlán nature metaphorically "as almost a religious experience, or a religious communication that man has with his earth when the two come to meet at one point and the power that is in each one is energized, no longer remaining negative and positive, but fusing together." The descriptive technique of presenting surrealist incidents as plausible and even normal reminds the reader of Latin American Magical Realism. Believing that anything is possible in nature, the narrator understands that the man who found a pistol perished because of enigmatic natural powers: "When one is alone, the hum of the earth becomes a mantra whose vibration works its way into the soul. Maybe the man was sucked deeper and deeper into that loneliness until there was no escape."

Anaya's use of the fantastic is most visible in the story's unexpected ending. Although the reader knows from the beginning that the man who found a pistol is dead, a twist in that information is revealed by Procopio, a believer in supernatural happenings. The man who found a pistol, Procopio adds rationally, was killed by himself, by his double. The ending helps to emphasize a crisis related to the main metaphysical theme: how to achieve knowledge of the self through understanding of nature. As that moment of self-recognition is brief and evasive, the myth, defined by Anaya as the truth in the heart, provides an answer to the spiritual quest. Through the use of the fantastic, the story's ending provides a lesson in the best Jungian folktale tradition, provoking in the reader an alluring sense about the meaning of life: "What is the future, I thought, but a time which comes to swallow what we make of life."

Rafael Ocasio

THE MAN WHO INVENTED SIN

Author: Seán O'Faoláin (John Francis Whelan, 1900-1991)
Type of plot: Social realism
Time of plot: 1920 and 1943
Locale: Rural Ireland
First published: 1944

> *Principal characters:*
> THE NARRATOR, a student of Irish at summer school
> SISTER MAGDALEN,
> SISTER CHRYSOSTOM,
> BROTHER VIRGILIUS, and
> BROTHER MAJELLAN, students of Irish at summer school
> LISPEEN, the village curate

The Story

In the 1920's, the Irish struggle for independence was waged on a cultural level as well as on a political front; on their summer vacations, Irish schoolteachers, many of them members of religious orders, flocked to the countryside to learn Irish. "The Man Who Invented Sin" is set against this background. As the story opens, it is the summer of 1920, and the narrator is staying in a mountain village that is crowded with summer students. He eventually finds lodging at the Ryder place, two miles out of town, down by the lake. He shares his new quarters with two monks, Brother Virgilius and Brother Majellan, and two nuns, Sister Magdalen and Sister Chrysostom, whose monasteries and convents have filled to overflowing.

At first these religious lodgers behave in a decorous, reserved fashion, keeping to themselves and observing "convent hours." As the summer progresses, however, they become increasingly friendly with one another and with the narrator, and bit by bit strict propriety is set aside. They give one another nicknames, sing together, and play "pitch-and-toss along the garden path."

One evening, they are gathered in the drawing room. The narrator is playing the piano while Chrysostom sings "like a blackbird," Virgilius enjoys a tankard of beer, and Magdalen and Majellan try to waltz. On this gay scene bursts the village curate, nicknamed Lispeen by the students, thundering fire and brimstone at the sight of such wild abandon. He sends the nuns to their rooms and scolds the monks, threatening to report them to their superiors.

Apparently, the matter is hushed up by the parish priest and Mr. Ryder, for no disciplinary action is taken. However, word of the encounter spreads among the summer students, who are sympathetic to the culprits, and soon the Ryders' house becomes a frequent gathering place for the students. The modest gaiety of the early summer escalates to "concerts in the garden" and "surreptitious boating parties," and the "bed-at-nine rule" becomes "bed at eleven."

The summer of forbidden pleasure climaxes with a late-night boating party of some twenty students on the religious quartet's last night in the village. They are out on the lake until midnight, and as they row toward shore, they see a black figure standing on the causeway. It is Lispeen, determined to catch the foursome in this blatant violation of ecclesiastical conduct. The students row to the other side of the lake, but Lispeen races around by the bridge and is waiting for them when they reach the other side. After a midlake conference, the students manage to outwit Lispeen. The nuns remove the religious trappings from their apparel, and all four don overcoats. When they land, the four slip past Lispeen while the other students crowd around him.

However, when the last student has departed, Lispeen stands alone on the causeway staring down at "a nun's starched gimp" and contemplating the damage that he will be able to wreak with this evidence. He carries it home but is immediately called out on an emergency, which proves to be a prank. When he returns home, the gimp is gone. The narrator admits to knowing something about this strange occurrence.

The narrator closes his tale by recounting how, twenty-three years later, he runs into both Majellan and Lispeen, separately but on the same day, in the city. Majellan has become stooped and gently puritanical. Lispeen, however, has become quite jovial.

Themes and Meanings

Seán O'Faoláin alertly prevents "The Man Who Invented Sin" from being merely a critique of the stunting of Irish cultural life. Interesting as this theme may be, and vocal as O'Faoláin has been on its behalf elsewhere, the richness of this particular story is attributable at least as much to its pastoral conventions as to its ideological analysis.

By setting the action deep in the heart of rural Ireland, O'Faoláin emphasizes the characters' idealistic return to a source of cultural well-being. (Inasmuch as it does this, the story is an important exemplar of a subgenre of Irish short fiction in the 1930's, the pilgrimage story.) In addition, however, O'Faoláin also creates an unspoiled environment—in effect, a prelapsarian world. "The Serpent had come into the garden" is how Lispeen's interference is described. The effect of his crude and unharmonious interruptions is to make the nuns and monks self-conscious.

Until Lispeen's intrusions, the "four saints" are free to express themselves, as the unlikely discovery of Sister Chrysostom's sweet singing voice confirms. Despite the curate's overshadowing presence, the religious foursome continue to behave as though they were free spirits. O'Faoláin subtly contrasts the natural and religious connotations of spirit. Lispeen, in effect, sees to it that the former sense must be suppressed in the interests of the latter. The narrator, on the other hand, facilitates the idea that both senses may coexist.

By doing so, the narrator unobtrusively reveals the story's ideological and political implications. The final encounters in the city show the narrator's desire to honor the naïve but spirited romanticism of youth. He alone remains faithful to the spirit of renewal and naturalness. He alone embodies the possibility of an actively critical perspective on events. However, perhaps he, too, has been eclipsed by the Prince of Darkness, Lispeen, his critical potential internalized, an agent of irony rather than a caster-out of demons. His intellectual emasculation is a bitter testimony to Lispeen's potency, as is his ultimate isolation, so strikingly at odds with the story's earlier sense of community. The story's concluding notes of loss, timidity, and dispersal cry out for a means of putting Lispeen where he belongs.

Style and Technique

The story's plain style articulates its promotion of openness and simplicity. The narrative is so direct and accessible that its artistry risks being taken for granted. "The Man Who Invented Sin" contains, however, a number of subtle connections between style and conceptual structure, which is appropriate, given its thematic concern with the interrelationships between spontaneous behavior and rigid judgment, between naturalness and discipline, between the individual and the institution.

These concerns are quietly but effectively dramatized by subtleties in the story's verbal texture. For example, befitting his role, Lispeen is consistently associated with blackness. Even at the end, irradiating well-being and arrogance, he casts an ominous shadow. The rest of the story's world, however, is typically a place of light: Lighted houses betoken vitality; moonlight lends romance. In the final confrontation between Lispeen and his victims, it is the white components of the latter's dress that are emphasized (gimps and Roman collars).

Perhaps the one word of Irish that all concerned will never forget is the curate's nickname, Lispeen, which in Irish means "frog," an arguably exaggerated contrast to the grandiose and somewhat implausible names of the nuns and monks. (The narrator's anonymity connotes his eventual cultural disenfranchisement.) More incisively, as though to underline the falseness of the curate's position, there is a significant discrepancy between his perception and the other characters' experience of the pastoral. The discrepancy is enacted by various means—contrasting Lispeen's noisiness with Sister Chrysostom's singing, for example, or juxtaposing the quartet's attainment of ease and informality and the priest's shock tactics. In the latter case, such tactics are not what the shepherd—the original meaning of pastor—wants for his flock.

The story's episodic nature also contributes to the critique of Lispeen's stern rigidity. The seemingly unplanned development of the plot, which the restrictions of first-person narration underscore, maintains a sense of openness and lightheartedness, as well as an absence of teleology. A general airiness of mood is attractively grounded in the story's use of landscape. Acquaintances with, or visions of, the landscape are episodic. Lake and mountain complement the human sphere. They echo the characters' singing. In the special moments when this occurs, the story assumes a knowingly illusory, but nevertheless charming and wholehearted, feeling of timelessness, of time beyond history. By the delicacy but firmness of touch with which O'Faoláin insinuates such effects, "The Man Who Invented Sin" becomes a model of what culture might mean, a model that his characters are prevented from fully, confidently, and permanently embodying.

George O'Brien

THE MAN WHO KNEW BELLE STARR

Author: Richard Bausch (1945-   )
Type of plot: Psychological
Time of plot: 1985
Locale: New Mexico
First published: 1985

> *Principal characters:*
> McRae, the protagonist, recently released from military prison
> Belle Starr, a young woman who has murdered several people

The Story

McRae, a twenty-three-year-old loner, is driving a beat-up Dodge Charger across Texas with a vague notion of starting over his failed life, hoping that in the West people will not require as much from a person, because there is so much room. He is soon proven wrong—much will be required of him, primarily from a hitchhiker he picks up on the way, a young woman holding a paper bag containing a small pistol. The woman calls herself Belle Starr after the female gunslinger from the Old West. McRae is bemused by the strange woman. She is not a talker, but the gesture she uses to show him who the original Belle Starr was is revelatory: "She put her index finger to the side of his head and said, 'Bang.'"

As the car rolls through Texas, the woman falls asleep, and McRae recalls his recent past. He has just been released from Leavenworth prison after serving a four-year sentence for striking an Air Force officer while drinking beer on duty. He remembers giving his name to the officer as "trouble" just before hitting him in the face. While in the Air Force, he had briefly visited his dying father, with whom he was not on good terms; all the father could say to his son from the gurney he was lying on was, "Getting into trouble, stealing and running around."

McRae is complacent about his own character and thinks he just might turn out all right after all. He is happy to be out of Leavenworth and the Air Force, and on his way west—and he had picked up a girl. The girl, however, is greater trouble than McRae can guess. The two stop for a hamburger at an isolated diner somewhere in the desert of New Mexico, and they speak briefly to the owner and cook, who has had no customers all week because the place is so far from the interstate highway. He tells his story: Retired from the army, he and his wife bought the diner, few people came, and his wife took off for Seattle, leaving him to sell the place. He decides to treat the two to hamburgers, but the woman is offended, pulls out her gun, tells him to open up the cash register, and then shoots him dead. McRae is stunned by what he sees, and what he does not want to know—that she is a psychopath, and that he is her next victim.

They return to the car unseen and McRae, driving with the pistol pointed at him, begins to talk to her in a desperate way, claiming that he wishes to join her gang, run with her from the police, and supply her with the information that she might need—after all, he is a former convict, wise in the ways of the criminal. Belle Starr is unimpressed. She tells him that she has already killed five and a half people: "A kid who was hitch-hiking, like me; a guy at a gas station; a dog that must've got lost—I count him as half—another guy at a gas station; a guy who took me to a motel and made an obscene gesture to me; and the guy at the diner. That makes five and a half."

Now McRae knows how much trouble he is in. He drives on through the night, talking about his past, the pain and neglect he has had, his difficult father, and the bad food at Leavenworth. He thinks he might convince her that he is her friend and accomplice, not another victim. McRae becomes a desperate Scheherezade; he knows that once his tale is done, he is too. Then she starts to talk, revealing her own bitter past, full of sexual abuse, yet she tells it in a detached way, even using the third person for her story. Their words suspend the inevitable, but eventually Belle Starr orders him at gunpoint to pull over and get out of the car. He runs for the desert, hoping to hide from her, but she fires at him, then reloads and, holding a flashlight, walks slowly toward him. He has injured his ankle in the rush from the road, and lies waiting for her to find him, his real essence somehow evaporated, leaving only "something crippled and breathing in the dark, lying flat in a winding gully of weeds and sand."

Themes and Meanings

The theme of "The Man Who Knew Belle Starr" emerges through retrospection: McRae's knowledge is in the past tense, signaling several ends—his life, of course, but also his self-delusion that now that he is free from prison with a few thousand dollars in his pocket from his father's life insurance, his life will take on a more meaningful direction. Driving his Charger across the blankness of the West, he thinks of himself as free, strong, and seasoned by his prison experience. His chance encounter with the strange young woman who calls herself Belle Starr, just as he once named himself "trouble," shows him he never had control over his fate, that even though he is sorry for everything he had ever done, it doesn't matter. He is reduced to a mere something by Belle Starr's random tale about her life and then her fusillade of shots in the desert. The story forces an enlightenment on McRae, who is not a self-reflective character, but who acted on impulse in bashing the officer and learned little from his prison punishment. He still thinks of himself as put on, friendless, not appreciated by his father; but when he witnesses the murder of the cook, he knows that until that moment he didn't know what the word "trouble" meant. He is forced to learn, and his attempts to outwit Belle Starr by posing as her sidekick, by spinning his tale of prison knowledge and past wrongs against him, and by feigning an eagerness to join her gang, are all pathetic, and he knows it. McRae is thrust into an unwelcome self-awareness, an awareness that is a genuine discovery, if a brief one.

Style and Technique

Richard Bausch's style is deliberately low-key and direct, using a vocabulary that is simple and even banal, to reflect the somewhat limited capacity for self-reflection and expression that characterizes both McRae and Belle Starr. Their conversations are filled with stereotyped phrases such as, "What I'm after is adventure" and "You want to hide out," but the strain of McRae's desperation is enhanced by the simplicity of phrasing. McRae uses every cliché he can think of because it dawns on him that she believes in clichés and possibly is one. He suggests that they hide out from the cops. Then he finds himself telling her his true story: "He was telling her everything, all the bad times he'd had: his father's alcoholism, and growing up wanting to hit someone for the anger that was in him; the years of getting into trouble; the fighting and the kicking and what it had got him." Belle Starr counters with her own painful story, which seems true and moving to him; they are each moved by the other's stories, but words are not enough to save McRae. Belle Starr follows him into the desert night shooting calmly, determined to get her man, to complete the cliché.

Paul R. Lilly, Jr.

THE MAN WHO LIVED UNDERGROUND

Author: Richard Wright (1908-1960)
Type of plot: Psychological
Time of plot: The 1930's
Locale: A metropolitan area in the United States
First published: 1942

> *Principal characters:*
> FRED DANIELS, a fugitive
> LAWSON,
> MURPHY, and
> JOHNSON, police officers

The Story

After Fred Daniels, a young black man unjustly accused of murdering a woman, is forced into signing a confession, he escapes from the police by going underground—into the sewer system beneath the city—where a series of adventures leads him to self-knowledge, maturity, and, ultimately, death.

Daniels's adventures include visits to various places that he observes through chinks in the floors of the buildings above him, the first of which is a black church. From his protected perch, Daniels watches the choir in their white robes singing and asking God's mercy. As he glimpses these singers, Daniels also gets a glimpse of his own situation, for he recognizes that these people should not have to state their innocence—they are struggling, hardworking people who are guilty of nothing, just as he himself is an innocent fugitive.

Daniels's next adventure also sheds light on his situation, literally, as he gropes in the darkness to find his way. He comes on an undertaker's embalming room and chuckles at the notion of watching, unseen, the embalming process. There he comes on a tool kit, light bulb, and electric wire that help him equip his temporary home, a cave he discovers in the depths of the sewer system.

In his next visit, Daniels comes on a movie theater. Like the embalming room, this place offers him a boon—sandwiches belonging to an old man working in the coal bin, as well as more tools for his effort to transform the cave into his lodging.

The next stop—at a radio shop—provides him with a radio for his new abode. Daniels hooks it up in his cave, expecting to hear music that will soothe him as he pauses from his frenetic adventures. Instead, he hears a catalog of news events, all of which suggest the irrationality of a world of war and destruction and hatred. Daniels adds this information to his growing sense of himself and the world he has momentarily left, not behind him, but above him.

He has more adventures before he returns to the surface world, two more visits to places that give him objects necessary to both his journey and his self-knowledge. The first place, a butcher shop, provides him with more food and a meat cleaver, and the other, a jewelry shop, gives him the most significant experience of his underground life. When he spies the jewelry shop, he also observes a safe and learns its combination by watching and listening to the employee open it. After the shop is closed, Daniels opens the safe himself, stealing money, watches, rings, jewels, and diamonds. He manages to do this without awakening the night watchman, who is obviously more compelled to sleep than to keep his watch.

Daniels returns to his cave and decorates his refuge with the loot he has stolen from the jewelry store: On the walls he puts the money and watches and rings and jewels; on the floor he puts the diamonds. The effect is both bizarre and revelatory. Daniels sees the meaninglessness of these symbols of wealth, and he recognizes the absurdity of a world consumed by a hunger for such symbols. When he returns to the jewelry store to spy on it once again, he has an insight into the notion of guilt in this absurd world. He sees the old night watchman being interrogated by the police officers who had interrogated him and forced him to sign the false confession. These officers attempt the same thing with the watchman; when they momentarily leave him, the innocent man commits suicide. Daniels sees himself in this man, especially when he knows that not only had he stolen goods from the store's safe, but so had the worker who had opened and closed it, unaware that Daniels could see him stuff wads of money in his shirt sleeve. Thus the guilty people go free and the innocent are condemned in this world above ground, a world to which Daniels decides he must return so that he can confess his guilt regarding his underground life and assert his innocence regarding his aboveground life.

Daniels emerges from the sewer system to return to the police station from which he had escaped after being forced to sign the false confession. He finds the three officers who interrogated both him and the night watchman in the jewelry store. Lawson, Murphy, and Johnson are momentarily surprised at seeing Daniels, but they quickly dismiss him, telling him that they have discovered the real criminal in the murder he was alleged to have committed. They burn his confession, taking this action as lightly as their interrogation of the night watchman. Their cavalier attitude persists as they attempt to ignore Daniels's announcement that he saw the suicide of the night watchman, that the watchman did not steal from the jewelry store, and that he himself was the robber.

Begging the police officers to come with him to his underground cave so that he could show them what he did with the stolen goods, thus vindicating both himself and the unjustly accused suicide victim, Daniels convinces the police officers that he has information that is dangerous for them. After he leads them to his underground world, they murder him, saying, "You've got to shoot his kind. They'd wreck things." Fred Daniels, the boy who had become a man as a result of his journey underground, could indeed wreck things by telling the truth. Instead, he falls into the underground that had been both his refuge and his place of revelation, and the world aboveground continues as it always had, punishing the innocent and protecting the guilty.

Themes and Meanings

An organizing theme for Richard Wright's story is Fred Daniels's quest for identity, his journey to discover who he is and how he fits into an absurd world in which people are both victims and victimizers. The opening line suggests this theme: "I've got to hide, he told himself." Although this line suggests that he is literally hiding himself by fleeing into the bowels of the underground, it also suggests that he is hiding from himself, the self that will become visible and apparent by the end of the story.

Each adventure reveals something to Daniels about himself, whether it is the innocence that he shares with the black churchgoers and the night watchman in the jewelry store, or the responsibility for himself and others that is prompted by his seeing the unnecessary suicide of the night watchman.

One particularly telling episode suggests how tentative is the self that Daniels is trying to discover. Sneaking into a jewelry store, he notices a typewriter on a desk. Although he has never used a machine like this before, he inserts paper into it and pecks out his name: freddaniels. When he looks at his name—his identity on the sheet of paper—he laughs and promises himself to learn to type correctly someday. He does indeed learn, not merely to type correctly, as he demonstrates later, but to spell his name and announce himself freely and innocently as the boy who goes underground to find himself and to accept himself.

Style and Technique

If a major theme of this short story is the quest for identity, then Wright's techniques reinforce that classical motif of the journey. Using devices found in myths and folk narratives, Wright shows how Fred Daniels must go through a mazelike underground world until he emerges with a clear sense of who he is. Like the hero with a thousand faces or the knight searching for the Holy Grail, Daniels must overcome obstacles that are placed in his way. When he visits the butcher shop, for example, he is mistaken for an employee, and he must turn the obstacle of mistaken identity into an opportunity.

The classical hero is also given magical instruments to aid him in his journey. For Fred Daniels, these instruments are numerous: a tool kit, light bulb, electric wire, radio, typewriter, and meat cleaver. He uses all of them to assist him in his quest, realizing that his success depends on his ingenuity and his courage.

Finally, in the archetypal quest story, the hero ultimately must seize a guarded treasure, whether it is the Holy Grail, or money and diamonds and watches in the safe of the jewelry store. Daniels successfully captures the treasure, eluding the night watchman, and realizes the significance of his success. The meaninglessness of the wealth symbolizes the meaninglessness of his flight. Just as he has nearly forgotten why he is a fugitive, so he understands the absurdity of a world in which people are both victims and victimizers, pursued and pursuing, innocent and guilty. He emerges from his underground hiding place with his newly found identity: a man who sees the light both literally and figuratively.

Marjorie Smelstor

THE MAN WHO LOVED ISLANDS

Author: D. H. Lawrence (1885-1930)
Type of plot: Symbolist
Time of plot: 1928
Locale: Several unspecified islands
First published: 1927

> *Principal characters:*
> MR. CATHCART, a man who loves islands
> FLORA, his servant, later his wife

The Story

Mr. Cathcart was born on an island. It does not suit him, however, because there are too many other people on it. His life purpose becomes to own an island that he can make into a world of his own. The would-be islander acquires an island, four miles around, with three cottages on it. It has a smaller island lying off it, which also belongs to him. He loves his island, but there is a sinister side to it. It is a timeless world in which the souls of the dead live again, pulsating actively around the living. At night, places and things that seem uncanny in the day become threatening.

To escape such awareness, Cathcart concentrates on the material aspect of the island. He tries to fill it with his own gracious spirit and render it a minute world of pure perfection, made by man himself. He begins by spending money. He brings a housekeeper and butler from the mainland, and installs a bailiff in the farmhouse. He acquires a herd of cows and a yacht. He fills the cottages with tenants, all of whom display a smooth and deferential manner to "the Master." The Master visits his tenants and is treated almost with adulation, but after he leaves, they have subtle, mocking smiles on their faces. It is doubtful that any of them really likes him, or whether he likes any of them.

At the end of the first year on the island, the bills flood in. Cathcart is shocked at how much money the island has swallowed. He thinks up projects to make the farm more efficient and conveys them to the bailiff, who watches him as if he were a strange, caged animal but does not register any of his suggestions. There is a good harvest and, at the harvest supper, everyone toasts Cathcart, dances, and seems happy. Underneath the gaiety, things are not well. A cow falls over the cliff. The men haul her up the bank and bury her, as no one will eat her meat. This incident is symbolic of the periodic malevolence of the island. More catastrophes happen: A man breaks a leg, a storm drives the yacht on a rock, the pigs get some strange disease, families come to hate each other.

Cathcart begins to fear his island. He feels strange, violent feelings he has never known before. He now knows that his people do not love him. Several of them grow discontented and leave, including the housekeeper. At the end of the second year, the island has lost thousands of pounds. The housekeeper has swindled him. He gives notice to the butler and the bailiff.

In the fifth year Cathcart sells the island to a hotel company, which plans to turn it into a honeymoon-and-golf island. He then moves onto the smaller island, which still belongs to him—taking along a few faithful staff—an old carpenter, and a widow and her daughter. The island is a refuge, with no human ghosts. The islander no longer has to struggle and believes himself free from desire. He begins a book on flowers, which he does not mind if he never publishes.

Cathcart and the widow's daughter, Flora, become lovers, and immediately he feels disturbed. Caught in the automatism of sexual desire, he resents losing the state of desirelessness that he had achieved. Eventually, even his desire for Flora dies, and he is left feeling that his island's purity is soiled. He leaves the island to travel but receives a letter from Flora saying she is going to have a child. At an auction of islands, he buys another tiny island to the north. This island is even smaller and more barren than the last, with no buildings or trees on it.

Cathcart marries Flora, but as soon as the child is born, he escapes, as if from a prison, to his new island. He builds a hut and lives on the island with a few sheep and a cat. He is glad there are no trees or bushes, as they assert their presence too strongly, and this would offend him. He loses interest in his book about flowers and avoids contact with anyone. When he watches the mail steamer on the horizon, his heart contracts in fear lest it molest him. He becomes shocked by the sound of his own voice and irritated by the mew of the cat and the bleating of the sheep. He wants only the sound of the sea and silence.

One day, the mail steamer comes and Cathcart talks to its men. He resents their intrusion into his neatly ordered environment. He cannot bear to open the letters they bring because any contact is repulsive to him. The cat disappears, for which he is glad. Sometimes he gets ill, but he knows this only because he falls down; he has ceased to register his own feelings.

In winter, the snow walls in the house. Cathcart tries to get on his boat, but he is too weak and is overcome by the snow, so that he must crawl back inside. When he reaches the boat, there is a great storm. He digs himself out, and when he emerges, the island has changed, with great white hills where no hills had been. He is repulsed: He cannot win against the elements. He climbs a hill, and, as the sun feels hot, he reflects that it is summer, the time of leaves. However, he already senses the snow rolling in over the sea.

Themes and Meanings

At the beginning of this story, the narrator comments that it will show that an island must be tiny before it can be filled with any one person's personality. The islander, who dreams of creating the perfect world, ends up being his islands' victim, not their master. It is as if the islands have a life and power of their own. The narrator comments that going to an island is like jumping off a secure little point in time into a timeless world in which the present moment begins to expand in great circles and the solid earth is gone: The usual crutches of time and space are knocked away. The myriad spirits and infinite rhythms of centuries dwarf and overwhelm the individual who tries to assert his individuality over the island.

On the first island, his perfect world crumbles when the island's people, events, and spirit prove beyond his control. On the second island, he attempts to create around him a still and desireless space but is defeated by his sexual desire. On his third and last island, he wishes to avoid contact with anyone or anything that disturbs his isolation or intrudes on his perfectly ordered existence.

Each island is more bare and less populated than the last, but Cathcart still fails to impose his own identity on them. His circle of influence decreases to the size of his tiny hut, and even then, he constantly feels under threat from outside influences. As his environment progressively slips out of his control, he becomes angrier and more malevolent. He ends up a sick, shattered wreck of a man, vainly struggling against the ebb and flow of life.

Style and Technique

The development of the imagery of flowers throughout the story is indicative of Cathcart's long-drawn-out spiritual death. In a happy interval on the first island (which has many flowers and bushes growing on it), he is described as opening out in spirit like a flower. As soon as this happens, some ugly blow falls and crushes him. On the second island, which is more barren than the first, he works on a book about flowers and marries Flora (Latin for "flowers"), who has a child by him. This continues the theme of birth and blossoming of life, but in both these cases, the islander abstracts these elements from the vastness of nature and tries to bring them into his tiny sphere of influence. Then he retreats even from these abstracted representatives of nature: He withdraws from Flora and the child and loses interest in his book. He is interested only in taking refuge on a smaller, more barren rock of an island, from which he excludes all remaining life—the sheep, the cat, the mailmen. In his tomb-like world, even his final vision of the leaves of summer is a transient mirage, instantly overshadowed by the coming snows of winter.

Other images contribute to the sense of the island's being a living, threatening entity: its resentful spirit coiled on itself like a wet dog coiled in gloom; its invisible hand that strikes malevolently out of the silence; its tendency to pick money out of pockets like an octopus with invisible arms.

Claire J. Robinson

THE MAN WHO STUDIED YOGA

Author: Norman Mailer (1923-   )
Type of plot: Social realism
Time of plot: The 1950's
Locale: New York City
First published: 1959

> *Principal characters:*
> SAM SLOVODA, a continuity writer for comic magazines
> ELEANOR, his wife
> ALAN SPERBER, their guest

The Story

Sam Slovoda writes for comic magazines and feels overworked and underappreciated. He dreams of writing a great novel but cannot seem to organize his thoughts. Every time he begins to write fiction, he is overcome with the feeling that what he wants to say is too complex and his way of saying it is not focused enough.

A frustrated, middle-aged man, Sam also fancies himself a great lover and feels hampered in his marriage. He yearns for affairs with other women but does not act on his desires, feeling stymied by his wife, Eleanor, who does not appreciate how much he has to offer other women. He values intensity of feeling, yet his life is flaccid. He considers leaving Eleanor, going off to an unheated loft, and living alone as a man in quest of his genius and manhood. In other words, he is confronting a midlife crisis. He questions his mode of life and laments what he has failed to accomplish. He criticizes himself for lacking the will and courage to accomplish his ambitions.

Sam generalizes from his plight to a conception of the modern hero. He contemplates writing an essay about a hero who would be both a man of action and a thinker, but he doubts that any contemporary man could be such a hero. This is, in part, why Sam has so much trouble writing his novel: He cannot imagine a character who could fulfill his heroic potential.

One evening, Sam invites a group of friends over to watch a pornographic movie. Instead of doing something daring, Sam contents himself with this rather passive and voyeuristic activity. On a second showing of the film, alone with Eleanor, he makes love to her reasonably well, but without any sense that he has furthered his plans to write or to lead a bolder life.

Before the first showing of the pornographic movie, one of the guests, Alan Sperber, tells the story of the man who studied yoga—the legendary Cassius O'Shaugnessy. He is presented as the type of hero Sam has sought. During World War I, Cassius served in France as an ambulance driver with the writers Ernest Hemingway and John Dos Passos. He was one of the founders of the Dadaist school of art. He is said to have influenced the poet T. S. Eliot and been involved in anarchist and then pacifist politics in World War II. He is, in short, one of the heroic questers of his age.

Sperber builds up O'Shaugnessy's biography, noting that he went to India to seek a mystical revelation about the meaning of life: There he contemplated his navel, believing that by giving it a counterclockwise twist he would receive the ultimate knowledge of things. All that happened after he unscrewed his navel was that his rear end fell off. It is a silly and anticlimactic joke that irritates Sam and his friends, who are ready to watch the pornographic movie.

Sperber's trivial ending to the big buildup of his story is paralleled by Sam's banal evening. After showing the film, after his friends leave, after he makes love to his wife, he retires to bed, a man who lives not by finding pleasure, but by merely trying to avoid pain.

Themes and Meanings

Sam Slovoda is presented in a sociological frame: He is an urban type—well-educated, sophisticated, jaded, and dissatisfied. He yearns to create great art, yet he capitulates to his defeatist sense that life is too complicated and that he cannot dominate it with his own vision. Sam and his friends speak in the psychological jargon of the 1950's, seeing people as inhibited by a conformist society. This aspect of the story becomes clearer when it is read in the context of Norman Mailer's essay "The Meaning of Western Defense," which argues that Americans have become increasingly passive, anxious, and guilt-ridden.

Sam is the hero of "The Man Who Studied Yoga" because he realizes more acutely than his friends that his life is a series of compromises, what the existentialists of the 1950's called bad faith, in which the individual becomes inauthentic, that is, untrue to himself, to what he could become through seizing experience and making it an expression of his will to create. Sam's job as a writer of continuity for comic magazines reflects his fragmented existence. He does not even write whole stories but rather fills in gaps. He is part of the machinery of comic magazine writing, not an independent creator.

Gathering to watch a pornographic film also exposes Sam's and his friends' passivity. They are observers, not actors in the dramas of their own lives. They follow the script society writes for them. They even mock their own desire to believe in heroes. Thus Alan Sperber's story about Cassius O'Shaugnessy makes a rather lame joke out of the hero's quest for spiritual fulfillment.

The story is a portrait of American ambivalence. Americans want to fit into society, to be well liked. They also want to believe that they are heroes, uncompromising individuals free from societal strictures. The psychological jargon in the story reinforces the sense of ambivalence. Louise Rossman, one of Sam and Eleanor's friends, remarks: "Artists, writers, and people of the creative layer have in their occupational ideology the belief that they are classless." Louise expresses what she thinks of as her insight in the cant of the day; that is, she talks like everyone else who has absorbed the tenets of Freudian psychology. She thinks she has put artists in their place by pigeonholing them in her jargon. She has, in fact, lost touch with reality by overlaying it with scientific-sounding but bogus phrases such as "the creative layer" and "occupational ideology." She is a critic without distinctive language or insight—the opposite of an original thinker.

Style and Technique

Much of the meaning of "The Man Who Studied Yoga" is conveyed through the confidential, yet elusive and reserved, tone of the anonymous narrator. The story begins: "I would introduce myself if it were not useless. The name I had last night will not be the same as the name I have tonight. For the moment, then, let me say I am thinking of Sam Slovoda." Is the narrator meant to be taken as one of the author's personas? Is this why the narrator's name changes? Is there a new name for every new story the author writes? This is a distinct possibility, because "The Man Who Studied Yoga" is included in *Advertisements for Myself* (1959), which is Mailer's self-professed scrutiny of his personality as a writer. In this book he discusses his writing successes and failures, and his effort to write a great novel just as Sam dreams of doing.

The narrator has an existential identity (that is, one without references to his past or future) that makes him superior to Sam, and seems to make himself up as he goes along. The narrator's turns of phrase and his light, deft irony suggest the very mastery of character and circumstance that eludes Sam. However, the narrator is sympathetic with and wryly amused by Sam, as though the narrator has gone through similar struggles to define himself and to stand apart from a conformist society. The narrator is something like a psychotherapist, except that he studiously avoids psychological jargon—indeed, he mocks characters such as Louise Rossman who use it.

A wonderful teasing undercurrent in the narrator's comments creates a fascinating sensation of being immersed in the immediacy of Sam's experience—not by an omniscient intelligence but by a literary mind literally thinking of the character at hand. "I know what Sam feels," the narrator says matter-of-factly. "It is just that I, far better than Sam, know how serious he really is, how fanciful, how elaborate, his imagination can be."

The narrator is confident because he has created Sam in his own words, which is to say that Sam lives as an independent creation speaking his words but also as a projection of the narrator's ability to grasp reality. Thus "The Man Who Studied Yoga" is about the process of storytelling, of narrating. It is a primary act of creation Sam would dearly like to achieve, and it is the act of creation that his narrator celebrates in his own distinctive voice.

Carl Rollyson

THE MAN WHO WAS ALMOST A MAN

Author: Richard Wright (1908-1960)
Type of plot: Psychological
Time of plot: The 1930's
Locale: The American South
First published: 1940

> *Principal characters:*
> DAVID GLOVER, a seventeen-year-old black laborer
> DAVID'S MOTHER
> JIM HAWKINS, David's employer

The Story

"The Man Who Was Almost a Man" is an initiation story, a tale of a teenage youth struggling to break free of childhood and enter the world of adulthood. Frustrated by being young, poor, and black, David Glover wrestles with the tension of wanting to be an adult yet being viewed as a child by the adult community. In David's case, the action that he takes to acquire manhood merely reinforces his elders' beliefs that he is still an adolescent.

When the story opens, David is thinking about his quest for manhood, which he connects with owning a gun. Because he is "almos a man," he believes that he should own the symbol of manhood: a gun. Borrowing a mail-order catalog from a local store owner so that he can look at the pictures of revolvers, David becomes obsessed with thoughts of guns, becoming a man, and, most important, the strategy that he must use to persuade his mother that he should be able to buy a gun.

Employing all the typical maneuvers of a child who knows how to manipulate his mother—David knows that he should work on her and not his father—he begins by slipping his arm around her waist and telling her how much he loves her. These strategies break down her initial resistance to the idea, and when David proposes that the gun be given to his father, she relents, telling the boy that he may purchase the gun but that he must bring it back immediately and give it to her to turn over to Mr. Glover.

Elated with his victory, David buys the gun for two dollars but delays his return home until after dark and after the family is in bed. That way he is able to keep the gun, put it under his pillow that night, and take it with him when he leaves to work on Jim Hawkins's plantation early the next morning. He arrives at work, hitches the mule, Jenny, to a plow, and starts across the fields, delighted that he will be able to get far enough away from the other laborers so that he can shoot the gun without anyone hearing.

Telling himself that he is not afraid, he shoots the gun and is nearly knocked off his feet by the power of the weapon. He is angry at the revolver for its deafening noise and its violence, which nearly tears his right hand from his arm. He kicks the gun, then looks over at Jenny, who is tossing her head and moving wildly. When he comes over to her, David discovers that he has shot her, not intentionally but nevertheless fatally. He leaves the mule, trying to decide what kind of lie he can tell to protect himself from the truth that, in a disobedient act, he has murdered Jenny.

His lie does not convince anyone. Jim Hawkins, the townspeople, his mother—all know that the story David tells of Jenny's falling on the point of a plow is unbelievable. At his mother's insistence, David tells the true story and elicits laughter from the crowd gathered around the boy and the dead mule. That laughter, which echoes in David's ears even after he leaves the scene, is more painful to him than the monetary punishment, having to pay for the mule from his wages on Hawkins's plantation. The laughter reminds David of the adults who are forever ridiculing him and thereby excluding him from their ranks.

David lies again, saying that, after the fatal firing, he threw the gun in a creek, whereas he really buried it for safekeeping. He makes a decision based on that buried treasure; he decides to dig up the gun and fire it again, because he believes that firing the revolver one more time will finally show people that he is truly an adult. He thinks to himself, "Ah'd like t scare ol man Hawkins jusa little. . . . Jusa enough t let im know Dave Glover is a man."

Standing on top of a ridge, looking down on Jim Hawkins's house and thinking about his next firing of the gun, David hears a train whistle, a sound that beckons him to flee his current entrapment and move toward a new environment. He feels his pocket and is reassured that the symbol of his manhood, his gun, is there. He jumps on top of a railroad car and projects into the future: "Ahead the long rails were glinting in the moonlight, stretching away, away to somewhere, somewhere where he could be a man."

Themes and Meanings

The question of how one becomes initiated into adulthood pervades this story, beginning with the first paragraph, in which David tells himself that someday he is "going to get a gun and practice shooting, then they couldn't talk to him as though he were a little boy." Because he is seventeen, he muses, he is "almos a man." Almost a man, however, is a dangerous age to be, for David is neither child nor adult; he is in that painful transitional period between the two.

Although he is neither fish nor fowl, neither child nor adult, David demonstrates characteristics of both stages of life, sometimes simultaneously. When, for example, he decides to purchase a gun, a step that will symbolize and initiate him into manhood, he resorts to the childish manipulation of his mother to persuade her to allow him to make the purchase. When he actually fires the gun to demonstrate that he is indeed a man, he is literally overpowered, as a child would be, by the power of the weapon. His final action also demonstrates this paradox of a childish adult or an adult child, for he hops a train, suggesting that he is making an independent, adult decision to set off on his own; yet he reveals his immaturity when, in the final lines of the story, he connects the gun in his pocket with the dream in his soul. To have a revolver is to be a man, he believes; the boy who is almost a man is still a child.

Style and Technique

"The Man Who Was Almost a Man" is one in a collection of eight stories, written at various times and published under one cover in 1961. The word "man" appears in all eight titles, and four of these begin with the phrase, "The Man Who . . . ," suggesting that each protagonist is a universal figure, a kind of Everyman. Thus David Glover is representative of the adolescent dimension of humankind, and Richard Wright employs various techniques to elevate the main character to a level of universality.

One technique is the use of interior monologue to reveal David's psychological state. Instead of relying on the omniscient narrator's description of the adolescent's turmoil, Wright presents David's own thoughts about, for example, his growing up:

> Shucks, Ah ain scareda them even ef they are biggern me! Aw, Ah know whut Ahma do. Ahm going by old Joe's sto n git that Sears Roebuck catlog n look at them guns. Mebbe Ma will lemme buy one when she gits mah pay from ol man Hawkins. Ahma beg her t gimme some money. Ahm ol ernough to hava gun. Ahm seventeen. Almos a man.

Revealing David's state of mind through his private thoughts—in David's own southern black dialect—creates a sense of immediacy as well as identification with the character's dilemma. Readers are not simply reading about the protagonist's struggle; they are witnessing it as it occurs in David's mind.

At times, Wright uses figurative imagery to dramatize this psychological turmoil. For example, David is said to be "like a hungry dog scratching for a bone" as he paws up the buried gun. For the most part, however, the story relies less on imagery than on dialogue, interior and exterior, to convey the inner struggles of an adolescent trying to become an adult, the struggles that make David Glover more than simply a seventeen-year-old character in a Wright story, that make him a universal figure, an Everyman.

Marjorie Smelstor

THE MAN WHO WOULD BE KING

Author: Rudyard Kipling (1865-1936)
Type of plot: Allegory
Time of plot: The late nineteenth century
Locale: India and Afghanistan
First published: 1888

> *Principal characters:*
> AN UNNAMED NEWSPAPERMAN, the narrator
> PEACHEY CARNEHAN, a vagabond adventurer who survives to tell
> the story
> DANIEL DRAVOT, his companion, who is made king of a small
> principality

The Story

"The Man Who Would Be King" is told by a first-person narrator who one can assume is Rudyard Kipling as a young newspaperman in India. Meeting Peachey Carnehan, an adventure-seeking vagabond, on a train, the narrator learns that Peachey and his fellow vagabond, Daniel Dravot, are posing as correspondents for the newspaper for which the narrator is a real correspondent. After the narrator returns to his office and becomes "respectable," Peachey and Dravot interrupt this respectability (characterized by the narrator's concern for the everyday reality that constitutes the subject of his work as a newsman) to tell him of their fantastic plan to make themselves kings of a small country and to try to obtain from him a factual framework for the country where they hope to achieve this incredible adventure. "We have come to you to know about this country," says Peachey. "We want you to tell us that we are fools and to show us your books." The mythic proportions of the two vagabonds, or rather their storybook proportions—for "mythic" is too serious a word for the grotesque and comic adventurers—are indicated by the narrator's amused observation that Dravot's red beard seems to fill half the room and Peachey's huge shoulders the other half.

The actual adventure of the two companions begins with Dravot, pretending to be a mad priest, marching forward with whirligigs to sell as charms to the savages. As the two vagabonds go off, they again leave the newsman-narrator to his respectability. Three years later, Peachey returns, a "whining cripple," to confront the narrator with his story: He and Dravot have been crowned kings in Kafiristan, and "you've been sitting here ever since—oh, Lord!" Peachey's story of their adventures is thus posed against the pedestrian story of the narrator's dealing with the lives and obituaries of real kings. The narrator's mundane world pales in comparison to the storylike world created by Peachey and Dravot, who have set themselves up as fictional kings in a real country.

The story Peachey tells, of Dravot being crowned king of Kafiristan, while Peachey himself was made head of the country's army, recounts how the two men, first through fighting and then through Masonic rituals, convince the local people that they are gods and kings. In a parody of British imperialism, Dravot says that he will make an empire: "These men aren't niggers; they're English. . . . They're the Lost Tribes, or something like it." His plans become so grandiose that he oversteps his bounds. Wanting to make a local woman his wife and thus reaffirm his reign through heirs, Dravot breaks the original "contrack" that he and Peachey established. When his future bride bites him and draws blood, the people watching the ceremony realize that he is human and not a god. They then kill Dravot, cut off his head, and crucify Peachey. This is the story that—along with the withered head of Dravot—the physically broken Peachey brings back to the journalist-narrator.

Themes and Meanings

"The Man Who Would Be King" is, among Kipling's stories, the one most reminiscent of Joseph Conrad; that is, although it is a typical Kipling adventure story, it seems to have more serious implications—much as does Conrad's *Heart of Darkness* (1902)—than most of his other stories do. Moreover, it attempts to sustain these philosophical implications on the structure of a typical Kipling social parable about British imperialism in India, just as *Heart of Darkness* is about imperialism in Africa. Both stories embody a strange combination of the serious and the absurd and a subtle mixture of reality and dreamlike fantasy. Although "The Man Who Would Be King" does not contain the philosophical generalizations of Conrad's story, nevertheless it should be seen as something more than merely an adventure story or a simple social parable.

The basic theme of "The Man Who Would Be King," which undergirds the social theme of British imperialism, is that of the dichotomy between two different kinds of reality—the "realistic" realm of the journalist who deals with the everyday world of "real kings" and the fantastic, make-believe world of Dravot and Peachey, who create their own fantasy and then live in it. The clue to this basic theme of the reality of pretense is announced when the narrator first meets Dravot and Peachey, characteristically playing roles, for the two men play roles throughout, not only as newspaper correspondents but also as mad priests and real kings. More comic, mythic characters than real people, Peachey and Dravot create stories for themselves within which they then live.

The storylike nature of their adventure is indicated in Peachey's account, first by his frequent confusing of himself with Dravot and second by his frequent references to himself in the third person: "There was a party called Peachey Taliaferro Carnehan that was with Dravot. Shall I tell you about him? He died out there in the cold." As Peachey tells his tale, he insists that the narrator continue to look him in the eye. Thus he becomes an image of Samual Taylor Coleridge's Ancient Mariner, who holds the wedding guest by his glittering eye and links the listener and teller in a story-made bond. The fact that the theme of the story transcends an obvious social parable about imperialism to focus on the dual nature of reality can be attributed to the fact that

Kipling was trying to combine the techniques of romance adventure with the techniques of realistic social fiction. The result is that the contradictory conventions of romance and realism are held in self-conscious tension.

Style and Technique

The basic stylistic technique of the story is Kipling's structuring it in a sort of parody of biblical history, complete with numerous biblical allusions. The purpose of these allusions is to give Peachey's tale an externally imposed story framework, indeed the most basic and dignified story framework in Western culture. Once Dravot projects himself into the role of god as king and thus assumes a position in the kingdom as the fulfillment of prophecy and legend (although it must be remembered that Peachey and Dravot are themselves the authors of their own legend), he is bound to this particular role. It is only when he wishes to escape the preestablished role and marry an Indian girl that his world falls apart. When he is bitten by his frightened intended bride, the cry, "Neither God nor Devil, but a man," breaks the spell of the story world and propels Dravot and Peachey out of the fictional reality of their own making and back into reality again.

Peachey and Dravot are not so much two separate characters as they are double figures; this is indicated not only by Peachey's references to himself as suffering Dravot's fate, but also by the fact that if Dravot is the ambiguous god-man, then it is Peachey who must be crucified. Kipling finds it necessary to make this character split in his story, for he must not only have his god-man die but also have him resurrected. Thus, it is necessary to have two characters in order to create the mythic substructure of the story and still make it realistically plausible. Peachey is the resurrected figure who brings the head of Dravot, still with its crown, back to tell the tale to the narrator.

Kipling creates in this story a burlesque version of a basic dichotomy between two different kinds of reality—the real world and the story world. The narrator, who deals with real events, tells a story of one (Peachey) who in turn tells a story of fantastic events in which the real world is transformed into the fabular nature of story itself. Dravot-Peachey project themselves into a purely self-created story world, but once accepted there, they cannot break the code of the roles that they have assumed. When Dravot makes an effort to violate this code (their own "contrack"), the story they have created and thus the roles they have played become apparent as just that—fictional roles.

The man who would be a king can be a king only in the pretend world of story itself, and then only as long as story-world, or story-reality, is maintained. It is little wonder that "The Man Who Would Be King" has such a comic tone, for truly what Kipling is playing with here is not only the nature of empires but also the nature of story itself. If one wishes to read "The Man Who Would Be King" as a parable of the tenuous and fictionally imposed nature of British imperialism, then such a reading is possible, but only because the story primarily is about the essentially tenuous nature of the fable world itself.

Charles E. May

THE MAN WITH THE DOG

Author: Ruth Prawer Jhabvala (1927-   )
Type of plot: Sketch
Time of plot: The mid-twentieth century
Locale: New Delhi, India
First published: 1966

Principal characters:
THE NARRATOR, a wealthy Indian widow
SHAMMI, her oldest son, a military officer
BOEKELMAN, an aging Dutch expatriate
SUSI, his little dog and constant companion

The Story

The narrator imagines herself as she was in earlier days: a beloved and respected Indian wife and mother, faithfully fulfilling her household duties. Now, however, her visits with her children and grandchildren degenerate into bitterness because references to her current relations with a European man named Boekelman are unavoidable. She alternately laughs and cries when she considers, at her age, that she has such passion for a man who is as advanced in years as herself. She reminisces about their first meeting. It happened, significantly enough, as the result of an accident, when her chauffeur drove into the rear bumper of Boekelman's car. Flushing angrily, Boekelman emerged from his car, with a little, barking dog in his arms. Once he caught sight of the narrator, gorgeously arrayed in the back of her Packard, he stopped shouting and cast her an admiring glance.

The narrator reflects on how her married life was spent quietly in the countryside with a much older husband and young children. Once she was widowed and her children were grown, she moved to the city, reveling in shopping and being invited to parties and teas. At one such function, she again met Boekelman. His foreignness is what most interested her. Unlike Indian men, he talked freely and familiarly with women and showed them little courtesies, such as opening doors for them.

Boekelman now no longer opens doors for the narrator, which she considers proper now that they live in the same house. Boekelman insists on paying rent for his suite of rooms, but by calculating the amount in his favor, he pays little. He originally came to India for the ivory trade but failed to acquire a big fortune, and his former wife returned to Holland. Although India is home to him, his friends are all Europeans. Sometimes Boekelman gives parties for them in his rooms, to which the narrator comments she may or may not be invited.

The narrator describes their daily routine: Boekelman appears at noon, shaved and dressed, his umbrella in one hand, his dog's lead in the other. Annoyed to find the narrator indolent on the verandah, still in her nightclothes, he complains about some minor irritation and grows incensed at her indifference. For emphasis, he pokes holes in the ground with the tip of his umbrella. After she accuses him of ruining her garden, he retreats out the gate, with her, agitated, in pursuit. By the time he returns in the evening, all is forgiven. Occasionally he allows her to stay in his rooms overnight. On these occasions, the narrator is rapturous as Boekelman sleeps next to her, toothless and snoring; she is convinced that no one else knows him so completely. All that prevents her perfect happiness is the constant presence of his dog, Susi, which watches her with old running eyes. The narrator senses a mutual resentment.

The narrator's relationship with Boekelman nearly ends during a visit from the narrator's oldest son, Shammi, when Boekelman's railing over some failing by a servant escalates to a general tirade against India. Shammi, a lieutenant-colonel in the Indian army, indignantly leaves the room. The narrator begs his forgiveness and promises to send Boekelman away. She maintains her resolve until she learns that Boekelman— who is unable to find as financially accommodating a landlord as she—is moving in with a shameless European flirt. She breaks down and pleads with him to stay.

As the story closes, the narrator muses that, despite going against society's rules and her children's wishes, she is fortunate in her happiness with Boekelman.

Themes and Meanings

"The Man with the Dog" explores the themes of social and cross-cultural tension that recur throughout Ruth Prawer Jhabvala's work. It appears in her collection *A Stronger Climate: Nine Stories* (1968). The three stories in this book's "sufferers" section focus on Europeans who have stayed on in India after independence. They are left experiencing the bitterness of being old in a country that is alien to them.

Boekelman and his circle of European friends know only a few words of Hindi and remain determinedly aloof from the life of India and ordinary Indians. The narrator explains that they are really more like family than friends, "the way they both love and hate each other and are closely tied together whether they like it or not." Having no other family, they cling to one another with all the blind loyalty and resentment that forced dependency breeds. They celebrate birthdays and holidays together and visit their sick friends. Nevertheless, they may not be on speaking terms with each other for months, even years, and are given to gossip and backbiting.

When the narrator is alone with Boekelman, he readily ridicules various women friends but will not tolerate her saying anything against them. He draws a rigid distinction between those who are in his circle and those who are outside it—for whom different rules apply. Even Boekelman's intimacy with the narrator fails to blur this distinction.

Jhabvala's ideas about Europeans in India are summed up in her essay "Myself in India," which introduces *Out of India: Selected Stories* (1986). All Europeans who encounter India, she writes, pass through three stages: First, "everything Indian is marvelous"; second, "everything Indian is not so marvelous"; third, "everything Indian is abominable." For some, the cycle ends there; for others, it renews itself.

The cycle of attraction, disillusion, and repulsion in which Europeans in India find themselves appears to parallel the relationship between Boekelman and the narrator, with its daily ritual of quarreling and making up. As in much of Jhabvala's fiction, sociopolitical and personal spheres mirror one another. Like the English author E. M. Forster, to whom she is often compared, Jhabvala uses love as a tool for investigating the manners and beliefs of different cultures and social classes.

Critics have suggested that because of Jhabvala's own experiences as a refugee and expatriate, her characters tend to be marginalized in some way. Alienation invariably defines them. If Boekelman is a foreigner in India, the narrator's relationship with him defies Indian tradition, which expects an aging widow to lead a life devoted to prayer and self-sacrifice. These characters' evidently foolish actions, it may be argued, are alternatively the stuff of comedy or tragedy.

Style and Technique
"The Man with the Dog" is essentially a character sketch. However, its portrayal of character extends beyond the single dimension; Jhabvala manipulates the first-person narrative so that it not only presents a third-person portrayal of Boekelman but also allows the reader insight into the narrator herself. The author again uses this technique, though in a more sophisticated form, in her novel *Heat and Dust* (1975). The narrator of this work uncovers the scandalous story of her grandfather's first wife, revealing much about herself in the process. The novel's narrator, like that of "The Man with the Dog," remains unnamed—her anonymity increasing her potential to reflect her environment and the people in it. What the reader in each case learns about the narrator and her subject generates other awareness, including the nature of relationships and also social and cultural contexts. The technique thereby provides the reader with a multilayered experience of the story. It also allows Jhabvala to present her characters and their situations with a certain amount of irony.

Critics have compared the complex of satire and familiarity found in Jhabvala's fiction with that of English novelist Jane Austen. Jhabvala's particular blend of intimacy and objectivity is generally traced to her geographical and cultural rootlessness. The title of a 1973 essay on her by Ramlal Argarwal, "Outsider with Unusual Insight," gives a clue to her singular vision. While living in India, Jhabvala was in the unusual position of being simultaneously an outsider, as a foreigner, and an insider, as a member of an Indian family.

Critics have also identified the influence of Jhabvala's screenplay writing on her later fiction. "The Man with the Dog," in its unfolding of character and situation, apparently draws on cinematic techniques such as the dissolve and the flashback. Throughout the story, the narrator constantly—and almost seamlessly—shifts back and forth in time.

It is worth noting that Jhabvala includes "The Man with the Dog" in her retrospective collection, *Out of India*. When asked how she selected the fifteen stories for this collection, she responded that because they were the ones that she "remembered most vividly," they "must be the ones that somehow came out the best."

Amy Adelstein

THE MAN WITH THE LAPDOG

Author: Beth Lordan (1948-   )
Type of plot: Domestic realism, psychological
Time of plot: The 1990's
Locale: Galway, Ireland
First published: 1999

> *Principal characters:*
> LYLE, a sixty-seven-year-old American retired in Ireland
> MARY, his Irish wife
> MARK, a vacationing American
> LAURA, his wife

The Story

Lyle, the man in "The Man with the Lapdog," has been living in Galway, Ireland, for two years after his retirement. He does not particularly like the Irish people, who he thinks stand too close, but there is a lot about Ireland he does like: He likes going for walks and he likes being a foreigner. Moreover, he feels displaced and distant from his Irish wife.

One morning he meets an American couple on one of his walks with his dog. Although it is March, not the regular tourist season, Mark and Laura are on vacation for three weeks. The couple is friendly, and Lyle is particularly taken by the woman, who is just entering middle age with "none of the artificiality of so many American women." Mark, who is obviously ill, has lost his hair and his face looks swollen, but something about the way the couple looks together makes Lyle remember the pleasure of walking with his wife in the same way, a pleasure he no longer feels.

When Lyle tells his wife about the American couple, he wants to avoid any reference to their sons, especially Jimmy, who lives in the United States and does not visit often. Although Laura told him that Mark was dying, he does not tell his wife that. While his wife chats about how she hates motels and sleeping in other people's beds, for she could feel the warmth of those who had slept in them before, Lyle can only feel the sweet warmth that a woman left in a bed, and he knows the woman is Laura. He makes a nasty retort to his wife, hurting her feelings.

When Lyle goes for a walk the day before St. Patrick's Day, he watches Mark put his head against a wall like a child playing hide and seek as Laura comes out of a shop and runs to him. He thinks about the inevitability of Mark's death and how men will be lining up to take his place. He thinks that if Laura comes back in a year or two, she will be over the death; he imagines walking along the river and meeting her or going to Idaho, where she lives.

The next day when Laura says they are going to drive to the Ring of Kerry because they have heard it is so beautiful, Lyle thinks "you are beautiful" and is afraid he may say it aloud and make a fool of himself.

That night as his wife takes a bath and talks to him from the bathroom, he looks for a roadmap for Laura, getting angrier and angrier when he cannot find one. When his wife realizes he is looking for the map for the Americans, she turns tender toward him, and the next morning she gets up before him for a change, makes coffee, and gives him the map. She offers to walk along with him this morning, and when they meet Mark and Laura, she is shocked at how sick Mark is. After an amiable chat, she invites them to tea.

When they walk away, Mary says, "Such lovely people," and Lyle wants to say, "So are we." He wants to say that he is not a young man but that he is not dying and that for them the end was still far off, with "difficulties and complications still to come." Instead he presses her wrist against him and says, using an Irish inflection, "They are so. And it's a sad thing it is."

Themes and Meanings

Beth Lordan's basic theme in "The Man with the Lapdog," second-prize winner in *Prize Stories, 2000: The O. Henry Awards*, is the rediscovery of connections between a man and a woman who have lived together long enough that they take each other for granted. The sense of loss of intimacy and connection is particularly felt by Lyle, an American living in retirement in Ireland, who feels a triple displacement. First, he is not in his home country and thus feels alien among conventions and traditions foreign to him. For example, he says he would feel foolish saying "half-five" instead of five-thirty, and saying "toilet" instead of bathroom would be unthinkable to him. He has frightened himself by trying to drive on the wrong side of the road, and he has trouble understanding what the Irish say. Second, he is retired and thus deprived of any work to make his life meaningful. Third, he feels alienated from his wife of many years, who, being native to Ireland, feels comfortable and at home.

When Lyle meets the American couple on vacation, he develops a romantic fantasy about Laura. Lyle has no intention of doing anything about the fantasy. He feels drawn to Laura, not only because she is an American and thus reminds him of the comfortable at-home feeling he has lost but also because he feels protective of her because of her imminent loss of her ill husband. His fantasies about meeting her after the death of Mark are harmless and unfocused, suggestive only of his sense of loneliness and his need to rekindle some sense of romance in his life.

It is not until he becomes frustrated while looking for a map to give Laura that his wife, Mary, understands something of his sense of alienation and his need to do something for his American friends. When Mary sees Mark and realizes that he does not have long to live, she reveals a tenderness and sympathy that Lyle feels he has not seen for some time. At the end of the story, when Lyle and Mary walk away and she says, "Such lovely people," Lyle wants to give her some sense of how much he values her and their relationship. He wants to say that although he is no longer young, still he is not dying and they still have a life together, a life, like any other, filled with difficulties and complications, but still a life to be lived with meaning and value.

Style and Technique

"The Man with the Lapdog" is essentially a retelling of Anton Chekhov's famous short story "The Woman with the Lapdog." In Chekhov's story, a Russian man meets a woman while on vacation and begins an affair with her. When the man returns to Moscow and the woman returns to St. Petersburg, the man cannot get her out of his mind and resumes the affair, arranging to meet her whenever he can. The man feels that he is living two lives: a public life at his work and with his family, which he feels is empty and unreal, and a private life with the woman that he loves, which he feels is the only true reality, the only time when he is truly himself. Lordan's story similarly presents a man who meets a woman on vacation for whom he develops romantic feelings. However, as opposed to Chekhov's story, in "The Man with the Lapdog," the man ultimately discovers that his real life lies with his wife.

Like Chekhov's famous realistic style, Lordan's style is deceptively simple. Although the story seems a classic example of domestic realism, in which the focus is on everyday experiences of ordinary people, the language, which focuses on the thoughts of Lyle, emphasizes how powerfully the imaginative life supersedes the ordinary world of everyday reality. A central image in the story is Lyle sitting alone in his home with his dog on his lap, entertaining romantic fantasies about Laura. In this sense, Lordan's story actually parallels Chekhov's. The important difference is the final realization or acceptance by Lyle that there is much to treasure with his wife. He accepts that even though he is not young he still has the feel of her hand on his arm and he still has a life to value, in spite of its difficulties and complications—maybe even because of those difficulties and complications.

The brilliance of Lordan's story is her ability to get inside the mind of Lyle so thoroughly and to express his sense of alienation and loneliness. Lordan's treatment of Lyle makes it clear that he has no desire to transform his fantasies into action. She knows quite well that the fantasy life of men is more often like that of Lyle—a vague longing rather than a call to action—than that of Chekhov's adulterous protagonist.

Charles E. May

MAN, WOMAN AND BOY

Author: Stephen Dixon (1936-   )
Type of plot: Impressionistic
Time of plot: The late twentieth century
Locale: Somewhere in the United States
First published: 1992

> *Principal characters:*
> AN UNNAMED MAN
> HIS WIFE
> THEIR SON

The Story

An unnamed husband and wife are in the middle of a fierce domestic battle that threatens to break up the family and lead to the dividing up of household items. Both parents are concerned with what will become of their son after they divorce. The scene turns out to be an imagined one, however, as both parents are merely reading quietly as their son works on a puzzle.

At times, the husband and wife argue over the division of domestic duties such as cleaning, dusting, and cooking. Because the wife works as a teacher and spends much of her time correcting papers, the house sometimes appears chaotic, a condition that her husband frequently mentions. He is highly concerned with order and the responsibility and division of domestic duties; he would like his wife to work on these periodically—that is, in a scheduled way. Their quarrel over dividing up duties leads him into an obsessive attempt to remember the origins of his concern over her sloppiness. As the narrative moves back several hours to a scene in which the wife promises to try harder to be neat, his memory again forces him to account for why he has taken her to task for her failures as a housewife. He admits that he has taken it out on her because of something that happened at work that has been bothering him all day. Not content with that explanation, he traces his resentment even further back to the early hours of the morning, when he wanted to have sex and she complained that she was too tired.

Not satisfied with the sexual explanation, the husband delves back still further into earlier conflicts over his wife's accusation that he is too quick sexually, a situation that leaves her frustrated. Interwoven throughout his relentless memory tracings, the husband constantly declares his love for his wife and admits that their sex life is, most of the time, very fulfilling.

The husband's memory then returns to the exciting sex they had the previous night, and from there back to his son's birth, then to when he and his wife met. His memory's almost autonomic regressive system then takes over as he recalls his first girlfriends in grade school; his parents' violent domestic squabbles—in which he, like his own son, asked them to stop; and finally to the womb experience itself, in which he remembers his father and mother screaming: "Filthy rotten bitch." "And you. Stupid, cheap, pig-headed, a pill. Get lost. I hate your guts." The disturbing flood of memories returns the husband to the present and creates within him feelings of deep gratitude for what he is presently experiencing—a loving wife and a sweet son.

Later there is an interior monologue in which the husband is preparing himself to make love with his wife, followed by his satisfied washing up after their lovemaking. It is crucial, though, for him to say to himself that he loves his wife and that he consciously admits to himself—for only words make it real—that he has a happy life. The story concludes as he surveys his memory for anything else to surface and, finding nothing, gratefully falls asleep.

Themes and Meanings

The title of the story, "Man, Woman and Boy," starkly presents the subject matter of the story without the father-narrator's meaning-making imagination. The theme of the story—what the author says about the subject and, therefore, what it means in his life—is precisely what Stephen Dixon demonstrates throughout the story. The reader receives the elements of the story only from the father's perspective—what he hears, sees, and, most important, remembers. The narrative delineates the process of creativity as the father relentlessly traces, in memory, how all the discrete actions in the story and related incidents in his life come together to formulate the most profoundly meaningful events in the man's life. By allowing his imagination to follow his memory in its most literal operations, he discovers that his life has been, and continues to be, happy, fulfilling, and rich in spite of the normal domestic difficulties that every family experiences. Whether or not he actually remembers his own parents' violent battles in the womb memory is beside the point. His imagination shows him that he is capable of becoming like his brutal father, a warning that reinforces his feelings of gratitude for the wonderful wife and sweet son he has.

One of the reasons that Dixon is considered a foremost postmodernist writer in late twentieth century American fiction is his ability to make the mental and psychological processes of the imagination the actual theme of many of his stories, and this story is one of his most impressive accomplishments. There is certainly nothing new in writing about a man, a woman, and a boy in terms of content. Dixon's fecund imagination, however, transforms a common family story into a reenactment of how the mind probes its own complex processes in creating meaning and, thus, understanding the evolution of the value of family love. Without the imagination's constant effort to understand and explain to itself the primacy of the value of the family as the center of a civilized community, the man perpetually runs the risk of falling into the chaos and terror of a world of mere natural process. Consciousness of the self as it operates within a specifically human and loving world is both the theme and the process that Dixon brilliantly explores in this unique story.

Style and Technique

The principal technique used throughout the story is the process of memory as it regresses from one event to another, until the narrator finds himself back in his mother's womb witnessing one of his parents' violently abusive battles. Dixon, carrying that technique to its most extreme applications, makes it comic and even absurd. Dixon is not concerned with literal events in this story; he explores in brilliant ways how the imagination, through memory, creates significance and meaning in one man's life. The process of projection, used in the opening scene in which they are dividing up the household goods in preparation for a divorce, enables the man unconsciously to test what such a disaster would feel like, which allows him to appreciate the domestic tranquillity he now enjoys. His son is shown throughout the narrative working on a puzzle, an image that becomes a metaphor for the fictive process that the story is exploring.

As the son is working on a puzzle, the father is experiencing how memory and the imagination unconsciously work out the most complex puzzles in everyday life. The narrator finds only clarity and meaning in interior monologues, where he must articulate in words what his life means to him. He dimly understands that meaning evolves only in words, and that words are the boundaries that protect him from the chaos and despair of what painter Francis Bacon calls "the brutality of fact." The stark personas of the title become, by means of the humanizing force of Dixon's imagination, a grateful husband, a loving wife, and a sweet child. Much of the adventure for the reader is following the complex turns of the man's mind as it regresses and projects and again regresses further and further into the history of his own consciousness. The climax of the story occurs, though, when the husband's regressive memory comes directly into contact with the rather frightening precincts of the unconscious as he recalls hearing his parents' battle from within his mother's womb. Dixon makes that scene simultaneously a comic and deeply disturbing one, because beyond that frontier lay the ultimate abyss of madness.

Patrick Meanor

THE MANAGEMENT OF GRIEF

Author: Bharati Mukherjee (1940-   )
Type of plot: Psychological
Time of plot: The late 1980's
Locale: Toronto, Canada; Ireland; and India
First published: 1988

> *Principal characters:*
> MRS. SHAILA BHAVE, the narrator, an Indian Canadian woman
> who has lost her husband and sons in a terrorist bombing
> KUSUM, her neighbor and friend, who has lost her husband and a
> daughter in the same disaster
> JUDITH TEMPLETON, a counselor of survivors

The Story

The narrator, Mrs. Bhave, is attempting an impossible task. She has just lost her husband and their two sons in an airplane crash caused by a terrorist bomb, and she carefully reports the interactions going on around her in an effort to understand and communicate her own experience. She seems at a great distance from her surroundings, yet anything can bring her back to the disaster and thoughts of her family. For example, while she lies in bed, a stranger making tea in her kitchen brings back the days when her sons made her breakfast.

Mrs. Bhave relives the disaster in a stream-of-consciousness monitoring of the constant activity surrounding her. As some people listen for the latest theories on why the airplane blew up, such as space debris, Russian lasers, and a Sikh bomb, she suddenly realizes that the radios she hears in the background belong to her sons. This thought leads her to recall how funny her neighbor Kusum looked as she ran to her door to tell her what had happened. Mrs. Bhave becomes aware of the voices of preachers speaking on the television, going on as though nothing had happened, yet cannot voice her own thoughts about this phenomenon. She hears the phone ringing and realizes that someone is talking about her condition and her medication. She feels like screaming but cannot. Instead, she hears the voices of her family screaming.

Mrs. Bhave speaks out very little and seems unable to judge anything, in view of the disaster. She appears to question her own customs, remarking to Kusum that she never once told her husband Vikram that she loved him. Kusum replies that modern women have to say it because their feelings are fake. As if to emphasize this judgment, Kusum's youngest daughter, Pam, who dates Canadian boys and works at a McDonald's, appears, urging her mother to dress herself for the reporters. Pam expresses survivors' guilt, part of her own grief, accusing her mother of wishing that she herself had died instead of her sister.

Soon, Judith Templeton, an appointee of the provincial government, visits the household. She describes her job to Mrs. Bhave, requesting her assistance in communicating with other survivors, having heard that Mrs. Bhave has taken it more calmly. Mrs. Bhave represents the human touch that Judith needs in order to manage the grief of all the survivors. She represents a bridge between the Canadian government and the Indian Canadian culture. From the beginning, there is a gap between Templeton's and Mrs. Bhave's understanding of the experience of the survivors. For Mrs. Bhave, it is true only in Templeton's judgment that some of the women survivors are hysterical, in contrast to Mrs. Bhave's calm. Mrs. Bhave nevertheless agrees to another meeting with Templeton, to be held after her return from Ireland, where the survivors journey in order to identify family members.

Four days later, Mrs. Bhave joins Kusum on a rock overlooking the Irish Sea. Kusum appears bewildered and stranded. The survivors and the people helping them try to find explanations that will make the disaster possible to cope with, but these pieces, when placed side by side, are of no comfort. In fact, they become a pool of endless pain and irony. The passengers had just finished eating breakfast; Mrs. Bhave's boys loved eating on airplanes. They were only a half hour from the airport when the bomb exploded. Someone assures them no one suffered. Someone else believes it possible that there were survivors. Mrs. Bhave's boys are good swimmers. Sharks are mentioned, and the fact that women float better than men because they carry more body fat. Another man reminds them all that it is a parent's duty to hope. Kusum tells Mrs. Bhave that her swami says it is fate. Mrs. Bhave thinks of her tranquilizers.

Mrs. Bhave never identifies her family among the photographs. She reports that many of the photos look like her boys, but none of them are. She cries but claims not to know why; she is ecstatic, she says, because she cannot be certain of her loss. She flies to India with Kusum, becoming suddenly vocal as she screams at airport officials who might want to search the coffin of Kusum's husband. Once in India, Mrs. Bhave tries to lose herself in travel. She realizes that she is caught between two worlds, the Indian and the Indian Canadian, too old to start over but too young to give up.

Mrs. Bhave sees others making changes in their lives. Some of the men remarry, as is expected of them. One day, as she offers prayers in a temple, Mrs. Bhave's late husband, Vikram, appears to her, urging her to continue the life they began together in Canada. She plans to leave India, but Kusum remains there while her daughter, Pam, moves to Hollywood. Soon after Mrs. Bhave returns to Toronto, Templeton visits again. She tells Mrs. Bhave that most of the survivors, after six months, have moved into the two middle stages of grief, which, according to her textbook, consists of four stages: rejection, depression, acceptance, and reconstruction. Mrs. Bhave does not tell Templeton that her family is no less real to her now than when they were living.

Mrs. Bhave agrees to help Templeton with a Sikh couple who refuse to sign anything that implies their sons are no longer alive. Templeton cannot understand the cultural duty to hope, and Mrs. Bhave cannot explain it to her. Unable to relate to Templeton's frustration and categorization of the couple as stubborn and ignorant, she parts company with her, refusing to explain. For a while, Mrs. Bhave tries other measures to make sense of the disaster, writing letters, selling her home, and looking for charities to support. Then one day, she hears the voices of her family again, this time telling her to go and be brave. She begins walking.

Themes and Meanings

The title of Bharati Mukherjee's "The Management of Grief" suggests that grief is something that can, indeed, be managed. Judith Templeton represents the authority for such a claim. She carries a textbook on grief, she has taken a degree in managing grief, and her job, created by the provincial government, is to manage grief. The ways in which individual survivors cope with the disaster might also be interpreted as management of grief. The whole story also demonstrates the opposite of the title's assumption: Mrs. Bhave cannot manage her grief; she can only experience it, move through it by some inexplicable process of mourning, and move on.

The assumptions that Templeton makes about the management of grief are not accurate when applied to the survivors. To a great extent, this misreading stems from cultural differences, which Templeton cannot see, even though her intentions are to do exactly that. Templeton becomes frustrated with survivors who refuse to accept the fate of their family members because they believe it is a parent's duty to hope. When the men begin to remarry, she shows surprise at how little time has passed. Templeton's judgment and ignorance is expressed in the labels she uses for surviving mothers, such as "hysterical" and "a real mess," and in her references to the parents' stubbornness and ignorance. Moreover, Templeton's concern for her own discomfort over the discomfort of the survivors is too apparent. She makes jokes about how her bladder will fare because the job requires the frequent ritual of drinking tea with her clients, and she complains that although the people are lovely, they are driving her crazy.

Style and Technique

Mukherjee uses the technique of reporting in the story to produce distance between the narrator, Mrs. Bhave, and her surroundings. This conveys the shock and thus the surreal quality of the experience of loss. She also uses stream of consciousness and chains of thought to convey the experience of loss in the narrative, linking seemingly unrelated events or words, such as the women making tea and Mrs. Bhave's sons making breakfast.

Mukherjee employs juxtaposition as well. One fact or event is placed alongside another, in seeming agreement or concordance, yet the effect of such placement is to pose irreconcilable disagreement between ideas, people, and cultures. An example of this is Kusum describing how modern women are fake because they must declare their love out loud, and then her own daughter Pam coming out into the living room and demonstrating modern and fake as defined by the preceding conversation. A more chilling example is the woman who makes tea; she is pregnant with her fifth child, all sons, and all living.

Jennifer Vinsky

MS. FOUND IN A BOTTLE

Author: Edgar Allan Poe (1809-1849)
Type of plot: Adventure
Time of plot: The 1800's
Locale: The high seas
First published: 1833

Principal character:
THE UNNAMED NARRATOR

The Story

The narrator begins his frightening tale with a one-paragraph introduction of himself. Although he does not give his age, he is probably middle-aged, for he has spent many years in foreign travel. Time and "ill usage" have estranged him from both his native country and his family. He has been well educated, especially in the natural sciences, but has been accused of "a deficiency of imagination." He describes himself as a person who cannot be lured from "the severe precincts of truth by the ignes fatui of superstition."

The narrator sets sail on a merchant ship from Batavia, Java, to the Archipelago Islands, for no reason other than a "nervous restlessness" to which he is addicted. For days the ship rides off the coast of Java, waiting for a favorable wind. One evening, he observes strange changes in the sea and the sky: an unusual cloud to the northwest, a red moon, and an extremely hot, spiral atmosphere. He suspects a simoom, but the ship's captain does not share his fears. Soon after, the ship quivers; the sea hurls it on the beam-ends and washes over the decks from stem to stern. Despite the whirling ocean, the ship rights itself. The narrator is saved from being washed overboard by being thrown between the sternpost and the rudder. Only he and an old Swedish sailor, however, survive the storm; everyone else on board is lost, many drowning in their cabins. The two survivors cannot control the ship as it flies for five days in violent winds on a course southeast by south. Cold and darkness envelop the ship, which the narrator believes to be farther south than any previous ship has ever been. He loses hope and prepares himself for the death he considers inevitable.

As the ship is trapped in a maelstrom, a huge vessel of four thousand tons is sighted at the top of the abyss, under full sail, with brass cannon and lighted battle lanterns in the rigging. When the two vessels collide, the narrator is thrown into the rigging of the strange ship. Escaping notice of the crew, he hides at first in the hold. Gradually he beings to explore. The crew, old and infirm, speak a language he cannot understand. The instruments and navigational charts are ancient; the ship itself is very old, but he thinks that it is not a warship. The narrator soon discovers that he is invisible to the crew. He can go anywhere he wishes. From the captain's quarters he takes writing materials, intending to write "this journal," which at the last moment he will put into a bottle and cast into the sea in the hope of communicating his adventure to the world. The ship withstands battering by high seas, which the narrator attributes to its being caught in some strong current or undertow. The crew glide about like "ghosts of buried centuries."

When he observes the captain in his quarters, the narrator discovers him to be quite old and of the same stature as he himself. On the cabin floor are iron-clasped volumes, obsolete charts, and scientific instruments. The captain is poring over a paper, which the narrator takes to be a commission with the signature of a monarch. Like the crew, the captain speaks an unfamiliar tongue and seems to be a ghost from the past.

Meanwhile, the ship continues to endure blasts of wind and ocean beyond belief. Black night and chaotic waters surround it, and huge formations of ice tower on both sides of it. As the narrator thought earlier, the ship is riding in some strange current roaring to the southward. The narrator's sensations and fears are so horrible that he can barely express them. However, his curiosity overrides his despair and will, he says, reconcile him to even a hideous death. He believes that he is rushing to "some exciting knowledge—some never-to-be-imparted secret, whose attainment is destruction." The current, he suspects, is carrying the ship to the South Pole.

In the last journal entry, the narrator notes that the storm is worse than ever and the ship is sometimes "lifted bodily from out the sea!" On the faces of the crew there is hope rather than despair, but the narrator reacts with horror as topless ice opens on each side of the ship and it spins in huge circles. The circles grow smaller; the ship plunges wildly in a whirlpool. He knows that he has little time to contemplate his fate. Then comes his final sentence: "The ship is quivering—oh God! and—going down!"

Themes and Meanings

This adventure story is suggestive of the unbelievable tale told by the haunted narrator of Samuel Taylor Coleridge's *The Rime of the Ancient Mariner* (1798). Edgar Allan Poe's narrator is similar to other misanthropic characters found in his stories, but like Coleridge's mariner, he experiences physical phenomena that no one else has experienced and lived to tell. Poe bows to reality by having the narrator killed at the end but has provided for the survival of his journal through the ingenious manuscript-in-a-bottle device. The story can be read purely as a fantastic adventure story, full of danger and mystery that cause psychological reactions in the narrator that he finds nearly impossible to describe. It is perhaps for these qualities that the story won for Poe a fifty-dollar prize in a contest conducted by the Baltimore *Saturday Visiter* in 1833. The three judges of the contest praised all the stories that Poe submitted for their "imagination," "style," "invention," and "learning." The explorer's narrative was a popular genre in the 1800's; the heavens and the depths of the ocean were settings for numerous stories by Poe and other writers.

In addition to its characteristics as an adventure tale, the story can be read as an allegory, according to some critics. In reviewing Nathaniel Hawthorne's *Twice-Told Tales* (1837), Poe has little to say in defense of allegory. He insists that if used at all, allegory should be merely a suggestive meaning that readers can call up if they wish, but that it should never interfere with the main current of the story. However, Maria Bonapart and Daniel Hoffman, two Freudian critics, believe the story can be interpreted allegorically. The adventure, in the narrator's words, toward "exciting knowledge," toward a secret "whose attainment is destruction," is a voyage of the soul backward in time to its beginning. Man has always been curious about the details of his existence before birth and after death. The ghost ship, which seems to swell like a living being, is the mother's womb, with the narrator hiding briefly in the hold. The terrifying fascination of the adventure that holds the narrator "in awe" is the subconscious desire of the human soul to know its existence before birth. The captain, so similar physically to the narrator (and to Poe himself), is the father. The commission that the captain studies in his cabin is signed by a monarch: the Lord of all, or God. These events are made possible by the hurling of the narrator into the rigging of the ghost ship and thence to the deck. This action signifies a change of state for the narrator. He is now beyond the ordinary state of ratiocination; he can attempt to describe his feelings and his surroundings but cannot explain them. They take on allegorical meaning if viewed as an expression of the soul's yearning to understand its preexistence; such yearning, however, can never be fulfilled in this life, and thus the narrator finally meets his death, leaving behind only a manuscript that records the awesome experience.

Style and Technique

Poe is highly skilled in combining the natural and the supernatural in adventure stories told by a narrator who struggles to express his horror at what he is experiencing and who believes that he is in the grip of some strange physical and/or spiritual power. Rational explanation is to varying degrees always beyond the narrator's power. Poe's attempts at analyzing the narrator's sensations reach their height in his story "Ligeia"; by combining the supernatural with the natural, he encourages the reader to suspend rational belief and let the story as a whole cast its spell over him, and only after the climactic closing lines does the reader return to the reality of his or her own world. In "The Philosophy of Composition" (1846), Poe stresses the importance of a story's emotional impact on the reader. In such stories as "Ms. Found in a Bottle," the reader identifies emotionally with the narrator (other characters are shadowy and undeveloped) and experiences the danger, horror, and terror with him.

The narrator is presented as an intelligent, educated man, not given to wild imagination or hallucinations. Moreover, he is a seasoned traveler who would not be easily surprised or frightened. His nautical vocabulary shows his great familiarity with ships and the ocean. All the narrator's characteristics are designed to persuade the reader to accept the truth of the strange adventure he records in his journal and communicates to the world immediately before his death. Even the headnote to the story (*"Qui n'a plus qu'un moment a vivre/ N'a plus rien a dissimuler,"* or "Anyone with only a moment to live has nothing to hide") encourages the reader to accept the narrator and his tale. Because of the reader's willing suspension of disbelief, this adventure story, like others of Poe, has engrossed readers for more than a century.

Louise S. Bailey

MANY ARE DISAPPOINTED

Author: V. S. Pritchett (1900-1997)
Type of plot: Naturalistic
Time of plot: 1935
Locale: The south of England
First published: 1937

> *Principal characters:*
> SID BLAKE, the protagonist
> HARRY NEWTON, the leader of the group
> TED, the oldest of the group
> BERT RICHARDS, the youngest
> THE WOMAN AT THE TAVERN
> HER SMALL DAUGHTER

The Story

Four men are cycling up a deserted road in the country, battling a wind from the hidden sea. The youngest, Bert Richards, is dreaming of a mythical, affectionate girl he will meet at the pub that finally comes into view. It is a small, red-brick house with outbuildings and a single chimney giving out smoke. The four men are delighted at the prospect of getting a beer after ten miles of mostly uphill pedaling. They look at the four windows with their four curtains and the varnished door. When Ted, who has walked the last thirty yards, catches up, they read the black sign over the door: Tavern. It is an old-fashioned word, according to Ted.

Harry Newton, contrary to custom, knocks. All are surprised to find a woman waiting behind the door, a frail, drab woman not much past thirty. She shows them into a sitting room with a sign in the window that says "Teas." When the men order beer and ask for the bar, she admits that despite the sign over the door and the notation on Harry's map, the house is not a pub. "Many are disappointed," she says.

Her tiny, frail daughter comes to cling close to her mother, who is happier now, and the men begin to speak more gently. The mother says that the nearest pub is ten miles behind them. There only Ted had wanted to stop. The woman, fearing that they are about to leave, informs them that she serves teas. Sid Blake is sitting on the arm of a chair, and the child is gazing at a gold ring he is wearing on his little finger. After checking with Harry, Sid orders four teas, and the woman is timidly delighted.

The men wait a long time in the cold room with its bare linoleum on the floor and its almost empty china cupboard while the wind blows sand along the empty road and over the rows of cabbages. The woman and child enter from time to time bringing a cup or a saucer; it seems to Ted, the married man, that she does not know how to set a table. Harry, who has planned the route and is keenly interested in old Roman roads, goes down to the gate to check the Roman road he has come to see. The woman points it out to him from the doorway. When he returns to report that it is only grass, Ted remarks, "No beer and no Romans," at which the woman says that there are seldom Romans in the neighborhood. When the laughter stops, Sid explains that she means gypsies and tells the woman to take no notice of the men's laughter. After her retreat to the kitchen, Bert and Ted say that she is "dippy," but Sid asks them to speak quietly.

While the men are eating their bread and butter, the child comes in with a written message from her mother, and after the girl's departure Sid remarks that he thinks he has seen the woman before. That, say the young men, is Sid's trouble: He has seen too many girls before.

When Sid goes to the kitchen to pay for the teas, he finds the woman sitting drably at a table covered with unwashed plates and the remains of a meal. The chairs are festooned with dirty clothes and a man's waistcoat. In the ensuing dialogue, Sid learns that she has been in this tavern only three years, although it seems to her longer, that she has been very ill, that her husband has given up his job to bring her here on doctor's orders, and that she is better now but lonely. Sid agrees that a woman wants company. Then he feels the child's hand touching the ring on his finger. Sid laughs and says, "You saw that before." He takes off the ring and, putting it in the palm of his hand, bends down so that his head nearly brushes the woman's arm. Saying that the ring is lucky, he slips it on the child's little finger and declares that it keeps him out of mischief. Then he takes the ring back, telling the child that her mother wants it and winking at the woman. "She's got hers on the wrong finger. Little one luck, big one trouble." With shining eyes the woman laughs and blushes. When he moves toward the door, she pouts and then, taking the child by the hand, hurries over as if both of them would cling to him. Avidly they follow him to the other room.

As the four men zip up their jackets, Harry gives the child a sixpence. The woman and the child, hand in hand, standing in the middle of the road, wave for a long time. Sid is in the lead with the ring shining on his finger as the men head for a real pub.

Themes and Meanings

The main theme of "Many Are Disappointed" is the vulnerability of women and the indifference of men to their suffering. This in no way means that the author has a didactic purpose; this is not a plea for social reform. The plot—sketchy as it is—is there to reveal character. Pritchett has said that he finds drama in human personality rather than in events. The tale consists of character revelations in a narrative simple in itself but complex in its implications. The nameless woman in the story is condemned to a desolate existence and virtual solitude following an unexplained and near-fatal illness. One is not told directly that Sid is in any way responsible for this, but one surmises that it is so because Sid remembers having seen her before, the child remembers his ring, and the woman sends him a written message and reacts to him emotionally. As she stands in the road waving good-bye, it is evident that she accepts her helplessness, is grateful for Sid's gentleness, and acknowledges his right to go happily off with his friends. She is the chief one who has been disappointed.

Other disappointments are comparatively minor: The tavern is not a pub, no beer is available, Bert sees no girls, the teas consist merely of bread and butter and tomatoes, and the Roman road is only grass. The men's disappointments are trivial and will be forgotten at the first pub they find. The woman's disappointment is devastating and will undoubtedly be lifelong. Pritchett conveys here his sense of the futility of human life and his conviction that the very persistence of people in their struggle demonstrates their essential courage.

Style and Technique

This story is the "slice of life" type. It is a series of word-photographs that readers must interpret for themselves. The author sets the stage very precisely with a few pertinent, evocative descriptions of the road, the characters, the sitting room, and the kitchen. He tells the reader very little about the four young men: Bert daydreams of girls, Ted tires the fastest, Harry plots the routes of their expeditions to gratify his interest in Roman roads, and Sid is dark and lanky with a high forehead and a Hitler mustache. He is a cocksure man with a gentle voice. The woman is frail and nervous. Her child resembles her.

Pritchett does not tell what his characters are thinking or feeling; this must be gathered from their conversations and actions. He has an acute ear for how people speak. His early life in trade equipped him for imitating the exact speech of the lower-middle-class section of English society. His keen perception of people's motives and reactions allows him to put revealing remarks into the mouths of his characters. In a 1980 essay, Pritchett says that he was accustomed to boil down one hundred pages to twenty or thirty. Thus, he leaves only the most distinctive and typical speeches. This is not to say that the characters are one-dimensional: Sid, for example, is a complicated, contradictory sort of person. He appears both gentle and ruthless. "Many Are Disappointed" is a fine example of naturalism by a master craftsman.

Dorothy B. Aspinwall

MARGINS

Author: Donald Barthelme (1931-1989)
Type of plot: Antistory
Time of plot: The 1960's
Locale: New York City
First published: 1964

> *Principal characters:*
> CARL MARIA VON WEBER, an African American panhandler and
>   former convict
> EDWARD, a white street person

The Story

Carl, an African American man, is standing in front of a men's store on Fourteenth Street near Broadway in New York City. He has brown sandwich boards over his shoulders, and on the boards is a handwritten message. It says that the wearer has spent five years in an Alabama jail for stealing a dollar and a half; that he did not steal the money; that while he was in jail his brother was killed; that his mother ran away when he was little; that in jail he learned to preach; that he bears witness to eschatological love; and that because no one will give him a job because he has been in jail, he is asking for handouts. Some of the sign does not make perfect sense; sentences are run together, and in one place, the words "Pepsi Cola" appear for no apparent reason.

Carl must be proud of his sign, however, because it ends with the statement that a patent has been applied for. In the same sentence he remembers his preaching and asks God to deliver humankind from evil.

Edward, a white man, criticizes the margins around Carl's handwriting on the sign and tells Carl that those margins reveal personality. In Edward's hand is a book about handwriting analysis, from which he reads about the meaning of wide and narrow left and right margins. Ignoring Carl's disbelief in such things, Edward tells him that a sign with wide margins all around it reveals a person of delicate sensibility who is a loner, loves color and form, and lives in a dream world of good taste. Because Carl's sign matches that description, he must be that kind of person.

When Carl asks Edward if he is sure that he has it right, Edward tells him that he feels as if he is trying to communicate across a huge gulf of ignorance and darkness. Carl resents being darkness, so they spar about that, then Edward begins to criticize the way that Carl makes his letters. His *m*'s and *n*'s are pointed rather than rounded, indicating aggressiveness and energy, but the fact that they are pointed at the bottom shows negative traits such as sarcasm and irritability. His capitals are small, which shows humility, and the big loops on his *y*'s and *g*'s suggest exaggeration and egoism.

Edward asks Carl his full name and then asks him directly if he is a drug addict. Carl says that he is not. Next, Edward asks Carl if he is a Muslim. To answer that, Carl shoots back a question to Edward: He wants to know if Edward has read *The Mystery of Being* (1951) by Gabriel Marcel. This probably is meant as a "yes" answer to Edward's question because Marcel believes that human experience can be understood only by participating in it, but Edward does not get it and asks the question again. Carl avoids the second question by making a crazy statement about the government. When Carl complains that the present location is bad for hustling, Edward tells him that the location is all right, but that Carl looks crummy and people like neatness.

The conversation turns to skin color. Carl says that white is the color of choice. Edward admits to being a fool but asserts that at least he is a white fool, which makes him lovely.

Carl asks Edward if he has read *The Cannibal* (1949) by John Hawkes, a contemporary American author. Edward ignores the question and continues to advise Carl on self-improvement, telling him that he needs to get a haircut and an Italian suit. Edward also wants to know about Carl's inner reality, but Carl says that his reality belongs to him and begins talking about other books by John Hawkes. Edward then asks Carl whether he stole the dollar and a half mentioned on his sign. Carl repeats what is on the sign, that he did not, and says that it is cold on Fourteenth Street. Edward tells him that the coldness he feels is from his being a despised person.

The conversation continues in this vein until Edward asks Carl what the term "eschatological love" means. Carl tells him that it is the kind of love that happens after death, and that black people talk about such things to make themselves happy.

Edward asks Carl where he steals his books, and Carl tells him that the best place to steal books is in drugstores. Stealing books is different from stealing money, Carl asserts, and quotes the author François Villon. Edward asks if that quote was from "If I Were King." Carl asks Edward if he has ever stolen anything.

Edward says not to remind him of his life, which shocks Carl, who supposes that all whites have nice lives. Edward tells Carl that he needs to improve his handwriting and that such a move might even help him end up as vice president. Carl thinks that better handwriting is only superficial self-improvement because it has nothing to do with character. He asks Edward to hold his sign for him while he uses the bathroom in the men's store.

When Edward puts the sign over his shoulders, he finds it heavy. On Carl's return, they slap each other in the face with the backs of their hands.

Themes and Meanings

This unemotional verbal encounter between street people appears devoid of deeper meaning. It happens in the present, and there is no beginning or ending as in a typical short story. As one tries to make sense out of what has been written, one theme begins to emerge: that racial stereotypes are foolish.

The title introduces the main symbol in the work. Margins are the actual areas around the writing on Carl's sign, but Edward makes them symbolize those pretentious ideas that people often have as answers to life's problems. In a sense, margins also help delineate the narrowness of perception that people have about each other.

Furthermore, these two characters might be called marginal human beings. They are outside the mainstream of society, so their allusions to literature and to psychological self-help books seem out of place.

The two characters are readers, an unexpected trait in street people. Carl has read Marcel and an avant-garde modern author named John Hawkes, who, like Donald Barthelme himself, does fragmentary sketches that have been called artistic lunacy. One assumes that Edward reads only self-help books until Carl refers to François Villon's ideas on stealing and Edward shoots back, "Is that in 'If I Were King'?"—referring to a poem that was done to resemble Villon's "Ballad of Dead Ladies."

The fact that nothing is revealed about the background of these characters, except what is written on Carl's sign, makes the reader almost painfully aware of the incongruities and prejudices of modern life and sharpens the images in this story. Both men deal with each other using stereotypes, although reality tells them that stereotypes do not apply here. As they talk, neither really processes what the other says. It might be said that this is a description of late twentieth century life in the United States.

At the end, each man gives the other a backhanded slap to the face, a probable insult. It would certainly be an odd way to show friendliness.

Style and Technique

"Margins" first appeared in *The New Yorker* in 1964 and was collected in that same year with thirteen other Barthelme stories into a book called *Come Back, Dr. Caligari.* This story and other creations by Barthelme can be categorized as contemporary experimental fiction. He calls his stories collages, but the literary critic Granville Hicks described them as "controlled craziness." They are exaggerated satires that allow glimpses into human life, but the incongruous dialogue and strange subject matter amuse at the same time that they appall. The humor can be termed black humor. There are absurd elements and mutual incomprehensions that are ludicrous. "Margins" uses a form of parody that imitates life to a certain extent but distorts it until it becomes ridiculous. Fun is poked at those humans who hope to control destiny by the modern "magic" of such things as handwriting analysis.

Plot is missing and character development does not occur. Dialogue is disjointed. Characters use slang as well as little-used words such as "eschatological," a term dealing with humankind's ultimate destiny.

Josephine Raburn

MARÍA CONCEPCIÓN

Author: Katherine Anne Porter (1890-1980)
Type of plot: Social realism
Time of plot: The 1920's
Locale: Mexico
First published: 1922

> *Principal characters:*
> MARÍA CONCEPCIÓN MANRIQUES, an eighteen-year-old Catholic
> wife
> JUAN DE DIOS VILLEGAS, her husband
> MARÍA ROSA, a fifteen-year-old beekeeper and Juan's lover

The Story

María Concepción, a hardworking young bride, is on her way to deliver food to her husband, Juan, and his boss, Givens, at an archaeological site on the outskirts of town. María is entirely contented in her work, her marriage, and the coming birth of their first child. Careful to avoid the thorns along the path, she ignores the live chickens swung across her back, concentrating only on her task. The reader soon discovers that María has done much to rise above the circumstances of her early life. She is a Christian and, unlike other members of the community, was married in the church. She can drive a hard bargain and always has money to pay for what she requires. She does not believe in the old ways of medicine, even though she cannot read the directions on the bottles of medicines she purchases from the drugstore. All of her accomplishments cause the townspeople to respect her but simultaneously to suspect her of having too much pride.

Ironically, it is a sudden superstitious craving for honey that begins María Concepción's troubles. Although she does not believe in the old ways of medicine, she does believe her child will be marked if she does not obtain the honey she craves. So she journeys out of her way to the house of the old medicine woman, Lupe, and the fifteen-year-old beekeeper, María Rosa. When María Concepción arrives, she is met by silence. She peers through the cactus into the small yard, then hears the sound of laughter, first a girl's, then a man's. María Concepción smiles to herself at the thought of María Rosa's having a lover, only to discover that it is Juan de Dios Villegas—her own husband.

María Concepción is overcome by learning of Juan's infidelity, yet manages to make her way back to the road and continue on to the archaeological site, where Givens awaits his noonday meal. Givens is Juan's patron and often saves him from trouble, referring to his frequent infidelities as "pickles." From this moment, María Concepción becomes increasingly divorced from her own emotions, perhaps because they cannot exist inside the civilized world that she has created for herself and her family without destroying it. Although her anger at Juan disappears by the end of one day, it is transferred to María Rosa, and she hears herself saying that María Rosa should die for what she did. She is now her enemy. Even Givens, who often thinks of María Concepción as royalty in exile, takes note of the ease with which she cuts the head off of the chicken that she prepares for his lunch.

Juan and María Rosa leave the next day so that he can join the army, and María Concepción's child is soon born but dies. Again, she does not react emotionally. She rejects Lupe's offers of charms to preserve the infant, and instead continues with her routine of hard work and visits to the church. Before long, the townspeople, who assume that María Concepción is being punished for her pride, regain their admiration and respect for her. Even Lupe begins to side with María Concepción over María Rosa, now that the abandoned hives no longer prosper. Despite this communal approval, however, María Concepción grows more and more gaunt, and her butchering knife is seldom out of her hand.

One day, Juan and María Rosa return. Juan is arrested for desertion, and María Rosa's baby is born immediately afterward. This child is also a boy, and unmistakably healthy. Predictably, Juan is once again saved from real consequences by Givens. Although he is warned against taking his predicament too lightly, Juan continues life in boyish fashion, visiting his new child and celebrating with *pulque* in town. He ends up in María Concepción's house, trying and failing to beat her, and finally falling asleep in a corner.

María Concepción attempts to resume her daily routine, making ready to go to the market, yet finds herself instead heading toward the house of Lupe and María Rosa, a crazy panic in her head. Her emotions overcome her, and she relives all the suffering since the discovery of her husband's infidelity and the loss of her child. Then she becomes calm. Whether she commits the outrageous act of violence before or after her emotional outpouring is uncertain, but there is no mistaking that something has happened as she crawls toward Juan after she arrives home, carrying a knife and murmuring to him about what has happened.

Juan is uncertain why he protects his wife against the gendarmes' questions about the murder of María Rosa, but he does, rehearsing with her about what they will say, and ridding the house of evidence. María Concepción is at first uncertain why the women of the town protect her in their testimony, but she soon realizes that whereas María Rosa forfeited her place among them, she, María Concepción, stayed, and so can rely on their communal sympathy and protection. The gendarmes are left without a case, even though they are certain of her guilt. María Concepción is free to take María Rosa's child home with her, and she does. The story ends as it began, with a picture of María Concepción's contentment and strength.

Themes and Meanings

Katherine Anne Porter uses the character of María Concepción primarily to represent the sense of social and moral order thought of as civilization; hence her devotion to her family, to her church, and ultimately to the community. In contrast, María Rosa's honey and seduction represent passion or the temptation to disrupt or destroy social and moral order. In the resolution of the deadly conflict between the two women, Porter seems to suggest that civilization and the mores of Christianity serve more as a facade than as an actual basis for social order. Ultimately, María Concepción relies on or returns to a more fundamental and primitive code of justice than her new religion teaches.

Porter shows as well the power a community has over people, and how a community will protect or reject a person for the sake of the larger organization. This communal rule is accomplished by the old women who watch María Concepción's actions throughout the story—especially María Rosa's guardian, Lupe, who is at first against María Concepción, yet later protects her from the gendarmes.

Finally, Porter comments on patriarchy and patronization in the characters of Givens and Juan. Although Givens claims to care for his workers, he neither understands them nor takes them seriously. Juan, who is often saved and jokingly warned against infidelities by Givens, is incapable of taking his own actions to heart. The only time he becomes a man is when María Concepción's power, derived from the religion of the patriarchal structure they must live in, breaks down. When the danger is past, he returns to his passivity, and María Concepción to her rightful household rule.

Style and Technique

Porter is known for her rich, descriptive narratives. The detail and highly symbolic imagery in the story contribute immensely to the story's themes, as well as providing suspense and enjoyment for the reader. Much of this imagery sets up ironic contrast, producing even more tension in the story. The civilized world of María Concepción, for example, includes ancient, thorny cacti, representing the customs, superstitions, and dangers that María Concepción herself cannot escape. María Rosa's honey is something that even María Concepción desires. The butchering of animals throughout foreshadows and intensifies the violent form María Concepción's revenge takes. Religious imagery underpins the action as well. Juan is simultaneously posed as a boy and as a Christ-figure, to underscore his irresponsibility as well as his innocence or victimhood in the hands of Givens and María Concepción. María Concepción is likened to the Virgin Mary as she holds María Rosa's son, creating a chilling, thought-provoking picture of her newfound "strange, wakeful happiness."

Jennifer Vinsky

THE MARIJUANA PARTY

Author: Mary Helen Ponce (1938-   )
Type of plot: Domestic realism
Time of plot: The late twentieth century
Locale: Los Angeles, California
First published: 1992

> *Principal characters:*
> PETRA, a Mexican American housewife celebrating her fortieth
>   birthday
> TOTTIE and
> EMILY (AMALIA), her friends and neighbors

The Story

It is the fortieth birthday of Petra, a lower-middle-class Mexican American housewife living in Los Angeles. The plump, graying mother of two school-age children, she lives a life filled with cooking, cleaning, shopping, and caring for her family. Looking for excitement to mark this significant day, she wants to do something dangerous and prohibited—something that her children would call "far out." The only thing that she can think of, however, is to go shopping, which would scarcely provide the excitement that she craves, particularly because she has just done it the day before. Petra decides, therefore, to invite two good friends, Tottie and Emily, to join her celebration, even though Emily, the younger of the two, is "Goody Two Shoes." Before calling them, she bakes pumpkin bread and dusts her already spotless house. While dusting, she rediscovers the marijuana cigarette that she found in the patio after a recent visit from her nephew, a rock musician, and decides that sharing the joint with her friends will provide the perfect celebration.

While waiting for her friends, Petra carefully applies makeup and dresses in a blouse and K-Mart polyester pants. Tottie and Emily appear almost simultaneously, each curious about what surprise Petra plans to share with them. Petra, stalling for dramatic effect, first serves them chips, salsa, and wine. Although outwardly a prim and responsible housewife, Petra drops all of her inhibitions and uses raunchy slang and makes repeated references to sex, calling her birthday "the birth of the biggest sexpot in history!" Emily, embarrassed, tries to change the subject by discussing the new PTA drug awareness committee; however, Petra swiftly cuts her off by leading her friends into the bedroom to see her surprise. When her friends wonder what the strange, wrinkled cigarette is, she calls it a miracle drug from Lourdes. Emily smiles her approval, but when Tottie cries out that it is marijuana, Emily is shocked by the idea of using an illegal substance. She is even more horrified to discover that both her friends have watched porno movies that Tottie once found in her son's car. She runs from the bedroom to get another glass of wine but quickly returns.

As the friends attempt to get high on the marijuana cigarette, unexpected visitors interrupt their party. First the mail carrier knocks, expecting to have a cup of coffee and chat as he often does. Then Petra's obstreperous daughter storms in, having forgotten her lunch. No sooner does her daughter leave but another neighbor shows up, complaining about rowdy children ditching school and smoking pot outside her back fence. Each visitor notices a strange odor, despite Emily's constant, frantic attempts to mask the smell with pine-scented spray; however, Petra deflects their curiosity and sends them on their way.

The final intrusion personifies Emily's greatest fear—a police officer. The officer is patrolling the neighborhood encouraging the residents to be on the lookout for a man in a blue car who is suspected of dealing pot to the local kids. Noticing the strange odor in the house, he insists on investigating, but Petra suddenly remembers having seen a strange blue car cruising the street a few minutes earlier, and she also reports that her neighbor has complained about pot-smoking truants behind her house.

By now, the marijuana joint is spent and the three friends are sure they are high, so Petra suggests that they watch a porno film. Emily, despite earlier professing shock that her friends would watch such things, agrees to join them in order to evaluate the film because she has recently joined Catholic Mothers Against Pornography.

The story ends as Petra invites her friends to return two hours earlier the next Friday, promising to stay on the lookout for a blue car.

Themes and Meanings

Two basic themes pervade "The Marijuana Party": the conflict between what people appear to be on the surface and their true inner selves, and the fascination that people have in what they profess to condemn. In her spotlessly clean house, wearing polyester pants, baking pumpkin bread, Petra appears to be just an ordinary, well-behaved middle-aged housewife—but she treats her friends to marijuana and porno movies. Tottie, nearly fifty years old, is an active Roman Catholic, but professes no shame about searching her son's car for contraband, and then enjoying the porno films that she finds. Although Emily (apparently the youngest of the three) seems to be shocked by Petra's earthy behavior, she gets along "famously" with Petra and apparently spends considerable time with her two less inhibited friends. When offered marijuana, she runs from the room, only to return immediately to participate. She seems already to know how to smoke pot but claims to have learned these things only from the drug awareness programs at school. She insists that she is not enjoying the pot but is sampling it only to make her a more effective member of the school's drug awareness committee by teaching her the drug's dangers. Similarly, when she agrees to watch the porno video, she insists that she does so only in order to give a talk on the subject to her sister's antipornography group.

Style and Technique

The first part of Mary Ellen Ponce's story utilizes an omniscient narrator who reveals Petra's inner thoughts; it then switches to a more distant narrator who presents the characters only through their outward appearances, behaviors, and dialogue. The story is more successful in its latter part, in which the characters' behaviors are allowed to contrast with what they say and how they act. This dramatic irony leads the reader to infer the story's central themes, rather than spelling them out.

A rather strained coincidence sets the story's plot in motion: Petra, who supposedly has never smoked marijuana, found a marijuana cigarette on the patio only a week earlier; she saved it instead of throwing it away but then totally forgot having done so. After this contrived opening, however, the story flows more smoothly, with its various incidents proceeding in a more organic fashion.

"The Marijuana Party" does not emphasize its setting, either as to place or time. Petra's musing about cutting her hair with bangs, because "bangs make me look younger. Like Mamie!" allude to Mamie Eisenhower—the First Lady of the United States from 1953 to 1961. The police officer is concerned that the odor he smells may come from trash burning in an incinerator, which had been "banned in 1958, or thereabouts." These references suggest that the story could be set around 1960; however, other references—such as the allusions to "movies" that must be videotapes—suggest a much later date. In the first two sentences, the reader learns that the characters live in a foothill community in California, but it is not until the end that an allusion to the "LAPD" (Los Angeles Police Department) suggests that the setting is Los Angeles. This lack of specificity enhances the universality of the story.

The story's characterizations, however, work against that same universality. The three friends are clearly identified as Mexican Americans in the traditional mode: All are Catholic wives, mothers, and homemakers. Petra begins her day listening to a Tex-Mex radio station, and her speech is laced with Spanish expressions and Mexican slang. The extensive use of such slang makes the story less accessible to readers who do not share the characters' background; nevertheless, any reader can appreciate the comic scenes of the women trying to cover up their transgressions. All readers will also recognize the hypocrisy of the anti-sin crusader who is so eager to enforce her morality on others—even after she tastes the forbidden fruit herself.

Irene Struthers Rush

MARIO AND THE MAGICIAN

Author: Thomas Mann (1875-1955)
Type of plot: Symbolist
Time of plot: About 1929
Locale: Torre di Venere, a fictional town in southern Italy
First published: "Mario und der Zauberer," 1930 (English translation, 1930)

Principal characters:
THE NARRATOR, a middle-aged German tourist
HIS WIFE
THEIR TWO YOUNG CHILDREN, a boy and a girl
CAVALIERE CIPOLLA, a traveling magician and illusionist
MARIO, a waiter and café attendant
SILVESTRA, Mario's girlfriend

The Story

Torre di Venere is a bustling but faintly decaying resort village on the Tyrrhenian Sea. It shares fine white sands and high pine groves with other beachside towns along the way. By the middle of August, it is awash in humanity; during the day hordes of sunburned vacationers of all ages, both sexes, and several nationalities converge at the water's edge. The narrator acknowledges his disappointment with these surroundings, which are no more auspicious than those of other southern Italian retreats. He and his wife are beset by redundant hotel and restaurant functionaries; a subtropical heat wave has set in. Their daughter is caught up in an unpleasant and slightly indecent incident when she adjusts her bathing suit at the seaside. For a brief time, their son is ill with what they fear may be whooping cough.

For a diversion, the narrator and his family decide to attend an evening performance by Cipolla, a traveling conjuror and prestidigitator whose reputation has preceded him. By nine o'clock, throngs of townspeople and tourists have gathered at a cinema hall built into a ruined castle. The audience is kept waiting for some time until, with calculated abruptness, the magician appears. Cipolla appraises them with small, hard eyes and clipped lips; he flashes his ragged, uneven, sawlike teeth. His hands, which are like long yellow claws, clutch a silver-handled riding crop. As he performs, he smokes cheap cigarettes and downs neat glasses of cognac. Bantering with the audience and slashing his whip through the air to make his points, the magician induces individual spectators to perform feats that they think impossible or initially refuse indignantly.

One youth extends his tongue to the farthest limits and then retracts it, hardly knowing what he has done afterward; another young man is drawn up and convulsed in a colicky spasm, and when he returns to an upright position he is unaware of his previous plight. Cipolla produces a slip of paper and then has members of the audience supply numbers; when he has added all of them—fifteen entries, yielding a sum of nearly one million—the magician shows the spectators that he had written down precisely that figure beforehand. He also demonstrates a series of card tricks, in which without looking he takes three cards from one deck and then, on all but a few occasions, is able to show that they are the same as those members of the audience have chosen at random from another deck.

The narrator comments that the magician's predilection is for harsh, mean-spirited challenges that subject the participants to physical and intellectual humiliation. As entertainment it is not entirely suitable for children. The magician styles himself Cavaliere, an honorific title often conferred for distinguished military service, and he wears the sash customarily given with this award. However, the Italian government has honored him only for his stage performances; he is oddly humpbacked and was exempted from wartime duty because of this deformity. Perhaps he is simply an illusionist, or a charlatan, but an unnaturally clever one.

After a painfully long intermission—of at least twenty minutes—Cipolla returns and seemingly mesmerizes other members of the audience. A woman is rendered briefly insensible to her husband's voice; one after another young men rise and dance to the magician's bidding, until he commands them to cease. Finally, Cipolla calls on Mario, a young man who is twenty years old, with heavy-lidded eyes and thick plain lips; by day he works unstintingly and without complaint as a waiter in a café, where he brings chocolates and biscuits to the guests. Disdainfully the hunchback inquires about Mario's work among the tourists and displays an uncanny knowledge of his female acquaintances. The magician discovers the name of the youth's beloved Silvestra and probes Mario's secret affection. As a final grotesque trick, the magician, in the girl's voice, asks Mario to kiss him, and when this is done the youth recoils in horror. The audience is still spellbound, and it is more than several moments before it hears two detonations: Mario has shot Cipolla with a homemade, short-barreled revolver and is scurrying away into the throng. Then the narrator can only describe summarily the collective sense of horror—but strangely also of liberation—felt by those looking on in the hall.

Themes and Meanings

The audience, whether as spectators or participants in Cipolla's rude jests, are drawn to the magician by an unseemly combination of fascination and curiosity. Some seek to uncover his secrets; others vainly attempt to assert their own strength and endurance against the magician's powers. There are also those who, while remaining aloof themselves, seem amused at the discomfiture of others. Once they have come, many in the audience feel compelled in spite of themselves to remain and acquiesce to Cipolla's clever but cruel pranks.

Shortly before the intermission, Cipolla delivers a disquisition on will. He claims to have begun as the audience's guide, pointing the way for them and correcting their course as he discovered the feats they wished him to perform; now he has become merely a suffering, passive instrument of their common will. To command and to obey are but two complementary principles of a single idea; submission and self-control ultimately are transferred from the people to himself, as their leader. This self-serving justification does point to the audience's perverse acceptance and growing tolerance of Cipolla's sway over them. There are subtle but unmistakable political allusions here, notably in some fervid patriotic references to the Italian Fatherland. Benito Mussolini's dictatorship, which was firmly in power when the story was written, is mentioned once. It is clear that in this instance the masses are led by an ingenious and beguiling, but essentially self-centered performer, whose concerns lie no deeper than the imposition of his authority on others.

In calling this incident to mind, the narrator comments on it as a comedy that became a tragedy; he is troubled by "the peculiar evilness of the situation as a whole." This work is more than a political allegory or a study in mass psychology; it suggests that personal dignity and freedom may be trampled on only to a point. The deformed charlatan may ridicule and humiliate selected members of the audience, but he cannot intrude on the intimate life of the least of them. It is for this reason that his demands on poor Mario arouse a distinct revulsion—in which the reader's sympathies are decidedly with the poor lad—and that the violent and unexpected end of the magician is received with relief as well as with shock.

Style and Technique

Stage magic consists of improbable feats for which other practitioners may find explanations. The extraordinary quality of this story is the manner in which the author recounts the stages by which individual spectators, much of the audience, and eventually the narrator himself seem to fall under the magician's spell. Lengthy descriptive passages preface each of Cipolla's challenges; increasingly the narrator refers to more abstract problems of volition and self-control. The atmosphere is conveyed by repeated references to the audience's reactions, from disbelief to laughter to applause, and ultimately to horror. The oral sparring that precedes each test of will is reproduced at length: Peculiar features of the magician's speech, the use of quaint south Italian dialect among the audience, and Cipolla's jibes at slow and unresponsive spectators highlight the dialectical tension that develops more and more. Palpable periods of silence, when the audience is breathlessly enthralled by the magician's performance, are interspersed with descriptions of the magician's piercing hypnotic eyes and the rhythmic crackle of his whip through the air to ensure obedience. Eventually the narrator himself can only present his impressions; at some points he loses track of the precise sequence of events as he becomes transfixed by the trial of wills on the stage.

Vague foreboding is communicated by a number of details in the story, from the beaches swarming with tourists and the musty, moldering castle, to the weary, jaundiced, yet preternaturally alert features of the magician. The audience's susceptibility to mesmerism and conjuring tricks is underscored by the author's evocation of character, from callow youths and simple, weatherbeaten fishermen to stern, upright soldiers, all of whom fall under Cipolla's spell. Mario, seemingly the most docile and obedient, is sketched in features that hint as well at the ultimate inviolability of his human dignity.

J. R. Broadus

MARJORIE DAW

Author: Thomas Bailey Aldrich (1836-1907)
Type of plot: Domestic realism
Time of plot: Late summer, 1872
Locale: New York City and New Hampshire
First published: 1873

> *Principal characters:*
> JOHN FLEMMING, an impatient young man with a broken leg
> EDWARD DELANEY, his correspondent
> MARJORIE DAW, a charming young woman, who is actually
> Delaney's fictional creation
> DR. DILLON, the elderly physician who prescribes Flemming's
> recovery regimen and enlists Delaney's help

The Story

The story unfolds through a series of letters exchanged between John Flemming and his friend Edward Delaney, a young attorney vacationing with his invalid father. The first letter, however, is from Dr. Dillon to Edward Delaney. It explains John Flemming's situation and the terms of his convalescence.

After slipping on a lemon peel and breaking his leg, Flemming has been ordered to remain at his New York City home for three to four weeks, confined to a couch. A robust, normally active young man of twenty-four, he finds his confinement at best tedious, at worst intolerable, and becomes extremely moody. When his sister Fanny comes home from the family's summer resort to care for him, he drives her away in tears. Flemming's servant Watkins then bears the brunt of his melancholy and sudden, unreasonable anger. The convalescent repeatedly pelts Watkins with volumes from the complete works of Honoré de Balzac. Hoping to calm his patient, Dr. Dillon encourages Delaney to write to him to buoy his spirits and still his rage.

The exchange of letters between Delaney and Flemming begins shortly thereafter, on August 9, 1872. Part of Flemming's frustration arises from the fact that he was to have spent the late summer months with his friend in New Hampshire and that his accident has ruined their plans. Delaney, noting the quiet, uneventful life he leads at the Pines, his rustic retreat, innocently speculates what he might do, were he a novelist like the great Russian Ivan Turgenev. Then, without making it entirely clear that he is doing so, he begins to spin a story about imaginary neighbors—the Daws, who live in an imaginary colonial mansion across the road from his own cottage.

Delaney starts by describing a young, graceful, and fashionably dressed woman of about eighteen. She has golden hair and dark eyes and lies in a hammock in the neighbor's piazza. The portrait that he creates fascinates Flemming, who hungers for more information about the young woman. Delaney innocently provides such information in his succeeding letters, drawing Flemming into his fictional web with realistic accounts of the young lady, Marjorie Daw, and her family. He has no inkling that his friend is accepting his account as entirely factual.

Delaney describes the girl's father, Richard W. Daw, as a banker, retired colonel, and widower, providing vivid details. He also identifies a brother who is a Harvard student and writes that another brother died at the Battle of Fair Oaks during the Civil War. The Daws, he explains, are a rich family of good lineage, who reside in Washington and Baltimore most of the year but summer in New Hampshire.

Hooked by Delaney's account, Flemming pleads for yet more information about Marjorie. Delaney obliges, writing about the idyllic relationship between Marjorie and her father and about a dreary party at the Daws's house that was attended by two dull men, a naval lieutenant named Bradley and an Episcopal rector, as well as two engaging women, the Kingsberry sisters from Philadelphia.

After writing just a few letters, Delaney has unwittingly made Flemming totally entranced by his depiction of Marjorie, a young lady of great beauty, charm, and grace. In response to Flemming's demands, Delaney piles detail on convincing detail, eventually adding a complication that leads to a humorous climax. Delaney writes that, in telling Marjorie and her father about Flemming and his unhappy accident, he has inadvertently piqued her interest in his friend.

Flemming is now totally captivated. After establishing that his friend has no amorous designs on Miss Daw himself, Flemming presses him to act as his intermediary with the young woman. When he asks for a photograph of Marjorie, Delaney declines to steal one from the Daws's mantlepiece but holds out the hope that he can get a print made from a recent negative. Meanwhile, he continues to paint his written picture of Marjorie, adding some sauce to her character. Although Marjorie is sweet and gracious, she is not without an occasional petulance that Delaney finds "disagreeable." He also indicates that Lieutenant Bradley has been courting Marjorie with her father's blessing but with little encouragement from her. She remains, Delaney reiterates, far more interested in Flemming, although she has never met his friend.

Matters come to a head when Flemming ends his convalescence and writes that he is making arrangements to come to the Pines to meet Marjorie. Finally realizing that his friend has been completely bamboozled, Delaney tries to talk him out of coming, but Flemming is not to be denied. He arrives at the Pines, only to discover that Delaney has skipped to Boston, leaving him a letter in which he confesses that "there isn't any colonial mansion on the other side of the road, there isn't any piazza, there isn't any hammock—there isn't any Marjorie Daw!"

Themes and Meanings

A comic tour de force, "Marjorie Daw" is an amusing story that is not concerned with illustrating lasting insights into the human condition. However, it does reveal the great power of words both to convince and deceive, particularly when a person, like Flemming, is susceptible to their suggestion. Knowing his friend well, Delaney sets out in all innocence to create a woman who will attract Flemming's interest. As a well-read attorney, he also knows the pen's might, but he initially assumes that he has made it clear that the story he spins about the Daws is just that—a story.

For his part, Flemming, an eligible bachelor of twenty-four, ripe for a husband's role, is easily drawn to a woman of Marjorie's reputed beauty and charm, particularly because he is not distracted by his normal pastimes, such as horseback riding. Instead of reading Balzac, who might enlighten him and give him some stoic resolve to bear his brief convalescence with cheerful fortitude, he hurls the novelist's works at his servant, then lapses into melancholy, mulling over his misfortune.

No wonder Delaney's portrait of Marjorie Daw so quickly intrigues Flemming. She looms in his mind as his reward for suffering through the misery of his convalescence—as fate's compensation for depriving him of his normal pleasures. Instead of receiving that reward, however, he eventually pays a comic penalty for his spoiled, moody ingratitude, an aspect of his character that allows the reader to feel he deserves to have his delusion shattered.

Style and Technique

Epistolary technique is what makes "Marjorie Daw" succeed. After some initial exchanges, involving a letter by Dr. Dillon and two by Flemming, the letters are all from Delaney to either Flemming or Dillon. However, near the end, there is a flurry of telegrams exchanged between Flemming and Delaney and a brief, necessary narrative under the heading "The Arrival," describing what happens when Flemming finally reaches the Pines and discovers his friend's unintentional hoax, which is explained in Delaney's final letter to Flemming, left to be delivered by a servant.

Thomas Bailey Aldrich adroitly alters the pace of the story by beginning with letters that are relatively long, desultory in content, and relaxed in tone. As Flemming's interest in Marjorie grows, the letters from Delaney grow both more focused and shorter, paralleling Flemming's mounting anticipation. Finally, on the eve of Flemming's arrival at the Pines, correspondence is reduced to terse, cryptic telegrams, exploding with Flemming's urgency and resolve and Delaney's insistence that he remain put. Placed just before the climax, the moment of recognition, these messages provide a pronounced staccato contrast to the earlier epistles and mark the moment of highest emotional pitch. In its structure, "Marjorie Daw" thus offers a textbook illustration of how the traditional, well-made formula story should work.

Equally important, the details about the Daws that Delaney invents are convincing and make his deception believable. First-time readers of the story might also find the Daws real, although from the start there are hints that Delaney's account is suspect. There are, for example, odd inconsistencies, such as the unlikely location of an old colonial mansion across the road from a rustic cottage, and Delaney's own stated disinterest in Marjorie—a woman whom he depicts as the ideal embodiment of beauty, charm, and grace. Such hints foreshadow the final revelation, making it not so much a surprise twist as the necessary and logical outcome of this carefully crafted story.

John W. Fiero

THE MARK ON THE WALL

Author: Virginia Woolf (1882-1941)
Type of plot: Psychological
Time of plot: 1917
Locale: England
First published: 1917

Principal character:
THE NARRATOR

The Story

This story of one individual's mind under pressure begins casually: "Perhaps it was the middle of January in the present year that I first looked up and saw the mark on the wall. In order to fix the date it is necessary to remember what one saw." However, what the narrator saw in the external world moments before seeing the mark—that is, the shade of light on the pages of the book she was reading, the three chrysanthemums in a bowl, and the smoke of her cigarette—serve as definite landmarks by which she may locate herself; such location of self becomes increasingly important as the narrative progresses.

The first hint the reader is given about the importance of the narrator's sense of place occurs in the initial paragraph, when she recalls looking at (besides those other things already mentioned) the "burning coals" in her fireplace, and how this sight caused "that old fancy of the crimson flag flapping from the tower" and the "cavalcade of red knights riding up the side of the black rock." This fancy is one that she believes was formed in her childhood, and one with which she is not comfortable (presumably because it reminds her of war). Although she does not explain why the fancy is discomforting, it is clear that it is when she says, "rather to my relief the sight of the mark interrupted the fancy." For a moment, then, she is able to focus on, and to locate herself by, this "small round mark, black on the white wall, about six or seven inches above the mantlepiece."

What is this mark? she wonders—a nail hole made by the people who lived in the house before her? Here she recalls a discussion about art she was having with one of these people when they were suddenly "torn asunder, as one is torn from the old lady about to pour tea and the young man about to hit the tennis ball . . . as one rushes past in the train." For the moment, she decides that neither what the mark is nor its cause is important enough for her to get up and walk across the room to inspect it more closely; besides, she reflects, "once a thing's done, no one ever knows how it happened." Nevertheless, it soon becomes apparent that the narrator is troubled by the "ignorance of humanity," by "what an accidental affair . . . living is after all our civilization," by how many things she has lost over the years, and—again—by how quickly time passes, as life is similar to being "blown through the Tube at fifty miles an hour" or similar to being "pitched down a shoot in the post office! . . . Yes, that seems to express the rapidity of life," she thinks, "the perpetual waste and repair; all so casual, all so haphazard."

Paradoxically, while letting her thoughts drift away from the mark on the wall to unpleasant reflections on the perpetual dissolution of life and order, and while such reflections prompt her to focus again on the mark and to wonder what it is, by not getting up to inspect it definitively she begins to realize a certain intellectual freedom from the mental constraints of tradition. Resisting the urge to define the mark reminds her that, during her childhood, there were rules for everything. "The rule for tablecloths," she says, "was that they . . . be made of tapestry with little yellow compartments marked on them." Anything different in the way of a tablecloth was not considered, by society in general, "real." Nevertheless, although "shocking," she recalls that it was also "wonderful" to discover that "real things" (such as tablecloths, Sunday luncheons, or Sunday walks) "were not entirely real, were indeed half phantoms, and the damnation that visited the disbeliever in them was only a sense of illegitimate freedom." Her reflections on such freedom notwithstanding, she is suddenly reminded that, in her and England's present moment, the "real standard things" are determined by "the masculine point of view which governs our lives, which sets standards, which establishes Whitaker's Table of Precedence." Such a table of precedency is for British society, like the narrator's urge to define the mark on the wall at the same time she continually locates herself by it, destructive to original living. Thus, she hopes that Whitaker's Table, synonymous with the masculine point of view, "will be laughed into the dustbin where phantoms go . . . , Gods and Devils, Hell and so forth, leaving us all with an intoxicating sense of illegitimate freedom—if freedom exists."

The narrator's preceding "if" clause sends her attention back to the mark on the wall, her own uncertainty about what is and is not fundamental to her existence prompting her to seek the mental anchor the mark has become. However, her mental focus widens again, she reflects on the long debate between various Englishmen about some ancient barrows, and whether they are tombs or forts; she concludes, "No, no, nothing is proved, nothing is known." After all, she says, England's learned men are "the descendants of witches and hermits who crouched in caves," and the only reason they are honored is that the British people are superstitious and do not yet respect "beauty and health of mind" enough. Even so, she believes a better world could be possible, "if it were not for Whitaker's Almanac—if it were not for the Table of Precedency!"

Suddenly, she realizes that it is her instinct toward self-preservation that causes her urge to get up and see what the mark actually is, for by sitting still and allowing the mark to serve as a catalyst for independent thoughts and incisive questions about herself and her society, she risks having a "collision with reality" and the masculine minds in power. With this realization she decides to end her "disagreeable thoughts" and focus on the mark as "something definite, something real" compared to the Archbishops and the Lord High Chancellor (who are, she says, as insubstantial as "shadows of shades"). This tactic works for a time, as she imagines herself as a tree and feels "full of peaceful thoughts, happy thoughts"; she then feels lost, however, forgets what she was thinking about, and is troubled by how everything seems to be "moving, falling, slipping, vanishing." What causes this sudden change in her reality is a heretofore unmentioned second person in the room who, as an "upheaval of matter," stands up and tells her, "I'm going out to buy a newspaper," even though "it's no good buying" one because "nothing ever happens. Curse this war; God damn this war! . . . All the same, I don't see why we should have a snail on our wall." As a matter of fact, the narrator now knows, the mark on the wall is a snail.

Themes and Meanings

"The Mark on the Wall" is the gradually unfolding revelation—through concentrically associative rings of thought—of one female character, the nameless narrator. However, it is not merely the revelation of one person's mind, as it also reveals the collective mentality and ethos of England at a crucial time in its history—that is, during World War I. Indeed, the time during which this story takes place is essential to understanding its central conflict, and this, again, concerns the narrator's state of mind.

In 1917, Britain, like most of the other European countries, is fighting a war; also like the other countries, it is ruled by men, "men of action—men, we assume, who don't think." However, the narrator does think about and question "the mark" these men are leaving on the wall of the thinking person's mind. Thus, Virginia Woolf bases her story on Plato's allegory of the cave, which describes—in Socrates' words—humans chained to one wall in such a way that they are prevented from looking in any direction other than straight ahead at the cave wall in front of them; on this wall are shadows of stick figures cast from behind the wall to which the humans are bound. Shadows, then, are all that these prototypical humans know as reality. Even so, Socrates says, if one of these people is set free, taken out of the cave and shown the world of light and three dimensional forms, and if—after discovering that what he thought was real in the cave was only shadows—he returns to tell the other people that what they think is reality is insubstantial, then the others would kill him if they could.

Like Plato's allegory, Woolf's story concerns the nature of truth, justice, and wisdom. In like manner, as Plato believed that truth consists of ideas that can be discovered and understood only through systematic thinking, Woolf's narrator thinks about the mark on the wall—thinks, that is, about the nature of reality and self. What she discovers is threatening to her existence because it goes against the grain of a table of precedency and what it ("the masculine point of view") points to as the "real standard things." This is why Woolf introduces the second character into the story at the end, as this is a person who believes in action and who is—unlike the narrator—bored because "nothing ever happens." Such a person serves as a foil, illustrating the profound difference between those people who live by the dictates of external facts ("a snail on our wall") and precedents, and those individuals who save themselves and their visions of a better, healthier life than a table of precedency offers a society.

Style and Technique

At one point in this story, the narrator remarks how "dull" fiction is which gives the reader only an external description of a given character; if "only that shell of a person . . . is seen by other people," then the world will be made to seem "airless, shallow, [and] bald." No, she says, people are more than one-dimensional shells, and "the novelists in the future will realize more and more the importance of . . . reflections [as those seen in mirrors], for of course there is not one reflection but almost infinite numbers; those are the depths they will explore . . . leaving the description of reality more and more out of their stories." By "reality" here she means that which is external to a character's inner self. "The Mark on the Wall" is itself a paradigm of such a narrative attempt to communicate numerous "reflections" of one character's being, and this was an important accomplishment for Woolf.

The style of this story came as an artistic breakthrough for Woolf, as it proved to be a decisive break away from the relatively traditional fiction she had written prior to 1917. Indeed, in one of her journals she noted that this story showed her how she could embody her deposit of experience in a shape that fit it; this discovery, she believed, led to the creation of her novels *Jacob's Room* (1922) and *Mrs. Dalloway* (1925). The narrative technique used in both of these novels, like that used in "The Mark on the Wall," is essentially impressionistic and circuitous, as the narrative focus in all three reveals its subject as ultimately indefinable and only describable through concentric rings of associations. Whether these various associations belong to the narrator in relation to a given character or to a character in relation to others and life, they all express Woolf's view that life and people are mercurially mutable.

David A. Carpenter

MARKHEIM

Author: Robert Louis Stevenson (1850-1894)
Type of plot: Psychological
Time of plot: Christmas Day during the nineteenth century
Locale: London
First published: 1887

> *Principal characters:*
> MARKHEIM, a murderer
> THE DEALER, his victim
> THE VISITOR, his hallucinatory double

The Story

At Christmastime, Markheim, the protagonist, comes to a dealer's shop, pretending that he is looking for a present for a lady. His real plan, however, is to murder the dealer so he can steal his merchandise and money. Markheim rejects the dealer's suggestion of a hand mirror for the lady, referring to it as a "hand conscience." Presumably, from his reaction to the mirror, Markheim feels twinges from his conscience even before he commits the murder. While the dealer is still in the midst of assisting him in finding a present, Markheim stabs and kills him.

The action of the story after the murder is limited, with most of it taking place inside Markheim's mind; the setting is restricted to the dealer's shop and house. The murder has intensified Markheim's nerves and consciousness; as a result, he is easily startled and alarmed by the external noises and shadows he hears and sees inside the shop. Ticking and striking clocks, footsteps running past the shop, shadows cast by flickering candles and the dim light outside, and falling rain all unnerve him and make him even more overwrought.

Internally, he reproaches himself for how he has carried out his crime and imagines that his neighbors somehow know of his crime and are planning his punishment. All these alarms and fears eventually lead him to believe that he is not alone in the shop; he becomes increasingly convinced that there is some presence lurking somewhere, even though he had seen the dealer's servant leave earlier, and he knows the dealer was alone in the shop.

His fears and imaginings are interrupted by a gentleman beating on the door and shouting for the dealer; he departs when he receives no answer. This interruption reminds Markheim of his purpose, and he realizes he must act quickly before he is interrupted again. He gets the keys from the dealer's dead body and enters the dealer's drawing room to gain access to the money cabinet. He is momentarily calmer and more relaxed as he searches for the key for the cabinet but is jarred suddenly by the sound of footsteps mounting the stairs.

He is surprised to see a friendly, familiar face appear at the door. He concludes that his visitor is not human but rather a spirit. This visitor—perhaps a devil, perhaps an angel, a hallucination of Markheim's conscience, or his double—proceeds to urge Markheim to move on with his crime because the servant is returning home. It also claims to know Markheim rather well. Markheim refuses to acknowledge any connection with this being, which he perceives as evil. He claims to hate evil and love goodness; he also excuses away his murder because of poverty. Markheim and the visitor continue to debate Markheim's connection with evil.

As they argue, Markheim gradually weakens, although he struggles hard to distance himself from evil and maintain his goodness. In the end, Markheim acknowledges and accepts his evil nature through his realization of the extent to which he has fallen morally. The doorbell rings just then; the servant has arrived, and the visitor encourages Markheim to murder the maid and finish his crime quickly. Markheim, with his new self-knowledge, decides to act to redeem himself. He determines that the way to salvation lies in confessing his crime and accepting his eventual execution. At this assertion, the visitor's features transform; they brighten, soften, and then disappear. When Markheim acknowledges his evil nature and acts to redeem himself, his visitor's work is done.

Themes and Meanings

The plot of "Markheim" could be regarded as simply the story of a murder and its aftereffects on the murderer that lead him eventually to confess his crime. It is more than the story of a murder, however; it is, more significantly, the story of the process a man goes through to first face and then accept the evil side of his nature. The development of self-knowledge and the conflict between one's good and evil sides are the central themes in "Markheim." Markheim experiences an insight about his true self when he finally accepts that he has fallen morally. Before this point in the story, he has suppressed and denied his evil side.

Immediately after he murders the dealer, he appears not to feel remorse for his crime; he is more fearful of being caught and punished. Even after he has a flashback, as he looks at the murdered dealer's face, to the revulsion he felt while looking at a famous crimes exhibit in his childhood, he claims not to feel penitent about his crime but rather feels only pity for the dealer.

Next, as he climbs the stairs to the dealer's house above the shop and reaches the top floor, Markheim continues to fear being caught as he wonders if the laws of nature will expose his crime. At this point, he still feels his crime is justified, believing God understands and accepts his excuses for committing murder.

In the dealer's drawing room, when he is in a calmer frame of mind, he hears children singing hymns nearby and recalls his churchgoing days in the past. When his mind is focused on a time when he was more religiously oriented, he hears the step on the stair. It is as if the memory of a time when he was a better and more moral person causes him to externalize his evil side and literally come face to face with it. The story can be seen then as an inward journey from denial and repression to acceptance and ownership of his evil nature.

Style and Technique

Two literary techniques, atmosphere and the use of the *Doppelgänger* or double, are notable in "Markheim." Most of the story is taken up by Markheim's inner conflict in coping with his guilt and the evil in his nature, and the eerie atmosphere accentuates and externalizes this conflict. The shop is lit by candles that waver and cast weird shadows, the overall light is dim so that mirrors and pictures appear strange, clocks sound in the dimness, and rain causes a variety of startling noises sounding like footsteps and echoes. This dim, rainy setting works to unnerve Markheim, who already is overwrought internally by committing murder and repressing his guilt about his crime.

The use of the double also helps to emphasize as well as externalize Markheim's conflict. The double or *Doppelgänger* is a technique that Robert Louis Stevenson uses in a number of his works, the most famous being *Dr. Jekyll and Mr. Hyde* (1886), and it is an effective way to indicate the duality in man's nature. In "Markheim," the use of the double and the debate between Markheim and his other self also help bring the story to its climax: Markheim's moment of self-knowledge. It is only when he sees his double face to face that Markheim begins to accept his evil nature. Before he encounters his double, he believes he is justified in his crime, but his double makes him face his crime and forces him to question the good side of his nature, which he asserts still exists. When he finally admits that he is beyond grace, he realizes that his only chance at redemption is to confess his crime. The technique of the externalized other side of his nature visually represents for the reader and for Markheim how he resolves his conflict.

The identity of the double, however, has been debated among critics. Some maintain it is a devil, others an angel, still others assert that it is a hallucination brought on by Markheim's overwrought nerves. One additional interpretation, stressed in the earlier discussion of the theme, is that the double is the result of externalizing Markheim's repressed guilt and limited self-knowledge.

The similarities between Markheim's story and the story of Raskolnikov in Fyodor Dostoevski's *Prestupleniye i nakazaniye* (1866; *Crime and Punishment*, 1886) are obvious. Both stories deal with the murder of a pawnbroker and the aftereffects of the murder on the murderer, as well as the criminal's eventual punishment. In addition, both stories have similar dim, eerie atmospheres.

Anna B. Nelson

THE MARQUISE OF O——

Author: Heinrich von Kleist (1777-1811)
Type of plot: Psychological
Time of plot: The early nineteenth century
Locale: The northern Italian town of "M——"
First published: "Die Marquise von O——," 1808 (English translation, 1960)

> *Principal characters:*
>> GIULIETTA, the Marquise of O——, a widowed lady of
>> distinguished family and excellent reputation
>> COLONEL LORENZO G——, her father, commandant of the
>> garrison at M——
>> HIS WIFE, the marquise's mother
>> COUNT F——, a lieutenant colonel in a rifle unit of the Russian
>> forces

The Story

A lady of high social standing and irreproachable reputation, the widowed Marquise of O——, announces in the newspaper in the town of M—— that, without knowing how it came to be, she is expecting a child and, out of consideration for her family, is resolved to marry the father if he will come forward to acknowledge his paternity.

After the death of her husband three years earlier, Giulietta (the marquise) and her children lived with her parents at the fortress of M——, where her father was commandant. During an attack by Russian troops, several enemy soldiers assaulted the terrified Giulietta but were driven off by one of their officers before they could do her harm. Giulietta fell unconscious at this point, and her rescuer returned her to the care of her servants. Her father was forced to surrender the garrison, but he and his family felt indebted to Giulietta's protector, a Count F——, and thus they learned with sorrow that on the same day as his departure from M—— he had fallen in battle. Giulietta regretted not having insisted on seeing Count F—— to thank him for his gallant deed, and several months passed before she could forget him.

In the meantime, she experienced physical discomforts that she jokingly described to her mother as oddly similar to those of pregnancy. These passed, however, and were soon forgotten. Then, to the entire family's astonishment, Count F—— reappeared, not at all dead as first reported, and now fully recovered. He showed great concern for Giulietta's well-being and abruptly asked for her hand in marriage. Giulietta and her parents were speechless, and the commandant assured him that his daughter's marriage in such haste would be unthinkable. At a loss to explain the sudden proposal, the family agreed that Count F—— should depart on the important mission for which he was already overdue in Naples, with the understanding that on his return in four to six weeks his request might be favorably considered. During his absence the commandant would make the necessary inquiries about Count F——'s status and character.

Within a few days, Giulietta was again indisposed and expressed concern over her condition. When a doctor was called and diagnosed her complaint as pregnancy, she reacted with disbelief and indignantly sent him away. Confiding in her mother, she denied that she had engaged in any erotic adventure and even began to question her own soundness of mind. A midwife was summoned and unhesitatingly confirmed the doctor's findings, whereupon Giulietta's parents banished her from the house, and she moved with her children to the isolation of their country residence.

There she recovered her pride, accepted her family's rejection and the "great, sacred and inexplicable order of the world," and reconciled herself to a life of seclusion and devotion to her two present children and the third soon to be born. Only the thought that this child would suffer disgrace in good society brought her to the idea of placing the newspaper announcement with which the story opens. If anyone should respond to it she could only imagine him to be of low standing and base character.

Count F—— returns from his mission in Naples, hears with consternation what has transpired, and sets off at once for Giulietta's retreat to renew his proposal of marriage. She resists his advances and flees, however, insisting that she will not hear what he has to say. That same evening the count sees Giulietta's advertisement appealing to the father of her child.

Meanwhile, Colonel G—— has been petulantly nursing his wounded pride and denouncing his daughter's disgraceful conduct, and her notice in the paper only makes him angrier. The next issue brings an anonymous reply announcing the offender's wish to visit Giulietta in her parents' house on a particular day and at a particular hour. The commandant is furious and interprets this as a deceitful scheme of his daughter and some secret lover to ingratiate themselves with him and to extract his forgiveness and blessing on their shameful union. Giulietta's mother, however, goes to visit her daughter and returns finally convinced that Giulietta is as ignorant of the offender's identity as the rest of her family. She brings Giulietta triumphantly home to receive the apology of Colonel G——, who is at first skeptical, then abjectly contrite, and finally overcome with devotion to his daughter—in a scene of unmistakably erotic reconciliation.

The family decides that Giulietta shall marry the man who replied to her advertisement and is to come to the house the following day, provided that he is not of hopelessly low station. Giulietta reaffirms her readiness to marry any but a complete scoundrel. At the appointed hour it is Count F—— who appears, and she recoils saying she was prepared to meet a depraved man, but not a devil. The commandant can only persuade her to keep her word and agree to the marriage under condition that Count F—— will renounce all conjugal rights and fulfill any duties imposed on him. The marriage is thus performed, and the count immediately retires to live in separation from his family. He is not invited into his wife's company until the day of their son's christening but is then gradually permitted to call more often at the house, and in the course of time, he begins a second courtship of Giulietta. When a year has passed, she consents a second time to marry him, a second wedding is celebrated, and they move into the country residence at V——. Only later does the count ask his wife why she rejected him as a devil when he appeared in response to her newspaper notice. Her answer is "that he would not have seemed a devil then if at their first meeting he had not appeared to her in the likeness of an angel."

Themes and Meanings

"The Marquise of O——" is a web of the known and unknown, that of which its heroine is either conscious or unconscious. ("Knowing," "consciousness," and indeed "conscience" are all closely related words in the vocabulary of Heinrich von Kleist's German text, a fact not always evident in the English translation.) What the marquise knows and acknowledges in the story is the clear implication of the empirical evidence that the doctor and the midwife have confirmed: the fact that she is pregnant but not the explanation for it. The power of consciousness is both destructive and redeeming. Giulietta owes her condition to a state of unconsciousness (the fainting spell during which Count F—— violated her), and she can rise above it only by the strength of consciousness of her own innocence.

Feelings, as Kleist understands and portrays them, are Giulietta's means of dealing with the empirical, "known" evidence and the foundation for her self-knowledge and sense of her own blamelessness. Of course, the conflict of physical evidence with knowledge of self is a valid issue in this story only if one believes that Giulietta is as unconscious of her sexual encounter as she professes to be. Her confusion and self-questioning seem genuine, but the reader may wonder exactly what she means in telling Count F—— that his first appearance seemed to her angelic; was it only because he arrived as her gallant rescuer? It bears remembering that Kleist himself scoffed (tongue in cheek?) at the idea of the lady's crucial fainting spell as a "shameless farce." Having merely "kept her eyes shut" would also make a farce of Giulietta's reputed virtue, but it obscures a question of greater importance and interest: that of repressed memory. Kleist was clearly psychologist enough to know and exploit the mind's capacity to conceal from itself the conscious knowledge of a forbidden act.

There is a difference between questioning Giulietta's innocence of what befell her and condemning the act itself. Kleist's own morality seems to have been sufficiently ambiguous to preclude his censure of Count F——, the impetuous perpetrator of the deed. Nor does any other person in the story condemn the count. He is one of those typically Kleistian characters who act impulsively, without reflection, and this is both his virtue and his vice. He is alternately called bestial and godlike, devilish and angelic. To Kleist's mind, the self-conscious, questioning majority of individuals have lost their intellectual innocence and are condemned to grope for certainty in a world of conflicting realities and appearances, while both the dumb beast and the god (and Count F—— is called both) are free of the self-consciousness that marks the fallen nature of ordinary humanity. The marquise and her family acknowledge the "great, sacred and inexplicable order of the world" and seek their answers in the social and moral conventions derived from that understanding of it. Count F—— is not defeated by the search, for at the beginning of the story he takes by storm what he could not have for the asking, and at its end "His instinct told him that, in consideration of the imperfection inherent in the order of the world, he had been forgiven by all of them."

Style and Technique

The point in the story at which Giulietta seems to take control of her situation, her decision to advertise in the newspaper for the father of her child, may be considered one of its hinge points. It occurs roughly three-fifths of the way into this novella, but the reader has known since the story's opening sentence the full content of the advertisement and Giulietta's reason for writing it. In the same opening sentence Kleist manages in addition to tell the locale, the heroine's social and family status, and her high reputation. It is a device at which he excels: the combined exposition and anticipatory revelation in such compressed form that it galvanizes the reader's attention in order to learn what events could have prompted the lady's unusual course of action—not to mention the source of her inexplicable pregnancy.

One would expect that a reply to her announcement in the paper will resolve the question of the father's identity and disclose the details of the sexual encounter. By the time the respondent presents himself, however, his identity is no longer much in doubt, and the attentive reader has already noted enough hints of what occurred during Giulietta's swoon to make any further account of it unnecessary. Instead of an answer and an explanation, Kleist sends the story off at once in another unexpected and baffling direction: The marquise refuses to accept the man whom her advertisement obviously describes. If one learns anything at all from this turn of events, it should be that one may have been asking the wrong question all along. What matters in "The Marquise of O——" is the process of "regaining consciousness"—not physically but cognitively.

To this end, Kleist employs a narrative perspective on the level of his characters rather than an omniscient one. The reader must thus experience the events and observable evidence in the same way as Giulietta and her parents and share in their confusion as they try to interpret them. As if willfully compounding their perplexity, Kleist—in his typical fashion—pushes the story forward as rapidly as it will go, relying most of the time on indirect discourse, eliding the rape scene with a mere dash in the punctuation of the crucial sentence, and joining one development to the next with forms like: "at once," "already," "just as," "even before," "meanwhile," "in the act of . . . when." All these devices generate an inexorable rush of events that the players are powerless to control or arrest.

The story's unifying metaphor is the stronghold besieged by one side and defended by the other. Count F——'s first objective is to storm and capture the garrison at M——; at the same time, he assails and overpowers the marquise's defenses as well. The rules of war oblige the commandant to surrender the fortress; his adversary in battle reappears as his challenger for the other prize as well: the widowed daughter whose virtue Colonel G—— is expected to guard and for whom his paternal devotion borders on illicit desire. Count F——'s characteristic approach is to rush ahead. Thus, he enters the room in the commandant's house; thus, he delivers his ardent marriage proposal; and thus, when denied entrance to Giulietta's country retreat, he breaches the garden wall to gain an audience with her. The beleaguered commandant's rules of social conduct are no match for the count's impetuous application of "military" tactics, and the fall of the citadel at M—— only prefigures the victorious siege of an eroded and crumbling system of social conventions.

Charles E. May

MARRIAGE À LA MODE

Author: Katherine Mansfield (Katherine Mansfield Beauchamp, 1888-1923)
Type of plot: Domestic realism
Time of plot: The early 1920's
Locale: England
First published: 1922

> *Principal characters:*
> WILLIAM, a London solicitor
> ISABEL, his wife
> PADDY and
> JOHNNY, his children
> MOIRA MORRISON, Isabel's friend and houseguest
> BOBBY KANE,
> BILL HUNT, and
> DENNIS GREEN, other houseguests

The Story

William is a hard-working, affluent solicitor who spends his weeks in London and his weekends in the countryside where his wife, Isabel, and their sons, Paddy and Johnny, live permanently. About to leave for his weekend at home, William frets because he has neglected to buy presents for the children. For several weeks in a row, he has given them candy that he bought just before his trains pulled out, but they prefer other gifts. This time, he decides to take his boys fruit—a melon and a pineapple—assuming that Isabel's perpetual houseguests will not invade the children's bedrooms to eat the fruit, as they have done with most of the candy in past weeks.

As his train speeds toward his destination, William fantasizes about Isabel's meeting him at the station. Consistent with his fantasy, Isabel is waiting for him, apart from the crowd. She has engaged a taxi to take him and her four houseguests—Moira Morrison and three young poets—home. William has grown to expect aesthetic, freeloading houseguests during his weekends at home.

William and Isabel formerly lived in the city, until Isabel felt stifled by that life. William doted on her, so he agreed to her moving to the country with their sons, whom he would be able to see only on weekends. In those days, he considered Isabel enticingly fresh, associating her with his childhood habit of rushing into the garden after a rainstorm to shake the rose bushes so that he might be drenched in the freshness of the newly fallen rainwater.

After William gets off the train, Isabel leads him to the taxi in which Bill Hunt and Dennis Green are already ensconced, as is Moira, wearing a hat that resembles a large strawberry. It is Moira who originally "rescued" Isabel from her city life, took her to

Paris, and introduced her to young poets. She refers to Isabel as "Titania," the mythological queen of the fairies.

Isabel tells William where to sit in the taxi, as though he were a child. At that moment, Bobby Kane emerges from the sweets shop with his arms full of packets. The shopkeeper is close behind reminding Bobby that he has not paid for the items. When Bobby says he forgot, Isabel pays the shopkeeper and Bobby is again ecstatic.

The weekend proceeds with William feeling isolated from Isabel and her guests. His children are not there, having been taken somewhere by their nanny. At every turn, Isabel's guests are condescending to William, who is made to feel like a stranger in his own home. He has no time alone with Isabel until just before he prepares to return to London.

On the train, William decides to write to Isabel. Before the day ends, he has written and mailed a long letter telling her that he does not wish to be a drag on her happiness, suggesting that they should end their marriage. When Isabel receives the letter, she reads it to her guests, who are still there. It takes her a while to realize that William is talking about divorce. Once she understands what William has in mind, she sits on the side of her bed saying, "How vile, odious, abominable, vulgar." She knows that she should reply to William immediately. She also realizes that she is shallow and vain.

As she contemplates writing to William, her guests call her to go swimming. After a moment's indecision, she joins them, vowing to write to William later.

Themes and Meanings

Born in New Zealand, Katherine Mansfield married English literary critic and journalist John Middleton Murry although she was a lesbian. She lived most of her life in England, where she closely associated with such literary figures as D. H. Lawrence and Virginia Woolf. Through these associations, she came to understand in considerable depth the hangers-on in the artistic and literary worlds. She also had a penetrating insight into the sham that marriage was for many of her friends and, most probably, for herself.

Although it would be inaccurate to read "Marriage à la Mode" as directly autobiographical, the story certainly depicts many elements from Mansfield's life with Murry. In this story Mansfield is essentially concerned with the ways in which married people grow apart. Neither William nor Isabel is a terrible person; the two have simply become unsuited for each other.

This story satirizes the civilized ways the British have for dealing with unpleasantness. They remain unflaggingly polite, sidestepping unpleasantness by deferring controversy. Very little is communicated directly in this story. William and Isabel do not fight. William voices no complaints, even though he is essentially excluded from the activities of the weekend and is inconvenienced to the point that he cannot even do the work that he brought home.

His children's absence is another disappointment, but William does not even complain about their being away. Isabel snatches for herself the pineapple William has brought for Paddy, telling William that he can bring the children other gifts the following weekend. Isabel's guests demean William's gifts; Bill Hunt calls them decapitated heads.

The young poets who have become a fixture in Isabel's house (for it is clearly her house, not their house) live in a world apart from William's. Ironically, however, it is his world—the one that the poets look down on—that provides the wherewithal to support Isabel and her collection of aesthetes.

William is an unromantic, dependable character. Seemingly unimaginative, he retreats more and more into himself. However, small details suggest that he has not always been like this. His shaking the raindrops from rose petals and, in a sense, cleansing himself with these scented drops, suggests someone who once had spirit and imagination.

Mansfield chooses to end this story without any real resolution. Isabel is going swimming with her friends, but in all likelihood she will eventually write to William. One can only speculate on the outcome. It would not be outlandish to guess that William will be back in the country place with Isabel and her entourage the following weekend and for a long procession of weekends to come.

As Mansfield presents him, William is a defeated man but one so used to the rut in which he finds himself that extrication seems unlikely. In *The Cocktail Party* (1949), T. S. Eliot presents a similar couple, Edward and Lavinia, who go so far as to separate, but they finally realize that the rut they are in is comfortable for them, probably better than any alternatives they are likely to find. In "Marriage à la Mode," Mansfield seems to be heading toward the same conclusion that Eliot reaches in his play a quarter of a century later.

Style and Technique

Much influenced by the short-story writing of Anton Chekhov, Mansfield wrote stories that are psychologically accurate and convincing. She understood life's ironies and the small personal tragedies that accompany them. She had a substantial grasp of the social milieu in which she and many other artists lived during the first quarter of the twentieth century in England.

This story is particularly strong in its use of physical detail, especially toward the beginning when William is in the first-class smoking compartment of the train departing for what he hopes will be a relaxing weekend with his family. He takes work with him, expecting to get it done in the relative quiet of his home. Mansfield depicts in considerable detail William's leaving London. A red-faced girl runs along beside the train carriages, waving and calling desperately. A greasy workman at the end of the platform smiles as the train passes him.

William settles in, thinking to himself that it is a filthy life. He needs the spiritual cleansing that the raindrops from the rose petals once gave him. William has grown up. He is no longer a boy, but rather a father and husband, a man with responsibilities that have stripped him of the romance in his life.

Mansfield skillfully juxtaposes William to Isabel's friends, irresponsible spongers who have preserved the romance in their lives. They are antipodal to William who, in some ways, comes off as the heavy, although not as an unsympathetic heavy. Mansfield tells the story from William's point of view. We can only guess how Isabel feels about his weekend visits, which, after all, interrupt her social life.

Isabel and her friends are frivolous. The friends hang on while it is pleasant and profitable for them to do so. It is not Isabel who has attracted them but rather what she can offer them materially. In his letter to Isabel, William offers her the freedom to continue the shallow existence she has created for herself.

R. Baird Shuman

THE MASQUE OF THE RED DEATH

Author: Edgar Allan Poe (1809-1849)
Type of plot: Gothic
Time of plot: Unspecified, but probably the Middle Ages
Locale: Unspecified, but probably a European country
First published: 1842

> *Principal characters:*
> PRINCE PROSPERO, a nobleman who attempts to shut out death
> THE RED DEATH, the disembodied, allegorical figure of death
> VARIOUS COURTIERS OF THE PRINCE

The Story

The allegorical nature of this very brief and well-known Edgar Allan Poe story is indicated by the fact that its only named character is Prince Prospero and its only real conflict is the symbolic one between Prospero and the Red Death. The Red Death is a mysterious pestilence that has ravaged the countryside; no pestilence has ever been so fatal and hideous. It manifests itself on the victim with bleeding at the pores, especially on the face, and inevitably ends with death in the space of half an hour. After half of his people have died from this plague, Prince Prospero takes many of the knights and ladies of his court into his castle and welds shut all the doors and windows, determined to escape death. In a supreme gesture of self-willed pride, Prospero assumes that "with such precautions the courtiers might bid defiance to contagion. The external world could take care of itself. In the meantime it was folly to grieve, or to think."

The main action of the story centers on a masked ball given by Prospero, during which those within can forget the reality of death outside. The buffoons, actors, dancers, and musicians who dominate the ball create an inner world hermetically sealed off from external reality: "All these and security were within. Without was the 'Red Death.'" In this very static and stylized piece of fiction, Poe spends approximately one quarter of the story detailing the interior of the ballroom, the primary characteristics of which are seven rooms so arranged that one cannot see them in a long vista, but only one at a time.

Each room has Gothic windows of stained glass, which match in color the decor of the rooms themselves. The order and color of the rooms and windows are blue, purple, green, orange, white, violet, and black. Only in the last room, shrouded in black, does the color of the windows differ from the color of the rooms, for here the windows are blood red. In the corridor outside the windows, a brazier of fire projects rays through the windows to create fantastic appearances within. In the final, or western, chamber, the fire throws such grotesque images through the red windows onto the black curtains that no one wishes to enter it. In this room also is an ebony clock that, when the hour is struck, makes everyone at the ball stop their dancing to listen to the sound in somber meditation or reverie.

Much of the remainder of the story describes the arabesque and grotesque figures who inhabit the rooms, characters who seem less like real people than fancies created by a madman: "There was much of the beautiful, much of the wanton, much of the bizarre, something of the terrible, and not a little of that which might have excited disgust. To and fro in the seven chambers there stalked, in fact, a multitude of dreams."

The ball reaches a climax at midnight, when, with the striking of the clock, a new presence makes itself known among the masked revelers—a figure dressed in shrouds, whose mask resembles the face of a stiffened corpse dabbled with blood to assume the appearance and type of the Red Death itself. Prospero cries for his courtiers to seize the figure so he might be hanged, but the mysterious guest inspires such awe that no one will touch him. Thus, Prospero himself chases the figure through the six chambers until they reach the final one, in which the prince, in the act of raising a dagger to kill the stranger, falls instantly forward in death himself. When the rest of the revelers seize the figure, they find that the shrouds and the corpselike mask hide no tangible form at all. With this discovery, all the courtiers fall down in death one by one, while the flames of the tripod expire. The story ends with the ominous last line: "And Darkness and Decay and the Red Death held illimitable dominion over all."

Themes and Meanings

The theme of Poe's allegory quite clearly focuses on the impossibility, regardless of one's power, wealth, and influence, of escaping mortality. However, the story is somewhat more complex than this easy moral statement would suggest. First, the particular nature of the Red Death itself creates a basic irony. The metaphor of a "Red" death, because it suggests blood, is the conventional image, not of death, but rather of life itself, for the presence of blood on the face of a person suggests the life within it. In this sense, every living person wears a mask of red—the blood visible beneath the skin. However, it is precisely this sign of life that ironically suggests death. For Poe's point is that it is the very presence of life that inevitably means death. Thus, Prospero does not simply try to escape death; rather, by enclosing himself within the castle and shutting out the outside world, he attempts to escape life into a realm hermetically closed off—in short, into a world very much like Poe's notion of the art work itself.

In this sense, Prospero is a reflection of William Shakespeare's character of the same name in *The Tempest* (1611), similarly an aesthetic magician who creates an alternate world of imaginative reality not susceptible to the contingencies of external reality. Indeed, Poe's emphasis in "The Masque of the Red Death" is that the abbey within which Prospero retreats is his own "creation," a result of his "own eccentric yet august taste"—phrases that echo Poe's own aesthetic theory—a Platonic notion that celebrates the ideal of the artwork as a self-sustained experience of absolute and immutable beauty. In effect, Prospero creates the image of a self-contained artwork within which he tries to live. However, the seven rooms within the abbey seem to reflect the inescapable temporality of human experience.

The sequence of rooms perhaps represents the seven ages of man—from the blue, which suggests the beginning of life and light in the east, to the black, which suggests the darkness of night and death in the west. Consequently, even though Prospero attempts to create the illusion of art as eternally protected from the contingencies of life, the final realization of the reader is that, because all art works inevitably reflect life, one cannot escape, even within the artwork, the inevitable implication of process and thus mortality. The image of the clock in the final room suggests why this is so: Both life and the literary work exist within time, and it is indeed time that makes life end inevitably in death.

Style and Technique

The style of "The Masque of the Red Death" focuses primarily on the pictorial rather than on narrative. Poe attempts to create the sense that the story exists as a painting does, within space and outside time. The story has been called Poe's most pictorial composition, an arabesque that attempts to create an intricate geometric spatial pattern. Thus it is quite static, lacking in narrative plot and emphasizing instead the spatial arrangements of painting. However, the irony is that because "The Masque of the Red Death" is a story and therefore exists in time, time triumphs. Thus the conclusion of the story emphasizes that the artistic effort to transform temporality into spatiality is doomed to failure. Even the seven rooms, which suggest a geometric pattern of static positioning, become transformed into an image of the time span of life when Prospero follows the Red Death through a temporal progression from birth to youth to maturity to old age and finally to death. It is when Prospero must confront the reality of the temporality of life that he inevitably must confront the death that life always insists on.

Thus, although the story is ostensibly about the moral lesson of the human inability to escape death, it is actually an aesthetic allegory or fable, in which Prospero represents Poe's image of the artist who insists on creating an ideal artwork, but who is always trapped by the time-bound nature of life. "The Masque of the Red Death" embodies an aesthetic theme common to much of Poe's short fiction. Such stories as "The Fall of the House of Usher," "The Tell-Tale Heart," and "Ligeia" also focus on man's attempt to find refuge from death in the immutable realm of art. However, while these other stories attempt to create a world of psychologized obsession to embody this theme, "The Masque of the Red Death" is a striking example of Poe's attempt to deal with it in the conventional genre of allegory. Like much of Poe's fiction, "The Masque of the Red Death" should not be dismissed as a simple gothic horror story, but rather should be understood in terms of the aesthetic theory that dominated Poe's work.

Charles E. May

MASTER AND MAN

Author: Leo Tolstoy (1828-1910)
Type of plot: Allegory
Time of plot: The 1870's
Locale: Provincial Russia
First published: "Khozyain i rabotnik," 1896 (English translation, 1899)

> *Principal characters:*
>> VASILI ANDREVICH BREKHUNOV, an innkeeper, a merchant, and a landowner in the village of Kresty
>> NIKITA, a day laborer in the employ of Brekhunov

The Story

Brekhunov has a passion to acquire a grove of oak trees in the nearby village of Gorachkin. He fears that unless he gets there as soon as possible, someone else will buy it before he can. The enterprising Brekhunov intends to have the trees cut down to make into sledge-runners; the leftovers will be sold for firewood. From this deal, he hopes to realize a tidy profit. He figures that the grove of trees is worth more than twenty thousand rubles. The owner is asking only ten thousand but will probably take seven thousand, with three thousand on account. Brekhunov will use seven hundred rubles of his own money for the down payment and make up the rest with some church money that he has in his safekeeping. Brekhunov is a church elder.

It is winter and the ground is covered with snow. It is now past two o'clock in the afternoon, and the day is "windy, dull, and cold," and twenty degrees below zero. Nevertheless, Brekhunov orders his horse and sledge made ready for the trip. His motto in business is, "Lose an hour and you can't catch it up in a year." His wife is apprehensive about his leaving, especially alone, and gets him to take his willing servant, Nikita, with him just in case.

The two men set off together. The going is fairly easy at first, despite the snow-covered roads. However, soon the wind becomes much stronger than either has anticipated, and the blowing snow diminishes visibility. The sledge comes to a fork in the road. Although both turnings go toward their destination, one road, the longer of the two, is better traveled and marked with a double row of high stakes. Brekhunov asks Nikita which fork they should choose, but the question is rhetorical, as he has already made up his mind to take the straighter, not-so-well-marked route. Brekhunov wants to get to Gorachkin as soon as possible, despite the risk.

After they have been jogging along for about ten minutes, however, it becomes obvious that the sledge has strayed off the road. They halt, and Nikita gets off to look around. The snow is still not too deep, except in certain places, but the wind is as fierce as before. It has now begun to snow, and the horse is becoming exhausted. After a prolonged search, the horse manages to stumble back on a road, but on a road that leads to another village, one off to the left of their original direction. They enter the town, and Brekhunov asks directions. However, no sooner is the sledge headed toward Gorachkin than they become lost again. Nikita again makes an effort to set things right, but the road is not easy to find, being completely covered with a snow that even hides the marker stakes. It is now getting dark, and the wind is blowing in their faces. They let the horse try to find the way. Some time passes, but the animal does manage to come onto a roadway again. This leads to Grishkino, the same village that they have recently left. They have been traveling in circles.

Brekhunov stops to get his bearings in front of a large, brick-fronted house, and the owner invites him to stay the night. Brekhunov insists that he must go on. "It's business and can't be helped," he explains. He agrees to come inside to warm up, and he and Nikita are served food and tea and vodka. Nikita, a onetime heavy drinker, refuses the vodka. Brekhunov tells his host how they have twice lost their way but says that he is confident that things will now go well, if he can have someone see them as far as the turning.

They get started again, but by now the weather is worse than before: "The wind was so strong that when it blew from the side and the travelers steered against it, it tilted the sledges and turned the horses to one side." They are taken to the intersection leading to Grishkino and bid their host farewell. It becomes more and more difficult to keep to the road, and they are soon lost for a third time. As they plough through the drifts, trying to find the right direction, the horse plunges down an incline into the bottom of a hollow. They manage to get the sledge moving along the ravine, but the exhausted horse soon can go no farther. Nikita realizes that they are stuck there, and he makes preparations to spend the night. He takes off the horse's harness. Next, he ties the shafts of the sledge together with a strap and sets them in front so they can project out of the snow; he puts a handkerchief around the strap to act as a flag. He covers the horse with a small blanket and then digs out a hole in the snow to shelter himself.

Brekhunov is still thinking of the money he will make from the forest grove, now regretting that he will lose one day. He thinks that it would have been better to have spent the night in Grishkino. Soon his thoughts change to fear, a fear that is increased by the howl of a wolf. Brekhunov becomes restless and asks himself what is the use of remaining here and waiting for death. He decides to try to escape on the horse, leaving Nikita to his fate. He reasons that for his servant, "It's all the same to him whether he lives or dies. What's his life worth? He won't grudge his life, but I have something to live for, thank God."

Brekhunov unties the horse, manages to climb on its back, and rides through the powdery snow in the direction of what he believes is a village. The dark patch in the distance, however, is only a stand of wormwood. He continues to ride but soon discovers that he is again traveling in circles. The horse stumbles and falls, tossing Brekhunov free, and struggles on alone. Brekhunov follows, trying to catch up. The horse leads him back to Nikita.

The half-frozen servant has crawled into the sledge to keep warm. Nikita tells his master that he feels that he is dying. Brekhunov stands silent and motionless for half a minute, then suddenly begins to brush the snow off Nikita and push it out of the sledge. He then opens his fur coat and lies down on top of Nikita, covering Nikita's body with the warmth of his own. He no longer feels any terror. He lies that way, protecting his servant for the rest of the night, until death comes to him just before dawn. Nikita awakes to find his dead master lying on top of him.

It is not until noon that some peasants find the sledge, discovering it from the improvised flag hanging above. They dig out its occupants. Both the master and the horse are frozen stiff, but Nikita survives. He spends the next two months in a hospital, losing only a few of his toes. He lives for another twenty years and dies at home in bed, "sincerely glad that he was relieving his son and daughter-in-law of the burden of having to feed him."

Nikita is convinced that he is entering a better life. However, whether, after death, he finds what he expected, the author comments, "we shall all soon learn."

Themes and Meanings

Vasili Andrevich Brekhunov is the quintessence of greed. Making money is his *raison d'être*, his fundamental dynamic, his only obsession. For this he will risk and ultimately lose his life. If the wages of sin are death, then he is rightly doomed, because even when in mortal danger he still thinks of all the wealth that will be his. He "thought ever of the one thing that constituted the sole aim, meaning, pleasure, and pride of his life—of how much money he had made and might still make, of how much other people he knew had made and possessed, and how those others had made and were making it, and how he, like them, might still make much more."

Materialism corrupts his entire vision. He cheats and shortchanges everybody, especially Nikita. He is supposed to pay his servant eighty rubles a year but gives him half that amount, in reluctant driblets and often in the form of payment in kind, for which he charges Nikita too much. However, Brekhunov can still hypocritically pose as Nikita's benefactor, "If you need anything, take it," he says to him, "you will work it off. I'm not like others to keep you waiting, and making up accounts and reckoning fines. We deal straightforwardly. You serve me and I don't neglect you."

Nikita is bound to his master symbolically as well as practically. He knows that he is being cheated but figures that such is his lot in life and accepts it: "He felt that it was useless to try to clear up his accounts with him or explain his side of the matter and that as long as he had nowhere to go he must accept what he could get." It is this spirit of resignation that makes him fearless in the face of death, accepting fate calmly. Nikita is Leo Tolstoy's noble savage, the perfect fool, one of the meek who shall inherit the earth. His master is the self-centered egotist, the epitome of a wasted life. His values are so bound up with getting and possessing that he is utterly defenseless in the presence of death. He rationalizes his desertion of Nikita by contending that he has so much more to live for, because he is a man of property and his servant is not.

Brekhunov's sacrifice produces his redemption. However, in the context of the plot, although not in terms of Tolstoy's *Weltanschauung*, this is accidental—indeed, almost whimsical. Before death comes, Brekhunov begins to hallucinate; he tries to move his arms and legs but cannot; then he understands "that this was death, and [he] was not at all disturbed by that." He wonders why he has been troubled with all the material things in his existence. Death now seems as natural—not an interruption of one more business deal—and as acceptable, as much a part of the flow of life, as his symbiotic relationship with the man he saves.

Style and Technique

Tolstoy's characters are clichés: the greedy master and his long-suffering, submissive servant. Brekhunov sets off on his pilgrimage to satisfy his lust for riches; Nikita comes along because it is his duty. The action takes place in a world increasingly devoid of landmarks, a world becoming increasingly alien. Tolstoy throws his characters back on themselves. However, although the crisis affects Nikita very little, save for the loss of a few toes, it completely changes Brekhunov.

The author is hard-pressed to make his main character's spiritual conversion convincing. He does so by toning down Brekhunov's hard edges, making him less of a stereotype. He makes him good-natured even while being the most unreconstructed of cheats, presenting him as more intrinsically manipulative than really evil. He becomes recognizable in the same way as, say, a shyster lawyer or a smiling used-car salesperson who tells one that the wreck he is selling has only been driven to church on Sundays. On this level, the reader can more readily come to terms with his character. However, Tolstoy is still exposing the reader to his own set of values; he is trying to persuade the reader to accept his view of the necessity of service to other human beings. He is showing the reader, through allegory, the sterility of materialism.

Tolstoy has a hopelessly lost Brekhunov going around in circles trying to find the path to salvation. Where Brekhunov believes his safety lies turns out to be nothing but wormwood. Liberation from such a hollow existence can come only through spiritual transformation. The death scene is not entirely convincing, but Tolstoy makes it more believable by making it mundane. The merchant gives up his life in the same manner that he has previously shown in his business deals: "Suddenly, with the same resolution with which he used to strike hands when making a good purchase." The spiritual result is not diminished, for such *joie de vivre* is in perfect keeping with exhilaration shown by saints in the hour of their martyrdom. As Brekhunov is dying, he is overcome with an ecstasy that is so pedestrian that the story's great theme seems as natural as the snowstorm that serves as its setting.

Wm. Laird Kleine-Ahlbrandt

MATEO FALCONE

Author: Prosper Mérimée (1803-1870)
Type of plot: Social realism
Time of plot: The early nineteenth century
Locale: Corsica
First published: 1829 (English translation, 1903)

> *Principal characters:*
> MATEO FALCONE, a Corsican shepherd and expert marksman
> GIUSEPPA, his wife
> FORTUNATO, his youngest child and only son
> GIANETTO SANPIERO, a bandit
> TIODORO GAMBA, an adjutant leading a band of government
>   troops; a distant relative of Mateo Falcone

The Story

On an autumn day, Mateo Falcone and his wife visit the fields to inspect their flocks, leaving their home under the care of Fortunato, their ten-year-old son. While they are away, Fortunato hears a burst of gunfire and then sees a man in ragged dress, wounded in the thigh, emerge from the underbrush not far from the house. The man is Gianetto Sanpiero, a bandit who has been raiding the area recently who is now being pursued by government troops. Fortunato is reluctant to help Sanpiero until the bandit offers him a five-franc piece. Fortunato hides Sanpiero under a haystack and arranges a cat and her kittens on top of it so that it looks as though the hay has not been disturbed. Shortly thereafter, government troops arrive at the house and the adjutant, a distant relative of Mateo named Tiodoro Gamba, asks Fortunato if he has seen a man in the area. Fortunato claims that he has been asleep but makes his excuse in so clumsy a manner that Gamba refuses to believe him. The adjutant threatens the boy several times, but Fortunato will not provide any information, merely repeating the words "My father is Mateo Falcone!" over and over.

The government troops search the house and even thrust into the haystack with their bayonets, but Fortunato displays little concern. Finally, Gamba holds up a fine silver watch worth at least ten *écus* and offers to give it to Fortunato if he will tell him where he has hidden Sanpiero. Fortunato is strong enough to resist temptation only for a few moments. He then takes the watch in one hand, gesturing toward the haystack with the other. Immediately, the troops begin to remove the hay, find Sanpiero, and take him into custody.

As the guards prepare the litter on which they will carry Sanpiero back to town, Mateo Falcone and his wife return. Assuming that the troops have come to arrest him, Mateo orders Giuseppa to get behind him and help him load the weapons. Gamba, aware of Mateo's skill as a marksman, advances toward him, speaking in as friendly a manner as he can. Gamba explains that he has arrested Sanpiero who, as Giuseppa knows, has been raiding Mateo's own herds recently. In an effort to flatter Mateo, Gamba praises Fortunato for the help that he gave him. Without the boy's assistance, Gamba claims, Sanpiero would certainly have gotten away.

As the soldiers lift Sanpiero in the litter, the bandit sees Mateo, spits toward the house, and calls it the "home of a traitor." Although such an insult would ordinarily provoke an immediate response, Mateo does nothing. Now aware that he has done something wrong, Fortunato offers Sanpiero a drink. The bandit, however, contemptuously refuses it and requests that he be given a drink by the soldiers who have arrested him. When the adjutant and government troops have gone, Mateo remains silent for a long time. Fortunato tries to speak to him, but Mateo immediately orders the boy out of his sight. Giuseppa then notices the chain of a watch hanging out of Fortunato's pocket. She asks Fortunato where he had received such an expensive gift. At once, Mateo understands what has happened. He pounces on the boy, smashes the watch against a stone, and wonders aloud whether such a child can really be his.

Mateo then becomes resolute. He sets off toward the underbrush and orders Fortunato to follow him. Giuseppa runs after Mateo, pleading for mercy on the grounds that Fortunato is his son. Mateo retorts that he is Fortunato's father, sends his wife away, and leads Fortunato toward a remote spot. He orders his son to kneel down and say his prayers. Fortunato, sensing what is about to happen, begs for his life, but Mateo takes aim and kills him with a single shot. Without even glancing at the body, Mateo returns to the house and finds a shovel. Giuseppa asks him what he has done. "Justice," Mateo replies and, as he leaves to bury Fortunato, says that their son-in-law must now come to live with them.

Themes and Meanings

"Mateo Falcone" is the product of Prosper Mérimée's lifelong fascination with bandits, outcasts, and the code of honor among thieves. These same ingredients also appear in Mérimée's most famous stories, "Carmen" (1845) and "Colomba" (1840). Mérimée loved tales of primitive justice and the desperate men who lived by a code remote from that of conventional law. Like many Romantic authors, he set his stories in exotic locations, such as Córdoba and the Basque countryside in "Carmen," Lithuania in "Lokis" (1869), the African coast in "Tamango" (1829), and Corsica in both "Colomba" and "Mateo Falcone."

The characters of Mérimée's stories often adhere to a brutal code of justice, at once impressive in its severity and appalling in its cost to human life. The character of Mateo Falcone was the author's first embodiment of such a code. Although he lives in a cabin that consists of only a single room, Mateo Falcone is transformed by Mérimée into a descendent of the caesars, a *paterfamilias* (head of the household) who literally has the power of life and death over everyone who lives in his home.

Mérimée—who was something of an antiquarian and classical scholar—based "Mateo Falcone" on a legend of ancient Rome. The first Roman consul, Lucius Junius Brutus (late sixth century B.C.), who freed the Romans from the tyranny of the Tarquin kings, is said by the historian Livy to have executed his own sons when he learned that they were conspiring with his enemies. Interest in this legend was revived in Europe during the French Revolution by the artist Jacques-Louis David, who, in a painting entitled *Brutus* (1789), depicted the consul at the moment when the bodies of his sons were brought home for burial.

By elevating Mateo Falcone to a modern equivalent of this severe *paterfamilias*, Mérimée has created a character whose code of honor transcends even parental affection. Although Mérimée expects his readers to be shocked by Mateo's actions at the end of the story, he also wants them to understand the Corsican's strange system of values. By the end of the tale, readers may even begin to feel awe for this man whose stern sense of justice leads him to do what they themselves could never do.

It is ironic that Mateo Falcone's strong sense of his family's traditions ultimately compels him to kill a member of his own family. To draw attention to this theme, Mérimée alludes to Fortunato's heritage frequently in the story. When Fortunato initially refuses to hide Sanpiero, the bandit insults him by saying "You're no son of Mateo Falcone." The only reply that Fortunato makes when Gamba threatens him is to repeat the name of his father. When Giuseppa finds the watch that Fortunato has accepted from Gamba, Mateo wonders whether the boy can really be his son. Giuseppa pleads for mercy on the grounds that Mateo is Fortunato's father. Mateo's response, however, is that that is precisely why justice must be done. By accepting a bribe and betraying a fellow Corsican, Fortunato has proven that he does not deserve his father's name. Fortunato's own actions have irrevocably alienated him from his family and its protection.

Style and Technique

The publication of "Mateo Falcone" in 1829 is often regarded as the start of the modern short story in France. With the tale's combination of exotic settings and realistic details, this story paved the way for the work of Gustave Flaubert, Guy de Maupassant, and the later stories of Mérimée himself. Although Mérimée filled "Mateo Falcone" with detailed descriptions of the Corsican countryside and its inhabitants, he himself did not first visit the island until ten years after the story was written. "Mateo Falcone" thus fits into the tradition of imaginative Romantic exoticism that also includes the historical novels of Victor Hugo and Alexandre Dumas, *père*, the mythological paintings of Eugène Delacroix, and the operas and orchestral works of Nicolai Andreyevich Rimsky-Korsakov.

Although generally realistic in tone, "Mateo Falcone" contains several symbolic elements. The name "Falcone" (falcon), for example, suggests Mateo's ferocity and clear sight, details that are mentioned several times in the story. The name "Fortunato" contrasts with the boy's disastrous fortune in the story. The silver watch with which Gamba bribes Fortunato is reminiscent of the thirty pieces of silver by which Judas Iscariot was bribed by the chief priests to betray Jesus in the Bible.

Jeffrey L. Buller

MATRYONA'S HOUSE

Author: Aleksandr Solzhenitsyn (1918-   )
Type of plot: Social realism
Time of plot: 1953
Locale: Tal'novo, a village "somewhere in central Russia"
First published: "Matrenin dvor," 1963 (English translation, 1963)

Principal characters:

MATRYONA VASILIEVNA GRIGORIEVA, the protagonist, an elderly, ailing widow, the narrator's landlady

THE NARRATOR, called Ignatich by his landlady, a former prisoner, now a teacher of mathematics

ILYA MIRONICH GRIGORIEV, Matryona's first love, the older brother of her eventual husband, Efim

KIRA, the daughter of Ilya and his wife, given by them to the childless Matryona to rear

The Story

The story of Matryona Grigorieva's life and death is told—and remarked on—by a narrator whose full name is not given, but whom one may take to be a spokesperson for the author. That is, like Aleksandr Solzhenitsyn, the narrator has served time in labor camps and has now taken up residence in a village where he will teach mathematics in high school. As the author taught in several places during his exile from 1953 to 1957, following his release from prison, the setting of "Matryona's House" is a composite of villages in Uzbekistan and in the Ryazan and Vladimir districts of the Soviet Union and is thus a generalized Soviet village, here given the fictional name Tal'novo. The village of Tal'novo is set in contrast to the nearby Soviet collective farm of Torfoprodukt ("Peatproduce"), with its processing factories.

As time passes from summer to winter, one learns from the narrator that his landlady, though a childless widow, has a foster daughter, Kira, who is now married. Anticipating her own death, she has bequeathed to Kira one of the several small structures that make up her dwelling place (the Russian word *dvor* means "homestead," rather than merely "house"). The actual cottage in which Matryona and her boarder live, though built within living memory of the villagers, seems almost ancient. The caulking has come loose from the logs, and in its walls live myriad mice and cockroaches. The cottage has begun to decay, just as Matryona has become old and sickly.

In a series of casually introduced flashbacks, one learns that Matryona had loved Ilya Grigoriev before he went away to war in 1914. When he failed to return at the expected time, she married his younger brother Efim (an act that, the reader will find, invokes the adage "Marry in haste, repent at leisure"). When Ilya returns at last from a

German prisoner-of-war camp, he tells Matryona that if Efim were not his brother, he would murder the pair of them. He then scours the area for another woman named Matryona and marries her.

The other Matryona bears her husband six children, all of whom survive to maturity. Matryona-married-to-Efim also has six children, but none lives longer than six months. Then comes World War II, and Efim is called up for military duty. Unlike Ilya, Efim does not return. Matryona thus becomes a widow; she would have been childless but for Kira, the other Matryona's youngest daughter, given to her to rear.

As the reader grows more and more sympathetic to the decent, tolerant, and passively suffering Matryona, he becomes increasingly aware of the tension created by the vindictive and greedy Ilya. Ilya insists that the promised outbuilding be given to Kira (who is, after all, still his daughter), and finally Matryona agrees.

The process of numbering, dismantling, and moving the logs of the hut is a lengthy one, complicated by February snows, the necessity of transporting the lumber some thirty-five kilometers to Kira's village, and the ritual requirement of drinking great amounts of moonshine vodka before departing. Matryona accompanies the men to the railroad crossing—and there she is killed when one of the sledges hangs up on the tracks and is smashed by a train. Through his greed, Ilya's threat of murder is thus implicitly fulfilled.

Ilya may be seen as representing the newer, urban values of ambition and materialism, while Matryona embodies the older Russian spirituality, fatalistic acceptance, and naturalness. The narrator recognizes Matryona's essential goodness as a kind of revelation or epiphany at the end of the story: "None of us who lived close to her perceived that she was that one righteous person without whom, as the saying goes, no city can stand. Neither can the whole world."

Themes and Meanings

The central theme of "Matryona's House" has its focal point in Matryona herself. She is presented by her didactic author not so much as a generalized moral ideal as the embodiment of all that is worth preserving in the old ways of the Russian peasant. Solzhenitsyn looks primarily to prerevolutionary ideals (those of Matryona's childhood) and thus implicitly criticizes the new mores under the Communist regime. The author's attitude toward the values of contemporary Soviet society determines the second important theme of the story.

It will be seen that Matryona's homestead—with its wooden shingles and weathered logs, its withered garden and potted plants, its Russian tile stove and icons in the corner, and its nanny goat, large cat, mice, and cockroaches—constitutes an extension of Matryona herself. The dismantling of the outbuilding symbolizes or anticipates the death of the old woman; more than that, it warns of the death of rural Russia, of its ancient, time-tested ways that must not be forgotten. This extended symbolism is reinforced by the author's failure to tell the exact location of Matryona's village. He speaks of his desire "to go somewhere in central Russia . . . and vanish in the very heartland of Russia." He emphasizes the fundamental Russianness of

Tal'novo by placing it in the context of a whole series of villages with ancient names that stretch out from the railway deep into the interior. The author writes, "The names wafted over me like a soothing breeze. They held a promise of the true, legendary Russia."

Among the Russian virtues practiced by Matryona are her passive acceptance of her fate (including her tendency not to complain when suffering illness or adversity); her willingness to help others without thought of compensation—in general, her self-sacrificing nature; her ability to live easily in the world of nature (for example, being on good terms with the mice and cockroaches); her practicing of old folkways, such as weaving on a hand loom; and a nonostentatious piety that includes displaying icons in a corner of her cottage but not praying aloud or in public. Solzhenitsyn refers to her also as "pagan" and superstitious, but this merely enhances her idealized Russianness. The fact that she is not very intelligent, not very ambitious, and does not like "new things" similarly marks her as typically Russian.

Another trait that Solzhenitsyn especially admires, and that he seems to feel is very Russian, is Matryona's willingness to work—"an infallible means of restoring her good spirits." In addition to collecting peat, scrounging tree stumps, and gathering hay for her goat, she picks bilberries and bottles them for the winter. She also works for the collective farm when asked. About work, she says, "Now to my way of thinking, when you work, you work—no gossiping, but get on with the job, and before you know where you are, it's suppertime." These views are precisely those of the protagonist in Solzhenitsyn's *Odin den Ivana Denisovicha* (1962; *One Day in the Life of Ivan Denisovich*, 1963).

Matryona's virtues are held up to the defects of Communist civilization, embodied here in the manners and morals of the "Peatproduce" collective farm, with its smoke-belching peat factories, its rumbling tractors, and even the railroad track that it has lured into the once virgin land. Also attacked are the uncaring regional bureaucracy, the indifferent medical clinic, and the careless teaching practices in the high school. The toilers in these institutions seem to have lost all feeling for the work ethic. That, together with the greed, selfishness, and "materialism" exhibited by many of the peasants—and by Ilya in particular—is perhaps meant to characterize the moral failure of Communism. The author is probably aware, however, that such pervasive social defects are as much a characteristic of the Soviet Union's transition to an urban society—occurring at a very rapid pace in the 1960's—as of Communism per se.

When he wrote this story, Solzhenitsyn was at least theoretically willing to hope that Soviet Communism was capable of positive change. Thus, when he gives the time of the story as 1953, he reminds the reader that the tyrant Joseph Stalin is dead and the time of the thaw has begun. A similar hope is expressed in the replacement of a black leather door in the education office by a glass partition: the diminishing of paranoid secrecy. Thus, although the tone of the story, especially at the end, takes on the character of an apocalyptic warning, the author nevertheless provides a basis for hope that the new society may be at least somewhat receptive to Matryona's virtues.

Style and Technique

Despite the later mutual hostility between Solzhenitsyn and the Soviet Union, "Matryona's House" has been a powerful influence on other Soviet writers. Although similar stories extolling rural virtues had already appeared by 1963, Solzhenitsyn's story must be regarded as the paradigm of the new literary genre that came to be known as "village prose." This genre is basically noninnovative in style while setting forth the sentimental philosophy of Slavophilism, or Russian nationalism. It appeals to the essential conservatism of Russians—including those at the helm of the Communist Party, who have tended to revive strictly Russian values as other national groups in the Soviet Union have increased in number relative to the Russian population.

In its details, Solzhenitsyn's style reflects the larger Slavophile philosophy. For example, he strives to use only Russian words and to avoid all those of Western origin. One reason he rejects the collective farm is that it bears an ugly, Westernized name— "Torfoprodukt."

Solzhenitsyn employs several motifs that act as omens of Matryona's death: the mice and cockroaches rustling in the walls, the dismantling of the house, the death of the old woman's cat, the coming of winter, and the several negative references to the railroad. When Matryona is finally killed by the train, one suddenly recognizes the parallel with Anna Karenina (1875-1877; English translation, 1886). In her character, Matryona is rather like Pasha in Leo Tolstoy's "Father Sergius," while Ilya seems to have his origin in Tolstoy's moralistic play about peasants, *Vlast tmy* (1888; *The Power of Darkness*, 1902).

Other brief allusions to Russian literary works may be seen in the overcoat that Matryona has made for herself when she finally starts to receive her pension (Nikolai Gogol's famous story) and the frequent references to Matryona's three sisters (Anton Chekhov's play). The extreme symmetry of the story (two Matryonas, with six children each) echoes the structure of folktales. The final words of the story, quoted above, seem to reflect a Russian version of the Hasidic myth of the thirty-six just men (called the *lamed vav*), without whose anonymous virtue the earth would be destroyed.

Further emulating the manner of folktales, Solzhenitsyn employs groups of three in a significant manner. The story itself is divided into three parts; three people are killed when the train crashes into the sledge; the coffins lie in the village for three days; a song is repeated three times in the funeral service; and so on. The fact that three people are killed perhaps suggests the three who died on Calvary; this reading is supported by the fact that the coffins remain in the village on Friday, Saturday, and Sunday, and that Matryona died in the ninth hour. The concluding description of her as that one righteous person without whom no city can stand marks her as a most interesting female symbol of Jesus Christ. She is sacrificed in Solzhenitsyn's tale so that the Russian ideal for which she stands may live.

Donald M. Fiene

MAY DAY

Author: F. Scott Fitzgerald (1896-1940)
Type of plot: Parody
Time of plot: May 1-May 2, 1919
Locale: New York City
First published: 1920

>*Principal characters:*
>GORDON STERRETT, a Yale graduate
>PHILLP DEAN, a former classmate of Sterrett
>CARROL KEY, a draftee, one of the drab set
>GUS ROSE, another drab draftee
>GEORGE KEY, Carrol's brother, a waiter
>EDITH BRADIN, a date of Yale men
>PETER HIMMEL, a Yale student
>JEWEL HUDSON, a woman of the drab sort
>HENRY BRADIN, Edith's brother, a writer for a Socialist paper

The Story

This story employs the May Day rioting of 1919 as the historical reality that impinges on characters existing at different social levels and about to collide. The double plot brings together the privileged and a drab underclass and reflects the multiple standards of an apparent democracy. Irony in this story is always near the surface, but as action mixes levels, judgments are urged increasingly. Romancelike, the story's plots are interlaced.

The main plot involves a Yale group reunited by an event less important than political unrest, the Gamma Psi dance. Most secured by privilege is Philip Dean, who was graduated immediately before the fight for democracy's sake. Dean radiates physical comfort, spending his first scene in the story polishing his body and the rest enjoying unfettered self-indulgence. He is rich enough to play at will, callous about others' needs, and self-righteous. Near the bottom of this group and slipping fast is Gordon Sterrett. His once expensive suit is shabby now, announcing his need before he does in Dean's room at the Biltmore. Since returning from France, he has lost a job and has become involved with Jewel Hudson, a common woman whom he cannot love. He needs money to study art and to break from Jewel, to whom he is attached by drunken letters. This whining failure would probably gain no sympathy at all if Dean were less insensitive toward him. Even so, his fall is parody.

Edith Bradin is more interesting. As she nears the end of her May days, accompanied by Peter Himmel, the quintessential awkward undergraduate, she is given the chance to rekindle her affection for Gordon as a love from his better-dressed and less-drunk days. The successful floater through social events cuts herself loose from her clumsy escort and, after an attempt to regain the past, from Gordon, too, hoping only to save some pieces of experience for future lovers. If there were no more to this character, she might be dismissed as mindless; she experiences an anxiousness, however, that leads her to admit to her brother, Henry Bradin, that she sees an incongruity between her party life and his radical causes.

Along the way, a subplot pushes members of the lower orders toward encounters with the privileged. Carrol Key and Gus Rose, two "human beings" temporarily released from service, desert an anti-Socialist mob and prowl for alcohol, which it is illegal to sell to servicemen. They find Carrol's brother, George Key, a waiter at Delmonico's, where the Yalies have easily gotten too much alcohol. George, the soldiers' link to booze, brings them inside the club to a broom closet, the only place for them among the dissipated privileged. When Himmel spots them there, the distance separating social levels is painfully clear, as is the irony of Himmel's drunken toast, "We're all Americans! Have another." From this camaraderie, Himmel can escape whenever he tires of slumming.

Minor foils contribute much to plot and theme. Jewel Hudson, appearing briefly at a crucial moment, sees Edith leave the Biltmore and judges accurately the other's freedom to move about unimpeded by protective waiters. When Jewel hauls Gordon down and presses her claim, she shows more feeling for him than have his lofty friends; when the marriage he commits with her drives him to despair, the judgment is more against his weakness than her tenacity.

Another important character appearing only briefly is Henry Bradin. Having had the privilege of education and experience as a teacher, he works at social causes. Though he is realistic about the difficulty of effecting change, he has trouble making positive contact with the masses; rather, it is when anti-Socialist soldiers storm his second-story office that the social orders collide, breaking Henry's leg and forcing soldier Key out the window to his death in the street below.

The chaos moves to Child's, where the shards of the upper-class partygoers meet in early morning. From there, Dean and Himmel rampage through other restaurants, demanding drink and breakfast and finally arriving at a parody of their high place, "heaven," atop the Biltmore. On the way, they pass Edith in the company of the "plain stout man" she has picked up at the dance—her form of slumming—and a "puzzled, spellbound" brute of a soldier. The shifting omniscience that glimpses these passings rests finally on Gordon Sterrett as he awakes to marriage and puts a bullet in his head.

Themes and Meanings

In much of his fiction, F. Scott Fitzgerald treated the real barriers lying beneath the illusion of access to opportunity. Henry Bradin, the philosophical spokesperson who labors amid New York City's incongruous mix of glittering fantasies and bleak social realities, tells his sister, "The human race has come a long way . . . but most of us are throwbacks. The soldiers don't know what they want, or what they hate, or what they like." Like others in American literature since Mark Twain's mobs, "They're used to acting in large bodies, and they seem to have to make demonstrations."

Fitzgerald understands social categories and knows that the type, "most" who are "throwbacks," includes not only George Key and Gus Rose but also many near the top and certainly Edith Bradin, the recipient of the lecture. The privileged also move in crowds and demonstrate: Consider Philip Dean and Peter Himmel's drunken prance, complete with placards—a hollow parody of the upsurging frustrations of society's servants. Money isolates in their illusions the "most" who have it; only a few, Henry and perhaps Edith, combine some awareness and the power of position. They are potentially tragic. Jewel Hudson, arguably the most abused of all, though intelligent and sensitive, lacks the privilege to rise above the pathetic. Gordon Sterrett cannot bear reality; the others, high and low, have hardly glimpsed it.

Violent dislocation is imminent because all can walk through the marketplace and most can purchase baubles; happiness eludes them, however, and those who have acted as society's servants are reaching for more in a blind way that does most damage to themselves. As pressure for access builds, however, means will be found to accommodate it, democratic or otherwise, by those who will tell the crowds "what they want" and "what they hate" and "what they like." Democracy is failing, and renewal seems unlikely because society lacks the critical mass necessary to transform it.

Style and Technique

Sharp contrasts stress social cleavage in an apparent paradise. Most noticeably, Fitzgerald's spatial rhetoric customarily pushes the lower orders down and out, while the privileged sort roam practically anywhere in any shape. Also underscoring separations are the language levels among the speeches. Drab talk is abbreviated utterance typified by repetition of monosyllables, contractions, and careless stops and endings: A street-orator presses his mob-audience to consider, "What have you got outa the war? . . . Look arounja, look arounja! Are you rich?"; Rose says loosely of Himmel, "He's sittin' lookin'"; Key thickly proclaims, "We gotta get another li'l bottle. . . . "; the police captain belongs to this order, too, as he shows by pleading, "Here now! This is no way! One of your own sojers got shoved out the back window an' killed hisself!"

These habits join in a brotherhood of sloppy speech some of the elements of revolution, ironically set against themselves. Even Himmel, lowered by alcohol, can sound drab: "A fight?—tha's stuff . . . Fight 'em all." Upstairs in Delmonico's, however, Himmel sets himself above the drab by a mocking interrogation: "May I ask why you gentlemen prefer to lounge away your leisure hours in a room which is chiefly furnished, as far as I can see, with scrubbing brushes," going on from that to a parody of how "the human race has progressed." In contrast to this rhetoric, Henry Bradin, the privileged person most concerned with human progress, sounds casual, a fact that supports the idea that he is the best hope for communication across the gaps.

Repeated imagery also teases together what cannot yet stay joined. A series of attempted embraces shows Peter's clumsiness, Gordon's spasmodic clutchings, and Jewel's taking command, with sudden grace, of a love she can hold only briefly, until his weakness reduces their marriage to a one-night stand.

Perhaps the most effective preparation for ironic cleavage is the exuberant fabular style of the beginning. New York appears to be the great city, of any realm, where all the ranks triumphantly celebrate in a vast materialistic binge, accompanied by bands. However, merchants from the outlands capture the furs, the varicolored slippers, and the bags of golden mesh, leaving little for ordinary folk to buy in celebration. The bag that Jewel Hudson carries measures her distance from acceptance by identifying her acceptance of a substitute: It is mesh, plain mesh, and she takes from it a dollar and bribes the drab waiter Key to bring her lover Gordon down to her.

William P. Keen

MEDUSA'S ANKLES

Author: A. S. Byatt (Antonia Susan Drabble, 1936-   )
Type of plot: Domestic realism, women's
Time of plot: The early 1990's
Locale: England
First published: 1993

> *Principal characters:*
> SUSANNAH, a middle-aged literary scholar
> LUCIAN, the owner of the salon she frequents
> DEIRDRE, a hairdresser

The Story

"Medusa's Ankles" presents a third-person narrative featuring Susannah, a literary scholar who frequents a hair salon featuring a print of the *Pink Nude* by the French artist Henri Matisse. The story relates Susannah's recognition of middle age. Her ongoing relationship with her hairdresser Lucian underscores her physical decline and brings Susannah literally to the breaking point.

Susannah was first attracted to Lucian's salon when she noticed the Matisse artwork through the plate-glass window. Cautious at first, she allows the salon owner to cut and blow-dry her hair. Susannah gradually finds a sense of ease in the salon, which looked like "the interior of a rosy cloud." The colors embodied in the Matisse nude, comforting shades of pink, blue, and cream, are reproduced in everything from the muslin curtains to the combs, brushes, and coffee cups.

Susannah enters the salon after decades of wearing a long, straight style because her hair is becoming lifeless. Its ends are split, broken, and frizzed. She is pleased to find the business of hair care greatly advanced from the 1950's when her mother's generation emerged from beauty parlors with artificial curls rolled, fried, and teased into place. Lucian wins Susannah's trust by giving her hair a short, bouncy cut. He assures her that the new style is "natural-looking," and Susannah takes his term to mean "young."

Her relationship with Lucian becomes somewhat one-sided, however. She does not confide in him, yet he confides in her. She observes that he is shallow and faddish. He does not possess an affinity for art but likes the *Pink Nude* because the color scheme matches his salon. She is surprised when Lucian confesses that he is thinking of leaving his wife for a younger woman.

Subsequently, Lucian closes the shop temporarily to sail the Greek Isles with his mistress. Once the shop reopens, Susannah finds the *Pink Nude* and its accessories removed. The refurbished design sports a cold gray and maroon interior of glass and steel. Susannah must make a speech on television as the recipient of a translator's medal and wants her hair to look especially good. In the midst of cutting her hair,

Lucian punctures his thumb as an excuse to take a break. As Susannah awaits his return, she contemplates her image in the mirror. When Lucian reappears, he takes up the scissors "listlessly," then confesses he is leaving his wife for good. As justification for his decision, he complains that his wife's fat ankles disgust him; she has "let herself go." Moments later, he is called away and sends Deirdre, another beautician, to finish Susannah's hair.

While the substitute stylist works, Susannah remembers when she was Suzie, a young woman with a chestnut mane, who made passionate love to an Italian student in Perugia. Once Deirdre finishes Susannah's hair, she protests that the "hideous" hairdo makes her look like a middle-aged woman. Her ankles are swollen, and the salon mirrors accentuate her wrinkles and sagging cheeks. Struck by her physical decline, Susannah grows increasingly agitated. An uncontrollable rage rises inside her like a flood.

In her mounting fury, Susannah hurls bottles of hair products into the mirrors and windows. Her rampage leaves no surface undisturbed. The salon becomes a battlefield of broken basins, scattered hairpins, glass shards, and puddles of hair gel and coloring foam. Lucian and the other stylists move to console her. Shaken, Susannah offers to pay for the damages. However, Lucian assures her he has insurance. Perhaps he will close the shop, he tells her, and go into business selling antiques with his mistress.

Susannah returns home to regain her composure and soak the insulting curls from her hair. Though her husband usually pays little attention to her, on this particular afternoon, he compliments her hairstyle, saying it makes her look twenty years younger, and then kisses Susannah on the nape of her neck.

Themes and Meanings

In "Medusa's Ankles," A. S. Byatt dramatizes Susannah's mid-life crisis. The realization that she is no longer attractive generates within her a sense of loss, anger, and frustration. The relationship Byatt creates between her protagonist and Lucian, the hairstylist, shows the differing ways men and women confront aging. In addition, the invocation of the Medusa myth in the title amplifies Susannah's plight.

The salon serves as a figurative fountain of youth. Although Susannah understands that Lucian, the shop owner, is self-centered, she tolerates his weaknesses because she relies on his skills to enhance her appearance. He, in turn, enables her to avoid the fact that she is growing old. Like Susannah, Lucian is also in denial. He is nearing middle age himself because he admits to having a teenage daughter, but conveniently, her exact age slips his memory. He bedecks his salon with glossy photos of youthful faces and surrounds himself with young employees. When he recognizes physical aging in his wife, he deserts her for a younger girlfriend.

Lucian's actions, which serve as an undercurrent to Susannah's dilemma, animate her calamity. In the pivotal scene when Susannah enters the remodeled salon, she sacrifices her own views to appease Lucian. When he solicits her opinion of the renovations, she claims it looks "very smart." However, Lucian has discarded the feminine décor of the salon in favor of harder, colder images. Black-and-white prints of adolescent models have replaced the painting of the *Pink Nude* with which Susannah identified. The gentle tones of pink and cream have been usurped by steely shades of chrome and maroon that make Susannah's complexion look gray rather than rosy.

The crisis arises when Lucian announces his divorce. As the hairdresser complains of his wife's fat ankles, Susannah observes her own swollen ankles rubbing against her shoes. In like manner, he ignores Susannah's urgency to look attractive for her television appearance and callously passes her to another stylist. When Lucian abandons Susannah, she feels the sting of rejection in symbolic sympathy with Lucian's forsaken wife.

Although Susannah is described as a linguist, university teacher, and classicist who can recommend insightful art books and gallery lectures, those attributes fade amid the glitzy lights of the salon. Susannah sees only an aging face that sags into "opulent soft bags." Even the pride that she ought to feel in receiving the translator's medal in a televised ceremony withers. She is convinced the camera will so magnify her imperfections that her words will be ignored. She has lost the "desire to be looked at."

In the Medusa myth, a beautiful maiden with dazzling tresses incurs the wrath of the jealous god Athena, who changes ravishing Medusa into a snake-headed monster. Similarly, Susannah's rage at her apparent disintegration transforms her into a violent creature who destroys the institution that cannot restore her lost youth or beautiful hair. She goes berserk and shatters the salon mirrors, splintering and distorting the reflections of Lucian and herself. Just as those who looked directly at the gorgon Medusa were turned to stone, Susannah finds that in middle-age, others have ceased to look at her. She has grown ugly and irrelevant. In contrast, Lucian pretends he is unaffected by time. Thus in "Medusa's Ankles," Byatt considers the significance of female body image and illustrates the inequities in the ways aging affects men versus women.

Style and Technique

Byatt's stories are well-constructed, clear narratives, rich in metaphor and vivid images. Her multilayered plots often incorporate references to specific artworks and are amplified by literary allusions. "Medusa's Ankles," for instance, is part of *The Matisse Stories* (1993), a collection of three tales inspired by particular Henri Matisse paintings. In addition, the volume includes a reproduction of a different Matisse drawing on each title page. The drawing for the "Medusa's Ankles" frontispiece is *La chevelure* (1931-1932) and features a woman's head inverted so that her long hair flows in opulent curves from the center to the bottom of the print. The drawing reinforces the setting of the beauty salon and also pictures Susannah's sense of loss in mourning the change age has brought to her once beautiful fall of chestnut hair.

In the text of the story, Byatt includes the description of Matisse's *Pink Nude*, which coaxes the protagonist into the beauty salon. Susannah is plump and therefore admires the "huge haunches" and "monumental knee" of the Matisse figure. However, her bond with the painting is brief because Lucian, the salon owner, eventually discards the artwork to suit his transitory tastes. The narrative describes the nude's round breasts as circular "contemplations" and "reflections on flesh and its fall." Susannah's physical decline is in opposition to the unchanging beauty the *Pink Nude* embodies. The beauty of the painting is eternal, but hers is not. She must come to terms with her mortality, a result of time's relentless movement and the fall of humankind.

In addition, Byatt constructs inherently ironic plots that incorporate unexpected events that produce a moment of discovery or revelation for the characters. For example, in the closing scene of "Medusa's Ankles," Susannah, the neglected wife, returns home after her destructive salon rampage still sporting the offensive middle-aged hairdo when, in a wry turn, her husband arrives. In uncharacteristic fashion, he actually notices her, praises the hairstyle that she despises, and bestows an unexpected act of affection by kissing her neck. Thus, the closing scene reinforces Susannah's sense of isolation, suggesting that no one, not even Susannah's spouse, understands how the woman perceives herself.

Paula M. Miller

A MEETING IN THE DARK

Author: Ngugi wa Thiong'o (1938-   )
Type of plot: Psychological, postcolonial
Time of plot: The early 1960's
Locale: Limuru, a village in Kenya
First published: 1964

> *Principal characters:*
> JOHN, a college-bound youth from a Kenyan village
> STANLEY, his father
> SUSAN, his mother
> WAMUHU, his girlfriend

The Story

"A Meeting in the Dark" tells the story of John, a young Kenyan man who worries most about what others, especially his father, think of him. John is consumed by a moral dilemma that he eventually fails to face with dignity.

The story begins with John thinking about the stories his mother used to tell him, particularly the story of the young girl who was deceived by an Irimu, an ugly ogre that had disguised itself as a handsome man. Unfortunately, John cannot remember the ending, and his mother no longer tells him stories.

John's father, Stanley, sees John and questions him about his upcoming trip to college in Uganda. John has been tense the whole time, worrying that his father will realize he has a secret. Overhearing the conversation, John's mother, Susan, rebukes Stanley for his harsh treatment of their son. Susan married Stanley before he converted to Christianity. Since his conversion, he has refused to let Susan tell John the tribal stories, and he blames Susan for their conceiving John out of wedlock.

John encounters a village woman who asks about his impending trip. She is pleased that John, although more educated in modern ways than most of the villagers, treats her with respect. John is pleased that she approves of him.

After a tense dinner with his parents, John sneaks out to visit his secret girlfriend Wamuhu. Unfortunately, only her parents are home. The mother is happy to see him, for she feels sure John is trustworthy and means to establish a long-term relationship with Wamuhu; the father is afraid that John will fail to respect Wamuhu because she has been circumcised. Female circumcision is traditional for their people, but now the educated young men did not want circumcised wives.

After Wamuhu arrives, John and she walk outside to be alone. Wamuhu assures him that nobody else knows that she is pregnant, but she also gives him only one more day to tell his parents. He thinks of the story of the young girl who followed the Irimu, and he promises to tell his parents that night.

Attempting to return home, John is sick with fear. He slumps to the ground in a cold sweat. He cannot face his parents and tell them of his mistake. He cannot say that he needs to marry Wamuhu, yet he does not know why he should not marry her. He does not even know to whom to pray: Would the Calvinist god believe him? Would the traditional god still listen?

John wakes up on the ground and remembers his discussion with Wamuhu. He walks home in the dark, contemplating the ways that marrying Wamuhu could ruin his life. In his mind, he blames her, her lack of education, and her tribal circumcision.

Back in his hut asleep, he dreams of being circumcised and initiated into the tribe. In the dream, he ends up in a strange land with two ghosts fighting over him, and as more ghosts enter the fray, he becomes nothing. Suddenly he is looking at the girl who followed the Irimu. He wants to help her but gets lost and afraid. Once awake, John tries to dismiss his dream. He considers the beauty of Limuru village, but he is going to Makerere, Uganda, to go to college as his father wishes.

He and his father shop for John's trip. John wonders why he has always feared his father. However, everybody fears Stanley, who has become a hell-fire preacher. He is strict with his flock, his family, and his villagers.

In the final scene, John desperately tries to convince Wamuhu to take money to say that someone else was the father of their unborn child. She refuses, and John becomes more and more upset and excited. Animal-like, he becomes breathless and foams at the mouth. He grabs her shoulders to persuade her. Images of his father and the villagers fill his mind. He violently shakes her. She runs away, but he catches her. He tries to hug her, but as she stops struggling, he realizes that he has killed her and can no longer keep any of it a secret.

Themes and Meanings

In this story, as in many of his other works, Ngugi wa Thiong'o explores the conflict of cultures brought about by British colonial rule in Kenya. John struggles because he does not feel comfortable in either the traditional Kenyan lifestyle or the educated, colonial lifestyle. With a strict Protestant preacher for a father and a Calvinistic headmaster at school, John feels restricted. He envies both the uneducated youth of the village, who he believes have more freedom than he, and the elder tribal folk, who seem to have a clear focus.

John's sense of alienation is reflected when he attempts to pray: He does not know which god to address in his prayers. He does not feel worthy of either the British god or the tribal gods. The tribal gods might be angry that he has not been initiated into the tribe. This makes him feel that he is not yet a man. His final action in the story, killing Wamuhu and their unborn child, contributes to his emasculation, for siring children is an important male trait. Instead of contributing to life, he has taken it.

Stanley represents a colonial paternalism: Just as Stanley has been convinced to blindly reject the traditions of his people, he tries to convince John to blindly reject those same traditions and espouse the new culture. Already, John has adopted his father's attitude toward his premarital sex, not merely the guilt, but the shifting of all blame to the female partner. John's attempt to pay Wamuhu off rather than marry her continues this refusal to take responsibility for his actions.

On the other hand, Wamuhu's family has remained tribal and apparently happy. Significantly, their hut is right in the middle of the village, suggesting that their lifestyle is central to the spirit of the village. However, following the old ways is not enough, for it does not prevent their daughter from being killed.

Style and Technique

The conflict between cultures is conveyed through a variety of techniques. For example, the characters' names suggest the dichotomy between cultures: John and his parents use Western names, while Wamuhu and her family use traditional African names. Ngugi considered names so important that in the 1970's he changed his own name from James Ngugi to the traditional name by which he is now known.

The setting, too, reflects the conflict between the traditional and the colonial cultures. Limuru village is contrasted with the new ugly villages (like Makeno) that developed during the emergency called the Mau Mau Rebellion against the British. John thinks of Limuru as a magical land of mist and hills and valleys; Makeno village enrages him and makes him feel trapped.

The initial tribal tale of the Irimu is the key to the story. The fact that John cannot remember the end of the story about the Irimu foreshadows the fact that he will not be able to find a suitable answer to his dilemma: He needs the traditional stories to help him cope with new situations, but he cannot remember them and his mother is not allowed to repeat them.

The Irimu emerges again when Wamuhu's father fears that John will not treat his daughter fairly. Her father knows that colonially educated boys often sleep with unmarried girls, leaving them pregnant and alone. He compares the situation of the tribe following the ways of the colonizers to the girl who chased the Irimu. She had nowhere to go, and in this refashioned world, neither does the tribe.

The importance of the traditional tale is emphasized at the end of the story, when John himself turns into the horrible Irimu: John foams at the mouth and his voice becomes hoarse; he chases Wamuhu, and a terrible anger wells up in him as he unwittingly shakes Wamuhu too hard. He seems to have a second mouth, and this double mouth offers her increasing amounts of money rather than appropriate assurances of marriage. Rather than becoming an enlightened, educated man, he has become an exploiter and murderer of his own people.

Kathryn A. Walterscheid

MELUNGEONS

Author: Chris Offutt (1958-   )
Type of plot: Regional
Time of plot: The 1990's
Locale: Rocksalt, Kentucky, a small Appalachian town
First published: 1993

> *Principal characters:*
> EPHRAIM GOINS, the town deputy and jailer
> HAZE GIPSON, a mountain man who has returned home after
>   many years in a northern city
> BEULAH MULLINS, an eighty-four-year-old member of an
>   opposing clan

The Story

Making use of the folklore tradition of mountain feuds, "Melungeons" focuses on Deputy Ephraim Goins, who, like the other two characters in the story, is a member of the mixed-race group that gives the story its title. The story begins when an elderly man comes into the town jail and asks Goins what he needs to do to get incarcerated. When Goins suggests, "defacing public property," the man urinates on the jailhouse steps and is put behind bars.

The man identifies himself as Haze Gipson, who Goins recognizes is a Melungeon, a member of a mixed-race community (Native American, African American, and white) who live in the Appalachian Mountains of Kentucky, Virginia, and Tennessee. He also recognizes the name "Gipson" as being the family name of a clan involved in an ongoing feud that began sixty years earlier over the carcass of an accidentally killed bear. Goins, also a Melungeon, has avoided involvement in the feud by joining the army during the Korean War and then living in town since his return.

Gipson explains that he has returned after all these years because he has missed every wedding and funeral his family has had. He tells Goins that he has gone up to the mountains to see his grandchildren and great-grandchildren, but that because he is the last of the old Gipsons still alive, he does not feel safe there.

The story then shifts to Beulah Mullins, an eighty-four-year-old member of the opposing clan, who, although she has not been off the mountain in fifty years, begins a long walk into town. When morning comes and Goins returns to the jailhouse, the old woman arrives. She reaches into her bag and takes out a blackened pot filled with squirrel stew, which she offers to Goins to prove the pot does not contain a file or a pistol. When Goins allows her to take the stew into Gipson's cell and goes back to his desk to eat, he hears a blast. The old woman has hidden a sawed-off shotgun under her long coat and has taken one last revenge against a member of her enemy clan. She willingly enters another jail cell to await her trial. After Goins locks her up, he opens the jailhouse door and begins walking toward the hills that are his ancestral home.

Themes and Meanings

Melungeons are a mixed race of dark-skinned people living in the mountains of Appalachia whose ethnic origins are mysterious. One recent theory is that they are descended from Moors who came to the New World in the sixteenth century with Portuguese explorers and then moved into the interior and intermarried with indigenous people. Some research has suggested that the word "Melungeon" comes from a Turkish word that means "abandoned by God." The dark-skinned, mixed-race people were often scorned by white settlers and driven out of the valleys and into the mountains where they lived relatively secluded lives.

Deputy Goins has suffered racial prejudice because of his mixed-race background. When an army dentist noticed that his gums were tinged with blue, he was assigned to an all-black company. Both black and white soldiers treated him with open scorn; thus he was doubly exiled and marginalized. This subject matter—a mixed-race person who suffers from prejudice—fits in with the 1990's literary focus on multiculturalism and racial conflict. However, this is less Chris Offutt's central thematic interest than it is a general thematic background for the sense of isolation and alienation that pervades the story.

"Melungeons" also is a variation of the oldest subtype of the Kentucky mountain story—the family feud, à la the Hatfields and McCoys in the late nineteenth century. Whereas the feud between the Gipsons and the Mullins started over disputed bear meat, the famous Hatfield-McCoy feud started over a dispute about a pig. The original cause of such feuds does not matter after a time, for other, more powerful elements take over: the tendency to never forget ancient grudges, the total devotion to one's family, and the stubborn insistence that there must be revenge for a past wrong.

When Beulah Mullins, one of the last old members of her clan, hears that Gipson, one of the last of his clan, has returned, it seems inevitable, given the characteristics of the mountain feud, that she will strike a blow for her family. Beulah—whose birth was never recorded and who has never voted or paid taxes and has not been off the mountain in fifty years—makes the trip into town in answer to a bone-deep demand; over thirty people from the Mullins and the Gipson clans have died in the feud that started sixty years earlier. She goes to the jail with a sawed-off shotgun hidden in her skirt, implacable in her duty, kills the last of the old Gipsons, and takes his place in the jail cell.

A related theme of the story is the contrast between the old ways of the mountains and the increasing modernization that Beulah observes when she makes her first trip to town in many years. On her last trip, there were wagons and mules, but now there are automobiles and neon signs. Beulah, now eighty-four years old, is a living icon of the old mountain life, and just as it is inevitable that she will kill Haze Gipson, it is also inevitable that she and all that she represents is destined to pass away. At the end of the story, Deputy Goins walks out of the jail and heads toward the nearest slope, having been called by this primitive revenge ritual back to the hills from whence he came.

Style and Technique

Although heavily dependent on the rural area of the eastern Kentucky mountains, "Melungeons" is not a conventional regional story, complete with phonetic spelling of dialect words and a heavy emphasis on rural folkways. Nor is it a political story about social injustice or rural poverty. It is less realistic than it is stylized and classical in its structure and rhythm. The story does not exist to exploit regionalism but is meant to be a story about the nature of tragic inevitability and thus is told in the restrained classical tones of a mythic story. Offutt tries to capture the life of the people of the mountains of eastern Kentucky, not by realistically depicting their everyday lives, but by penetrating to their universal humanness. He understands and respects his characters and does not exploit them as trendy exotics or revel in their local color quaintness.

Consequently, rather than trying to present a tape-recorded reproduction of mountain speech, Offutt tries to capture the simple, almost sixteenth century rhythms of that speech. The restrained style of the story also gives the three characters a sense of dignity that makes them larger than life. Deputy Goins is a man of few words, living very much alone amongst people he has know for years but has never really known. Haze Gipson has returned from his exile, knowing that he will probably be killed, but resigned and dignified as he waits in jail for the inevitable. Beulah Mullins is presented as a silent implacable avenger of past wrongs. When she visits the jail and waits for Goins to let her in Gipson's cell, her eyes are slow and patient, as if she could wait a month without speaking or moving, "oblivious to time and weather."

Some critics may accuse Offutt of not focusing sufficiently on the poverty-stricken status of mountain folk, presenting them too poetically. However, as "Melungeon" suggests, Offutt is not a modish socialist with a multicultural message about marginality, but a carefully controlled craftsperson who knows how to use language to reflect the essential humanness of his characters. In this story, he aligns himself more with the lyrical beauty of Eudora Welty than with the coarse cruelty of Erskine Caldwell. He is not a sociologist playing back a tape recording or illustrating political abstractions, but an artist, transforming mere external reality into poetic meaning.

Charles E. May

MEMORIES OF THE SPACE AGE

Author: J. G. Ballard (1930-   )
Type of plot: Apocalyptic and catastrophe, science fiction
Time of plot: The future
Locale: Cape Canaveral, Florida
First published: 1982

Principal characters:
> DR. EDWARD MALLORY, a former National Aeronautics and
>   Space Administration (NASA) doctor
> ANNE MALLORY, his wife, also a former NASA employee
> HINTON, an astronaut imprisoned for murdering a colleague in
>   space
> GALE SHEPLEY, daughter of the astronaut Hinton murdered

The Story

"Memories of the Space Age" is presented through the consciousness of Dr. Edward Mallory. Most of the story is narrated in the third person, although a few passages, ostensibly taped by Mallory, present events in the first person and illustrate his increasingly troubled mental state.

Once employees of the National Aeronautics and Space Administration (NASA), Mallory and his wife, Anne, have returned to a deserted Cape Canaveral for the most ambiguous of reasons. Both Florida and the space program have been abandoned, casualties of a spreading "space sickness" brought on by a "psychic fissure" in time and space apparently resulting from space flight itself. Both Mallory and his wife are suffering from the sickness, which seems ultimately to leave its victims in a timeless trance. As a result, their journey from Vancouver, British Columbia, took them two months and their drive down the Florida coast several more weeks. However, while Anne, the sicker of the two, wants to flee, Mallory insists on remaining. Behind their ambivalent behavior looms the mysterious figure of Hinton, a one-time astronaut responsible for the first murder in space.

Mallory and Anne are staying in a deserted hotel near Cape Canaveral, and it is from there that Mallory watches a pilot flying antique aircraft over the empty space center day after day. Mallory comes to suspect that the pilot is Hinton, who has recently escaped from prison. Subsequent events seem to confirm his suspicions, for when he ventures out in a police car to scavenge food from an abandoned supermarket, he is first buzzed by a glider and then strafed by a triplane.

Suffering a return of the space sickness, Mallory wanders through an abandoned theme park into a small zoo containing a tiger and other animals. This is the home of Gale Shepley, who identifies herself as the pilot of the glider. She is also the daughter of Alan Shepley, the astronaut Hinton murdered. It was Mallory who had teamed

Shepley with the unbalanced Hinton on the fateful flight; therefore, he bears some of the responsibility for the crime. Now Gale is waiting in Florida, hoping that the decaying orbit of the capsule bearing her dead father will cause it to crash nearby. She has even forged a peculiar pact with Hinton, who she now believes may not have killed her father after all.

After Mallory leaves Gale's compound, Hinton catches up with him and flies him to the heart of the deserted space center. Leading Mallory to an upper deck of the last remaining launch platform, Hinton apologizes for shooting at Mallory, who he had assumed was a police officer. More abstractly, he explains that flight and time are connected and that "to get out of time we first need to learn to fly." When Hinton fails to throw Mallory off the deck, he instead kidnaps Anne, the one person who seemed attracted to him in their years at NASA. Soon afterward the center is destroyed in a spectacular fire, presumably set by Hinton, and he and Anne leap into the flames. Do they perish? Victims of the space sickness, they may be locked forever in fiery flight.

As the story ends, time is slipping away from Mallory. He waits in Gale's compound while the young woman patrols the beaches for the long-awaited capsule. Once it crashes, he anticipates that he and Gale will go away together. However, his thoughts are on the tiger cage, whose keys he holds in his hand. He envisions opening the cage and embracing the flames of the tiger's pelt "in a world beyond time."

Themes and Meanings

Unlike most of his fellow science fiction writers, J. G. Ballard has seldom dealt with the technology or hardware of space travel. His interests lie not in outer space but in inner space, in the interplay between technological change and the human psyche. Therefore, "Memories of the Space Age" is a psychological and symbolic drama little concerned with gadgets.

At one point Ballard likens Mallory and Anne to Adam and Eve returning to paradise. His portrait of Florida—its marinas and parking lots empty, its shopping malls abandoned—is an ironic version of such a paradise. Mallory even sees the animals of Gale's tiny zoo as inhabiting a Garden of Eden, a state of existence drained of time in which the lamb really can lie down safely with the lion. However, Ballard alters this central metaphor to suggest that Mallory and Anne are like Adam and Eve suffering from a sexually transmitted disease. However, the exact nature of this modern couple's disease is at first unclear.

"Memories of the Space Age" repeatedly suggests that paradise is static and unchanging. Such a state recalls the common human experience of childhood (and the common human image of life in the womb) as a timeless golden age. The space sickness, whose symptoms include increasingly frequent periods of abstraction and vagueness, seems to restore this state. Mallory even calls the sickness the "dreamtime," a reference not only to sleep but also to the period in which, according to Australia's native peoples, the gods created the world and everything in it. The memory of this state, Mallory believes, is retained in the most primitive parts of the human brain.

If these suggestions are taken seriously, then the plague that has driven millions of people from Florida represents not a disease but a recovery from disease, an escape from human awareness of the passing of time. Consciousness itself may constitute the Fall, in which Adam and Eve defied God and were driven from the Garden of Eden. Hinton's suggestion that the space program was really aimed at escaping time becomes not the nonsensical raving of a madman but the insight of a visionary.

Style and Technique

Like many of Ballard's stories, "Memories of the Space Age" is scarcely believable by realistic standards. It is resolutely nonrational. However, it succeeds, thanks largely to Ballard's visionary imagination and to his persuasive skill in conveying his meaning with metaphors and similes. His language is often abstract, yet capable of embodying strikingly poetic ideas. "Time had flowed out of Florida," he writes in a typical passage, "as it had from the space age. After a brief pause, like a trapped film reel running free, it sped on again, rekindling a kinetic world." On other occasions, Ballard creates jewel-like images so striking that their significance is almost secondary.

"Memories of the Space Age" relies on a complex imagery of birds and flight. Ballard has used such imagery again and again, most extensively in the novel *The Unlimited Dream Company* (1979). Space flight itself is linked to the sickness spreading from Florida (if indeed the timeless present it offers its sufferers can be called a sickness). Hinton flies a series of planes through the skies above Cape Canaveral, and Gale (who calls herself Nightingale) soars through the story in a human-powered glider. Before Hinton attempts to push Mallory off the launch platform, he assures him that they will join the birds in flight. Ballard has routinely equated flight with freedom, and here he links those two states with timelessness as well.

Ballard makes use of another potent image, that of fire. Anne and Hinton throw themselves into the flames, and Mallory dreams of a similar kind of life in death, embracing the flames of the tiger's pelt. This imagery is probably suggested by English poet William Blake's poem "The Tyger" (1794), which opens with the famous line, "Tyger, tyger, burning bright." As presented by Blake, the tiger is a being both evil and passionately beautiful, a creature whose ambiguity Ballard exploits in the final lines of his story.

Grove Koger

A MEMORY

Author: Eudora Welty (1909-2001)
Type of plot: Psychological
Time of plot: The 1930's
Locale: A lake near Jackson, Mississippi
First published: 1936

> *Principal characters:*
> THE NARRATOR, a woman looking back on her youth
> A FAMILY of ugly people

The Story

The narrator remembers herself as a young teenager, lying beside a lake after her usual morning swim. In early adolescence, she judged everyone and everything and reacted so timidly to the physical world around her that she could bear to observe things only through a frame she made with her hands.

Through this frame she sees herself projected onto the world. Every leaf that falls, every bird that flies overhead, she imagines is trying to signal her, to leave her some message. Each moment is fraught with the heightened significance adolescents impose on their environment. Like most adolescents, this girl is obsessed with a secret love, a love hopelessly unexpressed that appears "grotesquely altered in the outward world."

Her love sent her a signal one day on the stairs; she allowed herself accidentally to touch his wrist as they passed, and he pretended not to notice. Since that day she has cherished the memory of their touch, a memory that she can bring to mind at any moment and burnish with longing until it "would swell with a sudden and overwhelming beauty, like a rose forced into premature bloom for a great occasion."

Since that day she has worried over him, watched for him, wondered about him, but has never spoken to him or made any direct contact. Her love, she confesses, made her both an observer and a dreamer. She obsesses over the dangers she imagines he may face, and when one day in Latin class he gets a bloody nose, she falls over in a dead faint. "I saw red—vermilion—blood flow over the handkerchief," she remembers, and adds, "I recognized it."

Lying on the beach, she polishes the memory of the day on the stairs and ponders the sense of mystery and danger that surrounds this memory in her mind. The reality of children running on the beach vies with the reality of the memory: Which is the real moment? She cannot distinguish.

While she is in this state of half-dream and half-wakefulness, a family of bathers comes and lies down too close to her. Once she notices them, she cannot look away or escape their physical presence. They are loud, squirming people whose bathing suits "did not hide either the energy or the fatigue of their bodies, but showed it exactly." It is as if the ugly physical reality of life has penetrated the careful frame the teenager has constructed around her world, and re-created her careful, static world of incredible beauty as a caricature of itself.

The family consists of a man, two women, and two boys. One boy is so grotesquely fat that he protrudes from his costume at every turn. In the manner of young boys, he runs about wildly, pinches his brother, and kicks up sand. The other boy is younger and skinnier; he avoids his brother by throwing himself into the lake whenever he is threatened.

The adults lying on the sand also are unruly by the careful standards by which the narrator judges the world. The man lazily scoops sand against the older woman's legs. She is fatly terrifying, a mountain of flesh that may disintegrate at any moment. Her breasts loom large and droopy; her arms teem with fat that hangs "like an arrested earthslide on a hill."

The younger woman wears a bottle-green bathing suit and embodies a jealous rage directed at the man and woman. When the man heaps wet sand into the older woman's bathing suit "between her bulbous descending breasts," the angry young woman cannot keep from laughing derisively. The teenager wishes fervently that they were all dead.

The scene suddenly erupts with action. The angry younger woman joins the boys in running and jumping along the beach. They scream, the fat woman smirks, and the sounds of frantic squeals and "the fat impact of all their ugly bodies on one another" take over the teenager's consciousness so completely that she sees that family's antics even with her eyes closed. She tries desperately to withdraw into herself, into her dream-memory, but even while she feels the familiar heavy sweetness the memory always brings, she cannot bring the stairs or the touch back to life.

She looks up once more, only to see the fat woman stand up and casually dump the sand out of her suit. The narrator wonders with horror if that fat woman's breasts themselves had turned to sand. The family is gone before she can bring herself to look up again, and when she does, although she tries to frame the world again within the safe boundaries of her hands, she cannot. This hour on the beach, she understands, must now be added to the memory of her old love, accompany it, and give it added sweetness.

Themes and Meanings

Most people experience a moment in life when they understand, for the first time, the physical realities of the world and their own relationship to them. Eudora Welty presents that moment here with objective clarity and great emotional depth. When the story begins, the teenager is a child. By the time it ends, she has entered adulthood. The difference lies in her new perception of the world. The ugly family on the beach breaks into a world that centers around the young girl. This world is neat and well ordered, almost fanatical in its insistence on conformity. Within it lives a moment, a memory, that embodies perfection.

Just as the young boy is betrayed by his physical body when he suffers a nosebleed, the memory is betrayed by a world that contains the ugly reality of the family of bathers. Life is not perfection, nor is it orderliness; instead it is a messy span of seventy or so years, where age reduces beauty to wrinkles and fat, and where the cherished perfection of a newly budded body must be replaced by the casual indifference the fat woman shows as she dumps sand from her bathing suit. Her body is no longer a shrine, but merely a home for her spirit, filled with cracked linoleum and peeling paint.

This is the mystery the teenage girl dimly glimpses when she thinks of the boy, and what she finally understands as she lies on the beach, overcome with horror at the other bathers. Opening and closing her eyes, she sees light and dark as two sides of the same coin and understands that "the sweetness of my love seemed to bring the dark." Still physically innocent, she has nevertheless glimpsed one of the primal mysteries of the universe.

Style and Technique

Welty grew up in Jackson, Mississippi, and has seldom left its confines, yet manages to address in her fiction, with quiet stealth, human issues that transcend time and place. This bittersweet summer memory, recalled by the narrator over the distance of some years, is as quiet as the summer day it depicts, wrapped in the same sultry air, and illuminated by the same glaring, steely sun as the memory itself.

A plot, Welty has mused in her essays, "is not a pattern imposed; it is inward emotion acted out." She strives in this story, as in all of her work, to write the depths of human character and emotion, to find in the small moment the motives that drive everyone. The vermilion red of the blood running across the white handkerchief, reminiscent of menstrual blood gushing unbidden, is so instantly recognizable to the young girl that she faints. A surreptitious touch, never acknowledged, becomes the object of passionate fantasy. The young girl's body lies unexplored, so alien to its owner that she never relates a single physical sensation throughout the entire story. However, she is fascinated and horrified by the sagging, obvious body of the fat woman.

Welty expresses the change in the girl in the symbol of the white pavilion that lies near the lake. At the beginning of the story, it has a "clean pointed roof," while at the end, it lies "small" and "worn," so pitiful that the girl bursts into tears. The framed world she saw through her hands has changed irrevocably, and she, like the boy she loves, must face the world "solitary and unprotected."

Susan E. Keegan

MEN UNDER WATER

Author: Ralph Lombreglia (1954-   )
Type of plot: Domestic realism
Time of plot: The 1980's
Locale: Cleveland, Ohio
First published: 1986

> *Principal characters:*
> REGGIE, a writer who works as an aide and scriptwriter-assistant
>   to a wealthy man
> TINA, his wife
> GUNTHER, a newly rich real-estate baron
> LUKE and
> OTIS, members of the rock band Acid Rain and Gunther's tenants

The Story

In the Peter Pan Diner in Cleveland, Ohio, Reggie and Gunther struggle to write a screenplay. They are trying to make money and to create an artistic project, but they are also trying to make sense of their own lives. Their collaboration is marked by both a sense of desperation and a certain companionship, but their relationship is not one of equals. Reggie is a professional writer who, like the vast majority of his peers, cannot adequately support himself through his writing. Gunther is a newly wealthy real-estate baron who is seeking to parlay his riches into fame in cinema. Reggie originally answered an advertisement for a handyman, but when he revealed himself to be a writer, Gunther was determined to exploit his new employee's talent on behalf of his nascent ambition to make it big in motion pictures.

Gunther reveals his darkest aspects in an incident with a Pakistani woman. The woman, one of Gunther's tenants, complains that the heat is not working in her house but to no avail. As a way of striking back at Gunther, Reggie gives the woman her landlord's unlisted telephone number. This act is the high point of Reggie's resistance against Gunther and almost causes Gunther to sever the collaboration with Reggie.

Gunther's treatment of the Pakistani woman outrages Reggie's wife, Tina, and makes her realize she can no longer tolerate the tradeoff between the financial rewards her husband gets from Gunther and the loss of integrity these rewards entail. In other words, she feels she is stained by association because of Reggie's subordination to Gunther.

The members of the rock band Acid Rain live in a renovated Victorian mansion owned by Gunther. Luke, the band's lead singer, and Otis, its blind keyboard player, complain about the plumbing in their house in a petulant way that does not show them to their best advantage. Reggie persuades Gunther to call Roto-Rooter, the famous plumbing concern, admitting that he cannot handle the task alone and that he needs outside help to do the work. Otis, the musician, is not convinced that the problem will be solved, but Gunther and Reggie manage to make him accept this outcome without further confrontation. In the process, Gunther thinks of an idea for a motion picture—the ultimate film about a rock-and-roll band.

Gunther introduces Reggie to Joseph, an elderly Hollywood tycoon, and Willie, the tycoon's chauffeur. Gunther and Reggie pitch the idea for the rock-and-roll film to the men from Hollywood. They try to persuade Joseph that such a film would appeal to the average American moviegoer. Joseph, whose musical tastes lean more to classical works, appears unconvinced. However, Gunther holds out hope that his Hollywood ship will come in one day.

At the end of the story, Reggie and Gunther have come to a reluctant compromise. Gunther has admitted his wrongdoing with respect to the Pakistani woman. Reggie, for his part, has accepted his continuing status as Gunther's subordinate and has come to appreciate the material comforts Gunther provides. The story's final image, of Reggie and Gunther's splashing around in a swimming pool playing with a scuba tank, illustrates both their material comfort and their spiritual and moral submergence. As "men under water," they are protected by the same factors that confine them psychologically.

Themes and Meanings

The most important aspect of a Ralph Lombreglia story is that a plot summary is not adequate to even sketch its lineaments, much less render its full meaning. The cliché of the talented but struggling writer compromising himself by accepting a rich man's money may at first seem to fit Reggie's relationship with Gunther. However, Gunther is not a conventional character. He has become rich only recently, is immature rather than deliberately evil, and has some genuine creative instincts.

The other characters also are individuals, not types. Willie and Joseph are presented on equal terms, even though one is a chauffeur and the other a tycoon. This mirrors some of the anarchic strangeness of real life, all too often neatened in order to suit fictional formulae. The treatment of Willie and Joseph also signals Lombreglia's treatment of issues of social class. The characters themselves are not working class, despite the initial setting of the diner as the source of artistic inspiration.

The rock band Acid Rain is the wild card in the story's menagerie of personages. The truculence of Luke and Otis is testimony to their ignorance and narcissism. Otis has no interest in anything outside himself, even a film about his vocation. However, the way Gunther and Reggie see rock music, as a subject for a film and an untapped market, betrays their exclusively entrepreneurial perspective on creativity. In a way, the musician's surly lack of interest in a money-making film is a guarantee of artistic integrity.

The irony is that no one involved in the production of the screenplay likes rock and roll; Reggie cannot stand Acid Rain, the rock group, either as performers or as people. The filmmaker-landlord is a symbol of the person who wants to have his cake and eat it too—to have the fun of creativity without taking the risks because the person always maintains control. What Gunther offers Reggie is not prestige but an almost narcotic sense of assurance, a promise that Reggie will be taken care of, that he will not have to assume the burden of living by his own convictions.

Lombreglia's combination of subtle observation of contemporary life with a cogent knowingness and a freewheeling sense of humor garnered his work acclaim, particularly in the early to mid-1990's, although he has not gained the high visibility in contemporary literature that he deserves.

Style and Technique

Lombreglia's writing style is adaptable, informal, and not restricted to one setting or tone. In his works, Lombreglia presents life as actually lived among his own social class and type of people, as far as such categories can be strictly defined. He does not romanticize his milieu, but he is not entirely cynical about it either.

The exploitation of the Pakistani woman shows that there are some things that Reggie will not tolerate. The idealism that the struggling writer displays in dealing with this incident is his finest moment. Gunther's money has not brought him satisfaction. His interest in the motion pictures is a combination of wanting fame and his name in lights and a legitimate need to express himself creatively in a way that his business and real-estate concerns do not permit.

The story's closing image of men under water is soothing, spiritual, and transcendent as well as lulling. It shows a kind of apathy, a willingness to accept the easy way out, and a certain complacency. There is a false sense of spiritual comfort about this scene, which in fact represents a kind of moral quiescence.

There are frequent references by commentators on Lombreglia to the jazziness of his style. This jazziness is a result of the sense of improvisation in his work, the way in which he sets out a given situation and then riffs around it with dialogue and anecdote. Lombreglia does not state but shows. Even some of the basic exposition in "Men Under Water" occurs within direct quotes: For example, all the discussion of the rock-and-roll film, one of the story's key elements, transpires within quoted speech.

Lombreglia is difficult to place within the prescribed history of the American short story. He shares with the minimalists or "dirty realists" of the 1980's an interest in domestic situations, the complexities of friendship and marriage, and a zest for the telling detail. However, his works do not have the air of deliberate, ascetic suppression of affect often found in minimalist stories. Similarly, though his vocabulary is not extravagant, it is not constricted or pared down. His style is conversational, with both the colloquial verve and the occasionally extravagant rhetoric found in everyday conversation. This enables Lombreglia to give a view of his character's inner life, as refracted through their external speech. There is, indeed, a fascinatingly "outgoing" quality in Lombreglia's introspection.

Nicholas Birns

MENESETEUNG

Author: Alice Munro (1931-   )
Type of plot: Psychological
Time of plot: 1854-1903
Locale: A small town in rural Ontario, Canada
First published: 1988

Principal characters:
ALMEDA ("MEDA") JOYNT ROTH, a young, unmarried woman
JARVIS POULTER, her neighbor, a widower

The Story

"Meneseteung" begins with a description of a book of poems, dated 1873, and of its author, Almeda Joynt Roth, as she appears in a photograph. In her preface to the book, Almeda explains that in 1854, when she was fourteen, her family moved to a part of Ontario, Canada, that was then just being settled. There her father's business prospered, and he built a comfortable home for his family. However, within the next six years, her sister, her brother, and her mother all died, leaving Almeda to keep house for her father until his death twelve years later. According to her preface, she wrote poetry to occupy her time and to help assuage her grief. The unidentified narrator concludes this section of the story with summaries of several poems and a brief comment on verse forms.

In the second section of the story, the narrator draws on the local newspaper, the *Vidette*, for details about daily life in 1879 in the small Ontario town where Almeda lived. It is then pointed out that Almeda's house faces on a respectable street, but that the back bedroom, where she sleeps, looks out on a section into which no decent woman would venture. The researcher also relates information in the *Vidette* concerning Almeda's neighbor, Jarvis Poulter, a prosperous widower.

The narrator notes that though Poulter often walks Almeda home from church, he has not yet made a declaration of his feelings. Almeda often wonders what marriage to him would be like. Then one hot Saturday night, she is awakened by noises in the street below. A woman is being beaten. Although Almeda feels she should do something to help, she cannot find the courage to venture into that back street. When the sounds stop, she fears that the woman may have been killed, but in the end, Almeda goes back to sleep. At daybreak, she looks out of the window again, and to her dismay, she sees a motionless figure on the ground just outside of her fence. Hastily putting on a robe over her nightclothes, Almeda goes down to investigate. The woman is not moving. Certain that she has been killed, Almeda runs next door to get Poulter. However, when he prods the woman, he discovers that she is not dead but just dead drunk. Contemptuously, he gets her up and sends her away.

The episode has an odd effect on Poulter. Seeing Almeda in her night clothes, her hair flowing free, for the first time, he can imagine her as his wife, and he takes a significant step in courtship by announcing that he will return later that morning to walk her to church. However, Almeda is both physically ill and emotionally disturbed. She leaves a note on the front door, informing Poulter that she is too unwell to go to church and then locks herself into the house. All day she sits motionless, while words and images flood into her mind. She concludes that she must write poems, or a poem, called "The Meneseteung." Finally she goes up to bed. She knows what her future holds.

The final section of the story begins with two death notices from the *Vidette*. One announces Almeda's death in 1903, the other, Poulter's, in 1904. "Meneseteung" ends with the narrator's uncovering Almeda's grass-covered tombstone, on which is carved only one word, "Meda," a name used in one of her poems.

Themes and Meanings

Like much of Alice Munro's other fiction, "Meneseteung" focuses on isolation and alienation. In the small, highly conventional Ontario towns that the author so often uses as her setting, to be a nonconformist is to be a social outcast. In her obituary, Almeda is measured against her society's ideal of what a woman should be. In her early years, when she attended church regularly, took part in church activities, took care of her parents, dressed neatly, and did nothing to surprise the other townspeople, they approved of her. The fact that this society based its judgments purely on appearances is reflected in the early Almeda's being labeled a profoundly religious person, while the later Almeda, whose inner life was far richer, is assumed to have been mentally ill simply because she was unkempt and unpredictable. Although the writer does not approve of the way Almeda was mocked in those later years and deplores the cruel prank that probably resulted in her death, there is in the obituary a subtle suggestion that women who ignore society's expectations do so at their own risk.

What the *Vidette* cannot know is that Almeda did not just drift into eccentricity but chose to be different from others in her community. Almeda seems to have no doubt that she could slip into a wife's role as easily as she had that of the dutiful daughter and even that of the pious community leader. However, although she believes that married life with Jason Poulter would not be unpleasant, it would require Almeda always to play a part. What she realizes on that fateful morning is that in a patriarchal society, no woman who is attached to a man can ever be free. Even though as the wife of Jason Poulter she would never be abused and beaten, as the drunken woman had been, if she married him or anyone else in that small town, Almeda would have to sacrifice her own identity. The price of protection would be a life of pretense.

Although the *Vignette* does commend Almeda for writing poetry, the obituary writer clearly does not understand that though in the very conventional preface to her book Almeda called her poetry merely a pastime, the truth was that poetry was her whole life. By writing poetry, by utilizing her imagination to see beneath the surface of life and then capturing her discoveries in words, Almeda can enter a world that the townspeople do not even know exists. Ironically, although in later life Almeda is isolated from the rest of the community, it is not she, but the community, that is out of touch with reality.

Style and Technique

Munro's use of everyday details for symbolic purposes is amply illustrated in "Meneseteung." For example, the fact that the Roth house faces onto a street of undeniable respectability but backs up to a street that terminates in a slum not only makes it possible for someone as genteel as Almeda to come into contact with a drunken, dissolute woman, thus furthering the plot, but also it symbolizes the choice Almeda herself must make, between conformity and freedom, between mindless propriety and alienation from respectable society.

Munro strengthens her symbolic effects by filtering details about her characters either through their own minds or through the minds of others. Thus it is Almeda who notices that Poulter's clothes are like those her father wore and that, also like her father, he smells of wool and tobacco and shaving soap, all of which Almeda equates with both masculinity and authority. Almeda's appearance at Poulter's door in her nightclothes leads Poulter to think of her as a wife because ordinarily no one but a husband would see her so informally dressed, and under the circumstances, there can be no question about her respectability. Later, when Almeda is on the way to bed, she notes that she has remained in her nightgown all day, that she has not washed herself, and that she is tracking grape juice through the house. Almeda herself sees these details as symbols of the dramatic change that has taken place in her mind and spirit. As she says, they show that she now has a different definition of reality.

Munro's superb craftsmanship is also demonstrated by her handling of voice. The story begins and ends with an unnamed narrator, presenting whatever objective details can be found about a woman who lived more than a century before. Soon, however, the author begins to report Almeda's thoughts, occasionally making a brief foray into Poulter's mind. In the final section of "Meneseteung," the narrator-researcher returns with the two obituaries, a report of the search for Almeda's tombstone, and finally, an admission that much of what has been presented has been mere guesswork, not fact but fiction. What Munro means the reader to realize, however, is that given Almeda's definition of reality, the fictional version of what made a woman into a poet may in fact be the truth.

Rosemary M. Canfield Reisman

METAMORPHOSES

Author: John Cheever (1912-1982)
Type of plot: Fable
Time of plot: The 1960's
Locale: New York City, its suburbs, and upstate New York
First published: 1963

> *Principal characters:*
> LARRY ACTAEON, an investment banker
> MRS. VUITON, another partner in Actaeon's firm
> ORVILLE BETMAN, a singer in television commercials
> VICTORIA HEATHERSTONE BETMAN, his wife
> MRS. PERANGER, a society matron
> NERISSA PERANGER, her daughter
> BRADISH, a New Yorker intent on stopping smoking

The Story

"Metamorphoses" consists of four related sketches. In the first, Larry Actaeon is a partner in the New York investment-banking firm of Lothard and Williams. One day he charges into Lothard's office to find Lothard and another partner, the stunningly beautiful Mrs. Vuiton, naked. From that point, "Some nameless doom seemed to threaten his welfare." Going into a bar to kill time before a directors' dinner meeting, he is almost attacked by a dachshund belonging to one of the regular customers. The bartender tells him that the dog is there every day but has never so much as barked at anyone. Arriving at the apartment house where the meeting is to be held, Actaeon is mistaken for a delivery person by the elevator operator. At the dinner meeting, no one seems to notice this boisterous, energetic man who is accustomed to commanding attention. The conductor on Actaeon's train home thinks that he recognizes the banker as a waiter. Arriving home, Actaeon is set on and apparently killed by his dogs.

Orville Betman, in the second sketch, is a singer in television commercials: "Whatever he praised in song—shoe polish, toothpaste, floor wax—hundreds and thousands of men and women would find his praise irresistible. Even little children heeded his voice." Betman falls in love with Victoria Heatherstone the first time he sees her, and he tells her that he wants to marry her. She eventually succumbs to his pursuit of her but cannot marry him because she thinks that her invalid father, an Anthony Trollope scholar, will die if she leaves him. When the old man has a stroke, is told by his physician to leave the city, and moves to Albany, Betman and Victoria marry, but she keeps the marriage secret from her father and spends every summer with him at Temple Island near Lake St. Francis. One summer, Betman is overwhelmed by his love for his wife and goes to retrieve her. When a maid refuses him entry, he begins singing an air by George Friedrich Handel, and Victoria comes to him. Although she says that her father is dying, Betman begs her to come with him, and she does. Because he loves her so much, her smile distracts him; their car veers into the wrong lane and is crushed by a truck; she is killed. Betman goes on singing in commercials.

The third sketch is the story of Mrs. Peranger, who dictatorially rules the social life of her community, wielding "the power of rudeness so adroitly that she was never caught in an exposed position, and when people asked one another how she got away with it they only increased her advantage." A widow, her only son dead, Mrs. Peranger lies about the beauty and accomplishments of her daughter, Nerissa, a "wasted spinster of thirty," who seems "burdened with the graceless facts of life." Nerissa constantly falls in love with janitors, mechanics, and tree surgeons only to have her outraged mother end her romances. After they swim in the marble swimming pool built by her grandfather, Nerissa falls in love with a veterinarian. When Mrs. Peranger uses her influence to have the veterinarian's hospital closed, grief-stricken Nerissa dies. A few weeks later, Mrs. Peranger begins hearing Nerissa's voice from her daughter's beloved pool: "Mother, Mother, I've found the man I want to marry."

In the final sketch, Bradish decides to stop smoking and almost immediately begins to see himself as "more sagacious, more comprehensive, more mature." The next day, however, Bradish becomes obsessed by what he has given up. At a cocktail party, he sees a young woman as having hair the color of Virginia tobacco, wraps his legs around her, and buries his face in her hair until he is pried loose. Everyone he encounters looks and smells like some variety of cigarette, cigar, or pipe. His final undoing is mistaking a child for a Lucky Strike: After attacking her, he is arrested.

Themes and Meanings

John Cheever frequently makes direct and indirect allusions to the figures of classical mythology in his fiction: to Jupiter and Venus in "The Country Husband," Hecate in "The Music Teacher," and Odysseus in "The Swimmer." In "Metamorphoses," Larry Actaeon is named for the hunter who, according to Ovid's *Metamorphoses* (c. 8 C.E.; English translation, 1567), accidentally sees Artemis bathing, is changed by her into a stag, and is pursued and killed by his own hounds. Orville Betman is based on Orpheus, who was endowed with superhuman musical skill. After the death of his wife, Eurydice, Orpheus goes to the land of the dead to attempt to regain her. Hades, dazzled by Orpheus's music, allows him to have her if neither looks back when they leave the underworld. Orpheus, seeing the sun again, turns back to share his delight with Eurydice, who disappears. Nerissa, described as "nymphlike," is inspired by the myth of Nereus, who could change his shape, and his water-nymph daughters, the Nereids. Cheever invokes mythology to underscore the universality of his characters' joys and agonies, and to convey the permanence of the human condition.

In addition to recalling Ovid, Cheever's title brings to mind Franz Kafka's *Die Verwandlung* (1915; *The Metamorphosis*, 1936), a disturbing vision of modern paranoia. Like Kafka's Gregor Samsa, Cheever's characters deceive themselves about their ability to control their lives, only to end in disaster. Larry Actaeon plays with the natural order of the world by breeding a Finnish wolf to a German shepherd, and the

American Kennel Club refuses to recognize his new breed, labeling it a "monstrosity." Just as unnaturally, Actaeon has no true identity of his own. When the elevator operator insists that he looks like a deliveryman, Actaeon replies, "I am worth nine hundred thousand dollars. I have a twenty-two-room house in Bullet Park, a kennel of dogs, two riding horses, three children in college, a twenty-two-foot sailboat, and five automobiles." Because he can define himself only through his possessions, he would be nothing without them.

Orville Betman is also a materialist, prostituting his talent in television commercials, growing wealthy with little effort. His work defines the superficiality of his life without Victoria: "He always sings of inessentials, never about the universality of suffering and love, but thousands of men and women go off to the stores as if he had, as if this was his song." Mrs. Peranger also perverts nature and love by claiming that everyone loves and adores the homely Nerissa, by insisting that "she is too attractive for words," and by refusing to let her daughter live her own life and find the love that she so desperately needs. Bradish, in the only nonmythological sketch, allows his weakness for tobacco to change his perception of the world.

All four protagonists are punished for their inability to understand themselves and their relations to their world. In their willingness to settle for half-truths, they lose their sense of proportion, their perception of reality. Cheever's tales, through their connection with ancient myths, show mankind's perpetual absurdities but also how people's follies make them human.

Style and Technique

Each sketch in "Metamorphoses" demonstrates Cheever's surety of style and tone. His description of Larry Actaeon, after seeing the nude Mrs. Vuiton, emphasizes Actaeon's commonplaceness and foreshadows his impending change of appearance: "He spent the last of the afternoon at his window, joining that vast population of the blunderers, the bored—the empty-handed barber, the clerk in the antique store nobody ever comes into, the idle insurance salesperson, the failing haberdasher—all of those thousands who stand at the windows of the city and watch the afternoon go down." An additional irony is that as the day declines, so does Actaeon.

Cheever deftly varies the tone from Actaeon's absurd story, to Betman's tragic one, to the more comic yet still pathetic account of Mrs. Peranger and her daughter, to the slapstick silliness of Bradish's obsession. Realizing an abrupt shift is necessary after Victoria's death, Cheever opens the third sketch with "To watch Mrs. Peranger enter the club was a little like choosing up sides for a sand-lot ball game; it was exciting." Cheever's approach to fiction, a skillful melding of literary tradition, insight into contemporary life, and distinctive style, is also exciting.

Michael Adams

THE METAMORPHOSIS

Author: Franz Kafka (1883-1924)
Type of plot: Psychological, fantasy
Time of plot: The early twentieth century
Locale: Prague
First published: "Die Verwandlung," 1915 (English translation, 1937)

> *Principal characters:*
> GREGOR SAMSA, a traveling salesperson who finds himself
>   transformed into a bug
> MR. SAMSA, his father
> MRS. SAMSA, his mother
> GRETE SAMSA, his sister
> THE CHIEF CLERK, the office manager of Gregor's firm

The Story

The first sentence of "The Metamorphosis" has become one of the most famous in modern fiction: "As Gregor Samsa awoke one morning from uneasy dreams he found himself transformed in his bed into a gigantic insect." Franz Kafka thus subverts narrative tradition by stating his climax in his initial declarative sentence. He then organizes three subclimaxes in three frustrated attempts by Gregor to escape from the imprisonment of his bedroom. The novella's three sections divide it into three clearly identifiable parts, showing Gregor in relation to his occupation, his family, and his divided psyche.

In the first section, Gregor accepts his fantastic transformation matter-of-factly, perhaps wishing to bury its causes in his subconscious mind. Instead of worrying about the mystery of his metamorphosis, he worries about the nature and security of his position as traveling salesperson for a firm whose severity he detests. Even though his boss treats him tyrannically and overworks him, Gregor needs to keep his degrading job because his father owes his employer a huge debt. He can only dream of walking out into freedom in five or six years, after having slowly repaid it from his earnings.

The firm's chief clerk appears in the Samsas' apartment at 7:10 A.M. and inquires why Gregor failed to catch the 5:00 A.M. train to work. He yells at Gregor that he is "making a disgraceful exhibition" of himself, exploiting his anxiety and insecurity by telling him that his sales have slackened to the point where he faces dismissal. Gregor responds with an agitated speech replete with a succession of special pleas that contradict one another: He is only mildly indisposed, yet cannot rise from his bed; he feels all right, yet is struck down with a sudden malady. "Oh, sir, do spare my parents!" he cries hysterically—but the chief clerk cannot understand him: Gregor has lost his capacity for human speech. Frantic, Gregor manages to open his bedroom door by painfully turning its lock key with his toothless mouth. When he scuttles into the clerk's sight, however, ostensibly to reassure him about his health and competence, he instead puts him into panicked flight, with the clerk relinquishing his cane as he leaps down the stairs. This will prove Gregor's sole triumph over authority; it is short-lived. His father snatches up the cane and "pitilessly" drives his son back into his bedroom, with Gregor bleeding heavily from the agony of squeezing his broad, clumsy body through its half-door.

In the second section, Gregor's isolation and alienation intensify. The reader learns about his relations, past and present, with his family; they have been characterized by concealment, mistrust, and exploitation on the father's part. Gregor now discovers that, contrary to what he was led to believe, his father did not go bankrupt when his business failed but managed to save and augment a tidy sum while relying on Gregor's income to sustain the Samsas. Ever the dutiful son, Gregor "rejoiced at this evidence of unexpected thrift and foresight." Gregor's mother is gentle, selfless, weak, and shallow; in the story's development she becomes increasingly her husband's appendage. His sister Grete is his favorite; he once hoped to subsidize her violin training in a conservatory. However, though she now ministers to his animal needs, she fails him emotionally, suggesting that his furniture be removed from his room—thereby stripping him of the last vestiges of his humanity. Desperately, Gregor scurries about the room trying to protect his possessions; his mother faints; his sister shakes her fist at him; then his father, now vigorously self-confident, joins battle with his son again and bombards him with apples, one of which grievously wounds his back. As Gregor is about to faint with pain, he sees his mother, her clothes in disarray, embracing his father "as she begged for her son's life."

In the third section, Gregor, defeated, yields up all hope of returning to the human community. His parents and sister form a triadic unit that shuts him out, as Gregor's miserable existence now slopes resignedly toward death. The wound in his back festers agonizingly; his room becomes a repository for the household's discarded articles and rejected food; he eats almost nothing. He does erupt from his room for what turns out to be the last time when he hears his sister perform a violin recital for roomers the Samsas have taken in; horrified by his appearance, they give immediate notice and threaten the family with a lawsuit for damages. Grete thereupon presides over a family conference in which she brusquely announces her determination to get rid of Gregor: "If this were Gregor, he would have realized long ago that human beings can't live with such a creature." Gregor agrees with her, and that night dies a sacrificial death, reconciled with his family as he thinks of them "with tenderness and love." The next morning the relieved Samsas make a holiday of his death day, review their promising prospects, and admire Grete's blooming young womanhood, bursting with crude health as she stretches her body in the spring sunshine.

Themes and Meanings

Kafka's art is so profoundly ambiguous and multivalent that no single analysis can completely comprehend it. This evaluation will stress a psychoanalytic, expressionistic interpretation.

Gregor's metamorphosis accomplishes several of his aims: First, it frees him from his hated job with an odious employer by disabling him from working; second, it relieves him of the requirement to make an agonizing choice between his filial duty to his parents—particularly his father—and his desperate yearning to emancipate himself from such obligations and dependence. It thus enables him to "bug out" of his loathsome constraints yet do so on a level of conscious innocence, with Gregor merely a victim of an uncontrollable calamity. Moreover, Gregor's fantasies include aggressive and retaliatory action against the oppressive firm. He accomplishes this by terrorizing the pitiless, arrogant office manager, who tells him, "I am speaking here in the name of your parents and of your chief." On the conscious level, Gregor pursues the clerk to appease him and secure his advocacy for Gregor's cause at the office; subconsciously, his threatening appearance and apparently hostile gestures humiliate his hated superiors.

Gregor's change also expresses his sense of guilt at having betrayed his work and his parents, at having broken the familial circle. It is a treacherous appeasement of this guilt complex, inviting his isolation, punishment, and death. His loss of human speech prevents him from communicating his humanity. His enormous size, though an insect (he is at least two feet wide), his ugly features, and his malodorous stench invite fear and revulsion. Yet his pacific temperament and lack of claws, teeth, or wings make him far more vulnerable than when his body was human. His metamorphosis therefore gives him the worst of both worlds: He is offensive in appearance but defenseless in fact, exposed to the merciless attack of anyone—such as his furious father—ready to exploit his vulnerability.

"The Metamorphosis," then, can be seen as a punishment fantasy with Gregor Samsa feeling triply guilty of having displaced his father as leading breadwinner for the family, for his hatred of his job, and resentment of his family's expectations of him. He turns himself into a detestable insect, thereby both rebelling against the authority of his firm and father and punishing himself for this rebellion by seeking estrangement, rejection, and death. Insofar as Gregor's physical manifestation constitutes a translation of the interior self to the external world, "The Metamorphosis" is a stellar achievement of expressionism.

Style and Technique

This novella is an extended literalization of the implications of the metaphor used in its initial sentence. Gregor is metamorphosed into an insectlike species of vermin, with Kafka careful not to identify the precise nature of Gregor's bughood. German usage applies Kafka's term, *Ungeziefer,* to contemptible, spineless, parasitic persons, akin to English connotations of the work "cockroach." Gregor's passivity and abjectness before authority link him with these meanings, as Kafka develops the fable by transforming the metaphor back into the imaginative reality of his fiction. After all, Gregor's metamorphosis constitutes a revelation of the truth regarding his low self-esteem. It is a self-judgment by his repressed and continually defeated humanity.

By having Gregor become a bug, Kafka has also accomplished a bitterly parodistic inversion of a traditional motif in fairy tales. In folktales the prince is rescued from his froghood by the princess's kiss; beauty redeems the beast with love. In Kafka's version, however, the "beauty," the sister Gregor loves, is horrified by her beastlike brother and condemns him to die rather than changing him back through affection. The most poignant aspect of the story is the inextinguishable beauty of Gregor's soul, as he consents to his family's rejection of his humanity and dies on their behalf.

Kafka illustrates Gregor's subjection to his father by the implied parable of the episode involving the lodgers. This triad duplicates the Samsa triad that excludes Gregor, with the middle lodger, like Mr. Samsa, exerting authority over his supporters. Initially they intimidate and threaten the Samsas. After Gregor's death, however, Mr. Samsa curtly orders these boarders out of the apartment, and they accede without a struggle—their apparently awesome power proves spurious. Equivalently, had Gregor found the self-confidence to revolt openly against both his firm and his father, had he walked out on his job and asserted his autonomy against his family's clutches, he, too, could have matured into triumphant adulthood and would not have needed the disguised hostility of his metamorphosis.

Gerhard Brand

MIDAIR

Author: Frank Conroy (1936-   )
Type of plot: Psychological
Time of plot: 1942 to the 1980's
Locale: New York City, Boston, and Philadelphia
First published: 1985

Principal characters:
SEAN KENNEDY, a writer and teacher
MR. KENNEDY, his father, a mental hospital escapee

The Story

Sean Kennedy's father is nearly a stranger to him; his mother has told him and his older sister, Mary, that he is in a rest home. When Sean is six years old, his father inexplicably shows up one day and takes the children home to the apartment where they live with their mother. Neither child has a key; Mr. Kennedy, who is dangerously and frighteningly exuberant, climbs with them to the roof of the four-story building to break into the apartment through the fire escape. Once inside the apartment, he excitedly begins to rearrange books and then insists on washing the windows. The fearful children stay with him, not knowing what else to do.

When the doctor and orderlies from the asylum arrive to take the father back, Mr. Kennedy grabs Sean and climbs with him to the windowsill. Sean stares down at the cracks in the sidewalk for a time, until they are finally pulled back in.

Sean apparently has forgotten the incident when the story encounters him next as a college student. Terrified of being alone, he is determined to find a wife. He marries a reserved and intelligent young woman, and for four years they drift, never becoming closer. They have two sons, John and Philip.

The next two scenes show Sean's attraction and aversion to his father's imbalanced pattern: Drunk and determined to get into his mistress's apartment, Sean climbs to the fifth story to try to break in. Gradually he comes to his senses and gives up. Later, a friend talks about the tragic death of a baby who fell from a window. Sean reacts violently, rushing home to see if his sons are all right. Neither incident, in Sean's mind, has any connection to the event in 1942.

His oldest son is six when Sean finally realizes that his marriage is foundering. He is heartbroken over what he fears will be the loss of his sons. Twelve years later, as Sean commutes between his two jobs, readers see that he has remained close to his sons. In the last scene, Sean is trapped in an elevator between floors with a young man much like Philip. When the young man panics, Sean comforts him and gives him confidence until the elevator moves.

After this incident, Sean remembers his father carrying him out on the windowsill more than forty years earlier. He has never thought about this incident before, and the resurfacing of this memory might explain much about his past he does not understand.

Themes and Meanings

Frank Conroy's autobiography, *Stop-Time* (1977), uses the concept of time as focus. In "Midair," time seems to freeze around certain events in Sean's life. The story also compresses time to show how a long-forgotten childhood event causes Sean to retreat from those closest to him. Sean so dreads spending his life alone that he marries a woman whom he does not love; his chosen work, writing, suffers from his inability to understand himself and the outside world. He acknowledges that the world is dangerous but hopes that he can find strength there. His wife, fearful for reasons of her own, wants to withdraw. It is only when their two sons are born that Sean begins to write about his childhood and to have some incidents slowly revealed to himself. Here time begins to unravel for him.

Time, as a theme, is closely connected to Sean's strength as a father. He begins to see his children as part of a continuum through time, and to reject the out-of-control behavior shown by his own father and by himself early in his marriage. The pattern of hanging over the edge of sanity shown so vividly in the first scene is repeated when Sean climbs his mistress's roof, obsessed with the idea of finding sanctuary and safety inside her apartment. Unlike his father, Sean recognizes reality and is able to save himself. When he hears the story of the baby falling from the window, his horror takes a more positive form: He vows to protect his sons.

The midair phenomenon appears again in his memory of John leaping through the air to catch a baseball. Unlike the other scenes, this suspension was a thing of beauty, joy, and pride to Sean. He begins to understand that being on the edge can be controlled. He was once afraid of flying but now commutes weekly by air because he has conquered his anxiety. Similarly, when the elevator breaks down, he is able to comfort the young man in a fatherly way. His fear of falling—emotionally and physically—has let him identify with the stranger. The incident in the elevator triggers powerful memories of his father putting him in grave peril years ago.

Conroy's portrayal of Sean as a committed and strongly protective father is rare in fiction. Although Sean is inarticulate about his feelings for his sons, he has a trusting and complex relationship with them. The fathers and sons in the story often reverse roles: Mr. Kennedy's insanity makes him behave in an irrational and childish way, while young Sean tries to find a way out of the situation; years later, when Sean breaks down at the thought of leaving his sons, Philip knows without being told that his father has been crying. When Sean mistakes the young man in the elevator for Philip, he feels a rush of inexpressible love for him, and time seems to slow down.

Style and Technique

The structure of "Midair" is unusual. Its collapsing of time has the effect of rushing the reader forward. The story begins in 1942, when Sean is six, and ends when his oldest son is twenty. Brief incidents from the 1960's, when Sean marries, has an affair, and has two sons, are framed by the two longer sections, which show Sean's father and Sean in midair. The forty years between these two incidents elapse with the barest of explanations; readers are told that nothing happened for the first four years of

Sean's marriage; that the marriage founders, but not why; and that Sean eventually teaches in a university, but not what happened in the intervening years. The emphasis is on the lightning-like depictions of Sean on the edge. These incidents illustrate the frightening precariousness and fragility in Sean's physical and inner life.

The pattern of a character hanging in the balance—between danger and safety, insanity and sanity, recklessness and control—is established with the first appearance of Mr. Kennedy. Sean's father, so vividly portrayed, gives Sean a nightmare vision of a person who has completely lost touch with reality, one who is in danger of falling over the edge. The pattern is cemented with later incidents: Sean's climbing on the roof, John suspended in the air, and Sean and the young man trapped in the elevator. Even Sean's wedding, so briefly reported, encompasses the two extremes: While the ceremony is being performed, a building is being demolished outside, foreshadowing the disaster of the marriage. Sean's tendency to distance himself from others because he fears losing control is shown through these patterns.

The issue of balance is shown through Conroy's careful use of tone. Sean's tears at the thought of losing his boys is the only highly emotional scene; the rest of the story has a deliberately flat and tightly controlled tone, letting the reader analyze the significance of certain events. The language is also restrained; for example, Sean is reported as being exultant at the births of his children, but any other reaction must be found through observing his relationship to his sons throughout the story.

Conroy leaves out long stretches of time in order to focus on incidents that made Sean the kind of man, husband, and father that he is. He shows that a repressed childhood trauma can repeat itself in adult life; the story's last line shows Sean's astonishment at the resurfacing of the memory of his father. There is a suggestion that acknowledging this memory will pull Sean permanently back into the world.

Michelle Jones

THE MIDDLE YEARS

Author: Henry James (1843-1916)
Type of plot: Fable
Time of plot: The late nineteenth century
Locale: Bournemouth, England
First published: 1893

Principal characters:
DENCOMBE, a middle-aged writer who is dying
DOCTOR HUGH, a young physician
THE COUNTESS, a wealthy matron
MISS VERNHAM, the countess's companion

The Story

A middle-aged writer, Dencombe, is ill and feels his strength ebbing irrevocably. He has just had a novel published, *The Middle Years*, and is reading it on a cliffside bench in the sea resort of Bournemouth, on the English Channel coast. As he meditates on his waning energy, he is distracted by three people who are walking slowly along the beach. He imagines that the young man is the son of the large, opulent matron, and that the humble young woman, possibly a clergyman's or officer's daughter, is secretly in love with the man. The object of her affection seems, however, more absorbed in a book he is carrying than in her.

Dencombe's surmise, although wrong in detail, turns out to be essentially right regarding the trio's relations. He learns that the older woman, wealthy and childless, has taken a strong liking to the young man, a recently graduated physiologist called only "Dr. Hugh." Although she will probably leave him a considerable inheritance, she exacts from him absolute devotion and attention. The young woman is her paid companion, whose only prospect is to promote Dr. Hugh's cause with his employer, so as either to marry him after the countess's death or else pressure him into buying her off.

The main concern of the story is introduced as the young doctor separates himself from the ladies, sits on Dencombe's bench, and each man discovers that the other is holding a copy of *The Middle Years*. Dencombe decides not to reveal his identity immediately: He wants an uninhibited evaluation of his novel by the young man. He quickly gets it: Dr. Hugh is wildly enthusiastic, convinced that it is the best thing the author has done yet.

Dencombe is equally enthusiastic. He believes that he has finally achieved the maturity of style and craft toward which he has labored all of his life. He is painfully conscious of the deadly irony that his struggles and sufferings have finally resulted in mastery at the point when his life is slipping away. Dencombe asks himself why his growth as a writer has been so arduously slow, why he has groped his way for too many years. He believes it has taken too long to produce too little art.

Dr. Hugh is the greatest admirer Dencombe can possibly wish for among the younger generation. When the doctor notices that Dencombe has corrected at least a dozen sentences in his copy of the novel, he is shocked at such desecration of his idol's text. When the doctor discovers Dencombe's identity, he offers not only his admiration but also his friendship and his medical services. Dencombe is flattered and seizes the opportunity. He would love to live longer, to have a masterful late phase to follow his middle years.

Dr. Hugh assures Dencombe that he will live, but then Dencombe hears that the countess has fallen ill, out of jealousy that the young man has neglected her for the writer. An agitated Miss Vernham visits Dencombe to charge that he was injuring the doctor's prospects of inheritance, so Dencombe should leave Bournemouth. Dencombe, although willing, is too ill to get away. He then learns from Dr. Hugh that the countess has died, after having cursed and disinherited him. The doctor assures Dencombe that he has made a good choice, preferring literature to wealth.

The effect on Dencombe is profound. The free and sensitive choice that Dr. Hugh has made shows that his writing has made someone care deeply. His life has been successful, after all. The dying author then gathers his strength to speak his testament:

> A second chance—*that's* the delusion. There never was to be but one. We work in the dark—we do what we can—we give what we have. Our doubt is our passion and our passion is our task. The rest is the madness of art.

Themes and Meanings

Henry James wrote "The Middle Years" at a crucial period in his own life, when he had failed as a dramatist on the London stage but had already produced a considerable body of distinguished fiction. He was already being surrounded by a group of gifted young men who wanted to be acolytes and hail him as a master. This relationship between an older author and young persons whose spirits are strongly touched by his art is reflected in such tales, composed in the 1890's, as "The Death of the Lion," "The Figure in the Carpet," and, as shown, "The Middle Years."

In this tale, James, as always, sees art and life as unalterably opposed, and creates a fable of the artist. Dencombe, as James's artist-hero, asks himself two important questions: How well has he done his work, and how valuable is it? The crucial question behind these meditations is whether his life has been well spent, or whether his apprenticeship has been too long, his mature achievement too brief.

Through his friendship with Dr. Hugh, Dencombe has the opportunity to get answers to his anxious questions. He discovers the hard truth that he is to be given only one chance in life—the one he has already had; that whatever the pearl of artistic perfection he could have created, were he granted longer years, it will never be realized. He also discovers his ability to embrace this truth, however ruefully, because his work has persuaded Dr. Hugh to choose between two ways of living and valuing, and to prefer the density and depth of experience manifest in art to the surface glitter represented by the countess's riches. In Dr. Hugh's sharing of what Dencombe has cared for, he has received a reassuring demonstration of his own life's meaning.

"The Middle Years" also dramatizes a concern that James treated in a number of other stories: the life unlived. Dencombe has lost his wife and only son to illness. He has outlived his older friends. He joins the group of estranged and solitary men, forlorn and anxious, in such tales as "The Pupil," "The Altar of the Dead," "The Birthplace," and what may be James's greatest artist fable, "The Beast in the Jungle." "The Middle Years," haunted by Dencombe's sense of the failed life, anticipates ironic fables of the artist by Franz Kafka and Thomas Mann.

Style and Technique

"The Middle Years" is a title James chose for not only this tale but for an autobiographical reminiscence that he began in 1914 but left unfinished, intending it as a companion work to his *Notes of a Son and Brother* (1914). The phrase is richly as well as ambiguously connotative, spanning an unspecified center of an individual's life. James may well have had in mind the famous opening words of Dante's *La divina commedia* (c. 1320; *The Divine Comedy*, 1802), "Midway in our life's journey . . . ," where the protagonist has lost his way and finds himself in a dark wood. The resonance of the title spans both Dencombe's life and last work.

The story's imagery serves to illustrate Dencombe's—and James's—sense of the artist and the proper concerns and value of art. When he creeps to his favorite bench at Bournemouth, it becomes his bench of desolation as well as reflection. His lack of interest in using external nature in his work is illustrated by his response to the sea, which strikes him as "far shallower than the spirit of man." In contrast, it is the "abyss of human illusion that was the real, the tideless deep." A little later, James pursues a water image by referring to Dencombe's awareness of his ebbing time. Later still, Dencombe has dived into his novel, drawn down to the dim underworld of fiction, to its tank of art. When he hears Dr. Hugh express his unreserved devotion to his writing, "The sense of cold submersion left him—he seemed to float without an effort."

The text's style and concentrated imagery are integrated meticulously with its theme in this haunting tale of art's rigors and trials.

Gerhard Brand

MIDNIGHT MASS

Author: Joaquim Maria Machado de Assis (1839-1908)
Type of plot: Sketch
Time of plot: The early 1860's
Locale: Rio de Janeiro, Brazil
First published: "Misa de Galo," 1894 (English translation, 1963)

> *Principal characters:*
> MR. NOGUEIRA, a young man studying for his college entrance examinations
> CONCEIÇÃO, the wife of Chiquinho Menezes, the notary in whose house Nogueira is staying

The Story

The narrator, Mr. Nogueira, is of indeterminate age as he tells his tale, but he was a young man of seventeen when the events occurred. A country boy from Mangaratiba, he has come to Rio de Janeiro to stay with Mr. Menezes, a notary whose first wife was Nogueira's cousin, in order to prepare for his college entrance examinations. The Menezes household is composed of the notary, his wife, Madame Conceição, her mother, Madame Ignacia, and two female slaves. Nogueira spends some months living quietly with the family, which he refers to as old-fashioned. The only exception to the nightly routine of a ten o'clock bedtime is the weekly visit that Menezes makes to the theater. Nogueira would like to join him, as he has never been to the theater, but he discovers that going to the theater is a euphemism that allows Menezes to spend one night a week with a married woman who is separated from her husband. Conceição accepts her husband's mistreatment of her passively, as she seems to respond to everything.

The events of the story occur on Christmas Eve, which coincides with the notary's weekly theater outing. Nogueira has remained in the city to see the special midnight Mass. He sits reading in the silent house. The clock strikes eleven, he hears footsteps, and Conceição appears, dressed in her negligee. Without greeting him she asks, "Haven't you gone?" Nogueira replies that it is still too early, and asks if he has awakened her. Conceição claims to have awakened naturally, but Nogueira notes that she does not appear to have slept. He discards the notion that she might be lying: She is, after all, a saintly, long-suffering, uncomplaining woman whose husband neglects her. A conversation ensues, which the mature narrator claims he never quite understood, and the rest of the story moves between their dialogue and the narrator's reflections and close observations of Madame Conceição. He refers to her as thin and notes her rocking gait, suggesting her difficulty with carrying her weight, then observes her exposed forearm—not as thin as he had thought—with blue veins visible through translucent skin. He gradually realizes that the passive, thirty-year-old wife of Menezes is a very beautiful woman. The conversation ranges from novels to the paintings of women her husband has hung on the wall; from her patron saint, Our Lady of the Immaculate Conception, to her childhood trips to the island of Paquetá in the Guanabara Bay near Rio de Janeiro. When the conversation dies out, they sit in silence until Nogueira's expected companion knocks on the window to call him to go to Mass.

The next day, when Nogueira reports to Conceição on the Mass, she expresses no interest, despite the seeming intimacy of the previous evening. He goes home to Mangaratiba a few days later. When he returns to Rio in March, the notary has died of apoplexy, and Conceição has moved to another district and married her husband's apprentice clerk.

Themes and Meanings

On first reading, this story may appear to be little more than a detailed sketch of the customs and manners of a typical bourgeois family in nineteenth century Rio de Janeiro. Nogueira reads a translation of Alexandre Dumas, *père*'s *Les Trois Mousquetaires* (1844; *The Three Musketeers*, 1846) originally published in serial form in an important newspaper, and the reader recalls the importance of French literature, language, and culture during this period of Brazilian history. The mention of the two female slaves suggests that, although published in 1894, the story was written somewhat earlier, for slavery was legally abolished in Brazil in 1888. The social arrangements are also typical. Nogueira's stay with the husband of a deceased cousin demonstrates the strength of family ties, however distant the relationship, as well as the importance of hospitality. The presence of Conceição's mother, Madame Ignacia, is also common to the period. The late-night conversation on polite and trivial topics is a model of social taste.

On further reading, however, the reader sees beneath the sketch of manners to the real-life situation of Conceição and the sexual awakening of Nogueira. The latter is evident in the gradual change in Nogueira's observations of Conceição. Early in the tale, his descriptions of her are somewhat distanced, even muted. As their evening together progresses, he awakens to her physicality, noting her shining teeth, her pale skin, her eyes, the tips of her slippers beneath her long gown (at a time when women were completely covered but for their faces). She suddenly becomes beautiful in his eyes and speaks "so graciously, so gently that it drugged [his] soul." Conceição is transformed from a thirty-year-old, nondescript married woman to a siren who mesmerizes Nogueira with her beauty and the song of her conversation.

Conceição has married late—at the age of twenty-seven, suggesting she was not a good catch—and perhaps not physically well. Her husband's choice of art is more fitting to a bachelor apartment, and he is conducting an affair with a married woman with the clear knowledge of the entire household. She refers to her household and family responsibilities as nothing. She has not slept this theater night, and she no doubt awaits the arrival of her lover by whom she is with child—the apprentice clerk whom she marries soon after her husband's death. Numerous details suggest this: the careful mention of three keys to the house (Menezes has one, Nogueira another, and the third remains in the home); Conceição's surprise at finding Nogueira still there when she comes to the living room; Nogueira's remark that the design of the house makes it possible for him to leave for midnight Mass without disturbing anyone; Conceição's comment that Madame Ignacia's room is quite a distance away; her loosely tied negligee that reveals nothing of her body; her not-so-thin arm; the translucent skin with visible blue veins; and most of all, her rocking gait "as if she carried her weight with difficulty."

Menezes dies of apoplexy, or a stroke, but in this period death by apoplexy could easily be the result of a tremendous shock, such as discovering that the wife you have ignored is expecting the child of another man. Menezes's death seems sudden, but Conceição's marriage and change of district also is remarkably sudden. Her marriage so soon after her husband's death is entirely contrary to accepted practice in the social milieu of the time, when any wife would mourn her husband for at least a year and indicate her grief by dressing in black throughout the year.

Style and Technique

Joaquim Maria Machado de Assis is well known for writing between the lines. The quintessential example of this technique is his most famous novel, *Dom Casmurro* (1899), which centers on a similar theme of adultery. Dom Casmurro is certain that his wife, Capitú, has been unfaithful to him by committing adultery with a mutual friend. The novel is written in such a way, however, that the reader is never certain of either her guilt or her innocence. Indeed, the question remains the central debate among critics of the novel.

In "Midnight Mass," Machado tells two stories in one: a sketch of the period, and the story of a woman who eventually finds happiness despite her present circumstances. It is the gradual accretion of careful detail that both creates the sketch of manners and culminates in Conceição's personal story. Although each detail alone seems unambiguous, their accumulation results in an ambiguous narrative that leaves both the narrator and the reader in a quandary, wondering if Conceição was unfaithful, if her husband did die of shock, why Conceição married so soon after being widowed, why she moved, and if she was pregnant. Machado once again uses detail, fact, if you will, to create a narrative resistant to factual interpretation, a narrative of ambiguity.

Linda Ledford-Miller

MIDSUMMER NIGHT MADNESS

Author: Seán O'Faoláin (John Francis Whelan, 1900-1991)
Type of plot: Social realism
Time of plot: 1920
Locale: The countryside near Cork, Ireland
First published: 1932

Principal characters:
JOHN, the narrator, a young Irish revolutionary
ALEC HENN, an old Anglo-Irish bachelor
STEVEY LONG, the commander of a guerrilla battalion
GYPSY GAMMLE, a maidservant in Henn's mansion and the lover
of both Henn and Long

The Story

A young guerrilla leader leaves his headquarters in the city to investigate the recent inactivity of a battalion out in the countryside from which his parents had moved when he was a young boy. As he sets off, nostalgic images of that place occupy him, and he anticipates a period of freedom from the tension of his underground life in the city. His pleasure in the sights and sounds of the countryside is mixed with his ambivalent childhood impressions of a legendary Anglo-Irish gentleman, Alec Henn, who "lived by the things of the body—women, wine, hunting, fishing, shooting." This "madman" and his mansion, the "Red House," are associated with images of ogres from fairy tales, but the narrator now reflects on what may have become of him after so many years. He wonders if the old Don Juan of Henn Hall is still alive, or if he is, what female company he could have; perhaps he has been reduced to finding a woman of the passing tinkers. This thought of the humiliation of Henn and of the end of a once prosperous Anglo-Irish family pleases John, for he has "nothing in my heart for him but hate" because Henn is a member of the establishment class against whose interests and their allegiance with English power in Ireland the revolution is directed.

As the narrator draws near Henn Hall, where his comrade Stevey Long will secretly accommodate him, he is confronted in the semidarkness by a woman, Gypsy Gammle, who mistakes him for Stevey. From her anxious questions, he discovers that she is having a love affair with Stevey. She forces John to admit that Stevey may have another girlfriend, and she vows not to marry him. The narrator is reluctant to become involved in this "unpleasant, real life," and when he sees Gypsy and Stevey embracing without inhibition in the kitchen of the hall, he is angry. As "investigator of Stevey's shortcomings," he has realized that Stevey's energy and attention have been going into this affair rather than into the revolution, but he is also jealous of Stevey's personal freedom in the countryside.

Henn now appears, a rather infirm and heavy-drinking old man who confronts the narrator with "I suppose you're another one of our new patriots." In spite of Henn's sarcasm, the narrator is courteous to him and Henn invites him to stay. Henn tells him that the revolutionaries are naïve to assume that they can create a new people whose attitudes will reverse the material and social decay in the country. From his cosmopolitan European experience, Henn has concluded that, unlike the Anglo-Irish and other European nations that value practicality and enterprise, the Irish prefer a self-pitying passivity and have little interest in the pleasures of material things. John is angered by such comments and skeptical of the "old libertine's" talk, for the culture and prosperity of Henn's family have served his life of pleasure seeking rather than a life of creative industry. When Gypsy returns, John realizes how much the old man is charmed by her beauty, but when Henn's desire for her becomes evident, a violent argument erupts between Henn and Stevey. The young Don Juan confronts the old Don Juan in a battle for Gypsy, but the narrator feels drawn to the lovemaking of Henn and Gypsy. He continues to think with "bitterness" of Henn as a pathetic figure, whose desire for beauty and pleasure is mocked by the decay of his body and of his house, and he discovers that Henn has taken in Gypsy, a tinker from the roads.

Later, in the middle of the night, John follows Henn out of the house and finds him comforting the distraught Gypsy; John realizes that she is pregnant. At first, John is frustrated by the impossible dilemma of discovering which of the men is responsible but soon realizes that their complex experience of passion and sorrow is more real than his self-centered wish for peace and freedom in the countryside.

Following this realization, the narrator becomes witness to the sudden revolutionary activity of Stevey's battalion of "incendiaries." First an old mansion across the valley is set on fire and its old virginal inhabitants driven out, and then they come to burn Henn Hall. It is evident to John that the political justification for the burning—as a reprisal for actions of the British Army—is not the truth; Stevey's action has been motivated by his personal anger against Henn. Gypsy is shown to be the frightened victim of the men's personal war. The narrator now finds himself more in sympathy with Henn than with Stevey when they discover that Stevey's intention is to blackmail Henn into marrying Gypsy. Henn refuses at first to give into the blackmail but agrees eventually when he sees that Gypsy would prefer to marry him rather than Stevey, who has betrayed her.

John leaves a few days later, unwilling to pass judgment on Stevey and Henn, having no cause "to believe or disbelieve anybody." It is evident that he has become bitter and disillusioned by the egotistical and romantic desires that made "madness" of his "dream" on political and personal levels. However, he is forced to admit later that the passionate madness of this night that he remembers so vividly has more of the truth of life in it than does the ideological simplifications that inspired him earlier.

Themes and Meanings

Although this story has a limited number of characters and a limited time frame, its plotting, characterization, and dialogue are as elaborate as in a novella. Its themes are developed through many scenes, and Seán O'Faoláin presents a complex truth of the overlapping and conflicting elements within his Irish situation. This is a story of individual and social passions that are more destructive than creative, more anarchic than harmonizing.

The background conflict is the opposition between two cultural traditions that has given rise to political and military hostility; this hostility will continue and intensify after the time span of the central actions. The narrator has grown up with his family's critical attitude toward Henn's caste and toward his individualistic and hedonistic lifestyle. John's passionate belief in his political stance, however, is undermined by the skeptical social analysis of Henn and by the sordid violence of the incendiaries. Turning from the conflicts in the social and political context, the picture of individual and interpersonal life is remarkable for its contradictions. The young woman is paired off with the old man; romantic dream and visceral impulse, logic and prejudice, hatred and love exist side by side. Underlying this tangle of personal and political desires is a sense of the impurity of human actions. All the central characters are described in animal images, and the instinctive impulses as well as the graceless decline into old age are emphasized.

The title recalls the anarchy of desire and the harmony of love in William Shakespeare's *A Midsummer Night's Dream* (1600), but the element of realism in O'Faoláin's story makes the Shakespearean echo an ironic one. Certainly, there are dreams, and the story's fast-paced action has elements of nightmare, but the marriage of Henn and Gypsy is overshadowed by John's melancholic awareness of the lasting incongruities of life's fabric. Life itself goes on until death, and the behavior of people more often resembles the blind impulses of animals than the beatific visions of romantic comedy.

Style and Technique

The story is in three parts, each with its own particular style corresponding to stages in John's initiation into the truth of the human condition. In the opening paragraph, the naïve young revolutionary leaves the city where he has been "seeing the life of men and women only through a peephole." His deprived and insulated perception accounts for the predominantly subjective and lyric style of the first part. He is inclined to grant an integrity and reality to what he sees and to his sensual impressions of nature; the "tiny beacons," the lights of the city, "were winking and blinking beneath me to their starry counterparts above," and "the heavy leaves of the chestnuts . . . scattered benediction on us." The narrator's romantic outlook blinds him to the irony of his own perception, for example, that Henn's house assumed a passionate red color like the sky behind it, "a most marvellous red as of blood." He thinks in either childhood images or ideological principles that allow him to categorize and contain the reality of Henn's existential revolt against sensual impoverishment.

When the narrator arrives at Henn Hall, the dominant style becomes more social. The three characters, Gypsy, Henn, and Stevey, are introduced and their relationships are suggested. There are many scenes of dialogue, much less description than before, and the narrator becomes almost self-effacing as each character is allowed to assume his or her own reality through dialogue and action. It is as if the narrator becomes more tolerant and wiser as he observes this complex social world.

Part 3 begins when the narrator awakens in the middle of the night. The narrative style becomes appropriately nightmarish or, perhaps, operatic. The social world of indoors is abandoned for the outdoors. Against the backdrop of a mansion on fire, the sexual intrigue is heightened, and the lovers are taken from moods of romance and tragedy to a rather cynical and crude bargain over the fate of Gypsy. Realism gives way to a genre that accommodates psychological and social extremes and accommodates also the bewildered response of the narrator. Pathos and compassion come close to cynicism and disgust; innocent belief is drowned in this dark world of passion. The human drama becomes almost mythical, introduced by Henn's recording of Wolfgang Amadeus Mozart's *Don Giovanni* (1787).

In a brief coda, the narrator thinks of the absurd image of the decrepit old man showing the sights of Paris to his young wife. He finds the image painful and pitiable and appears to draw back to a distance from which reserve and detachment are possible.

Denis Sampson

MIGRANTS

Author: Elizabeth Tallent (1954-   )
Type of plot: Psychological
Time of plot: The mid-1980's
Locale: Colorado
First published: 1986

> *Principal characters:*
> SISSY, a high school senior
> RAFER, her father, a sales representative of farm irrigation
>   equipment
> A MEXICAN FARMWORKER

The Story

Sissy, a high-school senior, is living with her father in a rented farmhouse near a small town in Colorado, after moving there from Iowa after her mother ran away with her boyfriend to Los Angeles. Sissy is alone much of the time while her father, Rafer, roams the open land selling "Rain Cats," giant circular sprinkler systems, to farmers. Sissy misses her mother, wonders what Los Angeles is like, and hates the place in which she lives. She has an affectionate relationship with her father, but it is not enough: "All spring in Wheaton, where she knows no one and nobody seems to be under forty anyway, Sissy has been lonely: all spring Rafer has been on the road." When he comes home on weekends, he takes Sissy to shoot at bottles lined up in an arroyo. When he is away, Sissy roams the empty fields with her dog, Joe, and stares off into the thousand-mile space between herself and Los Angeles.

Once, while Sissy is riding her bike, a caravan of beat-up cars drives past her, filled with migrant Mexican farmworkers. She is astonished at this sudden burst of exotic vitality: "Sissy loves them for having appeared behind her, out of nowhere. The dusty dashes hold groves of plastic saints, and rosaries wag from the rearview mirrors. A child sucking on its fist pushes aside a pair of fluttering pantyhose and gazes out at her." She knows that these migrants will probably stay near her town for a while and will not be welcomed by its white residents. Delighted by their sudden presence, she decides to pedal alongside one of the slow-moving cars. To her astonishment, the worn-out Cadillac she is keeping pace with slowly accelerates and then edges into her lane to cut her off. She wonders why she has been rejected without being recognized. The caravan slowly recedes in the distance.

When Sissy visits the local post office, the small room is crowded with Mexicans who are there to send money to Mexico. The men move away from her, permitting her to be first in line. She is embarrassed, but Mr. Cox tells her she might as well take advantage. Sissy does not want to take advantage, revealing her sympathies for the migrants. Seeing one who is their apparent leader, a young man, she smiles at him.

A few days later, hunting in the field with her dog, Sissy shoots a rabbit. She walks over to an irrigation ditch and finds a young migrant bathing there, his white shirt hung up in a branch to dry in the sun. She is touched by his care for his clothing: "He had wanted to keep it dry, or air his sweat from the cloth, and this is a revelation of his fastidiousness, of something as private as his nakedness. She loves the half-floating, half-sagging shirt." She wants to speak to him, thinking he might be the same man she smiled at in the post office. She knows no Spanish, however, and he no English, and he is naked, embarrassed. He silently hints that she should back away while he gets his shirt, but for a moment she senses she wants to see his nakedness: "She almost wants, so silently instructed, to do so yet she wants—it is so exquisitely clear what she wants that she can't, for the fraction of an instant, condemn herself for wanting it—to watch him rise from the water." She tries to talk to the young man, but there is nothing to say. Her pathetic attempt to talk reveals the depth of her loneliness.

That night her father takes her to the movies in Wyoming, forty miles away. He knows something is wrong with her but is unprepared for her soft-spoken request for a bus ticket to Los Angeles as they sit down together in the theater.

Themes and Meanings

The simple story contains two revelations. First, Sissy, longing to look further at the bathing migrant, realizes the extent of her loneliness and the degree to which she is missing life. Her only escape is the thought of her mother living in the big city, Los Angeles, and it is this image she nurtures as her salvation. The second revelation is for Rafer, who has managed to convince himself that he is succeeding in raising his daughter, whom he regards as having been abandoned by his wife. His life on the road as a sales representative is as lonely as Sissy's, but his consolation is that he can return to his daughter, fill up her life with his presence. Her unexpected request for a bus ticket to Los Angeles destroys the illusion that he can keep her with him and foretells the even greater loneliness that he will be facing soon.

The story resonates with inferences and implied meanings. Nothing is said of Sissy's mother, the boyfriend, or Sissy's life before the recent move to this forsaken patch of Colorado farming country. Sissy's character is revealed in short impressions—her joy at the sudden sight of the caravan of Mexicans, all poor but sustained by their large families; her instinct for justice when she sees she is being preferentially treated by the post office clerk; her dutiful writing to her mother; her sexual longings brought out by the sight of the bathing migrant; and her desperate need to talk to the migrant.

Much of the story relies on richly ornate description of the land Sissy sees or walks through as she hunts with her dog. The delicacy of Elizabeth Tallent's observations help to reveal the sensitive mind of the young Sissy. A sense of her wonder at the unexpected vision of the naked man bathing in the field emerges in sentences such as, "Coins of light reflected from the current float over his dark shoulders like minute spotlights." The spotlights of bright sunlight enhance the sight of his body; the value of what she sees increases like coins dropped from the sky. She cannot back away from him, as she knows she should.

Style and Technique

Tallent's gift is to illuminate character by accumulating unexpected, even lyric detail. One can see Rafer's Rain Cats working in the fields not as tools but as quiet revelations of beauty: The sprinklers throw off "a thin, prismatic spume, or entire moving rainbows no bigger than birds' wings." Sissy, riding her bike along the lonely farm roads, finds a hail of grasshoppers pattering against her legs: "When the wings flick open, oval dapples form glaring eyes precise down to the honey iris and darker pupil." Alone in the grasslands she sees a windmill, and its motion without apparent wind serves as a model of her status, alone, seemingly static, but moving within the world of her fantasy, her imagined life in far-off Los Angeles. "Though there seems to be no wind, the windmill blades keep turning, and blades of shadow switch with light on Sissy's face."

The flutter of light and then dark on Sissy underscores the dark and light side of her life—the few pleasant times with her father, perhaps shooting at glass bottles, and then the overwhelming emptiness of her life, the shadow cast by her missing mother. Her father once said, "We're in this together," referring to the unspoken flight of Sissy's mother away from her father, and the phrase offers her a temporary refuge but also a feeling of oppression, a sense of marking time. Sissy wants to break out of this sense of being placed in an empty space, and her thoughts of flight, joining her mother in a second abandonment of Rafer, are implied in the delicacy of description of which Tallent is such a master. The night of the movie, for example, finds her sitting in the car driven by Rafer, watching him, but apparently not speaking. She is mesmerized by the reflection of a car's taillights in Rafer's eyes. "She watches the lights of the car before them blink and elide into the corner of his eye like a tear swept sideways by the wind." The description implies a silence, a deferred speaking about Sissy's real feelings. It is only a later gesture—Rafer's holding her hands at the movie—that prompts the revelation that had been waiting behind those silent moments when Sissy watched a tear-shaped red light in her father's eye come and go. "Daddy, I want a bus ticket to L.A." ends both Sissy's silence and the story.

Paul R. Lilly, Jr.

THE MINISTER'S BLACK VEIL

Author: Nathaniel Hawthorne (1804-1864)
Type of plot: Parable
Time of plot: The seventeenth century
Locale: Puritan New England
First published: 1835

> *Principal characters:*
> THE REVEREND MR. HOOPER, the protagonist and minister of Milford
> ELIZABETH, his fiancé
> THE REVEREND MR. CLARK, the minister from Westbury who presides over Mr. Hooper's funeral

The Story

One Sunday, at the early morning service, the Reverend Mr. Hooper appears before his congregation wearing a black veil that extends from his forehead down over his mouth. The parishioners are shocked; some suggest that he has gone mad, and others speculate that perhaps the veiled figure is not the Reverend Mr. Hooper at all. What is clear, however, is that the veil has a tremendous impact on the congregation. Women with weak nerves must leave the service. Old Squire Saunders, who ordinarily invites the Reverend Mr. Hooper to dinner after the service, even forgets to extend his invitation. That afternoon, the Reverend Mr. Hooper conducts a funeral service for a young lady, and the veil again affects his audience. A "superstitious old woman" supposes that when the Reverend Mr. Hooper bends over the coffin, the corpse of the young lady shudders as his face is slightly unveiled, and two of the mourners in the procession to the grave say that they saw the spirits of the minister and the maiden walking hand in hand.

Finally, that night, Milford's handsomest young couple are married by the minister, and his veil casts a pall over the whole ceremony. When the Reverend Mr. Hooper catches a glimpse of himself in a mirror at the reception, he shudders and spills some wedding wine on the carpet, then leaves abruptly.

By morning, the minister's black veil is the central topic of conversation in the village of Milford, and it seems that no one can solve the mystery. A deputation from the church is sent to the minister's home to question him about the black veil, but they return entirely disappointed. Only one person can solve the mystery, Elizabeth, who is engaged to be married to the Reverend Hooper. At the first opportunity, she approaches him on the subject of the black veil, and to her questions his reply is enigmatic. "Know, then, this veil is a type and a symbol, and I am bound to wear it ever, both in light and darkness, in solitude and before the gaze of multitudes, and as with strangers, so with my familiar friends." Though Elizabeth asks him to let her alone see his face, it quickly becomes apparent that he has no intention of ever removing the veil, not even for Elizabeth. As Elizabeth starts away, the Reverend Mr. Hooper catches her arm, pleading with her to have patience. "Lift the veil but once . . . ," she says, and he replies "Never!" With that, she leaves him, and they are never married, though Elizabeth provides a surprise at the conclusion of this tale.

After the interview with Elizabeth, no one attempts again to persuade the Reverend Mr. Hooper to remove the veil. Through the remainder of his life, the veil has many negative effects. His parishioners see him with dread, and children flee at his approach. Rumors and tales abound concerning why he put on the veil in the first place. Many speculate that his conscience is tormented by some horrible crime and he is a lonely man separated from others. Besides all the negative effects, there is one positive result of the veil: It makes him a very effective preacher, for the veil is a symbol of the sins of all and gives the Reverend Mr. Hooper a special power over sinners. They call out for him in their last moments and will not expire until his appearance. However, basically, the veil casts a sense of gloom before the Reverend Mr. Hooper, so much so that when he preaches an election-day sermon before the governor and the legislature, the legislation for that year is characterized by an unusual gloominess.

Other than the veil, the Reverend Mr. Hooper's life is exemplary. At length, he lies dying, attended by Elizabeth, who has been secretly faithful to him throughout his life. The Reverend Mr. Clark of Westbury arrives to attend the Reverend Mr. Hooper in his dying hour, and he attempts to remove the black veil from the Reverend Mr. Hooper's face. Exerting all of his will and strength, the Reverend Mr. Hooper clasps the veil to his face, and he tells the people crowded around his deathbed that he is not alone in wearing the black veil. "Why do you tremble at me alone?" he said. "Tremble also at each other! I look around me, and lo! on every visage a Black Veil!" With this, the Reverend Hooper dies, and all who knew him shudder to think that his face will molder in the grave, beneath the black veil.

Themes and Meanings

The major theme of "The Minister's Black Veil" is revealed in the Reverend Mr. Hooper's remarks to Elizabeth when she attempts to discover why he has chosen to put on the veil. She assumes that he has decided to wear the veil only because of some secret sin or crime, but as part of the development of the major theme, he tells Elizabeth that his veil is additionally a "symbol."

As the story progresses, the exact meaning of the veil as a symbol becomes clear. In his interview with Elizabeth, the Reverend Mr. Hooper suggests that all mortals could cover their faces just as he has because all have some secret sin or sorrow. At the end of the story, as he lies dying, the Reverend Mr. Hooper says that he sees a veil on all the faces of those who are attending his deathbed. In this way, the major theme of the story is developed; that is, it is suggested that everyone wears a black veil, that everyone has a secret sin or sorrow that is hidden from all others. Everyone could, like the Reverend Mr. Hooper, cover his face with a black veil. The Reverend Mr. Hooper has chosen to make his black veil visible while others have kept their secrets in their own hearts. However, to acknowledge one's secret sin or sorrow exacts a high price, which is the second major theme of the story. When the Reverend Mr. Hooper dons the black veil, he is immediately set apart from his parishioners in a very special way. They no longer accept him among them as they did before the advent of the veil. The veil that so distinguishes him from his fellow villagers strikes fear in the hearts of all and causes them to dread his approach and to withdraw their friendship and companionship from him. Even his fiancé, Elizabeth, cannot marry him and must, until he is on his deathbed, love him in "secrecy" and "solitude." Thus, because he chooses to make his secret visible, the Reverend Mr. Hooper becomes a lonely man. The black veil "separated him from cheerful brotherhood and woman's love." Hence, one of the major themes of "The Minister's Black Veil" is that those who acknowledge the secrets of their hearts and those who choose to stand apart from their fellows will often find that they are ostracized and may well lead lives of loneliness, prisoners in their own hearts.

Style and Technique

Like many American Renaissance writings, Nathaniel Hawthorne's works are generally symbolic. *The Scarlet Letter* (1850) is one of the major symbolic novels of nineteenth century American literature, and Hawthorne often developed his short stories around a symbol. This is clearly the case in "The Minister's Black Veil."

When the Reverend Mr. Hooper first wears the veil, his parishioners think that it represents some secret sin or crime that the Reverend Mr. Hooper has committed. This impression in encouraged by Hawthorne's footnote to the story concerning an actual person, the Reverend Mr. Joseph Moody of York, Maine, who wore a black veil because he accidentally killed a dear friend. Hawthorne explains that the Reverend Mr. Hooper's veil has a different meaning, but the impression still remains that he is wearing it because of some secret sin or crime that he does not care to confess. Again, the sense of this is increased by the speculation that the young lady's corpse shuddered when the Reverend Mr. Hooper's veil fell forward over her as he bent over her coffin and also by the suggestion that the two mourners saw the minister's and the maiden's spirits walking hand in hand toward the graveyard.

It becomes clear in the interview with Elizabeth that while the veil may represent some secret sin or crime, for the Reverend Mr. Hooper its importance lies in its symbolic value, or the value that it has as a moral lesson to all. Throughout his life as well, the veil functions as precisely such a symbol, for it strikes terror in the hearts of sinners, and they hang on to life at the end until the Reverend Mr. Hooper can be by their side, for he knows they harbor sins and sorrows. At the Reverend Mr. Hooper's death, the full symbolic significance of the veil is revealed as he says that he sees a veil on the face of all gathered around him. In this manner, Hawthorne's symbolic style and technique are at the center of the development of the tale; yet the alternative significance of the veil as the representative of a specific crime or sin of the Reverend Mr. Hooper is also part of Hawthorne's narrative technique.

Although the black veil is clearly a symbolic device, there is a strong suggestion in the story that it also hides a secret sin or crime committed by the Reverend Mr. Hooper. In addition, other details of the story seem to link him to the death of the young maiden. He conducts her funeral on the very day he first wears the veil, and there is the speculation that the maiden's and the Reverend Mr. Hooper's spirits are seen walking hand in hand. The effect of all this is to create in the reader the sense that he is being given clues to a puzzle that he can solve; that is, if he reads the story carefully, he may be able to discover exactly the nature of the Reverend Mr. Hooper's sin or crime. As a result, the reader is drawn into the story and is given reason to read the story again and again. There is no answer to the puzzle, but the technique is effective and one that Hawthorne used in other stories, such as "Young Goodman Brown" and "Ethan Brand."

Michael D. Reed

MINOR HEROISM

Author: Allan Gurganus (1947-   )
Type of plot: Psychological, domestic realism
Time of plot: 1942-1972
Locale: North Carolina
First published: 1974

Principal characters:
RICHARD, an insurance sales representative and World War II
    veteran
HELEN, his wife and the mother of their two sons
BRYAN, his elder son, a furniture designer and would-be writer
BRADLEY, his younger son, a conformist

The Story

"Minor Heroism" is a story in three parts. The first part is essentially a biographical sketch of Richard in his prime, from his stint in the military in the 1940's to his young fatherhood in the 1950's.

Along with most of the members of his fraternity at the University of Virginia, Richard enlists in the Army Air Corps in 1942; he subsequently serves as a bombardier during the controversial Allied firebombing of Dresden, Germany, in February of 1945. On his return from that mission, he is "decorated for minor heroism" and photographed being kissed by actress and pin-up girl Betty Grable. It is this photograph and others featuring his handsome face that accord Richard a certain "local glamour."

After the war, with a debutante bride in hand, he returns to his native North Carolina, where his residual celebrity is useful in setting up his insurance business. Richard and Helen settle into an apparently comfortable middle-class life and become, at least on the surface, a typical suburban couple of the 1950's. They raise two children and join the local country club.

The narrative's second part focuses on Richard's relationship to his two sons. In contrast to his younger son Bradley, who has followed in his father's footsteps by graduating from the same college, marrying a girl from a good family, and establishing a comfortable career, Bryan is, in Richard's eyes, an enigma. Richard's worries begin when Bryan's teachers start praising his artistic talents. Other boys begin to pick on Bryan, and he gradually retreats indoors to draw and listen to records. Over the years, in Richard's eyes, Bryan grows "paler, taller, and more peculiar."

Now twenty-seven, Bryan writes for the magazine *Dance World* and lives in New York City with an actor-model roommate who paints his fingernails black. He rarely comes home to North Carolina, and when he does, he causes his parents distress.

The climax of the story's second part occurs when Bryan is home for a short visit after an absence of two years. Fresh from a party at the club, where their contemporaries regale them with stories of their children's engagements and pregnancies, Richard releases his pent-up resentment against his elder son by smacking him "across his fashionable haircut" so that he falls to the floor. The next day, Bryan accompanies his parents to church to make a public display of his injury and then leaves for New York, apparently with no intention of ever returning.

The narrative's third and final part focuses on a single incident from Bryan's childhood. While his brother plays outdoors, Bryan is in the dining room, drawing a picture of a tall uniformed man holding the hand of a small boy. When his father begins nagging him about going outside, Bryan tries to diffuse his anger by telling him that the drawing is a picture of him. When Richard now insists on seeing his son's work, Bryan resists long enough to blacken out the representation of the child, leaving only the adult figure intact. In essence, he is keeping himself to himself.

Themes and Meanings

Family life is a prevailing subject in the works of southern writers. Born and raised in North Carolina, the setting of "Minor Heroism," Allan Gurganus knows firsthand the significance of the often-complicated, cross-generation relationships that mark the southern family.

In this regard, Richard is the standard bearer of his family's values. His mother's contention that silence is "always in good taste" becomes, in Richard, the inability to articulate any of his feelings, particularly his fear concerning the truth of his son's sexual orientation.

Conformity lies at the heart of Richard's life. Except for his war years, when he temporarily befriended men who were "dark," "hairy," and "sooty from the city," Richard knows only the values of his time and place, a world marked by a mild Episcopal faith and manicured lawns. Perhaps much of his negative reaction to his son's lifestyle comes from his suppression of his own individuality. In essence, Richard returned from a great war in defense of freedom only to lead the most conventional of lives.

The family also provides the dramatic context for one of the staple narratives of gay literature, the coming-out story. At the moment that he admits his sexual orientation to members of his family, the gay man not only affirms the full range of his selfhood but also challenges the expectations of his parents and siblings by making his heretofore secret identity public. The claim has been made that "Minor Heroism" was the first story about homosexuality ever to be published by *The New Yorker*. It was also the first story published by Gurganus, and as such, it represents the author's own attempt to map out the perplexing place of gay people within the context of the traditional family.

The title "Minor Heroism" signals the story's operative irony. The father is an individual whose military service is marked and commemorated more by his photogenic good looks than by any extraordinary personal bravery. In fact, if anything, his princi-

pal contribution to the war effort is the fact that he followed orders and bombed a
largely civilian target. On his resumption of civilian life, Richard confines his innate
aggressiveness to the arena of domestic tyranny.

In raising his sons, Richard wanted little soldiers with automatic "Yes, sir" responses to his commands. When Bryan, however, fails to live up to his father's expectations, when he begins displaying "certain mannerisms" and cultivating his artistic
talent, Richard barks orders and physically lashes out against his elder son, slapping
him with a "hand the full size of [his] head." He tries to justify his harshness by explaining to himself and to the reader that he did not want his son to turn out like the
"thin, peculiar fellow" he "knew slightly in the army."

In contrast, Bryan, even as a "minor," exhibits courage beyond his years by standing his ground against his father's wishes and pursuing his own creative agenda. It
would be so much easier, so much less painful to surrender to his father's demands,
but Bryan already has a strong sense of both his own identity and his father's inability
to accept him for who he is.

Style and Technique

Much of the story's impact rests on the author's skillful use of point of view, which
shifts in each of the narrative's three parts.

All of the information provided to the reader in the first part of the story entitled "At
War, At Home" is filtered through the memory and imagination of the son Bryan. It is
clear to the reader that this is the adult Bryan trying to draw a picture of his father during the war years and after his own birth in 1947. In the portrait of his father before
and during the war, Richard is referred to in the third person as if he were some historical figure; but as the narrative progresses to a time when Bryan could bear witness to
his father's behavior, the "he" becomes "you" as if Bryan were trying to address his
father in his now adult voice.

In the second part labeled "My Elder Son," Richard gets an opportunity to tell his
side of the story. He uses the second person as if he is addressing other fathers and asking for their sympathy. "You start off with a child, a son, and for the first six years he's
on your side." As he moves toward puberty and beyond, however, "you're afraid of his
next phase—afraid of how the finished product will compare with the block's other
boys." In essence, Richard is looking for absolution. He admits making mistakes, but
he wants the reader not to think of him as a "tyrant" or a "villain." He keeps repeating
that he wanted "too much" for his son, but he never admits that he wanted Bryan to be,
at least on the surface, just like him. The tone of this section becomes progressively
angrier and angrier as if Richard were storing up his resentment over a catalog of
Bryan's offenses. The climax comes when he strikes his grown-up son with his "best
golfer's swing" in a final outburst of that mute rage that characterizes his reaction to
Bryan since his childhood.

The final section entitled "Addendum" provides a gripping conclusion to the narrative because of its immediacy. Here Bryan speaks in the first person and in the present
tense of an incident that occurred when he was eight. Even at that age, Bryan is ex-

traordinarily self-possessed, and despite the sheer physical menace of his exasperated father, it is the boy who holds the upper hand. As he "controls" his crayons, he controls the situation.

There is a longing here, a boy's poignant desire to have his father hug him "more than anything." However, this moment passes, and Bryan instinctively realizes that he must make his own way. Ironically enough, Richard wanted his son to be a little soldier, and he is. Outside the comfort zone that his brother Bradley will find in his conformity to his parents' and society's expectations, Bryan will have to depend on his own creative resources. That is a hard lesson for a little boy to have to face, but it is one that Bryan begins to grasp at the age of eight.

S. Thomas Mack

MIRACLE BOY

Author: Pinckney Benedict (1964-   )
Type of plot: Regional
Time of plot: The 1990's
Locale: A small town in the Seneca Valley
First published: 1998

> *Principal characters:*
> MIRACLE BOY, a boy whose feet have been cut off in an accident and reattached
> LIZARD, a boy who teases him and repents
> GERONIMO, Lizard's friend and fellow bully
> ESKIMO PIE, Geronimo's brother and fellow bully

The Story

"Miracle Boy," told in the third person by an omniscient narrator, revolves around four young boys living in a small rural town. On their way home from school, Geronimo, Lizard, and Eskimo Pie bully and strip a classmate whose feet were cut off and reattached after a farming accident. The newspapers named the boy Miracle Boy after the eight-hour surgery, and his peers, having heard the old Bible tales of the burning bush and Lazarus, are interested in seeing what a miracle looks like.

They knock him down, remove his clothing, steal his walking cane, and pitch his therapeutic shoes high in the air, where they catch on the electric line overhead. As the boys examine his ankles, knotty with pearly white scars, Miracle Boy does not say a thing. The scarred and purple feet are not what the boys expected, and they claim that the feet are not the work of a miracle. However, Miracle Boy contradicts them, telling them that there are miracles around all people every day.

Although his friends receive corporal punishment for their part in the abuse, Lizard's penalty is perplexing: He is made to invite Miracle Boy to his home to watch a film. Confused by this arrangement, Lizard watches Miracle Boy rather than the film. The two boys never say a word, but a fascination begins to grow in Lizard. He becomes preoccupied with Miracle Boy and with his old shoes weathering and dangling from the electric wires up above. His friends tell him to leave well enough alone, but Lizard devises a plan to retrieve the shoes.

Under the cover of darkness, Lizard drives penny nails into the utility pole that leads up to the rotting shoes, stands on each progressive nail, and ascends the pole. The transformer at the top of the pole, though charged with a deadly current, is a haven for Lizard after his treacherous climb, and he finally gains purchase on the prize. He takes the shoes to Miracle Boy's house and is surprised when Miracle Boy appears at the end of the darkened hallway with a slow inward smile and calls him into the house. Lizard slowly responds to the boy's invitation and offers the shoes to him as a gift.

Themes and Meanings

There is a legend about the black locust tree of which Miracle Boy's cane is made: It has such a will to live, it is said, that when used for fence posts and put into the ground, the posts grow roots and sprout limbs again. Like the cane, Pinckney Benedict's "Miracle Boy" reflects the cruelty of being uprooted from safety, as well as the powerful forces of renewal and redemption.

Like many of Benedict's stories, "Miracle Boy" deals with loneliness and isolation. Boys grow up without parents, physical differences are shunned, and children are cruel to one another. However, through his character Lizard, Benedict finds in this story a way to breech the desolation: compassion. Caught in an act of moral corruption, Lizard awakens to the humanity of Miracle Boy and begins to see beyond the walking stick, heavy brogans, and small-town infamy.

Unlike many of Benedict's stories, "Miracle Boy" is filled with strong religious symbolism. Following in the southern grotesque tradition, the title character serves as a deformed, disempowered, yet transformational figure. His slow shuffling gait and calm and forgiving behavior demonstrate wisdom beyond his years. Although he never preaches, his actions speak to Lizard in a way that prompts a change in the boy's behavior. This transformation culminates when Lizard creates a ladder from nails, climbs to the top of the post, and clasps onto the powerful electric transformer. This ladder picks up on a Christian symbol referenced in a flashback that immediately follows Lizard's climb. Of the wooden toys Lizard's father used to make him, his favorite was a Jacob's ladder, alluding to the biblical story in Genesis about a dream in which a ladder is set on the earth and the top of it reaches to heaven.

When Jacob awakens from his dream, he realizes that the ladder symbolizes the Lord's covenant with the people and that God is present in his land even though Jacob had not known it. Likewise, Lizard creates a ladder that serves as a covenant with Miracle Boy: Although the boy can never use the shoes again because of their physical deterioration, they serve as a promise that Lizard will never engage in another act of such cruelty. Also, as was the case with Jacob, when Lizard reaches the top of his ladder and looks on his homeland, he realizes he lives "in the cupped palm of a hand."

Lizard's new perspective on his world provides for his own transformation and redemption. As Lizard hands the shoes back to Miracle Boy, he hears in his head the song his father used to sing to him: "Was an old man near Hell did dwell,/ If he ain't dead yet he's living there still." Lizard's actions have turned him away from being such a man.

Style and Technique

Perhaps more than any of Benedict's other stories, "Miracle Boy" pays homage to the vast southern literary talent that informs modern-day writers. Like Flannery O'Connor, Benedict uses a terse, deceptively simple prose, displays a keen ear for southern dialect, and portrays violent, grotesque, and bizarre characters.

The world in which "Miracle Boy" is set is full of elements that are familiar and natural and yet take on a suspenseful and at times ominous feel. For example, having left the reader with the powerful image of the young disabled boy violated by his peers, Benedict turns to the first of three important flashbacks, to the moment when the tragic accident happened. He captures the infinite possibilities for human persecution by momentarily implicating the father as the cause of the boy's accident. Benedict's style of presenting "the facts" carries an emotional punch that effectively keeps the reader on guard throughout the story's telling. Whom does a person trust? Who is not capable of hurt and betrayal? Who has not sinned?

The second flashback effectively uses the present tense, for the only time in the story, to highlight the moment preceding the accident, the time before the boy is Miracle Boy. Benedict brings the reader even more into this moment by placing the action on a crisp fall afternoon and describing how Miracle Boy soon will be bird-dogging whitewings out of the stubble of the field. The reader is there with him and can effectively know the life he would have known with his father. The pair plan to drop a salt lick and wait together to shoot the deer that comes to the salt. In fact, the reader knows that they will not be able to do this. This is the life the farming accident has prevented the young boy from pursuing. However, according to Miracle Boy, this is the life before Jesus made him walk again. Although Miracle Boy does not lend a nostalgic tone to his life before the accident, Benedict's use of the present and immediate tense brings a fullness to the boy's loss and makes his courage in light of such events all the more miraculous.

Karin A. Silet

THE MIRACLE OF THE BIRDS

Author: Jorge Amado (1912-2001)
Type of plot: Fable
Time of plot: The timeless present
Locale: Piranhas, a town in Alagoas, Brazil
First published: 1982

> *Principal characters:*
> UBALDO CAPADÓCIO, a popular balladeer and lover
> SABÔ, the seductive town beauty
> CAPTAIN LINDOLFO EZEQUIEL, Sabô's jealous husband, a hired
> killer

The Story

The narrator begins by declaring that the miracle he is about to relate was witnessed by hundreds of townspeople, as it took place on a market day. In addition, the illustrious visitor being fêted that day, the widow of the renowned regional novelist Graciliano Ramos—a notoriously truthful woman—can testify to its veracity.

The reader is then introduced to the protagonist: Ubaldo Capadócio, widely celebrated as a lover, minstrel, and composer of popular ballads. His antagonist is also identified: Captain Lindolfo Ezequiel, who is best known as a hired killer and the husband of Sabô, the latter occupation demanding constant vigilance. Sabô is distinguished not only by her beauty and desirability but also by the lack of respect that she pays to her husband's position. She flaunts herself in front of all, but given the captain's violent possessiveness, none dare respond—that is, until Ubaldo arrives in town. Ignorant of local custom and ever ready to accommodate a lovely woman, Ubaldo will find himself, the narrator divulges, dressed in her nightgown, braving her husband.

Following this brash preface, the narrator details Ubaldo's reputation as a minstrel and ladies' man. His talents as an entertainer are such that he coaxes laughter from the deceased at a wake. As a lover, he is so constant that he never sends a woman away—any of them. He has three women to whom he is devoted, if not lawfully wedded, and nine children, three of them not biologically his. One came with the comely mulatto woman who, though she relented and left her husband for him, would not be parted from her little boy. Another was adopted after being left motherless at six months; the third was picked up by the side of a back-country road.

Ubaldo arrives in Piranhas, scene of the miracle, flush from a successful tour of the rugged Alagoan backlands. The narrator injects that the balladeer has gotten into trouble over women before. He has jumped out of windows and over fences and walls and has plunged into rivers; once a bullet grazed his jacket. Undaunted while the captain is out of town on business for some congressmen, Ubaldo finds his way to Sabô's bed.

Ezequiel inexplicably doubles back on his tracks. With a curious crowd gathering behind him, he storms into his home, threatening death preceded by castration in the public square. In his haste, all Ubaldo can find to cover himself is the top half of Sabô's pink baby-doll nightgown, which barely reaches his navel. Leaping through the window, he is pursued by the cuckolded captain. Ezequiel is determined to dispense with Ubaldo as with countless others whose intentions toward Sabô he has distrusted.

Worn out from a long night of love, Ubaldo is losing ground to his pursuer. In his path stands the bird market; he is unable to veer around the piles of cages fast enough. He crashes into them, and birds, freed from their cages, fill the air. They pick up their liberator by his nightgown and fly away with him. Crossing the state line, they set Ubaldo down in a convent, where the nuns welcome him and ask him no questions.

The captain, meanwhile, is rooted to the spot in the middle of the square, where, according to the narrator, he remains. He turns into a horntree, a source of raw materials out of which artisans fashion combs, drinking cups, and other useful items. Thus, the narrator concludes, the feared killer has been "transformed into an object of real public utility."

Themes and Meanings

Jorge Amado has developed his work, he says, "around the reality of Brazil, discussing the country's problems, touching on the dramatic existence of the people and their struggle." Imprisoned as a member of the Communist Party in 1935, Amado was exiled on two occasions; in 1937, after a national ban, his books were burned in a plaza by the Brazilian military.

"The Miracle of the Birds" is representative of the author's writing after 1958, which followed his break with the Communist Party in 1955. Although his focus remained the lives of the marginal classes, grim examinations of their plight yielded to humorous and highly sensual works. According to some critics, Amado tempered his social criticism with satire, irony, and ribald comedy. Others contend that Amado's commitment to social reform inevitably dissolved into a greater passion, that is, indulging in the local color and exotic mix of peoples and cultures in his native region of northeastern Brazil.

This passion links Amado with Modernism, which dominated Brazilian literature and art beginning in the 1920's. Modernism was less a cohesive "school" than a movement rejecting European influences and finding inspiration in the "real" Brazil, that is, in the backlands of the Northeast. A product of Modernism, the consciously "regional" novel became a staple of northeastern writers, probably based on the belief that the culture of this region was enriched by the racial admixture of its inhabitants.

For some critics, Amado's works do not so much call for reform as promote a certain nostalgia. Daphne Patai, for example, asks how the writer can "seriously wish to change a society" in whose "foibles"—he "so obviously delights?" Patai interprets Amado's humor less as satire than as burlesque. Such humor exploits rather than threatens the status quo.

A component of the status quo that Amado distinctly exploits, in the eyes of feminist critics such as Patai, is the ideology of Brazilian machismo. This view reasserts a primal claim of sex and biology on women. Arguably, one theme of "The Miracle of the Birds," as of other works by Amado, is female sexual appetite. Although the author may claim that he depicts women as free agents in sex, Patai counters that he presents the stereotype of the woman "in heat," unable to do without sex. They may be free in the sense of unrestrained sexual beings, but otherwise they are "dominated" by men. Amado's female characters in the story are clearly dependent on men economically.

Patai is not alone in her assessment that Amado's desire to entertain often overwhelms his ambitions as a writer of social protest. It is generally agreed that Amado is essentially a romantic writer, given to softening the hard edges of the squalor and injustice that he depicts. Whether making social protest palatable strengthens its effectiveness or in fact turns it into something else, critics continue to debate.

Style and Technique

Critics characterize Amado as an instinctive writer. His comparative lack of reflectiveness and defects of craftsmanship are compensated by his ability to captivate the reader with his storytelling skills. If his work is marked by a certain glibness, there is also an undeniable vividness to the scenes in his stories and novels, and "The Miracle of the Birds" is no exception.

Amado characteristically uses the device of authorial narrative in his fiction, that is, of a storyteller reporting and commenting on events. Widely used for centuries, this framing device is evident in Henry Fielding's *Tom Jones* (1749) as well as Miguel de Cervantes's *El ingenioso hidalgo don Quixote de la Mancha* (1605, 1615; *The History of the Valorous and Wittie Knight-Errant, Don Quixote of the Mancha*, 1612-1620; better known as *Don Quixote de la Mancha*). Producing the sense of immediacy and "presentness" made possible by a first-person narrative, the technique also permits the writer to exploit such privileges of third-person narration as intrusion and commentary, thereby directing the reader's interpretation of events. The device aims, ultimately, at convincing the reader of the "reality," or authenticity, of the story being told.

The authorial narrative relies largely on simulating the spoken word, enabling Amado's fiction to bridge the worlds of folklore and myth. The "realism" of Amado's style, then, seeks to approximate that of popular literature. Indeed, his narrative pose is that of a chronicler of "the people," rooted in the oral tradition of popular folklore and song. In keeping with this tradition, sustaining action is his forte. His characters, following E. M. Forster's categorization, are more apt to be "flat" than "round"; that is, they are readily identifiable and should not be expected to develop or to display complexity. As with the characters in popular literature, they are iconographic.

Amado's intermingling of the real and the super- or supra-real links him not only to local folklore and myth but also to the technique of Magical Realism so prevalent in modern Latin American fiction. This style serves to reinforce the irrationality of Amado's work, infused as it is with the romantic temperament of the author. Although Amado's use of the marvelous may be considered symbolic, as well as highly effective in terms of the storyteller's art, it also implies to critics such as Patai the inability to affect the true causes of events. It has been suggested after all that in societies, including many still in Latin America, in which the gap between the "have" and the "have nots" remains great, the influence of magic, as one of the few weapons left available to the latter, remains strong.

Amy Adelstein

MIRIAM

Author: Truman Capote (Truman Streckfus Persons, 1924-1984)
Type of plot: Psychological
Time of plot: 1944
Locale: New York City
First published: 1945

> *Principal characters:*
> MRS. H. T. MILLER, a lonely old widow
> MIRIAM, a sinister little girl

The Story

Mrs. H. T. Miller is a widow who lives alone in a small apartment near the East River in New York City. She dresses simply and wears no makeup. She spends her days cleaning her apartment, fixing her own meals, tending her canary, and smoking an occasional cigarette. One evening, she decides to go to the movies.

While waiting in line at the box office, she becomes aware of a thin little girl standing nearby. Mrs. Miller is struck by the girl's old-fashioned clothes and her silver-white hair. The girl hands her some money and asks her to buy a ticket for her. Mrs. Miller complies without really knowing why and even feels guilty, as if she has done something wrong. Inside the theater, Mrs. Miller gets a closer look at the girl and decides that her most distinctive feature is her eyes, which are large, unblinking, and adultlike. During the few minutes before the film starts, they have a brief conversation; the girl says that her name is Miriam, which happens to be Mrs. Miller's first name, and that she has never seen a film before.

One snowy night a week later, just as Mrs. Miller curls up in bed with a hot-water bottle and a newspaper, the doorbell rings. She tries to ignore it, but when the noise becomes one unceasing ring, she goes to the door to put a stop to it and finds Miriam on her doorstep. The girl barges into the living room and takes charge. As at their last meeting, her dress is old-fashioned, but this time it is white silk. Mrs. Miller marvels over such a costume on a cold February night. She marvels even more over Miriam's rude behavior as the girl goes around the room pronouncing judgment on various items. Miriam tries to uncover the cage of the canary to make him sing, but Mrs. Miller stops her. When Miriam says she is hungry and demands food, Mrs. Miller agrees to feed her on the understanding that Miriam will eat and then leave.

While she is in the kitchen fixing sandwiches, Mrs. Miller hears the canary singing and is furious. When she returns with the sandwiches, she finds the canary cage still covered and Miriam snooping in her jewel case. Miriam says there is nothing good there but a cameo brooch and demands that Mrs. Miller give it to her. At that moment, Mrs. Miller realizes just how much she is at the mercy of this sinister little girl. Once she has eaten, Miriam is about to leave, wearing the cameo brooch, when she asks Mrs. Miller for a kiss good-night. When Mrs. Miller refuses, Miriam seizes a vase containing paper flowers and hurls it to the floor, where it shatters. Then she stamps on the bouquet, walks to the door, gives Mrs. Miller a look of "slyly innocent curiosity," and leaves.

Mrs. Miller spends the next day in bed, but on the following day, she awakens to springlike weather and decides to go shopping. She is in a holiday mood until she encounters a deformed old man who stalks her until she escapes into a florist's shop. On an impulse, she buys six white roses, then stops by a glassware store to buy a vase, and a bakery to buy some sweets. Throughout this escapade, she feels that she is following some prearranged plan.

At home, she sets things out as if she is expecting someone; promptly at five, the doorbell rings. When Miriam demands to be let in, Mrs. Miller lights a cigarette and refuses to open the door. After the ringing stops and she thinks the coast is clear, she opens the door a crack, only to find Miriam sitting on a cardboard box with a doll cradled in her arms. Miriam interprets the flowers and sweets as a sign of welcome and announces that she plans to move in. The box, she says, as Mrs. Miller obediently drags it inside, contains her clothes.

Distraught, Mrs. Miller runs down the hall for help, but when a neighbor checks out the apartment, he can find no trace of Miriam. Fearfully, Mrs. Miller returns to her apartment and, seeing that Miriam and her belongings are not there, begins to wonder if she has ever really known a girl named Miriam. With a sense of relief, she realizes that with the apparition gone, she can reclaim her identity, for she is sure she has been suffering only a temporary lapse. Just as she is giving in to this contented feeling, she is aware of sounds from the next room, of drawers opening and closing, followed by the murmur of a silk dress moving toward the doorway.

Themes and Meanings

Truman Capote's own interpretation of this story is that Miriam is a part of Mrs. Miller herself, the terrifying creation of a woman drifting into schizophrenia. The story presents evidence of a woman who, in her grief and loneliness, conjures up images from her own childhood. Miriam's clothes are like those that Mrs. Miller would have worn in her childhood, a time when there would have been no films. It is possible that Mrs. Miller was once demanding and impertinent. There is much more to this story, however, than the mere case study of a split personality.

It is clear from the outset that Mrs. Miller is not a stereotypical recluse living behind locked doors in dark, untidy rooms. Her apartment is described as a pleasant one in a recently remodeled building. She is a widow, but there is a mention only of adequate insurance, not of insurmountable grief. Although she may have narrow interests and no close friends, she gets out to the grocery store once in a while, occasionally takes in a film, and even goes shopping. Her life is no different from countless other lives, especially in a big city. Capote says that "her activities were seldom spontaneous," that she rarely does more than clean house, fix food, tend her canary, and smoke an occasional cigarette. It may sound like a life of quiet desperation but not one of impending madness.

Miriam's initial appearances occur under fairly normal circumstances: while Mrs. Miller stands in line at a movie theater and just after she curls up in bed with the newspaper. These are not moments of stress or depression. In both instances, Mrs. Miller seems sane enough and quite contented. It is only on the occasion of Miriam's last visit to the apartment—when the girl arrives with a box of clothes, prepared to move in—that Mrs. Miller becomes filled with anxiety. Rather than give in to Miriam, Mrs. Miller does the smart thing: She goes for help. The neighbors do not take her for a crazy woman. Instead, they comfort her and offer to check things out for her.

It is not until Mrs. Miller returns to her apartment alone and finds Miriam still there that her mental state suggest psychosis. From the next room, she hears the rustle of a silk dress moving nearer, swelling in intensity; she feels the walls trembling with vibrations and the room caving under a wave of whispers. As she stares into the face of this fragile child with the hair and eyes of an old woman, she may either be surrendering to some sort of madness, or she may be facing the overwhelming reality of what has come to be, for her, a meaningless existence.

Style and Technique

Capote likes to deal in ambiguity. A favorite technique of his is to introduce a bizarre element into an ordinary scene or story and let it fester. Miriam is such an irrational element, one that can intrude on an orderly life for no apparent reason, the capricious agent of diabolical fate, blithely defying one's insistence on rational explanations.

Another irrational element in the story is the deformed old man who stalks Mrs. Miller while she is on her shopping spree. Whoever he is, he serves as a catalyst in the story, propelling it to a harrowing conclusion where all the bizarre elements unite to push Mrs. Miller over the edge. It is not until Miriam mentions having lived with a very poor old man that Mrs. Miller finally breaks down and runs for help, for she knows intuitively that it must be the same old man. This means that both he and Miriam can only be figments of her imagination—demons of her deepest dreads.

Thomas Whissen

MIRRORS

Author: Carol Shields (1935-2003)
Type of plot: Psychological
Time of plot: The late twentieth century
Locale: Big Circle Lake
First published: 1996

> *Principal characters:*
> A HUSBAND, a sixty-year-old retired management consultant
> HIS WIFE, a fifty-eight-year-old housewife

The Story

"Mirrors" is told in second person. The narrator explains to the reader the thoughts of a man and woman about their thirty-five-year marriage. Their contemplations center on the symbolic meanings of mirrors and what banning them from their summer home has meant over the years. The action consists of the revelations of the characters. The story includes many details about what has happened to the couple over the thirty-five-year period but does not contain any action beyond their memories and observations.

The story opens with the husband thinking about how many of the people he has known have sacrificed something—television, sugar, neckties. His friends have the idea that making a sacrifice will improve them in some way. He and his wife have sacrificed mirrors in their summer house; for two months of the year, they have rejected what the husband perceives as a basic human need to observe themselves. The wife even removes the mirror from her compact when they go to the house.

When asked by friends how he manages to shave, the man replies that he does it by feel. The woman does her hair and makeup by feel also. The man has watched her put on her lipstick so many times that he sometimes wants to stretch his mouth the way she does when he is watching her; this is one of many details in the story that show the husband and wife mirroring each other in both literal and figurative ways.

The man's meditation on his life is triggered by his retirement a week earlier from his management consulting company. His wife has been a housewife and volunteer, and they are described as being extremely typical except for their rejection of mirrors for the summer.

After the introductory material sets the scene, the story jumps back in time to explain how the man and women decided not to have mirrors in their summer home. The couple bought the cottage when they were newlyweds and childless. They spent weeks cleaning and fixing it. After shopping for a mirror and not finding one they liked, they decided to go without. The decision was, then, made somewhat by chance.

Although the two thought they knew each other well before marriage, working quietly together on the cottage helps them get to know each other better. The husband has a moment when he wants to tell his wife that working hard all day and waking up in the morning with her is just what he has always wanted. At the end of the summer, they see their reflections in a mirror at a restaurant. They are surprised not to recognize themselves but are pleased by what they see.

The story then jumps to a later summer, when the children are six and eight. The daughter looks for a mirror before remembering that there are none in the cottage. This incident triggers for the wife the thought that at one time new purses contained rough mirrors wrapped in tissue paper. She thinks they were like good luck charms or like compasses for finding yourself.

During a later summer, the husband is glad there are no mirrors. He has had an affair and is too ashamed to see himself. His wife contemplates mirrors while worrying about her husband's possible infidelity. She is reassured by noting the simplicity of mirrors—only glass and silver are required to make one. Because the construction is so simple, a mirror can be constantly renewed. If the glass breaks, it can be replaced. When the mirror gets old, it can be resilvered. Like a mirror, a marriage, also made of two parts, can be renewed.

Returning to the story's present time, the husband reflects that his children seem to envy him for having such a settled life with a long marriage, old friends, and a paid mortgage. However, his life is not as settled as it seems. He and his wife sometimes seem like strangers to each other, and he still has doubts about many things. For example, he wonders about going without mirrors. He finds this sacrifice, made on a whim, to be inconvenient and even childish.

The story ends with the husband and wife looking at each other, seeing themselves in the other's eyes, and, as the narrator perceives it, becoming each other for a moment; each is the mirror of the other.

Themes and Meanings

The husband's and wife's meditations on mirrors and on the meanings of living without them raise issues about how people see and define themselves. The husband notes a need people have to observe themselves. However, both the man and woman find freedom in avoiding mirrors. He feels better not having to see himself after having an affair, and she, frustrated with her inability to lose weight, enjoys not catching sight of herself in a mirror in her bathing suit.

Beyond this, the wife notes how a mirror can function like a good luck charm or even a compass for finding oneself. In the absence of such a compass, the man and woman must find themselves in other ways. In the simplest sense, they learn to rely on touch rather than sight, for fixing their hair or shaving, for example. However, ultimately, they find themselves in each other instead. At first, this takes the form of noticing small things that the other cannot know without a mirror, for example when the wife notices that her husband has a smudge on his face for several days. Ultimately, the couple realize that they share some bond, like twins. In the final scene, they see themselves in each other's eyes, literally becoming mirrors of each other.

Above all, the theme of mirrors is used to fashion the story as an affirmation of marriage. The story's ending, in which the husband and wife for a moment, looking into each other's eyes, feel as if they are under the skin of each other's faces, offers a perspective on the value of marriage in forming the identity of the spouses. Not only is the story, then, about actual mirrors but also is about the husband and wife as mirrors of each other.

However, marriage is more complex than merely an opportunity for the completion and definition of each spouse. This final moment of revelation occurs right after the man has thought about how he and his wife are still sometimes strangers to each other after thirty-five years of marriage. He has lain awake wondering who his wife really is when their eyes meet. Marriage is affirmed not only through what it reveals to the spouses but also through the mysteries that remain between a husband and wife.

Style and Technique

Carol Shields uses the central symbol, the mirror, to show meaning in a marriage that the story's details make seem typical. The piling up of mundane details about the ordinary characters contrasts the revealing details from the characters' contemplation of mirrors and the mirror-free state.

The details the man and woman remember of their thirty-five years of married life portray the couple as extremely ordinary. They are political moderates and members of the middle class. The lack of names for the characters leaves them with a type of anonymity that suggests that they could be anyone. Even the location of the summer home—Big Circle Lake—has a generic sound. The location is left vague so that this story could take place anywhere in Northern America.

The contrast of mundane and revealing details shows not only that meaning can be found in people and events that could be easily overlooked because they are so common but also that the most ordinary lives are filled with meaning. The man's thought that most of his friends have sacrificed something suggests that each has a story filled with significance.

The second-person point of view contributes to the generic feel of the characters and keeps the reader from forming an emotional connection with those characters. The direct address of the narrator to the reader accentuates that a story is being told and that the narrator and the reader are interpreting the information provided. This use of point of view separates the reader from the characters in the story by reminding readers that they are not being given direct access to the characters' thoughts but are instead having their access to material mediated by the narrator.

Although both the husband and the wife reflect on mirrors and on marriage, they never discuss their thoughts with one another. Their separate but parallel reflections support the theme of marriage containing mystery and secrets at the same time as it allows couples to mirror each other.

The notion of reflection, in both its literal and figurative forms, is explored through the characters' thoughts. The story's name, "Mirrors," suggests that it itself is a type of reflection of the events it records.

Joan Hope

MISERY

Author: Anton Chekhov (1860-1904)
Type of plot: Psychological
Time of plot: 1861 to 1886
Locale: St. Petersburg, Russia
First published: "Toska," 1886 (English translation, 1920)

> *Principal characters:*
> IONA POTAPOV, a poor sleigh-driver
> HIS HORSE

The Story

Cab driver Iona Potapov is physically miserable, sitting motionless on his sleigh, bent double with falling snow covering him. His horse also is motionless, and the snow covers her, too. She is lost in thought, psychologically miserable, as anyone would be who finds herself taken away from her quiet country home and cast into the chaos of busy St. Petersburg.

After a long wait, Iona gets a fare, a military officer. Iona appears to be a bad driver, weaving through the street and obstructing other travelers. His clumsiness comes from lack of attention; what he really wants to do is tell the officer about the death of his son. He cannot drive and tell his story at the same time, so the officer, who seems somewhat sympathetic, insists that he attend to driving.

After a few more hours, three young revelers demand his services. They are less sympathetic than the officer. In fact, they treat Iona much as they treat his horse: Both must take them quickly to their destination, or be beaten if they are not fast enough. Iona may prolong this trip unconsciously in order to have their company longer. Although they abuse him, he would rather be with them than alone. When he confides in them, one of the passengers, who may be trying to avoid facing his own case of consumption, generalizes that we all die and reiterates his wish to hurry to the destination where more pleasure awaits him.

When Iona is left alone again in the falling snow, he finds his suffering unbearable. He is silent and isolated in a crowded, noisy city. He realizes that he cannot appeal to these people to listen. He returns to the yard and his fellow drivers who are off duty but finds no one among the exhausted drivers who will listen to him. Everyone is absorbed in his own life, getting a living, and resting from it. Again alone in a crowd of people, Iona pictures what he wants, to tell the whole story of his son's life and death to sympathetic listeners who will help him to habituate himself to this breach of his sense of life's order.

Finally, he goes to his horse, the nearest he is able to come to finding a sympathetic listener. He imagines the horse as one who has suffered loss, thus creating a small community. Having done this, he cannot help but tell her the whole story.

Themes and Meanings

Readers unfamiliar with Russian history may easily miss a crucial dimension of Anton Chekhov's story. It is set in the period after the Great Reforms of the 1860's. These reforms included freeing the serf farmers from virtual enslavement, followed by a long, complex, and often chaotic process of redistribution of land. Most of Chekhov's fiction and drama is set in this period before the Revolution of 1917, which corresponds with his life span. The main features of this period were social ferment and disorderly economic change, and one major change was dislocation. Many rural people were forced to move, and among them were many peasants who went to cities to find work.

Iona is one such peasant who has come with his horse to St. Petersburg to drive a cab. His wife has died. His son, Kuzma, has followed him to take up the same work, and his daughter, Anisya, remains in the country. Iona, then, is an exile in the city. He comes from an old and comparatively rich peasant culture but now finds himself alienated and lost in a city that offers him none of the social support that his background has led him to expect. What culture he finds in St. Petersburg cannot meet his needs. The story is about Iona's need to grieve. He is miserable because his son has died, and he needs someone to listen as he shapes this event into a story that will give it an orderly place in his experience. In the lost community from which Iona comes, the proper way to grieve includes telling the story of his son's life and death to sympathetic listeners who will echo his sorrow and so help him to express it and begin to deal with it.

It is painfully ironic that in a city full of people, Iona must find sympathetic community with his horse. By coming to work in St. Petersburg, Iona has lost his community. A consequence of this loss is that he no longer has access to the resources of that community for dealing with the death of his son. Iona's attempts to deal with his grief by talking about it are not appropriate in the urban culture where he now works. There is a pronounced class barrier that prevents his passengers from sympathizing with a peasant cab driver. The reader might be tempted to condemn the people of the city for their failure to sympathize, but that does not seem to be Chekhov's point in the story. Clearly there is something wrong with this state of affairs, where basic human needs are not met, but Chekhov tends to locate the causes of these divisions between people in structures and processes over which individuals have little control.

The glimpses that Chekhov offers of other characters show them as like Iona, in that each is more or less absorbed in his personal concerns. A main difference is that they seem unaware of any obligation they might have to listen to Iona. Such an obligation would seem more natural in a small, rural community organized communally with church and family at its center, the kind of community from which Iona comes. How do people meet each other's spiritual needs in a large urban community of many competing interests, in which capitalism and individualism are the more powerful driving forces? A number of Chekhov's works lead to this question, which was on the minds of many Russian intellectuals at the end of the nineteenth century.

Style and Technique

Perhaps the most distinctive feature of Chekhov's style in this story is that it is narrated in the present tense, which heightens the sense of immediacy of the events. The contrast with more conventional past-tense narration seems to suggest a closeness to events and an intimacy with Iona and his horse. One suggestive irony of this intimacy is that it tends to place the reader in the imaginary position of Iona's horse, a silent and sympathetic listener. If the story as a whole works as it seems intended to, the reader may feel an intense wish to offer Iona the comfort he needs, a wish heightened by the immediacy of the unusual use of the present tense. In this way, Chekhov's story might in a small way contribute to solving the general social problem that Iona's plight illustrates, by stimulating the wish for the kind of community in which people of all classes and from all parts of society are sympathetic toward one another.

Another important and more characteristic feature of Chekhov's style is his understated, almost laconic approach to the telling. This approach prefigures Ernest Hemingway's characteristic style of conveying deep feeling in ways that avoid sentimentality. The story of a poor old man unable to find sympathy in a cold, hard world easily could become excessively pathetic, but Chekhov controls his tone carefully. He uses the setting and dramatic episodes to convey Iona's suffering at first. As Chekhov gradually reveals Iona's thoughts and feelings, the descriptions are spare and flat, explaining simply what he feels and what he needs. One result is that the story evokes the appropriate response from the reader without overspecifying what the reader should feel. One relates to Iona more as a person in a predicament than as a character created to elicit an emotional response for its own sake.

Control over tone is important to Chekhov's purpose in the story, which includes helping his contemporaneous Russian readers to understand and sympathize more fully with one another. It also contributes significantly to the story's continuing power to speak to readers who no longer fully recognize the story's historical moment, leading them to consider, for example, the fundamental needs that draw individuals into communities.

Terry Heller

MISS BRILL

Author: Katherine Mansfield (Katherine Mansfield Beauchamp, 1888-1923)
Type of plot: Character study
Time of plot: About 1920
Locale: A coastal city in France
First published: 1920

> *Principal characters:*
> MISS BRILL, a middle-aged woman living in exile
> A YOUTH AND HIS GIRLFRIEND, whose conversation Miss Brill
> overhears

The Story

An aging, lonely woman living in Paris and maintaining herself by teaching English is the subject of this character portrait by Katherine Mansfield. Miss Brill's life is one of shabby gentility and pretense; this impression commences in the opening paragraph as she lovingly takes an old-fashioned fox fur out of its box for her usual Sunday outing to the gardens. Looking forward to the new Season, she is, however, distracted by a peculiarly ominous feeling that seems to be in the air and for which she does not know how to account—"like the chill from a glass of iced water before you sip." Maternally caressing the fur, she looks into its "dim little eyes," hearing its fearful question: "What has been happening to me?" With this question, the narrator submerges the point of view into the psyche of Miss Brill, and the reader beholds her pathetic attempt to build a fantasy life to protect her from the harsh facts of her existence. Like the insidious illness that seems to be creeping to life inside her, Miss Brill is abruptly forced to confront the reality that her imagination seeks to escape: She is growing old and lonely in her exile, and the world is an unfriendly place for such people.

Occupying her "special seat," Miss Brill gives only partial attention to the band music, for it is obvious that her main interest in coming to the park each week is to participate in the lives of people around her—in fact, she prides herself on her ability to eavesdrop on the conversations of those nearby without seeming to do so. This is her escape from a dreary existence—a dark little room "like a cupboard" in a rooming house from which she emerges four afternoons a week to read to an invalid and cadaverous old man until he falls asleep in his garden.

At first, an elderly couple share her seat but prove uninteresting. Miss Brill recalls last Sunday's old Englishman and his complaining wife, whom Miss Brill had wanted "to shake"—presumably because the wife scorns the companionship Miss Brill lacks in her life. Soon, however, she turns her attention toward the crowd of passersby: raucous children, an old beggar who sells flowers from a tray, and laughing young girls in bright colors who pair off with soldiers. Hovering just beyond the threshold of a conscious reflection is the knowledge that all the people who meet in the Jardins Publique Sunday after Sunday, occupying the same benches and chairs, are nearly all old and look as though they, too, have just come from the same dingy little rooms.

As if the thought were too painful for close scrutiny, Miss Brill focuses on the crowd once again, and this time she notices a woman wearing a shabby ermine toque approach a dignified, elderly gentleman. Miss Brill's sudden, intense identification with the woman blurs her literal point of view: "Now everything, her hair, her face, even her eyes, was the same color as the shabby ermine, and her hand, in its cleaned glove, lifted to dab her lips, was a tiny yellowish paw." Immediately, Miss Brill projects a fantasy aura around the pair; next, however, she sees the man rebuff the woman, crudely blowing cigarette smoke in her face. The woman—whom Miss Brill has come to identify by her toque—covers her humiliation by smiling brightly and retreats out of Miss Brill's sight. As usual, whenever a painful thought comes too close, Miss Brill turns her attention outward to the sights and sounds around her.

Now, however, a new perception has been awakened in her as a result of this slightly sordid encounter, and it fills Miss Brill with elation: "Oh, how fascinating it was! How she enjoyed it! How she loved sitting here, watching it all!" She conceives of life as all theater and playacting, and she herself as a participant—one of life's actresses, no longer a mere eavesdropper and spectator. The premonitions that tugged at her spirits at the beginning of the story are dispelled by this vision; she even imagines a future dialogue with the old man to whom she reads, in which she pronounces herself an actress.

Like the ominous leaf drifting from nowhere out of the sky, a warning chill fills her with sadness and presages the story's denouement. A young, well-dressed couple appear nearby; inescapably, Miss Brill prepares to overhear, first having assigned them their romantic roles as hero and heroine fresh from his father's yacht. Their dialogue overwhelms Miss Brill with its blatant cruelty:

> "No, not now," said the girl. "Not here, I can't."
> "But why? Because of that stupid old thing at the end there?" asked the boy. "Why does she come here at all—who wants her? Why doesn't she keep her silly old mug at home?"

The youth continues to importune her, but the girl breaks off in a fit of giggling, derisive laughter—at Miss Brill's fur, which to the girl looks like "a fried whiting."

The narrator then summarizes Miss Brill's return home, commenting only that she bypasses her usual stop at the baker's for a slice of honeycake. Back in her room, mortified like the woman in the shabby toque, she hurriedly replaces her fur in its box without looking at it; as the full shock of her rejection strikes, the narrator concludes the story in a manner reminiscent of the opening: "But when she put the lid on she thought she heard something crying."

Themes and Meanings

Characteristically, Mansfield imports a term from her native New Zealand for effect: "brill" is a common fish without culinary or commercial value. However, clearly, Miss Brill is not a figure of contempt; her self-deception is a very human response to what she feels is becoming an intolerable reality; moreover, her apprehension of something at work inside her, alternately numbing and tingling, explains her displaced feelings and her need to fantasize.

Mansfield herself knew well the plight of a woman on her own living in exile: The last years of her life were a frenetic search for health on the Continent. The pleurisy that afflicted her in 1917 was later aggravated into tuberculosis; she died at the age of thirty-four near Fontainebleau, France, in 1923, when a coughing fit ruptured blood vessels.

In addition to the theme of exile, there is Miss Brill's achingly human need to belong. The narrator's adroit mediation between what Miss Brill literally sees and what her imagination invents accounts for her somewhat hysterical attempt to participate in life as more than a spectator. It is equally obvious, however, that to retreat into a fantasy world is merely to delay truth; Miss Brill's shrill efforts to coerce others into her fantasy, such as the man and woman who meet in the gardens, becomes a way for her to participate in life without risking her emotions. What may in fact have been a man rejecting a prostitute's solicitation becomes the basis for a rendezvous, until Miss Brill's sense of identification with the woman in the toque reminds her too much of herself in the outward signs of aging and the losing struggle with poverty.

Finally, chastened by the snarling young man and the young woman's mockery, Miss Brill is left without any defense other than the false sense of buoyancy she has conjured to protect her from reality. Alone in her room, she is unable to deceive herself, nor can she yet accept full knowledge of her condition. Still detached from her feelings, Miss Brill thinks that she hears the fox weeping. Mansfield's husband—the author and editor John Middleton Murry—has said that Mansfield's obsession for truth dominates her later, more mature stories, of which "Miss Brill" is an example.

Style and Technique

Mansfield's influence on the structure of the short story is comparable to that of her more famous contemporary James Joyce on the novel. Crucial to each is a sense that point of view must be controlled from within the character and that the elusiveness of life's meaning can be captured through an epiphanic moment. Here, mental access has been restricted to Miss Brill, but mere selective omniscience cannot account for the artfulness of the technique. The manipulation of time is important because the story tends toward the exploration of a few moments in a character's life.

These highly compressed moments, therefore, reveal psychological time instead of clock-time, and they are everywhere marked by Miss Brill's colloquialisms and features of her private language. Mixed with this language, however, is the narrator's phraseology (narrated monologue), so that even the most neutral observations are reinforced by a kind of lyric intensity: "And sometimes a tiny staggerer came suddenly rocking into the open from under the trees, stopped, stared, as suddenly sat down 'flop,' until its small high-stepping mother, like a young hen, rushed scolding to its rescue." It is this rich mixture of interior monologue, narrated monologue, and narrator summary that enables the reader to perceive the very reality Miss Brill seeks to deny in her fantasies.

Like Joyce, Mansfield rejected an intrusive commentary, allowing the reader to form a reaction to the character in more subtle ways. As Miss Brill reflects on the past, or once, notably, anticipates a future time in the imagined dialogue with her reading companion, she reveals herself and her anxieties most fully. Using Miss Brill's eyes to look outward on the world of the story enables the narrator to infuse her vision with a stronger vision so that themes of isolation, exile, and aging in a hostile world appear to evolve naturally from the character herself.

In this way, the intermingling of scene, narrator summary (or withdrawal), and the modes of Miss Brill's mental life work in harmony to preserve the flavor of Miss Brill's own phraseology and to keep the narrative fabric smooth and seamless. The end result is that Miss Brill's life tends toward a moment in which she can no longer deny the reality she so greatly fears.

Terry White

MISS CYNTHIE

Author: Rudolph Fisher (1897-1934)
Type of plot: Social realism
Time of plot: The 1920's
Locale: Harlem, New York City
First published: 1923

> *Principal characters:*
> MISS CYNTHIE, a seventy-year-old southern grandmother
> DAVE TAPPEN, the grandson whom she raised
> RUTH, Dave's girlfriend and show partner

The Story

Miss Cynthie has just arrived in New York City from Waxhaw, the author's frequent prototype of the rural South. She has come to visit her grandson, Dave Tappen, whom she raised after his mother's death. Dave has apparently done well for himself since coming to the city, as evidenced by his sending money to his family back home in Waxhaw. It is clear from the beginning of the story, however, that Miss Cynthie does not know in what type of employment her grandson is engaged. Miss Cynthie, as she insists on being called, is seventy years old, yet she is very spry and quick-witted, in contrast to what might be assumed from her bumpkinish appearance and outlandish baggage.

In the opening scene, Miss Cynthie engages in a good-natured banter with the redcap who offers to assist her with her luggage. During her climb from the train depot up to the street level, Miss Cynthie turns the topic of conversation to her grandson, who is to meet her at the station. She shares with the man her hopes for her grandson's success, but she is clearly apprehensive about the type of work in which he is engaged.

When Dave Tappen arrives to pick up his grandmother, he is immediately recognized by the redcap as someone with a wide-ranging reputation, although the redcap does not reveal why Dave is so well known. The redcap's subsequent chuckle at Miss Cynthie's hopes for her grandson's accomplishment—a preacher, a doctor, or an undertaker, at least—heightens the suspicion that Dave is engaged in some activity of which Miss Cynthie would not approve. Dave's elegant mode of dress, his exquisite "robin's egg blue open Packard with scarlet wheels," and his luxurious, well-appointed apartment in one of the best areas of the city add more mystery to the source of his income.

The next evening, Dave and his girlfriend Ruth take Miss Cynthie to the Lafayette Theater, where crowds of people compete for his attention. Still unbeknownst to Miss Cynthie, Dave has become a celebrated singer and dancer and will perform in the show's debut later in the evening. As Miss Cynthie watches the opening act of the show, she is a mixture of incredulity, amusement, disgust, and pious outrage because she inwardly considers the theater a sinful enterprise. Although the show's scenes of cottonfields, the good-natured humor, and the music awaken some interest in Miss Cynthie, they are not enough to cover her shock and embarrassment when her beloved grandson dances onstage amid a group of scantily clad dancing girls. Miss Cynthie can hardly contain the heartbreak of seeing the boy whom she raised "from a babe" turn into a "tool of the devil." For the remainder of the show, Miss Cynthie withdraws as she bemoans her grandson's activity and her own failure and complicity in what he has become.

At the close of the show, however, Dave comes onstage alone and sings a song that Miss Cynthie taught him as a child. To the delight of the audience and the pride of Miss Cynthie, Dave acknowledges his grandmother as his inspiration and attributes his success to her wise and wholesome teachings. He gives her one of the many floral bouquets tossed to him onstage. Miss Cynthie, through an epiphany of sorts, comes to understand that neither entertainers nor theatergoers are necessarily "tools of the devil." She realizes that she has not lost Dave to the city's vices but that he is engaged in a wholesome expression of his art, and she becomes reconciled with her beloved grandson. As the story closes, Miss Cynthie is singing and tapping her foot to the little jingle that she taught Dave as a child and that has now made him famous.

Themes and Meanings

Rudolph Fisher frequently reused certain themes in his short stories. Among the recurring themes in "Miss Cynthie" are the ineptitude of newly arrived rural southerners to New York City, the centrality of the grandmother figure, and the wonders of Black Harlem of the 1920's.

In Fisher's best-known short stories, which include "Miss Cynthie," the author seems fascinated with how southern blacks who arrived in New York City during the Great Migration of the early part of the twentieth century were, for the most part, ill equipped to deal with the city's sophistication and fast-paced life. Although for most of these characters the city failed to reveal itself as the proverbial "Promised Land," Miss Cynthie seems to challenge Fisher's typical southern character in that she possesses a keen wit and much wholesome, old-fashioned wisdom that characterize her as being able to handle herself in the city. Furthermore, the fact that she fares well during her stay and has several life-affirming experiences while there demonstrate that her visit to the city has been an edifying experience. Her naïveté notwithstanding, Miss Cynthie is presented as a character with spunk, one from whom Dave Tappen, her grandson, has obviously learned his lessons well.

Similarly, Miss Cynthie is an example of the grandmother figure who appears in several of Fisher's stories. These characters are presented as strong, enduring, often long-suffering women who struggle to pass on their sense of the sanctity of life to their second-generation offspring. In the case of Miss Cynthie, she has raised Dave from infancy and has sought to endow him with the virtues of good, clean, moral living. She is, then, understandably disappointed with his involvement with the theater. However, although Dave has not landed in one of the professions that she wished for him, Miss Cynthie comes to realize during his moving testimonial to her at the close of the show that her lessons were well learned and that her hopes were not misspent. Dave has indeed followed Miss Cynthie's admonition to "do like a church steeple— aim high and go straight," and for that, he has achieved stunning success.

Another theme common to Fisher's fiction that is found in "Miss Cynthie" is the focus on life in black Harlem during the 1920's. Although Fisher is frequently noted for pointing out the vice and nightlife of Jazz Age Harlem and the sordidness and corruption of city life, his portrayal of Harlem in "Miss Cynthie" is more a celebration of the best of Harlem. As Dave drives Miss Cynthie through Harlem on her arrival, for example, he is careful to point out the best the city has to offer—the throngs of well-dressed blacks enjoying a leisurely summer day, the numerous handsome edifices owned by blacks, and the several manifestations of his own affluence. Absent are the elements of the lowlife that often are integral to Fisher's short stories. Although a departure from Fisher's norm, the portraiture in "Miss Cynthie" is nevertheless presented with power equal to, if not exceeding, his other stories.

Style and Technique

"Miss Cynthie" is a prime example of the stylistic economy that earned for Fisher the admiration of his contemporaries during the Harlem Renaissance of the 1920's. Its tightly controlled plot, dynamic presentation of character, and deft use of literary devices are all evidence of the consummate artist at work. For example, the reader is intrigued by the way that Fisher develops the mystery surrounding the nature of Dave Tappen's employment. Miss Cynthie's expressed hopes for her grandson, the redcap's suggestive response, Dave's obvious wealth, and Miss Cynthie's distrust of the theater all contribute to the developing notion that Miss Cynthie will not be amused with her grandson's vocation.

Another element of style is the warm, good-natured humor that abounds—from Miss Cynthie's early insistence on carrying her umbrella to ward off snakes, even in the city, to the final scene that shows her tapping her foot and singing to the tune of the song she had taught her grandson as a child. Fisher's tone, while focusing on ways and manners of the folk, is neither condescending nor mean-spirited; rather, it is a tone of wonderment and appreciation—hallmarks of vintage Rudolph Fisher.

Warren J. Carson

MISS LEONORA WHEN LAST SEEN

Author: Peter Taylor (1917-1994)
Type of plot: Social realism
Time of plot: The 1950's
Locale: Thomasville, Tennessee
First published: 1960

> *Principal characters:*
> MISS LEONORA LOGAN, an elderly retired schoolteacher
> THE UNNAMED NARRATOR, a fifty-year-old man who was one of
> her favorite students

The Story

Miss Leonora Logan, a lifelong resident of Thomasville, Tennessee, and retired school teacher of English, Latin, and history at the local high school, has left on one of her frequent automobile trips. The narrator, her former pupil, now a middle-aged man, is concerned that she will never again be seen alive. Indeed, the city fathers have condemned her house to build a new school on the site.

Miss Logan's house, "Logana," is not really the best site for a new school, but racial integration is coming to Thomasville, and the townspeople want to avoid zoning problems by clearing away the small houses belonging to blacks on her property. Perhaps more important, however, is the grudge the town has held against the Logan family for several generations. They feel the Logans tried to keep the town unspoiled and thereby retarded progress; Logans prevented the town from becoming the county seat, prevented the railroad from coming through the town, and prevented other manifestations of change. Now the town has gotten revenge on the last remaining Logan, elderly Miss Leonora, who taught the town's children for fifty years.

As weeks pass with only an occasional postcard from Miss Leonora, people in town worry about her. They feel guilty about their role in her departure and project their guilt onto her: She is making the town look bad.

The narrator goes back in time to recall Miss Leonora's youth, her intellectual interests—which were not shared by the town—her teaching, and her automobile trips. A beautiful young woman, Miss Leonora started her teaching career at the Thomasville Female Institute, which burned in 1922; then she taught at the consolidated high school. Over the years, she adopted promising young men as her protégés and encouraged them to go to college, mostly unsuccessfully. The narrator is one such former protégé. Miss Leonora was constantly instructing her pupils and the town, even when she seemed to digress in her classes, and continues this role after her retirement.

Periodically, Miss Leonora goes on automobile trips to various byways in the South. On the road, she affects the role of a grande dame in pearls and gloves or a farmer in overalls. She stays in antiquated tourist homes and loves to tell their owners about her town, Thomasville. Now Miss Leonora is gone again, perhaps for the last time. The narrator has been sent with other former students to break the news to Miss Leonora that her house has been condemned. The narrator is surprised to find her packed and ready to leave on a journey. She has also dropped the grande dame and farmer attire for a new persona as a modern, elderly, white gentlewoman. She has cut and blued her hair and wears a stylish dress. As she and the narrator have tea for the last time, she tells him she appreciates him and her other pupils and apologizes for trying to instruct them with her ideas. Then she leaves. The townspeople are left to worry about Miss Leonora and their role in running her out of town. The narrator worries as well and ponders Miss Leonora's role in Thomasville.

Themes and Meanings

"Miss Leonora When Last Seen" exemplifies the complexities of community life and the pettiness that often informs public decisions. Thomasville has loved having the Logan family to revile and use as an excuse for their own lack of progress. Although Miss Leonora is old-fashioned in some respects, she is the one who gave African Americans work and homes on her property. Shortly before her final departure, she gives a small black boy a book she is reading when he expresses an interest in it. The town does not approve of her different ways and finds a way to cast her out by condemning her house.

The city fathers of Thomasville disguise their cruelty to Miss Leonora by calling the new school progress and projecting ancient grievances against Miss Leonora's ancestors onto her. They are also uneasy about her kindly treatment of blacks and nervous about the coming of integration. Will Miss Leonora side with the blacks who live on her property? The town decides not to take a chance and drives her out. Miss Leonora cuts her losses and leaves, not giving the town the satisfaction of knowing where she is going. Now it is their turn to feel left out of the decision-making process.

The English poet William Blake said, "Then cherish pity, lest you drive an angel from your door." The city fathers of Thomasville do not heed Blake's admonition. In the thankless, pitiless treatment of Miss Leonora, they have driven from their midst an essential ingredient to the health of the town. In "Miss Leonora When Last Seen," Peter Taylor challenges the reader to examine the role of eccentrics in communal life and exposes the petty cruelty of blind group decisions.

Style and Technique

The voice of the first-person narrator plays an essential role in conveying the meaning of this story. This unnamed denizen of Thomasville is perhaps a more insightful person than he might have been thanks to Miss Leonora's influence. In the narrator's genteel southern style, one notices Miss Leonora's solid grounding in English and Latin in his use of future perfect tenses and the subjunctive mood. He displays wit in his description of the recalcitrant Logans, who fended off progress and the railroad in the nineteenth century. The narrator is, however, a product of the town and can understand both the city fathers and Miss Leonora. This delicate balance is one of Peter

Taylor's best stylistic achievements. The reader is alternately directed toward sympathy with Miss Leonora and understanding of the town's point of view throughout the story. One must draw one's own conclusion about the justice of the matter, although Miss Leonora seems to have the edge. In the end, Miss Leonora has more than an edge and the town's reasoning is seen as specious but fallacious, as well as uncharitable. Taylor, the puppeteer of the story, engineers these shifting reactions.

Verisimilitude is also an important stylistic feature of the story. Thomasville is typical of a sleepy southern town of the 1950's; it complacently enjoys its present, while harboring grudges dating from the nineteenth century and worrying about the coming of integration. Although the milieu that Taylor depicts is southern, the types of human nature displayed in the town are universal. The town fathers cloak their cruelty toward Miss Leonora in civic piety and the law. This universality, which is more reminiscent of William Faulkner than it is of other writers of manners to whom Taylor has been compared—such as John Updike and John Cheever—makes "Miss Leonora When Last Seen" one of his strongest stories.

Because much of the story is retrospective, Taylor's narrator employs the selective nature of memory in telling Miss Leonora's story, somewhat in the manner of Tennessee Williams's outstanding memory plays, such as *The Glass Menagerie* (first performed in 1944). Vivid scenes such as the one in which she gives the black child the book stand out; less vivid scenes recede or are not told to the reader at all. In a real sense, this is the story of the narrator as well as Miss Leonora. She touched his life early, and she will continue to be an influence. The town is upset about Miss Leonora at the time of the story, but it will salve its insensitive conscience and go on. Taylor leads the reader to see that his narrator will be faithful to Miss Leonora in memory and in life, much as Tom is faithful to the memory of Laura in *The Glass Menagerie*. The lens of memory may be a selective one, but it endures. The last literal sighting of Miss Leonora in Thomasville will not be the last sighting in the narrator's mind. Taylor shows the reader that Miss Leonora accomplished more than she realized, a life beyond life in the mind of the narrator.

Isabel B. Stanley

MISS OGILVY FINDS HERSELF

Author: Radclyffe Hall (1880-1943)
Type of plot: Allegory
Time of plot: After World War I
Locale: England and France
First published: 1934

> *Principal characters:*
>> MISS WILHELMINA OGILVY, the protagonist, a woman with a troubled nature
>> SARAH AND FANNY OGILVY, her dependent sisters and frequent antagonists
>> MRS. NANCESKIVEL, a hostess at an isolated hotel on a sparsely inhabited island
>> A NEOLITHIC MAN, part of Miss Ogilvy's dream or previous incarnation
>> A NEOLITHIC WOMAN, part of the same dream or incarnation

The Story

"Miss Ogilvy Finds Herself" begins with the protagonist, Miss Wilhelmina Ogilvy, watching the disbanding of her World War I Red Cross Allied Ambulance Unit at the busy port of Calais in France. The vehicles, only recently back from the front lines, and suddenly expendable, are being unceremoniously hauled onto a freighter bound for England—the same freighter that will transport Miss Ogilvy from her glorious war experiences back to her narrow life in Surrey, England, with her sisters, Sarah and Fanny Ogilvy.

On the train home from Dover, Miss Ogilvy reflects on her troubled youth and her strong need to serve, more actively than most women, in the Great War. She was, it appears, an odd little girl, in a world that valued conformity. As a child, she had a marked predilection for boyish pursuits. As an adolescent, her physical prowess became an embarrassment to her; muscles and muslin did not mix. Even so, as an eligible young woman, she was courted, much to her mother's surprise, by three different men. She could not, however, generate an enthusiasm for any of them. She felt only fellowship with men, and her nature made it impossible for her to take part in the feminine life going on around her. When she moved aside, socially, for her younger sisters—who were avid for matrimony but, ironically, destined to a life of irritable spinsterhood—she became even more isolated.

Then Miss Ogilvy's father died, and she, who as a child had wished ardently to be called William, not Wilhelmina, found herself in the role of paterfamilias. In quick succession, her mother died and then her aunt. Although the aunt left a small fortune, Miss Ogilvy was too worn out from struggling with her unusual nature and her unsympathetic sisters to do anything more adventurous than to buy a small estate in Surrey and settle there. At fifty-five, her energies waning, shy and essentially friendless, she had become content simply to tend her own garden.

Then World War I roused her latent temperament. She despised the work given to women in the war effort. She would not be satisfied until the English officials allowed her to lead a group of women to the frontline trenches of France to do ambulance duty. Once there, "she was competent, fearless, devoted and untiring. . . . Could any man hope to do better?"

Returning to Surrey was a great trial for Miss Ogilvy. Sarah and Fanny had become, in her words, "two damn tiresome cranks!" When a young girl from her ambulance unit visited her and announced an impending marriage, she left Miss Ogilvy with "strange . . . unbidden, thoughts." Growing old no longer seemed a solace. Miss Ogilvy, whose hair had been cropped during the war, refused to grow it back, and Sarah and Fanny began to circulate the rumor that she was suffering from shell shock. She even began to doubt herself.

It is at this point that the story takes on a metaphysical dimension. Quite unexpectedly, Miss Ogilvy packs her kit bag and departs for a small island near the south coast of Devon. This island, seemingly chosen at random and never seen by her before, is rich with *déjà vu* experiences. Before she even disembarks, she "remembers" a cave about which she could not possibly have known. Her "remembrance" is verified by the boatman.

Once at the only hotel on the island, Miss Ogilvy falls into conversation with Mrs. Nanceskivel, her hostess, who offers to show her the island's treasure: The skull and thighbone of a neolithic man unearthed on the island during the digging of a well. Ominously, the man's skull shows that he had been killed by a bronze ax. Miss Ogilvy's response to seeing the bones is disproportionately passionate, and she retires to her room.

What follows may be interpreted by the reader as a dream, a hallucination, a symptom of shell shock, or evidence of a previous incarnation; it most assuredly illuminates the difficulties of Miss Ogilvy's nature. Miss Ogilvy envisions herself living at the dawn of the Bronze Age, as a powerfully built neolithic man, a leader of his tribe, much beloved by a sturdy and beautiful neolithic woman. Though there is danger from another tribe with weapons of "some dark, devilish substance," the primitive man and his mate find consolation with each other and eventually consummate their love in the dark womb of a cave. The man's love for the woman is inarticulate, but profound, and finally fatal: He "put by his weapon and his instinct for slaying. And he lay there defenseless with tenderness," soon to become, as the reader knows, Mrs. Nanceskivel's treasured relic. The next morning finds Miss Ogilvy herself, inexplicably, at the mouth of the island's cave, quite dead.

Themes and Meanings

Radclyffe Hall believed, along with Henry Havelock Ellis, and others of her time, that "sexual inversion" was a congenital condition and a kind of biological tragedy. A lesbian herself, Hall wished to make explicit in her art the frustrations of the congenital invert. She believed that what cannot be helped cannot be censured; thus, her works argue for sympathy, rather than persecution, for those who are different. "Miss Ogilvy Finds Herself," like Hall's more famous novel *The Well of Loneliness* (1928), is an exploration of the psyche of a woman who wishes to be conventional but whose masculine nature makes such an accommodation impossible.

"Miss Ogilvy Finds Herself" has attracted criticism in the twentieth century because of its somewhat antiquated view of homosexuality, yet it was an unusually courageous and explicit work for its time. The reader should not overlook that the protagonist, Miss Ogilvy, is presented in a strikingly favorable light in comparison to her self-indulgent and conventional sisters and her painfully dependent mother. In situations in which her true nature can manifest itself, for example, in managing her estate or serving in the ambulance corp, Miss Ogilvy is decidedly admirable. It is only in her thwarted personal life that she experiences pain and confusion, which Hall attempts to elucidate for the reader through her own version of the allegory of the cave.

Style and Technique

An allegory is the figurative treatment of one subject under the guise of another. It is understandable that in writing about a relatively taboo subject such as lesbianism, an author might gravitate to allegory in an attempt to imply more than can be said. "Miss Ogilvy Finds Herself" is very much in the tradition of Nathaniel Hawthorne, the master of allegory and ambiguity, whose stories are always engaging at the plot level, but whose real richness usually lies just beneath the surface.

The beginning of "Miss Ogilvy Finds Herself" is handled realistically enough, with considerable sophistication of style—as in, for example, this elaborately repetitive sentence from the opening of section 2: "The soft English landscape sped smoothly past: small homesteads, small churches, small pastures, small lanes with small hedges; all small like England itself, all small like Miss Ogilvy's future." The story gathers momentum only on the tiny island off Devon, where everything is both strange and familiar at once. Here the style becomes less consciously rhetorical, and the reader's interest is focused on the meaning of the neolithic love story, which is told largely through metaphor. The warrior describes his lover as a "hut of peace for a man after battle . . . ripe red berry sweet to the taste . . . happy small home of future generations." This change in style, as much as the switch in time, place, and gender, suggests to the reader multiple layers of meaning, layers that permit Hall to develop her ideas about inversion while maintaining a necessary artistic distance.

Cynthia Lee Katona

MISS TEMPY'S WATCHERS

Author: Sarah Orne Jewett (1849-1909)
Type of plot: Social realism
Time of plot: The late nineteenth century
Locale: A small New Hampshire farming community
First published: 1888

> *Principal characters:*
> MRS. CROWE, one of the watchers, a wealthy married woman and
> friend of the deceased Miss Temperance Dent
> SARAH ANN BINSON, the other watcher, a poor spinster and
> friend of the deceased

The Story

The two main characters, Mrs. Crowe and Sarah Ann Binson, fulfill the request of their deceased friend, Temperance "Tempy" Dent. Before she died, Tempy asked that the two, who had been schoolmates and her friends, "come together and look after the house, and manage everything, when she was gone." The story, which has very little plot, is about what is revealed about the women through the commentator or narrator, through their conversations, and through their reactions to each other and to the immediate environment in which they find themselves.

Mrs. Crowe and Sarah Ann Binson pass the hours of their long watch over Tempy and her things by talking, knitting, sewing, eating, and sleeping. Their conversation touches on Tempy: her virtues, her life, and her good deeds. As they reminisce, they reveal Tempy's character along with their own dominant character traits. Each shares secrets she did not intend to share. Each reveals a part of herself never shown before. As the night and the conversation progress, these women, between whom there are numerous differences, are drawn together.

Mrs. Crowe, mentioned first in the story, is considered superior to Sarah Ann Binson. Mrs. Crowe, who enjoys the respect of being referred to as "Mrs." throughout the story, is married to a wealthy farmer. She is stingy, rigid, composed. Sarah Ann, who is called "Sarah" throughout most of the story, is also referred to as Sarah Ann Binson, Sister Binson, and "Miss Binson." Sarah, a spinster, is poor. She is exploited by a widowed sister and six nieces and nephews whom Sarah supports. Sarah is self-sacrificing, hospitable, and sympathetic. She fixes supper for Mrs. Crowe and herself. She is "moved" by Mrs. Crowe's confession that Tempy "has been a constant lesson to me." Mrs. Crowe is uneasy about death and indicates her dread of it several times. The conversation and keeping the vigil help to alleviate some of her fear.

The references to a babbling and then silent brook that runs by the house and to Tempy's spiritual presence suggest that the work has four characters, the brook and Tempy's spirit being the other two. These two "minor" characters seem instrumental in closing the gap between Mrs. Crowe and Sarah Ann, in helping each woman to re-solve other problems. For Mrs. Crowe, the additional problems resolved are her in-ability to give generously and her fear of death.

"Miss Tempy's Watchers" does more than provide portraits of two women and show how they have overcome differences which prevented their enjoying a sister-hood. The work also documents social customs, the language of the region, lifestyles, values, and attitudes.

Themes and Meanings

A number of subjects are explored in this work. The values of sisterhood and of a community are major topics. Mrs. Crowe has lived in her very restricted world, barely extending a helping hand to the many needy in her community. Sarah Ann Binson has worked alone to support her sister's family. Keeping the watch demonstrates how these two women can work together and are able to form a community to serve a friend. The changes in them, especially in Mrs. Crowe, suggest the end of an era, a way of life, and the ushering in of the new. The importance of nature in the form of the brook and a whistling wind, and of one's obligations to one's fellow human beings, are also dominant themes.

Style and Technique

The language in this work is simple, direct, and precise, a blend of the local idiom, incorrect English, and formal English. In addition to mirroring the speech patterns of the region, the language reflects the temperament, the unfolding sensitivity of the women, and the social class of each character. The conversation is the vehicle for un-raveling the personalities and for bringing together parts of the narrative, for unifying the story.

The major pattern in the story is the movement from summary to dialogue and back to summary. After providing information about the setting and the reason for the two women being together, the narrator focuses on the social status and the personalities of Mrs. Crowe and Sarah Ann Binson. The exposition provides a natural introduction to the conversation.

Another major pattern is the use of contrasts, personalities, social status, language, values, and attitudes. Silence is juxtaposed to the noisy brook and the whistling wind. The three provide a contrast with the conversation of the women. Temperance Dent's life and goodness serve as a backdrop for the conversation and any changes these women may make. The relationship between Mrs. Crowe and Sarah at the beginning of the work and that which they appear to have at the conclusion are different.

Ora Williams

MOCCASIN GAME

Author: Gerald Vizenor (1934-   )
Type of plot: Parody
Time of plot: The late twentieth century
Locale: Point Assinika, an imaginary island nation
First published: 1993

> *Principal characters:*
> STONE COLUMBUS, the founder of Point Assinika
> PELLEGRINE TREVES, a rare-book collector from London who is
>   investigating the death of Felipa Flowers
> THE WIINDIGOO, a child-eating evil spirit of Chippewa legend

The Story

In the opening scene, Stone Columbus and other residents of the new sovereign nation, Point Assinika, wait at the marina for the floatplane carrying Pellegrine Treves, bearer of the moccasins worn by Felipa Flowers when she was murdered. Treves is also transporting the purported remains of the long-dead Algonquian princess, Pocahontas, to be interred alongside the remains of Felipa Flowers.

Treves's arrival initiates a series of unusual scenes, during which details of the murder are disclosed. Treves also reveals that federal agents (presumably of the United States government) have deliberately spread believable disinformation about Point Assinika and some of its citizens. One lie in particular, concerning a Jewish Holocaust survivor working as a scientist and healer among the people, emphasizes the disturbingly accurate parallels between the fate of European Jews during World War II and the fate of Native Americans at the hands of European immigrants to America.

Stone Columbus knows, however, that his people thrive on opposition—the more, the merrier. Fully aware of the opposition such an act will generate, Stone and his people are considering a plan to annex the United States—an example of reverse assimilation—if the federal government refuses to meet their demands. Opposition indeed intensifies, as federal agents unthaw and thus release the evil wiindigoo, who returns to Point Assinika to resume the deadly moccasin game that he was about to win many years ago. To combat the wiindigoo, Stone deploys a war herb so powerful that even when unused it shows up on satellite radar as a radiant shadow. In the end, the mutually assured destructive power of the terrible soldier weed war herb creates a Dr. Strangelove kind of scene within the ultimate contest that the moccasin game has become. The fate of the entire human race now lies in the balance.

Themes and Meanings

Stone Columbus, who has had the Trickster of Liberty made and placed at Point Assinika, is the master trickster of the story. The local radio show host, Luckie White, says Stone is a healer in his stories, and healing through humor is his only mission in the world. Such is also the mission of the author, Gerald Vizenor, the trickster behind the trickster.

The story refers once to the patriotic U.S. color scheme of red, white, and blue; however, the only color appearing consistently throughout the story is blue, a color held in high religious regard by many Native American cultures. For example, the blue statue named the Trickster of Liberty, an obvious link between the Native American trickster figure and the U.S. Statue of Liberty, sits prominently in the bay by the Point Assinika marina. Many other blue things, both living and inanimate, also appear: birds called "blue puppets"; a blue child named Blue Ishi; blue medicine poles; "the blues that heal," possibly the music known as the blues; many blue moccasins, including those worn by Felipa Flowers when murdered and those worn by the children of Point Assinika as a sign that they have been healed; Admire's blue tongue; Miigis's blue robe; blue spirit-catchers; and the vault in the House of Life, which turns blue when Blue Ishi touches the stones and the Trickster of Liberty statue outside the vault.

Names are also important in "Moccasin Game." The central character, Stone Columbus, is purportedly a direct descendant of Christopher Columbus, as are all the other residents of Point Assinika. Those residents include Truman, Eleanor Roosevelt, and Lady Bird Johnson, apparently all refugees from some sort of historical time-warp and, perhaps more important, representative of the ongoing, large-scale genealogical experiment that Native Americans and American immigrants have engaged in since the times of Christopher Columbus. Caliban, William Shakespeare's deformed being, is also present on the tempestuous island scene, here as a "great white mongrel." Judge Beatrice Lord is a possible echo of the regionally famous Minnesota jurist of the 1970's, Judge Miles Lord. Most notably, the name of the great Oglala medicine man, Black Elk (with reference also to John Neihardt, Black Elk's biographer), is used to introduce the great war herb used—and yet not used—against the wiindigoo.

Several names seem to appear simply because they fit the characters or things so named: Felipa Flowers, who is plucked from life before the story begins; Binn, who hears containers, or bins; Pellegrine Treves, the peregrinator from London; Teets and Harmonia, whose names simply sound suggestive and euphonious; Carp Radio, the talk radio forum for carping callers and an outlet for truth in the night; and its host, Luckie White, who wants answers (ends), in Caucasian contrast to the other residents of Point Assinika, who dream only of starts (questions).

The cacophony of names and characters finally comes together in a symphonic performance illustrative of a basic pan-human interdependence and interrelatedness. At the climax of the moccasin game, a light show of famous figures flashes in a laser-lit sky, featuring a cast of Jesus Christ, Christopher Columbus, Pocahontas, Crazy Horse, Black Elk, and Louis Riel, the nineteenth century Native American-French Canadian revolutionary.

Finally, the shell game that is the moccasin game conceals (or reveals), within the word "moccasin," the source of the name given by early explorers to Vizenor's Native

American ancestors, the Ojibwa (or Ojibway). "Ojibwa" was the name of the distinctively gathered moccasins made and worn by members of the Algonquian tribe who called themselves Anishinaabe; a variant pronunciation of Ojibwa later gave rise to the tribe's other common name, the Chippewa. As Pellegrine Treves observes, "Language is our trick of discovery, [and] what we name is certain to become that name." Although almost a linguistic cliché, an awareness of that creative trick, which both conceals and reveals, is a rewarding requirement for the reader of Vizenor's "Moccasin Game."

Style and Technique

The title of "Moccasin Game" hints at the playful, gamelike approach the author brings to the serious conflicts humans have with one another and with various natural and supernatural adversaries. The opening line, which begins with the words "The Trickster of Liberty," underscores the devious quality of fate and of human nature, and draws attention to the trickster figure found throughout much of Vizenor's and other Native American literature. The line also provides an obvious allusion to the Statue of Liberty, thereby setting the stage for a story with political overtones as well.

Vizenor's language and plot twist along chaotically, sentences straining the bounds of grammar, and the creative, often alliterative, wordplay and names are reminiscent of Kurt Vonnegut. Freely mixing the names of factual historical figures with his fictional characters, Vizenor makes it impossible to know what is real and what is not; possibly the point being made is that it does not matter, for the real and the fictional also interweave throughout real life. Despite the ever-present threats to humanity, including the story's allegorical parallels to late twentieth century doomsday threats to all life, Vizenor's vision and wordplay ultimately affirm life.

Clearly satirizing human foibles in the nuclear age, Vizenor also parodies, but much more gently, the often naïve visions of those who would create a modern, conflict-free Utopia. For Vizenor, there is no perfect world free of trickery, free of conflict. Without conflict—that is, without humans—there is no moccasin game for the wiindigoo or anyone to play. This is the ultimate irony within the ultimate game, like the game of strategic nuclear standoff, wherein the winner takes all. All is nothing; therefore, as long as no side tries to win, no one loses. The object thus remains what it has always been: to keep playing the only game in town.

William Matta

THE MOLE

Author: Yasunari Kawabata (1899-1972)
Type of plot: Epistolary
Time of plot: The twentieth century
Locale: Japan
First published: "Hokuro no Tegami," 1940 (English translation, 1956)

> *Principal characters:*
> SAYOKO, the narrator and protagonist
> HER HUSBAND
> HER MOTHER

The Story

The text of "The Mole" is an undated letter written by Sayoko to her husband of some years. She tells him about a dream that she has had. The night before, during a visit to her mother's home, Sayoko reports that she dreamed of the mole located high on the upper right side of her back, near her shoulder. Through her reflections on her marriage and life and her account of her dream about her mole, Sayoko reveals both her past and present. She knows that her husband will know about the mole about which she has dreamed because it has been the focus of dissension between them from the earliest days of their marriage. When she lay in bed, her left arm across her chest, playing with the mole, her husband scolded her. It was a bad habit. The mole would grow larger. She should have it removed.

Sayoko's letter tells her husband of the shame she felt when he first began scolding. Even more important, she says that she first became faintly conscious of the oppression of her marriage; her lack of privacy, her lack of refuge, her total vulnerability to his control. Although she then tried to dismiss his attention to her habit of playing with the mole as inconsequential, now that she has been away from him for many years, she sees its importance.

Thinking through her life as she writes, Sayoko tells her husband the history of her relation to her mole—a history that is also the story of her own inner life. As a child she began to play with the mole, perhaps because her mother and sisters had noticed it—perhaps even finding it charming—and drew her attention to it. She remembers, however, that her mother also scolded her during puberty for her habit of rubbing the mole and staring absently into space. Her husband's dislike for her habit grew during their marriage until it became a metaphor for their relationship. Sayoko tells her husband, "it was as though I were warding you off, as though I were embracing myself." All attempts by her husband to change or stop her habit failed, and his dislike for her habit grew into a dislike for her. Conflict over the mole turned into abuse. Her husband beat and kicked her. Nonetheless, her habit continued. His caring ceased. One day Sayoko realized that her habit had disappeared of its own accord, but by then her husband no longer cared one way or the other.

Now regarded as a bad wife on the verge of divorce, Sayoko is surprised to find herself thinking of her husband and feeling grief. In her mother's home she is again free to play with her mole but cannot. When she sleeps she dreams of the mole. Drunk and pleading with her husband in her dream, she touches her mole and it comes off in her hand. She beseeches him to put her mole in the pit of the mole beside his nose. Awake and weeping, she finds that her mole is still on her back. She imagines her husband's mole swelling with the addition of hers; she imagines with pleasure that he might dream of her mole.

Her letter concludes by suggesting to her husband that playing with her mole began in her childhood as a fond expression of her connection to her family. Perhaps, she suggests, playing with the mole was a young girl's expression of a love that she did not know how to speak. Perhaps the mole is a symbol of her love that has gone unrecognized and that has turned malignant and destructive. Like the countless "little things" that might combine to poison a relationship, the mole, seemingly insignificant in itself, has been a sign that cannot be deciphered, a language that cannot be understood.

The letter resolves nothing; like the mole, it does not appear to be read by its intended audience. Like the mole, the letter remains visible but mysterious, contemplated but never fully understood.

Themes and Meanings

Like many of Yasunari Kawabata's stories, "The Mole" captures the mind and heart of a woman at a critical moment—here the moment that a woman is breaking with her husband. First-person reflections on her body, her family, her marriage, and her life blend in this brief letter to reveal her maturing awareness of herself, her motives, her anger, and her love. Unaddressed, perhaps unsent or unanswered, this letter written in painful isolation captures the loneliness, estrangement, and failures of communication that have characterized the woman's life with her family and with her husband. The letter without an audience also represents her own powerlessness and inability to communicate her feelings. Even the message of her dream itself is cryptic, condensed, and—like her letter—her dream cries receive no response.

In her letter Sayoko is working on her life, trying to make sense of it, trying to explain how it is she has come to be defined as a bad wife. She struggles against long years of feeling worthless and searches her life for some experience or emotion that might redeem her self-esteem. The letter, however far removed from direct communication of her feelings, is at least an attempt to reach out, to tell her husband what she has felt and thought and how she is trying to come to terms with her feelings of loss and failure.

The central image of the story is the mole. During Sayoko's exploration of her own experience, the mole gains many levels of meaning as it comes to represent the woman and her relationship to her own body. The mole represents a kind of deformity that makes her the object of others' pity and disgust. It elicits others' arbitrary negative assessments of her and her body that are destructive of her well-being. The mole comes to represent the way in which she is turned in on herself, unable to communicate, as well as her husband's refusal to accept and love her and the failure of their marriage. Although physically harmless, the enigmatic mole is emotionally malignant in Sayoko's life.

Style and Technique

The story's epistolary form offers Sayoko distance to put her experience in perspective and gives her privacy for serious reflection. The letter that she writes does not at first glance appear well organized. Its purpose is to report a dream to her husband, but she begins it by discussing her married life and her husband's physical and emotional abuse. The epistolary form evokes an intense awareness of the audience addressed while at the same time preserving the interiority of the narrator's stream of consciousness. The letter reveals how little the husband with whom she has lived so long knows of her life. Even her mother has never seen any of the misery, uncertainty, shame, guilt, or love that is revealed in the letter.

Although the structure of the letter initially appears chaotic, it is quite logical, even though the dream that is its declared subject is not described until very late. Meanwhile, by describing her husband's familiarity with her mole and their conflict, the letter establishes context for him and provides the reader with an essential comprehension of the dream itself. Sayoko shows her husband how strongly she thought and felt and suffered as the result of his annoyance with her habit. She now sees that the habit of wrapping herself in her own arms absently was itself a defense against him, a form of self-protection.

The change of scene that occasions the letter also provides the perspective that Sayoko needs to investigate the original cause of her mole. She has been able to go back in time and question her mother on the origin of the mole. When did it begin to grow? Babies do not seem to have moles. Moles seem to develop with age, as stigmata of experience. Perhaps her mole grew as her sense of worthlessness grew, bit by bit during childhood, until it was "bigger than a bean." In this second component of Sayoko's letter, she offers her husband and the reader the additional context for the dream in her dialogues with her mother on body image and feelings of self-worth.

Only near the end of the letter does Sayoko tell her husband the story of her dream that she mentions in the first line. Although the dream's message is cryptic, it reveals Sayoko's pain and anger. Her offer of the liberated mole "like the skin of a roast bean" and her demand that her husband take it into his own body express the beginning of her new capacity for physical and emotional self-assertion. Truly the dream is the climax of her life to this point, just as it is the climax of her letter.

Virginia M. Crane

THE MONKEY

Author: Isak Dinesen (Baroness Karen Blixen-Finecke, 1885-1962)
Type of plot: Gothic
Time of plot: The nineteenth century
Locale: Northern Europe
First published: 1934

> *Principal characters:*
> CATHINKA, the prioress, who is co-protagonist with the monkey
> THE MONKEY, co-protagonist with the prioress
> BORLS, a young nephew and godson of the prioress
> ATHENA HOPBALLEHUS, a strong, freedom-loving girl
> COUNT HOPBALLEHUS, Athena's father

The Story

Cathinka, the virgin prioress who governs Cloister Seven, a nonreligious convent in northern Europe, and her little gray monkey play a sinister role to bring about the marriage of Boris, her favorite nephew and godson, and Athena Hopballehus, the freedom-loving daughter of a neighboring nobleman, Count Hopballehus. From the story's title, the reader expects the monkey to be the central character, but the creature is absent during most of the story. The reader therefore has the ominous feeling that the monkey is up to some potent machinations behind the scenes, or is present in another guise. This constant presence of an unidentified evil lends to the eeriness of this gothic tale.

One October when the monkey is away for a few weeks (as is its practice every autumn) to enjoy the freedom of the outdoors, Boris comes to his aunt, the prioress, in a desperate state. To avert the wrath of the authorities, he must get married in a hurry, for the voice of moral indignation has been raised against him: It is implied that Boris is homosexual. His resourceful and energetic aunt promptly sends him off to Count Hopballehus with a letter proposing the marriage of Boris and Athena. She allays Boris's doubts as to Athena's consent and, to his wonderment, adds that if Athena will not have him, she herself will.

The count, having that very day won an old lawsuit (a victory that makes him immensely rich), is delighted to share his jubilation with Boris, for he has been a great admirer of the latter's mother. He also receives with philosophical joy the proposal for his daughter's marriage to Boris, who is very handsome in his white uniform. Athena, eighteen, six feet tall, fair-skinned, and strong, makes Boris uneasy; he thinks of the ballad of the giant's daughter who could break a man—a foreboding of things to come. His return at night through the forest is full of terror. A crashing branch, his shying horses, the wind and the shadows, and "glinting" eyes in the dark—all suggest the presence of strange powers.

The next morning, the count informs Boris in a letter, in words full of pathos and poetry, that Athena has rejected his suit; indeed, she says that she will never marry. Boris finds himself torn by the opposing wills of two determined women: a young "fanatic virgin" and an old woman who would not be crushed by a "vacuum." Boris understands beyond a doubt that his aunt wants him to suffer, in order to make her own (unnamed) torture bearable.

Hearing the news of Athena's refusal, the prioress suddenly goes to the window as though to throw herself out but returns ready with a plan; she invites Athena to supper, urging her to give her answer in person to Boris, the playmate of her childhood. Confident that Athena will respond to duty, the prioress delights in her strategy for his "happiness." Athena must not leave the next day, she tells Boris, without being "ours."

The prioress, decked in jewels and finery, presides over an elegant dinner and convivial conversation. The wine flows freely until the three diners are drunk. Athena, though conscious of danger, feels confident of walking out to freedom. Boris, who finds the theater more real than life, sees Athena and himself as tragic players. The prioress is drunk with a mysterious joy that "glints" in the dark.

After Athena leaves for her room, the prioress shows Boris a letter from the capital naming him as a corrupter of youth; there is now no salvation for him but a hasty marriage. She urges him to follow Athena and helps him with a mysterious potion. Even with that, however, he is not able to overpower Athena, who knocks out two of his teeth. He presses his mouth, full of blood, on her mouth, and they grapple with each other in a revolting scene, while Boris decadently imagines the beauty of Athena's skeleton. Predictably, and true to her classic namesake, Athena wins, and Boris retreats defeated.

The next morning, however, the prioress informs the puzzled but still self-possessed Athena that, now that she has been seduced under the roof of the convent and will no doubt bear Boris's bastard child, and furthermore, because the repentant Boris is ready to make amends, she must not leave without making two promises: to keep the night's happenings secret from her father out of concern for his health and to marry Boris for the sake of honor.

Incredulous that she would be with child from the events of the previous night, Athena is nevertheless unsure of what happened, or whether she was drunk or clearheaded after the supper. The reader cannot resist an amused smile at Athena's pastoral innocence. Concerned though she feels, Athena still resembles an invincible martyr who may not be possessed by her torturers. She makes not two but three promises, adding to the other two that as and when possible, she will surely kill Boris after the wedding.

Just as things come to this impasse, the monkey returns. The prioress, far from welcoming it, dashes about in fear. A wild struggle ensues between the two. Boris and Athena witness a strange metamorphosis: The monkey is transformed into the gentle prioress they have known in the past, and the prioress of recent events turns into the monkey.

Their shared experience brings Boris and Athena together and divides them from the rest of the world. Through unnatural means, inscrutable and incredible as well as uncanny, the two are bound to each other for life. The prioress declares serenely in Latin, "*Discite justitiam, et non temnere divos*": "Learn justice, and [learn] not to spurn the divine ones." What is divine to her, however, is demonic to the others, and to the reader.

Themes and Meanings

Apart from its absorbing interest as a story, "The Monkey" explores, through a decadent romanticism, the theme of captivity: the struggle between those who would be free and the demonic intelligence that would bind them. Everyone in the story is a captive of Christian morality and bourgeois convention, or threatened by them. Those who accept their lot are pathetic: The women at the convent—a sanctuary that is also a place of confinement—live in their memories or on news from the outside; Pastor Rosenquist, shackled to poverty, finds solace in the credit for virtuous behavior that, he trusts, he has accumulated in the other world; the count, a prisoner to family name and obligation, forgets to live in the present and escapes into poetry. Boris and Athena are different: They are young and assert their freedom. However, they, too, are finally bound.

Boris prefers the chaotic to the ordered world, the romantic and theatrical to the mundane and customary. The constellation of The Great Bear teaches him the lesson of preserving individuality in a crowd. His bid for freedom, of which his unsanctioned sexual behavior is the most flagrant expression, backfires; circumstances force him into the bondage of matrimony.

Athena, like the virgin goddess after whom she is named, is a huntress, invincible and strong, not a female who may be pursued and caged into matrimony by men, especially not by Boris, the decadent, imaginative, halfhearted suitor. She prefers championing the rebel's cause to losing her own freedom by getting married. She is a more challenging freedom lover than Boris for the prioress to lure into the captivity of marriage.

The prioress, the protagonist, is herself oppressed by captivity. Though extolling austere duty, she surrounds herself with exotic, foreign things; the very wallpaper of her parlor depicts Oriental sensuousness and mystery, a world of escape. So desperate is her need for freedom that she switches personalities with her monkey to escape from the confines of the convent to a life of abandon in the forest.

In another story, "The Dreamers," Isak Dinesen has Pellegrina speak of having a little ease of heart, a little fun by not being any one person for long. In "The Monkey," the prioress and her monkey not only switch personalities but also function simultaneously like the ancient Wendish idol of the goddess of love, who has the face of a woman turned one way and the face of a monkey turned the other. Far from being the goddess of mercy, Kwan Yin, as Boris initially imagines her to be, the prioress is a cruel manipulator who finds her own relief in bringing about the bondage of Boris and Athena.

Style and Technique

In "The Monkey," repeated motifs, observations, allusions, and images indicate character and foreshadow action. For example, The Great Bear, the bear hunt, Athena fighting like a bear—all reveal Athena's strength and prepare the reader for her victory over Boris. The monkey as the prioress's Geheimerat or privy councillor, the monkey taking an intelligent interest in a game of cards, the monkey scattering pages dealing with witches' trials and marriage contracts, the monkey sitting in the place of Cupid's statue, the identical monkey of the count's lawyer, the double-faced Wendish idol of a woman and a monkey—these suggest the sinister movement of the story without robbing the reader of the thrill of suspense.

The third-person narrative is varied and adequately adjusted to the writer's purpose throughout the story. It starts out with a detached, matter-of-fact description of people, places, and events, building up to a world of romance into which unicorns might step, as Boris imagines on his way through the forest to the count's house. The romantic and hopeful mood changes on his way back, for the forest becomes threatening with fearful forebodings conjured up by shadows and sounds, frightened horses and glinting eyes. Then, through the supper scene, the bizarre fight, the next morning's climactic dialogue, and the shocking finale, the sense of evil keeps mounting. The "hard" look of the prioress, indicating cruelty, is mentioned more than once. Her thin, pointing finger—a familiar gesture of a witch—and her odd habit of scratching herself here and there with that finger—a familiar gesture of a monkey—link the dual roles, unmistakably and mysteriously. Dinesen thus has the reader gripped in suspense throughout.

Sita Kapadia

THE MONKEY'S PAW

Author: W. W. Jacobs (1863-1943)
Type of plot: Horror
Time of plot: The late nineteenth or early twentieth century
Locale: An English suburb
First published: 1902

> *Principal characters:*
> MR. WHITE, a retired businessperson
> MRS. WHITE, his wife
> HERBERT WHITE, their only surviving child
> SERGEANT-MAJOR MORRIS, a soldier recently returned from India

The Story

One rainy evening, Mr. and Mrs. White and their son, Herbert, wait at their home, Laburnum Villa, for a visitor who knew Mr. White before going to India as a soldier twenty-one years earlier. When Sergeant-Major Morris arrives, the Whites serve him whiskey and seat him before the fire as he relates his experiences in the exotic British territory. Eventually Mr. White returned to the subject of the monkey's paw that Morris mentioned earlier, but the old soldier tries to put him off, which only excites the family's curiosity.

The sergeant-major produces the little mummified paw from his pocket, remarking that it had a spell cast on it by an Indian holy man who wanted to illustrate that those who interfere with fate do so to their sorrow. The spell would allow three men each to have three wishes from it. When Herbert asks him why he does not take three wishes himself, the sergeant-major responds soberly that he has. He adds that the first man had had his wishes as well, that the third was for death, and the paw thus had passed on to him. With this explanation, he throws it into the fire. As Mr. White retrieves the paw from the coals, the sergeant-major tells him that he does so at his own peril but reluctantly explains the appropriate manner for making the wishes. Dinner then follows.

After their guest leaves, the Whites discuss the paw. After some thought, Mr. White remarks that he has everything he wants and is unsure what to ask for. Herbert suggests that he wish for two hundred pounds to pay off the mortgage on the house, and Mr. White, with some embarrassment, does so. As he makes his wish, it seems to him that the paw twists in his hand, and he throws it down.

The next day, Mrs. White notices a mysterious stranger hesitating at their doorstep. When he is shown in, he announces to the Whites that Herbert has been badly hurt at the factory but is not in any pain. After the briefest of pauses, Mrs. White realizes that Herbert is dead and falls to comforting her husband. The stranger insists that the company that owns the factory denies all responsibility but is anxious to present a sum of money to Herbert's parents in consideration of their son's services—the sum of two hundred pounds.

One night after the funeral, Mrs. White suddenly realizes that there is a way to undo their misery. Begging her husband to fetch the monkey's paw, she reminds him that there are two wishes left, and urges him to bring their son back to life. Mr. White falteringly explains that not only has Herbert been dead ten days but also that his body had been mangled beyond recognition. Nevertheless, he makes the wish.

The two wait in vain in their bedroom until the candle gutters out. Eventually Mrs. White gives up and creeps back into bed. Now Mr. White cannot sleep. He slips out of the bedroom, and as he reaches the foot of the stairs, a gentle knocking sounds at the door. It is repeated and repeated again more loudly. Mrs. White hears the knock and rushes downstairs to unlock the door, explaining that she has forgotten how long a walk it is from the cemetery and that Herbert has now returned to them.

Mr. White searches frantically for the monkey's paw, fearful of what is pounding ever more stridently. As he hears his wife slide open the bolt, he finds the talisman and makes his last wish. The door swings open and the two rush out onto a quiet, deserted road.

Themes and Meanings

Sergeant-Major Morris's remark that the monkey's paw is intended to show people that fate rules their lives and that it is unwise to interfere with it is true. Judging by the sergeant-major's testimony, both he and the first owner of the paw have chosen badly. When Mrs. White jokingly suggests, as she sets the table, that her husband might wish for three extra pairs of hands for her, Morris forcefully points out to Mr. White that if he must wish, he should wish for something sensible. Despite the fact that he does so, fate exacts a terrible retribution.

The magnitude of this retribution is difficult to account for in conventional terms. After all, Mr. White wishes for a relatively insignificant sum of money and with little enthusiasm; he is far from being a greedy man. Traditional ghost stories tend to establish a comfortable balance between mortal transgression and supernatural retribution. "The Monkey's Paw," on the other hand, suggests that fate, whatever meaning one chooses to read into the word, operates beyond such familiar concepts as fairness and justice. The author refrains from comment, but his opening and closing scenes—a night "cold and wet" and a road "quiet and deserted"—suggest that humans may be at the mercy of an indifferent, if not actually malevolent, universe. It is these suggestions that render "The Monkey's Paw" so chilling.

Style and Technique

W. W. Jacobs was well known during his lifetime for his light, humorous novels and stories about England's dockyards but is now remembered only for "The Monkey's Paw." Although this story exhibits traces of Jacobs's characteristic humor and insight into the prosaic lives of his subjects, it seems to have been rejected by *The Strand*, which regularly published his work. Whatever that magazine's reservations about its unpleasant content, it is recognized today as one of the best supernatural stories ever written and is frequently anthologized.

"The Monkey's Paw" is effective not only for what Jacobs does but for what he refrains from doing. A master of economical, unobtrusive prose, he sets a cozy scene—a chess game in front of a fire, a cold and windy night outside—in a few strokes. Only later does one realize how closely the rest of the story recapitulates the elements of this first brief scene, as the Whites make their moves in a fateful and fatal game while the forces of darkness swirl just beyond the comfortable circle of their lives.

Alongside Jacobs's gently humorous touches are macabre examples of what since has come to be known as black humor. One such moment occurs when the sergeant-major panics at Mrs. White's suggestion that she be granted extra hands—a wish that the reader later realizes might have had a grotesque fulfillment. Another such moment occurs immediately after Mr. White's first wish, as his son, having set up the situation, tries to relieve the ensuing tension: "Well, I don't see the money, and I bet I never shall." These words turn out to be literally and bitterly accurate.

Jacobs introduces the paw into the story through a device familiar from folklore—the figure of the traveler who has returned from distant and exotic lands with a strange story to tell. He also uses the number three, a number traditionally associated with mystery in superstition and folklore. As part of his curse, the holy man has specified that three men shall have three wishes each, as if to intensify the number's troubling power. In addition, there are three visitors to the Whites' home: Morris, the man from the factory, and the final visitor.

"The Monkey's Paw" is most effective for what Jacobs leaves unsaid and accomplishes offstage. Nothing is known of the first man to utilize the paw, except that his third wish was for death. Morris admits that he, too, made three wishes, and his grim manner implies that he regrets his choices, but the details are never explained. The reader learns what the Whites wish for but never witness the gruesome results. A diffident lawyer for the factory brings news of Herbert's death, but Herbert's condition is only implied by Mr. White's reluctant admission that he could only recognize him by his clothing. Of the condition of the being—several days dead—who knocks at the Whites' door, the reader can only guess. In each case, Jacobs leaves the reader to imagine something much worse than he can effectively describe.

Horror writer Stephen King based his 1983 novel *Pet Sematary* on "The Monkey's Paw." Readers may want to compare its more expansive and more graphically explicit treatment with Jacobs's concise, understated approach.

Grove Koger

THE MONSTER

Author: Stephen Crane (1871-1900)
Type of plot: Realism
Time of plot: The early twentieth century
Locale: A small town in New York
First published: 1898

Principal characters:
DR. NED TRESCOTT, a respected doctor in a small town
GRACE TRESCOTT, his wife
JIMMIE TRESCOTT, their son
HENRY JOHNSON, the Trescotts' carriage hand

The Story

In its barest details, Stephen Crane's "The Monster" is the story of a black carriage hand who saves the young son of his employer, a respected small-town doctor, from certain death in a fire that destroys the doctor's home. In the process of the rescue, the black man, Henry Johnson, is horribly burned. When he recovers under the doctor's healing hands, besides apparently losing his mental capacity, Henry loses his face as well; in fact, the only recognizable feature in his scarred countenance is a single "winking eye."

Because of his debt to Henry, Dr. Trescott insists on arranging for the injured man to be cared for by a black family. This family, however, as well as everyone else in the town, is terrified by Henry's monstrous appearance. Eventually, Henry runs away from his caretakers and frightens a number of people whom he encounters in town before he is caught and returned to Dr. Trescott. Henry lives relatively undisturbed with the Trescotts, but his presence in their household has repercussions for the doctor, his wife, and his son. The boy, Jimmie, gains notoriety among his peers through the strange figure of Henry that inhabits his yard. Dr. Trescott, however, steadily loses business so that his practice and status in the community noticeably decline, and Mrs. Trescott is subjected to the scorn of her lady friends, who refuse her customary invitation to tea on Wednesday afternoon.

Although Henry, via his radical change in appearance from a dapper young man sporting lavender pants to a grotesque figure, is central to Crane's story, its main action involves the change in relations among various figures in the town—a change wrought by Henry's metamorphosis. Of primary importance is the alteration in Dr. Trescott's relation to the town. Dr. Trescott appears initially as a benevolent judge in matters of human conduct. When, in the story's opening episode, little Jimmie breaks a peony in the family garden while pretending to be a locomotive, the doctor renders a gentle but just punishment: "Well, Jimmie," he says, "I guess you had better not play train any more today." Both Jimmie and Henry, to whom Jimmie retires when he suffers an "eclipse" from his father's favor, perceive Dr. Trescott as "the moon"—a beacon of right behavior, a moral eminence. Trescott, moreover, enjoys similar admiration within the town where he is, in the beginning, "the leading doctor." The fire and disfiguring of Henry Johnson, however, change this.

Feeling duty-bound to employ his skill as a physician to heal the man who saved his son, Trescott becomes a kind of Dr. Frankenstein. An old friend, Judge Hagenthorpe, advises him against intervening in the natural course of events:

> He is purely your creation. Nature has evidently given up on him. He is dead. You are restoring him to life. You are making him, and he will be a monster, and with no mind.

The doctor, however, sees only that Henry "saved my boy." His sense of moral obligation springs from this immediately self-evident and incontrovertible fact; he acts morally, without fear of Henry's image or concern for the town's fears or opinions. For everyone else, though, Henry is a monster and a devil. His escape, made ironic by his apparent lack of self-consciousness—his seeming ignorance of or innocent disregard for the way he looks to others—utterly (and, from the narrator's perspective, humorously) disrupts the town's secure complacency. Subsequently, the doctor and his wife bear the burden of Henry's image. The menfolk of the town approach Dr. Trescott, asking him to send Henry away; it is not they who really want this, they say, but the women. Moreover, they do not want to see the doctor further ruined by Henry's presence; he has already slipped from being the town's leading doctor "to about the last one." Dr. Trescott, however, holds resolutely to his sense of the good. He refuses to send Henry away.

In the story's final episode, Dr. Trescott experiences in full measure the moral isolation of the monster. Arriving home on an autumn day, he finds Jimmie alone indoors absorbed in a book. His wife, half-hidden in her drawing room, cries softly. Going to her, Trescott notices the serving table set with dishes and uncut cakes. The gentle but godlike authority with which he assuaged Jimmie's guilt in the story's opening episode gives way in this scene to the muted solace he offers his wife. Completely immersed in the moral dilemma occasioned by his creation of "the monster," Dr. Trescott holds Grace's head on his shoulder and tries to count the unused teacups—"there were fifteen of them."

Themes and Meanings

Self-effacement emerges as a primary theme in "The Monster." It is first explicitly mentioned when Jimmie, having broken the peony and received his father's punishment, feels "some kind of desire to efface himself." The most graphic instance of self-effacement occurs when Henry's face is literally burned away. This event comprises the imaginative center of the story, for it is Henry's monstrous image that disrupts the town's original unity and propels it, and particularly Dr. Trescott, into their moral predicament. Trescott, too, undergoes a process of self-effacement. His moral stance with regard to Henry leads him to lose face within the town and to lose his face as a "moon," or moral authority issuing judgment from on high—as he is seen from Jimmie's perspective in the opening episode—and to become a man brought morally down to earth when he must confront the pain that his actions cause his wife.

In the story, to lose face is to lose the persona by which one is recognized within the general community. It is to lose that characteristic that marks one as a known quantity. Society ascertains the individual by his face, and when that face is gone—as it graphically is with Henry—certainty and security go with it. Consequently, Henry, who begins in the story as a genial compatriot of Jimmie and as a delightful spectacle for the town as he embarks on his Saturday night courting ritual, becomes in the general eye a horrifying monster devoid of human qualities. Without a recognizable face, he cannot be conventionally known, and so the town assumes a conventional attitude toward him. Fearing and despising as the ultimate evil that which is different or novel, they seek Henry's removal while they progressively ostracize Dr. Trescott and his family.

Aside from a few townspeople—Judge Hagenthorpe, who tries to reason with Dr. Trescott about saving Henry's life; Martha Goodwin, herself a kind of old-maidish outcast, who, as "a woman of great mind," defies the town's opinions of Henry; and the barber Reifsnyder, who tries to imagine what it would be like to live without a face—only Dr. Trescott sees the good in Henry. For him, the impulsion to save Henry operates beyond reason; it is not an action rationally decided or argued—in fact, as the story progresses, Dr. Trescott offers fewer and fewer reasons for keeping Henry—it is simply the inherently moral thing to do. In opening himself to a moral relation with Henry, the monster, Trescott opens himself to what is creative and life-affirming. Restoring Henry to life (as Henry has restored Jimmie to life by rescuing him from the fire), Dr. Trescott becomes, literally, a creator. However, in the process, he effaces himself and his family—thrusting them all beyond the safe rule of judgment and beyond the town's customary certainties, into the moral unknown where life enters on "monstrous" novelty.

Style and Technique

As in other of his major short stories—notably, "Death and the Child," "The Open Boat," "The Blue Hotel," and "The Bride Comes to Yellow Sky"—Crane employs a narrative voice in "The Monster" that directs attention away from its point of view and toward the inner, or moral, life of the events that it narrates. Such a voice, merging with the act of narrating, effaces itself. In this way, self-effacement becomes not only a dramatic and thematic concern in "The Monster" but also a stylistic method that surpasses the conventional notion of point of view.

Point of view, in fact, cannot adequately account for the narrative feat that Crane performs in this and other stories because there is no single point or definable consciousness from which events emanate. The narrator has no "face" as a character or mind either within or outside the dramatic events of the story. What appears as omniscience—the narrator's ability to see the outside as well as the inside of characters—is more accurately described as a relative or conditional perspective. The narrator does not, for example, comment with "all knowing" intelligence on what characters think, but instead shows how they "seem" to feel or what "might" have passed through their minds. In "The Monster," this conditional attitude occurs grammatically when Jimmie tries for a second time to point out the broken peony to his father:

> After a period of silence, during which the child may have undergone a severe mental tumult, he raised his finger and repeated his former word—"There!"

Here, the narrator's relative perspective, expressed grammatically in the conditional verb "may have undergone," allows that the boy's naïve but profound sensitivity to his father's stature may not, in fact, give rise to "severe mental tumult"; yet such a condition is, in fact, morally and imaginatively true for Jimmie in this moment.

Crane's narration, moreover, does not pass judgment on the characters or their actions. In rendering them from the inside, it effaces conscious opinion and becomes—instead of a voice that intellectually knows character—a mobile eye that focuses on dynamic centers of action visualized concretely as "Jimmie," "Henry," or "Trescott." Given Crane's self-effacing method, these names refer to identities much less than they give individual form, or an image, to complex moral powers involved in growth and change. The episodic structure within which these powers collide enables the story's moral perspective—its attitude toward the events it narrates—to evolve naturally out of the narrative process rather than being imposed on those events from the outside. Consequently, Crane's moral or narrative perspective in "The Monster" cannot be reduced to a thematic statement about what happens in the story; it is, rather, coextensive with the whole story—emerging only in and through the narrative moves that transform Jimmie's imaginative life as a train in the opening episode into the moral unknown, the "monster" that his father contemplates in the fifteen teacups.

Critics have called Crane's narrative technique "impressionistic," a term borrowed from the visual arts. In painting, it refers to the fleeting impression struck in one converging instant of space and time. For Crane, impressionism is a way of seeing in a particular moment the soul or moral genius of a man. Through his self-effacing method in "The Monster," he brings that genius to light—in Jimmie, in Henry, in Dr. Trescott, and most surely in his narrating.

S. Elaine Marshall

MOON AND MADNESS

Author: Isaac Bashevis Singer (1904-1991)
Type of plot: Fable
Time of plot: The early 1900's
Locale: Radzymin, Poland
First published: 1980

> *Principal characters:*
> ZALMAN, a glazier, the first storyteller
> LEVI YITZCHOK, the second storyteller
> MEIR, a eunuch and Cabbalist, the third storyteller
> COUNT JAN MALECKI, a landowner
> MACIEK SOKAL, a corrupt lawyer
> WOJTEK, a notorious criminal
> STACH SKIBA, a peasant
> STASIA SKIBA, his daughter
> STEFAN, the peasant youth whom Stasia marries
> STANISLAW KARLOWSKI, a rich, litigious landowner
> RABBI JOSEPH DELLA REINA, a rabbi and conjurer
> PTIMA, the wife of a Spanish caliph and Rabbi Joseph's mistress
> GRISHA, the beautiful wife of the Grand Vizier and Rabbi
> Joseph's other mistress

The Story

One winter night in the Radzymin study house, three Jews swap stories about pity. Zalman begins by telling of a Count Jan Malecki, who freed his serfs long before Czar Alexander abolished serfdom in 1861. Dividing his land among the peasants, Malecki worked as hard as any of them. Meanwhile, all of his relatives lived idly from his earnings. Despite Malecki's egalitarian sentiments, the Russians who rule the area appoint him district judge. Because he is so tenderhearted, however, he never sentences anyone. As soon as he hears the flimsiest excuse, Malecki not only frees the criminal but also gives him money from his own pocket.

One felon who repeatedly appears before him is Wojtek, a robber, murderer, and rapist. Malecki can do nothing about this criminal because no one will testify against him. Finally, however, Wojtek goes too far. He is in love with Stasia Skiba, but she rejects him for the honest Stefan. As they are celebrating their wedding at her father's house, the building burns down. Among the twenty dead are Stasia and Stefan.

This time there are witnesses to accuse Wojtek of arson and murder. The peasants jail him, but Maciek Sokal, the defender of all the local criminals, appeals to Malecki. The weak judge accepts Sokal's claim of Wojtek's innocence and signs the order for his release. Enraged, the peasants kill Sokal, Wojtek, and Malecki.

Zalman's story reminds Levi Yitzchok of a similar one about the rich landowner

Stanislaw Karlowski. In Kozienice, he was known as Crazy Karlowski because he squandered his money on foolish lawsuits. Everyone but Karlowski knew that his wife was having affairs, but he insisted on her chastity, even fighting a duel with someone who spoke against her.

At last she tires of him and runs away with a lover, taking with her as much money as she can find in the house. When she returns with a bastard three years later, everyone expects that her husband will recognize his wife's true nature and kill her. Instead, he welcomes her and her child; when her lover reappears, he takes him into his household, too.

The lover does not continue his affair with Karlowski's wife—not because he has reformed but because he considers her too old. He begins a new liaison with a servant and one day robs both Karlowski and his wife before fleeing with this new mistress. Shortly afterward, Karlowski and his wife die.

After a long silence, Meir the Cabbalist responds to this story with a tale of Rabbi Joseph della Reina, who was so powerful a magician that he succeeded in chaining Satan. The Redemption was at hand; then Rabbi Joseph offered "a sniff of tobacco" to the devil. This misplaced compassion undid all the spells; Satan freed himself, and the Redemption could not occur. Rabbi Joseph then fell into despair and abandoned himself to sensuality. He used his powers to secure two beautiful women: Ptima, the wife of a Spanish caliph, and Grisha, the wife of the Grand Vizier. Each night he would conjure demons to bring Ptima, whom he enjoyed until midnight. They would then return her to her husband and fetch Grisha, whom he enjoyed until dawn.

Eventually, Ptima learns of Grisha, and she also discovers the magic word that gives the rabbi his power. She uses her knowledge to kill Grisha. She also orders the demons to bind Rabbi Joseph and then bring her the Fallen Angels and the giants before the Flood. As Rabbi Joseph is forced to watch, she makes love to them. After three days, Rabbi Joseph secures his release and banishes the demons.

He is about to kill Ptima for what she has done, but she tells him, "We two can conquer the world. You will conjure the most beautiful women, and I the richest men. We will put them to sleep and rob them. . . . You will become king of the netherworld and I will be your loving queen." Their first joint effort is also their last. Ptima agrees to revive Grisha, but resurrection is the one power denied to conjurers. Therefore, their attempt to recall Grisha costs them their magic powers. Ptima dies a beggar; Rabbi Joseph dies and is reincarnated as a dog.

Themes and Meanings

All three tales treat the subject of misplaced pity. Malecki feels sorry for the criminal rather than the victims and so loses his life. Karlowski pities his wife and her lover, neither of whom deserves his sympathy, and so loses his fortune. Rabbi Joseph pities Satan and thus postpones the coming of the Messiah. Later he pities Ptima and destroys himself. The blind Jeremiah provides a pointed commentary as he recites Psalm 135, which speaks of God's mercy in slaying the wicked kings of Og and Sihon. Even God does not always forgive, at least not in this world; punishment is sometimes necessary if society is to endure.

Isaac Bashevis Singer does not reject compassion. Zalman says that "pity is virtuous," and Meir reminds the reader that "the doors of repentance are always open." Still, to be forgiven one must walk through them. Malecki's pity would have been commendable had the criminals reformed; because they did not, however, Malecki does harm rather than good.

For each of the characters, pity is really a form of self-indulgence. Malecki's motto is, "Each man should do what he wants." Rabbi Joseph wants to revive Grisha only because he lusts for her; he refrains from killing Ptima because she promises him sensual pleasure. Singer warns the reader to examine his motivations, for behavior that seems virtuous may not be. Malecki's blindness to the wickedness around him and Karlowski's lack of perception are symptoms of still greater ignorance, that of their own folly. Singer's message is the age-old warning, "Know thyself." In Poland as in ancient Greece, the failure to heed that warning produces tragedy.

Style and Technique

Singer presents his parables not as stories themselves but as stories within a story. This technique allows him to introduce pointed commentary, suggesting the rabbinic glosses on biblical and Talmudic texts. Sometimes these reflections are subtle, as when Jeremiah recites Psalm 135; Singer trusts that the reader will recall that psalm's refrain, "For His mercy endures forever." Elsewhere the comments are explicit. Thus, after listening to the first two stories, Meir observes, "What Squire Malecki was doing had nothing to do with pity."

At the same time that the various observations highlight the theme, they emphasize the fact that Singer is offering fiction, not reportage. The artifice of the story-within-a-story calls attention to itself, as do the comments. When Levi Yitzchok questions the truth of Meir's account of the life and death of Rabbi Joseph, Meir concedes that he has made up the narrative. When Zalman says that the stories have frightened him so that he hesitates to go home, Meir laughs at him: "The moon is shining. The heavens are bright. Evil is nothing but a coil of madness."

As is often true in Singer's stories, the last words are not really the last words. Meir is sane when the moon is waxing but crazy while it wanes. Before beginning his story, Meir looks outside to be sure that the moon is not yet full; because he does look, though, it must be close. Is this the night that divides the month? Can one trust Meir's pronouncements? He has said that Malecki took money from the thieves and that Karlowski delighted in his wife's infidelities. The text offers no support for these conclusions. Hence, his easy dismissal of evil at the end of the story is also suspect. The tales themselves are not reality, but they reflect reality as the moon reflects the sun and shines even though the moon produces no light of its own.

Singer chose this story to conclude *The Collected Stories* (1982). The selection is appropriate, for "Moon and Madness" combines artifice and truth, fiction and reality, in a manner that Singer has made his hallmark.

Joseph Rosenblum

MOON DELUXE

Author: Frederick Barthelme (1943-   )
Type of plot: Social realism
Time of plot: The early 1980's
Locale: An unnamed southern city
First published: 1982

> *Principal characters:*
> EDWARD, the protagonist
> EILÉEN, his neighbor
> PHIL, Eileen's boyfriend
> LILY, another neighbor
> ANTONIA (TONY), Lily's roommate

The Story

"Moon Deluxe" is a brief story in which nothing of significance happens. Edward, the protagonist, is referred to throughout as "you," starting from the story's opening sentence: "You're stuck in traffic on the way home from work, counting blue cars, and when a blue-metallic Jetta pulls alongside, you count it—twenty-eight." The driver of the Jetta is a young woman whom Edward has seen before. A little later he stops at a drugstore, not to buy anything in particular but because he is restless and at loose ends. He looks at "red jumper cables, a jigsaw puzzle of some TV actor's face, the tooled-leather cowboy belts," and some other items, and finally buys "Curad bandages, because the package is green." On the way out of the parking lot, he "drive[s] too fast and nearly hit[s] a teen-ager."

When he gets home to The Creekside, the apartment complex where he lives, he is invited by Eileen, a neighbor and casual friend, to come by later. At the end of the first of the story's four sections, Edward rinses and sugars some lettuce leaves, "the way your mother did when you were a child, then eat[s], looking at the local news." He observes that his teeth need brushing, strips and runs water for a bath, and looks at his skin in the mirror.

Phil, Eileen's boyfriend, opens the door to her apartment, and refers to her as "Ivy"—Edward does not know why, nor does the story ever explain. Also present is Lily, dressed in "green slacks, a red belt, a shiny violet undershirt, a white jacket," who, Eileen says, moved into Carmen's apartment. She tells Lily that Edward "and Carmen had a thing. . . . Only a small thing, but definitely a thing." Lily flirts with Edward, but he does not respond. Meanwhile it begins to rain. There is a reference to Tony, Lily's roommate, then some inconsequential chatter, followed by an anecdote about Eileen's sister, who was thought to have a serious circulatory illness but whose skin discoloration turned out to have been caused by eating too many carrots.

At the beginning of the third section, Lily invites Edward to walk her home: "Outside, the air is sweet and dense after the rain, the sidewalks are still wet, and as the two of you bend to go under a tree limb that hangs low over the path, Lily slips her hand into yours." She makes a further overture—"You're not anxious to rush to my apartment and keep your record intact?"—but Edward stalls by proposing that they take a walk first. Lily begins "a rambling account of where she was born, what her parents were like, where she went to school, how much she loves her brother Rudy," then says that she has to get home: "I told Tony I'd be back by nine, and it's already ten."

The final section consists of a scene in Lily's apartment, involving Edward, Lily, and Tony (Antonia), who turns out to be the woman Edward saw on his way home from work. Antonia is "huge, extraordinary, easily over six feet," and wears "a white T-shirt with 'So many men, so little time' silk-screened in two lines across the chest." Lily says that the message on the shirt is ironic, and introduces Edward as "tonight's Mr. Lucky." The women's apartment looks like "the inside of a fifties-movie spaceship."

There follows much talk, nominally casual, out of which a degree of veiled tension emerges. If Lily and Tony are not actually lovers, Tony clearly wishes they were, and she regards Edward as threatening. Edward, however, is too indecisive, too disengaged, evidently too alarmed even by the minimal commitment implied by a single night with a woman, to contest actively for Lily. Abruptly he announces that he is leaving, then wonders what it would be like to spend the night on the couch, and briefly becomes part of the women's routine. They walk out with him, and by the pool they both kiss him "with their lips awkwardly, resolutely shut," then return to their apartment hand in hand. The story ends with Edward standing there, alone as he was when it began: "There is a moon. . . . Pool lights are waving on the sides of the buildings."

Themes and Meanings

Edward, like other protagonists in Frederick Barthelme's works, has been wounded in some ill-defined way and as a result is unwilling or unable to engage himself in any significant aspect of life. The encounter Barthelme describes here can be assumed to be typical, in that it comes about without having been planned, offers no particular pleasure or interest, and then dwindles away without altering Edward's inner or outer life. "Moon Deluxe," therefore, can be seen as a parable of the rootlessness and meaninglessness of American life in the late twentieth century. What gives significance to human existence, ordinarily, is work that matters and serious, lasting relationships. Here both are missing. Barthelme does not say what Edward's job consists of; the reader can deduce only that it provides him with enough income to live well in material terms and that he is not sufficiently interested in it to think or talk about it. As for relationships, he had only a "small thing"—as opposed to a full-fledged, fully committed love affair—with Carmen, and when she moved out, the "thing" ended. He could not find interest or energy enough to pursue her; to one or both of them, then, it was simply an affair of convenience.

He shows no real interest in Lily, though she is attractive and eager; he is willing to be pursued, however, and might even drift into another Carmen-like affair, but then Tony enters the picture. At that point, with little at stake anyway, he runs. The hint of competition, complication, perhaps real emotional danger, is too much for him.

Edward has lost his innocence. He merely drifts through life, apathetic and perpetually a bit unnerved. Life holds no real possibilities for him because he is unwilling or unable to take risks. In "Moon Deluxe," as in his other fiction, Barthelme has painted a bleak (and decidedly one-sided) picture of modern life.

Style and Technique

Barthelme tells his story in the present tense, a technique that was relatively common by the time of the story's publication in 1982. The effect is to negate the ordinary sense of a story as history unfolding in time; instead, it is all very flat and immediate, like a cubist painting. There is no attempt, that is, to provide any sense of historical perspective, of Edward's past bearing down on and shaping his present. The story says: This is what life is for Edward today; then today vanishes, leaving only the faintest trace.

The use of the second-person point of view is much rarer, and the effect is problematic. First-person narration invites the reader's identification with the narrator; second demands it. This is not simply Edward's life, the persistent "you" seems to say, but yours, the reader's. The danger is obvious, and explains why "you" is hardly ever used in this way in fiction. Most readers will resist, deny emphatically that their lives and Edward's have anything significant in common.

Just as significant as the details Barthelme provides are those he omits. He never mentions Edward's last name, the city in which he lives, the work he does, anything about his past except the "thing" with Carmen, his age, what he looks like, or what he may be thinking. Edward is Everyman living anywhere; in this world, all that matters is surfaces. Thus, the reader sees "Eileen's stiff hair, like a giant black meringue, ris[ing] over the top of the fence" and gets a detailed catalog of the items that Edward looks at in the K & B Pharmacy. Barthelme describes the interiors of apartments but not of people. The inner lives of his characters are only hinted at—and that hint suggests that there is little within them that is worth mentioning.

Edwin Moses

THE MOONS OF JUPITER

Author: Alice Munro (1931-   )
Type of plot: Psychological
Time of plot: The 1980's
Locale: Toronto, Ontario
First published: 1982

> *Principal characters:*
> JANET, the narrator, a writer
> HER FATHER, a retired working-class man
> JUDITH, her younger daughter

The Story

"The Moons of Jupiter" is narrated in the first person by Janet, a woman whose father has been hospitalized and faces the possibility of dying during heart surgery. The story focuses on the narrator's reflections on, and reevaluation of, her relationship with her father, as well as her relationships with her two daughters, Judith and Nichola.

The story begins in September in the Toronto General Hospital, where the father's condition is being monitored. Flashbacks then inform the reader that Janet, whose real home is Vancouver, arrived in Toronto from England two days earlier. She was met at the airport by her younger daughter, Judith, and Don, her daughter's live-in companion. Judith and Don left for Mexico the next day, leaving the narrator in their apartment during their absence. During a casual telephone call to her father, residing in a small town outside Toronto, she discovered that her father's doctor was sending him to Toronto for an emergency medical examination, so she rented a car and drove her father to the hospital.

When a young doctor advises immediate surgery for a defective heart valve, the father resists, especially when an older doctor says that rest and medication might take care of the situation. Without surgery, he would die shortly anyway, so in the end, he decides to have the operation despite the risks.

What emerges during the story, from the dialogues between Janet and her father and Janet's multiple, brief excursions into the past, is a portrait of her father. He is a working-class man—who is also a reader of poetry and history books—who cares for his daughter (and other family members) but is unable to express his love and constantly comes across, instead, as somewhat critical. As he prepares psychologically for death, he briefly toys with the idea of the existence of the soul and the afterlife but rejects that possibility. In a calm, matter-of-fact manner, he informs his daughter about details concerning his house, his will, and the cemetery plot.

During the five days before the operation, Janet visits her father daily and fills the rest of her time with random shopping and other superficial activities. (She had coped in this same manner many years earlier when there had been a possibility that Nich-

ola, at the age of four, had leukemia.) She would like to see her older daughter, Nichola, who lives in Toronto, but does not know how to reach her, and Nichola never calls
although she had been told that her mother is in town. She attempts to call an old
friend, but he is gone for all that month.

On the day before her father's operation, in an ongoing effort to distract herself
from the pressure of the uncertainty of her father's future, the narrator visits a museum
and attends a show at the planetarium. Feeling she cannot take in the immensity of the
universe as described by an overwhelming stream of mathematical facts listed by the
show's narrator, she concentrates on the facts about the solar system.

The solar system is the focus of the last conversation between the narrator and her
father. Jupiter and its moons finish out the conversation as her father tells what he
knows about Jupiter and is able to name some of its moons. The narrator and her father touch lightly on some of the mythological characters for whom the moons are
named (Ganymede, Io, and so on), and the daughter says she will see him the next day
after the surgery.

The story ends with a flashback to her time at the museum's Chinese garden. As she
sits on a bench watching passers-by on the street, she is reminded of the emotional
distance between Nichola and herself. She then returns to the hospital for what turns
out to be the last time she sees her father.

Themes and Meanings

This story gives its title to a volume of eleven short stories with a variety of female
narrators. Unlike many other female narrators in these and other Munro stories, Janet
bears a strong resemblance to Munro in a number of ways. Janet is a writer by profession whose father dies in a Toronto hospital, whose marriage (to Richard in Vancouver)
has broken up, and whose two daughters live in Toronto. Similarly, Munro's father died
in a Toronto hospital in the 1970's after a heart operation at a time when her marriage
to James Munro in Vancouver had broken up and she had moved back, with two of her
three daughters, to Ontario. Although there are differences between the two (Janet has
two daughters, not three), the parallels are too blatant to ignore. This award-winning
Canadian author is known for drawing on her experiences in southwestern Ontario for
many of her characters and stories, so this event in her personal life becomes a resource for at least some part of this story of a daughter's remembrance of her father.

On the other hand, Janet is typical of many of Munro's female narrators in that she
combines multiple perspectives as she weaves retrospective views of her life and relationships around a core event, in this case, of the father's hospital stay. From her triple
vantage point as daughter, mother, and former wife, she is able to review—and revise—
her understanding of past events and her past perceptions, especially of her father. Her
status as a parent enables her to reevaluate some of her own experiences of being a
daughter and to sympathetically adjust her perception of her father. Theirs was not a
warm relationship: Both as a child and as an adult she felt either blamed or disap-
proved of by her father. Ironically, as a parent now herself, she has daughters who are
emotionally distant and remind her of herself at their ages: There are tensions with Ju-

dith, and Nichola does not visit or even call during the time her mother is in Toronto.

In the opening line in the story, Janet reports she had found her father on the eighth floor of the hospital, and indeed, during these five days of hospital visits, the daughter comes to understand—to "find"—her father in a new way before he dies. The constant display of the father's heart activity by the monitor in his hospital room becomes a symbolic externalization of the psychological drama played out in the story. Her father's inner heart becomes better known by his daughter as he expresses his true feelings on many issues, however briefly, and as she reviews memories concerning her father. Janet is able to realize that despite the distance, misunderstandings, and tensions between them, there is also a bond of love between them.

Style and Technique

Although the father's five-day hospital stay before the operation is presented as a linear event, the majority of the narrative is circular. The reader is later told of events that immediately precede the opening event (driving her father to the emergency room), of events in the distant past (her childhood, her early married life), and even of events in the future (cleaning out her father's house after his death). The intermingling of past, present, and future allows multiple perspectives to coexist simultaneously and conveys a multidimensioned picture of Janet's father. The various angles of perception about her father at different stages in her life converge to help nuance and clarify a more balanced, compassionate and nonjudgmental presentation of her father's character.

The circularity of the narrative functions as a literary parallel to the movement of Jupiter and its moons. The single, focused event of the preparation for surgery by the father—Jupiter—precipitates the narrator's mental excursions to explore and reevaluate family relationships. These short digressions, explanations, and memories of other events and other dialogues—like Jupiter's moons—revolve around the main event. Each dialogue during the narrator's time in Toronto stimulates commentaries or mirror-events from Janet's past that shed light on and give a more complete picture of a family member. These digressions—these time-travel journeys into the past and even once into the future—are presented as compressed vignettes, revealing a major character trait or expressing a quality in a particular relationship. The father—in his current medical condition—functions as the center of gravity that holds all these satellite digressions together and harmonizes them.

Jupiter and its moons become an ironic symbol of the narrator's ambiguous relationship with her father. The difficulty of family members who love another despite their differences and yet cannot express their love verbally is highlighted by the last conversation between the narrator and her father before he dies. The discussion is factual and impersonal: a review of some of the moons' names and their mythological namesakes. It is as removed from earthly life as it could possibly be, but it is something they can share together without the tension of differing perspectives that had so long characterized their relationship.

Marsha Daigle-Williamson

THE MOOR

Author: Russell Banks (1940-   )
Type of plot: Regional, realism
Time of plot: The 1990's
Locale: Concord, New Hampshire
First published: 2000

> *Principal characters:*
> WARREN LOW, a middle-aged plumbing supplies sales
>   representative
> GAIL FORTUNATA, an eighty-year-old woman, once his lover

The Story

"The Moor" tells of a man and a woman whose paths cross again after thirty years. Warren Low, a middle-age plumbing supplies sales representative, and two buddies, one in real estate, the other in car sales, are heading for drinks after taking part in an induction ceremony at the Masonic Hall. Warren's face still shows traces of the makeup he wore for his role as an Arab prince. His red-painted lips and black-smeared cheeks elicit teasing racial slurs from the two, which the narrator, self-admittedly less prejudiced than they, dismisses as just idle, unthinking talk.

On entering the Greek restaurant, they head to the bar in back, enjoying the comfort that comes from being regulars and ordering the usual. They pass a table of celebrants, with an elderly, lively eyed woman, four dour but dutiful adults, and a bored teenager. A spark of recognition passes between Warren and the woman, but she is old, with thin silvery blue hair, liver-spotted cheeks, and wattled jowls, and he cannot imagine any kind of acquaintance with her. He checks to see if the bartender knows her, but not even the information that the men are named Fortunata and they are celebrating their mother's eightieth birthday helps.

The three men have their drinks and talk about the weather and their wives and former wives and grown children, comfortable and familiar with one another, out late and guiltfree, and then prepare to leave. Warren passes the woman, who tugs at his sleeve and clears up the mystery. She is Gail Fortunata, the woman with whom he had shared a few months of love when he was a twenty-one-year-old plumber's apprentice and she a lonely fifty-year-old housewife.

At her urging, he stays behind to have a quick drink after promising her sons that he will drive her home shortly. They talk hesitantly, almost shyly, at first, but then she dares ask the question that has been on her mind all these years: Was he a virgin when they met? She reassures him that he does not have to answer, that she had not asked at the time because he was so insecure about what they were doing and she had not wanted to embarrass him. He pauses, they laugh, and then he gives her a gift of an answer: Yes. She is clearly delighted and confesses that both at the time and whenever she recalled those days, she had imagined that she was his first sexual partner. He was special to her, so sensitive and filled with potential, and she had wanted to encourage him with her love and their shared conversation about the theater and his possible acting career.

The lateness of the evening and the growing storm force them to finish their drinks and head for home. They drive silently for a while; the snow is more forceful, and most people are already out of the elements. Then Warren asks his question: Had she otherwise been faithful to her husband, both before and after him? Without hesitation, she says yes. She had loved just two men in her life. He is sure that this is not true, but he understands the answer. At her door, he kisses her, gently at first, but then, spurred by the power of memory, with greater warmth. They stand there in an embrace, each remembering an earlier time filled with life and promise. Then he leaves, beginning his lonely drive home. Close to crying, he looks into the storm, aware that the past is gone, the present fleeting, and that all he has is what lies ahead.

Themes and Meanings

Russell Banks writes of ordinary people who suffer the joys and sorrows of ordinary life. His stories are populated with working men and women who marry, have children, sometimes divorce, live by modest means, and grow old. His characters love as grandly and despair as profoundly as those who, by chance or fortune, are able to express their emotions more eloquently through creative endeavors. They do not write poetry or sad, tragic novels; instead, they live with their altered circumstances and adjust.

"The Moor" covers much of two lives in a span of no more than three hours. It is a sweet moment in time, a time filled with memories of youth and health, of a tall older woman with porcelain skin and thick red hair and a twenty-one-year-old boy testing his powers. In the dark of the restaurant and then in the snowy night, these two people find that the spark of their initial love and attraction remains, with all its drawing power. The man searches for the woman he once knew, looking carefully into her now cloudy but still intense blue eyes, knowing that if that woman is no longer there, then the boy he was is gone, too. For just a short time, they are able to capture the energy of an earlier time. He is reluctant to leave this memory of youth, wanting to stand on Gail Fortunata's doorstep all night, watching their footprints fill with snow. However, he has to get up early for work the next day.

His observations on the drive home echo with the loneliness that most people feel when struck with the awareness that life is fleeting. He thinks of how the past is gone and how all that is left is the future. What is ahead of him may not seem like much, containing emptiness perhaps, but maybe some small joys as well, similar to that which he just experienced with the eighty-year-old Gail.

Style and Technique

Snow and long, dark New England winters figure heavily in much of Russell Banks's fiction. The vagaries of the weather enable him to capture the bittersweet qualities of everyday living. At the start of "The Moor," the snowflakes are light, growing in intensity as the evening passes. Snow, so beautiful in reflected light, embraces the landscape, but the inherent dangers of a snowfall—sleet, massive accumulations, enforced isolation—are always there. Snow might represent aging, impending silence, and death. People's personal weather forecasts are as changing, as fraught with the potential for good or bad, as any that a meteorologist might provide.

Banks is a storyteller and, therefore, engages the reader in a dialogue. Warren, the main character, addresses the reader in the first line, saying that he is middle-aged. The reader instantly knows who is being called on to look age squarely in the eye and identifies with his uneasiness. Warren takes the reader on a journey into the past and to the uncertain future as though holding the reader's hand instead of that of the eighty-year-old love of his youth. These two people are still lovers in the sense that they each want to give something to the other, perhaps just the "right" answer to a question. The pure happiness and gratitude that fill Gail's face when Warren says that she was his first love justifies the prevarication. Her love is expressed through the simple gesture of covering his hand with hers. When she tells Warren that he was the only other man she had loved, he encircles her hand.

Banks's eye for detail and his terse, exact prose cut through to the essence of what is important. The reader understands the unthinking banter of Warren's cronies, the need they feel for a place to belong, and the everyday quality of their lives. The bartender's small gesture of providing the two old friends' last drinks on the house speaks volumes about caring and kindness. Although Warren notices his former lover's dewlaps, bagginess, liver spots, and crackled old hands, they do not detract from the tender love he feels or make the kiss goodbye seem implausible. Repeated references to her age do not negate the fact that she is ageless to him—and concentrating on the small kindness they shared will help him along that snowy, lonely road.

Gay Pitman Zieger

MOSBY'S MEMOIRS

Author: Saul Bellow (1915-   )
Type of plot: Psychological
Time of plot: About 1962
Locale: South-central Mexico
First published: 1968

> *Principal characters:*
> WILLIS MOSBY, a former Princeton professor
> HYMAN LUSTGARTEN, a Marxist turned capitalist
> TRUDY LUSTGARTEN, Hyman's wife
> ALFRED RUSKIN, an American poet
> KLONSKY, a Polish Belgian, Lustgarten's associate

The Story

Dr. Willis Mosby is in Oaxaca, Mexico, on a grant from the Guggenheim Foundation, writing his memoirs. Mosby's memoirs depict him as one of the brightest, most observant people in the twentieth century. He is "erudite, maybe even profound; [had] thought much, accomplished much—had made some of the most interesting mistakes a man could make in the twentieth century."

Mosby thinks that he must now put some humor into his memoirs. He has told about his early life: shaking hands with Generalissimo Francisco Franco during the Spanish Revolution; having experiences in the Office of Strategic Services, the U.S. organization for intelligence gathering and secret operations created during World War II; and describing President Franklin Delano Roosevelt as having limited vision during the war. During the war, Mosby argues, "the Nazis were winning because they had made their managerial revolution first. No Allied combination could conquer, with its obsolete industrialism, a nation that had reached a new state of history and tapped the power of the inevitable, etc." Although Mosby admits that the concentration camps had been deplorable, he thinks they show that Germany had rational political ideas. After the war, he expected a high government appointment but was disappointed. Princeton University also fired him because, he thinks, his mode of discourse upset the academic community.

Now Mosby begins to write about 1947 in Paris and Hyman Lustgarten, whom he considers to be a funny man. An American from New Jersey, Lustgarten was a follower of the communistic philosophy of Karl Marx. In 1947, Lustgarten was in Europe trying to make a fortune as a capitalist. When Mosby met him, Lustgarten was working for the U.S. Army, doing something involving cemeteries, although Mosby is not sure what. On the side, Lustgarten invested all of his and his mother's money in an illegal dental-supply business with a German dentist in Munich who cheated him. Lustgarten next borrowed money from his brother to import a Cadillac into France because Cadillacs could then be sold without taxation at enormous profit. The day his Cadillac arrived, new regulations went into effect, making it impossible for him to sell the car. Lustgarten and his wife, Trudy, moved out of the hotel at which they were staying. Trudy stayed with friends; Lustgarten lived in the Cadillac and used Mosby's place for washing and shaving. Lustgarten next decided to sell the Cadillac in Barcelona. As Klonsky, his associate, was driving the car south, Lustgarten received a marvelous offer for the car from a capitalist in Utrecht in The Netherlands. He took the train south, caught up with Klonsky, and started to drive the car himself to Utrecht. He fell asleep at the wheel, wrecked the uninsured car on the side of a mountain, and landed in the hospital.

While Lustgarten was in the hospital, he heard a rumor that his wife was going out with Alfred Ruskin, an American poet. Mosby, in fact, had arranged for Trudy and Ruskin to be seen in public to mask his own affair with Trudy, of whom Mosby also made fun.

Lustgarten then went to Yugoslavia, thinking he was to be a guest of the communist government of Marshal Tito, the prime minister. Lustgarten was, Mosby wrote, a candidate for resurrection. Instead of being resurrected, however, Lustgarten found himself trapped in the mountains in a labor brigade that he described as being just like a chain gang. Lustgarten returned to Paris sick, disillusioned, and penniless. In the meantime, Trudy had divorced him. Nevertheless, as Lustgarten walked away from Mosby, Mosby noticed that Lustgarten had a certain dignity.

Mosby next saw Lustgarten five years later. Lustgarten had gotten on the wrong elevator trying to find the offices of *Fortune* magazine to sell them the story of how he had made a fortune running a coin-operated laundry with Klonsky in Algiers. He also had married Klonsky's sister and had children. Later the Algerians expelled the French and the Jews, so the one Mosby called "a sweet old Jewish Daddy" and "Jewish-Daddy-Lustgarten" had to move on.

While Mosby is writing about Lustgarten, a car arrives to take him to the ruins at Mitla. Along with two elderly Welsh women, he travels to Tula and then to Mitla. They look at the temples where the Zapotecs—members of a large tribe of Indians who now live in the Mexican state of Oaxaca—once practiced human sacrifice, under Aztec influence. Mosby and the women enter a tomb, where Mosby finds himself oppressed and afraid. The story ends with Mosby telling the guide he has to get out, and admitting to the women that he finds it very hard to breathe.

Themes and Meanings

A central theme in this complex, revealing story involves the conflict between the intellect and the emotions or passions. Mosby, a fanatic about ideas, is all intellect. As a result, he is unattractive, as his ideas about Nazi Germany show. Saul Bellow describes him as pondering with hate the mistakes of political and military leaders and being intolerant in his conversations. He is "stone-hearted Mosby, making fun of flesh and blood, of these little humanities with their short inventories of bad and good." The narrative style leads the reader to believe that these really may be Mosby's opinions of himself. Mosby realizes that he should feel compassion for Lustgarten, in whom Mosby sees no harm, but he feels none. Mosby also abhors unmasked emotion. In contrast, Lustgarten is a man of emotions. The first syllable of his name indicates passion. Although Lustgarten fails so spectacularly, he is ultimately a much more attractive figure than Mosby. When he calls Lustgarten "Jewish-Daddy-Lustgarten," Mosby seems to see even Lustgarten's Jewishness as ridiculous.

"Mosby's Memoirs" also contrasts Mosby with nature and the ruins at Mitla. Bellow characterizes nature in terms of an aggressive vitality. When Mosby goes to Tula, he looks at the Tule tree, which Bellow describes as being older than the religion represented by the church in the yard in which the tree stands. According to Mexican guidebooks, the tree is one of the largest and oldest in the world. Bellow also writes about the kind of passion, bloody though it was, that led to the building and use of the temples and tombs at Mitla. When Mosby thinks of Lustgarten's "Toltec, Mixtec, Zapotec look," this connects Lustgarten to three Mexican tribes, including those associated with the ruined temples and tombs at Mitla. In contrast to nature, especially the Tula tree and the ruins, and in contrast to Lustgarten, Mosby lacks passion and vigor: The French, Mosby recalls, considered him to be a dry fellow.

Mosby, who usually laughs at human tragedy, faces his mortality in Mitla. The name "Mitla" means city or abode of the dead. Entering a tomb at Mitla, Mosby recalls a fantasy in which he died in an automobile accident but continued to live. "His doom was to live life to the end as Mosby. In the fantasy, he considered this his purgatory." In the tomb, he thinks, "To be shut in here! To be dead here! Suppose one were! Not as in accidents which ended, but did not quite end existence. *Dead*-dead." Facing his mortality, Mosby is terrified, for his existence has been empty, and his life has been a kind of living death.

Style and Technique

The story is told for the most part from a limited third-person point of view that reflects Mosby's ideas and opinions. At times, the narrative becomes first-person when Mosby writes. However, the third-person narrative may also involve Mosby writing his memoirs, because Bellow writes that at times Mosby speaks of himself in "third person as Henry Adams had done in *The Education of Henry Adams*," a book first published privately in 1907, one of the most important American autobiographies.

The structure of the story is very complicated, switching from third-person to first-person narrative. This complexity mirrors Mosby's mind. The story is also highly allusive: Mosby's references to various philosophers, statespeople, anthropologists, and scientists show his feeling of superiority to his fellow human beings.

Bellow uses symbolism in connection with the Tule tree and the tombs at Mitla to show the way in which their vitality contrasts with Mosby's lifelessness. The symbols show that heartless, lifeless Mosby deserves to be in what he considers purgatory or even a kind of hell.

Richard Tuerk

THE MOST DANGEROUS GAME

Author: Richard Connell (1893-1949)
Type of plot: Adventure
Time of plot: The mid-1920's
Locale: "Ship-Trap Island," in the Caribbean
First published: 1924

> *Principal characters:*
> SANGER RAINSORD, the protagonist, a famous American hunter
> and author
> GENERAL ZAROFF, the insane owner of Ship-Trap Island
> IVAN, the deaf and dumb servant of General Zaroff

The Story

The title immediately introduces the ironic implications of the story. The word "game," in a tale about two hunters, signifies both the competitive nature of their sport and the victims of it. The most dangerous game is one in which the lives of the hunter and the hunted are equally at risk, and this occurs only when both are men. Rainsford presumes that hunting is a sport involving no more moral consequences than a game such as baseball; he further demonstrates his naïveté by assuming that his victims, big-game animals, have no feelings. These two beliefs, based as they are on Rainsford's certainty that man is superior to animal, are challenged when he encounters General Zaroff, who has pushed the same ideas to their inhumane limits in his madness.

When Rainsford falls off a boat near Ship-Trap Island, he views the sea as his enemy and the island as his salvation, despite the curious rumors surrounding the place. In the same way, he sees safety in the chateau of General Zaroff. Looming unexpectedly over an otherwise deserted landscape, the chateau represents civilization and Rainsford's hope of a return to New York. The image of civilization is confirmed when Rainsford meets the general, who wears clothes designed by a London tailor, drinks rare brandy, and serves gourmet meals on fine china. A man of refined taste, the general denies himself nothing, including the luxury of continuing his greatest passion, hunting. Rainsford, a skilled hunter himself, is intrigued. What kind of game, he wonders, can be hunted on an isolated island? When the general informs him that he stocks the island with the only animal that can reason, Rainsford is aghast to realize that Zaroff hunts men. This perversion of sport repels him, and he rejects the general's defense of manhunting even as he is fascinated by the man's madness.

Zaroff's insanity has a logic that parallels Rainsford's defense of hunting big-game animals. Asserting that "the weak of the world were put here to give the strong pleasure," Zaroff finds justice in hunting the "scum of the earth." Luring sailors and deserters to his island by means of lights that indicate a channel where none exists,

Zaroff imprisons his prey for as long as it takes to get them into excellent physical condition. Most victims choose to be hunted, because their only alternative is to be handed over to Ivan, who prefers prolonged torture to a swift kill. Zaroff believes these men have no rights and no feelings; like Rainsford, he assumes superiority to anything he can outwit and conquer.

Rainsford finds his assumptions shattered when his refusal to hunt another man with Zaroff turns him into the hunted. As he fights to stay alive for three days (the span of Zaroff's challenge), Rainsford feels the unreasoning fear of being trapped, and he saves his life by copying the instinctive behavior of hunted animals. He comes to recognize the inherent unfairness of Zaroff's game, and indeed, of all hunting; with only a knife and meager provisions, he must fight a man who has guns, trained dogs, knowledge of the island, and a safe place to retreat for rest. Trying to use the island's geography to his best advantage, Rainsford is ironically forced to return to the sea, his former enemy, in order to delude Zaroff into thinking that he has committed suicide. The final scene takes place in the most civilized setting, the locked bedroom where the general feels most secure.

In this last reversal of the plot, Rainsford refers to himself as "a beast at bay"; with nothing to lose, having trapped the general, Rainsford knows he must commit murder or be murdered. The scruples that prevented him from joining the general's game in the beginning dissolve under the imperative to defend himself. This encounter between the two, conducted in the language of fencing, further confuses the distinction between sport and killing, civilization and uncontrolled brutality. Rainsford's victory, within the terms that the general has defined, may be no victory at all: He decides to sleep the night in the general's bed and finds it comfortable; the hunted has succeeded, but only by becoming like his hunter—if not as mad, at least as morally suspect.

Themes and Meanings

Two ethical questions seem to dominate this story. First, what is the moral distinction between murder and such forms of killing sanctioned by society as self-defense during war? To kill at all, the story implies, the killer must first believe in his superiority to the victim. Rainsford's belief that animals cannot feel and the general's conviction that they cannot reason provide convenient justification for both men in their lifelong careers as hunters. However, the smugness of their attitude is demonstrated to be dangerous to both of them. Rainsford is forced to play the hunted and must rely on the instinctive behavior of animals to survive (indeed, his vision of himself as a beast at bay justifies the murder of Zaroff), and Zaroff has been driven into madness by the extremity of his sense that no animal is equal to his prowess as a hunter. Rainsford, who fought in World War I and claims not to condone "cold-blooded murder," has nevertheless learned to kill efficiently enough to fool the general and trap him in his own bedroom. There is certainly a suggestion at the end of the story that any experience with killing—through sport, soldiering, or self-defense—contributes to the idea that the victor deserves to survive and makes the idea of murder conscionable.

A second question raised by this story is how successful civilization really is at controlling or diverting the instinctive, often brutal, behavior of man. Zaroff, who appreciates the cultural opportunities of society (evident in his clothing, food, and the snatches of opera that he hums at bedtime), has perverted the civilized convention of the game and sportsmanship to achieve insane, self-indulgent ends. His idea that "life is for the strong, to be lived by the strong, and, if need be, taken by the strong" is in some measure reinforced by the society that has given him tremendous wealth and sanctions his passion as a hunter.

Rainsford, too, is the moral victim of a society that directs men to amuse themselves by intentionally risking death. The ease with which he oversimplifies the world into the hunters and the hunted parallels Zaroff's satisfaction with a world consisting of the strong and the weak. Forced to play the hunted for a time, Rainsford may learn empathy for the victim, but he never questions the dualistic thinking that allows him only to kill or be killed. The story thus forces the reader to question the civilization that assumes that man needs to kill, and at best will only provide him with equally brutal alternatives to murder rather than insist on more creative responses to conflict.

Style and Technique

The dominant technique of this story is that of ironic reversal. Not only does the plot contain reversals that challenge the surface meaning of the story, but also the characters, with their sometimes opposed, sometimes parallel visions of the world, establish expectations that are ironically reversed by the end of the story. The style intentionally directs the reader to think in terms of opposition: hunter versus hunted, strong versus weak, man versus animal, reason versus instinct, civilization versus brutality. However, these obviously opposed pairings disguise a greater complexity; the world is not really arranged so neatly. To be successful, the hunter must imitate the hunted, the man must act the animal, civilization must disguise its brutality.

The final irony, that Rainsford conquers a murderer by killing him, is a last trick on the reader, who has been led to believe that one of the values represented by half of each set of paired opposites is better than the other. No such certainty is possible in a story designed to challenge the conventional understanding of civilized behavior.

Gweneth A. Dunleavy

THE MOTE IN THE MIDDLE DISTANCE, H*NRY J*M*S

Author: Max Beerbohm (1872-1956)
Type of plot: Parody
Time of plot: About 1912
Locale: England
First published: 1912

> *Principal characters:*
> KEITH TANTALUS, the young protagonist
> EVA, his sister
> THE NARRATOR, a friend of the two children

The Story

As indicated by the abbreviated name in the title, this story is a brilliant parody of an incident as it supposedly would be described by Henry James. The plot is somewhat obscure regarding specific details. Two precocious children, a boy and a girl, awake on Christmas morning to find filled stockings at the foot of each bed. The principal story line, however, seems to be a rambling account and speculation by the boy, Keith, on the psychological implications and barriers to ultimate fulfillment suggested by the occasion. It is the idea of seeing beyond the "mote" that is the principal impediment to his view of every aspect of his experience. He periodically ponders Eva's motives for having dug into her stocking in her sleep before he was able to get at his own. This is followed by reflections on Eva's character. Her "remoteness" is discussed in considerable detail with comparisons to a telephone conversation.

Keith's analysis of Eva culminates in his annoyance at his sister's perverse attitude about a lifelike doll that he presumes is included in the contents of her Christmas stocking. This minor irritation is followed by admiration for her "magnificence" and his acknowledgment that the encounter has changed him. That, in turn, leads to the narrator's final sense of inferiority to his two friends, Keith and Eva, whom he occasionally visits even though he admits to never being able to come close to their standard of behavior or introspection. Thus, the story is filtered through the consciousness of a mutual acquaintance whose presence is merely suggested at the beginning of this sketch but is felt strongly in the final paragraph.

Themes and Meanings

Max Beerbohm was a master in his time not only of caricature but of parody as well. Though best remembered now for his cartoons of well-known contemporaries such as King Edward VII and Lytton Strachey, Beerbohm also wrote short stories, essays, and an amusing satirical novel of Oxford undergraduate life, *Zuleika Dobson: Or, An Oxford Love Story* (1911), probably his most famous single prose piece. "The Mote in the Middle Distance, H*nry J*m*s" is only one parody in a collection entitled *A Christmas Garland Woven by Max Beerbohm* (1912). This volume, in which each essay mimics the style of a famous contemporary writer, includes imitations of the writings of Joseph Conrad, H. G. Wells, John Galsworthy, Rudyard Kipling, George Meredith, and others. The unifying topic is the celebration of Christmas; they all concern the holiday season in some way. Beerbohm's deft aping of his "models," as he called them, almost all originally appeared in a London magazine, *Saturday Review.*

The central images of this short travesty are appropriately Jamesian. The two characters are typically left indistinct in both physical appearance and psychological makeup. As in many James novels and short stories, the actual plot seems secondary to the close mental and emotional examination of the characters. However, as in James, Beerbohm seems never to reveal the exact perspective of his protagonist (Keith Tantalus's very name suggests the condition of the reader eager for some more definite information from the author).

Eva, Keith's sister, is described ridiculously, as the "most telephonic of her sex." Keith's impressions seem contradictory as he finds Eva both "magnificent" and remote. The telephone symbol to suggest communication (or the lack of it) between the two children is particularly farcical, as James himself would have never used a machine metaphorically in any of his fiction.

The "mote" of the story is related closely to the impediment to real understanding and frank expression that Beerbohm suggests is the major flaw in the writing of James. The reader of James's fiction, Beerbohm suggests, is ever on the verge of clarification, but all is ultimately seen only "through a glass darkly." Thus, the physical presence of the two looming stuffed stockings at the foot of each bed is merely one manifestation of an impediment to a clear view of the situation. Others seem to be the reluctance of Eva to declare her intentions and the vacillation of Keith. Then there are his troubled relations with his sister and the broader suggestion that perhaps his admiration might have a physical as well as a psychological interpretation. The images of reading and attempting to touch and the additional metaphor of attempting to see beyond a barrier are noteworthy.

Style and Technique

Beerbohm simulates the Jamesian style amusingly and with considerable accuracy. The ponderous and lengthy metaphors here sometimes make either no sense or perverse sense ("talking to Eva you always had . . . your lips to the receiver"). Beerbohm, using lovely mixed metaphors, parodies the Jamesian ones: "pasted the windows of his soul with staring appeals." Sometimes, indeed, he almost overdoes his mocking of the great man's style: "There they are, and you know I know you know we wouldn't."

As with James, some words are repeated for emphasis ("watching," "seeing," especially "peered" and "peering"). The "mote" is echoed in variations such as "points" and "period" (used as a pun in the first sentence). The elegance of the Jamesian style is lacking here, but its essence has been captured in this clever parody.

F. A. Couch, Jr.

A MOTHER'S TALE

Author: James Agee (1909-1955)
Type of plot: Fable
Time of plot: Unspecified
Locale: Unspecified
First published: 1952

Principal characters:
A MOTHER COW, the narrator of the tale
HER SON AND DAUGHTER
THE ONE WHO CAME BACK
THE MAN WITH THE HAMMER

The Story

This story, a beast fable in the manner of seventeenth century French author Jean de La Fontaine or the nineteenth century German brothers, Jacob and Wilhelm Grimm, is a tale told by a mother cow to her son and daughter. It opens with her son running breathlessly up the hill to ask her about the immense cattle herd he has seen moving eastward, accompanied by men on horseback and barking dogs. What are they doing? Where are they going?

The persistence of her son and the other spring calves that have joined him cannot be ignored, and mother finally tells them that the herd is going on a long journey, to a railroad, great bars of metal on which run huge wagons pulled by a screaming, smoke-belching black machine. The cattle are put into these wagons and taken away. She assures her young companions that the herd is probably being taken to a nice place. The children, of course, all want to go, but mother assures them that it is a much greater honor to stay home. Only the ordinary, careless, and silly are taken to the trains. The strong, brave, and bright are allowed to stay at home where it is safe. The word "safe," a slip of the tongue, arouses her son's curiosity. Where are they going? Why is it not safe there?

The mother begins the story of The One Who Came Back, and the tale takes a decidedly darker turn. According to mother's great-grandmother, who heard it from her great-grandmother, The One Who Came Back found himself pressed tightly into one of the railway wagons on a dizzying and frightening ride to an unknown place. There was no food or water, and the cows had to stand in their own excrement, pushed and pulled this way and that, with the countryside rolling past them like a slow wheel. After a seemingly endless time, the doors of the wagon rolled open and the herd staggered out into the open air, where they had water and what seemed the most delicious food they had ever eaten. Their new home was beautiful and grand, with white fences and dark buildings in the distance as huge as mountains. The cows were now being treated so well, and their destination was proving to be so lovely, that there obviously was nothing to worry about.

Soon The One Who Came Back found himself being guided into an increasingly narrow gate that led into one of the enormous buildings. Suddenly the cow ahead fell down with a great sigh and was dragged away immediately. Looking up, The One Who Came Back saw for the first time The Man with the Hammer. The mother cries inwardly, seeing the terror in the eyes of the young ones, but it is too late: She must go on. The Man with the Hammer brought his hammer down on the forehead of The One Who Came Back, who sank into darkness and dreadful pain. He awakened upside down, hanging by the tendons of his heels from a great hook, and he could feel his hide being torn away inch by inch, his living flesh being sliced by sharp knives.

With a supreme effort, The One Who Came Back managed to tear himself from the hooks, charge the men with the knives, and escape from the building, leaping one fence after another. Some inner power seemed to guide him along the railroad tracks that took him to his recent horror. Traveling day and night, exhausted and in pain, The One Who Came Back staggered back home from the East. The hide was gone from his head and body, his flesh had been carved away, and in the middle of his forehead was an indentation that looked like a third eye. He could barely speak.

As his fellow cattle listened to him, some thought that he looked human, that he was perhaps even a man trying to disguise himself as a cow. Others doubted that he came from their ranch, for no cow could remember him. Still others concluded he was a lunatic. Eventually some men came along and shot him, whether out of kindness or to silence him was endlessly disputed. Some came to believe, however, that he died of sorrow for his fellow cows before the shots were fired. There was no argument about his final words. Each cow is himself, he told them, and not of the herd. Obey and depend on nobody. Break down the fences and kill Man. If you cannot kill him, avoid him. Kill your yearlings and calves, and bear no more young. You must save yourselves, for all who are put on trains will meet The Man with the Hammer.

Finished with her tale, mother sees the puzzlement on the faces of the young, especially on the face of her oldest son. He asks her if she believes all this, and mother evasively answers that some cows do. There are even rumors of some very old ones, in the distant corners of the range, who have never been taken to the trains, who are obsessed with the terror of the two sublime beings, The One Who Came Back and The Man with the Hammer. They even make up songs about them. Her son asks again if she believes it. Of course not, mother answers. It is merely a tale to frighten children. The son vows to find out the truth for himself. He will go on the train, make the great journey, and if there is The Man with the Hammer, he will charge him and kill him. That will make the son an even greater hero than The One Who Came Back. The littlest one, the daughter, skipping along to keep up with her mother, shyly whispers the question that has been troubling her all this time. Mother, she asks, what is a train?

Themes and Meanings

"A Mother's Tale" is open to a variety of interpretations. The manner in which cattle are herded into railway cars and taken to a destination of death and horror recalls the Holocaust, when thousands of human beings were herded in the same way to destruction. Just as many refuse to face the reality of such horror, the majority of the herd cannot face the incontrovertible truth of experience.

The tale also has religious implications. The capitalized Man with the Hammer is both personified human evil and the merciless God of destruction, the destructive force that murders the perishable body of everyone. The One Who Came Back, however, is an affirmation of Ernest Hemingway's famous statement in *The Old Man and the Sea* (1952) that "man can be destroyed but not defeated." There are several hints that this battered creature is Christlike—his arrival from the East, his stigmatic hooves, his suffering for his fellow creatures—but his newly acquired knowledge betrays only satanic hatred: Kill man, kill your offspring, bear no more children. Although humans may deserve such condemnation, James Agee's point seems clear: Violence breeds only further violence. The One Who Came Back is only a sad, beaten animal that has failed to learn through suffering, to become truly Christlike, to become Everyman—or, in his case, Everycow.

Style and Technique

As in all beast fables, Agee's animals have human characteristics, and his tale really is not about cows but people. The mother cow is given motherly qualities of bemusement, concern, and solicitude, while her children are inquisitive, impatient, and naïve. The One Who Came Back is heroic, tenacious, and suffering, while The Man with the Hammer is all that is cruel and inhuman in human nature. Agee begins the story like a fairy tale ("The calf ran up the little hill as fast as he could."), but by the end, we have listened to a horror story as harrowing as that of Dachau, site of the notorious Nazi concentration camp of World War II. The daughter's simple-minded question at the tale's end, "What's a train?" indicates that nothing of the story's import has gotten through to her.

Agee's style ranges from the poetic descriptions of the hillside and of the moving cattle herd to the brutal descriptions of the cattle train and slaughterhouse, told from the cattle's point of view. Readers are made to feel what the cattle feel, see what they see, and experience what befalls them, as though they are part of them. In a sense they are, for they too will fall to The Man with the Hammer, the nameless killer that will take the life of man and cow alike. The nobility of everyone, Agee says, is in humankind's feeble attempt to rise above mortality and suffering—to endure.

Kenneth Seib

THE MOTHS

Author: Helena María Viramontes (1954-   )
Type of plot: Magical Realism
Time of plot: The 1980's
Locale: Los Angeles, California
First published: 1985

> *Principal characters:*
> THE NARRATOR, an adolescent girl
> MAMA LUNA (ABUELITA), her grandmother
> AMÁ, her mother
> APÁ, her father
> HER SISTERS

The Story

When the narrator was fourteen years old, her elderly grandmother Abuelita (Mama Luna), who was dying of cancer, asked her to help take care of her. The girl felt this was a reasonable request, because Abuelita had taken care of her through illnesses, whippings, a broken arm incurred in the process of following a dare, her first lie, and puberty. Though she denies a special connection with her grandmother, it is clear that one has developed and that her grandmother has offered her a level of understanding that she never received at home.

Within her own nuclear family the girl was the odd member. She was too tomboyish for the girls, too rebellious for her father, and a trial for her mother. Although her sisters were ultra-feminine, with delicate hands and manners and fine embroidery skills, the narrator was awkward and large. She was violently defensive and boyish in her ways (she once struck a sister with a brick hidden in a sock when the sister teased her about her big hands). Throughout her childhood, her father, Apá, criticized her and beat her for not conforming to his notions of what a docile girl should be and for not attending church regularly.

The narrator's father directed some of this anger over his daughter's behavior at her mother, whom he blamed for poor parenting. To protect her mother from his wrath, the narrator sometimes dressed as if she were going to church, when she was actually going to Mama Luna's house, where she helped the older woman prepare food. As they worked together in the kitchen, tears streamed down her cheeks as she peeled and crushed chili peppers. On some days, the narrator's mother sent her out of the house to save her from a whipping by her father, and she went to Abuelita's to help her plant seedlings in coffee cans that were later transplanted to the grandmother's beautiful garden.

Now Abuelita, whose own hands have rubbed and healed and nurtured so many, is dying. She lies in her bed and looks out the open window at the Bird of Paradise blooming without. Her eyelids remain partly open even when she is sleeping, showing her one gray and one brown eye as if she is watching and remembering everything around her. The narrator has never kissed her grandmother but has held her hand for hours.

One day she goes out to the market and on the way stops in at a chapel, feeling utterly alone in its cold, vacant marble interior. After purchasing the few items that Abuelita needs at a store, she returns to the house to find her mother crying in the kitchen. She puts the cans of soup away in the cupboard, without kissing or comforting her mother, then stiffly pats her on the back, aware that her relationship with her mother is hampered by all the quarrels and beatings in their household and by her own feelings of oddness and helplessness. She goes and sits on the porch swing until her mother departs and the sun begins to set, then goes into the kitchen to prepare soup for Abuelita's evening meal. She notes the defiance of the sun just before it changes color and finally sinks below the horizon in the moment of illumination when sun and earth meet. She switches on the kitchen light as darkness falls—the very moment at which Abuelita passes away.

The narrator finds her grandmother lying dead on her side facing the window, her mouth open as if she is about to speak. "I heard you," she assures the dead woman, and strokes her cheek. She carefully undresses and bathes Mama Luna's body with a basin and towel, then fills the bathtub with steaming water. Stripping down to nakedness herself, she lifts her grandmother and carries her into the bathroom, lowering both their bodies together into the tub. There she cradles Abuelita, assuring her again that she had been heard, and comforting her with rocking motions as one would a child. The water from the tub overflows onto the floor, and moths flutter up out of the grandmother's mouth to the light of the bulb in the ceiling of the bathroom. The granddaughter wants to assuage the loneliness of dying. She wants to return to the womb again with her grandmother so as never to be alone. She wants her own mother. As the bathroom fills with moths the girl begins to sob, crying for herself, for her mother, for her grandmother, feeling the misery of being half-born, and in rocking and comforting the dead Mama Luna, comforting the traumatized child in herself as well.

Themes and Meanings

A story of transitions and transfiguration, "The Moths" traces the passages of a girl into a woman, day into night, birth into death and into rebirth again. It explores the themes of female adolescence, particularly the pain faced by a young girl who does not fulfill the conventional expectations of femininity, and of patriarchal violence within a household and its effect on three generations of women. Love and the power to take care and heal is another theme, particularly displayed in the links between grandmother and granddaughter. As in her other work, Helena María Viramontes uses careful characterization and irony to display her meanings. Here the adolescent branded as selfish, sacrilegious, and disrespectful engages in a private ceremony that is deeply imbued with respect, selflessness, and religious awareness.

Style and Technique

Told in the first person, "The Moths" revolves around rites of passage and religious imagery. The twoness of adolescence is captured in the girl's androgynous body and actions, in the transfiguring sunset uniting earth and sun that signals the old woman's death, and in the girl's own impression of being half-born.

Viramontes uses symbolic imagery in creating the specifics of the granddaughter and grandmother's closeness and the grandmother's powers to heal. Hands are both metaphors and physical means of connection. The defiant sun is like the grandmother's own life. The chili peppers that the girl prepares are like her own hot, tempestuous temperament. The tears evoked in roasting and crushing them brings a kind of spiritual remedy or release that is a spiritual substitute for churchgoing. In contrast to the cool and indifferent marble of the church, the grandmother's house is a true sanctuary for the abused girl. There her emotional turbulence is transformed from a state of agitation to the calmness of a rose petal floating softly in the breeze and coming to rest beside the finished bowl of chile on the table. The girl is also like the seedlings that the grandmother protects in a can and then transplants so that they can pursue their mature growth. As the plants mature, their roots burst from the bottom of the rusted coffee cans in search of a place to connect, in search of water. So does the protagonist at the end of the story burst through her contained emotions and connect with her dead grandmother, surrounded and nurtured by womblike water.

Viramontes uses techniques of Magical Realism in her references to the moths that give the story its title: They personify the grandmother's soul as they emerge from within her body and fill the room in the surrealism of the final scene. Earlier in the story the grandmother rubs dried moth wings, the stuff of transcendence, into her granddaughter's hands in order to cure their awkward heaviness, reversing the sensation the girl has of her hands being pulled down to earth.

The story's final scene is deeply imbued with religious meaning. The soul of the grandmother who in the last hours of life looked at a Bird of Paradise flowering outside her window metamorphoses into many moths fluttering toward heaven. The two naked women, one old and one young, are connected in a kind of osmosis, and as they float together in the water each generation of women is collapsed together in the girl's mind. The water breaks over the side of the tub signaling the process of birth/rebirth, and the old woman is converted to a babe rocked in her young granddaughter's arms. The water serves as a kind of balm and baptism. At the same time the girl whose positive emotions have been so repressed is able to express her terrible loneliness; she, too, is like a baby in need of her mother's rocking and nurturing arms, and her sobs convey the desperation she feels at being abandoned by her only protector through Abuelita's death.

Barbara J. Bair

THE MOUNTAIN TAVERN

Author: Liam O'Flaherty (1896-1984)
Type of plot: Adventure
Time of plot: 1919
Locale: The mountain country of Ireland
First published: 1927

> *Principal characters:*
> THE FIRST SOLDIER, Jack, a young man
> THE SECOND SOLDIER, the "commandant"
> THE THIRD SOLDIER, Curly, a very big man
> MRS. GALLIGAN, the proprietor of the tavern

The Story

Somewhere in Ireland during the time known as "The Troubles," the era of the civil war that led to the creation of the Irish Free State, three soldiers identified only as Republicans are struggling through a snowstorm in mountainous terrain. They are described only as a man with "grim young eyes"; a man referred to by the others as the commandant who has "a forlorn look in his eyes"; and a huge man walking bareheaded and erect who has a "proud, fearless face." The commandant is seriously wounded following an ambush in which their column was wiped out, and the three soldiers are trying to reach the sanctuary of a mountain tavern that the first man knows about. Snow has been falling steadily for many hours and the features of the countryside are hidden beneath a "bare, flat" landscape, a moorland that is "silent, oh, silent as an empty church." The setting is as bleak as the men's prospects. All that they can see as they search for shelter are "falling flakes of white snow, undeflected, falling silently on fallen snow," an image of desolation stretching toward infinity.

The commandant is very weak from the stress of his wounds, "blood on his coat, on his hand, and congealed on his black leggings," and the soldiers are aware that they are being pursued, but the possibility of finding safety and warmth in the tavern gives them the impetus to proceed. The first soldier recalls the tavern in better times to encourage his mates, "two storey high and a slate roof with sun shining on it," but when they abruptly come on it, it appears as a ruin, "a crazy blue heap," with smoke rising from its base. The soldiers are stunned, then enraged, but before they can make any kind of decision about what to do, a group of people appears around the house. The people have clearly been through some trial of their own, as indicated by the strange state of their dress. There is a woman with a "long overcoat buttoned over her dress and a man's overcoat on her shoulders" holding a hat with red feathers, two thin children "in queer clothes," and two men trying to salvage some items from the wreckage.

The two groups face each other, frozen by a kind of paralysis of despair, until the commandant suddenly cries out, "Stand fast. Stand fast boys. Stand." in a last instant of consciousness before collapsing in death. Rather than holding their ground, they are propelled by this terrifying incident into frantic grief as the youngest soldier implores the woman for some kind of assistance. Her response is to call them "daylight robbers" and to accuse them of burning down her house. The soldier's attempt to explain that it was their adversaries who are responsible is lost on the woman, who sees both sides as equally guilty. "Ain't I ruined and wrecked for three long years with yer fightin," she demands, giving tongue to a sentiment felt by many citizens of the country. Her anger is illuminated as one of the men from the tavern describes a fierce battle earlier in the day in which the house was used as a fortress and destroyed by a bomb, with the survivors of the explosion carried off in cars to an unknown fate.

In the aftermath of this explanation, both groups settle into silence and immobility, the two soldiers sitting exhausted and dazed in the snow, the family that managed the tavern for the previous twenty years unable to reconcile their fury with any recognition of the humanity of the soldiers. In an awful expression of the most grievous wounds of war, the gaze of the tavern owner is filled with "hatred" and "curious apathy," while the anguish of the soldiers over their comrade's death is regarded with "the serene cruelty of children watching an insect being tortured."

The narrative action of the story has been marked to this point by a steady decline in the fortune and spirit of the soldiers, but the third soldier has seemed indestructible until now. Finally, even his resolve is overcome. "Let them take us. I'm tired fighin'. It's no use," he says, but this wrenching admission of defeat is merely a prelude for further brutality as the soldiers of the Free State arrive. Their roundup of all the people at the tavern is brusque and pitiless, their leader expressing a cold pleasure at the discovery of the dead commandant. "So we got him at last. Eh? Heave him into the lorry, boys," he orders. The entire troop and their prisoners descend into the valley, with no sign of human pity, no mercy, no compassion. All that remains of the carnage is the "black ruin" of the tavern, and the "black spot" where the body of the commandant had fallen. The night and the snow, falling "like soft soothing white flower petals," provide a natural relief from the horror, a sort of benediction from the cosmos for a remnant of humanity that seems, temporarily, to have lost its capacity for the grace of forgiveness.

Themes and Meanings

It is impossible to consider a story about Ireland in which snow covers the land without thinking of James Joyce's masterpiece from *Dubliners* (1914), the concluding story entitled "The Dead." In Joyce's story, however, the snow "general all over Ireland" is a symbol of reconciliation and transcendence. For Liam O'Flaherty, the snow is an emblem of nature's power to restore tranquillity after man has devastated the realm (the white over the black), which has a tangential correspondence to Joyce's use of snow in that it represents a comforting return to a state in which all is unspoiled. The snow is also, however, a symbol of obliteration. His story is a rueful commentary on three centuries of internecine struggle that has accomplished nothing, and a sad, prescient vision of the Isle of Erin as a land suffocated by sectarian strife well into the late twentieth century and beyond. In this vein, the snow symbolizes the chill blankness of mindless hatred.

Throughout its history, in written literature and in great oral tradition, Ireland has proclaimed itself a land of talk, drink, and song. The tavern of the story's title is a figure for Ireland's hospitality and community, a place where the stranger is welcome from the storm and where men and women might gather to share words and feelings that inspire and give one the courage to face the burdens of an often harsh existence. Through famine, colonization, and grinding poverty, the "indomitable Irishry," as William Butler Yeats calls them, offered the world a version of communal civility and singing life. However, for O'Flaherty, the soul of this people is in danger because of the fierce hatred that threatens to overwhelm what Yeats called the "terrible beauty" born of revolutionary fervor. The tavern has been burned, its managers driven mad with grief, no longer able to offer comfort to their countrymen in time of need. The snow, with its persistent whiteness, is a chilling, suffocating substance that has transformed the Emerald Isle from its green, fertile, misty glory into a plain of blankness and featureless desolation. The story is a vivid presentation of the obscene stupidity and destruction of any war anywhere, and a lament by O'Flaherty for the losses wreaked on the people of Ireland, his countrymen, by a war that seems never to end.

Style and Technique

To render its impact in the broadest terms, O'Flaherty has fashioned "The Mountain Tavern" in the form of a folktale. All the primary characters are intensely concentrated but none of them is very complex. The "voice" of the narration is distant and removed, like a legend filtered through time in which the narrator is content to let the events speak for themselves and the details accumulate strength through directness. The lyric beauty of much of the descriptive writing is understated but extremely evocative. A poignant contrast between the supple poetic power of the writing and the stark and chilling events that are described is developed as a means of charging the mood of the story with dramatic tension. The entire story is like an unrelenting poem of force and fracture, in which a sustained, intense vision of a terrifying reality is created and held throughout the narration.

Leon Lewis

THE MOVING

Author: James Still (1906-2001)
Type of plot: Social realism
Time of plot: The 1930's
Locale: A coal-mining camp in eastern Kentucky
First published: 1941

> *Principal characters:*
>> THE NARRATOR, a boy leaving Hardstay camp
>> FATHER, a resolute coal miner
>> MOTHER, a plain, good-hearted woman
>> HIG SOMMERS, a dimwit
>> SULA BASHAM, a widow

The Story

A boy and his mother are standing by their loaded wagon while his father is nailing the windows of their house shut and spitting into the keyholes to make the locks turn. The mine has closed for all time, and idle men, their wives, and children—some of whom have stuffed their pockets with rocks—are watching the family leave. Only Hig Sommers, a dimwit who speaks things backward, is saddened by the boy's leaving; and only Sula Basham, a tall widow, walks over to say good-bye to Mother and tell her that she ought to be proud that her husband is not satisfied to rot in Hardstay. The crowd stirs uneasily, and Sill Lovelock, raising his arms like a preacher's, declares that the family is moving to nowhere.

With the key in his hand, Father walks from the house, now shut against their turning back. The boy, looking at the family's empty hull of a house and at the lost town, longs to stay in the place where he was born. Father asks if someone will deliver the key to the commissary, and Hig comes forward, his hands stretched out like a baby's, crying that he will "fotch it." Father explains to Hig that it does not need to be fetched, it needs to be taken. Sill then urges Father to stay in the shelter of the camp; Father replies that he would rather die hunting for work than die of dry rot by staying in Hardstay. Loss Tramble offers to take the key if Father will take Sula along and find her a husband, and Sula announces that, if she wanted to marry, she would have to go outside the camp to find a worthwhile man.

Mother, who has never owned any jewelry, begins to study Sula's locket, looking at it in wonder. Sula, with Loss still teasing her about widowhood, then offers to deliver the key for Father. Loss retreats and Sula turns back to Mother, who has climbed onto the wagon. With the two at an even level, Sula thanks Mother for comforting her when her husband died and says she wants to give her a keepsake.

The family now ready to leave, the boy climbs to the top of the loaded wagon, where, over the heads of the men, he views the whole of the camp. As he sees the shotgun houses and the smoke rising above the burning heaps, he is stricken with the pain of homesickness. Father then starts the mare, who walks right out of the wagon shafts, for a prankster has cleverly unfastened the trace chains. After fixing the harness, Father jumps back onto the wagon and drives away. At once, the boy hears the echo of Sill's final warning, "You're making your bed in Hell!" and sees hanging from Mother's neck Sula's gold locket, "beating her bosom like a heart."

The story ends as the boy glances back and notices the other boys shattering the windows of his home; sees the crowd move away from Sula, who has just knocked down Loss; and beholds Hig, holding up his breeches because his suspenders had just been cut, waving and yelling to the family, "Hello, hello!"

Themes and Meanings

On its broadest level, "The Moving" is a portrait of a community in severe straits because of the industrialization of a rural culture. The coal business is known for its boom and bust cycles, and clearly this story is set in a bust. Because of the economic situation, the people of Hardstay face two dismal options: They can either stay "where there's a floor underfoot and joists overhead," but possibly die of dry rot, or take their chances and migrate into a land where "they's no work anywheres." James Still's characters react in both ways, a division reflected by the repetition of "they" and "we" in the opening paragraph: Some stay "locked"—a resonant word in the story—in a place they know and trust, but where there is minimal opportunity; others try to unlock themselves from their hopeless condition, although to do so is to journey into the unknown.

The choices made inform the story's central tension between the community and the narrator's family. Father, Mother, and the boy, because they are moving, are no longer accepted by the community. With the exception of the widow Sula and the dimwit Hig—both community outcasts—the townspeople appear to turn against the family, mocking them, vandalizing their home, shunning them as they drive away. Once the family leaves, returning is not an option—a dilemma suggested by the narrator's description of Father locking the house and the boys breaking the windows at the end of the story.

The choice between moving and staying is portrayed by the narrator as a choice between life and death. The narrator describes the camp as a doomed place, a lost town. Thus the family is fleeing death and seeking salvation, a move charged with biblical implications. The story has direct references to the Israelites' journey into the wilderness, for example, Sill's warning, "There's no manna falling from Heaven this day and time." The narrator's descriptions of the town suggest a link to Sodom and Gomorrah—"I looked back upon the camp as upon the face of the dead"—and to Hell—"I could see the smoke rising above the burning gob heaps." These images emphasize the great irony of Sill Lovelock's last warning to the family, "You're making your bed in Hell!"

Sula Basham is a defender of the right. In sharp contrast to the immature and confined perspectives of Loss Tramble and Sill Lovelock, names that reflect the lost town and the sealed and locked fate of the crowd, Sula is a realist; her great height suggests her liberty to see what the others do not. Her dignity, strength, and loyalty counter the cruelty, powerlessness, and betrayal of the others. Giving her gold locket to Mother signals more than just her selflessness: The locket represents Sula's spirit, and if Sula herself cannot leave—perhaps because she has no means of leaving—then at least her spirit can. To the boy, the locket has the force of a heart—an organ of life, a symbol of empowerment and rebirth.

The townspeople embody misery. Loss's humor, funny as it is, cannot save them. Even Sula, the voice of reason, is drawn back into the morass and does not watch the family drive away. As the boy heads into the unknown, he is left with the final words, "Hello, hello!" a gesture at once symbolizing the backwardness of the town, as it comes from "backwards" Hig, and the progression of the family greeting a new life.

Style and Technique

Remarkable for its directness of contact with its subject, "The Moving" is a good example of a well-controlled and tightly compressed story. The first-person child narrator as reporter, common in Still's work, gives the reader an inquisitive, observant, trustworthy, and nonjudgmental perspective. The use of idiomatic language places the reader on location: Still is true to the culture's use of compound terms such as "pin-pretty" and "widow-woman"; its manner of using an "a" before a present progressive verb, for example, "a-setting" and "a-wanting"; and its folk terms and expressions, such as "roust" and "pulled a rustie."

Still, an acclaimed poet, was recognized for his use of exact, lean, concrete language grounded in nature and the practical world, for example, "We waited, restless as the harnessed mare" and "I say as long's a body has got a rooftree, let him roost under it." Still's prose often demands the same attention, and offers the same rewards, as poetry. A single sentence in the story's first paragraph evinces Still's use of prose rhythm and metaphoric implication: "They hung over the fence; they crowded where last year's dogtick stalks clutched their brown leaf-hands into fists." Here, Still suggests the men's immobility by the use of the word "hung"; signals that the time of year is fall, the season of death, by the color and state of the leaves; links the leaves to hands, suggestive of the men as hands or laborers, a synecdoche used later in the story; uses the word "fist," which introduces the crowd's brutality and foreshadows Sula's strike with her fist near the end of the story; and juxtaposes the men and the stalks, which are doomed to wither and die where they stand.

M. A. Grubbs

MOVING PICTURES

Author: Charles Johnson (1948-   )
Type of plot: Psychological
Time of plot: The 1980's
Locale: The Neptune Theater, a cinema
First published: 1985

> *Principal characters:*
> A MAN, a frustrated film viewer
> COATES, a film editor
> MEGAN or DAPHNE, the man's wife

The Story

Told from the perspective of a second-person narrator, who interprets the thoughts of a man viewing a film in a theater, "Moving Pictures" does not involve the usual interaction of characters. It is a roving excursion through the thoughts of the unnamed viewer of the matinee. At times, the man appears to be either a novelist turned screenwriter or simply a highly imaginative viewer who fantasizes that he has written the ninety-minute Western film. The narrator creates uncertainty about the identity of the man: "Perhaps you have written this movie. Perhaps not." The man's observations are filtered through the commentary of the narrator, who initially makes remarks about the American film industry.

The man is aware that the James Bond films have been seen by countless people, which indicates the immense popularity of films. The narrator notes the high status of film directors and the importance of movie houses as arenas of visual culture. The narrator also analyzes the motives of the viewer, who is a kind of Everyman in search of enlightenment and perhaps an experience of transcendence.

In probing the thoughts of the main character, the narrator informs the reader of the viewer's background. He grew up during the Aquarian age of the 1960's and now lives in the fast lane. Sanka, traffic jams, and hectic business schedules are part of his current existence, which contrasts with his earlier life when he was addicted to methadone. The man, who has a degree in English, uses the Neptune Theater as an escape from the tedium of his daily routine.

The background of the viewer is continually unraveled by the narrator. The man is experiencing a failed marriage to a woman, named either Megan or Daphne, who is a semiprofessional actress. The worlds of illusion and reality—especially concerning the man's identity—become indistinguishable. Details of the failed marriage are presented. The pending separation, resulting from disaffection on both sides, poses a series of depressing complications involving children from a former marriage, a tax audit by the Internal Revenue Service, mortgage payments, and alimony. There is also an allusion to the death of the man's mother.

These bothersome thoughts are shelved when the film begins with the usual trademark images, which become hopeful signs that the dream merchants will provide either a tragic or farcical experience of value. The narrator identifies the man as a screenwriter, who may have written the film he is watching. The man attempts to locate his name in the credits and recalls crew members and the difficulties in shooting on location in Oklahoma cow towns.

The narrator explores the man as screenwriter. His novel, which had been read by the director, resulted in his having been offered the scriptwriting assignment. The director's concern with sex scenes is contrasted with the screenwriter's goal of genuine depth. The man's educational background, his dissertation on literary theorist Jacques Derrida, are contrasted with the entertainment necessities of filmmaking. The film project caused the screenwriter to receive admiration from his friends, many of whom became distant after his success. As the credits roll, the man compares the demands of novel-writing technique with the easier task of scriptwriting.

The man makes a variety of observations unlike those of the average viewer. He knows the traits of the actors, the producer's motivations, and the casting suggestions with which the writer ultimately complied. The film business itself is critiqued as part of a corrupt industry in polluted Hollywood.

Uncertainty about the man's identity is furthered by the narrator, who continues to question whether the film was actually written by the man. The action of the film is described from the perspective of a screenwriter. The main characters of the Western, Bret and Bess, are part of the opening scene, which involves a funeral. This scene causes the man to choke up because he is reminded of his mother's funeral. He realizes that the true magic of film is that the viewer is the repository of the emotions that appear on the screen.

The man recollects the editing process and his interaction with Coates, the film editor. As the film ends and the final credits appear, the man realizes that the film can no longer fool him or transform his feelings. He recalls the technical aspects of the project rather than its emotional effect. Edited lines and visible microphones are the reality of the process that is connected to those parts of the film that evoked laughter from the audience. The happy ending, the marriage of Bret and Bess, is clearly ironic because they had disliked each other as actors. Furthermore, the man is experiencing an unhappy ending in his own marriage.

When the man leaves the theater, he discovers that his car has been broken into. His checkbook, spare house keys, and a report due the next day have been stolen. The photograph of his wife that falls out of the glove compartment reminds him of the tragedy of his life, the pending separation, the grinding boredom of his job, and the demands of his children. He releases the anger that is building inside him by banging his fists on the car. He finally climbs inside, cranks up the car's engine, and curses as he lowers his head to the steering wheel.

Themes and Meanings

True to the philosophical and multilayered nature of Charles Johnson's writing,

"Moving Pictures" explores a number of issues, which derive from an epistemological concern with illusion and reality in the postmodern world. Johnson complicates the act of viewing a film by probing the unspoken thoughts of the man. The monotony of routine American life is relieved through the imaginative escape of film and the dream of Hollywood success. Johnson explores the way a person can assume a different identity. The despair caused by death and the failure of love are two of the universal themes of the story.

On the one hand, Hollywood and the film product provide escape, which is useful because it interrupts routinized existence. The escape is itself an illusion, however, because the observer displaces his own dilemmas by creating a parallel identity on which these dilemmas are reinscribed. The film industry is presented as materialistic, shallow, and corrupt.

Another theme is the role of the artist as writer, especially the dilemmas faced by the serious novelist who must compromise in order to be successful. The artist must struggle to maintain creative integrity in the face of commercial realities. Although creative work is in itself an achievement, it is also a commodity, which can be altered and modified to meet the requirements of the marketplace of illusion and dreams.

Johnson is concerned with the way American life not only constrains the creative process but also promotes the assumption of counteridentities, which become survival mechanisms. The postmodern world has created a network of obligations that trap the individual. Maintaining marriages, meeting job requirements, and facing the congestion of urban life are signifiers of the postmodern condition.

Behind the illusion that Hollywood creates is the need for individuals to define their own reality. In assuming the identity of the screenwriter, the man creates a parallel script and consciously delves behind the obvious action. This counterscript is a form of empowerment. The ending of "Moving Pictures" implies that although the creative process is a form of empowerment, it is challenged by the realities of physical existence.

The postmodern dilemma is represented in the rifling of the Fiat's glove compartment, out of which fragments of the viewer's life tumble—especially the significant photograph of his wife. The unresolved tension of the failing marriage is inescapable. The story suggests the difficulties of escaping the problems of material existence and that one must pay a price for moments of illusion. Ironically, the experience of living is the paramount show.

Style and Technique

Johnson's use of the second-person narrator is a distinctive stylistic element. The narrative style, both linear and circular, affects the construction of the plot. The narrator is an alter ego or countervoice that both defines and informs the central character. Certain phrases are used to sustain ambiguity, to challenge the reader's conception of the main character.

Although the action is based on the act of viewing a film, this act becomes the locus for additional smaller narrative segments. When the man begins watching the film, the narrator presents a brief narrative involving the man's personal life, especially his relationship with his wife. This segment returns to the main story line. The looping of smaller narratives is part of Johnson's technique.

The setting is conceived as the interior landscape of the mind, and some of the characters are possibly imagined. The complexity of sentence structure replicates mental processes of recollecting and imagining. The absence of dialogue results from the emphasis on narrative perspective.

Joseph McLaren

MR. AND MRS. BABY

Author: Mark Strand (1934-   )
Type of plot: Parody
Time of plot: 1979
Locale: California
First published: 1979

Principal characters:
BOB BABY, a man who lives a shallow life
BABE BABY, his wife

The Story

The story presents a day in the life of Bob Baby and his wife, Babe, characterless characters leading entirely shallow lives somewhere in that nebulous place of modern existence: California. They get up, eat breakfast, wade through the blasé morning, skip lunch, cry, try to talk, go to what is supposed to be a party, then go back to sleep. This routine is how Bob and Babe spend their days and live their lives.

There is no conflict, external or internal, in the story. The two characters have been bought with bread and circuses in the sundry forms these things take in today's world: television, appliances, entertainment, and other diversions. Mr. and Mrs. Baby inhabit a world in which thought is unnecessary; like babies, they depend entirely on something larger than themselves to take care of them. They are helplessly and haplessly devoid of both pain and pleasure; they seek only to perpetuate their own existences through the boredom of routine.

The setting is California, appropriately a nameless town there, where the future happens first. Even the physical descriptions of Bob and Babe Baby lack any depth: Each of them is compared to some twenty movie stars—that is, to the personages these actors and actresses portray, and betray as humans—so as to reveal that they are completely lacking in any unique characteristics. In the shadow of Hollywood, they are as movie characters leading pointless lives.

Although there is little here that can be labeled as plot, action, characterization, or setting, there is movement in the work as readers slowly become aware of the pain of existence, not so much of Bob and Babe Baby, but in their own lives. Strand takes the couple through a day, showing them getting up in the morning, following their activities around the clock, then tucks them in at night. The story is one of a void in the life of human automatons.

Themes and Meanings

Mark Strand presents two main themes in "Mr. and Mrs. Baby." First, he wants to show that contemporary life has no plot, little movement, and no meaningful action; hence, his characters, reenacting their daily lives yet once again, perform only the most pointless of activities. Even so, this is the best they can do. Bob and Babe Baby are parodies of late twentieth century man and woman, male and female, husband and wife. They functionally exist in entirely pointless lives, oblivious to any lack of meaning, mobility, experience, and joy; even their attempts to feel pain fail. They remain babies, cared for on every hand by the artificial and technical mechanisms of a society and culture with no emotions, feelings, or values. Like the babies they are, they cannot move into an adult world where they can feel, think, love, hate, even just live their own lives.

They are overwhelmed by banality, by their inability to grow up and to move beyond dependency: When they awaken, there is no discernible difference between being asleep and being awake. When they are together at breakfast, they have no reason to talk—in part, because each already knows what the other one is thinking and, more important, because, being unable to think, they have nothing to say. When they try to think, it is too hopeless a process because they do not know how and, therefore, are only frightened at their attempt. When they try to talk, they mumble clichés. When they go to a party, they leave because it seems that nothing is happening. When they finish the day and go to bed, they do so knowing only that tomorrow will be another day just like the present one was.

The writer also attempts to convince readers that his depiction of modern life is accurate for everyone. The moral of the story is not so much that Mr. and Mrs. Baby have pointless, meaningless lives as it is that many readers also have similarly pointless, meaningless lives. By giving almost no identifying qualities or unique personality traits to the two characters, Strand makes them into versions of Everyman for those living just behind McDonald's somewhere in the suburbia of contemporary America, where everyone is homogenized as a baby in a world with no emotions.

"Mr. and Mrs. Baby" is not meant to be read as asserting that life has no meaning. Rather, Mr. and Mrs. Baby consciously and continuously choose not to experience any meaningful event, trying not to express any feelings. They remain content to let contemporary society take care of them, with entertainment for diversion and a sense of total acceptance of pointless lives, so long as their physical needs are met by technology and its concomitant cultural homogenization.

In the last section of the work, the author makes his point explicit: "Now, at day's end, the Babys slip naked into bed, their limbs overcome with weariness, their minds dimming, giving way to the power and grandeur of nothingness, the silent ohs and ahs of oblivion." The couple has come full circle, because their day has been described by many of the same words. Their lives are weary; there is truly no grandeur to the nothingness; and oblivion dictates only "ohs" and "ahs" that cannot be heard.

Style and Technique

Not a conventional story in any sense of the word, "Mr. and Mrs. Baby" is a work of fiction with little setting, plot, action, or characterization. These elements of writing do surface but are held at all times in a position of minimal importance: Mark Strand is concerned entirely with his theme—the blandness, circularity, and empty rituals of modern life.

What conflict there is in the story, and thus the matter that is of interest to the reader, is contained in the tension worked on the reader as he or she identifies with, or at least empathizes with, these two subreductive caricatures of life as we know it today. Strand does not create a story in which there is conflict within or among the characters; his characterizations cause internal conflict in the reader who must come to terms with just how close and accurate Strand is in his depiction of human experience.

Although Strand does not begin his story with "Once upon a time," he does leave it with the same atmosphere such stories exhibit. The work is a parody of modern life, in which adults never grow up and those who have reached physical maturity remain, in the vein of parody, only babies. This is no fairy tale, though, for Strand's message is too haunting, biting, satirical, and pessimistic to be rendered as such.

The story has a rather noteworthy absence of symbols and imagery. Once the reader realizes that Mr. and Mrs. Baby are the embodiments of contemporary man and woman, these are not necessary. Strand does tell his story with a great deal of attention to language. First, his style is purely in the shadow of Ernest Hemingway here; he writes terse, short, clipped sentences of simple vocabulary for a punchy, journalistic effect. Even sectional divisions of the story adhere to requirements of this device.

More important is Strand's use of poetry and its elements that are embedded within the prose. It is not that he waxes poetic, but that he consciously includes words, phrases, and ideas worthy of the form of poetry. This is most true, perhaps, at the end of the story. Consider this sentence:

> Among the celestial acts in the theatre of night, in the superdome of the firmament, where distance is a monotonous allegory of diminishment, a shifting of solar dust, a waltzing of matter to the tune of darkness, a grave passage of this and that, what does it mean that you are asleep, adrift in the spectral silt of the unknown?

The acceptable swelling of language and the very tuning of the wording here can both worthily be compared to the poetry of Walt Whitman or Allen Ginsberg.

Strand's satiric tone also pervades his word choice. These are people babies who have never grown up; hence there is a way in which they are deserving of the contempt of readers as well as of their sympathy. The story ends with Strand tucking the Babys into bed: "Sleep tight; another Baby day is on its way."

Carl Singleton

MRS. FORTESCUE

Author: Doris Lessing (1919-   )
Type of plot: Psychological
Time of plot: The 1950's
Locale: London, a small apartment above a liquor store
First published: 1963

> *Principal characters:*
> > FRED DANDERLEA, the protagonist, a sixteen-year-old boy
> > troubled by adolescent sexuality
> > JANE DANDERLEA, his more sophisticated, seventeen-year-old
> > sister, with whom he shares a room
> > MRS. FORTESCUE, their elderly upstairs neighbor, a prostitute

The Story

"Mrs. Fortescue" is the story of a boy's sexual initiation. Fred Danderlea, at sixteen, is beginning to feel uncomfortable about his own emerging sexuality. Up until this autumn, he has had an easy, friendly relationship with his sister. Now she seems to hate him and treat him like a child from her superior position as a young woman no longer in school, free to go out in the evenings. Aided by the flimsy partition his parents have used to divide their room, he tempers his erotic dreams with visions of a lovely, tender maiden, his sister's alter ego, who redeems him from his shame. One night, tormented by libidinous inner battles, he sneaks out of the house and accidentally discovers that the ugly old woman who lives upstairs is a prostitute. He is filled with fear that his friends must know, and anger at his parents for tolerating her presence above them. When he confronts his parents with his new knowledge, they fail to react as he expects and proceed to discuss Mrs. Fortescue, her working conditions, and her relationship with her visitors as if there were nothing the slightest bit unusual about her occupation. Such "casual back and forth chat about this horror" turns him scarlet; he gobbles down his meal and returns to his room listening to the sounds above with "an ashamed, fixed grin on his face."

The next evening he follows Mrs. Fortescue and then his sister, spying on both their activities. After he observes Jane admiring an advertisement for lipsticks made to look like bullets, he returns home, fetches a revolver his parents have hidden in their liquor store, and places it under his sister's pillow. In his new "craziness," he sees phallic symbols everywhere and even squirms at the sight of his parents' double bed. Fred goes back downstairs to the store, gets a bottle of whiskey, and lies in wait for Mrs. Fortescue. Already slightly tipsy, she accepts his invitation for a drink and leads him to her room commenting that his dad has often done the same on cold winter nights.

Doris Lessing describes Mrs. Fortescue's room in great detail as seen through Fred's embarrassed and shocked eyes. The brocade curtains and satin sofa reinforce his sense of shame. The photographs of a younger and even more garishly dressed and painted woman underscore the thirty years that such activities have taken place above his parents' apartment even before he was born. Worse yet, her cherry-red dressing gown reminds him of his sister's.

Once Fred knows that Mr. Spencer, Mrs. Fortescue's regular, will not be coming, he awkwardly pushes her into the bedroom. She resists, saying, "But, Fred. . . . I don't work here," then submits with her second casual reference to the fact that his father has asked for similar favors. At first she remains "inert," but slowly "her expertise revived in her, or at least in her tired hands, and he achieved the goal of his hot imaginings . . . in one shattering spasm that filled him with no less hatred." In a fit of disgust he strips off the cherry-red gown and calls her a "filthy old whore." Her response, a tame "That wasn't very nice, was it?" reminds him of his mother.

His initiation complete, Fred flees to his room where he finds his sister calmly doing her nails, the gun now lying out on her dressing table. He points it at her, an apparent repetition of his violation of Mrs. Fortescue; her casual reply is to call him "stupid," as she always has. Nevertheless, he is able to discover something in her glance that allows him to believe she has new respect for him, that she recognizes his manhood. Triumphant, he walks through his parents' bedroom "without thinking more than: 'Poor old things, they can't help it.'"

Themes and Meanings

Ostensibly, "Mrs. Fortescue" is the story of a sexual initiation told in Freudian terms. More broadly interpreted, it compares with other Lessing stories of adolescents attempting to prove themselves by accomplishing what at first seems impossible, whether staying underwater long enough to swim through a tunnel or "losing one's virginity." In these stories, Lessing adheres to a clear narrative pattern: The protagonist sets a goal for himself spurred on by sudden feelings of alienation; he circles around the goal and works toward eliminating the obstacles that stand in his way over a seemingly long and difficult period of time; in the end he achieves his goal and is returned to the sense of equilibrium he possessed before he set out to test himself. The significance of this apparent threshold experience is ultimately undercut by the emphasis on returning back, rather than leaping forward.

Lessing's great theme in many of her stories, whether about adolescents, middle-aged women, or aging men, is the existential moment. Each of her characters awakens one day to the reality that something is fundamentally wrong with his or her life. For whatever reason—the onset of illness, a husband's confession of adultery, the sudden realization of one's own mediocrity brought home by a critical review—these characters experience a profound sense of alienation from self and world. The split between thinking and feeling threatens to widen into a chasm that drives them to madness or suicide. The new self-awareness that follows is fraught with both danger and opportunity. It offers the possibility to change one's life, to transcend the conventions and habits that limit an individual's essential humanity, but also the risk of breakdown, the loss of the fragile self-control that allows one to function in the real world. Few Lessing stories depict characters with the strength to move beyond such a moment. Some ignore the truths they have learned and retreat into the safety of past patterns of behavior; others seek to deaden their senses literally or figuratively through suicide.

Lessing's men generally find it easier to regain their previous equilibrium for two reasons: Their relationship to life is less intense than that of their female peers, and the cause of the particular crisis is usually one over which they have more control. Fred never really questions the significance of his sexual feelings; he feels no guilt over his easy triumph. For him, Mrs. Fortescue's "old, rather kind face" is only a mask; he never sees her humanity, though the narrator makes sure that the reader does. As Fred settles back into his easy, bantering relationship with his sister, the reader suspects that he will, in fact, grow up to resemble his father and so many other Lessing men who do not value women and base their own self-esteem on a system of easy conquests. If there is profound truth to be gained from a confrontation with one's own libidinous instincts, Fred Danderlea manages to avoid learning it.

Style and Technique

Lessing writes in a cold, calculated style that makes her stories read as if they were case studies in psychology textbooks. Added to this style is the use of a classic, third-person narrator whose selective omniscience lets the reader see the protagonist from the inside and all other characters from the outside. The reader knows what Fred thinks about his sister and Mrs. Fortescue, but never what they think about him. Instead of using such a perspective to encourage sympathy with Fred's adolescent turmoil, Lessing allows Fred's thoughts, gestures, and words to reveal his own egocentricity and disregard for others. Morever, there is an ironic tension created between the violence of Fred's dreams and actions and the hard-boiled, realistic tone of the narrative. This irony further serves to mock his sense of triumph as the story ends.

Many Lessing stories also contain the apparent symbolism of an allegory that itself can be interpreted ironically. Thus, for example, in "To Room Nineteen" the female protagonist's irrational belief that a demon awaits her in her backyard expresses both her psychological fear of losing control over her life and a symbolic expulsion from paradise. The irony derives from the fact that the garden from which she feels driven is a prison she herself has constructed. Fred Danderlea is also plagued by demons who threaten to destroy him, but like so many literary men, he has a gun to help him regain control. In "Mrs. Fortescue," Lessing uses the gun both as a symbol of the real violence Fred has committed and in mockery of the archetypal allegory of killing as a male initiation rite.

Other Lessing stories may have more complex plots and characters than "Mrs. Fortescue." Most, however, share the same ironic tone, austere symbolism, carefully established narrative perspective, and grim endings. It is no wonder that so many critics and readers admire her work but few love it.

Jane M. Barstow

MRS. PLUM

Author: Ezekiel Mphahlele (1919-   )
Type of plot: Political
Time of plot: The 1960's
Locale: Greenside, a suburb of Johannesburg, South Africa
First published: 1967

> *Principal characters:*
> MRS. PLUM, a white widow in a Johannesburg suburb
> KATE PLUM, her daughter
> KARABO, a young black domestic working for Mrs. Plum
> CHIMANE, Karabo's best friend, another domestic
> DICK, Mrs. Plum's garden boy

The Story

"Mrs Plum" is told in the first person by Karabo, a young black South African woman who works for the title character as a housemaid and cook. The time is the 1960's, and South Africa is still under the strict system of segregation and oppression known as apartheid.

As the story begins, Karabo has been working for Mrs. Plum only a short time and is bewildered by her new employer. Unlike other whites for whom she has worked, Mrs. Plum seems to take a personal interest in Karabo and encourages her to read the newspapers, to learn to sew and to cook from recipes, and to eat her meals at the table with the family. All of this makes Karabo uncomfortable; for her, the boundaries between whites and blacks, between employers and servants, are clear and impermeable, and she does not understand why Mrs. Plum wants to upset things. As she reads the newspapers and attends lectures at the Black Crow Club, Karabo comes to understand that seemingly isolated beatings and arrests of blacks are part of a larger pattern. She learns that Mrs. Plum writes books and pamphlets calling for better treatment for blacks, but she cannot understand why the white woman feels qualified to speak for others.

Mrs. Plum has two dogs, Malan and Monty, on whom she dotes. The dogs have special food, and special beds with pink linen in Mrs. Plum's room. Dick, the gardener, is charged with feeding and brushing the dogs. Mrs. Plum constantly worries that he is not doing a good job, although he is honest and conscientious and much too afraid of white people ever to fail in his duties. To Dick and Karabo and their friend Chimane, the idea of white people talking to animals and worrying more about them than they do about other people is simply ridiculous, one more astonishing and incomprehensible thing about white people.

In Karabo's third year working for Mrs. Plum, several important things happen. Kate, Mrs. Plum's college-age daughter, goes through a period of rebellion, playing loud music and staying out late. When Kate falls in love with a black doctor who has been invited to dinner parties at her mother's house and announces that she will marry him, Mrs. Plum's liberal convictions are challenged. She will not allow her daughter to marry a black man, and the mother and daughter try to work out the tension between them by confiding separately in Karabo. Karabo refuses to be drawn into the dispute or to express her opinions about anything to her employers. Soon Chimane finds that she is pregnant and has an abortion. Karabo helps her friend through the operation and raises money to make up for her lost wages, while her employers remain unaware that Karabo has worries of her own.

One day, Karabo hears odd noises coming from Mrs. Plum's bedroom. Looking through the keyhole, she discovers Mrs. Plum on the bed masturbating and holding onto one of the dogs. Shortly afterward, Mrs. Plum fires Dick unfairly, and Karabo decides that she has had enough. She leaves Mrs. Plum and goes back to her village. After a few days, Mrs. Plum drives out to fetch Karabo back. Stronger and wiser now, Karabo negotiates better terms and more respect for herself and goes back to Greenside with Mrs. Plum.

Themes and Meanings

Part of Ezekiel Mphahlele's intention in writing "Mrs. Plum" was to show life under apartheid to a world that in the 1960's knew little about it. Several details of the story demonstrate the oppression of blacks under South African law: The only black people in Greenside are servants, blacks do not have the right to vote or to criticize the government, there is no protection for Karabo when her employer sexually harasses her, Dick has no right to oppose the police who want to search his quarters, and all blacks are required to carry identification passes that show through which parts of the country they may travel. Karabo does not realize the extent of her oppression until she starts reading the newspapers and attending lectures by Lilian Ngoyi of the African National Congress. Similarly, readers of Mphahlele's fiction in Europe and the United States (his writing was banned in South Africa and not available to South African audiences until 1979) were largely ignorant of what was happening in the author's homeland.

More pointedly, however, "Mrs. Plum" is an indictment of white liberals in South Africa who believed that they could change South Africa from within, without giving up their own power. This is a theme Mphahlele returned to again and again in his career, most notably in two other short stories, "The Living and the Dead" (1958) and "We'll Have Dinner at Eight" (1961). Mrs. Plum is a typical white liberal. She writes books and articles criticizing apartheid and demanding better protection for blacks. Karabo, however, cannot understand why Mrs. Plum feels capable of speaking for blacks. Mrs. Plum entertains educated blacks in her home, in violation of custom and of the law. She turns the hose on the police officers who want to search Dick's rooms and dramatically goes to jail rather than pay a fine. She believes in the cause.

While Mrs. Plum may love black people as abstractions, she does not respect them as individuals, as real human beings. She makes no attempt to understand Karabo or

Karabo's way of seeing things; Mrs. Plum wants Karabo to eat at the table with her as a gesture of equality, but she does not serve the foods Karabo is used to eating and uses utensils that make Karabo uncomfortable. When Karabo wishes to travel home for a funeral, Mrs. Plum refuses to see that Karabo's way of saying goodbye to a relative, while different from Mrs. Plum's, is important to her. When Mrs. Plum's daughter falls in love with a black man and wants to marry him, Mrs. Plum is adamantly opposed. A distinguished black doctor as a dinner guest is one thing, but as a son-in-law is something else entirely. Mrs. Plum's unnatural relationship with her dogs demonstrates Mphahlele's main theme: that white liberals are, at their core, corrupt. Blacks in South Africa should not look to people such as Mrs. Plum to hand them their rights. Instead, they must learn, as Karabo does at the end of the story, to demand better treatment.

Style and Technique

By its setting and its point of view, "Mrs. Plum" gives readers a realistic glimpse of life in a particular place and time—South Africa in the 1960's. Greenside, Johannesburg, is a wealthy suburb of a major city. By law, the only people who live there are white families, in large, walled-off homes, and their black servants, who live in small spartan quarters in the back. Like Karabo and her friend Chimane, many of these servants come from small villages. They send part of their wages back to support their families and are granted one brief vacation a year to visit. "Mrs. Plum" presents, through Karabo's eyes, vivid descriptions of the parts of Greenside accessible to the servants, the bus ride between city and village, and the segregated shops and schools in those sections of Johannesburg catering to blacks. Because of social and political impediments, there is little fiction depicting black South Africa under apartheid from a black writer's point of view. This scarcity lends "Mrs. Plum" a significance beyond its inherent qualities as a work of fiction.

Also striking in "Mrs. Plum" is the point of view. The story is told in the first person by Karabo, a humble servant girl from the village of Phokeng. Karabo's sentence structures and vocabulary represent the language of a particular class of people who are not often depicted in literature—and it should be noted that when Karabo speaks English to her employer she is using her second or third language. Everything in the story is filtered through Karabo's eyes. Her growing awareness of the system of apartheid becomes the reader's growing awareness. Things that seem strange to Karabo— including Mrs. Plum's choices of food and her attempts to be friendly with her servants—appear strange to the reader. Presenting small details of life under apartheid in the authentic voice of one of its victims is one of Mphahlele's most important accomplishments in "Mrs. Plum."

Cynthia A. Bily

MRS. RIPLEY'S TRIP

Author: Hamlin Garland (1860-1940)
Type of plot: Domestic realism
Time of plot: The late nineteenth century
Locale: A northern Iowa farm
First published: 1891

> *Principal characters:*
> ETHAN RIPLEY, an old Iowa farmer
> JANE RIPLEY, his wife
> TEWKSBURY ("TUKEY"), their grandson

The Story

On a stormy November evening in their Iowa farmhouse, Jane Ripley announces to her husband that he and their grandson Tukey will have to get along without her for a while because she is planning a Thanksgiving trip to New York state to visit family and friends whom she has not seen in twenty-three years. Since her marriage, she alleges, she has never had so much as a day to herself. When the surprised Ethan Ripley expresses his doubts as to their ability to finance such a long journey, she assures him that he will not have to pay, in the process ruffling his feathers by implying that she never would have expected him to. He, sensitive to criticism of his ability to provide for the family, responds angrily, and the two argue.

It is apparent that despite the wrangling, there exists a profound bond between the two, and, the next day, as she bustles around planning her getaway, Ethan, working in the field, decides that he will sell one of his pigs to provide the funds for her trip. That evening, after he sells the pig, Tukey worries that his grandmother is "mad" at them and may never come back. As she tries to explain her motive to the young boy, she begins to cry. Ethan then comes in with a load of wood and confesses that he and Tukey have been guilty of not adequately considering her feelings. He thereupon hands her a railroad ticket and ten dollars, causing her to retreat from the room, only to return shortly carrying a mitten full of the coins she has been saving for years to make the trip possible. She reluctantly accepts the ticket, however, when he informs her that it is not possible to get his money back.

The following day as Ethan drives Jane to the railroad station in their wagon, she informs Tukey and him of the provisions she has made for their welfare while she is gone, including some services from a neighboring woman. On their return home, they realize that she kissed neither of them good-bye. Ethan theorizes that she, "flustrated," has forgotten.

Without any transition, the final scene has her returning home, laden with parcels and greeting her grandson with hugs, kisses, and tears. When Ethan comes in from the barn, they merely acknowledge each other laconically. Although neither expresses any emotion, it is apparent that both are satisfied that she has accomplished her trip and is now ready to resume the usual household routine.

Themes and Meanings

Growing up in the later nineteenth century in what he referred to as the Middle Border—western Wisconsin, northeastern Iowa, and southern South Dakota—Hamlin Garland learned what it meant to live and work on a family farm. What gave him a perspective on this life, however, was his subsequent gravitation to Boston in the 1880's to work as a journalist and writer of fiction. When, after several years in the East, he twice revisited the Middle Border, he was struck anew by the bleakness of the life his family had led and was still leading. The stories in his *Main-Travelled Roads: Six Mississippi Valley Stories* (1891), of which "Mrs. Ripley's Trip" is the last, interpret the territory of his early life in the light of the possibilities for personal fulfillment of which he had since become aware.

In these stories, Garland highlights the physical characteristics of midwestern farm life and their effects on the human spirit. The weather, for instance, proved characteristically harsh and undependable. In November, the time of this story, a snowstorm descends on Ethan as he makes his way to town to raise the money for his wife's ticket. It is clear from the Ripleys' poverty—the only light they can afford in their house is a candle—that weather has often been no more propitious during the growing season. The physical demands on both have long since worn them down. Jane Ripley is described in the first paragraph of the story as "little, weazened, and hopeless." Amidst the withered corn rows on his farm, Ethan plods, his back stiff and bent.

What particularly appalled Garland was the acceptance of these conditions, the resignation that he saw in people like his parents. The Ripleys' backbreaking routine has extended over decades. Ethan has no more comfort to look forward to than the buffalo coat that after all these years he still has not accumulated enough money to purchase. When a neighbor learns that Mrs. Ripley is planning a trip East, she is "astonished." The possibility of such "gallivantin'" has hardly crossed her mind. These are people who for the most part can scarcely imagine, much less actually devise, plans for such an adventure.

Despite the numbing oppressiveness of such an existence and Garland's recognition that the overwhelming response of most farm families was a stolid and fatalistic acceptance, a story like "Mrs. Ripley's Trip" expresses his conviction that the human spirit is not always and necessarily overcome by the physical facts of life on a poor Iowa farm. Mrs. Ripley's body may be nondescript, but her eyes have a "peculiar sparkle." Strange as it seems to her neighbors and even to her husband, she has been planning this trip East for years. Knowing that it could never happen more than once, she has nevertheless determined that it will happen that one time. Ethan's spirit remains alive also, although in a different way. Poverty cannot destroy his generosity. He has very little, but when he recognizes how much this unexpected break in the routine of their lives together means to Jane, he is willing to break into his meager resources to help her accomplish her goal. His imagination does not permit him personally to con-

template a return to the site of his early years, but he is able to imagine what such a
visit means to his wife. Like her he retains, amid all afflictions, a sense of decent and
generous conduct.

Style and Technique

Several aspects of Garland's style enhance the effect of the story, especially his use
of details conveying the sense of sound. He captures the Ripleys' simple but salty conversation and the squeaks of Mr. Ripley's old violin. He vividly suggests the sounds of
nature: the "rattling" of the snow, the "moaning" of the cornstalks in the wind. His eye
for visual detail is equally proficient. As Jane Ripley struggles back home through the
drifts, Garland describes the wind's inflation of her skirt, which throws her off her
track into the deep snow. Back home she must remove kettle marks from the tablecloth at home and the "splotches" of pancake batter with which her husband has clum-
sily decorated the top of the stove. Garland's colorful imagery often emerges through
the voices of his characters, as when Ethan is portrayed as the type of man from whose
back troubles slide like "punkins off a haystack."

Garland relates the stories of *Main-Travelled Roads* economically, and "Mrs.
Ripley's Trip" is the shortest and perhaps the most economical of the six. He is a
writer who know what to leave out of his story as well as what to put in. Clearly wishing to keep the focus on the vicinity of the Ripley farm, Garland moves directly from
the leave-taking scene at the depot to one in which a neighbor looks out her kitchen
window and sees Jane Ripley walking back home from the station. Garland does not
attempt to describe Ethan's and Tukey's reduced state while Jane is gone but simply
has Mrs. Ripley sweep her practiced eye over their inept attempts at housekeeping on
her return.

The reuniting of husband and wife is deliberately understated. They are an old married couple clearly embarrassed by the prospect of revealing emotion, but the reader
realizes that it is nonetheless there, for their prior actions have already demonstrated
the love that these two crusty old characters feel for each other.

The controlling image of the stories in *Main-Travelled Roads* is the road itself. Literally it is the route—alternately dusty, snow-swept, and boggy—that the characters
must traverse; symbolically it is the road of life. The road that Mrs. Ripley travels mirrors the hardships of her life, but it is also the point of departure of an inspiriting journey back to the locale and the people of her earlier years.

Robert P. Ellis

A MUNICIPAL REPORT

Author: O. Henry (William Sydney Porter, 1862-1910)
Type of plot: Social realism
Time of plot: 1909
Locale: Nashville, Tennessee
First published: 1909

> *Principal characters:*
> THE UNNAMED NARRATOR, a literary agent
> AZALEA ADAIR, a poet and member of the Old South aristocracy
> "MAJOR" WENTWORTH CASWELL, an alcoholic remnant of the
> Confederacy
> UNCLE CAESAR, the driver of a horse-drawn cab and Adair's
> servant

The Story

"A Municipal Report" is introduced by two meaningful epigraphs: A verse from Rudyard Kipling sings the pride of mighty cities, while a paragraph from Frank Norris asserts that only three cities hold value for a writer—New York, New Orleans, and San Francisco—and easily dismisses the possibility of anything interesting ever happening in Chicago, Buffalo, or (most absurd) Nashville. This story, ironically, is set in unlikely Nashville. It fuses a sense of history, romance, and Rand McNally, and reveals a narrative of universal human interest irrelevant to geography.

The narrator, a literary agent who is visiting Nashville, arrives in this Tennessee city and, after being transported to his hotel, begins to inspect his surroundings. After strolling about the nearby streets and seeing that everything closes at sundown, he becomes bored with watching streetcars and listening to occasional laughter emanating from innocuous ice-cream parlors, so he returns to the lobby. Nothing of consequence, apparently, is going on in Nashville.

In the lobby, the visitor meets "Major" Wentworth Caswell, a red, pulpy-faced, sordid-looking man with a talent for ringing the brass cuspidor with tobacco chaw. A professional Confederate southerner, Caswell drags the visitor into the bar, authoritatively pounds the table for service, and launches into a rambling disquisition on genealogy, stressing in particular his own patrician background. The narrator, himself a southerner, brands Caswell a rat extremely offensive to him. The bogus major may have the standard accoutrements of southern aristocracy—string tie, slouch hat, Prince Albert coat—but he is crude and profane. The visitor's impression of the hard-drinking, annoying major is corroborated by the desk clerk, who identifies Caswell as a local nuisance and loafer with no known means of support, his presence reluctantly tolerated because he carries a pocketful of money and cannot, therefore, be legally thrown out.

The narrator is an agent commissioned by a northern literary magazine to sign Azalea Adair, a Nashville author, to a contract at two cents a word before another publisher offers ten or twenty. He embarks next morning on his mission. Outside the hotel, he meets Uncle Caesar, a black carriage driver. Caesar wears a remarkable, variegated overcoat that clearly once had been owned by a military officer, but now is stitched together with twine, its lone button, the size of a silver dollar, made of unique yellow horn. Stepping into Caesar's rickety carriage and giving the Adair address, the agent is startled when his driver demands to know what business he has at that number.

Angry at this affront and refusing to answer, the agent is satisfied when Caesar explains his prying by noting that Jessamine Street, located in a decaying part of town, is not a proper destination for a visitor. Arriving there, the agent is again puzzled and upset when Caesar, having set the fare at fifty cents, now demands two dollars, asserting that he needs this exorbitant amount because business has been poor. Furious, the agent pays with two single bills, one of them, old and torn, having been pasted garishly together with a strip of blue tissue paper.

A refined, fifty-year-old lady of the Old South, sensitive and soft-spoken, Azalea Adair lives in genteel poverty, surrounded by books in a decrepit house unpainted in twenty years. Her furniture and her home fixtures are in decay. Her exquisite character, though, lights and gives dignity to the squalid environment. In her poetic presence, the agent cannot bring himself to discuss so commercial a topic as a business contract, and decides to return the following day to address such crass matters. Azalea Adair speaks to him of her inner, imaginative life through which she has traveled the globe in dreams and in print, witnessing lurid events in Turkey and bizarre adventures in San Francisco.

This perceptive writer has seen similar excitements in East Nashville; she even describes a few human collisions happening in her humdrum town. Adair politely insists that her visitor stay for tea, and calling a little black girl to send to the store, the poet draws a dollar bill from her purse—a bill fastened with blue tissue paper. As the child leaves, Adair excuses herself to see to a noisy man in another part of the house. When she returns, having attended to one she calls her tenant, the invitation to tea is rescinded and rescheduled for the following day.

The bemused agent encounters the waiting Uncle Caesar and in somber conversation learns that the old man had been a slave of Judge Adair, Azalea's father; when questioned about the lady's present-day poverty, Caesar pointedly states that she has resources and that she will never starve. Saddened by Adair's economic condition and realizing that such a person will never haggle over money, the agent returns to the hotel and sets the contract figure at eight cents a word. The publisher accepts. After this transaction, he goes to the hotel bar where Major Caswell once more accosts him, usurps his company for a drink, and ostentatiously pays with two single bills, one of them, the agent notices, fastened with the now-familiar strip of blue tissue paper.

The next day, as a pleased Azalea Adair signs her generous contract, she turns pale and faints. The doctor who is summoned, an old family friend, diagnoses the lady's condition as malnutrition. He explains to the agent that Azalea Adair Caswell is unfortunately married to a worthless drunk who robs her of every cent that she has— even the small amounts donated by faithful servants. The woman was on the verge of starvation; this contract will be her veritable salvation. Shaken and stunned, the visitor leaves but not before he overhears Adair confess to Uncle Caesar that Caswell pilfered her last two dollars.

That evening the agent observes Caesar downtown near the hotel and notes that the remarkable coat has lost its only button. As the agent walks the city on his last night there, he is attracted by a crowd. Major Caswell has been murdered, evidently killed in a robbery attempt; the Confederate had struggled and fought but had lost. Unnoticed by the babbling group, the agent approaches the corpse to have a look; as he lingers momentarily, one dead hand suddenly relaxes, releasing a small object immediately pocketed by the agent. The next morning, as his train leaves Nashville, he throws the yellow horn button into the river.

Themes and Meanings

Pretense, disguise, the deceptions in everyday lives—these were essential themes exploited frequently by O. Henry, in whose tales nothing is ever what it appears to be. The cloak of Old South respectability Major Caswell tries to project in his apparel is belied by the insensitive and coarse persona under the clothes. Conversely, the picture of secure, comfortable aristocracy Azalea Adair endeavors to assume is immediately brought into question by her threadbare poverty. Uncle Caesar, at first suggested as a conniving opportunist looking to extort fares from strangers, is eventually revealed as philanthropic, even heroic.

The inner lives of ordinary people become correlated with the pulse of an ordinary American city where—as in the most glamorous, cosmopolitan places—the baseness and nobility of human nature are constantly in play. The repulsive, abusive husband, self-indulgent and animalized; the noble, if misplaced, silent martyrdom of the suffering wife; the devoted and loyal Uncle Caesar, who selflessly supports his mistress and finally liberates her from future victimization—these are all character types manipulated through their melodramatic moments in the so-called human comedy by the twists and turns of coincidence and fate, accident and destiny.

Evil is punished in "A Municipal Report" by a swiftly administered hand of justice; the simple juxtapositions of good and bad are easily discernible; the author brings about a popular catharsis. O. Henry, in sketching the triumph of good, reduces the complications of life inherent in the more complex moral dilemmas of living: Is Uncle Caesar morally defensible in his murder of Caswell? Is the agent justified in removing and disposing of incriminating evidence? Such questions serve to deflect the emotional focus of the tale, for the passionate response to the story on its most elemental level is in perfect agreement with the way the adventure turns out. Ordinary people react with their spontaneously engaged feelings. Thus, as the agent leaves Nashville musing, "I wonder what's happening in Buffalo," all is right in O. Henry's world.

Style and Technique

O. Henry once observed to Robert H. Davis, one of his editors, "I've got some of my best yarns from park benches, lamp posts, and news stands." With such mundane inspirations, he was able to elevate the ordinary vicissitudes of life into universal significance by the inventive, clever tricks that he incorporated. Indeed, a *New York Times* survey taken in 1914 judged "A Municipal Report" as "the greatest American short story." Although such an extravagant claim is critically indefensible, the story embodies the most effective devices and strategies of the author's technical virtuosity: realistic description of background and environment, precise rendering of vernacular in accent and speech pattern, accurate representation of easily recognizable character types, and the deftly fashioned surprise—some say trick—ending.

O. Henry's strength is not in presenting complex characters caught in psychologically challenging situations. "A Municipal Report" demonstrates his reliance on the heart over the head; the artificial and the sensational dominate. Realism is confined to the details of the tale and to its supporting literary adornments; the historic, geographic, and economic data about Nashville establish its essential reality amid the often incredible events that will be dramatized there. Despite the evident contrivances—the blue-pasted bill's appearance and reappearances, the horn button—and the puppetry involved in the forced and manipulated action, O. Henry's considerable ability as talespinner enables him to create and maintain narrative suspense, to convince the reader to accept as true the improbabilities just depicted.

Abe C. Ravitz

MURDERERS

Author: Leonard Michaels (1933-   )
Type of plot: Impressionistic, coming of age
Time of plot: The late 1940's
Locale: New York City
First published: 1971

> *Principal character:*
> THE NARRATOR, a man recalling a summer in the 1940's
> MELVIN BLOOM,
> ARNOLD BLOOM, and
> HAROLD COHEN, his friends
> A RABBI
> HIS WIFE

The Story

"Murderers" is a first-person recollection of a crucial summer in the late 1940's when the unnamed narrator was a young teenager. The narrator is of Polish Jewish descent, living in the tenements of New York City. The recent deaths of some family members, immigrants who never left their neighborhood once they settled there, prompt him to seek adventure by exploring the city. He takes subway rides to exotic locations—sports stadiums, night club districts, amusement parks, and beaches—in search of novelty and excitement. One afternoon he meets three of his friends, Melvin and Arnold Bloom and Harold Cohen. Harold tells him that the rabbi is home, and eleven-year-old Arnold suggests that they go up to the roof. The reader soon understands that spying on the rabbi and his wife from a nearby rooftop with a view of their apartment is an activity that the boys have engaged in many times before. All wait for the narrator to decide for them what to do. He assents and the boys begin to run.

To reach their perch, the boys must climb a steel ladder up the side of a tenement building to the ledge of its steep roof, holding on with fingers and feet to keep from sliding off. From there they have a magnificent view of the city—its great bridges, buildings, landmarks, and monuments. They also have a clear view of the young bearded rabbi and his attractive young wife. The wife's head is shaved, for religious reasons, but this also allows her a great measure of creativity and allure, for she has several wigs of different colors and hairstyles, which she has varied to great effect in the past. This particular day, she is a blond. The rabbi and his wife put a record on the phonograph and begin to dance to the sound of a big band orchestra of the 1940's. He is boldly naked and cavorting; she is demure and seductive. The boys watch in fascination as the rabbi and his wife dance erotically and begin to make love.

Harold Cohen, with only his feet keeping him precariously on the slanted, slippery roof, starts to masturbate with both hands. The narrator is terrified by Harold's action.

Melvin Bloom frees one hand and uses the other to tap the beat of the music on the narrator's head. Arnold Bloom squeals and squirms as the rabbi and his wife experience ever higher peaks of ecstasy. As the couple reach climax, Arnold slips and falls from the roof to his death. The other boys scream and begin to scramble down the ladder. The rabbi's wife hears and then sees the boys, and the rabbi runs to the window and shouts at them, calling them "murderers." The boys continue their frantic descent down the side of the tenement, while the rabbi shouts out their names.

Soon afterward, at the rabbi's insistence, the boys are sent to a summer camp in New Jersey, operated by World War II veterans. The emphasis in the camp is on outdoor sports and strict discipline. The boys feel shame and regret, particularly the narrator who, at night, listens to the owls and feels the darkness both outside and within.

Themes and Meanings

"Murderers" is an initiation story into the mysteries and complexities of life, sexuality, and death. At the beginning, the narrator rebels against his family's inertia and timidity by boldly and independently exploring the greater world outside his own run-down neighborhood. He seeks excitement, romance, and adventure, all of which are conspicuously lacking at home. This independence is the beginning of his maturity, and the narrator recalls feelings of optimism and confidence.

Then one day he meets three friends, and instead of descending, by subway, in search of excitement, he and his friends ascend to the top of a building for another sort of adolescent adventure, a vicarious experience of sex. At first, the narrator gazes from the couple to the sky above and senses the immensity of space with such intensity that he calls it the beginning of philosophy. The implication seems to be that there, suspended between earth and sky, he comes to an awareness of the infinite, an intimation of the vast backdrop to any human drama. As with the subway adventures, the primary feeling associated with adolescence at this point is excitement.

The naked, bearded rabbi and his chameleon-like wife with her wigs of many colors seem almost generically male and female. As the rabbi and his wife begin to make love, the boys respond intensely to the sexual display. This, too, is their inheritance, a reality emphasized by the generic aspect of the couple who are making love. However, just at the moment of orgasm, one of the boys slips and falls, and the others begin a desperate and noisy descent, alerting the rabbi and his wife to their observers. The rabbi runs to the window and calls them "murderers." With that accusation, the narrator's confidence and elation begin to give way to feelings of shame, guilt, and fear.

The narrator remarks that the rabbi could not have known what he was saying. However, the vehemence of the his accusation and its lasting effect on the narrator provoke speculation and interpretation. Perhaps the rabbi has seen Arnold fall and means to imply that they are murderers because they have contributed to their friend's death by their reckless adventure. Or he may mean that each new generation (the boys) is relentless in its eagerness to supplant its elders (the rabbi and his wife), and he cries out in pain and anger at the prospect of their sexual awakening. Perhaps he means to signify that their intrusion, like that of the snake in the Garden of Eden, brings a kind of death into the rabbi's and his wife's world, a death of spontaneity and unselfconscious sexuality. Or he may mean that the boys have murdered their own innocence. Whatever he means, his shocking accusation darkens his outlook.

The view from the rooftop provides an intense experience of budding intellectual and sexual power to the narrator, but it also brings an awareness of other realities— that actions have complex consequences, sometimes fatal in the real world. The feelings of excitement, freedom, and power of the early summer, and of adolescence, are soon tempered by a recognition of human weakness, vulnerability, and mortality. The narrator, in other words, is learning what it means to become an adult, and he faces the prospect with mixed emotions, the predominant one being a sense of foreboding.

Style and Technique

The incident recounted in the first person by the narrator is a formative, even defining experience in his adolescence recalled from the vantage point of the mature adult. The style is colloquial, witty, exuberant, and darkly ironic. The narrator moves effortlessly back and forth from sharply visualized scenes of the city, to humorous portrayals of adolescent longing and lust, to philosophical musing of considerable depth. The voice suggests a person of great wit, vitality, and intelligence, with a highly idiosyncratic view of the world, a person who finds speculative matter in unusual places.

At the beginning, the story is straightforward and realistic in setting, character, and mood. The narrator, recalling the energy and curiosity of adolescence, tells of eager trips by subway to exciting places that would attract most young people in search of adventure. With the next phase, and its focus on moral and psychological growth, the story becomes allusive to biblical, mythological, and psychological narratives.

The description of the rabbi and his wife makes them seem more like archetypes than particular individuals—a satyr and a nymph, or Adam and Eve, perhaps. The coupling itself is referred to as the primal scene. The watching boys are described as bathed in light, hovering in the air like angels beholding the couple as they make love. Once again the story of Adam and Eve is suggested. The fall of Arnold, who initiated the adventure, has overtones of Lucifer's fall from heaven, in view of the earlier reference to angels. The boys descent from the pinnacle of their building with its magnificent view of the city, along with their subsequent exile to the military-like camp, has overtones of Adam and Eve's expulsion from the Garden of Eden.

The story does not systematically employ symbolism; rather it teases the reader with allusions to well-known biblical, mythical, or psychological narratives to signal its movement from straightforward adventure into more complex realms of psychological and moral discovery. The result is a sense that the experience the narrator is recalling is unique, even highly idiosyncratic in its details, while also being universal in its implications. In other words, it is an archetypal coming-of-age story of an adolescent's growth from innocence to experience.

Michael J. Larsen

THE MURDERS IN THE RUE MORGUE

Author: Edgar Allan Poe (1809-1849)
Type of plot: Mystery and detective
Time of plot: The 1830's
Locale: Paris
First published: 1841

> *Principal characters:*
> THE NARRATOR, a man of some means, Dupin's companion
> C. AUGUSTE DUPIN, an impoverished aristocrat, a mysterious but
>   gifted analytical thinker
> LE BON, a French sailor recently returned from Borneo

The Story

This tale of ratiocination opens with a long discussion of the differences between the truly analytical mind and the mind that is possessed of great powers of calculation. What this long expository section sets up is the notion that persons possessed of this keen analytical faculty are different from other human beings. The story is narrated from the first-person point of view by a nameless young man who is residing in Paris during the spring and summer of an unnamed year sometime during the 1830's. He has come to Paris, it is implied, to make some discoveries about the world and about himself. During the course of his visit, he encounters in a bookshop Monsieur C. Auguste Dupin. About Dupin very little information is provided; the reader is given to understand, however, that Dupin is an individual who has fallen on hard times and who chooses to live a more or less shadowy existence. The narrator, fascinated by the general character and demeanor of Dupin, proposes that they spend much of their time together, and, because he has some financial independence, he and Dupin rent apartments together in an old deserted mansion in the Fauborg St. Germain section of Paris.

Together, the two of them develop a lifestyle that involves remaining indoors shuttered away from society during the day and venturing out to stroll the streets and boulevards of Paris only after dark. In the course of these nocturnal wanderings, the narrator describes a situation in which, while the two of them are walking along, each apparently alone in his thoughts, Dupin speaks aloud to the narrator a sentence that could only have been a response to something the narrator was thinking. Amazed at this apparent intrusion on his mind, the narrator asks for an explanation. Dupin then offers a step-by-step recounting of how he came to deduce what it was that the narrator was thinking about as the two of them walked along.

Having thus established the mysterious yet brilliantly analytical powers of Dupin, the narrator then moves on to describe the discovery not long afterward of an item in one of the local newspapers detailing grisly murders occurring on the fourth floor of a house in the Rue Morgue. Persons in the neighborhood heard screams issuing from the house, mounted the stairs, and attempted to enter the apartments; the door was locked, however, and though they could hear a terrible furor within, they were unable to gain entry by any means. When the door to the apartment was finally broken open, the would-be rescuers were confronted by a chaotic scene: furniture was broken, clothes strewn about, and a blood-smeared razor lay on a chair. Nearly four thousand gold francs were in bags in plain sight, but the windows to the apartment were all closed and nowhere was there a sign of life. On further investigation, the horrified persons discovered the body of a young woman, the daughter of the owner of the apartment, stuffed up the chimney of a fireplace. It took four or five persons to remove it from the flue into which it had been forced. Subsequent examination of the scene revealed the body of the woman's mother, the owner of the house, in the rear courtyard four stories below the apartment. The corpse was horribly battered and her head had nearly been severed from the body.

These are the essential circumstances with which the narrator acquaints the reader: a room locked from inside; two murders; and the police baffled. Dupin suggests that he and his companion pay a visit to the scene of the crime. When they do, Dupin makes a very careful investigation and discovers matters that the police have overlooked. He also offers brief lectures on the general failure of authorities to observe carefully the scene of a crime and to apply powers of reasoning to such a scene in order to make some deductions about what happened there. Too often, Dupin asserts, the police see but they do not observe.

On completion of his visit to the Rue Morgue, Dupin places an advertisement in a local newspaper, and he and the narrator return to their apartments. Dupin tells the narrator that they should prepare themselves for a visitor who might be dangerous to them. They therefore make pistols ready, and as they await the anticipated visit, Dupin launches into a long explanation of the means by which he arrived at his conclusions about what happened in the Rue Morgue. This detailed explanation of Dupin's analysis of the physical details of the crime scene and of the observations he made there provides concrete illustration of the differences between the reasoning powers of ordinary mortals and those of persons gifted in analysis, such as Dupin.

When the explanation is complete, and the narrator, and thus the reader, knows what Dupin knows, a sailor named Le Bon appears at the door in answer to the advertisement Dupin placed in a local paper. The sailor is the owner of an "Ourang-Outang," an animal Dupin has deduced to be the murderer. When Dupin informs him that he knows what happened in the Rue Morgue, the sailor's initial fright gives way to resignation. Dupin is not interested in turning the sailor over to the police but rather in verifying his solution to the murders. The sailor offers additional explanations, all of which coincide exactly with the deductions offered by Dupin. The story ends with Dupin visiting the prefect of police and explaining what happened in the Rue Morgue, an explanation that exonerates Le Bon and marks the case as closed.

Themes and Meanings

Edgar Allan Poe wrote three stories about C. Auguste Dupin; this was the first one.

Each of the Dupin stories contains essentially the same theme: the triumph of analytical reasoning over mere thinking. Again and again in "The Murders in the Rue Morgue," Poe, through the assertions of Dupin, makes invidious comparisons between the crime-solving methods of the police and the analytical powers of the highly trained mind. In this tale, it is necessary that the gifted Dupin visit the scene of the crime and make careful observations of the physical evidence in order to draw his conclusions. It is not always necessary, however, for the amateur detective to be on the scene, because most of what he accomplishes he achieves by careful analysis of the facts in the case.

In this story, the now classic locked-room mystery is introduced for the first time. Moreover, Poe created here the first detective story in American literature. In so doing, he also created the basic template that later writers in England and the United States would use to build their detective heroes. Thus, it was with the publication of this tale that Poe became the father of the detective story.

An important thematic element in this story is the use of reason as a kind of defense against unreason, of rationality against irrationality. The horror of the murders in the Rue Morgue disturbs the little universe of the neighborhood; Dupin's application of reason to the problem restores order. Thus, Poe, through the medium of this and other of his detective stories, seems to be arguing that reason is humanity's most potent weapon against acts of madness. However, because Dupin is depicted as an extraordinary human being whose behavior and analytical powers mark him as an outsider, it would seem that, for Poe, the forces of reason may be overcome in the long run.

Style and Technique

Inasmuch as Poe uses this story to define and extend his arguments about the application of rational analysis to the whole of problem solving, whether it be draughts or whist or murder, there are long expository and often tediously constructed passages in this tale. Moreover, the characterization of Dupin as a mysterious and brilliant outsider leads Poe to dot his story with words and phrases from French and Latin and with several classical allusions. Further, the use of the first-person narrator allows the reader to know only what the narrator knows about Dupin and does not permit a view of Dupin's psyche.

The somewhat stilted style of the expository passages in the story notwithstanding, the basic technique that Poe used has become the standard for the genre of detective fiction: the discovery of the scene of a crime; the visit to the scene by the detective; the collection of information that the police have overlooked; the discovery of the culprit as a result of the application of reason to the situation; and the final confrontation between the detective and the person or persons responsible for the crime. This pattern is now so familiar to readers that it is sometimes difficult to realize that it was Poe who created the formula less than a century and a half ago. Monsieur Dupin is the prototype of the gifted amateur detective. Arrogant, at home in the world of books and facts, he triumphs over evildoers whose machinations have stumped the best police minds.

Dale H. Ross

MURKE'S COLLECTED SILENCES

Author: Heinrich Böll (1917-1985)
Type of plot: Satire
Time of plot: 1955
Locale: An unnamed city in West Germany
First published: "Doktor Murkes gesammeltes Schweigen," 1958 (English translation, 1966)

> *Principal characters:*
> DR. MURKE, an employee of a radio station
> BUR-MALOTTKE, a frequent speaker on cultural matters
> DIRECTOR OF THE BROADCASTING HOUSE, his friend
> HUMKOKE, Murke's boss

The Story

Dr. Murke is introduced as a man who performs an existential exercise every morning on entering the radio station and riding the elevator to his office on the second floor. The elevator is the kind known as a *paternoster*—a continuous belt with open cages that remain upright like cars on a Ferris wheel as they pass the points where their direction of travel changes from up to down or vice versa. Normally, Murke feels the need to remain on the elevator and submit himself to his daily "anxiety breakfast" as it passes through the top housing with its greasy chains and groaning machinery.

For the past two days, however, Murke has been obliged to forgo this exercise. The Director has ordered him to edit two talks on The Nature of Art, which the great Bur-Malottke has taped for broadcast later in the week, and Murke has had to come in at eight in the morning on these two days and begin work right away. Bur-Malottke, who converted to Catholicism only in the religious fervor of 1945, has suddenly felt religious qualms and wants to omit the word God, which occurs frequently in each of the two half-hour tapes, and replace it with a more neutral formulation.

Murke has spent Monday afternoon and Tuesday morning performing the excruciatingly painful task of listening to the two talks three times each day and cutting out the word God. Now it is Wednesday morning, and Bur-Malottke arrives at the broadcast house to tape the substitutions under Murke's supervision. A complication that Bur-Malottke has not counted on, however, is that the case reference has to be made clear. Wherever God appears in the genitive, as in "God's will," for example, Bur-Malottke must say the noun in question followed by "of that higher Being Whom we revere." Of the twenty-seven occurrences of the word "God" on the two tapes, there are seven genitives and one vocative. Instead of "O God," he has to substitute "O Thou higher Being Whom we revere." Moreover, because the new formulation is much longer, the two programs will now require a total of one minute more airtime, so each of them will have to be cut by thirty seconds.

Bur-Malottke is greatly annoyed by these complications and begins to sweat profusely. Murke thoroughly enjoys the discomfort of the pompous windbag and revenges himself on him by purposely sabotaging the session. For example, Murke is able at one point to force his adversary to start again from the beginning by claiming that the tape is defective. He further aggravates him by suggesting that several of the takes are unsuitable for use—and they are, largely because Bur-Malottke is unable to mask his growing agitation. Later, Murke and a technical assistant splice the snippets of tape containing Bur-Malottke's "higher Being Whom we revere" twenty-seven times into the two talks on The Nature of Art. The technician has divided the snippets into individual small boxes according to grammatical case. A box marked "Pure Chocolate" contains two vocatives, a terribly botched version and a retake. "Now," says Murke, "comes the vocative; we'll take the bad one, of course." Humkoke advises Murke to go home and relax but cautions him to remain by the phone until it has been determined that the Bur-Malottke tapes are in acceptable form.

Murke's collected silences are the snippets of tape he saves when he has to edit periods of silence from program tapes. He splices them together and listens to them at home. Up to this point, he has been able to collect only about three minutes of silence, and the Bur-Malottke tapes did not yield a single second.

At home, Murke entertains his beautiful young girlfriend, Rina. Neither of them says a word, and a tape recorder is running on the coffee table. Finally, Rina breaks the silence by saying that Murke's request is indecent. She would be happy to put words on the tape, but "putting silence" on it strikes her as almost immoral. Murke begs her to continue. Rina agrees, but the silence is soon broken by a telephone call from Humkoke. The Bur-Malottke tapes are fine.

In the basement coffee shop of the radio station freelance contributors are overheard planning to do features on every conceivable topic, no matter how banal. One of them, Wanderburn, enters the room mouthing a hypocritical warning against the radio business, hypocritical because he has just picked up a check for a quick adaptation of the Book of Job into a radio program. It is because of the disparity between pretension and reality in the radio station that Murke feels compelled to put up a tacky picture in the hallway. It is a religious postcard that his mother sent him with the inscription: "I prayed for you at St. James' Church."

In the final scene of the story, the assistant drama producer and the same technician who worked with Murke on the Bur-Malottke tapes are editing a radio drama. In the radio play, an atheist poses a series of questions, such as: "Who will remember me when I have become the prey of worms?" Each of the questions is followed by a long silence, a weakness in the play. The assistant producer decides that what is needed is a voice speaking the word "God" after each question. He is amazed when the technician produces a small tin with the snippets Murke has saved from the Bur-Malottke tapes. The assistant producer remarks that it is, indeed, strange what one can find in this place, and produces from his pocket a crumpled picture he has found stuck in his door. The inscription reads: "I prayed for you in St. James' Church."

Themes and Meanings

On one level, "Murke's Collected Silences" is a satire on the German "culture industry" in the postwar period of the mid-1950's. The scene is dominated by "cultural priests" such as Bur-Malottke and characterized by rampant hypocrisy and venality. The small army of free-lance contributors who live from broadcast royalties will exploit any material for the sake of a paycheck. Humkoke, for example, must chide Murke for leaving a book on his desk when Wanderburn is likely to turn up, and Wanderburn is always likely to turn up. The reason is that he will immediately turn it into a two-hour feature. The broadcasting house is equally guilty, however, because it willingly accepts the most banal of programs merely to fill up the available broadcast hours. It is no surprise, then, that the young Murke, a blazingly intelligent young man whom the Director regards as an intellectual beast of prey, finds the rare moments of silence to be the station's most precious product.

On another level, however, Böll also satirizes the authoritarian mentality that he believes the Germans have apparently been unable to overcome in spite of that trait's dubious role in German history. The Director rules his fiefdom with an iron fist and has the motto "Discipline above all" painted on the wall. He is, however, the very model of obsequiousness when dealing with Bur-Malottke or even the most outrageous suggestions from listeners. Murke's only real success in his odd rebellion against this system comes in the scene where he briefly has the upper hand over Bur-Malottke in the recording studio. It is, however, a deliciously humorous scene and points to the possibility of a more critical attitude toward authority figures.

Style and Technique

Although Böll's satire is laced with critical barbs, the narrative tone is more one of amused resignation than caustic invective. The scene in the recording studio with Bur-Malottke notwithstanding, Murke is a man who has for the most part internalized his revolt and sublimated it in such idiosyncratic forms as his daily elevator ride or his collection of silences. In many ways he is therefore a poor model of a more positive social type. Böll uses the technique of ironic understatement to underscore the absurdity of the world he describes and leaves it to the reader to imagine alternatives.

One alternative to the authoritarian, hypocritical world of the radio station is, however, symbolically suggested in the contrast between the broadcast house itself and the basement coffee shop. This is the region to which Murke and others retreat for a momentary respite from the world "above." It is a sanctuary from the hierarchical order, a place where even a hypocrite such as Wanderburn can utter an honest opinion about the nature of the institution. The contrast between the two spheres is symbolized in the figure of the good-hearted, simple waitress, Wulla. Her real name is Wilfriede-Ulla, but for the sake of simplicity she has conflated it into the abbreviated form, Wulla. Thus, she provides the perfect counterpoint, in name as well as in personality, to the inflated, self-important Bur-Malottke.

Dennis McCormick

MY FIRST GOOSE

Author: Isaac Babel (1894-1940)
Type of plot: Impressionistic
Time of plot: 1920
Locale: Poland
First published: "Moi pervyi gus," 1924 (English translation, 1929)

> *Principal characters:*
> THE NARRATOR, the unnamed protagonist, newly assigned to the
> staff squadron of a Russian cavalry division
> SAVITSKY, the Cossack commander of the VI Division
> SUROVKOV, the Cossack platoon commander of the staff
> squadron

The Story

"My First Goose" is an early story in Isaac Babel's collection *Konarmiia* (1926; *Red Cavalry*, 1929), based on the author's experiences in the Russian campaign against Poland during the summer of 1920. Although this story is not precisely autobiographical, the fuller context of the collection clarifies that the narrator, like the author, is an educated Jew, newly appointed to the Division as "Propaganda Officer." Virtually all the soldiers in the Division are Cossacks, and anti-Semitic to the bone (as were the men of the historic First Cavalry in which Babel served).

The entire thrust of the first half of the story is to contrast the narrator, the newly arrived, bespectacled officer, with his little trunk full of manuscripts, to the Cossacks of the Division Staff. First, Commander Savitsky is described as a marvelous giant, all in purple and crimson, and beautiful, as he strikes his riding whip on the table. Not content to be merely imposing, Savitsky, on learning that his new propaganda officer can read and write, calls him a "nasty little object" and ridicules his "specs"—referring to him as "one of those [Jew] grinds." When the quartermaster takes the new officer to his billet, one of the five soldiers living there immediately tosses out the officer's little trunk, turns his backside to him, and emits a series of vulgar noises.

Mortified, the narrator withdraws and tries to read Vladimir Ilich Lenin's speech published that day in *Pravda*; he cannot concentrate, though, as the Cossacks continue to torment him. Finally he goes to the old landlady, who is half blind with cataracts and in a suicidal state because the soldiers have taken over her house, and demands food. Cursing, he shoves her aside, overtakes a goose in the yard, and cracks open its head beneath his boot. He digs into it with a sword and demands that the old woman cook it.

On witnessing this act, which, at its most trivial level, may be seen as an initiation rite common to any male group admitting or testing a new member, the Cossacks immediately open up to the propaganda officer. They invite him to share their cabbage soup and pork until his "goose" is ready. Well aware that his gesture of cruelty was essential to gain the confidence of the soldiers, the narrator nevertheless remains depressed. When the illiterate Cossacks ask him what is in the newspaper, however, he triumphantly reads aloud to them Lenin's speech. "I read on," he says, "and rejoiced, spying out exultingly the secret curve of Lenin's straight line." The platoon commander, Surovkov, praises Lenin's ability to strike at the truth "straight off like a hen pecking at a grain!"

Thus, the narrator's first day's duty is accomplished. He has won over the men and established a rudimentary but effective propaganda program. The fact that the Cossacks are all nominally Bolsheviks does not mean that they have an understanding of Marxism-Leninism. The propaganda officer's task is a difficult one, but at least he has begun well. That night, he and the five Cossacks sleep together in a shed, "warming one another." The narrator sees women in his dreams, but his "heart, stained with bloodshed, grated and brimmed over."

The ambivalence created by the final line is crucial to a right perception of this story: Violence is evil and must not be condoned. However, violence is necessary and cannot be avoided. The anguish of knowing that these conflicting realities can never be resolved is to be fully aware of the human condition.

Themes and Meanings

One of the most interesting themes in this story is the ambivalent character of the mutual relationship between the intellectual and the primitive man (whether peasant, "noble savage," or Cossack). The intellectuality of the narrator is stressed; he has a law degree; he wears glasses; the quartermaster tells him that there is "no life for the brainy type here" and suggests that he will not get on with the troops unless he "mess[es] up a lady"—that is, commits rape. Only when he has symbolically raped the goose (and its owner, also symbolically) is the new officer accepted—and then the soldiers are able to admit that they need him for his ability to read out and explain the truth. Their contempt has changed to respect, but the reader understands that these attitudes will continually alternate.

The narrator's attitude toward the Cossack Commander Savitsky seems to be one of almost irrational adoration; his desire to get on with the soldiers is more than simply a matter of wanting to succeed as a propaganda officer. He admires the primitive innocence of these men even as he is appalled by their vulgarity and cruelty. This ambivalence remains constant throughout the *Red Cavalry* stories.

Another theme is that touching on anti-Semitism. The narrator's Jewishness is not mentioned but only implied (though known in fact from the other *Red Cavalry* stories). As far as that goes, the Russian-Orthodox Christianity of the Cossacks is not mentioned, either, but the story manifests a strong sense of the mutual contempt between Christians and Jews. This contempt is not quite the same as that discussed above, between the intellectual and the primitive, but there is some overlapping. In any case, the anti-Semitic Cossacks are described as "heathen priests" (so much for

Christianity) sitting around their caldron in which "pork" is cooking. When the narrator joins them in eating the pork he becomes a terrible apostate, despite the fact that as a Communist he is supposedly no longer religious.

At a deeper level, the narrator and the Cossacks are linked together by the ritual of sacrifice, which reflects the daily, bloody offering of human victims in the war without. The killing of the goose, however contorted, is a ritual sacrifice that reflects Jewish, Christian, and probably "heathen" values. The goose is described as severe-looking (that is, dignified), inoffensive (that is, innocent), and white (that is, pure): an offering of adequate symbolic significance.

The ritual of the sacrificial act is emphasized by the narrator uttering the word (or curse) "Christ!" immediately before the killing and then again immediately afterward. This would seem to give the sacrifice a Christian character, but the original Russian here is: "*Gospoda boga dushu mat'*." This is a crypto-euphemistic expression for one too hideously vulgar to print, but the Russian reader understands it to be obscene. This is no longer religious, but antireligious, or blasphemous—or perhaps "heathen," like a Cossack curse. In fact, Babel depicts the Cossacks around their caldron as sitting "motionless, stiff as heathen priests at a sacrifice." Thus, the narrator has committed a heathen act to make friends with heathens. The white goose was sacrificed. It seems doubtful that the sacrifice can be justified, yet somehow it also seems to have been necessary. Even more disturbing is the realization, from the story's title, that there will be other such sacrificial offerings—and other victims of war and revolution.

Style and Technique

Despite the rich, multileveled significance of "My First Goose," style plays as great a role as meaning, and certain images are perhaps more memorable than any given idea. For example, there is the initial description of the beautiful giant Savitsky, ending with the line, "His long legs were like girls sheathed to the neck in shining riding boots." The erotic imagery could suggest a Freudian sexual element within the narrator's admiration of the Cossacks—all the more so as the story ends with a description of the narrator sleeping with the Cossack soldiers: "our legs intermingled. I dreamed: and in my dreams saw women." It is more likely, however, that erotic imagery is simply a casual motif in this story, as it is in other stories from *Red Cavalry*. Such imagery is commonly found in Russian fiction of the relatively liberal and experimental 1920's. The vivid literary imagery of that period, erotic or not, is often characterized as "ornamentalism."

Another "ornamental" image in "My First Goose" is the following, occurring early in the story: "The dying sun, round and yellow as a pumpkin, was giving up its roseate ghost to the skies." Possibly the dying sun suggests the coming sacrifice—all the more so as the concluding words recall those of Mark 15:37: "And Jesus cried with a loud voice and gave up the ghost." The most vivid portion of the image, though, is the sun, "round and yellow as a pumpkin." It seems futile to seek too deeply for meaning in such painterly, impressionistic prose.

It is common for Babel to decorate his stories with striking descriptions of heavenly bodies or of dawn, evening, and the heat of the day. Two other such images in this story deserve quoting: "Already the moon hung above the yard like a cheap earring," and "Evening wrapped about me the quickening moisture of its twilight sheets; evening laid a mother's hand on my burning forehead." Both images, especially the latter, reflect the narrator's moods and are thus integrated into the story, but the story must be seen as a brightly colored mosaic rather than as a traditional example of realism. This does not mean that its impact, as a commentary on war and revolution, is diminished. Indeed, critics generally agree that Babel's stories are the best Russian short stories of the twentieth century.

Donald M. Fiene

MY KINSMAN, MAJOR MOLINEUX

Author: Nathaniel Hawthorne (1804-1864)
Type of plot: Psychological
Time of plot: On the eve of the American Revolution
Locale: Massachusetts Bay Colony
First published: 1831

> *Principal characters:*
> ROBIN, the protagonist, a young man in search of his kinsman
> A KIND GENTLEMAN, who befriends Robin after the young man
> finds Major Molineux
> MAJOR MOLINEUX, the mysterious kinsman for whom Robin
> searches

The Story

Robin, an eighteen-year-old country boy, arrives by boat in Boston Harbor at nine o'clock in the evening to find his kinsman. Though poor and dressed in ill-fitting clothes, Robin has the confidence and buoyant optimism that accompanies youth, and he walks from the dock with enthusiasm despite the thirty miles his journey has taken him. He soon realizes, however, that he does not know where to look for Major Molineux, the kinsman who would be his protector. Even this does not disconcert Robin, for he believes that almost anyone he meets will be able to direct him to the home of such a prominent man.

Robin soon discovers that no one is willing to tell him where to find Molineux's dwelling and that often these refusals are accompanied by antagonistic replies or threats of violence. For example, the solemn man carrying a polished cane whom Robin first approaches threatens him with the stocks if Robin does not release him and let him pass. The man insists, amid "sepulchral hems," that he has "authority." Embarrassed by the man's evasiveness, his loud repulse, and the roar of laughter from a nearby barbershop, Robin determines to move ahead and continue his search.

Pleasant aromas from a tavern make Robin wish that he had enough money for a meal, but he consoles himself with the thought that his kinsman's home must be nearby and that he will soon have his meal there. The innkeeper's friendly greeting makes Robin think that the man recognizes in him a likeness to Molineux, but when he makes his inquiry the innkeeper reads aloud the description of a fled indentured servant and advises the boy that he had "better trudge." Though he would like to have struck the innkeeper with his oak cudgel, the evident hostility of the others in the tavern convinces him to go. As he leaves he again hears loud laughter, but he believes that it is because he had earlier confessed that he could not afford a meal.

Young Robin's patience wears thin as he continues the search for his kinsman. He sees the well-dressed young gentlemen of the town and once again hears the solemn old man with the "sepulchral hems," but Robin now seems aware of his own shabbiness and hunger. He determines to use his oak cudgel, if necessary, to get the information he wants, but just then finds himself before an ill-built house near the harbor and sees a flash of scarlet petticoat through the open door. When he asks the pretty mistress where he can find Molineux, she answers that this very house is his dwelling place. Robin resolves to enter; indeed, the mistress leads him by the hand, but just then the town watchman appears, threatens him with the stocks, and chases him away.

Robin now grows desperate. He even asks the watchman his question, but the only response is drowsy laughter as the watchman moves away. This further rejection causes Robin to seize a quickly moving stranger and threaten violence until he receives an answer. He had seen this stranger before at the inn, but now the man's face seems a blazing red on one side and midnight black on the other. It is as if two devils, of fire and of darkness, have joined themselves in a single face. The strange man tells Robin to wait and watch for an hour, and Molineux will pass by.

Robin sits on the church steps and considers the curious experiences he has had since his arrival. He notices a large mansion and wonders if this could be his kinsman's house but is distracted by the low murmur of voices he hears in the street. He now feels very much alone, and when he peers in one of the church windows, he wonders if his kinsman has died. He recalls, longingly, the happiness of his home and seems to see the church services and daily thanksgiving that had been part of his upbringing.

Determined to bring himself out of his reverie, Robin despondently confides his story to a kindly man who asks why he is sitting on the church steps. Robin's father, a poor country clergyman, had decided to accept an offer made a year or two earlier by his cousin Molineux to help the boy advance his prospects. The kindly man assures Robin that he is in the right place and should continue his vigil. The low murmurs have, all this time, continued to grow in intensity and are now accompanied by the sounds of a trumpet. When Robin suggests that they investigate the cause of all this merriment, that he would like to laugh too, the kindly man advises Robin to be seated and reminds him to wait for his kinsman.

Now all the windows fly open; the street is filled with a reddish glare, and people in fantastic costumes and Indian dress suddenly appear. A single horseman in military uniform is in the center of the mob, his one cheek a fiery red, the other a mourning black. Spectators stand along the way, shouting with combined mirth and terror. The horseman orders a halt to the march; absolute silence fills the street, and there, in an open cart where the torches blaze their brightest, is Major Molineux in tarred-and-feathered dignity. Church bells begin to peal; Robin sees the saucy maiden and hears the man with the "sepulchral hem," this time broken by hearty laughter, and the young man joins the general mirth. His own shout is the loudest there.

When the procession has passed, Robin asks the kind gentleman to show him the way to the ferry but receives from him an offer of shelter and the assurance that his youthful shrewdness will allow him to rise in the world without the help of his kins-man, Major Molineux.

Themes and Meanings

The historically uneasy relationship between Massachusetts Bay Colony and its appointed royal governors that Nathaniel Hawthorne sets forth in this story's first paragraph allows the author to write a complex tale that deals simultaneously with the popular overthrow of a governor and with the coming to maturity of a boy. Neither of these themes is sacrificed to the other, for Robin discovers as a result of his long and frustrating inquiry his personal independence and his American identity. Though co-lonial Boston's twisted roads lead him very close to the place from which he started his search, Robin's "initiation" has changed him considerably. He had hoped in the tavern that his resemblance to Molineux would assure his fortune; by the story's end, his laughter makes him one with the crowd, and his rejection of Molineux implies that the earlier rebuffs that he received as Molineux's kinsman were correct. It is, then, sig-nificant in the story's final scene that he exists as "Robin" rather than as Molineux's kinsman. He has overcome temptation (the maiden in the red petticoat) and despon-dency (on the church steps), has rejected pleasant but unconstructive memories of his past (when he recalls his Huguenot background), and has determined to seek his own place in the world.

The initiation theme applies equally to the story's sociological level. Just as a boy seeks his freedom and independence, so does a country. Robin can thus be seen as the slowly awakening American spirit that infuses and maintains the American Revo-lution. Correspondingly, Molineux can represent oppression that masquerades as family. He is Great Britain, but he is also whatever constrains the American spirit. The kind gentleman is, by extension, France, America's first ally, but he also repre-sents the respectful autonomy for which one should strive in any alliance.

Style and Technique

The symbols of Hawthorne's story blend masterfully to create its dual allegory. Robin arrives in darkness (doubt) with only the superficial confidence that his family background gives him. He wanders labyrinthine streets (the subconscious) in search of where he belongs. He fortuitously rejects temptation (the saucy maiden) and stares evil in the face (the man with the red-and-black countenance). He finally acquires the strength to laugh at the tarred-and-feathered Molineux's false dignity, realizing even as he does this that he needs others. This is what provokes an offer of help from the kind man with whom he watches the procession.

Hawthorne's story thus moves from the absolute darkness of its first scenes, repre-senting Robin's early state of mind, to the glare of torches at its conclusion when Robin sees Molineux's face. Significantly, Molineux's face is described in terms that make it resemble the devilish appearance of the stranger from whom Robin had ear-lier received an answer to his question. Thus, Robin finally sees the full reality of Molineux's evil.

Ancillary symbols support the story's legal theme. The Ramillies wig that the barber is dressing in one of the first scenes would be worn by a presiding judge. Also, the mansion that Robin thinks might be his kinsman's home is clearly described as a colonial courthouse, while the sober man with the "sepulchral hems" in his speech could be a judge. That some legal proceeding is under way while Robin waits for his kinsman to appear is plain, and this is most evident when the sober man reappears on the mansion balcony in time to see Molineux pass. This time the man's sober "hems" are interspersed with hearty laughter.

Robert J. Forman

MY MAN BOVANNE

Author: Toni Cade Bambara (Miltona Mirkin Cade, 1939-1995)
Type of plot: Domestic realism
Time of plot: 1970
Locale: New York City
First published: 1972

> *Principal characters:*
> MISS HAZEL, the narrator and protagonist
> ELO, her daughter
> JOE LEE, her eldest son
> TASK, her youngest son
> BOVANNE, an elderly blind man, a friend to Hazel

The Story

The title of Toni Cade Bambara's short story is ironic because "My Man Bovanne" is a meaningless, pat expression to all the people who utilize it in the story; to them it is merely a "hip" way to address an old, blind man for whom they have no real feeling. On the other hand, Miss Hazel, the story's narrator, who at the story's outset insists that Bovanne "ain't my man, mind you," by the end of the story has taken in Bovanne out of empathy and concern, qualities lacking in all the others who deal with Bovanne in the story.

The story takes place at a fund-raising, consciousness-raising party held by a black coalition in the hope of organizing and unifying the African Americans of a New York City neighborhood into a politically powerful organization. Hazel, however, does not focus on the speeches or the politics of the evening; in fact she starts off her account by informing her readers that all blind people have a "hummin jones"; they are often given over to humming as a natural consequence of "what no eyes will force you into to see people." Bovanne, a blind gentleman who has been invited to the party, is no exception to this rule. When Hazel asks Bovanne to dance, it comes as no surprise to her that they should soon reach a kind of humming, intuitive rapport on the dance floor. Hazel is not very interested in the ostensible reason for her presence at the party: to support the candidacy of her niece's cousin, Nisi, "who's runnin for somethin with this Black party somethin or other behind her." She has a difficult time understanding lofty causes, but she can appreciate individuals. She sees everyone passing by poor, blind Bovanne with a glib "My man, Bovanne," without any of them once offering to talk to him or get him a sandwich or something to drink. She therefore takes it on herself to be kind to him.

However, her dancing with Bovanne becomes a major point of controversy in the story. She admits that they danced closely, but in her account there is almost something sublime, and certainly nothing scandalous, in their closeness: "Touch talkin like the heel of the hand on a tambourine or on a drum." Hazel's children, however, take a very different view; in fact they physically escort her off the dance floor and into the kitchen to be reprimanded.

Hazel informs the readers why she, Bovanne, and a number of other elderly neighborhood residents have been invited to the function in the first place; it is a matter of "Grass roots, you see." Hazel is amused by the notion that suddenly her children and others their age want to get back to their "roots." Only a few years earlier they had complained about her "countrified rags," but they "now can't get black enough to suit 'em." All during her ensuing confrontation with her three children, she reiterates or rethinks this basic irony.

In the kitchen, the reader gets his first direct look at the perspective of Hazel's children through dialogue. They accuse her of having had too much to drink; they complain that her dress is too short and too low-cut; they note that her wig looks ridiculous, and they bluntly express their distaste for her too-close dancing with blind Bovanne: Her daughter Elo goes so far as to say that Hazel's behavior looked no better than "a bitch in heat." Hazel is dismayed by this reaction but insists that "I wasn't shame."

Hazel's children have very specific reasons for their negative reactions to their mother's behavior. They inform her in the kitchen that she was going to be expected to start up a "council of elders" and to ask the Reverend Trent for the use of his basement for party headquarters; clearly, in their minds, such responsibilities do not jibe with lewd dancing with a pitiful old blind man. Hazel reacts negatively to her children's demands in part because they treat her so harshly, in part because they have no empathy for Bovanne, and in part because they tell her of their plans only at the last second: "If grass roots mean you kept in the dark I can't use it." She also refuses to talk to the Reverend Trent, whom she considers a hypocrite, and intentionally misunderstands the tenor if not the intent of her children's request when she says, "You want me to belly rub with the Reven, that it?"

When further argument seems futile, the three children agree that a "family council" is needed, which they set up for the next evening's dinner, presumably at their mother's house, and again without her specific participation or permission. They then leave her alone in the kitchen. Bovanne wanders into the kitchen and Hazel decides to take him to buy some dark sunglasses and then to take him to her home for a "nice warm bath." Again her ironic humor shows forth when she notes that these actions will be her way of "doing her part" for the elderly of the neighborhood. She also informs Bovanne that he will be guest of honor at the "family council" the next evening. The story ends with her ironic reply to Bovanne's comment that she must be a "pretty woman": "I surely am; just like the hussy my daughter say I am."

Themes and Meanings

A principal theme of this story centers on an exchange between Hazel and her daughter, Elo. After Elo has referred to Bovanne as "that tom" and expressed her distaste for his lack of sunglasses, which forces everyone to "look into them blown out fuses," Hazel interrupts her with the question: "Is this what they call the generation gap?" Elo "spits" her reply angrily: "That's a white concept for a white phenomenon. There's no generation gap among Black people."

The events of the story prove that Elo could not be more wrong. The irony of the story is that Hazel's children, and presumably most of the other people of their generation at the party, ostensibly want to adapt an Africa-based system, in which much respect and attention is paid to a "council of elders." However, while they admire the notion conceptually and theoretically, in practice they are shamefully deficient because of their insensitivity and lack of a genuine respect for either Bovanne or Hazel. In fact, they are nothing short of abusive in their behavior and are disrespectful and condescending in their attitudes. Their treatment of the elders, particularly their desire to get on the Reverend Trent's good side merely to use his basement, constitutes an attempt to exploit the very people whom they are supposed to be helping.

The black generation gap is further underscored by the fact that the very things for which the children used to condemn their mother, such as corn-row braids or colorful clothes, are now what they praise her for. Bovanne, who all the neighborhood children used to like because he would fix their skates or bicycles, they now condemn as a "tom," blaming him for how he has been forced to eke out an existence instead of admiring him for having been able to survive, not only as a black man but also as a blind black man.

Although readers may debate over just how sexual Hazel's initial motivations were for dancing with Bovanne, and although readers may continue that debate over her motivations for finally taking Bovanne home with her, it is certain that Hazel is the only character who has really shown Bovanne a measure of attention or respect. Perhaps the final irony of the story is that Hazel and Bovanne have found a kind of intuitive, natural togetherness, while her children have condemned her in a very Puritanical, "white" mode.

Certainly Bambara was not condemning the Black Power movement as a whole; she was merely pointing out how easy it would be for people to get so caught up in a cause as to forget the purpose of genuine goals of that cause. Bambara's story has a universal message about the need for genuine respect and understanding among people. Her story shows that a cause that ignores or downgrades the individual can never really be right, no matter how righteous.

Style and Technique

Perhaps the single most interesting thing about "My Man Bovanne" is the way in which it is told. Hazel is the narrator of her own story, and Bambara creates a narrator who tells her story as if the reader were sitting on her stoop in New York, taking in every colorful word. Hazel speaks black English, in a highly colloquial, freewheeling style that might be characterized as ghetto stream of consciousness, particularly in the opening paragraphs. She also makes extensive use of metaphor and simile, as when she describes her dance with Bovanne: "chest to chest, like talking"; the way her son Task approaches her, "Like he the third grade monitor and I'm cuttin up on the line to assembly"; or the way her children manhandle her, "hustlin me into some stranger's kitchen . . . just like the damn police."

Hazel renders all accounts with tenacious honesty. She reveals the dialogue word for word, keeps back no vulgarity, seems always totally frank. It is precisely her honesty and her street poetry that make the reader side with her completely. Although it is possible to see the children's point of view and even to share their embarrassment over their mother's behavior to some extent, overall they are indicted by their own behavior, their disregard for their mother's feelings and wishes. The reader knows only Hazel, only she is speaking directly to the reader and being honest with him. Bambara's story would be radically different if anyone but Hazel narrated it. Hazel's point of view makes the story by engaging the reader in the particular problems and perspectives of an individual, real human being, instead of a theory or an idea. This technique works especially well in a story about children who cannot see the individual for the masses.

Joseph Benevento

MY MOTHER

Author: Jamaica Kincaid (Elaine Potter Richardson, 1949-   )
Type of plot: Magical Realism
Time of plot: About 1963
Locale: Antigua, the West Indies
First published: 1983

> *Principal characters:*
> THE NARRATOR, a teenage Caribbean girl
> HER MOTHER

The Story

A daughter, in characteristic teenage fashion, is wary of her mother and yet wants her acceptance. The distance that grows between them is portrayed several times in intensely lyrical images. For example, after her breasts develop, she says, "Between my mother and me now were the tears I had cried, and I gathered up some stones and banked them in so that they formed a small pond" of thick black liquid in which only invertebrates can live. She and her mother now watch each other cautiously, making sure to shower each other with artificial words of love.

The story moves from lyric image to lyric image, each scene embodying the problematic intimacy between them. The narrator describes herself and her mother on her mother's bed in a room lit by candles. Their shadows dance in the flickering candlelight, but a distance remains between them.

Many of the story's images illustrate not only the growing sense of confidence and ability that the daughter feels for herself, but also her longing for the days when she was closer to and more reliant on her mother. In one scene, the daughter turns to her mother for sympathy, but when her mother reaches out to rub her head, the daughter steps aside, roars with self-confidence, but then lets out a self-pitying whine. She is unable to completely accept or reject her mother's intimacy.

In another scene, the mother transforms herself into a lizardlike creature that crawls on its belly, and she instructs the daughter to do the same herself. Elsewhere, the daughter transforms herself into a lamblike creature. When the mother notes how cross she looks, the daughter builds a trap for her mother by building a house over a hole and inviting her mother to inspect it. When the mother walks in and out without falling, the daughter burns the home and fills in the hole.

The story returns to the image of the pond of invertebrates the narrator created with her tears. She sees herself as big now, but her mother as three times her size. She and her mother build houses on opposite sides of this pond, expressing both their connection and the distance between them. The daughter not only cries for the lack of closeness between them but also wears herself out with anger at her mother.

At the end, the mother packs the girl's things in a bag and sends her on a voyage, apparently to Great Britain for schooling. The physical separation between mother and daughter in fact leads to a renewed intimacy; when the girl arrives, she meets a woman who looks exactly like her mother, and she unites herself with this woman. Later, she describes herself as living in the same house with her mother, eating from the same bowl, and fitting "perfectly in the crook of my mother's arm." As they walk through the rooms, she says, "we merge and separate, merge and separate; soon we shall enter the final stage of our evolution." The temporary harmony between them is passing and illusory, quite likely the sense of similarity and intimacy born of a physical separation between them.

At the end, the girl imagines her mother as a goddess figure who has ensured the bounty of the sea for local fishermen. She herself is a grown young woman; she has perfumed herself with the blossoms from lime trees, and she has a woman's womb, which she describes as a nest a hummingbird built on her stomach. She and her mother have lived this way for a long time now, she says, but it is clear that this regression to the bliss of early childhood is the girl's fantasy of a temporary merging. Although the ending is ambiguous, it is entirely likely that the girl is now essentially separate from her mother, but closer to her in that she sees her mother everywhere in the world around her.

Themes and Meanings

The book in which "My Mother" was first published, *At the Bottom of the River* (1983), is a collection of short stories connected by theme, style, and content; each story challenges a reader's expectations of what a short story can be. The central concern uniting these stories is the intimacy between a young girl and her mother, an intimacy that becomes increasingly strained as the girl grows. The earlier stories trace the central character's movement not only away from her mother but also toward the edge of a nervous breakdown, which is represented in the story "Blackness." "My Mother" is about the narrator's recovery and her attempts to assert her own individuality to her mother, while still seeking her mother's affection. Critic Wendy Dutton has argued that *At the Bottom of the River* tells of the initiation of the young narrator into a world of matriarchal knowledge. Accordingly, in "My Mother," the narrator mimics many things that her mother does, such as growing larger, but is never able to surpass her. The peace she finds at the end seems to be a retreat to a preadolescent state of mind at finding herself continually bested by her mother.

A secondary theme relates to the narrator's position as a subject in a colonized land. When the mother sees a lamb, she remarks that the lamb is miserable because it lives in an unsuitable climate. The lamb represents British Christianity out of place in Caribbean soil; when the narrator tries to turn herself into a lamb, her mother remarks that she now looks cross and miserable, implying that she is trying to act British. The preadolescent bliss to which the narrator returns at the end is also marked by the presence of a lamb running across the pasture, implying that she has retreated to a state of cultural infantilism that cannot last.

Style and Technique

"My Mother," which begins with the narrator wishing her mother dead and then immediately regretting it, is the story of the growing sense of competition between the mother and daughter. It is written in a richly textured prose that aims to reveal emotional truth rather than to tell a conventional story.

Because of its densely lyrical and impressionistic prose, as well as its avoidance of conventional narrative, "My Mother" is likely to challenge a reader's expectations of what constitutes a short story. The strikingly original style of "My Mother" is likely to be what a reader first notices about the story. Although the separate vignettes are narrative in nature, perhaps the easiest way to approach each scene is as a densely composed fable, operating primarily on a figurative level, as opposed to a literal one. Rather than describe childhood experiences, Jamaica Kincaid creates lyrical images that evoke the feelings of being a child.

A careful reader of "My Mother" understands the basic story of intimacy and separation between the mother and daughter. Specific details of actions are hard to come by, though, because of the impressionistic style of writing. The strengths of Kincaid's writing are the emotional honesty it conveys, as well as the great compression that captures the emotional life of a relationship in only a few pages.

Shortly after publishing *At the Bottom of the River*, Kincaid also published *Annie John*, a novel of several closely linked short stories that, taken together, trace the course of a mother/daughter relationship in Antigua. Although the prose style in *Annie John* (1985) remains impressionistic and sensitive, the stories employ conventional narrative, and it is often recommended that the two works be read as companion pieces. The stories in *Annie John* try to reveal the inner life of its main character by observing her actions and thoughts, as is the more common narrative practice. "My Mother" and many of the other stories in *At the Bottom of the River* approach character from the inside out, by building vivid pictures of feelings. The images in "My Mother" are direct appeals to the heart, which have to be comprehended emotionally before they can be approached intellectually.

Thomas Cassidy

MY OEDIPUS COMPLEX

Author: Frank O'Connor (Michael Francis O'Donovan, 1903-1966)
Type of plot: Psychological
Time of plot: 1918
Locale: Cork, Ireland
First published: 1950

> *Principal characters:*
> LARRY DELANEY, the narrator and protagonist, who, as a young
>   boy, was home with his mother while his father was away at
>   war
> MICK DELANEY, his father, who returns home after the war
> MRS. DELANEY, Larry's mother
> SONNY, Larry's newborn baby brother

The Story

The story begins in retrospection. The adult Larry remembers his idyllic and blissful early childhood at home with his mother while his father was away during World War I. Larry, confident of his mother's full attention, accompanied her throughout each day, prayed unfailingly for his father's safe return, and urged his mother to brighten up the house by bringing home a baby. This Edenic existence is abruptly lost when his father returns home from the war. Suddenly, Larry finds that he has been demoted: His mother is attentive to his father and inattentive to him. He is repeatedly asked to be quiet while his father speaks and to be careful not to wake him up in the morning. In short, he finds that he must at all times play second fiddle to a rude and monstrous stranger whom his mother seems to favor for some reason mysteriously related, Larry concludes, to "that unhealthy habit of sleeping together." Larry regrets his many prayers for his father's safe return. "I couldn't help feeling that if this was how God answered prayers, he couldn't listen to them very attentively."

One morning, when Larry awakens his father by screaming, his father tells him to shut up. Larry is so shocked by this presumptuousness that he yells back, whereupon his father slaps him. Thereafter, the two of them are "enemies, open and avowed." They engage in a series of skirmishes: In one of these, Larry announces to his mother that he will one day marry her and they will have lots of babies. When she tells him that she will have one soon, he interprets her response as a sign of favor to him.

Just when Larry concludes that he has turned the tide, he is besieged by the noisy arrival of his brother, Sonny, who proves as much of a disappointment to him as his father was on his return. One day, his father overhears him muttering to himself that he plans to leave if another baby arrives. Thereafter, his father treats him more kindly. One evening, when Sonny is crying louder and longer than usual, his father seeks refuge in Larry's bed. Larry understands that now it is his father's turn to be dispossessed. "I couldn't help feeling sorry for Father. I had been through it all myself, and even at that age I was magnanimous." He attempts to comfort his father, asks him for a hug, and concludes that, it was "better than nothing." Thus, in their common displacement, Larry and his father are reconciled.

Themes and Meanings

The poignancy and humor of this story turn on Larry's personal and individual struggle with a universal dilemma. In the course of the narrative, Larry learns that, in family life, every son is ousted and every king deposed. As a result, he learns to feel compassion for his father, his former rival, and to enter the fraternity of males in which membership derives from exclusion. Although there is a gain in this awareness, there is also much loss. Larry wryly notes of his early childhood, before his father's return, "The war was the most peaceful period of my life. . . . Life never seemed so simple and clear and full of possibilities as then."

Like many of Frank O'Connor's finest stories, "My Oedipus Complex" centers on a key experience in the childhood development of Larry Delaney, O'Connor's semi-autobiographical protagonist. Much of the power of the story derives from the dual awareness that it provides of the immediate experience of the child and the larger, more distanced perspective of the adult. Although the adult Larry Delaney recalls himself as a child first struggling with his feelings of rivalry and jealousy toward his father and then toward his baby brother, the reader also shares the perspective and resignation of the adult who has come to terms with the material he presents. However, the reader always has the poignant awareness that the child and the adult are the same person, that the laughter of the adult modifies but does not eradicate the pain of the child. The story also confirms with understanding and compassion the universal struggle of sons with fathers and maintains that each son must reenact in the particular circumstances of his own life this age-old struggle. Only then can he also claim the experience as uniquely his own—thus the meaning of the title: "My Oedipus Complex."

Style and Technique

The greatest feature of this story is O'Connor's astonishingly accurate recollection of the feelings and perceptions of the child as he tries to make sense of the world; to run his own life, often unsuccessfully; and to understand the strange and bewildering ways of the adults who surround and control him. The extraordinary frustrations that the child encounters in these undertakings is most tellingly recalled by the adult Larry Delaney as he relates in detail his childhood efforts to understand and capture in his own person the mysterious and elusive charm that his father held for his mother. Accordingly, he mimicked his father by walking around the house with a pipe in his mouth and by making up news items to read to his mother out of the newspaper, all to no avail.

The futility of these efforts to regain his special position in the household takes its toll on him. He changes from a child who wakes up in the morning "feeling myself rather like the sun, ready to illumine and rejoice" to a displaced person who wakes up lonely and cheerless, awaiting the awakening of his parents to give warmth to his life: "I didn't feel in the least like the sun; instead, I was bored and so very, very cold!" In time, however, his egocentrism is replaced by understanding of his father ("I realized he was jealous too") and finally by sympathy, the sympathy of a boy who is taking an early step toward adulthood, one who is able to make the first overtures of friendship to his previous rival: "'Ah, come on and put your arm around us, can't you?' I said."

Throughout, O'Connor's style echoes the lilt, the drollery, and the pungency of Irish speech. Always chatty and colloquial, the narrative convincingly places the reader in the position of a chance listener to a tale, told perhaps in a pub, by an able but anonymous local storyteller. Accordingly, the narrator pauses to explain ("Father was in the army all through the war—the first war, I mean"), breaks off to exclaim ("Mind you, I meant that"), and continuously takes the reader into his confidence, as in this comment on his mother: "Sonny never had anything up with him, and only cried for attention. It was really painful to see how simpleminded she was."

In the straightforwardness and simplicity of his style and in the common humanity of his approach, O'Connor reminds the reader of the great traditional Irish storytellers, whom he so much admired. Always suspicious of the artist who calls attention to himself, O'Connor labored greatly, through many, many drafts of each story, for the effect of spontaneity and for the natural feel of everyday speech. "My Oedipus Complex" demonstrates the success of these efforts.

Carola M. Kaplan

MY OLD MAN

Author: Ernest Hemingway (1899-1961)
Type of plot: Social realism
Time of plot: The 1920's
Locale: Italy and France
First published: 1923

> *Principal characters:*
> JOE BUTLER, the twelve-year-old narrator
> BUTLER, a jockey and Joe's "old man"

The Story

Narrated by the title character's twelve-year-old son, Joe, the story begins in Italy, where the man works as a jockey. Joe recounts the difficulties his father had keeping his weight down and how strenuously he exercised to stay fit. He also recalls how fond he was of his old man as he watched him jump rope in the hot sun. Joe recalls once how tired his father appeared at a weigh-in and how he looked at a younger jockey with envy. Joe thinks that everything might have been better if they had remained in Italy riding at the easy courses in Milan and Torino. He remembers the big green infield at San Siro with the mountains in the distance and how much he loved the horses and the sweep of the race as they rounded the turns.

After winning the Premio Commercio, his old man has an argument in the Galleria with an Italian and a man named Holbrook, who calls him a "son of a bitch." This shocks Joe and he notices that his father is greatly upset by the confrontation, but he cannot quite figure out why. His father tells him that there are many things one just has to accept. Three days later they leave Milan for good on the train for Paris.

They arrive the next morning at the Gare de Lyon, and Joe remarks on the differences between Paris and Milan. They find a place to board with a Mrs. Meyers in Maisons-Lafitte in the district with the race tracks. It is the best place to live he has ever seen. His father hangs around the Café de Paris in Maisons with other jockeys waiting for his riding license to arrive from Milan, and Joe hunts rabbits with another boy.

Butler's license arrives and he begins to ride in local races but cannot get any full-time engagements. Once at St. Cloud, Joe witnesses his old man accepting information from George Gardner, another jockey, about a race that is being fixed. When the prohibitive favorite, Kzar, is beaten by Kircubbin, an eight-to-one long shot, his old man cleans up because he had bet five thousand on Kircubbin to win. Joe describes the race and admits his disappointment that such a beautiful horse should have been forced to lose. His father remarks that it took a great jockey to keep Kzar from winning. The knowledge that the race was fixed hurts the boy. The money allows his father to spend more time in Paris but does not bring him contentment.

After a race at Auteuil, his father, again a heavy winner, buys a horse, Gilford, and he enters him on the circuit. Joe remarks that riding for oneself makes an "awful difference." His father goes back into training. The second race his old man rides on Gilford takes place on a rainy Sunday at Auteuil, and, although in the lead, he falls on a water jump and is killed. George Gardner takes Joe in to see his dead father, and while they are waiting for the ambulance, Joe overhears a couple of spectators remark that Butler got what he deserved after all of the things he pulled. George tells him not to listen to them because his father was a swell guy, but after all that has happened, Joe remains unsure.

Themes and Meanings

The primary theme of "My Old Man" is Joe's youthful disillusionment with the values and behavior of his "old man." Young Joe must come to grips with the conflict between his love and respect for his father and the disappointment he feels about his father's connivance with a corrupt racing system. The boy's ambivalence, which has been of central concern to Ernest Hemingway's critics, sets up the problematic ending that has received much of their attention.

One of Hemingway's biographers, Michael Reynolds, identified "My Old Man" as the first story the writer began after leaving Chicago and as the first of many stories that feature a father failing his son. It is of great importance in the development of Hemingway's career. The story was thought at first to be little more than a slight early piece about a son's disappointments with his father. Later, however, it began to be seen to contain a highly complex experiment in narration, one that explores the nature of fictional observation and of the narrator's understanding of his father's successes as well as failures.

The narrative reveals Joe's skill at remembering detailed descriptions of places and events and contrasts those recollections, which he seems to comprehend, with those involving his father's actions, to which he frequently admits a naïve confusion. The key scenes that reflect the narrator's uncertainty are the Galleria episode when his father is called a "son of a bitch"; the time when the old man learns of the fix at St. Cloud and cashes in on it; and the ending, when the spectators are overheard saying that Butler got what was coming to him. Because of their ambiguity, these scenes add substantially to the story's complexity and, therefore, to its potential for richer interpretation.

Style and Technique

One of the great achievements of "My Old Man" is Hemingway's creation of Joe's voice, a pre-adolescent narrator who speaks like Huck Finn, Mark Twain's wise child. The narration is both knowing and naïve, reflecting Joe's position in the adult world. The story is further complicated by the fact that it is a tale told in retrospect, presumably by an adult Joe looking back on his childhood events in order to understand their significance for his life. At the conclusion of the story, he admits that he still does not know what it all means.

In this early story, Hemingway provides carefully rendered, highly evocative narrative events but withholds authorial comment about what they suggest. He was already following his famous dictum of not telling but showing. By not explaining what a scene means for either the characters or the audience, Hemingway engages the reader with the narrative in ways that not only elicit multiple possible meanings within the story but also invite an examination of the responses the story may call forth from life outside the fiction. This authorial technique became an important characteristic of Hemingway's prose and helped him to secure a place as one of the masters of the modernist movement in twentieth century literature.

Charles L. P. Silet

MY SIDE OF THE MATTER

Author: Truman Capote (Truman Streckfus Persons, 1924-1984)
Type of plot: Satire
Time of plot: The 1930's or the 1940's
Locale: Rural Alabama
First published: 1945

Principal characters:

THE NARRATOR, an ignorant sixteen-year-old who was recently married

MARGE, his pregnant wife, who is also sixteen years old

EUNICE, one of Marge's maiden aunts

OLIVIA-ANN, Eunice's sister, Marge's other maiden aunt

The Story

The first-person narrator records his side of the quarrel with his bride's family, in a household ruled by Marge's maiden aunt Eunice. He reveals his youthful egotism in the first paragraph by proclaiming his intention to reveal the facts to the "citizens of the U.S.A."

Though the setting and circumstances have some of the qualities of the seamier, possibly degenerate rural South popular in some southern literature, they hardly suggest any dark secrets. The two maiden aunts in their big old house, with "real columns out in front" and japonica trees lining the yard, are certainly eccentric, and Marge's maiden aunt Olivia-Ann may be, as the narrator puts it, a "half-wit," but the narrator himself is hardly an unbiased observer. He may overestimate the stupidity of others, because he is not overly bright himself.

The narrator reveals that he married Marge four days after meeting her—his first mistake. He does not know why, except that she is a "natural blonde," though he can find nothing else to recommend her. Marge has "no looks, no body, and no brains whatsoever." She soon "up and gets pregnant" (his second mistake, he says) and insists on going home to Mama—except that she does not have any Mama, only two aunts living in the country. The narrator gives up his job of clerking in the Cash 'n' Carry and accompanies his wife to her former home.

His reception in this all-female household is not comforting. The maiden aunts look him over like a piece of livestock and proclaim him undersized and effeminate in appearance. Olivia-Ann says, "The very idea of this little runt running around claiming to be a man! Why, he isn't even of the male sex!" He is not allowed to sleep with his wife but is put on a cot on the back porch, where the mosquitoes swarm and make sleep difficult.

Bad feeling between the idle husband and the houseful of women comes to a head one day when Olivia-Ann accuses the narrator of damaging her piano, even though the young man claims to be a "natural born musician." He, in turn, threatens to reveal a secret he had promised not to tell—that Olivia-Ann deliberately let Eunice's canary loose and shooed it out of the house. Eunice, however, is already on the warpath, charging him with stealing a one-hundred-dollar bill from her secret cache of funeral money. Even Bluebell, the old black maid, and Marge are against him. When Bluebell says that she is "sick and tired of carryin' his ol' slop jar," the narrator snatches up an umbrella from the stand and bangs her on the head. Although Marge tries to protect Bluebell from the assault, Eunice is appalled at his ruining her "real Japanese silk parasol."

The free-for-all seems likely to have more violent results because Eunice then comes after him swinging her father's Confederate sword, but at this point, Marge faints. The story closes with the husband barricaded alone in the parlor eating chocolates, while the women fuss with Marge upstairs.

Themes and Meanings

Truman Capote was twenty-one years old when this rather lighthearted story was accepted by *Story* magazine. He quickly moved into a darker, more complex treatment of such materials, introducing the mysterious and sometimes the ominous into his southern gothic settings.

Even if she is actually a "half-wit," there is nothing at all sinister about Olivia-Ann, as there is in the strange, feebleminded man in Capote's "A Tree of Night." Nor is the threat of violence a grim reality here, as it is in Capote's later "experiment in realism," *In Cold Blood* (1966). Capote is writing here more in the spirit of William Faulkner in his purely comic mode, found in such works as *The Reivers* (1962). Capote's adversaries are so evenly matched in their human frailty that they seem to deserve one another.

The story really has no serious theme, though one might expect from the plot line at least the theme of initiation into the mysteries of adult life. The young husband is apparently as self-centered and ignorant at the end as he is at the beginning, however, and offers no indication of increased maturity. When he first comes to the country estate, he makes the pregnant Marge carry their luggage because he presumably has some "terrible trouble" with his back. Months later, when he is accused of laziness, he protests some vague "scurvy condition" to explain his idleness. At the end, he is concerned only with his own well-being, not with whatever ails Marge in advanced pregnancy. Thus, the story does not reveal any growth in character. Experience does not necessarily make men wiser.

Curiously enough, the physical characteristics of even so unheroic a protagonist and such odd old ladies have certain autobiographical elements. Capote himself was only five feet, three inches tall and was berated by his mother for effeminate mannerisms. Perhaps he converted what may have been a personally humiliating experience into the purely comic in the following passage:

> While my back is turned, Eunice says, "You sure must've picked the runt of the lit-
> ter. Why, this isn't any sort of man at all."
> I've never been so taken back in my life! True, I'm slightly stocky, but then I haven't
> got my full growth yet.

Although in some circumstances, such an episode might lead the reader to condemn the verbally cruel aunt and excuse the foolish young man, it does neither here.
One imagines the protagonist as being happily impervious to serious insult. The colloquial phrase "taken back" indicates more surprise than psychological pain.

Capote was himself reared by aunts and a grandmother and has used pairs of elderly
ladies elsewhere, as in *The Grass Harp* (1951), with considerable affection. Even the
flawed females of "My Side of the Matter" seem more commendable than their miserable nephew-by-marriage.

The story demonstrates Capote's early facility with language, colloquial dialect,
telling imagery, and comic-folk tradition. In fact, Capote once asserted of his own
work, "The thing that's most important is style; not what I'm saying but how I'm saying it; manner over matter."

Style and Technique

One must look, therefore, to style as the paramount achievement of this story; its
sustained colloquial dialect, which reveals so much about the limitations of character,
cultural background, education, and expectations of the speaker. The protagonist reveals his ignorance and inflated opinion of himself, for example, by periodic reminders of his "perfectly swell position clerking at the Cash 'n' Carry." The story is appropriately adorned with trite phrases, such as "really takes the cake," "a drop in the bucket,"
and "if the shoe fits, wear it," but it also sports some variations on conventional
phrases, such as Marge's description of her husband as "free, white, and sixteen."

The old ladies, however, have a comic way of garbling conventional wisdom:
"Don't think you can pull the sheep over our eyes," says Olivia-Ann, and "We weren't
born just around the corner, you know," says Eunice. However, occasionally one of
them creates a peculiarly bizarre expression that has the spirit and cadence of familiar
phrases but is original in content: "If he's ever so much as driven a plow I'll eat a
dozen gophers fried in turpentine."

The narrator provides a vivid, though possibly biased, vision of Eunice as presiding
queen of the household:

> Eunice is this big old fat thing with a behind that must weigh a tenth of a ton. . . . She
> chews tobacco and tries to pretend so ladylike, spitting on the sly. She keeps gabbing
> about what a fine education she had, which is her way of attempting to make me feel bad,
> although . . . I know for a fact she can't even read the funnies without she spells out every
> single, solitary word. You've got to hand her one thing, though—she can add and sub-
> tract money so fast that there's no doubt but what she could be up in Washington, D.C.,
> working where they make the stuff.

Capote displays his ability here to reveal the ignorance, small-mindedness, and egotism of common people, a trait he shares with a number of contemporaneous southern writers. He has not here displayed the depth of humanity that often graces William Faulkner's comic works or the moral passion that burns in Flannery O'Connor's merciless exposes of everyday malice. Nevertheless, the story is an effective vehicle for the careful control of language, from which he could and did venture forth into realms of either gothic romanticism or increased realism.

Katherine Snipes

MY WARSZAWA

Author: Joyce Carol Oates (1938-   )
Type of plot: Psychological
Time of plot: 1980
Locale: Warsaw, Poland, at the First International Conference on American Culture
First published: 1981

> *Principal characters:*
>> JUDITH HORNE, the protagonist, a distinguished American culture
>> critic between her late thirties and early forties
>> CARL WALSER, her longtime lover and traveling companion, a
>> successful journalist
>> ROBERT SARGENT, an American poet attending the same
>> conference

The Story

"My Warszawa" is the story of a successful writer's progressive loss of self-control and self-confidence during a week spent in Poland. Early in the narrative, Joyce Carol Oates gives an account of the kind of gossip Judith Horne's celebrity has generated but then shifts the point of view to her protagonist's own self-doubts. Apparently, public curiosity about her ethnic background and essential femininity has already fueled Judith's "morbidly sensitive consciousness," and this "hyperesthesia" will be further aggravated by the experience of being an American traveling in a Soviet-bloc country.

The story is structured around a series of incidents that mark Judith Horne's growing sense of alienation and awareness of her Jewish roots. As a foreigner in Warsaw, she is particularly disoriented by ignorance of the Polish language ("not a word, not a phrase is familiar"), by the annoying haze of smoke that fills every meeting room and restaurant, and by her inability to make sense of the relationship between Poland's past and its present. Judith and her colleagues often describe Poland as a tragic country, an occupied country that is the victim of Soviet oppression. However, Judith, almost despite herself, keeps uncovering evidence of hypocrisy and anti-Semitism and cannot help remembering that there was a pogrom in Warsaw in 1946. At first, she feels guilty "for her freedom, her American spirit," the passport that allows her to travel anywhere. Later, she identifies herself as a victim who would have been despised and denied basic liberties had she lived in Poland "back then."

Two incidents in particular trigger Judith's emotional identification of herself as a Jew. A visit to Gezia Cemetery affects her profoundly, as she notes the row on row of graves marking the deaths of "fortunate" Jews who "were buried in their own soil" having died of "natural" causes. Toward the end of her stay, Judith confronts Marta, an interviewer, about her religious conversion; though Marta's features are clearly Jewish, she wears a small gold cross around her neck. Marta defends herself against

Judith's implied accusation by dissociating her wealthy family from those "other Jews." "You see, Miss Horne," she explains, "they were very slow—very ignorant—filled with superstitions—lazy. . . . They could have saved themselves. . . . But they did not try." Judith repeats this formula ("They didn't try") in utter disbelief at what she is hearing; then, after a "long, uneasy pause," she slaps the cigarette from Marta's fingers and leaves the room.

The depth of feeling aroused in Judith by these and other encounters takes its toll on her sense of self and her relationship with her lover, Carl. It is as if she has regressed to an adolescent stage marked by extreme mood swings and self-loathing. Her need to be in control constantly wars with her vulnerability and need to be loved. One moment, she accuses Carl of not loving her enough; the next, she is childishly screaming that she hates him and wishes that he were dead. Despite his evident understanding of her situation and his attempts to appease what he refers to as the "adversary" in her, the story ends (as it began) with them bickering even as their plane takes off for the return home.

Themes and Meanings

"My Warszawa" is one of a sequence of stories set in Eastern Europe that Oates wrote between 1979 and 1983 and later collected in *Last Days* (1984). Several of these stories depict characters whose experiences as Americans abroad seem particularly unnerving and serve to aggravate conflicts between personal and public selves. "My Warszawa" is by far the longest and most complex of these stories, and the one that probes most deeply into the theme of role confusion on the part of the highly successful American woman.

Despite her reputation as an astute and often provocative critic of American culture, Judith Horne finds her thoughts from time to time turning helplessly toward love, marriage, and a conventional life. "She is in love and suspects that her love is not returned. Not pound for pound, ounce for ounce," and she hates herself for what she perceives to be a "humiliating weakness." Oates identifies these emotions as adolescent and associates them with Judith's reading of Henry James's *The Awkward Age* (1899). Judith is clearly ambivalent about her own femininity—she throws away a bouquet she receives after a successful lecture because she dislikes its implications, yet wears an "inordinate amount of jewelry"; she wants to be thought handsome, yet defends her use of makeup as emphasizing the intelligence rather than beauty of her eyes. This ambivalence is further complicated by ambivalence about her Jewish heritage. Although her immediate family and her surname are English, her biblical given name, her dark, curly hair, and her dark, uneasy eyes suggest a Semitic past that no longer seems so remote. The two identities—woman and Jew—threaten to overpower Judith while in Warsaw. She feels weak, "And queerly Jewish. And womanly—in the old, rather sick sense of the word. A Jew, a woman, a victim. Can it be," she asks herself.

Judith's inability to integrate her public and private lives and to overcome the increasing dislocation of feeling from intelligence parallels Oates's description (through

Judith's eyes) of Poland's equally divided identity. The story asks whether the real Poland is Communist or Catholic, victim or oppressor, tragic or comic. Is the pervasive smoke—a cigarette in every hand—a political statement, a way of blocking out Soviet oppression, or is it simply a dirty habit compounded by poor ventilation? In particular, Judith questions the significance of Polish Catholicism, sometimes justifying it— "When one can't move horizontally, one must move vertically," she tells Robert—and other times associating it with "Censorship, repression, exploitation of women, anti-Semitism, pogroms. . . . The Church of Rot."

There is the official Warsaw of the 1944 Uprising, which has been rebuilt almost completely, a town of almost too perfect facades. There is also Judith's "Warszawa," an ugly town of long lines of people, "withered lemons," "small shrivelled apples," and poisonous pollution. It is here that Judith searches for her Jewish heritage, only to find it denied. No one seems to know how many Jews may still live in Poland; certainly there are few children. Even the so-called monument to the Jewish ghetto depicts five heroic, Aryan-looking male figures with nothing Jewish about them, the lone female figure relegated to the background. Judith's failure to master any Polish words is finally symptomatic of her inability to find any link between Warsaw's present and her own identity as a female Polish Jew.

Style and Technique

"My Warszawa" is a disturbing story, made more so by the apparent objectivity of Oates's narrative voice. The cold, highly analytic style, though an accurate projection of the destructive power of Judith Horne's intelligence, seems more typical of a Doris Lessing case study than the flamboyant, image- and symbol-laden fiction for which Oates has become famous. The reader understands and shares in Judith's mixed emotions about herself and Poland but is given little evidence of whether the author sympathizes with her protagonist's plight. The overall tone of ironic understatement may further alienate the reader, who finds him- or herself in the position of Judith's lover, wanting to like her but prevented from doing so by Judith's own self-hatred.

Even the character of Robert Sargent, whose experience in Poland seems a comic restatement of Judith's, offers little relief from Oates's cold objectivity. He, too, suffers from feelings of alienation and paranoia because of an insecure sexual identity and fears humiliation at the hands of his homosexual lover. He complains that his "toenails are growing wildly" with "wicked, razor-sharp" corners, just as Judith worries about the "tiny worms of dirt that roll beneath her fingertips." The difference is that Judith understands and fights against what Poland has done to her, while Robert appears to be the bumbling, naïve butt of a world that is beyond his comprehension. Judith's literal entrapment in the back stairway of her hotel finds its metaphoric equivalent in Robert's Kafkaesque vision of his own victimhood. Still, it is not clear whether Robert's role in the story is to validate or mock Judith's overly acute sense of self.

There is one metaphor that suggests that Oates does have a message for her readers. Early in the story, Judith Horne almost walks into a glass door that she mistakenly presumes will open automatically for her. The door would seem to represent the naïveté of Americans who assume that another culture is easily accessible to them without any effort on their part. It may also stand for the communication missing in Judith's relationship with Carl. It is at least indirectly because she chooses not to relate the incident to him, out of fear of looking foolish, that Carl later repeats her mistake, crashing into the glass "with a thud that reverberates through the lobby" as "she stands frozen, staring, appalled as any stranger." The moral might be that entry into good relationships with oneself, one's lovers, one's past, and other cultures depends on mastery of the language of honest and open communication—a seemingly impossible task for the insecure individuals who populate Oates's world.

Jane M. Barstow

MYSTERIOUS KÔR

Author: Elizabeth Bowen (1899-1973)
Type of plot: Psychological
Time of plot: World War II
Locale: London
First published: 1944

> *Principal characters:*
> PEPITA, a young London girl
> ARTHUR, the soldier whom Pepita loves
> CALLIE, Pepita's girlfriend and roommate

The Story

"Mysterious Kôr" is set in London during World War II on a night when, despite the bright moonlight, the sky is clear of bombers. Into the strange silence come a girl named Pepita and a soldier named Arthur, wandering through the night together, because in the crowded city there is no place where they can be alone. Pepita quotes from a poem about Kôr, an abandoned city, which she imagines London to be; it is a city from which all the people have long ago disappeared, a city free of the dominion of time, a city where Pepita and Arthur can be forever alone together. By contrast, Arthur must actually spend his leave on the living-room couch in the apartment that Pepita shares with Callie, and Callie intends to act as a kindly chaperon. At this point, the brief illusion of Kôr vanishes, and the lovers return to the apartment.

The second part of the story traces Callie's thoughts as she lies awake, listening for Pepita and Arthur. Virginal Callie cannot understand why Pepita and Arthur would like some time alone together; instead, she idealizes their love and vicariously enjoys it, as a spiritual experience. As she waits, the moonlight enters the room, and she thinks that the lovers are outside, in a different, moonlit world. At this point, they enter the apartment, hoping that Callie has gone to sleep, but Callie jumps out of bed to play hostess, revealing with every speech that she has no inkling of their desire for each other. At last, when the girlfriends are alone in the bedroom, Pepita is so cross that Callie cries. Later, when Pepita is sound asleep, Callie has a conversation with Arthur, who has wakened thinking about Pepita's periodic withdrawals to the nonexistent city of Kôr. When there is no place to go, comments Arthur, a couple might as well imagine Kôr.

By now, the moon has dwindled, and the magic that has held all London in its spell is gone. In her bed, Callie realizes that her own joy in love has gone, as well. Arthur had said that to be human was a terrible fate; Callie now recognizes that to be human in wartime is to miss out on living. Accidentally, in her sleep, Pepita slaps Callie's face. In her sleep, motivated by her need for Arthur, Pepita is wandering through the dream city to which she escapes whenever life is unbearable.

Themes and Meanings

"Mysterious Kôr" is a story about the contrast between two worlds, the real world of wartime London and the imaginary world of Kôr. The real world is described in the opening paragraphs of the story. It is a world of destruction, of bomb craters and of helmeted air wardens. It is a world in which private life has disappeared and nights are spent huddled in the Underground. However, it is a world of separation and isolation, even in the midst of crowds; thus the French soldiers, far from their own occupied country, unable even to find the place where they are to stay, are ignored by the wardens going off duty.

Pepita and Arthur are part of this real world. Although on the night of the story no bombs are falling, it is clear that this is merely a freakish respite, an exceptional night between nights when horror is normal. Arthur, too, has a respite, for he is on leave. There is no privacy, however, even for soldiers on leave. Although on this night he and Pepita do not have to go to the shelters, they cannot be alone, for in crowded London, Pepita must share a room with Callie. Thus, like the French soldiers, the lovers are homeless, and in the tiny flat with Callie, they are as much isolated from each other as they would have been had they been separated by miles.

In the real world, the love relationship itself is flawed. Arthur thinks that he would not ordinarily have been drawn to Pepita; she was not "his type"; their love had been a "collision in the dark." Perhaps this wartime romance has been merely a desperate attempt to break out of the horror, the isolation. Certainly it is not the dream romance that Callie has made it.

In the moonlight, however, Pepita enters the imaginary world of Kôr. It is a world without inhabitants, without history, and without vulnerability. Whenever the heartbreak around her becomes too much to endure, Pepita says, she escapes to Kôr, which contains no hearts to break. Imagining with her, Arthur thinks of a city in which no one would prevent their coming together. However, suddenly the dream is gone, and the lovers must return to the real world, where they cannot be together.

Later, when Pepita is asleep, Arthur tells Callie that Pepita has escaped to Kôr in her dreams. When the narrative penetrates Pepita's dreams, it is clear that Arthur is right. In her sleep, Pepita wanders through Kôr with Arthur. Arthur is not the end of her dreams, however, but the means by which Pepita can escape from wartime London. Somehow her love for him enables her to escape to her real love, the world without pain, without change, without life itself, the mysterious Kôr. Ironically, because Pepita has escaped from the real world, crowded with suffering people, into an imaginary world without people, she has rejected life for "Kôr's finality," itself a kind of death.

Style and Technique

Elizabeth Bowen's stories achieve their effect by the interplay of symbols and characters. For example, in "Mysterious Kôr," the moonlight transforms the scenery and influences the characters, to the point that it becomes almost a character itself. At the beginning of the story, the moonlight has invaded all of London, somehow keeping people indoors and thus enabling Pepita and Arthur to imagine the forsaken city, a city that Pepita yearns to find but that Arthur volunteers to populate. The moon has also invaded the room of the virginal Callie, who sees it as a symbol of the beautiful romance that she has created for Pepita and Arthur. Experiencing the romance vicariously, Callie will put only her hand in the moonlight.

Missing the point of what the moonlight means to Arthur, Callie saves the moonlit portion of her bed for Pepita, who will presumably be content with romantic dreams. When she sees her moonlit bed, Pepita says crossly that she cannot sleep in the moonlight; though she promptly falls asleep, her comment has made it clear to Callie that moonlight means something different to Pepita from what she had supposed. Later in the evening, when the moonlight is gone, Callie is relieved. However, if the moonlight of Callie's naïve idealization will not come again, that of Pepita's imagination has drawn her further and further along her separate road, for in the Kôr of her dreams, it is the only light.

On one level, then, Bowen has used moonlight in this story to symbolize the imagination. However, she has also used it to indicate the isolation of her characters; because moonlight means something different to each of them, because each imagination takes a different path with different goals, Callie, Pepita, and Arthur are doomed to live at cross-purposes. Finally, because moonlight causes the action of the story, it has the importance of a character, interacting with the human characters to reveal the human condition.

Rosemary M. Canfield Reisman

NAIROBI

Author: Joyce Carol Oates (1938-   )
Type of plot: Realism
Time of plot: An April during the early 1980's
Locale: New York City
First published: 1983

> *Principal characters:*
>> GINNY, a young and innocent model hired for a "companion"
>> job
>> OLIVER LEAHY, a man about thirty-four years old, who hires
>> Ginny for intrigue
>> HERBERT CREWS, highly placed in the Zieboldt Foundation, who
>> is Oliver's friend, the object of the intrigue
>> MARGUERITE CREWS, his wife

The Story

As the story opens, Oliver Leahy is taking Ginny to some exclusive shops on New York City's Madison Avenue to buy for her what he calls "an appropriate outfit." For what it is appropriate, Ginny does not know, but she takes great pleasure in the several hours of shopping. Ginny is very attractive, the kind of woman it would be hard for a man not to find captivating, though she seems unaware of that. Indeed, she is a rather young model.

It is only after the reader has finished the story, reflected on it, and considered the reverberations of the title, "Nairobi," that he or she comes to understand what is taking place. Ginny is innocently to get some information for Oliver. The information will come (although she will not know that) from Herbert Crews as a tribute to her beauty. Crews is highly placed in the Zieboldt Foundation, which has money to give away or invest.

In the first shop, Ginny loves a green velvet jumpsuit, but whether to buy it is not her decision, and Oliver chooses for her a navy blue blazer and a white pleated skirt, both in Irish linen, and a pale blue silk blouse. Oliver tells the clerk to take the tags off, that she will wear the clothes, and the clerk wraps Ginny's old clothes in a bundle. Out in the street, Ginny looks at herself in the shop windows and finds her image strange but not unpleasing. Oliver compliments her, saying that she looks like a convent schoolgirl.

In a jewelry boutique, Oliver buys for her more gifts to emphasize her look of expensive simplicity: silver earrings in conch shapes and thin silver bracelets with the heads of animals and birds. Ginny is puzzled about how to relate to this man who is buying her expensive gifts—in essence, costuming her—and when he asks if it hurts to put the earrings in her ears, she is conscious of him being close to her. She does not know whether to accept the intimacy or draw away. She draws away slightly, perhaps like a convent schoolgirl, as she answers him. In a shoe salon, Oliver chooses for her some vanilla kidskin sandals, which evidently please Ginny very much. The salesperson notes that Oliver's taste is "unerring."

Her costume is now complete. It makes no demands or claims, except the evident one, and it speaks, as her appearance and manner speak, of guilelessness. They take a cab, and Oliver gives her instructions in a low, "casual" voice.

Ginny is to speak and interact very little, and perhaps even wander away to skim a magazine or step onto the porch, if no one is speaking to her. She is to pay no attention to Oliver. Above all, she is to act as if nothing that any of the three of them say is important to her. He squeezes Ginny's hand and releases it, and he repeats that she is not to be concerned with any of them. She says yes, admiring her vanilla sandals with eight straps on each, and thinks that she has never owned any shoes so lovely. She reassures Oliver that she understands him.

The reader wonders why this lovely, innocent young woman is being made so irresistible and at the same time being instructed to be so cool and distant. For whom is she the bait, and for what purpose is he to be so tantalized? How will he demand intimacy?

The uniformed doorman is very accommodating about keeping the parcel that Oliver is carrying. In the elevator, Oliver shows some signs of nervousness. He assays that her costume is perfect, and he straightens his tie. Ginny regards him coolly as an old thirty-four-year-old, but she realizes that he is handsome and comes to see that they are an attractive couple.

Oliver introduces his friends, Marguerite and Herbert, their last name sounding like "Crews." Oliver says that they cannot stay and he cannot accompany them on their weekend holiday. They urge him to come out to the Point, as they had planned—and to bring his friend along. Ginny is noticed, and the trap is set.

Ginny moves politely away, and after a while Herbert comes over to her. Herbert begins to talk about his work and how it keeps him moving and makes him fatigued at times. Perhaps she has heard of the Zieboldt Foundation (he says, bragging), with which he is associated. He has been in Nairobi for the foundation and returned only two days ago. Oliver is about to succeed overwhelmingly. Ginny is not even sure where Nairobi is. Herbert speaks of the wild animals and of how it is worth going there.

Rushing things, Oliver insists that they must go. He knows his cast well. Herbert, however, goes on about the animals in Kenya. Finally, in a last demand for intimate interest, Herbert says that the trip was fatiguing and that he discovered—what the foundation suspected—that the microbiological research there had come to nothing and much money had simply disappeared. Ginny gives her sympathy but offers the suggestion that that sort of thing is going on everywhere. She does not guess the truth of what she is saying.

Herbert now tells the story to Oliver, and Oliver seems interested in it. Within five minutes afterward, Ginny and Oliver are down the elevator. On Fifth Avenue, Ginny slips her arm through Oliver's, but soon they have to walk at different paces. She realizes that he is not going to offer to buy her a drink even as a courtesy, and she resolves not to feel slighted. Her struggle to act appropriately toward an employer who has bought her such lavish gifts—and with whom she makes a lovely couple—continues to the end, and she is very sad that she cannot blow a kiss to Oliver from the taxi as she leaves. However, after all, she reflects, she has lost nothing but her pair of red shoes, abandoned at the shop when the situation seemed to call for it.

Themes and Meanings

The ostensible subject of this story, as the title suggests to the reader, is "Nairobi." The story appears to be a detective story, investigating what is going on in Nairobi, where Zieboldt Foundation money is being wasted and is disappearing. When Oliver finally learns that the Zieboldt officials now know this from Herbert's investigation, the mystery (from his point of view) is solved, and he can take the information to the people who wanted him to get it—presumably in order to perpetrate or cover up a crime, possibly theft.

Nairobi is metaphorically New York, and the story is about "Nairobi" in action—the scam, the cheating. It is going on in the actions of Oliver, one of Herbert and Marguerite's friends. Most important, it is going on in the actions of Ginny, who wonders what she has lost at the end of her day. She does not have any idea of what she is doing or has done. Ginny is an unwitting accomplice. Her payoff is in her regular salary for the day as a model and actress, and her expensive gifts, for which Zieboldt has ultimately paid.

There are others innocently involved, Third World citizens, the reader may guess. There is the uniformed doorman who has the secret of a package of plain clothes being left with him (if he has any idea what has been left, which he likely does not). There is the black elevator operator, who hears Oliver tell Ginny how to act.

However, the primary accomplice to Oliver in the Zieboldt theft is Ginny, even though the reader can see how far her thoughts are from theft and cheating. Her two major concerns are whether she looks pretty enough and whether she should not have some sort of emotional involvement—maybe even a hug—with the man who bought her such fine gifts. It is this juxtaposition of the role Ginny plays in an evident crime and her lack of concern for the significance of the role she is playing that points to the story's theme: the culpability of the willfully ignorant and innocent in the face of obvious wrongdoing.

Style and Technique

"Nairobi" is told in the third person, but entirely from Ginny's limited and rather self-centered point of view. The reader thus begins to discern what is going on in the story only gradually, perhaps not until after the second or third reading: that Oliver is getting the corporate leak that he wants and that it is indiscreet of Herbert to reveal.

This limited point of view serves to heighten the impact of the story's broader concern—with innocence and its corruption. By foregrounding Ginny's superficial preoccupation with clothes and the romance of the adventure (to the exclusion of any concern for that with which she is involving herself) and leaving unstated the obviously sinister implications of Oliver and his objectives, Joyce Carol Oates shows her protagonist to be a fool, willfully blind to the significance of what is going on around her. It is no wonder that, on descending in the elevator with Oliver after their meeting with Herbert and Marguerite, she "felt a pinprick of disappointment" in her disheveled (and symbolically significant) appearance, whereas Oliver had found her nearly perfect on their ascent in the same elevator. Ginny has lost more that she realizes—not merely her old shoes but also her integrity, a part of herself.

Leslie D. Foster

A NASTY STORY

Author: Fyodor Dostoevski (1821-1881)
Type of plot: Psychological
Time of plot: The early 1860's
Locale: St. Petersburg, Russia
First published: "Skverny anekdot," 1862 (English translation, 1925)

> *Principal characters:*
> GENERAL IVAN ILYITCH PRALINSKI, the Actual State Councillor, who is forty-three years old
> PORFIRY PETROVITCH PSELDONYMOV, a young clerk in his department
> TITULAR COUNCILLOR MLEKOPITAYEV, the father of the bride
> THE BRIDE, a seventeen-year-old girl
> AKIM PETROVITCH ZUBIKOV, the chief clerk in General Pralinski's department

The Story

Actual State Councillor Pralinski, a forty-three-year-old man recently promoted to the rank of general in the civil service, is a bachelor from a good family. As the pampered son of a general, he was educated in an aristocratic establishment and is generally considered to be a gifted person. The third-person narrator calls him "a kind man and even a poet at heart," one who is frequently overcome by painful moments of disillusionment. As the story opens on a winter evening in St. Petersburg, General Pralinski, while at a dinner party with two other generals, expresses his idealistic view that the privileged must have a love of humankind and must have consideration particularly toward their inferiors. This idea is in keeping with Pralinski's satisfaction at being known as "a desperate liberal, which flattered him greatly."

Leaving the dinner, Pralinski, who realizes that he is slightly drunk, begins to walk because his coach driver has disappeared. After going a short distance, Pralinski notes a wedding party taking place in a long, one-storied wooden house. When he inquires, he learns that this is the party for Porfiry Petrovitch Pseldonymov, a young clerk in his department. After briefly discussing with himself whether he should attend the party, he decides to do so. The narrator states that "he was being led astray by his evil star."

Entering into this party of about thirty guests, Pralinski instantly becomes the center of attention, as he had foreseen. After an awkward, stunned silence, Pralinski is welcomed by the young groom, Pseldonymov, who does not know what to make of his presence. The situation is briefly saved by Akim Petrovitch Zubikov, the chief clerk in General Pralinski's department. After Pralinski unsuccessfully tries to tell a humorous story, he is introduced to the bride. This seventeen-year-old girl, whose first name is never given, has a malicious look to her thin, pale face, a scraggy neck, and the body of a pullet. Her father describes her as having "seven devils."

Pseldonymov's mother, a very kind woman, makes the general at home by offering him a bottle of champagne, obviously intended only for the bride and groom. In his nervousness, the general consumes two bottles of the expensive champagne. By this time, the other guests return to normal, realizing that Pralinski is here only because he is drunk. As several young men begin to express themselves, Pralinski grows more uncomfortable. He manages to infuriate a young journalist, who also has had more than he is accustomed to drink.

Although he knows that he should leave before dinner, Pralinski allows himself to be persuaded to remain. Having never before drunk vodka, he drains "a huge wine-glass of vodka." After this, he is blindly drunk, and the narrator says, "From then on, events took their own course." The bride's mother appears, a spiteful-looking woman with an "irreconcilable hostility towards Pseldonymov's mother." At this time, Pralinski drunkenly decides to tell the guests some of his idealistic views, only to begin spitting on the table in his drunkenness. The young journalist can no longer contain his hatred, bursting out that the general has "disrupted everyone's enjoyment" and insulting him openly. As the journalist is evicted from the party, General Pralinski passes out cold. It is now three o'clock in the morning.

At this point, the narrator explains what is really the "nasty" part of the story, as if the general's embarrassment were not bad enough. Pseldonymov's true story is presented. He and his mother are extremely poor, he suffers from a sketchy education, and she is forced to wash clothes for other people to support their miserable living conditions. Now Titular Councillor Mlekopitayev is presented, a man who was in some way indebted to Pseldonymov's father. This Mlekopitayev, father of the bride, is "a vicious man": pigheaded, a drunkard, a petty tyrant. He was "sure to be tormenting someone all the time. For this purpose he kept several distant relatives in the house." The reader learns that the young bride is against this marriage and that Mlekopitayev favors the marriage particularly because it is against her will and because she is furious. This is the wedding feast that the general has chosen to attend.

Being unable to transport the general home by carriage, Pseldonymov must lodge him in this house for the night. The bridal couch being the only available bed, Pralinski is placed there. The hastily arranged substitute bridal bed crashes to the floor in the middle of the night, the bride trembles with rage, and Pseldonymov is morally crushed as the bride is led away by her shrewish mother. Pseldonymov realizes that he will have to change his place of work. He also realizes that he has not yet received from his vicious father-in-law any of the money and property promised as wedding presents.

With this, the focus again returns to the drunken General Pralinski, who spends the night with "headache, vomiting and other most unpleasant attacks." Even the tender care given him by Pseldonymov's mother cannot reduce the deadly shame he feels about his disastrous involvement with this affair. In the morning, Pralinski runs from the house and grabs a passing cab. He hides out in his own home for eight days, painfully ill "but more in his mind than his body." He realizes that this shameful affair will be talked about all over the city. He is particularly ashamed that he can find no excuse for himself.

When he finally returns to his office, he finds that nothing unpleasant happens to him. He hears no whisperings, sees no malicious smiles from those who work under his supervision. At last, chief clerk Zubikov appears, asking shortly afterward that clerk Pseldonymov be allowed to transfer to a different department. When the general begins to discuss the matter with Zubikov, the chief clerk becomes so upset that he quickly withdraws. The story ends with General Pralinski's sense of shame and heaviness at heart. He says in the final sentence: "I have failed to live up to my ideals!"

Themes and Meanings

Fyodor Dostoevski is primarily interested in presenting a man who must come to terms with his weaknesses and illusions—a difficult realization for anyone. General Pralinski, fond of idealism, professes the need to be humane to others, bearing in mind that his inferiors also are human beings. Pralinski believes that his humaneness will lead others to love and trust him. This in turn will lead them to believe in reform and to "settle everything fundamentally in a friendly spirit." To Pralinski's regret, one of his colleagues responds, "We shan't live up to it."

During his drunken visit to Pseldonymov's wedding party, Pralinski mentally rehearses various speeches about what he is attempting to achieve by his presence: "I must leave in such a way that they will all understand why I came. I must reveal my moral aim." The other guests, however, realize none of his idealism; instead, they understand that he is drunk and getting increasingly more drunk. Finally, after waking in the morning in the bridal bed, Pralinski himself realizes his inability to control his own appetites and desires. He does not love Pseldonymov and his shrewish bride as he thinks he ought; instead, he realizes that he detests them. Perhaps Pralinski may even have gained an insight into his own vanity and self-centeredness. He has accomplished quite the reverse of what he intended by his visit. He has forced Pseldonymov to transfer to a different department, and in his own eyes Pralinski has shamed himself before his department even down to the next generation. The story indeed ends with Pralinski's statement of his moral failure.

"A Nasty Story" is also about the evils of poverty. As in his novel *Prestupleniye i nakazaniye* (1866; *Crime and Punishment*, 1886), Dostoevski vividly portrays the great sufferings that the poor must endure. Pseldonymov and his kindly mother have no choice left to them but to marry into the evil Mlekopitayev family. The reader might hesitate to think of the wretched life that awaits them.

Style and Technique

Dostoevski skillfully organizes the story to place emphasis on his main theme. The focus at the opening is on Pralinski's idealism; after scattering a number of references to it throughout the story, Dostoevski concludes with Pralinski's sad realization that he has not lived up to his ideals. Dostoevski's focus on Pralinski's characterization also aids in presenting the idea because Pralinski often focuses on his introspective nature, his self-criticism, and his sense of shame.

Dostoevski also makes use of both revelations and the withholding of information in this story. Only after eighty percent of the story is finished is the "nasty" part of the story revealed: the miserable, arranged marriage of Pseldonymov. Pralinski's part of the story probably will not strike most readers as nasty. He is weak, perhaps, in allowing himself to get drunk and to act foolishly. However, this may prove to be a rare mistake for him. On the other hand, this disastrous marriage is destined to last for many years, considering the youth of the couple. Although General Pralinski's story parallels the Pseldonymov portion in its atmosphere of weakness and shame, it is the Pseldonymov marriage into the inhumane Mlekopitayev household that gives this story its title.

A. Bruce Dean

NATIONAL HONEYMOON

Author: Paul Horgan (1903-1995)
Type of plot: Satire
Time of plot: Immediately following World War II
Locale: Hollywood, California
First published: 1950

> *Principal characters:*
> GUSTAVUS ADOLPHUS (GUS) EARICKSON and
> ROBERTA MAY EARICKSON, a newlywed couple from New Mexico
>   and contestants on the *National Honeymoon* radio show
> GAIL BURKE, the suave host of *National Honeymoon*

The Story

Paul Horgan's "National Honeymoon" is divided into two sections; the first section shows the temptation, fall, and humiliation of the protagonists Gustavus Adolphus (Gus) Earickson and his new bride, Roberta May, and the second part reveals their redemption. The newlywed couple's innocence is pitted against the cheap vulgarity of Hollywood and the persuasive insincerity of its pitchmen.

Roberta May succumbs to the lure of radio-show riches and secretly arranges for the newlywed couple to appear on a regular radio program, *National Honeymoon*. She keeps her plans secret until the last moment, because she suspects that her husband would not submit to a public invasion of their private life. In her naïveté, she believes that they have nothing to lose and everything to gain.

Married for only several hours, Gus and Roberta May find themselves whisked away from their home in New Mexico to Hollywood, where they must confront the carefully orchestrated spontaneity of the show's professional host, everyone's "favorite father-in-law, Gail Burke Himself." Gus and Roberta May soon find that they have temporarily turned their lives over to the glib machinations of Burke, whose purpose is to pry and probe into their private lives, to titillate the audience, and generally to put them on display. Under the guise of jovial beneficence, Burke bullies and belittles the couple to reveal the details of their courtship, the intimacies of their quarrels, and the sincerity of their love for each other.

At first, he targets Gus, complimenting him on his good looks and making fun of his name. The disconcerted Gus reluctantly replies to Burke's sallies, but when Burke moves too close to an invasion of privacy with his sly insinuations about their honeymoon activities, he senses the danger of a scene in the "dry edge" that comes into Gus's voice. Burke quickly switches to the more vulnerable Roberta May, tempting her with "surprises for them that will take their breath away," and reassuring her with phony familiarity. Carried away by the moment, Roberta May tells Burke and the avid audience about the details of their courtship, how she realized that she loved Gus when she learned that he was missing in action, that two weeks elapsed before their first kiss, and that they had quarreled about whether she should keep her job. Her revelations are interspersed with roars of approval from the audience and the banalities of the slick host. Not wanting to humiliate Roberta May publicly, the unfortunate Gus unwillingly acquiesces to the public exposure of their private lives. They are duly rewarded with an all-expenses-paid honeymoon in Hollywood, lunch with the stars, monogrammed shirts, silk pajamas, silk negligee, silk sheets, and the fulfillment of Roberta May's secret dream, a special room done up in knotty pine with a fireplace and special furniture.

Later that night, Gus awakens to find Roberta May silently crying. She realizes that she has made the Devil's bargain and traded away "their very own love story" and "let it be given to everybody else." The inconsolable Roberta May berates herself for the irretrievable loss. Gus, however, tells her that if she will simply leave it all to him, he can make it right. The next afternoon after the show, Gus and Roberta wait for Gail Burke to appear. Gus tells Burke that they have come to return all the things that they had been given. The uncomprehending Burke is stunned. "'You can't do this to me!' snapped Burke. 'In all my years on *National Honeymoon* a thing like this has never happened to me.'"

Burke warns his usually obsequious attendants to keep things quiet, but he has been stripped of his polished veneer. Roberta May, sensing his vulnerability, seeks to reassure him: "'Never mind, Mr. Burke,' she said with sweetness." Her compassion and simple dignity in contrast to the now-befuddled Burke reveals him as a ludicrous marionette, and Gail Burke suffers the "final punishment" of the derisive laughter of his staff. The triumph of Gus and Roberta May over the polished professional host and the materialistic values for which he is a cipher is an affirmation of the humanistic values found throughout Horgan's work.

Themes and Meanings

Gus and Roberta May Earickson come face-to-face with one of American society's icons of greed, the "giveaway" show. They succumb to the blandishments of the show's host, Gail Burke, not so much out of cupidity as out of a comfortable innocence. In particular, Roberta May's perception of the *National Honeymoon* show is self-deceptively naïve. By keeping her plan to be on the show a secret from Gus, Roberta May protects herself from taking a closer look at what the *National Honeymoon* show does: exploits its contestants to sell a product. More important, she refuses to consider the idea that she and Gus will have to trade away the intimacy of their private lives for the promised prizes "that will take their breath away."

When she discovers that she has purchased the prizes at a very high cost, her suffering is made more acute by her realization that she not only cast away "the things that meant so much" to them but also has been duped into making her husband a part of their humiliation. It is at this point in the story that Gus takes charge of the situation and proposes his plan to remedy what appears to be irremediable.

The biblical parallel becomes apparent. Gus and Roberta May, like Adam and Eve, fall from innocence and grace, and like their biblical antecedents, the woman is the weaker vessel and the instrument of the fall. However, Horgan, a Roman Catholic writer, gives the Edenic tale a comic twist and a positive moral. Gus and Roberta May have the power of choice, and they decide to undo the damage. They are not dealing with Satan and an angry Jehovah but with the narcissistic Gail Burke and, more important, their own weaknesses and lack of knowledge. Horgan reminds his readers that the Earicksons have been willing participants in their downfall.

When Gus and Roberta May realize that they have chosen to violate the values they cherish, they also realize that they can redeem the special privacy of their love story by refusing to sell it.

Thematic resolution comes about when Gus and Roberta May return the prizes. Their act affirms their values and that these values are not for sale. Gail Burke becomes a figure to pity. He cannot understand Gus and Roberta May or why they returned "all the things," for he lives within the confines of a crass and exploitative world too narrow for the simple dignity of human affection. Moreover, Horgan makes it clear that in this temporal world the possibilities of the exercise of free will make redemption a matter of choice.

Style and Technique

Although "National Honeymoon" takes a satiric look at a uniquely American foible, the story is told without rancor. Paul Horgan has an accurate ear for the patter of the professional host and an understanding of audience manipulation. Gail Burke, the host of *National Honeymoon*, is a familiar figure. The happy hyperbole of praise and the implied self-love in Burke's favorite invocation, "People, do you love it?" reveal the confident pitchman at work. This deft portrait is biting, but it has none of the vitriolic quality present in most satire. Instead, Horgan chooses to set his characters in comic contrast to one another, the overly naïve newlyweds from New Mexico and the mainstream values they represent with the glib host of the radio show, the minion of coarse Hollywood hucksterism. These characterizations could easily have been a bit too pat, but all the characters reveal human weaknesses that endow them with a greater humanity than the stereotypes they are in danger of becoming. Even Burke has a damaged humanity that raises him above being merely despicable. Though it is obvious that the Earicksons become caught up in a process that overwhelms them, it is not so obvious that Gail Burke is inextricably enmeshed in the shallow banalities of the show he hosts. When Gus and Roberta May return the prizes, Burke becomes confused and angry and suffers a loss of confidence. He is humiliated when his underlings sense his vulnerability, and he becomes the recipient of their mocking laughter. Although he gets his "just deserts," he becomes a pitiable figure rather than a convenient scapegoat. Thus, Horgan reveals himself as a writer with a compassionate rather than a sardonic view of the human condition.

David Sundstrand

A NATIVE OF WINBY

Author: Sarah Orne Jewett (1849-1909)
Type of plot: Regional
Time of plot: About 1890
Locale: Maine
First published: 1891

> *Principal characters:*
> JOSEPH K. LANEWAY, a senator, general, and millionaire, and a
> native of Winby
> MARILLA HENDER, a schoolteacher in Winby
> ABBY HARRAN HENDER, her grandmother

The Story

When Joseph K. Laneway was thirteen, he and his family left the New England town of Winby and headed west. Laneway also left behind his first love, Abby Harran. He rose to the rank of general in the Civil War, was elected senator from Kansota, and became rich. Now, back in Winby, people still talk about him; Marilla Hender, a teacher, repeatedly reminds her pupils that Laneway attended their school, where he paid more attention to his studies than they do and thus began his rise to fame.

Abby's life is more difficult. The family farm always yielded more stones than crops. Her husband died young, as did her favorite son and his wife. To survive, she has had to work hard and live frugally.

One drowsy May afternoon, a stranger enters Marilla's classroom. He listens to student recitations for a time, then, to the astonishment of the children, sits at one of the benches. When Marilla informs him, as she does all strangers, that Senator Laneway once sat in that room, he—Laneway—introduces himself. He delivers an address to the students; then, as he prepares to leave, Marilla urges him to visit her grandmother, Abby Harran Hender, who was once a classmate and who still talks about him.

Laneway spends the rest of the day wandering around the old town. He is saddened to discover that his family's house has become a sheep meadow, and even the old walnut tree has been cut down. When he asks passersby whether any Laneways live in town, the response is always an indifferent no. This is hardly the triumphant reception he had anticipated.

Tired and disappointed, just after dark he arrives at the Hender house, where Marilla has been telling her grandmother about the surprise visit. Abby, hearing the knock, goes to the door to dismiss the stranger, for she wants to hear more of Marilla's story. As soon as she sees Laneway standing in the door, she recognizes him and invites him to come inside.

Through much of the night they relive their past. Abby prepares Laneway's favorite New England foods: rye drop-cakes, fried turnovers, broiled salt fish, brown-crusted loaf bread, and baked beans. Later they drink cider made from apples Abby picked herself. She proudly shows him the 106-volume library she has collected. Among the books are a few that Laneway sent and a campaign biography, which she has used to hold the "three or four letters" he wrote to her.

The next morning, Laneway departs. Before going, he gives Abby a bunch of pink anemones and tells her, "You mustn't put these in your desk." After almost six decades he still remembers giving the thirteen-year-old Abby a similar bouquet, which she left in her desk until they withered. She replies, blushing, that she still has those flowers pressed in a book.

Marilla drives the senator to the station and returns to report that the whole town has turned out to greet their guest. Then Marilla notices that Abby has been crying. Abby reassures her granddaughter that the visit has been pleasant; she is crying only because she realizes that she is aging.

Themes and Meanings

Repeatedly, Sarah Orne Jewett presents the conflict between past and future: the old, pre-Civil War America with its frugality and innocence on one hand; the new, prosperous, mechanized country heading into the twentieth century on the other. She recognizes the changes that are affecting even the small towns in Maine: The old Laneway house is gone; other children sit in Laneway's former place at school.

However, Jewett stresses the permanence of the land in the midst of these changes. Laneway finds that the air is still as sweet and fresh as it was in his youth. Though the Laneway house has vanished, the old rosebush his mother tended is still blooming, still putting out fresh shoots. Laneway's mother often wished that she had removed the sweetbrier to their new western home, but Jewett suggests that some plants, like certain virtues, cannot be transplanted.

Tied to the land, Winby is an idealized portrait of stability in the midst of flux. The old families still live in the same houses. They still cook the same foods, make and drink the same cider from apples that come "from the old russet . . . and the gnarly, red-cheeked ungrafted" trees, not the newer, human-made varieties. The school desks are the ones Laneway used and bear notches that he carved with his first jackknife almost sixty years before.

Jewett's nostalgia for the past extends beyond a desire to retain old plants and old furniture. For her, these physical objects symbolize traditional—and better—ways. The young Marilla does not recognize the senator she repeatedly invokes, but her grandmother recognizes him instantly. Marilla can cook "kickshaws" and "fairy gems" but not substantial fare. Indeed, Abby knows that "there ain't one in a hundred, nowadays, knows how to." Marilla wants to feed Laneway in the formal parlor, where he can see the best furniture and dishes, but Abby insists that they share the intimacy, warmth, and hospitality of the kitchen. Jewett believed that these homespun values were vanishing; yet these are the values she treasured and sought to preserve in her fiction.

Style and Technique

Jewett highlights the conflict between old and new by contrasting her two main characters, Laneway and Abby. The senator has left the old town for the young West because he has wanted the external things that the world offers: glory, fame, wealth. He has achieved these, but he has had to pay the price of their acquisition, the loss of simplicity and compassion. He no longer can get "a good, hearty, old-fashioned supper" whenever he wants, and he has neglected Abby when he might easily have helped her. As she shows him her small library, "His heart smote him for not being thoughtful; he knew well enough that the overflow of his own library would have been delightful to this self-denying, eager-minded soul."

Abby, though, has always remembered her first love. She not only saves the few letters he has sent but also uses some of the little money she has to buy a campaign biography of her old friend. Even though "the household stores were waning low," she fixes a feast for her guest. Nor is he an exception; she has always sought "to help and to serve everybody who came in her way." Though she has not prospered as Laneway has, he recognizes that she has held onto the spiritual values that are "the very best of life."

Hence, at the end of the story, Abby does not join her fellow citizens of Winby at the train station as they publicly celebrate their famous native son. Laneway is pleased with the adulation he receives, and Abby is happy that he has gotten what he wants. However, she believes that she "had the best part of anybody." Treasuring the homey and the simple, she prefers her private evening to any public recognition. For one night Abby has resurrected the innocent New England boy who has been buried inside the Kansota millionaire and has delighted in his company; Abby prefers the simple youth to the famous man.

She realizes, too, that her quiet life has been richer than Laneway's. Though Laneway and Abby have both lost their spouses, they do not rekindle their old romance because they have become too different. Abby has clung to the past, preserving even the faded flowers, and Laneway has chosen the new world. In opting for tradition, she has chosen "the best part."

Joseph Rosenblum

NEBRASKA

Author: Ron Hansen (1947-   )
Type of plot: Regional
Time of plot: The last half of the twentieth century with flashbacks to earlier times
Locale: An unnamed small town in Nebraska
First published: 1986

> *Principal characters:*
> VICTOR JOHNSON, a rummager
> KOCH, a chiropractor who coaches the Pony League in baseball

The Story

This story does not go anywhere in any conventional sense. Rather it quite exquisitely sets a tone, delicately sketches an environment, and projects a slice of history dealing with how the West was settled and with the generalized types of people who settled it. First published in *Prairie Schooner* and subsequently in *Harpers*, "Nebraska" is a story of place. The town in which it is set remains unnamed, although at the very beginning, Ron Hansen offers a catalog of place-names—Americus, Covenant, Denmark, Grange, Hooray, Jerusalem, and Sweetwater—any of which might identify the small town in which the story is set. These towns are too small to be on any but the most specialized regional maps. Hansen creates a prototype for a typical, tiny Nebraska town.

Although he names various people in his story, the author develops none of these people as rounded characters. He mentions their names, offers a fact or two about each, then moves on. If there is any looming character in the story, it is the small town that significantly shapes the outlooks and lives of those who live in it.

The town and the area take on lives of their own. They exist as discrete entities, flat bodies spread out on a flat landscape. The only outside life pulsing through them comes from the Union Pacific trains that lumber through the town several times a day, occasionally stopping just long enough to deposit a boxcar full of supplies on a siding. The railroad tracks are the arteries of the recumbent body that is the town.

Little happens in this story or to the few people who populate it. Just as the population of the small Nebraska town is sparse, so is the population of the story. Hansen relates how some people convert their porches to sleeping quarters for boys who will soon join the navy and find themselves on ships whose populations are as great as that of the town from which they come.

Most of the pioneers who settled Nebraska are of German, Swedish, Danish, and Polish stock. They journeyed west from the east coast ports through which they entered the country, finally reaching Nebraska, where many of them settled because, exhausted and disoriented, they compromised, following the path of least resistance.

Here they built their first dwellings, sod houses—largely holes in the ground with wooden supports to hold up the blocks of sod from which the walls and roof were made. Such dwellings were buried in snow during the harsh prairie winters and emerged crumbling with the spring thaw.

"Nebraska" is largely nostalgic. It briefly sketches salient details about each season: the hay trucks spraying the gray highway with hay in July; October with its full grain silos and trees stripped of their leaves; January with heavy snow obliterating the highways and freezing the water on the Democrat so solid that people can walk clear across the river; April with snow still "pettycoating" the tree trunks.

Victor Johnson goes rummaging in an old garage, again evoking feelings of nostalgia. He finds an antiquated, windup Victrola and stacks of records from the 1920's, abandoned farm equipment, high-topped shoes, and a wooden film projector painted silver, along with big cans of old film. There are pictures, including one of a daredevil aviator who walks on the wings of biplanes.

Hansen understands the effect small-town prairie life has on those who live in such an environment. Everyone knows everyone else and, more important, knows everyone else's business. As Hansen says, everyone in the town is necessary, everyone enjoys the sort of identity of which people who live in large cities are often deprived. He does not suggest whether this is good or bad. Indeed, it is difficult to judge its goodness or badness in absolute terms. It seems—on the surface at least—wholesome, although the undercurrents that pervade such communities can be pernicious. Hansen presents bare facts and invites his readers to arrive at their own conclusions.

Themes and Meanings

Although Hansen remains the objective observer for most of this story, he reveals some of his own reactions to small-town Nebraska life. He describes the one Protestant church in town—a crisp, white building with a steeple—but he juxtaposes it to the Immaculate Conception Catholic Church that he says holds the town at bay like a German wolfhound. Generally classified as an American Catholic writer who is sometimes compared to Flannery O'Connor, Hansen obviously finds Roman Catholicism a more daunting religion than the Protestantism that the crisp white church represents. Although he makes no direct comment about religion in this story, he suggests the outward differences that exist between the two major Christian religious forces in the United States.

He enumerates in a helter-skelter manner an intermixture of some of the people and businesses in town—the insurance agency, the country coroner and justice of the peace, a tavern, a post office, a secondhand shop, a handsome chiropractor named Koch who coaches the Pony League baseball team—but these are mere impressionistic enumerations. Hansen does not comment or expand on any of them, even though he has earlier stated that the town's citizens go to the Vaughn Grocery Store for their daily news—presumably gossip—and to the Home Restaurant for what he terms "their history class," very likely meaning conversations in which the elderly patrons reminisce about the town and their memories of its past.

Hansen also enumerates what the town lacks—book stores, film houses, a dry cleaner, a pharmacy, a jewelry store, a piano store, a motel, a hotel, a hospital, and, perhaps most tellingly, extreme opinions and philosophical theories about Being and the soul. The story contains numerous catalogs of place-names, people, and objects all calculated to help readers evoke memories of elements drawn from their own lives. Thematically, the implication is that life is composed of a surfeit of impressions, most of them occurring in no logical sequence, as people pass through their individual existences. The totality of these impressions makes people what they are. People become the sum of what they experience.

Style and Technique

Hansen is a consummate stylist, an author fully in control of the elements of effective writing. He is particularly strong in his physical descriptions of place, as he demonstrates in his early novels such as *Desperadoes: A Novel* (1979) and *The Assassination of Jesse James by the Coward Robert Ford* (1983).

His similes and metaphors are striking and memorable. He refers to the air as being as crisp as Oxydol and describes the town's water tower as being "belittled" by the sloppy tattoo of one year's senior class at the high school. He sees a heavy snow "partitioning" the landscape. The town's houses are very similar, each a "cousin" to the next. The area's fruit trees are planted so close together that they cannot sway without "knitting." Other trees, stripped of their leaves in winter, raise their gray limbs in "alleluia."

Hansen captures compellingly the isolation of small prairie towns and the insularity that is a consequence of this isolation. In the small town about which he writes, everyone, according to Hansen, is famous in the sense that everyone is known. The Kiwanis Club meets every Tuesday night and resolves petty sins, then empties the gumball machines and deploys the proceeds for the upkeep of the local playground. At the Home Restaurant, old people eat pot roast and gravy followed by lemon meringue pie. Everything is ordinary, everything middle of the road.

The Union Pacific trains, the town's one link with the outside world, do not stop regularly in the town. When they do stop, it is not to take on or disgorge passengers but merely to put on the siding a car containing the supplies the town needs for its sustenance.

Hansen captures fully the utter sameness of every day in the kind of small town about which he writes. The people who live there are as flat as the surrounding prairie. They dare not risk having extravagant emotions. They are solid, rock-of-Gibralter types, good citizens ready to help their neighbors when the need arises but not out to change society in any significant way.

R. Baird Shuman

THE NECKLACE

Author: Guy de Maupassant (1850-1893)
Type of plot: Social realism
Time of plot: About 1884
Locale: Paris
First published: "La Parure," 1884 (English translation, 1903)

> *Principal characters:*
> MADAME MATHILDE LOISEL, a lower-middle-class housewife
> MONSIEUR LOISEL, her husband, an insignificant bureaucrat
> MADAME JEANNE FORESTIER, her rich friend

The Story

Mathilde Loisel is attractive and pretty, but unhappy, very unhappy. She believes that life has played her false. She feels relegated to a lower station than she deserves. She wanted to be appreciated and loved by some rich gentleman from a good family, but instead, having no dowry, she had to settle for a junior clerk in the Ministry of Public Instruction. Her existence is one of constant frustration. She hates her plain apartment, its absence of pictures on the walls, its shoddy furniture. Even the sight of her maid, doing housework, fills her with hopeless regrets and provokes flights of fancy about more opulent surroundings. Though other women of her class may come to terms with their station in life, Mathilde never can.

She is so humiliated by her lower-middle-class existence that she even refuses to see one of her old friends whom she has known from her days at the convent school. Madame Forestier is wealthy, and Mathilde finds visits to her too painful to bear; so, she spends her days hanging around her drab flat, sometimes crying the entire time, overcome with worry, regret, desperation, and distress.

Her husband, on the other hand, seems better adjusted. He does not notice that the tablecloth has been in use for three days. When he is served a simple casserole, he can exclaim with pleasure: "Well, a good hot-pot. I don't know anything better than that." One day, he comes home from his office with an invitation to a party that is being given by his superior, the minister of public instruction. Instead of greeting the news with delight, Mathilde throws the invitation down on the table, saying that it is no good to her, because she has nothing suitable to wear for such an occasion. Her husband tries to convince her that it was very difficult for a junior clerk to get asked to such an event. "You will see the whole world of officialdom there," he says, suggesting that she wear that good-looking dress she once wore to the theater. She refuses and tells him to give the invitation to a colleague whose wife is better turned out than she.

Monsieur Loisel tries another tack. He asks her how much it would cost to get a proper dress. She thinks it over, trying to estimate what an old pinchpenny like him would be willing to spend. She decides on the sum of four hundred francs that, as it happens, is exactly the amount that he has put away to buy himself a gun so he could join some friends who go Sunday lark-shooting on the Nanterre flatlands. He is not happy to forgo his pleasure but agrees.

An appropriate dress is ordered and is ready before the date of the dance. Mathilde, however, is still depressed. Now she complains that she does not have any jewelry to wear with it. Her husband suggests flowers. She is unimpressed. He then suggests that she go to her rich friend Madame Forestier and borrow some jewelry. His wife thinks it a good idea and the next day goes and explains the situation to her. Madame Forestier is more than willing to comply and goes to a wardrobe to get a large jewelry casket. She tells Mathilde to take what she likes.

Such an embarrassment of riches makes it difficult for Mathilde to make up her mind. She asks to see something else. Suddenly, she discovers a black satin case that contains a magnificent necklace, "a river of diamonds." With tremulous voice she asks if she may borrow this item. "But yes, certainly," says her friend. Mathilde throws her arms around her friend's neck, and then joyously hurries home with her treasure.

At the minister's party, Mathilde scores a success. She appears to be the prettiest woman in the room; all men's eyes are on her. Even the minister notices her. She dances throughout the night, leaving her exhausted husband dozing in a small drawing room with three other husbands whose wives are also enjoying themselves. When the party breaks up at four o'clock, Mathilde wants to get away as fast as possible because she does not want the other women, who all wear furs, to notice her plain cloth coat. She runs out to the street hoping to find a cab, but the search takes her down to the Seine where, at last, she and her husband find an old dilapidated brougham stationed along the embankment. The ride back to their dismal apartment is sad for Mathilde with her fresh memories of her triumph.

Once home, as she is taking off her wraps, she discovers that the necklace is no longer around her neck. They search her clothes: nothing. Her husband goes out and retraces their path home. He returns several hours later having found nothing. The next day, he goes to the police and files a report. He then advertises in the lost-and-found in the papers, but still, nothing. To give them time to continue the search, they tell Madame Forestier that the clasp on the necklace is being repaired. After five days, however, when nothing shows up, they decide that the necklace is truly gone and they must have it replaced.

They take the necklace case from jeweler to jeweler to find a strand of diamonds that matches the one lost. They finally see one in a shop at the Palais-Royal. The price, with a four-thousand-franc discount, is thirty-six thousand francs. The Loisels pay for it with an eighteen-thousand-franc inheritance that the husband has received from his father, and by borrowing the rest in small amounts, thereby mortgaging their lives for the next decade. The replacement necklace is returned to Madame Forestier, who remarks rather coldly that it should have been returned sooner because she might have needed it. She does not bother to open the case.

The Loisels are left with their debts. They get rid of their maid. They move to a poorer apartment. The wife now has to do all the menial work herself: wash the sheets, carry garbage down to the street, carry up the water, do her own shopping, bargaining with everybody to save a few sous. The husband moonlights, working in the evenings for a bookkeeper and often at nights, doing copying at twenty-five centimes a page. This goes on year after year until the debt is paid. The time of penury has transformed Mathilde into a poor, prematurely old hag, with a loud voice, red hands, and neglected hair, but in her misery she often remembers the minister's ball, where she had her great success. What, she asks herself, would have been her fortune had she not lost the necklace?

One Sunday, as she strolls along the Champs-Elysees, she sees Madame Forestier taking a child for a walk. Jeanne Forestier is still young-looking and attractive. Now that the debt for the necklace has been satisfied, Mathilde Loisel decides to tell her old friend everything that happened. She stops to speak to her but is not recognized until she introduces herself. She explains that life has been pretty grim. She tells her about the lost necklace, how she had it replaced and for the past ten years has been slaving to pay for it. She is relieved that the long ordeal is over, and naïvely proud that her friend never knew that a different necklace had been returned to her.

Madame Forestier is deeply touched. Taking both of her friend's hands she says, "Oh! My poor Mathilde! But mine was a fake. It was worth no more than five hundred francs!"

Themes and Meanings

In this cruel tale about ridiculous social pretensions, the main characters obviously get the fate they deserve. This is the world of the Parisian lower middle class, but it could well serve as an allegory for French society as a whole, or at least those elements of French society where ambition, materialism, greed, and petty meanness are the main dynamic. Mathilde bears a striking resemblance to Madame Bovary. Both feel trapped in a provincially dull existence, made worse by the solid mediocrity of their husbands. Both long for deliverance, but the deliverance that only money can buy. The party attended by the Loisels at the town house of the minister is not unlike the soiree that the Bovarys attend at the chateau of the count. Even the descriptions of the opulence of both settings seems interchangeable.

Both heroines pay a terrible price for their inability to come to terms with their situation in life. In the case of Emma Bovary, the cost is her own life, ended by suicide; with Mathilde Loisel, the torture is more prolonged. She has thrown away her youth and will have to live with her misery for the rest of her life. The grand party whose pleasant memory has sustained her even while she has been drudging to pay off her enormous debt now becomes a hideous nightmare.

This, in one way or another, is the price to be paid for crass materialism and false pride. Had the characters been less superficial and been willing to admit the loss of the necklace, all of their misery would have been avoided. In accepting a code of conduct that befits their ambitions, not their real situation, they courted disaster. In this the husband is as much to blame as his wife. Although Guy de Maupassant seems to be saying that such people are the victims of the society in which they live, dominated by the status-conscious in the early days of the Third Republic, he never prevents his characters from exercising their free will. It is precisely their ability to make such choices that leads to their own damnation. Maupassant shows how the Loisels are imprisoned in their loneliness and their lack of self-worth. Their pathos is their inability to speak to avoid a whole lifetime of misery.

Style and Technique

Maupassant learned much from his godfather and mentor, Gustave Flaubert, displaying in his short stories the same precision and sobriety of language. Maupassant is particularly good in creating atmosphere by describing sights and smells, places and things. He likes to describe his characters through the way that they view their own surroundings:

> She dreamed of hushed antichambers cushioned with oriental fabrics and illuminated by tall bronze candle sticks, with two imposing footmen in knee breeches, made drowsy by the oppressive heat of the radiators, dozing in large arm chairs. She imagined great rooms bedecked with ancient silk, with splendid furniture decorated with expensive knick-knacks, and of smaller intimate perfumed rooms, intended for five o'clock gossip with the closest friends, the men well-known and sought-after enjoying the envy and attention of every woman.

Although Maupassant tried to suppress his own passions to achieve that objectivity of description for which the realists were known, his sententiousness, nevertheless, shines through:

> Women have no class and no breeding. Their beauty, their grace, their charm are substitutes for birth and family. Their instinctive shrewdness, their predilection for elegance, their suppleness of spirit are their only system of rank, and in this way the daughters of the common people are the equals of the great ladies.

In this rather pessimistic view of women, Maupassant has descended to the level of the cliché, something that he is rarely guilty of doing, but he also gives his main character a deterministic slant, making her more a victim of forces beyond her control than he undoubtedly intended.

Wm. Laird Kleine-Ahlbrandt

NEIGHBOR ROSICKY

Author: Willa Cather (1873-1947)
Type of plot: Social realism
Time of plot: The 1920's, with flashbacks to the 1880's
Locale: Nebraska, London, New York
First published: 1920

>   *Principal characters:*
>   ANTON ROSICKY, a Czech immigrant who is farming in Nebraska
>   MARY, his wife
>   RUDOLPH, his oldest son
>   DR. ED BURLEIGH, the family physician and a friend
>   POLLY, Rudolph's wife

The Story

"Neighbor Rosicky" begins with Anton Rosicky's having a medical checkup and learning from Dr. Burleigh that he has a bad heart. Sixty-five years old, Rosicky has worked hard all of his life, and the doctor urges him to take it easy, to cut back on farmwork and spend more time instead helping his wife around the house. Rosicky has five sons and one daughter, who can do the manual labor on their Nebraska farm. A contented man who enjoys his family, Rosicky is not a workaholic, and he follows the doctor's advice.

As Rosicky leaves, Dr. Burleigh thinks about the man and his family, for whom he feels deep affection. Rosicky has the knack of always being interested in things, of embracing life, taking the hard times philosophically, and not getting depressed. Those in his family have natural good manners and offer generous hospitality. Though they are far less affluent than most neighboring farmers, they seem to enjoy themselves more and are free from the mania of acquisitiveness.

However, life has not been easy for Rosicky, and several times he thinks back to the hardships of his youth. A Czech by birth and upbringing, Rosicky emigrated at eighteen to London, where for two years he experienced the harshness of Victorian poverty while he worked in a tailor's shop. With the help of some rich Bohemians, he sailed to New York when he was twenty and took up work as a tailor, enjoying his bachelor life and the cultural offerings of the city. For fifteen years, he was happy with this existence, but becoming increasingly restless and wanting to be the first of his family ever to own land, he went to Nebraska at thirty-five, married, and made a fresh start as a farmer, eventually owning his own farm, a place in which he takes pride, though the land is poor and produces less than that of his more prosperous neighbors.

Now Rosicky's oldest son, Rudolph, is married to a town girl, and Rosicky worries that his daughter-in-law may be so bored with farm life and his son so frustrated by bad weather and poor harvests that they will give up farming and move to the city, where Rudolph can find salaried work as a mechanic. Rosicky considers cities harsh and cruel to the poor and fears that Rudolph will lose his independence. Polly, Rudolph's wife, is a bit standoffish from her immigrant relatives but warms to Rosicky when he shows his affection and concern by arranging for her and her husband to borrow his car and go to town Saturday evenings, while he cleans up behind them.

The day before Christmas, Rosicky tells his family that they do not know what hard times are and relates to them the conditions of his youth. He is worried that the second generation may lack his patience and power of endurance, and he hopes that they can get through life without experiencing cruelty.

In the spring, Rosicky is at Rudolph's farm, raking up thistles that his son has ignored but that he fears will ruin the alfalfa crop, when he has a heart attack. Polly helps him to bed, sits with him, and realizes the depth of his love for her. The attack passes, and Rosicky goes home, seemingly recovered, but the next morning after breakfast, a second attack kills him.

Themes and Meanings

Like Willa Cather's novel *Death Comes for the Archbishop* (1927), her tribute to the heroic Catholic leaders of territorial New Mexico, "Neighbor Rosicky" is the account of an admirable life and the portrait of an idealized person, worthy of emulation. As the reader sees Rosicky through the eyes of his doctor, his wife and children, his daughter-in-law, and through his own thoughts, words, and deeds, he emerges as a kind, considerate, courteous, gentle, generous, soft-spoken, humorous, and self-reliant man whose life seems to Dr. Burleigh to be "complete and beautiful." The message for the reader is that one should try to have an equally admirable character, to accept life with amusement and interest rather than to complain of ill fortune or to compete with ruthless cruelty to get ahead of others. What Polly discovers about Rosicky is that he "had a special gift for loving people."

Despite that love and his deep loyalty to his family, Rosicky is self-contained and endowed with self-respect. The most disagreeable feeling he knows is embarrassment. He and his wife have agreed not to hurry through life skimping and saving. When there is a crop failure one year, Rosicky responds by having a picnic. There is no use feeling sorry for oneself, and he and his family survive the year better by keeping up their spirits rather than wallowing in self-pity, as others do. A good craftsperson, Rosicky takes his time with his work, taking pride in doing things right.

"Neighbor Rosicky" could easily have been flawed by sentimentality, but Cather avoids it by showing the grim details of Rosicky's youth and the continuing unpredictability and hardness of farm life. Rosicky is not simply a lovable old man; he is a survivor, like Ernest Hemingway's old fisherman Santiago. Having encountered evil, Rosicky is careful to avoid it and not to inflict it on others. Having finally achieved independence as a farmer on his own land, he sees the agrarian life as one of freedom and cities as places where the poor suffer and are exploited. Aware of "depraved and poisonous specimens of man," Rosicky sets an example to the contrary for his children and for the reader. He exemplifies what William Faulkner meant when he said that man will not merely endure but will prevail because he has a soul capable of pity, pride, compassion, sacrifice, and endurance.

Style and Technique

"Neighbor Rosicky" has a minimum of plot and a maximum of characterization. The story resembles the novel demeuble, or unfurnished, which Cather invented to strip the narrative of excessive characters and incidents in order to concentrate on a central character. Reduced to the bare facts, the narrative in the present consists only of Rosicky's medical diagnosis, his developing friendship with Polly, and his death. Cather provides a richer texture, however, by having Dr. Burleigh reflect several times on Rosicky's character, his family, and the values they represent, as well as by having Rosicky reflect on his own past and at one time tell a long story about his youth. Thus the reader sees the contrast between his difficult beginnings and the tranquil life he has accomplished as well as a conflict between the first generation of immigrants and their children, whose lives are easier and expectations, higher.

As in all of Cather's writing, the style is clear, spare, and uncluttered, an art that conceals its artistry. The writing has some of the austerity of the pioneer life that Cather admired.

Robert E. Morsberger

NEIGHBORS

Author: Raymond Carver (1938-1988)
Type of plot: Psychological
Time of plot: The mid-twentieth century
Locale: An American apartment house
First published: 1971

> *Principal characters:*
> BILL MILLER, a middle-aged bookkeeper
> ARLENE MILLER, his wife

The Story

The Millers and the Stones live in apartments across a hallway from each other. The two couples appear to have lives fundamentally alike. Bill and Arlene Miller, however, feel they are missing out on the better things in life. They believe that the Stones' lives are more satisfying, more exciting, than theirs. The Millers particularly envy the fact that the Stones frequently socialize and travel. When the Stones leave on a ten-day trip, they ask the Millers to care for their plants and cat. In the few days after the Stones depart, both Bill and Arlene are transformed by their explorations of the Stones' home.

The responsibility of caring for the Stones' household becomes an opportunity to take over their possessions, to occupy the spaces of their most private lives, to become the Stones. During the first evening of the Stones' absence, Bill Miller enters their domain, delights in its very air, ogles at their ordinary treasures, pockets a bottle of Harriet's prescription medicine, swigs their Chivas Regal, and stakes a strangely thrilling proprietary claim on their way of life.

Bill's initial incursion into the Stones' world arouses his sexual energy and leads him to break his own routines at home and at work. During a second visit to his neighbors' apartment the next day, Bill rummages through their cupboards, refrigerator, and bedroom. He takes a pack of cigarettes before he is interrupted by his wife, who is sharply curious about his long stay. The next day, Bill is so preoccupied he does not go to work. Again he enters the Stones' lives, and his violation of his neighbors' personal privacy is still bolder. Reveling in his dominion over their most intimate spaces, he locks up the cat and masturbates on his neighbor's bed, then dons Jim's clothing, and finally changes into Harriet's underwear, skirt, and blouse, losing his sense of his own identity in the process, or perhaps merging with their identities.

Bill's sexual arousal and long journeys next door do not escape Arlene's notice. She also takes a trip into the Stones' world. When she answers Bill's impatient knock and steps into the hall, she appears flushed and flecked with white lint as if she has duplicated Bill's indulgences in the pleasures of the Stones' bed. Standing close to each other, aroused, on the brink of thrilling sexual travel together in this magic realm of their neighbors' apartment to look at pictures that Arlene has found, Bill and Arlene discover she has left the key inside. Abruptly, they find themselves locked out of their new lives. They both appear stricken; Bill utters what seem to be inappropriate words, "Don't worry." One would think this is merely a brief delay of their gratification. However, they cling together, apparently paralyzed by emotions powerful but not explicit. Is it loss, fear, excitement, shame, guilt, or something else that they feel as they brace themselves for what is to come?

Themes and Meanings

Bill and Arlene Miller's violations of propriety and privacy may come as a shock to the reader. The trust given them by the Stones is betrayed by these pallid people in a series of abuses that escalate in offensiveness. Readers may experience a further shock as they recognize in the Millers' behavior their own suppressed impulses to snoop, their own persistent urges to know others' most intimate secrets. In this regard, the Millers mirror universal impulses. Indeed, to gain such knowledge is a kind of intercourse accompanied by a secret thrill, a psychic rape for the reader as it is for Bill and Arlene. Readers may even realize to their chagrin that as readers—literary voyeurs—they, like Bill and Arlene, are entering into and vicariously sharing the closely held secrets of others' lives.

The story seems to suggest, however, that this impulse to know, explore, and even take over others' lives is exacerbated in Bill and Arlene's case by the emotional and spiritual emptiness in their lives. The protagonists represent the condition of modern man and woman, hollow at their centers; they are humans who know they are missing something. They believe that what they are missing is possessed by others but withheld from them. Their belief is mistaken, it seems, for the story suggests that others may be in exactly the same condition.

The Millers, like so many others, seek to fill the void in their inner lives with things they can take possession of, such as drugs, alcohol, food, gewgaws, and clothes. These external stimulants arouse them but do not satisfy their inner hungers. Finally, the drive to consume those other people who have more satisfying lives takes over. The Stones themselves must be ingested, acquired, totally assimilated, obliterated, sacrificed to fill the awful emptiness. "What's gotten into you?" asks Arlene when she begins to sense that Bill has quite literally taken possession of the Stones and their lives. Both Bill and Arlene soon find that such psychic possession is arousing but not truly satisfying. They must return like addicts to the Stones' apartment. For a moment Bill becomes an adventurer, a rogue, a man capable of being thrilled, a man capable of thrilling his wife. He feels more alive, but the fix he has given himself does not last long. He must get more. At the end of the story, both Bill and Arlene have eaten of the fruit of the tree of the knowledge of good and evil, and they suddenly and inexplicably stand outside the entrance to their Garden of Eden, cut off. Clutching each other at the apartment door, they are a shaking Adam and Eve in exile, overwhelmed by their sudden loss and their unknown future.

The behavior of the Millers is not to be interpreted as sexually deviant. The perversity of their behavior is more disturbing than that. Their cramped, bland, lusterless, but comfortable lives mirror their inner emptiness, their spiritual vacuity. Beneath the muted surface of their lives is a seething restlessness and loneliness that, if confronted, could turn their lives from banality to horror. Perhaps it is against that horror that they brace themselves at the end of the tale, as they stand holding each other at the Stones' door, so close to looking at the terrible mirror in the other's eyes.

Style and Technique

Raymond Carver's fiction, especially his earlier stories, has been described as minimalist because of its remarkable flatness of tone, unadorned language, spare plot lines, and characters bereft of identity and affect. This was the story with which Carver first entered American popular magazines, and it launched his career as a major literary figure. In keeping with this minimalist style, "Neighbors" follows an ordinary couple whose lives have little pleasure, little drama, little distinction, through three days behind doors not just closed but locked. When the story ends, neither they nor the reader can say exactly what transpired, if anything. These are protagonists who live unexamined lives on deadend streets.

One recurring image is that of the mirror. Invading some new corner of the Stones' private realm, Bill frequently turns to a mirror as if he is uncertain who he is. Perhaps he is looking for an outward sign of the life transformation he seeks. Has the shadow of discontent that darkens his every moment been lightened? Perhaps he just wants to be sure he still exists. This dependence on a reflection to be assured of the status of his own being is a powerful metaphor for his inner emptiness and lack of sense of self. In contrast, Arlene is not seen looking into a mirror. Bill is her mirror. She responds to and repeats the changes in him. The Millers misunderstand the nature of their quest so badly that even when they symbolically appropriate others' lives, they expect that their transformations into more alive, more exciting, human beings will show up in the mirror.

Some critics have found Carver's flat prose, arid landscape, muddled and unhappy characters, and enigmatic endings nihilistic, vapid, or pointlessly bizarre. Others argue that such unhappy and empty people, unable to even articulate their own pains much less fix their own lives, are powerful evocations of the modern experience of living lives without significance.

Virginia M. Crane

NEIGHBORS

Author: Diane Oliver (1943-1966)
Type of plot: Realism
Time of plot: The early 1960's
Locale: A state in the South
First published: 1966

Principal characters:
ELLIE MITCHELL, the protagonist, a young black woman
TOMMY MITCHELL, her little brother
JIM MITCHELL, their father
MRS. MITCHELL, their mother

The Story

Set in the school desegregation period, "Neighbors" focuses on the conflicts faced by one black family, which has decided to defy custom and send its small son to a white school. The events of the story take place on the day before Tommy Mitchell is to go to the white school for the first time. Interestingly, the tensions are seen through the eyes of Tommy's older sister, Ellie Mitchell, who is old enough to fear for her brother but not old enough to make the hard choices that the parents must face.

In the first part of the story, Ellie is making her way home from work to her own house. Everything and everyone she sees remind her of the danger faced by Tommy and the family. When a well-dressed man on the bus stares at Ellie, she wonders whether her family is pictured in the newspaper he is reading. The foreboding weather and the silent main street, though not unnatural, seem ominous under the circumstances.

However, there is more than Ellie's imagination to make her nervous. A stranger in a Chevrolet calls Ellie over to promise revenge if Tommy is harmed; a friend signals with crossed fingers; an old man speculates on what will happen to Tommy. When Ellie reaches home, the strange cars in front, the locked door, the serious men in the living room, and the drawer full of threatening letters all remind her that Tommy is a marker in a game played for keeps.

Tommy, too, is apprehensive, clinging to his favorite book, asking whether he will be hurt. Nervously, Mrs. Mitchell asks Ellie to take her place in the group that will go with Tommy to the school, and Ellie agrees. Then, after Tommy is in bed and the men have all left, just as the family is ready to settle down for the night, the house is bombed. Although no one is hurt, the parents rethink their plans and at last decide not to send Tommy to the white school.

Themes and Meanings

The title "Neighbors" suggests that the story is about more than the conflict between blacks and whites. Through the still young eyes of the protagonist, Ellie, it reveals the fragmentation of a society in which everyone is increasingly alone, which because of racial tension has negated the homey notion of friendly neighbors.

One indication of the loss of community in society is Ellie's own increasing awareness of color difference. On the bus, she notices the proportion of blacks to whites. In the neighborhood, she notes that blacks and whites no longer play together once they have started school. Seeing a black car, she stops herself from laughing about its shiny blackness. Throughout the story, it is the "white people" who are threatening her little brother and her family. It is the white people who follow her family, photograph them, and write stories implying, for example, that the Mitchells are on welfare. It is the white people who write the threatening letters and who finally carry out their threats. Therefore, after the blast, Ellie concludes that white people cannot be trusted. By their own rejection of Tommy, the whites have produced in Ellie a rejection of them.

In the breakup of the neighborly ideal, the statement of the man in the Chevrolet is significant. He and his friends are ready to take revenge on the whites for anything that happens to Tommy. After the blast, after she realizes that ordinarily she slept under the now shattered window, Ellie recalls the man in the Chevrolet and thinks that the revenge he suggested would be only justice.

Aside from the growing hatred between whites and blacks, however, there is a loss of neighborliness within the black community. After the blast, no one comes to the Mitchell house; no one does the neighborly thing. Everyone is afraid to get involved.

In pleading with her husband, Tommy's mother points out what no one has remembered—not the white fanatics, not the black militants, not the frightened neighbors. Tommy is not a pawn. He is a little boy, too young to hate people or to understand why they hate him. At the end of the story, the parents make a very human decision. Feeling compassion for the child who has been ignored as a person by all those who think of causes, insisting that they alone must take responsibility for whatever happens to him, the Mitchells decide to keep him home. In the final analysis, they are a family under siege, and they will surrender rather than permit a small child to be harmed. It is an indication of the irony of the title that neither the neighbors on the street nor the "neighbors" in the community as a whole have thought about what is happening or may happen to little Tommy. However, the concept of neighborliness does indeed assume that one is accepted as an individual simply because one lives in proximity to another person—in other words, because of where one is and not because of who one is.

Style and Technique

Diane Oliver's style is simple and restrained, illustrating through the perceptions of Ellie Mitchell the real conflicts in one town at one time in history. Because the story contrasts the public issues with the private reactions of those people involved with the issues, Oliver sets up a pattern of objects that Ellie notices, some of which are familiar and safe, others of which are related to a new time for her family, a time of fear. By juxtaposing the images of everyday security and those of unusual danger, Oliver suggests the nightmare in which the family is involved.

For example, Ellie cannot keep her mind on the clothes in the store windows because of her apprehensions. Just as she has been glancing at the raincoat, the man in the Chevrolet assures her of his willingness to take violent action. Helping her friend Saraline to sneak out on a date, Ellie is reminded of the crisis by crossed fingers. On the familiar street, where Mr. Paul sits as usual, she is told that the whites may spit on her brother.

At Ellie's house, the familiar is once again juxtaposed to the unfamiliar. The geranium pot, the familiar sofa, a pitcher of ice water—all are everyday images, contrasting with the route plan on paper on which the men are working. The kitchen, the yellow sun on the wall, her mother peeling potatoes—all point up the horror of the threatening envelopes. However, although the evidences of the outside ugliness have penetrated the Mitchell home, it still seems a safe place until the bomb blast, which proves that geraniums, freshly ironed clothes, and Uncle Wiggily are all vulnerable. When the living-room window is shattered, the geranium pot broken, Ellie knows that the objects of everyday life can be destroyed, and so can the small boy.

At the end of the story, the fight is abandoned so that Tommy and the symbols of security can survive. Mrs. Mitchell begins to get breakfast and to straighten the kitchen. The table, the clock, the dishes, the oatmeal—all these objects are meant to reestablish the illusion of security that was shattered when the bomb exploded, though no one in the Mitchell family will now take the same comfort as before in those familiar objects. When they broke, a world shattered.

Rosemary M. Canfield Reisman

NEVADA GAS

Author: Raymond Chandler (1888-1959)
Type of plot: Mystery and detective
Time of plot: The 1930's
Locale: Los Angeles
First published: 1935

> *Principal characters:*
> JOHNNY DeRUSE, a gambler
> HUGO CANDLESS, a wealthy and powerful Los Angeles attorney
> NAOMI CANDLESS, Hugo's wife
> GEORGE DIAL, one of Hugo's employees
> FRANCINE LEY, George Dial's girlfriend
> MOPS PARISI, a mobster
> ZAPPARTY, a Reno gangster
> CHARLES "CHUCK" LEGRAND, a mobster
> NICKY, a friend of Johnny DeRuse
> KUVALICK, a house detective

The Story

Hugo Candless, a wealthy and powerful Los Angeles attorney, is playing squash with an employee, George Dial, at the Delmar Club. He goes outside to board what he thinks is his limousine. As his cigar smoke fills the passenger compartment, he reaches for the window handle and finds that there is none. There are no door handles or communication tube either, and as the limousine follows an unfamiliar course into the hills, the odor of almonds fills the passenger compartment. Candless is being killed with cyanide gas, the kind used to execute criminals in Nevada.

Meanwhile, George Dial visits his girlfriend, Francine Ley. He tells her to leave her other boyfriend, a gambler named Johnny DeRuse, for him, but Francine points out that George does not have enough money. George tells Francine not to worry: He has information about Hugo Candless that can get him some money. Candless double-crossed a Reno gangster, Zapparty, whose half brother was on trial for murder. The lawyer took twenty-five thousand dollars to defend the gangster's relative but instead made a deal on another case with the district attorney and allowed Zapparty's half brother to go to prison and be executed.

While George and Francine are talking and drinking, they are watched by Johnny DeRuse, who has come in quietly. After a time, Johnny bangs the door to make it appear that he has just entered, strides past the couple, and goes into Francine's bedroom, where he begins packing his suitcase. He also straps a small pistol to his leg. As Johnny packs, George departs. Johnny tells Francine that he is leaving her because he saw a mobster, Mops Parisi, who could give him trouble because Johnny once called the police when he knew that Parisi had arranged a kidnaping. Francine says that the real reason he is leaving is that he knows that he is losing her to George, who, in spite of appearances, is a tougher man than he.

As Johnny leaves Francine's apartment, he is accosted by two men who hold him at gunpoint, take the gun that Johnny has kept in a shoulder holster, and lead him into the limousine in which Hugo Candless died. However, the two men, one of whom is called Chuck, overlook the gun that Johnny has concealed on his leg, and, using this weapon, Johnny kills Chuck and shoots a hole in the thick glass. The car crashes, Johnny shoots and kills the driver, and searches the pockets of both men. He finds matches from the Club Egypt in one man's pocket, and the same kind of matches and a hotel key for room 809 at the Hotel Metropole in Chuck's pocket. Johnny drives the car back to town, parks it, and takes a cab back to Francine's apartment. He notes the license number of the limousine: SA6.

Johnny calls a friend at a newspaper to find out the name under which the car is registered and learns that it is Candless. Next, he calls Naomi Candless, who tells him that Candless is out of town but that she knows he left the Delmar Club earlier. Johnny then calls the Hotel Metropole and asks for Charles LeGrand in room 809. He is told that LeGrand is in 609. Driving to the Delmar Club, Johnny learns from the doorman there that Candless's limousine, license number 5A6, picked him up that afternoon, but his regular driver was not at the wheel. Johnny goes to Candless's apartment and visits the garage, where he sees Candless's limousine, license number SA6, and where the garage man tells him that the car has not been out all day. He also tells Johnny that Candless's chauffeur lives at the Hotel Metropole. Johnny goes there and finds the chauffeur in room 809, shot to death.

When Francine Ley returns to her apartment, Johnny is waiting for her. He explains that someone replaced Candless's car with an identical but deadly model, killed Candless's chauffeur and then Candless, and then tried to use the same execution method on him. Johnny tells Francine that he suspects her of setting him up because the men who tried to kill him knew where to pick him up that afternoon. Francine explains that George Dial knew that Candless had double-crossed Zapparty. Johnny tells her that Zapparty is the owner of the Club Egypt.

At the Club Egypt, Francine, Johnny, and his friend Nicky create a disturbance over a rigged roulette table in order to see Zapparty, whom they find in his office along with Mops Parisi. As Johnny talks to the two about the deadly limousine, a hand holding a gun appears in a secret panel and Johnny and his friends must now submit to Zapparty. Zapparty orders the person in the panel to go back to work downstairs. Zapparty and Parisi pistol-whip Johnny, but Johnny draws his leg gun and fatally shoots Parisi. Francine gets Zapparty's gun, and Johnny apologizes for not having trusted her.

Johnny sends Francine home in his car while Zapparty leads him and Nicky, in the murder car, to a deserted house, where Candless's body is hidden. Zapparty confesses that he and Parisi planned the kidnaping and murder of Candless as revenge for Zapparty's half brother's conviction and subsequent hanging. Candless's regular chauffeur was supposed to switch the cars and drive the murder car, but he got too drunk and had to be killed and replaced. Johnny still wants to know who set him up.

Johnny goes to Candless's apartment, sees George Dial's car outside, and asks for the help of the house detective, Kuvalick, in getting in to see George. When Kuvalick does not return from Mrs. Candless's apartment, Johnny breaks in and finds Kuvalick tied up. He had described Johnny to George Dial, and Dial has slugged him. Just then, Dial comes into the room with a gun in his hand. Kuvalick goes for his gun, and Dial shoots him. He confirms Johnny's theory that George and Mrs. Candless set up Candless and that George had also set the killers onto Johnny "for the hell of it." Johnny asks who told George that Johnny had escaped, and George tells him that Francine did but that she took too long to do it. Mrs. Candless appears and asks jealously who Francine is. She begins to struggle with Dial but Kuvalick, who wears a bulletproof vest, shoots them both to death.

Johnny returns to Francine's apartment and tells her the story, thanking her for her help. He falls asleep, murmuring about quitting the kind of life they lead. Francine soothes him to sleep and then looks at him for a long time.

Themes and Meanings

Although the superficial meaning of any murder mystery is contained in the answer to the questions of how the crime was planned and who did it, the great writers in this genre add something more, and in the case of "Nevada Gas," it is a chilling view of life in the amoral twentieth century. Unlike Raymond Chandler's later famous creation, the knightly Philip Marlowe, Johnny DeRuse is not interested in seeing that justice triumphs or in helping people. In Johnny's world, there is no good or bad, only the next piece of luck, be it the turn of a wheel, the flip of a card, or the draw of a gun. The only value is staying alive, and if that means killing someone else, so be it. When Dial shoots Kuvalick, apparently killing him, "no emotion showed in his face, not even excitement." However, Johnny is hardly better than Dial; he is only a bit cagier. He kills three people and also shows no emotion. In a world where there are no rules and everyone is out to get everyone else, there is a premium on staying one step ahead of the competition, as Johnny does by carrying one gun where it can easily be seen and taken, and then saving the day with his surprise leg pistol and, as Kuvalick does, by pretending to be dead until the right moment. The intellect is used not to enrich the mind and spirit but to defeat the next person, and cleverness is prized where there is no wisdom. Even Johnny's name, a pun on "the ruse," suggests trickery.

Johnny does not ask people for information; he pays them for it. The standard is economic, not moral. When Johnny speaks of changing his life, the reader cannot believe it, for there is no better life to achieve. Love is never even considered, even as a ghost of a youthful delusion, for Francine tells George that she will not leave Johnny for him, not because she does not love George enough but because he does not have enough money. Thus, when Francine stares at the sleeping Johnny at the end of the story, she looks at him not with love, which is impossible in the world they inhabit, but with admiration.

Style and Technique

Most of Chandler's works are written from the first-person point of view, enabling the reader to know exactly what the narrator is thinking about and planning to do. "Nevada Gas," however, is written from the third-person point of view, and, as a result, the reader sees Johnny and the other characters from the outside. Consequently, the reader is always a step or two behind the characters' motives and thinking and, thereby, behind the meaning of the action. For example, after Johnny's attempted murder, he immediately begins to search for the meaning of the clues he has, and the reader is left temporarily bewildered about his purpose. Part of the pleasure of a mystery story from the reader's point of view is to try to think along with the characters and thereby add life to the narrative. If the reader can figure out the mystery long before the sleuth does, then the writer has not done a good job.

The objective third-person point of view and rather unemotional characters of "Nevada Gas" are characteristic of the "hard-boiled" mysteries written by Chandler's contemporary, Dashiell Hammett, rather than of Chandler's wisecracking narrative style in the Philip Marlowe novels. Chandler's eye for the colorful detail that reveals a person's true nature is much in evidence, as when Johnny says, "When I lose I don't get sore and I don't chisel. I just move to the next table."

James Baird

THE NEW APARTMENT

Author: Heinz Huber (1922-   )
Type of plot: Social realism
Time of plot: The 1950's
Locale: Germany
First published: 1961

> *Principal characters:*
> THE NARRATOR, a middle-class German technician
> HIS WIFE
> MARX MESSEMER, his colleague
> KAY MESSEMER, his colleague's wife
> FRAULEIN KLIESING, a party guest

The Story

The narrator describes a bland and uneventful social gathering at the home of Marx and Kay Messemer, a young upwardly mobile couple who are proud of their newly acquired, completely refurbished apartment. Its wall-to-wall carpeting is graphite gray; its furniture is severely functional; and its walls are bare, except for a single painting. One of its few decorations is a leafless branch in a large glass vase. The effect reminds the narrator of the Italian artist Giorgio Chirico, whose surrealistic paintings of deserted city squares convey uncanny feelings of loneliness and melancholy.

The narrator, who admires his friend Marx, mentions that he considers such modest social gatherings to be significant in the development of a new society that is adapting to a changed environment. This comment is typical of the story's ambiguity and understatement. The hosts and their guests actually seem inhibited, determined to avoid any topics of conversation that might cause embarrassment. The apartment itself serves as a neutral topic that helps them evade more awkward or controversial matters.

The narrator describes Marx as a connoisseur of cool jazz, whose entire apartment suggests "cool jazz converted into armchairs, carpets, lamps (or rather light-fittings), and pictures." The Messemers boast about what they have achieved, spending much of the evening describing how they managed to get their place and how much time and thought have gone into its modernization. They reveal that the rooms were formerly occupied by two reclusive old widows, who lived among piles of accumulated junk and paid no attention to housekeeping or maintenance. This is thus not a new apartment in a modern building, but a modernized unit in an old building that has survived World War II.

After one of the widows died, the Messemers managed to have the other woman placed in a nursing home. From their descriptions of the maneuverings through which they went to get their apartment, it is clear that there has been an acute housing short-age since the surrender of Germany in the war. Embarrassed by this development in the conversation, the narrator states: "I had the feeling that Messemer now had really gone a bit too far."

Later in the evening, the host entertains his guests by playing some of his newest cool jazz records. Afterward, the narrator and his wife take a taxi home. He explains that they do not own a car yet but adds: "I'm quite confident we shall have one next year or the year after—provided that nothing comes in between, which I think rather improbable."

Themes and Meanings

Heinz Huber uses the symbol of a new apartment to represent the feelings of the German people in the years of privation, fear, and misery following World War II. During the war Germany was devastated by Allied bombing raids from the west and by relentless Soviet artillery attacks from the east. Millions of German soldiers and ci-vilians were killed, and Adolf Hitler's dream of a German empire evaporated. The German people were in the process of trying to reconstruct their country politically, socially, and culturally while cleaning up the rubble and rebuilding their cities. Ger-many was split into two sections and occupied by the armed forces of the United States, Great Britain, France, and the Soviet Union. The Cold War was threatening to erupt into a nuclear holocaust, and Germany was caught between the two hostile su-perpowers.

The people gathered at the Messemers' new apartment represent the new middle class emerging in postwar West Germany, where a free-enterprise economy was grad-ually bringing order, prosperity, and democracy, while East Germany stagnated under the oppressive rule of Soviet Communism. The Messemers and their guests wish to avoid talking about the horrors of the past and the uncertainties of the future. What they discuss is clearly of less importance than what they carefully avoid; they are afraid of all the emotions that lie just below the surface, emotions that include guilt, humiliation, anger, bewilderment, and grief. All of them undoubtedly had friends and relatives who were killed in the war.

Some of the men may even have had Nazi connections that might come back to haunt them. The men may have been involved in wartime atrocities. The past is thus a painful subject that they wish to avoid. The future is full of ominous uncertainty be-cause there was no way of knowing in the 1950's whether democracy and capitalism would survive, whether Germany would be engulfed by Soviet Communism, or whether the country might become the focal point of a nuclear Armageddon. The fact that the guests enjoy modern jazz suggests that they are pro-West, while their guarded conversation suggests that they are prepared to adapt to other standards, should the Soviets prevail.

The old widows who formerly occupied these rooms symbolize the old Germany. Both women lost their husbands during the war and had their lives ruined. Little can be done for such people. The younger generation who are taking charge of Germany's future would like to forget about them; they want to forget about the past. They would like the whole world to forget about what Germans did under Hitler, but they know it will take many decades for all the wounds to heal. They are a defeated people trying to build a new society without clear ideas as to how to go about it. Specters of the past and future seem to hang over the new apartment in an old building that has managed to escape destruction. The new apartment is the new Germany itself.

Style and Technique

The narrator makes repeated references to "cool jazz." This is one of many clues that Huber offers to the underlying meaning of his deceptively simple story. The writing style of "The New Apartment" itself emulates the techniques of modern jazz. Modern jazz is muted, flatted, understated, experimental, and emotionally subdued. Huber is writing the literary equivalent of what he calls "cool jazz." Modern jazz, like all jazz, emphasizes variations on a theme, which might be one of the so-called "standards" by composers like George Gershwin and Cole Porter, or a few bars of original notes that offer opportunities for improvisation. The theme must be known in order for the variations to be appreciated. In Huber's story the theme is the war and its aftermath; the text can only be understood by reference to the underlying theme of guilt, grief, fear, hope, and uncertainty—all of which are so well known to the Germans that their explicit expression is unnecessary.

Modern jazz musicians, like Huber's middle-class Germans of the 1950's, are searching for new directions; they are improvising. The choice of "cool jazz" as both a symbol and a literary technique is admirably appropriate to this short story. It is a brilliant overarching metaphor that, like all good metaphors, has ramified implications.

It is evident that Huber's characters are living in the western part of Germany, where democracy and free enterprise are putting down delicate roots. During the period in which the story is set, the Communist rulers hated jazz and did their best to suppress it, along with all other aspects of Western culture, wherever they held power. People in East Germany would have been afraid to gather to listen to jazz records. They also could not have lived in apartments like that of the Messemers, unless they were high-ranking Communist Party officials.

In order to be interesting, a short story must usually be dramatic. In order to be dramatic, it must contain conflict. There is considerable conflict in Huber's short story, but all of it is hidden, just as the old rooms formerly occupied by the bereaved widows are hidden under the new paint and neutral-colored carpeting. The guests are experiencing inner conflicts in their efforts to keep the party on a light, sophisticated plane and to avoid saying the wrong things. Hanging over their heads is the great psychological, ideological, economic, and military conflict of the two superpowers threatening each other with nuclear missiles and at the same time threatening to annihilate the fragile civilization that these postwar Germans are trying to create.

The five characters in the story are like members of a modern jazz combo. Marx Messemer is the lead soloist, the star performer. His wife, Kay, is a back-up soloist who merely echoes her husband's virtuoso improvisations without attempting to rival him or to break away on any new tangents. Marx might be compared to a jazz superstar, such as saxophonist Charlie Parker or trumpeter Miles Davis. Of Marx the narrator says: "When he's up to his style, his descriptions range themselves one on another like the colored flags that a conjuror pulls out of his mouth on a neverending string, gay and effortless." The same might be said of the great jazz stars. The other three characters might correspond to the drummer, the bass player, and the pianist, who merely provide the pulse and accompaniment that help the stars to shine at their brightest. The "song" on which they are all improvising might therefore be called "The New Apartment."

Bill Delaney

A NEW ENGLAND NUN

Author: Mary E. Wilkins Freeman (1852-1930)
Type of plot: Domestic realism
Time of plot: The late nineteenth century
Locale: New England
First published: 1891

Principal characters:

LOUISA ELLIS, a woman who has been engaged for fifteen years

JOE DAGGET, her fiancé

LILY DYER, a young woman who helps Joe's mother

The Story

Louisa Ellis's fiancé, Joe Dagget, has returned to marry her after spending fourteen years in Australia, where he had gone to make his fortune, so he could support her. Louisa, however, has become used to her simple single life and does not know what to do with this large male who seems always to be disturbing the order of her life. Louisa's meticulous ways are revealed as she takes care of her spotless house, her canary, and her old dog, Caesar, who, because he had bitten someone long ago, has been chained up approximately as long as Joe has been away. Then Joe arrives to court Louisa, a month before they are to be married. Joe tracks in dust and knocks things over, causing Louisa much discomfort. Both are relieved when the visit is over, he is outdoors again, and she can sweep up the dust and set the room to rights.

The narrator, omniscient but focused mainly on Louisa's reflections and experiences, traces the course of the relationship between Louisa and Joe. Louisa, when young, had considered herself to be in love with Joe, although it is clear that Louisa was never a passionate person. In his absence, she has inherited her mother's house and her brother's dog and learned to enjoy a narrow, peaceful single life. Now she is reluctant to give this life up for the very different life Joe would offer. He has a big house with his mother in it, a domineering, shrewd matron who would look down on Louisa's finicky housekeeping and her old-maid occupations, such as distilling the essences from herbs and flowers. One of Louisa's major fears when she thinks of the coming marriage is the possibility that Joe might set free her old dog, whom she pictures as ravishing the neighborhood. Joe, on the other hand, has fallen in love with a young woman, Lily Dyer, who has been helping his mother. Both Louisa and Joe feel honor-bound by their engagement, however, and intend to go through with the marriage.

With the wedding a week away, things change for Louisa. She is sitting outdoors in the evening, resting in the middle of a late stroll, when she overhears Joe and Lily discuss their feelings for each other and their intention to deny their feelings and part because of Joe's engagement. Now Louisa has reason to end the engagement and she does so, not mentioning Lily but claiming only that she has lived one way so long that she does not think she can change. Having made the break, she weeps a little, hardly knowing why, but on waking the next morning, she feels greatly relieved.

Now Joe is free to marry Lily, and Louisa is free to be herself, a New England nun who has created her own hermitage. She will not give up her cared-for home for Joe's disorderly one, and she will not have children or experience passion.

The conclusion contrasts the wide world she has given up—"Outside was the fervid summer afternoon; the air was filled with the sounds of the busy harvest of men and birds and bees"—with the narrow world she has chosen of linen seams, distilled roses, dusting, and polishing.

Themes and Meanings

"A New England Nun" is a rich example of local-color writing. It presents the people and occupations of a New England farming town in such a way as to capture the feel of the time and place involved. Louisa Ellis becomes real to the reader as a simple person who must choose between two clear and mutually exclusive options. The narrator, by giving snatches of Joe's perceptions but concentrating on Louisa's, takes the reader into Louisa's mind as she makes her choice.

The details are carefully chosen to reveal character and to emphasize elements of Louisa's dilemma. At home, for example, she wears three aprons—a green gingham apron for working, a calico apron for sewing, and a white linen apron for company. She removes the top two for Joe's visit. The three aprons suggest the defenses Louisa has put up against intimacy. Her attitude toward her two animals, old Caesar and her little yellow canary, represent how she regards feelings and drives. Old Caesar has been chained for fourteen years and is reputed to be dangerous because he once bit somebody, although now he is a sad, fat old dog fed only on light vegetarian fare to avoid inciting him to violence.

It is suggestive that Caesar has been chained for the length of time Joe was away. Now Louisa is afraid that Joe will set Caesar free to ravage the neighborhood. The little yellow canary goes into a panic whenever Joe enters the house, but when the threat of marriage is over, it will be able to "turn itself into a peaceful yellow ball night after night, and have no need to wake and flutter with wild terror against its bars." Louisa never will be subject to the ungovernable passions of love. She will remain in the exclusively feminine world she can control and will not need to fear the destructive elements of passion.

The narrator suggests that Louisa is giving up more than she is receiving, but that Louisa will never believe this, and compares Louisa's choice to the biblical Esau's selling of his birthright to his brother Jacob for some pottage because he was hungry. "If Louisa Ellis had sold her birthright she did not know it, the taste of the pottage was so delicious." The narrator implies that Louisa's choice is conditioned both by her natural inclinations, which have been given free rein by Joe's extended absence, and by the circumstances of her life.

The images of indoor versus outdoor life particularly illuminate the nature of Louisa's choice. Throughout the story she is associated mostly with well-cared-for rooms, well-ordered drawers, and seats safely behind windows, where she may sew a fine linen seam, looking out. Joe is associated with the out-of-doors, with its profuse and unmanageable life. The closing scene finds Louisa once more at the window, watching as "Lily Dyer, tall and erect and blooming, went past." Louisa will not bloom; she has chosen not to be a part of the world of natural fruition. She prefers to observe from a window rather than participate in the fullness of life; the sounds of the world outside, "halloos, metallic clatterings, sweet calls, and long hummings," neither disturb her nor incite her envy.

Style and Technique

Local-color writing provides a sketch of a particular time and place, usually with sympathetic portrayals of local types and suggestions of the interrelationship between a locale and those who inhabit it. "A New England Nun" does these things skillfully. Its descriptive passages capture the New England area Mary E. Wilkins Freeman knew so well. Freeman was born in Massachusetts in 1852 and remained in New England until 1902, when she married and moved away, but continued to write about her New England background and the remnants of Puritanism that still laced the society in which she grew up.

The details of Louisa's life suggest what the community she belongs to is like, and show the limitations of her options. Every small detail has its implication: that Louisa's neighbors talk about her daily use of her good china, for instance, suggests that there is little to talk about in the village and that there is not much room for individual eccentricity. It also indicates that someone who values privacy is going to have to work hard for it. The dialogue in the story also captures character, although it is not dialect, as it is in some local-color stories. It is clear that Louisa's more educated tones do not match Joe's plainer speech, giving another hint at the incompatibility of the two for marriage. The narrator's somewhat negative assessment of Louisa's choice of serenity and a peaceful narrowness does not reduce the reader's sympathy for a woman who has only two choices and a great deal to lose either way.

Janet McCann

NEW ISLANDS

Author: María Luisa Bombal (1910-1980)
Type of plot: Surrealist
Time of plot: The twentieth century
Locale: Buenos Aires and a country estate some distance from the city
First published: "Las islas nuevas," 1938 (English translation, 1982)

> *Principal characters:*
> YOLANDA, a beautiful and enigmatic estate owner
> FEDERICO, her brother
> JUAN MANUEL, a Buenos Aires lawyer visiting in the country
> BILLY, Juan Manuel's nine-year-old son
> SYLVESTER, the owner of a neighboring estate, and Yolanda's
> fiancé thirty years ago

The Story

On its most literal level, "New Islands" is an account of a city lawyer's four-day visit to an estate in the country a few hours drive from Buenos Aires. Juan Manuel, the lawyer, has been visiting at the La Figura hacienda and is part of a group of hunters from La Figura that goes to have a look at some new islands that have emerged in a lake. They stay at Yolanda and Federico's hacienda, and the story describes Juan Manuel's four-day relationship with Yolanda, which ends with his return to Buenos Aires. The new islands sink mysteriously back into the mud and algae out of which they were thrust. Yolanda, too, represents a mystery that cannot be fathomed rationally.

The story opens with one of Yolanda's dreams, one of a series of nightmarish dreams that recur throughout the tale. It is not clear whether her dreams mirror reality or whether reality mirrors her dreams. Attracted by Juan Manuel, she dreams a seduction scene with him as they gaze over the pampa at twilight. The exact scene occurs at dusk the next day. In her dream, Yolanda has struggled to resist Juan Manuel's caresses and in the mirror-image reality, she runs away. Juan Manuel is fascinated by her but baffled. She appears to be very young, yet Sylvester claims that thirty years ago, she jilted him only two weeks before their planned marriage, for reasons he has never understood. Yolanda is beautiful yet strange, frequently associated with a primeval earth of foliage, flowers, and animals. When she stands up, she seems to Juan Manuel to uncoil like a beautiful snake. Instead of walking, she glides, "pale, angular, and a bit savage," fragile, "aggressive yet hunted." Her feet seem far too small for her height. Dressed in diaphanous white one evening, she reminds Juan Manuel of a sea gull; she faints when he tells her so, as though he had discovered some mysterious secret.

Yolanda is associated repeatedly with camellias and with birds—gulls and magpies, for example—and with the natural world of the pampa. Made desperate with desire and bewilderment, Juan Manuel searches through the vast ghostly hacienda at three in the morning of the fourth day until he finds Yolanda, deep in a nightmare world; as she struggles to awake, she describes her dreamworld of prehistoric forest, giant ferns, "silence as green as chloroform," and the buzzing of giant insects. Once again, Yolanda appears to encourage Juan Manuel's sexual advances but then she cries out—in her husky, strange, sea gull cry, which has punctuated the whole story— and resists, shaming his passion with her tears, not trying to keep him when he leaves.

As Juan Manuel returns to the house at dusk on the fourth day, he sees Yolanda through a bathroom window, her naked body slender and white, her attention absorbed in the contemplation of her right shoulder, "on which something light and flexible looms, drooping down . . . a wing . . . the stump of a wing." Horrified, Juan Manuel jumps in his car and hurtles back to Buenos Aires to the safety of the rational city, the orderly, familiar company of his mother and young son. He dials Yolanda's number but hangs up when the phone is answered at the hacienda; he cannot bear to know more about her, either to confirm or to deny his horror. He perceives that there is no rational explanation of Yolanda or of man's relationship to the passage of time. His beloved wife, Elsa, remains frozen in time at the moment of her death, "preserved forever at age thirty-three. . . . And the day would come when Billy would be older than his mother."

Billy's geography book provides a description of the prehistoric world of giant ferns and enormous flying insects that Juan Manuel recognizes as the world of Yolanda's dreams, a world in which she perhaps still lives. However, Juan Manuel is unable and unwilling to deal with this; he

> feels incapable of soaring into the intricate galleries of Nature in order to arrive at the mystery's origin. He fears losing his way in that wild world with its disorderly and poorly mapped pathways, strewn with an unsystematic confusion of clues; fears falling into some dark abyss that no amount of logic will lead him out of.

He prefers a rational, tidy life, and he rejects the magnetic, instinctual pull of Yolanda's tumultuous mystery.

Themes and Meanings

The meanings of "New Islands" are not explicitly stated. The reader allies with Juan Manuel as he tries (and fails) to find rational explanations for Yolanda's appearance and behavior. Throughout the story, the irreconcilable opposition of rationality and instinct is stressed. The story is a collage or musical composition of repeating elements of this polarity. Descriptions of the howling wind, the wild pampa with its large insects, and Yolanda's primitive dream forest alternate with the sounds of the passing train (modern, dehumanized technology), the volleys of shots fired by the hunters (humanity destroying nature), and the orderly labyrinth of city streets where Juan Manuel's mother never gets lost. Images of Yolanda's long black hair recur again and again, wild hair that streams around her, hair that covers "her face like a latticework of luxuriant vines," a monstrous net that seems to trap her in her nightmare. Juan Manuel is entangled in this hair when he grapples with her in the night. It symbolizes passion, instinct, and untamed nature. In contrast to this, a repeated image of Juan Manuel is of him cleaning the mud off his boots, reestablishing order, aware of the precise hour (three o'clock, eleven o'clock) and of proprieties. Instinct, mystery, and dreams are contrasted with clarity, reason, and the valuing of analytical skills. The timeless disorder of the primeval past of Yolanda's dreams is set against four measured days of ordered time.

The emergence and disappearance of the new islands is a mystery that is parallel (but not explicitly connected) to Juan Manuel's attraction to Yolanda and his ultimate rejection of her. The four new islands are seen by the hunters on the first day, "still smoking from the fiery effort that had lifted them from who knows what stratified depths," depths that are comparable to the prehistoric landscape of Yolanda's dreams. When the hunters explore the islands on the second day, they are appalled by the oppressive, foul odor. They "advance, stepping in amazement on slimy weeds that seem to be oozing from the hot and shifty soil. They stagger on amid spirals of sea gulls that swoop around them, flashing by their faces and screeching as they dip and rise." Later on, the notes of Yolanda's piano scale—the passion of music reduced temporarily to methodical scales—seem to "beat against Juan Manuel's heart, striking where the sea gull's wing had wounded him that morning."

On the new islands, the hunters stomp along, "crushing under their boots frenzied silver fish stranded by the tide," tearing their hands in a futile effort to uproot eerie bushes of pink coral. These rational men, who cannot understand this mystery and can only destroy its fragile beauty, are ultimately defeated by the islands. Sea gulls swirl around them, low clouds dizzy them, and dense fumes nearly suffocate them. "Everything boils, shakes violently, trembles. . . . Disheartened and afraid, they flee to their boats." The violence and irrationality of the islands triumph over the hunters' desire to explore, to dominate, to tread with their heavy boots over this virgin land.

On the third morning, the islands have sunk without a trace. Juan Manuel peers into the water, knowing "that his eyes could never see the muddy bottom where, after its vertiginous plunge, the island sank into silt and algae." A small jellyfish is all there is to remind him of the islands, just as Yolanda's wing is the only vestige of her connection with the forest of her dreams. The Spanish name for jellyfish, *medusa*, is clearly associated with Yolanda's wild, Medusa-like hair. The jellyfish melts and cannot be studied by the rational Billy, who is puzzled by how the jellyfish could have gotten to the lake because it is a sea creature. Juan Manuel can only say that he does not know, just as he cannot understand the mystery of Yolanda.

Yolanda is associated with earth goddess and earth mother images of powerful instinct, timelessness, and nurturing. However, she is a sterile and frustrated earth mother, unwilling to bear a child because she would have to part with it, unwilling to succumb to physical desire with either Sylvester or Juan Manuel. Just as the islands reject the tread of humankind and sink back into the depths from which they came, Yolanda, too, will be unfulfilled, her mystery intact.

Style and Technique

María Luisa Bombal sustains an atmosphere of mystery and tension in "New Islands" by playing opposites against each other without resolving them. She suggests many possible connections and meanings but does not explicitly define her symbols. The boundaries between the real and the unreal, dreamworlds and conscious worlds are often hazy. One is left with questions: Is Yolanda really immune to aging? Does she really have a wing on her shoulder or does Juan Manuel imagine it (because he wants to escape from her or because he is overwrought and guilty about his assault on her)? Is Yolanda's passionate primitive realm of dreams and sexuality really out of reach for the rational young lawyer from the big city? "New Islands" evokes powerful images and contradictions, the endless seesaw of desire and frustration, emotion and intellect, lush vegetation and sterility, pampa and city, passion and reason.

Mary G. Berg

NEW YEAR FOR FONG WING

Author: Monfoon Leong (1916-1964)
Type of plot: Social realism
Time of plot: 1946
Locale: San Francisco
First published: 1949

>*Principal characters:*
>FONG WING, a dishwasher in a Chinese restaurant
>LEE MUN, his friend, the restaurant's chef
>THE GAMBLING HOUSE OPERATOR, a man who lost both legs in
>   World War II

The Story

It is the early morning of New Year's Day. After they close the restaurant, Fong Wing and Lee Mun collect their pay and leave. Lee Mun wants to go to the House of Ten-Thousand Delights, a gambling house, to celebrate New Year's, but Fong Wing fears that if he loses all of his money, his wife will be mad at him.

On the way to a Chinese grocery store, Fong Wing has a sad feeling. The streets littered with shattered red paper—the remains of thousands of exploded firecrackers— look as empty as his life. He and Lee Mun start to talk about children. Fong Wing had four children, but two sons were killed in France during World War I and the third son was killed during World War II. Now he has only one daughter left, and his friend wonders who will carry Fong Wing's name in the future.

Fong Wing becomes depressed. The fish bellies at the Chinese grocery store remind him of his third son because they were his favorite dish. He suddenly realizes that although it is New Year's Day, he can hope for no new beginning, as no grandchildren bear his own name. He laments that an old man has no tomorrow without sons and decides to go to the gambling house with Lee Mun.

Inside the gambling house, Fong Wing notices that the dealer at the fan tan table is very young; he appears not to be over twenty-five. Fong Wing cannot figure out why such a young man would be content working in a gambling house. In the old days, for such a young man to work in a gambling house was understandable. In those days, Chinese in America could find work only in restaurants, laundries, or gambling houses. Today, however, there is opportunity almost without limit. In disgust, Fong Wing complains to Lee Mun: "My boy died so he can waste life running bean game."

Fong Wing's luck at the table does not last long; he soon loses almost all of his money. His hand trembles as he pulls a five-dollar bill from his wallet. This bill came home with his youngest son's personal belongings.

Before he can place the entire five dollars on number three, he hears a heavy thumping and the splintering of wood: The gambling house is being raided by the police.

The young fan tan operator collects all the money on the table and begs Fong Wing to carry him to his hiding place in a closet. It is the first time that Fong Wing notices that the young man has no legs. He lost his legs during the war and army doctors told him that there was "not enough left to fit man-made legs." Fong Wing tells the dealer that his wife and he need a son, but the young man replies: "half a son is worse than none."

In the closet, Fong Wing tries to find the young man but cannot. There are too many people, and it is too dark. On the way home, he imagines what it would be like to have a son, even "half a son—."

Themes and Meanings

Many works in modern Asian American literature, especially those that become commercially successful, describe middle- and upper-middle-class Asian American experiences. Only a few touch on the lives of Asian Americans who struggle at the bottom of the social totem pole. Similar to Louis Chu's *Eat a Bowl of Tea* (1986), Chinese American writer Monfoon Leong's "New Year for Fong Wing" portrays a first-generation Chinese immigrant's struggle in the United States.

Fong Wing has been working hard all of his life to support his family, but he feels that his life is empty. In appearance, many of his problems, such as money and his relationship with his wife, are caused by his gambling habit. As the story develops, however, the reader learns that Fong Wing has lost three sons to two wars. After his third son is killed in World War II, he becomes despondent. When Lee Mun reminds him that his third son "returned from War on Fourth of July heroes' ship and received hero's burial," Fong Wing laments that there will be no sons, no grandson to "tell of his heroism," and there is no future for an "old man without sons" (traditional Chinese custom, similar to that in the United States, dictates that children adopt their fathers' surnames).

It appears that the only way Fong Wing knows how to handle his emotional problems is by gambling. It helps fill his spiritual void and numb his feelings of ennui and emptiness. Every time he goes to the gambling house, he hopes that winning money may "ease the emptiness, the barrenness of his existence." However, each time, he loses more money, as well as his respect for life and hope for the future.

Fong Wing's meeting with the young dealer at the fan tan table almost succeeds in rekindling hope in his heart. The young man lost both of his legs during the war and reminds Fong Wing of his third son. Fong Wing's implied offer to make the dealer his son is kindly rejected, throwing him back into an emotional abyss as dark and cold as the streets in the early morning of the New Year's Day.

Style and Technique

The tone of this story is as humorous as it is somber. When Lee Mun tempts Fong Wing to go to the House of Ten-Thousand Delights with him, the latter, after a long period of hesitation and deliberation, finally admits: "If I lose all my money again in fan tan game, old woman will nag me without rest." Lee Mun's inquiry about his daughter's age makes Fong Wing suspicious; he looks sharply at Lee Mun and rebukes him: "Too young for you." When the police raid the gambling house, Lee Mun refuses to run and hide, telling Fong Wing with a shrug of his shoulder: "I wait for police. They always wait at back door anyway—and I am too fat for closet door."

The story is, however, a comic-tragedy, using humor to create comic relief as the story pushes its conflicts to a tragic ending. It is tragic not in the sense of experiencing physical death but in an emotional one. For Fong Wing life without hope is like "a hollow gourd, there was left only the shell of the past." It is true that one must know one's past before determining where one is going. In Fong Wing's case, however, the memory of the past serves only to confirm the meaninglessness of the present and the hopelessness of the future. This tragic undertone of the story is accentuated by the fact that the beginning of a new year does not bring Fong Wing hope, but only agony; it does not bring him change, but only reminders of the emptiness of his life. Fong Wing ends where he starts, shuffling heavily along and "feeling the thick fog like an enormous weight on his shoulders, pushing him down."

In "New Year for Fong Wing," Leong's use of the setting to underline his thematic concerns is meticulous and effective. The setting mirrors and corresponds to Fong Wing's frame of mind. As Fong Wing and Lee Mun walk to the grocery store, the street is wrapped in a thick screen of fog, the few cars parked on it look like "shapeless monsters," and the street is "still and empty." Chun Bock, the Chinese grocery store, is also empty but for "a clerk drowsing on a stool behind the counter." The fish bellies in the store remind Fong Wing of his lost son; without the hope of having grandchildren to carry on his name, he sees the future as empty "as a hollow gourd." Fong Wing's meeting with the legless young man at the gambling house momentarily warms his heart, but after his attempt to make an emotional engagement with the man fails, he is thrown back into an environment that portentously reminds him of the loneliness of his empty life.

Qun Wang

A NEW YEAR'S EVE ADVENTURE

Author: E. T. A. Hoffmann (1776-1822)
Type of plot: Fantasy
Time of plot: The early nineteenth century
Locale: Berlin and Italy
First published: "Die Abenteuer der Sylvester-Nacht," 1815 (English translation, 1855)

Principal characters:
> THE TRAVELLING ENTHUSIAST, the narrator
> JULIA, the Enthusiast's lost love
> ERASMUS SPIKHER, the man who gives up his reflection
> GIULETTA, the woman for whom Spikher gives it up
> DR. DAPERTUTTO, a guise of the Devil, who wants Spikher's family and his soul
> PETER SCHLEMIHL, a character from another nineteenth century German fantasy

The Story

"A New Year's Eve Adventure" is partially E. T. A. Hoffmann's own romantic fantasy, but it is also a satire on the convention of the lost reflection or shadow familiar in other German fantasies of the early nineteenth century. It is typical of Hoffmann in that its reality seems to hover halfway between the real world and the world of fairy tale; thus the split in the central character, Spikher, both between himself and his reflection, as well as between himself and the Travelling Enthusiast, is reflective of the duality of the world as Hoffmann sees it—always half-actual, half-imaginative, always half-comic, half-tragic.

The basic nature of such a split is announced in the editor's foreword to the story, in which the Travelling Enthusiast is described as one who cannot separate the events of his inner life from those of the outside world. Suggesting that the reader is to enter a world where he cannot determine where inner world ends and outer world begins, the editor warns the reader that in this story he will be in a strange magical realm, where figures of fantasy step right into his own life.

The story opens with the convention, familiar in the stories of Edgar Allan Poe (who was highly influenced by Hoffmann's fiction), of the Enthusiast's sense of inexplicable fear and madness, the source of which is the fact that every New Year's Eve the Devil keeps a special treat for him. He goes to a party given by the counselor of justice and there sees Julia, a beautiful woman from his former life of love and poetry, only to discover that she is married to a spindle-legged little cretin with eyes like a frog.

Retreating from the grand party to a beer cellar, the Enthusiast meets a tall, sad man who looks like a character from a Peter Paul Rubens painting and a short, dried-up fellow who has a powerful antipathy toward mirrors. This second stranger has two different faces, one that of a pleasant young man and the other that of a demoniac old man. The reader discovers that this little man is Erasmus Spikher, who has lost his reflection, and that the tall man is Peter Schlemihl, the man who lost his shadow, the title character of Adelbert von Chamisso's 1814 novel. When the narrator goes to a room that night, he looks into a mirror and sees from the background of his own reflection the image of Julia, which then changes into the image of the little man, Erasmus Spikher.

The duality of the narrator and Spikher is made clear when Spikher tells him that he has lost his reflection because he earlier gave it to Julia, or Giuletta, as he calls her. When the Enthusiast awakes the next morning after having strange dreams of Julia as a demoniac figure out of the paintings of Pieter Brueghel, Jacques Callot, and Rembrandt, he thinks that it all must be a dream until he finds a manuscript that is "The Story of the Lost Reflection"—the story of Erasmus Spikher, which is now inserted into the text and becomes the greater part of "A New Year's Eve Adventure." This story begins with Spikher traveling from the cold North to the beautiful warmth of Italy. Leaving his wife in order to fulfill this dream of travel, he sets off for Florence, where he meets Giuletta, who looks exactly as if she were a woman from a Rembrandt painting, walking about. He immediately falls in love with her, saying that he has seen her in his dreams, that he has always been in love with her, that she is his life.

It is at this point that Spikher also meets the strange figure of Dr. Dapertutto and, in a madness of jealousy, kills a young Italian suitor of Giuletta. When he realizes that he must now leave her to avoid prosecution, she begs him to leave her his reflection. Spikher travels back home to his wife and child and gradually forgets Giuletta—that is, until his son and wife discover that he has no reflection and reject him as a demon. Claiming that Giuletta must now have him body and soul, he calls up Dr. Dapertutto, who tries to make him poison his wife and child. When he refuses, Giuletta tries to convince him to sign over his wife and child to Dr. Dapertutto, but this, too, he refuses at the last moment. Spikher's story ends with his wife telling him to go out into the world again to see if he can track down his reflection and get it away from the Devil. Spikher follows this advice, meets with Peter Schlemihl, and plans to travel with him.

The story ends with a postscript by the Travelling Enthusiast, who once again takes over the narration to tell Hoffmann that he is completely saturated with the manifestations of this New Year's Eve and that he now believes that Julia is a picture of a siren by Rembrandt or Callot.

Themes and Meanings

This is a story-within-a-story, which is sometimes published under the title "A New Year's Eve Adventure" and sometimes published only with Spikher's insert story and entitled "The Lost Reflection." It belongs within the Romantic tradition in nineteenth century Germany, a tradition of the novellas that begins with the works of Johann Wolfgang von Goethe and develops in more detail with those of Ludwig Tieck, Chamisso, and Hoffmann himself. American readers are most familiar with the tradition in the works of Edgar Allan Poe and Nathaniel Hawthorne, both of whom make use of the familiar convention of the double figure, which is based on the notion of the split in the self between the body and the soul. "A New Year's Eve Adventure" also makes use of the convention, made most famous by Goethe, of the man who falls in love with a beautiful woman, sells his soul to the devil, and is doomed to wander eternally in search of his lost self.

In this story, Hoffmann makes the convention a bit more complicated both by making use of it and by simultaneously making fun of it. Thus, one has a classic Romantic story of the lost self, even as one has a story that burlesques the theme. The fact that the story of the Travelling Enthusiast serves as a framework for the story of Erasmus Spikher suggests that Spikher similarly serves as a double for the Travelling Enthusiast, even as within his story one meets a character out of the fiction of Hoffmann's friend Chamisso. The fact that a fictional character such as Peter Schlemihl enters into the frame story as if he were a real character is indicative of Hoffmann's innovation of integrating the world of dream, fantasy, fairy tale, and psychological projection into the world of "as if" reality.

Style and Technique

The tone of the story is one of mock seriousness, for although it seems to take place in the real world and involve real people, the events are also described as if they were the events of the fairy tale. Throughout, there is a sense of mocking both the Travelling Enthusiast and Spikher, both for their obsession with Julia/Giuletta and for their taking themselves so seriously. The story draws from the fairy-tale convention of the reflection or shadow as that which divides the ego into truth and dream.

Indeed, this split between what is physically actual and what is an imaginative projection is both the theme and the technique of Hoffmann's story, for the style of the story itself is calculated to keep the reader off balance, never being quite sure whether he is reading a fiction that follows the conventions of realism or one that follows the conventions of the fairy tale, never being sure whether he is in the world of physical reality or in the world of pure psychological projection. The fact that Giuletta seems to be a character out of a painting by Rembrandt or Callot suggests further that the basis for this story is the realm of art. Nothing comes from external reality here; everything comes from art itself. The stories of Hoffmann mark the beginning of the Romantic insistence that reality is of the imagination only. Moreover, Hoffmann's combination of psychological realism and fairy-tale conventions is a key factor in the development of the short-story genre in the United States with the works of Washington Irving, Nathaniel Hawthorne, and Edgar Allan Poe.

Charles E. May

NIGHT-SEA JOURNEY

Author: John Barth (1930-   )
Type of plot: Allegory
Time of plot: Anytime
Locale: Anywhere
First published: 1966

Principal character:
THE SWIMMER, a spermatozoan, representative of all humankind

The Story

Story and theme are one and the same in this interior monologue by a spermatozoan swimming toward an ovum. He announces immediately that "it's myself I address" and that he has two aims: to "rehearse" the human condition and to disclose his "secret hope." As he considers his existence (and humankind's), he evaluates the various ontologies, or theories of being, that philosophers have conjured up; he meditates as well on some common, and uncommon, theodicies, or explanations of why the world is the way it is. He raises first the insoluble metaphysical conundrum represented in versions of epistemological idealism: Because one can know the world only through one's senses, does the external world really exist? As the swimmer puts it, "Do the night, the sea, exist at all? Do I myself exist, or is this a dream?" His answer is only conditional and raises another question: "And if I am, who am I?" Is he the "Heritage"—both genetic and cultural—that he carries?

He admits to his vacillation. At times he feels drawn toward the religious-humanistic faith that swimmers have a "common Maker" who has created the world with a master plan, but then the existential absurdity of his undertaking strikes him as he witnesses the many who perish as he flails on, and he suspects "that our night-sea journey is without meaning." At this point he rejects the well-known thesis of Albert Camus in "The Myth of Sisyphus," that humanity in its plight is like Sisyphus: Just as Sisyphus had to keep pushing the rock up the hill throughout eternity, always to have it roll back, so must humanity struggle against life's obstacles and find its only values and satisfactions in the struggle itself. The swimmer takes no solace in this vision of life: "Swimming itself I find at best not actively unpleasant, more often tiresome, not infrequently a torment."

Neither is he convinced by the argument from design—that because the creation reveals design and order, there must be a designer with an ultimate goal. "If the night-sea journey has justification, it is not for us swimmers ever to discover it." Even if there were a "Shore," a goal, a telos, what would it be? What would we do there? He imagines it as "the blissful state of the drowned."

The swimmer then quickly entertains some of the common options open to humankind. As for the Superman, for example, the Faustian individualist who goes his own way ruthlessly, the spermatozoan sometimes envies the forcefulness of this type and regrets his own weak vitality. The appeal, however, is short-lived: "In reasonabler moments I remind myself that it's this very freedom and self-responsibility I reject, as more dramatically absurd, in our senseless circumstances, than tailing along in conventional fashion." Other worldviews are rejected as they occur to him. The doctrine of survival of the fittest is "false as well as repellent," for it makes the night-sea journey "essentially haphazard as well as murderous and unjustified." The dandy's argument that "You only swim once" is answered with, "Why bother, then?" The swimmer quickly dismisses as "poppycock" the Christian admonition that "Except ye drown, ye shall not reach the Shore of Life."

The monologuist then ponders a number of cynical, perverse theodicies suggested to him by a "late companion." Perhaps, for example, the Maker made swimmers unknowingly and has no knowledge of their existence, or perhaps He knows and simply does not care. Perhaps the Maker even wishes swimmers unmade and is their adversary, working against their struggle to reach the shore. Worst of all, maybe the Maker is a monster whose end for swimmers is "immoral, even obscene." These visions suggest the speculations of the Marquis de Sade, of Voltaire, of Mark Twain in his most bitter moods, and of Herman Melville's famous God-hater, Captain Ahab.

In one wild conceit, thousands of Makers send millions of swimmers off into thousands of seas in which "both sea and swimmers were utterly annihilated." Occasional spermatozoa achieve a "qualified immortality," and so do the fortunate elect in theologies such as Calvinism. However, some drown at the outset and others are born damned, "created drowned," in a senseless orgy of creation that implies "impotent Creators, Makers unable to Make, as well as uncommonly fertile ones and all grades between." Another hypothesis is that Makers and swimmers generate each other, going on and on in a "cyclic process of incarnation" that constitutes their only immortality. In all these fancies, the allegory comes very close to the spermatozoa's own fate.

Themes and Meanings

After this summary of creation theories, the swimmer turns to "the point of my chronicling." This point turns out to be his tentative belief in a dimly sensed "She" that draws him "Herward," making the goal "a mysterious being, indescribable except by paradox and vaguest figure: wholly different from us swimmers, yet our complement; the death of us, yet our salvation and resurrection." He recalls, furthermore, his friend's speculation that every creation had two kinds of creator: "One of which gives rise to seas and swimmers, the other to the Night-which-contains-the-sea and to What-waits-at-the-journey's-end." (These two creators perhaps should be interpreted as Eros and Thanatos, the life urge and the death wish.)

The swimmer explains that the only "purpose" of his journey must be some kind of merging of identities with "Her," or so his friend had argued. However, if the "issue of the magical union" cannot remember the journey, then there is no satisfying immortality. The whole cyclical process thus becomes pointless, even anguishing eventually. Young swimmers, though, can only swim onward toward the figure that whispers, "I am all love. Come."

The monologuist, himself by now an older swimmer, feels the attraction "Herward" as strongly as the others do, realizes its source, and appeals passionately to "You who I may be about to become." What the monologuist begs of his progeny-to-be is nothing less than an end to life by a breaking of the cycle. He realizes that he is too caught up in Life, Desire, Love, Eros, or whatever, and cannot end "this aimless, brutal business" himself. Even as he goes flailing on to his fate, consummation with the ovum, he pleads:

> Whoever echoes these reflections: be more courageous than their author! An end to night-sea journeys! Make no more! And forswear me when I shall forswear myself, deny myself, plunge into her who summons, singing . . . 'Love! Love! Love!'

Style and Technique

John Barth has a reputation for flawlessly written allegories, playful, imaginative, and intricate. He has a superb sense of both structure and texture, and he puts these fictional skills to the service of philosophical reflection and complicated patterns of meaning and imagery. "Night-Sea Journey" enjoys all these standard Barth talents, and it reveals many literary sources that, although never mentioned directly, give the story resonance and offer the reader the pleasure of recognition.

To give examples, the lament that "I have seen the best swimmers of my generation go under" is a clear allusion to Allen Ginsberg's sensational Beat manifesto, the poem "Howl." The whole meditation on the virtues and satisfactions in swimming for its own sake derives from Albert Camus's *Le Mythe de Sisyphe* (1942; *The Myth of Sisyphus*, 1955), and behind that essay the myth itself. In another glancing allusion, Alfred, Lord Tennyson's poem on the Light Brigade is invoked in the assertion, "Ours not to stop and think; ours but to swim and sink." Neither Charles Darwin nor Friedrich Nietzsche is mentioned by name, but both come to mind in the swimmer's accounts of the Superman's philosophy and the creed of the survival of the fittest. Although no particular passages echo lines from Walt Whitman, the discussions of merging identities and immortality through transmission of life all evoke some common Whitman themes. Finally, the desire to end the cycle of life in a peaceful obliteration suggests Hindu doctrines about samadhi and the release attained in Nirvana. The effect of all these covert allusions is a knowing style that, combined with the many explications of theodicies and ontogenies, makes "Night-Sea Journey" a very literary work, more of a playful philosophical tour de force than an ordinary work of fiction.

One more technique should be mentioned: the use of the "friend" as a source of many of the philosophical systems explicated. This device makes the point of view more complex, and thereby enables the swimmer/narrator, and the author, to sustain his exposition with less danger of monotony and loss of interest. Some small bit of narrative tension develops in the attitude of the swimmer to his friend, thus creating additional fictional life in a work that is essentially a lecture on philosophy.

Frank Day

NIGHT SWIMMING

Author: Pete Fromm (1958-   )
Type of plot: Domestic realism
Time of plot: The 1990's
Locale: Pocatello, Idaho
First published: 1998

>*Principal characters:*
>JOE, a janitor in his mother's nursing home
>JENNY, his sister
>MOM, their mother

The Story

Joe, the narrator, relates how his mother was found up in the mountains frozen to death a week after she escaped the nursing home where she was staying. Joe tries to imagine what she was doing up there, perhaps fantasizing that she was skinny-dipping, taking her clothes off in front of some boy for the first time. Joe's fantasy about what his mother was doing in the mountains is based on a story she told him when he was just a child. She was swimming at night, when down deep in the blackness of the water, something touched her and frightened her, but she then realized it was only the boy with whom she was swimming. That is how it is when you are frightened, she tells him, "It's just something you haven't understood right."

When his mother began to get sick, Joe was barely passing his courses at Idaho State University and unable to care for her, so he dropped out, put her in a nursing home, and got a job at the home as a janitor. After his mother's funeral, Joe invites his sister Jenny over to the family house for coffee. Joe asks Jenny what kind of life his mother must have had before she met their father, but Jenny tells him she did not have the magical life Joe has always wanted for her. Joe tells Jenny where they found their mother, sitting on the bank of the stream wearing one red sock. Jenny tells him there was nothing he could have done and that he should not blame himself. When Jenny leaves, Joe searches one last corner of the attic, looking into a box he has saved for last, but it does not contain the secret love letters of his mother he fantasizes might be there.

A few days later when Jenny calls, Joe tells her he does not think his mother thought she was alone up there on the mountain. He tells her he thinks his mother was skinny-dipping with a man named Edward. The next morning when Jenny wakes up and insists there was no Edward with whom their mother could skinny-dip, Joe says perhaps she is right, for he has looked for some evidence of him and never found it. Finally, he says that his mother must have been waiting for Edward and that now he has finally come for her.

Themes and Meanings

The central theme of "Night Swimming" centers on the "magical life" that the protagonist/narrator Joe imagines for his mother. His belief or hope that his mother had a secret life, that she was more than just his mother, derives in part from the story she told him when he was small about swimming at night down in deep, black water that is "deliciously silent" and having something touch her beneath the surface, only to discover that it was the boy with whom she was swimming. As with most stories, this one has a lesson—that fear results when you encounter something you have not understood right. However, it is the magic of the mother's story, the metaphor of a secret hidden life under the surface of reality, not the story's moral lesson, that fascinates Joe and makes him urge his mother to tell it over and over again.

Based on this story, as well as his generalized Oedipal fascination for the mysterious mother, Joe develops fantasies about his mother's secret life, complete with packets of love letters he searches for but never finds and a mysterious man named Edward who leaves her for an exotic woman named Natasha. The Oedipal connection is suggested by the fact that the mother once whimsically introduced Joe and his sister Jenny to each other as Edward and Natasha. Thus, Joe is the mysterious man Edward, who competes with his father for his mother's attentions.

When Joe's mother develops Alzheimer's disease and must live in a nursing home, her detachment from reality further encourages Joe's fantasy about her secret life. Joe's intense need to know who his mother really was, as opposed to Jenny's acceptance that she was simply their mother, is based on his male sense of the mystery of the romantically distant female. "Wouldn't it be wonderful," he asks a skeptical Jenny, if there really were a stack of hidden love letters?

With this in mind, Joe explores one last section of the attic he has not searched and finds a box, but it contains only a few baby outfits and some clothing of his father, who died when he was very young. Joe has clung to the hope that his mother could not really destroy every trace of her past but now must accept that his mother became so overwhelmed raising him and Jenny that she simply had nothing to hide. Still he insists to Jenny that his mother must have been "night swimming" up on the mountain at Spirit Creek when she died.

At the end of the story, when Joe drapes his mother's old afghan over his sleeping sister, the identification of mother and son and sister and brother is complete. When Joe talks more about the story his mother used to tell of "night swimming" with a boy that Joe calls Edward, Jenny tells him once more that there is no Edward. Finally, Joe says he thinks she is right, that although he has kept on looking for some trace of Edward, he now thinks that Edward was not in his mother's past but in her future and that with her death, he has finally come. Thus the story ends focusing not on one young man's romantic dreams about his mother's past, but his mother's romantic dreams about her prince someday coming to rescue her from the ordinariness of her life.

Style and Technique

The key stylistic device of "Night Swimming" is the insistent, almost manic, voice of Joe, who is determined to hold on to his belief in his mother's secret romantic life. Regardless of the fact that he has the flimsiest of evidence on which to hang this hope—a story his mother told him when he was a child and her being found naked and frozen solid in the snow—Joe wants to believe that there was more to his mother than just being his mother.

Either consciously or unconsciously, Pete Fromm makes use of several well-known stories from American literature to create "Night Swimming." First, the mystery of how his mother had got that far into the mountains is an echo of the opening head note to Ernest Hemingway's famous story "The Snows of Kilimanjaro" (1936), which begins with the mystery of how a leopard, found high on the African mountain, reached such a high altitude. Related to this is the image that concludes Sherwood Anderson's short story "Death in the Woods" (1926), about a woman who spends her entire life caring for and feeding her family freezing to death in the snow on her way home with food on her back. When a young boy thinks about her body, stripped naked by wolves, lying pure and beautiful in the snow, she becomes a mysterious emblem of aesthetic beauty to him, elevated out of the realm of the merely physical into the realm of mystery and romantic inaccessibility.

Finally, Joe's realization at the end of the story that Edward is not someone from his mother's past but rather someone she has been waiting for is an echo of Katherine Anne Porter's "The Jilting of Granny Weatherall" (1930) in which the dying Granny recalls being jilted on her wedding day and then looking for a reunion with her lover at the moment of her death. All these literary allusions coalesce around the central metaphor of "night swimming" as an activity that represents leaving everyday reality and entering into a realm of pure desire, a world, that like the world of another famous American short story, Conrad Aiken's "Silent Snow, Secret Snow" (1932), is "deliciously silent." Fromm's "Night Swimming" is a tissue of intertextual motifs and themes from various other stories that focuses on a basic mystery of the hidden life.

Charles E. May

NIGHT WOMEN

Author: Edwidge Danticat (1969-   )
Type of plot: Realism
Time of plot: The late twentieth century
Locale: Ville Rose, a fictitious Haitian town
First published: 1995

> *Principal characters:*
> AN HAITIAN PROSTITUTE, the narrator
> HER SON
> EMMANUEL, a doctor and her client

The Story

The narrator, a twenty-five-year-old Haitian prostitute, provides a first-person account of a night in her life as a night woman. It is a hot tropical night, the time of day she most dreads but must endure in order to live. She has just put her young son to bed in her tiny one-room house, with only a curtain separating his "bedroom" from her place of business. She has let him wear, as usual, his Sunday clothes in bed, along with her blood-red scarf, worn in the daytime to tempt suitors; thus he will always have something of hers near him when her face is out of sight. In the dark, for a moment, she almost mistakes him for the ghost of his father, a lover long gone.

There are two kinds of women, she thinks—day women and night women—she being actually caught between the two. Her son mutters faintly in his sleep, and she fears he may climb out of bed to find her on the other side of the curtain.

She strokes his cheeks with her lips, his reaction telling her whether he is really asleep. Sometimes she sees in his eyes a longing for something more. "We are like far away lovers, lying to one another, under different moons," she thinks. Her finger caresses the cleft under his nose; sometimes he will lick her nails. She thinks of ghost women who "ride the crests of waves while brushing the stars out of their hair," wooing strollers and strewing the stars on their paths. She whispers stories in his ear about these ghost women with the stars in their hair, about snakes at one end of the rainbow and a hat full of gold at the other. His Sunday suit matches her own carefully made-up appearance. He must wonder why, she worries, and tells him she is expecting an angel to pay them a visit. Where angels tread, hosts must be beautiful as floating hibiscus.

Still asleep he runs his tongue over his lips, tasting some sugar candy he stole from her purse. She has forgotten to have him clean his teeth with mint leaves to whiten them. Some day when he is older, another woman may take pleasure in their whiteness. Should her son awake, she will tell him her client is a mirage, naked flesh a dream. When he becomes too old for such a subterfuge, she will say the man is her missing husband.

The doctor-lover Emmanuel is due tonight. She applies Egyptian rouge to her cheeks; the sparkles in the mixture help the doctor find her in the dark. The doctor reaches his climax, and she must cover his mouth to stifle his screams. At dawn he leaves. She returns to her son's bed, placing her face next to his lips to feel the heat from his mouth. He awakens and asks, "Mommy, have I missed the angels again?" She rocks him back to sleep, telling him, "Darling, the angels have themselves a life- time to come to us."

Themes and Meanings

Edwidge Danticat spent the first twelve years of her life in Haiti, toward the end liv- ing with her aunts, separated from her parents, who had preceded her in emigrating to the United States. She was an imaginative child in a land of strange religious voodoo rites, myths about spirits and ghosts, and customs that many outsiders can scarcely comprehend, and her work reflects those early years. Her upbringing presents a sharp contrast with her later life in the United States, which involved a bachelor's degree from Barnard College in 1990, membership in a sorority, and a master's of fine arts from Brown University three years later. This duality of outlook can be seen in her writing.

In "Night Women," among other concerns, Danticat touches on the problems of un- employment (high in the impoverished island of Haiti) and the beguiling choice of prostitution as a solution. There is also a hint of the author's reaction to the social breakdown that turns part of the heroine's life into something that she dreads.

"Night Women" is one of nine stories and an epilogue that make up *Krik? Krak!* Some of the other stories in this collection are much more bitter and socially aware. For example, "Children of the Sea" chronicles a failed attempt by a party of refugees to escape to Florida in a leaky boat, and "Nineteen Thirty-Seven" is about a woman dying from conditions of her incarceration in the state prison. What is simply men- tioned in "Night Women" is more centrally emphasized in these works.

One paragraph in "Night Women" mentions ghost women with stars in their hair. If the myth/folktale aspect of Danticat's work gets more frontal treatment elsewhere in the collection, perhaps most noticeably in the otherwise realistic "Caroline's Wed- ding," it is at least present here. "Night Women," however, treats a theme missing from the other eight stories: the prostitute's nearly incestuous love for her own son. The physical contact she describes—little details such as brushing her lips across the cleft of his nose—are the motions she would use to arouse her lovers. With the boy, she is experiencing the joy only feigned with her clients.

Beyond social concerns, myth and superstition, and forbidden sex lies the basic na- ture of Danticat's work: She is more than anything else, a realist. This trend is clearly evident in *The Farming of Bones* (1998), an unflinching, indictment of the 1937 mas- sacre of migrant Haitian farmers by the Dominican Republic military.

Some critics have lauded Danticat's charm as a storyteller, calling this her essential goal as a writer—a weaver of the picturesque lore of her native land. They note that *Krik? Krak!*, the title of the collection, is an expression that reflects a Haitian practice. In one interview, Danticat explained that storytelling is a favorite Haitian form of en- tertainment. The storyteller asks the audience "Krik?," inquiring whether they are ready for a tale. Their enthusiastic "Krak!" indicates they are. She is undoubtedly a most skilled practitioner of this age-old art, but she is much more. It is her realistic assessment of the strengths, weaknesses, and woes of her embattled land that will ultimately fix her place in its literature.

Style and Technique

Danticat is not merely a realist, but an impressionistic realist, perhaps best described as a poetic realist; her realism is clothed in the poetry of her picturesque language. She handles the English language not only with an assurance befitting a born teller of tales but also with a justness rare with foreign-born writers operating in a tongue they did not know from birth. One is reminded of Joseph Conrad or Vladimir Nabokov (and even Conrad is guilty of occasional clumsiness). The list is small, Danticat their worthy successor. Consider such felicitous turns of phrase as her description of one of the clients in "Night Women," who has a "breadfruit head," leaving the narrator "with his body soaking from the dew of our flesh."

Although she must often be tempted, she never lets her style interfere with the narrative. However rich and satisfying, it never overwhelms with pyrotechnics. A mark of authorial maturity is often said to be to know when to add and when to stop. The stories in *Krik? Krak!* vary in length from slightly under six to sixty pages. With a mere fifteen hundred words, "Night Women" is a complete, satisfying study of a prostitute's existence. The reader can picture not only the misery of prostitution but also what it means to a real woman, with a very special son, living in a carefully described milieu, servicing at least three carefully delineated customers (though just with short thumbnail sketches). She paints the setting, the odors, the heat, the darkness. As well, she envelopes the whole tale with the aura of a mother in a very special relationship with her son, thus setting her account apart from the usual social problem/prostitution story.

Danticat disdains common novelists' tricks for creating interest or suspense: unexplained details, Dickensian characters, coincidences, sexually explicit descriptions, and the like. Stylistic tricks are equally rare. She obviously depends on setting, realistic characters, and the tragedies inherent in most Haitian lives to move her stories. One device employed all through "Night Women" is relating present events in two ways: first, that they happen once, and second, that they are repetitive. In one paragraph, the little boy is asleep, his mother afraid he may wake up because Emmanuel makes noise. However, other events told in present time, such as the Sunday clothes he wears and her story about dressing up to greet angels, happen nightly. Mixing the unique with the reiterative imitates real life, emphasizing the fears and boredom, even the hopelessness of her existence. It helps the author create the little masterpiece in six pages that is "Night Women."

Armand E. Singer

NIGHTFALL

Author: Isaac Asimov (1920-1992)
Type of plot: Science fiction
Time of plot: Unspecified
Locale: Saro University on the planet Lagash
First published: 1941

> *Principal characters:*
> ATON 77, an astronomer and director of Saro University
> THEREMON 762, a reporter
> SHEERIN 501, a psychologist
> LATIMER 25, a member of the Cult

The Story

Theremon 762 is trying to get an interview from Aton 77 regarding the collapse of civilization, which Aton and his colleagues at the university have predicted will occur in a few hours' time. After some hesitation, Aton agrees to give Theremon the interview. This interview, with several digressions and interruptions, forms the bulk of the story. The first interruption is the entrance of Sheerin 501, a fat, jovial psychologist, who actually provides most of Theremon's information. He has just come from the Hideout, a refuge where some three hundred people with food, weapons, and scientific data will wait out the coming disaster and try to preserve the planet Lagash's civilization.

As Sheerin explains, civilization on Lagash is cyclic. Every two thousand years, something happens that causes the existing civilization to be destroyed by fire, from which a new order has to be rebuilt slowly. The "Book of Revelations" of a religious organization, the Cult, claims that periodically a great darkness engulfs Lagash and then things called Stars appear in the sky that cause men to go mad. In the current scientific age, this theory is largely discredited, but Aton and other members of Sara Observatory have been claiming for the past few months that such an event will occur. They have constructed the Hideout and are now preparing to record the coming of the Darkness for the use of the refugees.

The major difference between Isaac Asimov's planet Lagash and Earth is that Lagash orbits around a star that is part of a complex system of six stars. Regularly alternating nights and days are unknown on Lagash because there is almost always at least one sun in the sky. Lagash's scientists have only recently analyzed this situation, beginning four hundred years previously, when Genovi discovered that Lagash orbited the star Alpha, replacing the older geocentric cosmology. Since then, astronomers have been plotting the orbits of the six suns until the Law of Universal Gravitation was applied to account for their motions. Recently, unaccounted for variations have been observed. Using data supplied by the Cult, Aton has discovered a moon orbiting Lagash that had not been noticed because the light from the suns had rendered it invisible. Further research has shown that this moon will eclipse the sun Beta, a small red companion to Alpha, when Beta is the only sun in the sky and when the relative distances of Beta and the moon are such that the moon completely blocks out all light from Beta for more than half a day, so that all of Lagash is deprived of sunlight. These eclipses will coincide exactly with the collapse of Lagashian civilization.

Theremon asks how half a day of darkness could drive everyone mad, and Sheerin explains that human beings (at least those on Lagash, which has no night) cannot stand more than a few hours of darkness without going mad. Theremon himself is noticeably uneasy when the room he and Sheerin are in is cut off from sunlight for several minutes. The public reaction to the Darkness will be to burn anything in order to dispel it, and civilization will be gone.

Sheerin's discourse is interrupted when Latimer 25 breaks into the observatory and tries to destroy the photographic plates that will be used to record the Darkness and the Stars. Presumably acting under orders from Sor 5, head of the Cult, Latimer has tried to prevent scientific recording of the Darkness, that will turn it into a mere natural phenomenon and not a divine intervention, just as Aton's use of data supplied by the Cult for his research proved that the Cult's "Book of Revelations" was scientifically correct but in doing so destroyed its religious significance. Just as Latimer is subdued, the eclipse of Beta begins. The astronomers move to their assigned tasks, Sheerin tells Theremon of the probable origin of the "Book of Revelations," and Latimer begins prophesying from the book. The eclipse causes a panic in Saro City and at the instigation of the Cult, crowds swarm to the Observatory to destroy it.

Sheerin and Theremon barricade the Observatory against the mobs. The scientists speculate on the possibility that the Stars might actually be suns with planets orbiting them. There might even be a planet that experiences darkness as part of its normal routine. Life on such a planet could not exist, however, with that kind of environment. Finally Beta is completely gone from view. The Darkness descends and the Stars appear in a profusion greater than the scientists had ever dreamed of. Aton babbles in his madness about humanity's ignorance while the people of Lagash experience the Stars and destroy their civilization.

Themes and Meanings

"Nightfall" is one of the most famous and highly regarded of all science-fiction stories. This is not because of its highly conventional style and characterization but rather because of its theme of humankind's contact with an unknown universe. A quotation from Ralph Waldo Emerson prefaces the story. "If the stars should appear one night in a thousand years, how would men believe and adore, and preserve for many generations the remembrance of the city of God!" "Nightfall" puts this statement to the test and finds it inadequate. Asimov's universe is naturalistic, the stars are not the city of God but natural phenomena to be explained scientifically and this scientific knowledge is to be used to help humankind. This belief is held by Aton and Sheerin and is expressed by the various works at Saro University. They have learned of the disaster, built the Hideout, and are preparing to record the eclipse for future generations at the price of their sanity.

Opposing the scientists are the Cultists, represented by Latimer, and the masses, represented by the reporter Theremon. The Cultists know of the impending disaster. Indeed, their knowledge is greater than the scientists who suspect that the Stars are only a myth, but they know it through faith, not reason. Thus, they oppose scientific knowledge even when it validates their beliefs, because it destroys the need for faith. Rather than avoiding the disaster that will destroy civilization, they rejoice in it and try to stop anyone from doing otherwise. The mass of people on Lagash are neither Cultists nor scientists but simply those who accept familiar events as the natural order of things. Theremon, even when he has heard the scientific explanation for the eclipse, never really believes it until it actually happens. The other Lagashians, when their commonsense universe falls apart, join the Cult out of desperation.

"Nightfall" demonstrates how human beings are conditioned by their environment. People in a world that has no night would be frightened by it to the point of mass insanity. Not even Aton's devotion to science saves him from madness. It can, however, enable him to save others, those in the Hideout, who will not be affected by the disaster and can rebuild the world with a scientific rather than a religious account of the Darkness. Possibly when the Darkness comes again, they will be able to overcome its effects. If Lagashian civilization can be destroyed by something as trivial from an Earthman's viewpoint as nightfall, Asimov suggests, how easily could Earth's civilization be toppled. Physically, nightfall does no real damage to Lagash; it is the Lagashians' ignorance of the eclipse and fear of the dark that cause them to demolish their civilization. Only scientific inquiry as practiced by the Sara Observatory astronomers can help humankind overcome the dangers of the unknown universe. Though their astronomical knowledge is limited, they are willing to investigate the universe.

Style and Technique

"Nightfall" employs the technique, often used in pulp science fiction, of having one character, usually a scientist, give out the major elements of the story to another character, usually a reporter or someone else who represents the common viewpoint. In this way, the reader can receive a large amount of information without the tedium of a formal lecture. In "Nightfall," Sheerin furnishes for Theremon the information that is the crux of the story, because the actions of the story simply dramatize what Sheerin says will happen. Thus, the structure of "Nightfall" is like that of a lab experiment report within a highly dramatic context. This structure reinforces the main theme of the value of scientific inquiry. "Nightfall" creates suspense by exciting curiosity to know what is happening and why. "Nightfall" is a story that produces the sense of wonder that is the core of all good science fiction. This sense of wonder lifts that story above its trite dialogue, weak characterization, and numerous scientific improbabilities and justifies its place as one of the finest American science-fiction short stories.

Anthony J. Bernardo, Jr.

NO ONE'S A MYSTERY

Author: Elizabeth Tallent (1954-   )
Type of plot: Realism
Time of plot: The 1980's
Locale: Wyoming
First published: 1985

> *Principal characters:*
> JACK, a married man
> THE NARRATOR, a young woman

The Story

The narrator, an eighteen-year-old woman, is riding in the front seat of a speeding pickup truck next to the driver, Jack, an older man. For her birthday, he has given her a five-year diary with a little lock and key, and she is trying to work the lock, which is jammed. Suddenly Jack thinks he sees his wife driving toward them in her Cadillac. He pushes the narrator to the floor and keeps his hand on her head as the Cadillac approaches. The girl notices the dirt on the floor and smells the cigarettes in the ashtray. On the tape deck, she hears Roseanne Cash singing, and she observes the bottle of tequila from which they had been drinking as it nestles against Jack's crotch.

As the Cadillac passes and honks, Jack waves to his wife, commenting sharply on her obsession with driving exactly fifty-five miles an hour while he is barreling along at more than eighty miles per hour. The narrator scolds Jack for keeping his truck so filthy, especially for the beverage cans littering the floor, and for the muddy, manure-stained boots he always wears. Jack gently mocks her and orders her back into the seat. He knows, he tells her, that his wife will not see her, just as he knows that his wife always drives fifty-five miles an hour and that she will make him meatloaf for supper that night. Jack also says that he knows what the girl will write in her diary. Tonight, Jack says, she will put in her diary that she loves him; next year, she will record her wonder at what she really ever saw in him; five years from tonight, she will have forgotten his name.

Protesting, the narrator offers her own scenario. She declares that tonight she will write that she loves Jack deeply; next year, she will record her waiting for him to come home to a candlelight dinner; last, she will write of her joy at their little boy saying his first word while their little girl nurses at her breast.

The narrator's scenario pleases Jack, but he remains cynical and scoffing. He declares that the narrator's version of the future will never happen and that in her heart of hearts, she, too, knows that it will never be.

Themes and Meanings

"No One's a Mystery" is a brief, sharply detailed distillation of a doomed relationship between two people of contrasting personalities. In five minutes—the time it takes to read the story—Jack and his young lover not only come to terms with their relationship but also illuminate aspects of their own characters of which they themselves are not fully aware. The story is more of a character sketch than a traditional tale containing a beginning, a middle, and an end. The sequence of events is less important than the specific detail and the dialogue between the couple.

Jack is the older of the two; his marriage to a woman who always drives at the speed limit is one of boredom and safety. His breakneck speed and the general unkemptness of him and his truck are outward signs of his own emotional turmoil, his need to be free, irresponsible, socially and morally unsafe. He is a man of no illusions. He knows, as he tells the narrator, that their fling will not last; she will forget him in a few years' time. Jack is vague about details—details, after all, epitomize social routine. He knows what he will have for supper, knows what the narrator will write in her diary, knows that this affair is simply a matter of filling the empty time on his hands. Aside from these generalities, he makes no judgments and demands no commitment, even mocking the narrator's version of their future together. His remark that the sky is empty carries a double meaning: In the context of the dialogue, Jack is referring to the absence of aircraft monitoring the speed of traffic, but in the light of his own character, it is a statement of unbelief, of detachment from social, emotional, and moral values.

The young narrator, by contrast, has already acquired a set of values that make her a more sympathetic character. Her sharp eye for detail, her specific observations, lend her a solidity, a steadiness of purpose that is missing in Jack's life. Her observations of the embroidery on Jack's jeans and the glinting gold of his zipper show a woman who is not afraid of specifics, who is capable of physical commitment, honest about the pleasures of the flesh.

Even in her naïveté, the narrator reveals her traditional view of life. Her version of their possible life together is almost melodramatically romantic—candlelight dinners of trout à lá Navarre, her grandmother's linen and silver on the table, even her family of two children, Jack, Jr., and daughter Rosamond—the fair Rosamond of romance. Rosamond would be at her breast, as in a picture of a madonna. She is thus traditional, even conventional. Although she enjoys this adventure with an older man, she is not simply looking for a wild life. Her sensitive description of the Wyoming countryside—the fawn-colored wheat and the smell of water in the ditches—shows that she is committed to the life-asserting qualities of nature, love, and beauty. She is intelligent, sensitive, and affirmative, where Jack is irresponsible and destructive.

It is in this contrast between the two characters that the meaning of the story is clarified. Because the two are traveling in opposite emotional directions, their relationship is doomed, just as Jack predicts. Jack's world-weariness will win out over the narrator's idealism. Each has already become alienated from the other by an irreconcilable view of life.

Style and Technique

The story succeeds in capturing the intensity of the moment by a shrewd, deliberate economy of expression. In less than twenty-five hundred words Elizabeth Tallent delineates the action and the motives through a careful use of detail and language. When the narrator describes the five-year diary Jack has given her, she notes that it is "light as a dime." She means the expression to be a compliment—the diary is easy and convenient—but Tallent has skillfully converted the narrator's praise of the diary into a moral assessment of the relationship. It certainly is light for Jack, who has no intentions toward the narrator other than sexual play.

The title is another example of the fine choices of language that characterize the story. The title is from a song by Roseanne Cash, recorded in 1983. "No One's a Mystery" refers to the singer's refusal to get involved, to fall in love. Jack's choice of the song on his tape deck suggests that he, too, is unwilling to get involved and that, in truth, the young narrator is no mystery to him—he knows the affair will be short-lived. Conversely, Jack seems to be no mystery to the narrator, whose speculations on their future suggest that security found only in romance or youthful idealism.

The story employs the simple but effective journey motif. Stories in which the protagonist endures a journey and experiences a life-change are among the most profound and universal in literature. The journey is thus more than a physical movement from one place to another, but a spiritual progress of the soul, an engagement of the mind or the understanding. The protagonist thus gains insight by the experience.

The plot of "No One's a Mystery" centers around a journey—a seemingly aimless, reckless spree across the Wyoming desert. Unlike typical journey stories, the protagonist here does not gain insight at the end. The narrator remains idealistic. It is Jack who has the final line; it is his view that dominates. However, the reader becomes enlightened. The reader, as a kind of third passenger, understands the emptiness of the future for the two.

Edward Fiorelli

NO PLACE FOR YOU, MY LOVE

Author: Eudora Welty (1909-2001)
Type of plot: Realism
Time of plot: The late 1940's
Locale: New Orleans, the Mississippi River delta
First published: 1951

> *Principal characters:*
> A NORTHERN MAN, a guest at a luncheon in New Orleans
> A NORTHERN WOMAN, a fellow guest

The Story

Eudora Welty uses a limited authorial voice in "No Place for You, My Love," although on several occasions, she enters the consciousness of the two central characters. These characters reveal few facts about themselves, especially the woman, and the authorial voice reveals little more directly. However, although the facts of the characters' lives and their feelings are not revealed, the details of their drive through the delta are clearly described.

A man and a woman, both northerners and strangers to each other, are accidentally brought together at a luncheon in New Orleans by southern acquaintances. Looking at the woman, the man thinks that she is having an affair. She wonders to herself if her being in love makes her open to others. Conscious of their being outsiders and so somehow linked, the man invites the woman to escape by taking a ride in his rented car.

The man and woman set off to explore the delta land south of New Orleans, leaving the city at the intersection called Arabi—to which they will return. Hardly talking, they ride into flatness, oppressive heat and swarming insects. It is an alien yet fascinating land. On all sides, there are mysterious paths and roads; some are paved with shells, and one is a plank road that the man guesses leads to some oil production plant. At last, mounting the Mississippi levee, they find a ferry to take them across the great river. The ferry is crowded with people—young, old, mostly poor, but filled with life. For most of the trip across the river, though, the man and woman are separate; she spends her time above, while he is down on the deck with the cars. After the ferryboat docks, they get back in the car and leave this world of people behind, following the river farther south into a greater emptiness.

At one point, the man turns into a narrow road through a cemetery, filled with white-washed, raised tombs that their car barely avoids. Here in this place of death, she asks what his wife is like, and he responds only with a gesture. The authorial voice notes that they did not continue on to the subject of her husband, "if she had one." At last they come on the house of the local priest, a man living alone and, of course, without a woman, doing his own housework. Returning to the main road, they follow it until, just as night begins to fall, it ends in an isolated cluster of buildings, seemingly at the end of human settlement.

Here they eat at a "beer shack" where the locals gather. Slowly the little tavern fills up with people, the community coming together for their evening entertainment. Although treated with respect, the man and woman are outsiders, aliens twice over. At one point, they dance together, dancing with a skill that separates them even more from the others.

At last they return to New Orleans, driving through the still hot and oppressive night. At one point, the man stops the car and kisses the woman but that is all. Back in the city, he lets her off in front of her hotel. Here, he says, "Forgive . . . ," for kissing her, then she goes in. He is not sure, but he believes someone comes to meet her. As the story ends, he remembers, from his youth, the subway of New York, which is also terrible and alien and yet in its noise and movement holds "the lilt and expectation of love."

Themes and Meanings

"No Room for You, My Love" is a complex, even mysterious, story. The point of view, shifting subtly as it does, both reveals and hides the characters as well as the meanings. In a way, the two protagonists are as mysterious to the reader as the southern world is to them. That they are northerners in the South, especially Louisiana with its mixture of cultures that is so unlike the North, emphasizes the separateness of these two and the strangeness of their coming together.

Almost nothing of the woman's life is revealed except in that moment at the beginning when she thinks of herself as being in love. Certainly the man guesses at some truth when he thinks she is having an affair, but the actual truth is hidden. The man's relationship with his wife is presented only as mechanical facts in his memory, so that the reader cannot know how they really relate, except that there is a hint that the connection is without depth and intensity. However, the complexity and mystery of the story express its thematic subjects: What do we know of one another and how do we fit into the mystery of the world?

The two learn almost nothing factual in their journey. They do not know New Orleans. However, the Arabi intersection, from which they leave and to which they return, suggests the themes. The name calls up the mysterious and romantic "Araby" of the onetime American myth. However, nothing really happens as they travel into the delta land, into Araby. It is a disappointment, not because it fails, but because they cannot fully respond to it. Indeed, the images of life and death, of fertility and infertility, are images of a richness of life that is beyond them.

The woman jokingly says as they leave that she did not even know that there was anything south of New Orleans. Toward the end of the story, the man is struck with the "extremity of this place." It is extreme and strange, for it is a test of the two as well as, almost paradoxically, a presentation of a world of openness and of emotions. It does bring them together for the moment, especially as they dance, a dance that was, as the authorial voice says, what the two had wanted, "for themselves and each other." However, this is as close as they come, except perhaps for the kiss, which has no passion and seems more a gesture, and is, in the end, a danger.

Style and Technique

Welty's use of point of view is essential to what is told, both on the surface and below; however, her style is equally important. It is deceptively simple: There are no long, involved sentences, little subordination, and no difficult words. However, her sentences are richly but unobtrusively metaphoric and imagistic. For instance, heat thickens, and a singer is "mosquito-voiced," so that even the language makes sure the man and woman cannot escape the setting and people through which they move. Such language manages to suggest much more than the mere surface, deepening the complications of their relationship.

Because the authorial voice rarely comments on the emotions of the two, the story's tone seems almost dispassionate. The two talk very little, thereby keeping their secrets. However, the contrast—clearly deliberate—between the story's surface, with its brilliant visual imagery, and the hidden feelings paradoxically emphasizes those feelings. The two repress their emotions, but those emotions are therefore felt more strongly. Indeed, the story is one of contrasts: North versus South, the familiar versus the strange, heat versus (implied) cold, and emotional restraint against open emotion.

These contrasts also suggest that class, perhaps race, and certainly the expectations of age limit people's emotional freedom. The southerners, obviously well off and white, who bring the man and woman together seem languidly satisfied with their lives. The man and woman, both entering middle age and also apparently financially comfortable, seem restrained by what is acceptable to people in their positions in life. Set against them are the lower class southerners, African Americans, and Cajuns, who, though oppressed by heat and poverty, seem much more alive. The Cajuns at the "beer shack" are a close-knit community, who are polite to outsiders and willing, within limits, to accept them. Their lives, despite the limitations placed on them, have purpose and intensity. At the end of a day of labor, they are enjoying themselves without self-consciously holding back, for that is what life is about. It is also about humanity, in the form of a small black boy who waves at the man and woman as they leave New Orleans on their journey of discovery and the young, poor boys on the ferry who demonstrate their sheer delight in being alive.

L. L. Lee

NO TRACE

Author: David Madden (1933-   )
Type of plot: Social realism
Time of plot: June 4, 1968
Locale: A college campus in the Midwest
First published: 1970

> *Principal characters:*
> GORDON FOSTER, a college student who commits suicide at his
>   graduation
> ERNEST FOSTER, his father
> LYDIA FOSTER, his mother
> JASON CARTER, his roommate

The Story

On June 4, 1968, graduation day at Melbourne College in the Midwest, Gordon Foster, valedictorian of his class, has set off a grenade, killing himself and others at the ceremony. His father, Ernest Foster, now climbs the stairs to his dead son's dormitory room—which had been his own room at the college some twenty years earlier. He will enter ahead of the police in order to piece together reasons, if possible, for his son's actions.

The room is replete with psychedelic paint, beer-can pyramids, records in orange crates, colored lights, underground books, and rock music posters. The father, under the influence of a sedative, searches quickly through the remnants of the last four years of his son's life—understanding, misunderstanding, and unable to understand what has happened and why.

Most puzzling of all seems to be his son's relation with his roommate of four years, Jason Carter. Ernest learns that his son has been sleeping in Jason's bed, reading his books, and wearing his clothes. The father discovers any number of items that shock him: semen on his son's sheets, vomit on both his and his roommate's clothes, a picture of Jesus Christ that has been used as a dart board, and irrefutable proof that his son has plagiarized his senior thesis. What troubles the father most, however, is the fact that he can find the letters that Lydia, his wife, sent to Gordon, but not those that he himself sent.

While searching among Gordon's letters and books, Ernest slowly realizes why his son has killed himself and why he did so by setting off a grenade at his own graduation. His roommate had been an activist against the Vietnam War, participating in protests and peace marches. On being drafted, however, Jason had gone to Vietnam. Letters from the roommate cum soulmate had been written to convince Gordon that he, too, should join the army and go fight. Jason had written home about his activities in Vietnam, asserting that he liked the realities of warfare, that he was fighting on the right side, and that Gordon should follow his own example. One of the last letters Ernest discovers is from Jason's parents. Written three days before the graduation, it tells Gordon that Jason is missing in action and most surely dead.

As Ernest goes through his dead son's room, he begins to collect items, then steal them; that is, he begins planning to take them so that they will not be found by the police. Ernest tells himself that he is taking these things, all of which might reveal his son to be a cheater, a war activist, a hippie, or a psychopath, to protect his son's memory and reputation and to protect Lydia from additional heartbreak. The truth, however, is that Ernest is acting to protect himself from such information becoming public through the police or coroner. As the vice president of a large insurance company, Ernest is aware that this will likely occur. Moreover, the insurance company may not pay.

Hauling out boxes of items so as to leave no trace, Ernest escapes to the garbage dump where he buries them. When gunshots go off in the darkness, he hears hunters talking and realizes that they are shooting rats. His final realization as he himself runs is that perhaps he, too, has become a rat.

Themes and Meanings

On one level, David Madden's "No Trace" is about father-son relations, the Vietnam War, friendship, and the 1960's. All of these give way, however, to the one overriding question: What does one do with the truth, if the truth is terrible and will not set one free?

Ernest learns that nothing about his son, since his departure to college some four years earlier, has been what he thought. Gordon had become caught up in the alternative lifestyle of the 1960's, playing with drugs, participating in wanton sex, protesting for civil rights and against the Vietnam War. Moreover, he developed a strange relationship with his roommate, perhaps both operantly and covertly homosexual. The father is shocked that his son would sleep in his own vomit and semen, as well as the missing roommate's bed; that he would keep his mother's letters but not his own; and that he would kill himself and others intentionally with a grenade in some sort of misguided statement against the war and, presumably, his father himself.

At issue here is far more than merely the matter of civil protest. Setting off the grenade has nothing to do with the war itself, although it is arguably connected to Jason and Jason's involvement in the Vietnam War as a soldier there. Jason had become not only Gordon's roommate, but also his best friend, bosom buddy, and virtual family member—in short, the closest person in the world to him. Jason had been transformed from peace dove to warmonger; his letters to Gordon show that he enjoys this new role, that he likes killing Viet Cong men, women, and children.

Ernest can confront the horrible facts only by trying to hide them from the police, his wife, the public, and himself. All that is important to his son, all that would define and explain him and make his life—if not his death—meaningful, is carted away to a garbage dump and hidden among the rot, filth, and decay of civilization. Ernest decides that the truth about his son would not do anyone any good but would actually harm all concerned.

That the author intends for the story to be a comment about the nature of terror and truth and what to do with it is best revealed in the last paragraph. Ernest succeeds in hiding his son's secrets in the garbage dump, only to overhear hunters converse as, aided by flashlights, they shoot rats in the darkness. It is human nature for people to go on search-and-destroy missions whether there is a reason or not. The hunters find sport in death and killing, enacting and reenacting the behavior of the dead Jason Carter, and, now, Gordon Foster. One truth about Vietnam is that collective humanity will kill one way or another; that all people are hiding secrets in the garbage pit of life; and that all people are embodied rats searching in the dark in terror and with futility. The truth about Gordon cannot be hidden; it can only be relocated to a more appropriate place.

Style and Technique

Written from a limited third-person point of view, "No Trace" remains something of a puzzle for the reader to piece together. One's awareness of events unfolds so as to parallel that of the father. Readers see the evidence and learn the clues only as Ernest does; and Madden provides little insight into Gordon's motivations for killing himself with the grenade, or his father's response to this tragedy.

The pivotal action of the plot, Gordon's suicide, happens before the story opens. As is perhaps the case with all suicides, survivors are left only to ponder the question of why. There are many subtle clues, such as the poster of the Buddhist monk in Saigon burning himself on a street, the music cover of an album by the Grateful Dead, and Ernest's numerous references to an unknown person who died twenty years earlier in a fire on campus. More direct and clear-cut evidence is also provided by the writer, particularly the letters from Jason after his arrival in the battlefields of Vietnam.

Juxtaposed against these clues is the author's use of symbolism. Among these is the return of the seventeen-year locusts, caught up in a death cycle that follows the pattern set by father and son. Other symbols include the ascent and descent of the stairs, the cigarette burn in the desk made by Ernest years before, and the garbage dump itself in the last paragraphs. Gordon's vomit, dirt, and semen symbolically encapsulate the story's theme of wasted life.

"No Trace" is less about Gordon's death than about Ernest's reaction to that death. The truth cannot be hidden—it can only be reshuffled to a more central location of stench and deterioration. Ultimately, the wasteland is not so much the battlefields of Vietnam as it is the city dump of American life.

Carl Singleton

NOMAD AND VIPER

Author: Amos Oz (Amos Klausner, 1939-   )
Type of plot: Psychological, social realism
Time of plot: The late 1950's or early 1960's
Locale: A kibbutz in rural southern Israel
First published: "Navadim Vefsefa," 1964 (English translation, 1981)

>   *Principal characters:*
>   GEULAH, an unmarried twenty-nine-year-old kibbutz resident
>   THE NARRATOR, her former would-be suitor, a fiction writer and
>   member of the kibbutz's executive council
>   ETKIN, her kibbutz's rational and pacific secretary
>   AN ELDERLY MAN, the leader of a local Bedouin Arab tribe
>   ARAB GOATHERDER, a young man who is blind in one eye

The Story

In the first of its nine numbered sections, the story begins with a depiction of the northern flight, sanctioned by Israeli military authorities, of Bedouin Arabs from a famine in the drought-ravaged south to a kibbutz and of the appearance and behavior of the Bedouins, their flocks, and their camels. Typical encounters between the Bedouins and kibbutzniks (residents) are described, along with the eerie nocturnal Bedouin music and the baying of their dogs—all of which unsettles the kibbutzniks and their own dogs.

The story then describes animal diseases and crop losses from the Bedouins' flocks and an "epidemic" of petty thefts by Bedouins in the kibbutz. There is some physical retaliation by young kibbutzniks and an administrative confrontation between Etkin, the secretary of the kibbutz, and the elderly leader of the Bedouins. However, the meeting is unsatisfactory because the Bedouin leader admits his people's responsibility for only a fraction of the damage. After the Bedouins leave, Etkin coolly ignores the personal insults of the younger generation kibbutzniks and humanely argues against their retaliating against the Bedouins. However, he agrees to a vote of the secretariat, whose meeting he urges Geulah, a twenty-nine-year-old resident, to attend, asking her to bring a pot of her celebrated coffee and a lot of good will.

Geulah, irritable after being awakened from sleep by Etkin, is wandering around outside on a hot, humid night. She is short, energetic, and pretty from a distance but has acne. She makes coffee and cookies for gatherings and once had a relationship with the narrator, a writer and member of the secretariat. During their relationship, she often strolled with him to the orchard, mercilessly criticized his stories, and dropped flirtatious hints. Now, the narrator usually avoids her, although he anonymously gives her a book of poems for each birthday, but she continues to take walks to the orchard by herself.

A still-restless Geulah works at breaking a discarded bottle that has attracted her attention and then decides to go to the orchard before making coffee for the secretariat meeting. At the orchard, she sheds her sandals and unexpectedly encounters a similarly barefooted young Bedouin goatherd, who is there with his flock. As they casually converse in Hebrew and Arabic, Geulah notices the youth's rugged handsomeness and accepts his offer of a cigarette and light. She asks him if he is hot in his robe, accuses him of trespassing and doing damage with his flock, and watches him unsuccessfully discipline a goat for foraging. After urging him to give up disciplining the goat, she makes some suggestive remarks about his love life and watches him worriedly gather his goats and disappear with the flock. At the same time, she sees an Israeli warplane on maneuvers, panics, and runs home as if pursued, although she is not.

Back in her room, Geulah makes coffee and decides that Etkin's humane attitude toward the Bedouins is wrong. When she showers in the communal stalls, she imagines herself being assaulted by the Bedouin youth at the orchard and concludes that her imaginary mistreatment justifies the retaliation of the kibbutz youths against the Bedouins. Later, she starts back to her room to pick up the coffee and has an overwhelming emotional reaction as she thinks about the Bedouin. As she repeatedly thinks "there's still time" (which may refer to either preparing the coffee or fulfilling her own romantic desires), she hears the counterpoint of Israeli warplanes and Bedouin music.

Members of the secretariat wait in vain for Geulah's coffee and debate about the Bedouins until a dispute between Etkin and the younger generation breaks up the meeting. Although the narrator does not share the views of the young men, he accompanies them out of the meeting, feeling that he, too, has been unfairly deprived of his right to speak. In the next section, the narrator wonders if Geulah's attendance—along with her wonderful coffee—might have calmed the meeting, not knowing how Geulah has changed.

The focus then shifts back to Geulah, who lies outside in the bushes watching the airplanes, struggling between feelings of love and hate for the young goatherd. She feels the cut from a shard of the discarded bottle she broke earlier or a viper slithering among the glass fragments, and she wearily watches Israeli soldiers advance on the Bedouin camp as she caresses the dust with her fingers, her face calm and almost beautiful.

Themes and Meanings

"Nomad and Viper" is about how the world's or a country's polarities may have underlying connections, which if grasped may facilitate communication and communion and if not grasped may lead to miscommunication and hostility. Many polarities are revealed in the story: Arab versus Israeli, herder versus farmer, nomad versus settler, foreign language versus native language, poetic versus prosaic, wild versus domestic, old versus young, ancient versus modern, humanitarianism versus vengeance, male versus female, good traits versus bad traits in human nature, desert versus orchard, and nature versus technology.

Geulah herself, both within and without, exemplifies many of these polarities, which need to be, but are not, harmonized. Her sharp and acerbic intelligence contrasts with her love and writing of poetry. She feels (as do others) the poetic lure of the Bedouins but also finds them repellent. She yearns for romance but rejects it. She loves the orchard—a symbol of creation—but nevertheless feels a need to break a discarded bottle into smithereens—a symbol of destruction. Her very name, "Geulah," comes from a Hebrew word that means both "redeemer" and "avenger."

In contrast to the story's narrator, a writer whose fictional works Geulah criticizes as being polarized into black and white sides, Amos Oz suggests that the whole must be comprehended, that both Arabs and Israelis have their strong and weak points.

Style and Technique

Helping convey the idea of connections among persons and groups are frequent shifts in point of view in the story. These range from the third-person reports of the conversation between Geulah and the goatherd, to the second-person attribution of experience with the nomads ("sometimes you manage to catch them unawares"), to first-person plural that seems initially to be the kibbutz generally but then narrows down to the secretariat and then to the narrator, to direct first-person singular of the narrator, to the fragmented first-person interior of Geulah ("must go now").

Likewise, numerous ironic reversals of plot and character suggest a link underlying polarities, how something may contain or be transformed into its opposite. Metaphors of the nomads "trickling" and "streaming" northward ironically contrast the drought that drives them, as well as the damage they do to the kibbutz agriculture. The timeless nomads, whose ancientness is symbolized by the "wisdom of age" in their camels, sometimes dress in combinations of primeval robes and patched modern European jackets. They cannot afford cigarettes but have gold cigarette lighters. The poetry of their darkly draped tents and nocturnal music making contrasts with the prosaic damage they bring to the kibbutz.

At the story's end, an anonymous Bedouin shepherd, who is mentioned in passing early in the story as having been beaten and who is blind in one eye, seems to be the very one fleeing from Geulah, who will fantasize romance with and assault by him. Geulah herself is dedicated to social activities but cannot form the elemental social bond of marriage. She is attracted to the Bedouin youth, although her own brother was killed in a desert reprisal raid against Arabs. Glass slivers from the bottle she works so hard to smash cut her. The orchard she loves so much may be the scene of a fatal viper bite.

Biblical allusion is pervasive in the story and underlies many ironic contrasts. In a reference to the kibbutz's trouble with the Bedouins, Etkin alludes to the conflict between Cain and Abel in the Old Testament. The venomous snake that approaches Geulah in or near the orchard—the latter a recurrent symbol—recalls the Adam and Eve story of Genesis, in reference to Geulah generally and to her encounter with the Bedouin shepherd in particular. Ironically, however, the nomads in Oz's story would be equated with the innocent Abel, a keeper of flocks, while the kibbutzniks would be equated with Cain, a worker of the soil, and the murderer of Abel. In an ironic reversal, the initial tempter in the orchard is the Bedouin shepherd, who offers Geulah a cigarette. This incident itself is a reversal of an example at the story's beginning, when a kibbutznik offers an Arab a cigarette.

Further biblical symbolism is conveyed in the obscure motif of Geulah's need to smash the discarded bottle, which has overtones of Psalm 2 and its prayer to God of dashing Israel's enemies to pieces like a shattered potter's vessel. However, just as Geulah is cut by the bottle, this allusion suggests that the violence against a supposed foe may have rebound with disastrous consequences.

Norman Prinsky

NOON WINE

Author: Katherine Anne Porter (1890-1980)
Type of plot: Psychological
Time of plot: 1896-1905
Locale: Texas
First published: 1936

Principal characters:
> MR. ROYAL EARLE THOMPSON, a dairy farmer who is overly
> concerned about appearances
> MRS. ELLEN "ELLIE" BRIDGES THOMPSON, his sickly wife
> ARTHUR THOMPSON and
> HERBERT THOMPSON, their sons
> MR. OLAF ERIC HELTON, a Swede from North Dakota who works
> for the Thompsons
> MR. HOMER T. HATCH, a bounty hunter

The Story

One day in 1896, Mr. Olaf Eric Helton appears on Mr. Royal Earle Thompson's dairy farm in the southern part of Texas. Helton, who last worked in the wheat fields of North Dakota, asks for a job. Thompson decides to hire Helton for seven dollars a month, even though he is "practically" the first Swede he has ever seen.

Thompson takes advantage of his new status by going into town for groceries and a few drinks. Mrs. Ellen Thompson, his wife, in perennial ill health, is drawn out of the house by the tune that Helton is playing on a harmonica. She assumes that the new hired man is worthless, as is so often the case, and she is surprised to see that all the work has been efficiently done. Her husband, on his return, is also impressed with the work of the new employee. The only things that bother them about Helton are that he will not talk or eat enough, but his industry more than makes up for his faults.

Mr. Thompson particularly learns to enjoy the luxury of having Helton around to do the work that is below an employer's level. There are only limited fields of activity with which a boss ought to concern himself, according to Thompson. Most of the work on a dairy farm is fit for women or hired help. It would not look right, for example, for a man to be seen slopping hogs. He worries about his dignity and reputation, and, now that he has competent help, he can concentrate on manly work.

As a young man, Thompson had fallen in love with Ellen's charms, and, though they have disappeared over the years, he has learned to appreciate her. He accepts the burden of her illness, and, in fact, is proud of himself for doing so. Before the arrival of Helton, however, he had been resigned to failure. The miserable condition of the farm testified to this resignation. Helton changes things, however, and, as the years pass, the farm begins to prosper.

Mrs. Thompson learns to accept Helton, even if he is different. She invites him to go to church with the family once, and she is alarmed at the rejection of the Christian invitation and his accompanying anger. On another occasion, she is upset when she discovers him shaking the boys, Arthur and Herbert, ferociously, but silently, for playing with his harmonicas. They are the only things, besides his privacy, that he seems to value. Mrs. Thompson is puzzled by Helton, but because the farm is doing well, she decides to accept him even if he is not like ordinary people.

About nine years after Helton's arrival, another stranger appears on the farm. He introduces himself as Homer T. Hatch. He is looking for an escaped murderer whom he describes as a lunatic who disappeared from a mental institution in North Dakota. Thompson tries to defend his hired man, but Hatch says that Helton killed his own brother with a pitchfork after a quarrel over a lost harmonica. Thompson's dislike for the fat stranger grows when he discovers that he is a bounty hunter. Hatch, however, claims that he is for law and order. He had discovered the location of Helton because of a letter the Swede had sent to his mother in North Dakota, and now Hatch believes that he is only doing his duty. Thompson counters by saying that Helton has become one of the family. Hatch is trespassing, and Thompson orders him to leave. Then something strange happens. Thompson sees a bowie knife and a pair of handcuffs in the stranger's hands and, at the same time, spots Helton coming around the corner. The latter charges in between them, and Thompson thinks he sees the knife go into Helton's stomach. He responds by hitting Hatch with an ax. When Mrs. Thompson appears, he tells her that he had to knock out Hatch because he killed Helton. She points out, however, that Helton is running away. It is Hatch who is dead.

Mr. Thompson is acquitted at the trial, but that does not erase his guilt. He still thinks of himself as a possible murderer. His wife, who was persuaded to testify to the lie that she had witnessed the whole scene involving the killing, does not help to ease his torment. She blames him for ruining the lives of her sons and causing the death of Helton. The Swede had been captured by a posse. He apparently died in jail as the result of the rough treatment of his captors or perhaps because of a broken spirit. It is suggested that Helton might have escaped if he had not stopped to retrieve two harmonicas that had fallen from his pocket.

Thompson, meanwhile, spends his time trying to convince people of his innocence, but he cannot convince himself or his family. He is haunted by the question of whether he had to kill the man or if he only overreacted. One night, he jumps out of bed as he is wrestling with his conscience. It frightens his wife, and she faints. When the sons come charging in, they turn against their father and threaten him with violence if he frightens their mother again. This incident is the final humiliation for Thompson. He pretends to be going for a doctor to help with Ellen's fainting spells, but instead he writes a note that states that he killed Hatch only in defense of Helton. He then kills himself by pulling the trigger of his shotgun with his toe.

Themes and Meanings

"Noon Wine" deals primarily with human fallibility. For nine years, the Thompson farm is a virtual paradise. Then Hatch arrives and sets in motion the events that destroy the characters. The faults of the Thompsons and Helton, when brought into conflict with the amorality of Hatch, dominate their actions and lead to their downfall. Hatch helps to bring about his own death by his lack of respect for humanity, which turns Thompson against him. The farmer is consumed by worry over how he appears to others. His wife turns her stern moral code against herself by condemning rather than forgiving, and, in the process, divides and demoralizes the family. Helton, despite all that he does for the Thompsons, puts them in jeopardy with his silent madness.

Thompson's concern for appearances is his major fault. Before Helton takes over, he is unable to make the farm pay because of his aversion for most types of work. He limits his fields of activity according to what looks proper from the perspective of a proud landowner. Thus, when Hatch poses a threat to his happiness, violence follows. Thompson is not sure if he tried to protect Helton because of benevolence or self-interest. The legal exoneration does not eliminate the doubt. Although he cannot convince himself of his innocence, he literally goes crazy trying to convince everyone else. His family's failure to support him leads to the suicide.

Mrs. Thompson's illness represents her quarrel with a world that does not run according to her moral standards. A former Baptist Sunday school teacher, she is disappointed by her husband's vanity. Nevertheless, life is bearable for her until Hatch interposes. After that, her life becomes too much. Instead of comforting her husband, she remains silent and withdrawn. The lie that her husband forces on her (about seeing the fight with Hatch), and that she corroborates in the desperate attempt to look good to the inhabitants of the area, makes her feel guilty. Although she verifies her husband's innocence to others, she does not accept that verdict herself. In her moral blindness, she contributes to her husband's demise.

Homer T. Hatch hides his greed behind the respectability of law and order. As a bounty hunter, Hatch does not care about Helton as a person. He only wants to collect his money.

Helton's passion for harmonicas is his weakness. He cares more for them than life itself. The one song that he repeatedly plays is identified by Hatch as a Scandinavian drinking song about a worker who feels so good that he drinks all his wine in the morning rather than saving it for the noon break. This single tune, his almost total verbal silence, and his tendency toward violence indicate his uniqueness. He is an outsider who lives by his own rules. However, his refusal to yield to the rules of society eventually hurts him and the Thompsons.

The title, referring to Helton's single tune, suggests the happiness that is potentially available to humanity. The nine-year interlude on the Thompson farm is a step in this direction. This Edenic existence, however, is interrupted by human fallibilities. Hatch sets in motion the events that destroy himself and others.

Style and Technique

In "Noon Wine," Katherine Anne Porter brings people to life in scenes filled with physical detail and realistic dialogue. The characters are given human qualities in an attempt to make them more than abstract representations of fallibilities. Their actions, thoughts, and words make them seem like ordinary people. The general qualities that they represent are made more intense by the specific situations that are skillfully depicted. Each scene also foreshadows future events. Thus, the tragedy is made credible.

An early scene shows the intimacy between the Thompsons. A debate over the merits and faults of Helton leads to a mock quarrel. Mr. Thompson pinches his wife, suggesting that she is too lean for his taste in woman. She retaliates by pulling his hair and calling him evil-minded. This playful domestic episode illustrates the close relationship they share and increases the tragic effect of their inability to communicate at the end of the story.

Another revealing incident is Mrs. Thompson's witnessing of Helton's attack on the boys for playing with his harmonicas. Hatch later reveals that Helton's brother had been murdered for a similar offense. Helton's irrational response to the molestation of his harmonicas is a foreshadowing of the madness that recurs with the appearance of Hatch.

Even Hatch reveals a typical human trait when he engages Thompson in a discussion on tobacco. This subject, however, does not relieve the farmer's misgivings about the stranger. Hatch offends him by insisting that the use of sweetened tobacco is a sign of cheapness. Thompson likes sweet tobacco, and he thinks that the man is trying to humiliate him. He thinks about shoving Hatch off the stump in the hope that he might fall on the ax. Before long, the knife and the ax do come into play. Hatch's propensity for offending others appears even in casual conversation. Thompson, put on the defensive, reacts violently.

Every scene, then, leads to the confrontation between Hatch and Thompson and to the disastrous aftermath. The weaknesses of the characters make their downfall unavoidable; their individual traits make them credible as human beings. Although the pessimism of this tragedy of the human condition is dominant, the impact of its message is softened by the engaging manner in which the story is told.

Noel Schraufnagel

NORTH LIGHT
A Recollection in the Present Tense

Author: Mark Helprin (1947-   )
Type of plot: Psychological
Time of plot: The 1970's
Locale: Israel
First published: 1981

Principal character:
THE NARRATOR, a middle-aged Israeli soldier

The Story

The unnamed narrator is an Israeli soldier who fought in the Six-Day War and hoped his days of war were over. This morning, however, his unit has been called up and is watching from a ridge as tanks maneuver in a small valley, waiting until nightfall when they will be ordered into a battle. Although their comrades below are outnumbered, the Israeli command has decided that the unit should not enter into the valley until dark, because they have only two old half-tracks that could accomplish little against the Syrian tanks in the light of day.

It can be more difficult to wait than to fight. The narrator notes the differences between the older men who have experienced war before and the young soldiers who are facing enemy fire for the first time. The young do not know what the reality of battle will prove to be, but the narrator believes that because they are young—approximately eighteen years of age—they have little to lose even if they lose their lives, for they are responsible only for themselves.

The narrator and the other older soldiers who have been in battle before know the maiming and death of warfare. Unlike in their youth, they now have something to lose: their families and loved ones. The soldier next to the narrator sniffs his wrist. When asked why, he responds, "I can still smell her perfume on my wrist, and I taste the taste of her mouth." Another veteran soldier, about fifty years old, and with two sons fighting in the Sinai, constantly scans his watch, but he cannot tell anyone the time even after looking at the dial because of his fear and his fear of loss.

The narrator notes that for the young, going into battle is like being a member of a sports team waiting for the game to begin; their courage comes easily. With more knowledge and more to lose, the older men say to themselves, "I must not die; I must not die." It is impossible to be eighteen again, and for them courage is no longer a reflex but a conscious decision to act when one desires above all else not to step forward. In battle, however, conscious thought might lead to one's death. A soldier dare not be overcautious because warfare is like a dance where one's body must lead, not one's mind.

The waiting, the being held back, allows too much thought. In a kind of epiphany, the narrator remembers when he and his comrades were fighting the Egyptians in the

Six-Day War. The secret to courage is to be angry. Only when the soldier is angry should he join the dance of war. Paradoxically, although being held back gives one too much time to think, it also brings anger; against the Egyptians, the Israeli soldiers were forced to wait for weeks before their angry dance was allowed to begin.

A group of Israeli airplanes flies low over the ridge, dipping their wings in salute. The soldiers' anger increases, focused not only against the Syrians in the valley but also against the high command that does not allow them to enter the battle. Finally, in response to pleading by the sergeant, just before three o'clock, the order is given to proceed. All are ready, young and old. "We are shaking; we are crying. Now we stare into the north light. . . . Now we are moving."

Themes and Meanings

In "North Light," Mark Helprin explores the question of why soldiers willingly risk death in battle. War is the subject but not the actual chaos, pain, or even glory of battle. "North Light" concludes as the soldiers are ready to begin to join the battle they have been observing throughout the day. The closest they come to the sound and fury of war is when friendly Israeli planes fly over their ridge, although the older soldiers have their memories, their recollections of earlier conflicts.

The answer, Helprin implies, is not merely love of country. Patriotism and nationalism are not an explanation. The reader is aware that the narrator and his comrades on the ridge are Israelis and the enemy are Syrians, but neither one's own country nor war against a traditional opponent is sufficient to drive people toward possible death. Countervailing forces of love and responsibility for one's family would justify not chancing one's life in combat. Not even loyalty to one's fellow soldiers suffices as an explanation. The narrator in "North Light" concludes that people willingly enter the valley of death because anger, irrational anger, manifests itself, anger that is not necessarily focused or directed against a specific threat or opponent. When the order is given to descend into the valley, they are in a sustained fury, and those with families will obliterate thoughts of their loved ones until the battle is over.

Those feelings of anger are complex. After being ordered to advance, "For a magnificent half minute, we stare into the north light, smiling . . . and listen to the explosions below." Light is a consistent theme in Helprin's writings. He has used the expression "north light" elsewhere, and in this story there is no simple interpretation of its meaning. The soldiers wait on the southern ridge of a small valley with the sun shining from behind, so the north light cannot be the sun. Within the narrative, no other obvious physical or natural characteristic or event is suggested that might explain the story's title.

In the Middle East's hot desert climate, reference to north light might imply a consoling, comforting alternative, a renewal or redemption, from the burning heat of that region's sunlight. Helprin probably means the reference to north light to suggest a more transcendent possibility. In his novel *A Soldier of the Great War* (1991), Helprin has one of his characters comment "that all the hard and wonderful things of the world are nothing more than a frame for a spirit, like fire and light, that is the endless roiling of love and grace. . . . That beauty cannot be expressed or explained in a theory or an idea, that it moves by its own law, that it is God's way of comforting His broken children." The real or material sun is shining from a southern exposure. From the north, however, there is another light. It is not a false light, not merely a mirage, nor does it seem to represent futility or misguided finality. It does not simply prefigure the battlefield deaths that will be the fate of many in the unit with only their two inadequate half-tracks in the bright three o'clock light. Perhaps it expresses a totality, encompassing not only death but life, the young and the old, anger and love, aggression and sacrifice—a transcendent embrace, if not by God, then from humanity itself? Whatever the meanings of that north light, it adds to the richness of what might appear as a simple tale of men going into battle.

Style and Technique

The story is related in simple declarative sentences but with an intensity and emotion appropriate to a soldier waiting for battle to begin. More unusual as a literary technique, the story is told in the present tense. The narrator recites his observations and his feelings as they occur while waiting until the orders are given to engage the enemy. He is not relating the events after the fact.

The author successfully develops his themes over the course of the story. As noted, light is an important reference in "North Light." In the first paragraph "The sun shines from behind, illuminating with flawless light" and in the last paragraphs it is the north light that dominates. When the story begins, the prevailing emotion is fear, which gradually turns to anger before the company embarks into the valley.

Finally, there is the subtitle: "A Recollection in the Present Tense." Helprin tells the story through a first-person unnamed narrator using the present tense, but the use of the word "recollection" suggests that the narrator survives the coming battle in the valley to later relate the story, although in the present tense. The word "recollection" has another implication. The narrator's discovery that anger is the answer to the question of why men fight is recollected from his earlier experiences in the Six-Day War.

Eugene Larson

THE NORTHERN LIGHTS

Author: Joy Harjo (1951-   )
Type of plot: Psychological
Time of plot: The 1970's and 1980's
Locale: Ashland, Wisconsin and Vietnam
First published: 1991

> *Principal characters:*
> WHIRLING SOLDIER, a Native American Vietnam War veteran
> HIS FATHER, an alcoholic who drowned
> HIS MOTHER, the pillar of the family
> HIS DAUGHTER, a recovered alcoholic
> THE NARRATOR, who meets Whirling Soldier at a powwow

The Story

The story of Whirling Soldier, a Vietnam veteran and Native American, unfolds through a series of flashbacks, alternating between his war experience, his childhood, and his life after he is discharged from the military. As an unnamed narrator relates the story's beginning and end, the body of the story comprises a series of images that reveal the psychological and spiritual decline and subsequent recovery of Whirling Soldier.

The narrator meets Whirling Soldier at a traditional Native American powwow held on the shores of Lake Superior. In contrast to the natural phenomenon of the northern lights that blaze across the sky, the powwow takes place under the garish electrical lights of an auditorium. From his physical appearance it is apparent that Whirling Soldier still suffers the psychological trauma of war. However, despite his suffering, his attendance at the powwow demonstrates that he has reintegrated into the Indian community. The narrator and Whirling Soldier engage in small talk and look on proudly as the latter's niece and eighteen-year-old daughter, a recovering alcoholic, dance joyfully before their relatives.

Whirling Soldier confides to the narrator that he has suffered much pain because of his war experience and because of his father's death. Memories of his Vietnam experiences intertwine with those of his childhood. His first Vietnam memory is sparked by the appearance of the northern lights on the night of the powwow: At one moment during the war, he and a white companion take cover in a ditch. Gunfire from an unseen enemy reminds him of the northern lights. In his confusion, he cannot tell whether the gunfire originates with his ditchmate or with the enemy Viet Cong.

Whirling Soldier's confusion concerning the enemy gunfire is symptomatic of a deeper cultural conflict. The Vietnam War—which was orchestrated by white men in Washington—violated the "warrior code" with which he was brought up. He was disturbed by the wailing of children that the war left fatherless. In his own culture, the conquerors would have cared for the orphans. The distress of the children brings to mind events from his own childhood. Although he grew up in a poor family, his parents did the best they could to provide for their children. He fondly remembers his mother cooking breakfast for him and his sisters and days when he skipped school in order to be with his father. Images of Whirling Soldier's father frequently come to his mind as he fights in Vietnam. He remembers how his father got drunk while ice-fishing and drowned in an ice-covered lake. The image of his father's death haunts him as he daily faces the possibility of his own death. To dull his fears and pain, he becomes addicted to heroin and performs his duties in a drug-induced haze. Finally, he is wounded and discharged from the military as a hero.

After Whirling Soldier leaves the service, he does not return home even though he imagines his mother beading a blanket in honor of his status as a returning warrior. Instead he ends up in Kansas, becomes an alcoholic like his father, and pawns his medals to buy liquor. After a night of drinking, he wakes up one morning to a day that reminds him of his childhood. He remembers his mother making a venison sandwich and his father just waking up and asking him where he is going. The question takes on a deeper meaning as he wanders the roads of Kansas with only a bottle as his companion. As he walks, he notices a sunflower that reminds him of his two-year old daughter. He takes his last drink from his nearly empty gin bottle and reflects on the fist fight he had in a bar the night before. The contrast between his status as a war hero and his meaningless barroom brawl points up the extent of his decline. He begins to hallucinate and sees a vision of a "relative that he never met." The image of the relative spiritually reconnects Whirling Soldier with his family and ancestors and is the beginning of his rehabilitation.

The story ends where it begins—at the powwow in Ashland. The narrator does not tell of the intervening time between Whirling Soldier's vision of his ancestor and his return to his family. However, it is clear that returning home, the presence of his family, and rediscovering the importance of his Native American heritage have helped to heal his mind and soul. Whirling Soldier is not only surrounded by his human family but by his spiritual ancestors. The northern lights are perceived as relatives returned from the war. It is an unusual moment of grace and reconciliation for Whirling Soldier.

Themes and Meanings

Cultural and personal survival are recurrent themes in Joy Harjo's writing. Harjo herself notes that her prose and poetry are imbued with this theme "both on a personal and a larger, communal level." In "Northern Lights," the psychological and spiritual survival of Whirling Soldier is accomplished by the healing effect that Native American tribal traditions have on the individual.

Whirling Soldier is aptly named; not only is he a Vietnam veteran, he must overcome an inner conflict as well. The war that rages in his psyche is the result of the cultural battle between Anglo American society and his Native American heritage. For example, in Native American traditions, the warrior is an honored member of the community. However, the war in Vietnam so divided the country that American soldiers felt alienated from their own people back home. Whirling Soldier is doubly alienated; he not only is fighting in an unpopular war, he is fighting at the command of another enemy—the Anglo Americans who have oppressed his people.

White conquest has severed Native Americans from their ties with the land, suppressed their traditions, and forced them to conform to European ways of life. One result of this cultural violation is alcoholism. In "Northern Lights," three generations have been affected by this disease: Whirling Soldier, his father, and even his teenage daughter. Alcoholism is a visible symptom of the deeper psychological war that is raging inside the minds of these characters. The suffering of Whirling Soldier symbolizes the problems that many Native Americans presently face as a marginalized people. Such psychological conflict threatens the survival of the individual as well as the Native American culture.

Hope for personal survival as well as a "larger, communal" survival lies in reconnection with traditional customs, values, and religion. The northern lights represent the importance of recognizing the natural world and the spiritual realm in achieving this reconnection. The northern lights appear at the beginning, middle, and end of the story. At the beginning, their appearance lends a spiritual aura to the proceedings at the powwow. When the northern lights are mentioned in connection with the gunfire in Vietnam, their meaning is both salutary and somewhat ambiguous. Though Whirling Soldier perceives them as "mercy gathering on the horizon," he also associates their flashing light with the dangerous situation in which he finds himself. At the end of the story, the beauty of the northern lights is associated with ghostly warriors coming to join with their living relatives in the dance. This "moment of grace" reflects the Native American belief that the extended tribal family includes living members and the spirits of ancestors. Whirling Soldier's healing is aided by a loving community in which past and present merge and tradition is valued.

Style and Technique

Harjo, who is a gifted painter as well as a writer, has commented that she approaches writing in much the same way as a painter creates a painting. Her use of flashbacks is similar to a painter's technique. Just as a painter covers a canvas with a series of images that suggest something deeper than the images themselves, Whirling Soldier's memories are images that indicate his deep pain, his inner conflict, and need for wholeness. Although his memories of war, childhood, and early adulthood seem to describe very distinct periods of his life, the central image of the northern lights connects them together. Because the story shifts back and forth in time, the appearance of the northern lights is important in lending continuity to the story. Telling a story in nonlinear fashion is a common characteristic of Native American literature. In the case of "The Northern Lights," this mode of storytelling also mimics the way the human mind thinks and remembers and is an effective way to reveal Whirling Soldier's psychological state.

Pegge Bochynski

THE NORWEGIAN RAT

Author: Naguib Mahfouz (1911-   )
Type of plot: Domestic realism
Time of plot: The early 1970's
Locale: Cairo, Egypt
First published: "Al-Fa'r al-norwiji," 1984 (English translation, 1991)

> *Principal characters:*
> MR. A. M., the senior householder of an urban apartment house
> THE NARRATOR, a resident in the building
> A GOVERNMENT INSPECTOR

The Story

Mr. A. M., the senior householder in an urban apartment house, calls a tenants' meeting in his flat to discuss the threat posed by an acute rat infestation that they are expecting. The media, both print and broadcast, have warned about the scope and destruction likely to follow the invading rodents. Reportedly, the aggressive rats are attacking even cats and humans. Accordingly, Mr. A. M. tells the ten tenants in attendance that they should meticulously carry out both his instructions and those from the authorities regarding preparations to meet the threat. He urges them to set traps, spread rat poison, and to have as many cats as possible in the stairwell, on the roof, and even in their apartments because cats are useful no matter what.

The source of the rat infestation is a matter for speculation. Some suggest that the rats originated from the evacuated Suez Canal towns, which were heavily shelled by Israeli guns positioned on the eastern bank of the waterway in 1969 and 1970 during the War of Attrition. Others believe that the explosion of the rat population is a negative consequence of the Aswan High Dam, which affected the irrigation canal networks downstream. Another suggestion is that the surge in the rat population is due to bad public administration. Some attribute the problem to Allah's anger on account of his servants' refusal to accept divine guidance.

At a subsequent tenants' meeting in the building, Mr. A. M. expresses satisfaction with the residents' preparations, though some of them complain about the expense of feeding the numerous felines. New rat poison ground up in corn is to be distributed, Mr. A. M. announces, warning the tenants to protect their children, pets, and poultry (often kept on roofs or verandas in Egyptian urban areas). However, in the meantime, the anticipation—indeed, the dread—fueled by some earlier horror stories is causing tension and even taking control of people's lives. The threat comes to dominate the tenants' other existential worries, their conversations, and even their dreams.

At the third tenants' meeting, Mr. A. M. reports progress in their preparations to confront the rats. He relays the expressed gratification of the governor at these measures. He gives further directives about the need to seal windows, doors, and any other openings and possible points of entry. Although he tries to pacify some tenants' complaints about the restraints that these measures impose on them, some of the tenants are bothered by weariness, boredom, and depression, which affect their domestic relations.

Soon, the government inspector from a previously announced team of experts shows up and gives the building's preparations a passing grade, commenting favorably on the large number of cats roaming around, even in the garage. A week later, the official returns to inspect the narrator's apartment. The civil servant inspector is a middle-aged man with a thick mustache and a glassy stare and reminds the narrator of a cat, a resemblance that he considers appropriate under the circumstances. The official finds only a minor deficiency. However, because the apartment is now redolent of the meal just prepared by the narrator's wife, the inspector's compliments trigger an invitation to partake. The inspector sits down and begins to wolf down his lunch with extraordinary voracity. When the narrator returns to serve another helping, the tenant is struck by the appearance of the official's face: It is now reminiscent of a Norwegian rat. The dazed narrator returns to his wife and asks her to look in on the man. She, too, is dumbfounded by his facial metamorphosis while gobbling down the food. Soon, a cheerful blessing by the inspector sounds from the hallway. When the departing figure turns around to bid the couple goodbye, he gives a "fleeting Norwegian smile."

Themes and Meanings

A number of Naguib Mahfouz's short stories deal with problems involving the human condition—anxiety, fear, uncertainty, frustration, crisis, and conflict—which he often describes ambivalently. In this story, although the residents of the apartments, with the assistance of the authorities, have the actual capability to prevent rats from entering the building and to destroy them if necessary, they are traumatized by rumors of the rodents' aggressiveness, destructiveness, and danger to public health.

As the story unfolds, the protagonists' frame of mind becomes phobic to the point that their entire existence is monopolized by the mere anticipation of this latter-day plague, which the narrator equates with the great flood and the birds turning on humans, quoting the Qur'an, the holy book of Islam. By the time of the denouement, even the narrator and his wife have become infected with the hysteria, fantasizing that the government inspector has ratlike features. Thus, the condition of psychological transference—and the perverseness of the situation—become evident when the couple project their fixation on the very individual whose job it is to deal with the problem. The rats may well be a metaphor for the numerous social and political problems plaguing Egypt and about which Mahfouz has written extensively elsewhere.

Even though the characters are not developed in the brief scope of the story, Mr. A. M. comes through as a real individual. He is the senior householder. He has the most senior position, presumably in his professional life, but is also the most affluent and oldest in the building. Arabs have great respect for age, which is equated with having the experience essential for survival in a hostile environment. He is authoritative not only by virtue of what he is but also in what he says. At one point, he curtly puts an end to a tenant's complaint regarding frayed nerves. Mr. A. M. also implies his closeness to the governor, the head of a large administrative district. The take-charge attitude of this middle- or upper-middle-class individual is in stark contrast with the fatalistic acceptance of Allah's will by the lower social strata of a Muslim community whenever calamity strikes.

Style and Technique

This short story, which appeared in a collection entitled *Al-Tanẓīm al-sirri* (1984; the secret organization), is told chronologically. As in Mahfouz's other works, there is more narrative than dialogue. The story is brief and explicit, a skill that the author attributes to his having written many film scripts during his career. The dialogue emerges from the mouth or consciousness of the anonymous narrator with whom the author may well identify.

The context of this work, as with all of the writings of Mahfouz, is distinctly Egyptian. The Nobel Prize-winning author does not like to travel abroad. With one or two exceptions, all his stories are set in his hometown, most often in the familiar neighborhoods in which he has spent most of his life. This local focus and Mahfouz's specifically Egyptian frame of reference may make it hard for some readers to relate to some of his works. For example, in "The Norwegian Rat," readers need some geopolitical background to understand the speculations raised about the possible causes of the rodent invasion, ranging from an episode in the Arab-Israeli War to ecological changes caused by the construction of the Aswan High Dam located more than four hundred miles to the south.

However, none of this detracts from a story that proposes that even as commonplace a pest as the brown house rat—the *Rattus norvegicus*, often called the Norway rat—can bring consternation to a community and cause it to resolve to organize to deal with the physical and psychological threat. As usual in political contexts, Mahfouz is supportive of leadership and action to meet crises. In the story, "the estimable Mr. A. M." and "our revered Governor" epitomize both.

The dry humor evident in this story about one of the many tribulations that Egyptians have had to face bespeaks of the latter's habit of making fun of their circumstances. However, on this occasion, a frequently bungling government comes through with flying colors.

Peter B. Heller

THE NOSE

Author: Nikolai Gogol (1809-1852)
Type of plot: Satire
Time of plot: The 1830's
Locale: St. Petersburg, Russia
First published: "Nos," 1836 (English translation, 1915)

Principal characters:
 COLLEGIATE ASSESSOR PLATON KUZMICH KOVALYOV, a
   government clerk
 IVAN YAKOVLEVICH, his barber
 PRASKOVYA OSIPOVNA, Ivan Yakovlevich's wife
 IVAN, Kovalyov's manservant
 PELAGEYA PODTOCHIN, a widow whose daughter Kovalyov is
   courting
 A POLICE OFFICER

The Story
 "A most extraordinary thing happened in St. Petersburg on the twenty-fifth of March." Ivan Yakovlevich, a Russian barber in St. Petersburg, wakes up in his house and prepares to eat the breakfast prepared by his wife. As he cuts into a fresh loaf of bread, he finds a human nose inside. Although confused and distraught by the discovery, the barber recognizes the nose as that of Collegiate Assessor Platon Kuzmich Kovalyov, a government clerk whom he shaves every Wednesday and Sunday. Fearing his wife's wrath and further complications, Ivan Yakovlevich gets dressed and goes out with the idea of disposing of the nose. The streets are crowded, however, and there is little opportunity to get rid of his grotesque burden, which he has wrapped in a rag. He finally manages to throw the nose into the Neva River, but as luck would have it, he has been observed by a police inspector, who summons him to explain why he was on the bridge. Here, the story continues, "the incident becomes completely shrouded in a fog and it is really impossible to say what happened next."
 On the same morning in March, Kovalyov, a bachelor, wakes up in his St. Petersburg apartment and immediately goes to the mirror to check a pimple that had appeared on his nose the previous evening. Instead of a nose with a blemish, he sees only "a completely empty, flat spot" on his face where his nose had been.
 Kovalyov dresses and goes out with intention of reporting his loss to the police. As he is making his way to the police station, he notices a gentleman in a gold-braided uniform jump out of a carriage and enter a private house. This gentleman is none other than Kovalyov's nose, dressed as a State Councillor, a rank three degrees higher than Collegiate Assessor. A few minutes later, the Nose/State Councillor comes out from the house and drives to a nearby cathedral, with Kovalyov in pursuit. Inside the cathe-

dral, Kovalyov sees the Nose saying his prayers and decides to confront him (or it), in spite of the protocol involved in addressing a civil servant of a higher rank. When Kovalyov finally musters enough courage and presence of mind to speak to the pious Nose, he can only blurt out the obvious: "You are my nose, sir!" The Nose, in turn, rebuffs any such suggestion by insisting, "My dear fellow, you are mistaken. I am myself."

Kovalyov does not know what to think or say, but at this moment he is distracted by a slim young girl in a white dress and straw-colored hat who is standing near him in the congregation. Kovalyov smiles at this "spring flower" with "semi-transparent fingers" and "dazzling white chin," but suddenly realizes that he is exposing his noseless face to the young beauty and retreats.

While Kovalyov is engrossed with the unknown girl, the Nose leaves the church. Kovalyov gives chase but loses the Nose in the crowd on Nevsky Prospect. Afraid that his quarry will slip out of town, Kovalyov goes for help to the Police Commissioner's house, but finding the official out for the evening, he decides to go the newspaper office to place a "missing nose" advertisement. At first the newspaper clerk does not understand the nature of the advertisement Kovalyov proposes to print. Finally, after realizing that this is not a usual lost-and-found notice, the clerk rejects it because it is, to his mind, absurd and potentially libelous. The clerk feels sorry for Kovalyov and tries to calm him by offering him a pinch of snuff. Kovalyov angrily responds by reminding the clerk that he does not at the moment have the appropriate organ for taking snuff.

Kovalyov returns to the Police Commissioner's house, this time finding the Commissioner in, but the official is sleepy after a big dinner and in no mood for Kovalyov's problem, adding that "a respectable man would not have his nose pulled off." Insulted and upset, Kovalyov returns to his apartment, where he muses on what has happened to him. He dismisses the possible explanations that he is dreaming or drunk; applying some strange logic to the situation, he concludes that a Mrs. Podtochin has engaged a witch to put a curse on him and make his nose disappear. This, he is sure, is the lady's revenge for his refusal to marry her dowryless daughter, with whom he has been flirting.

As Kovalyov reflects on how to deal with Mrs. Podtochin, a police officer arrives to announce that he has found Kovalyov's nose. According to the officer, the Nose was trying to escape the country on a stagecoach for Riga, using a bogus passport. The police officer further explains that luckily he was wearing his glasses at the time of the incident and recognized that the Nose was not the gentleman he pretended to be. The police officer also announces that the barber from the first part of the story was somehow mixed up in the affair and is now in jail. Kovalyov picks up the officer's hint that a gratuity would not be refused and gives him a lavish tip.

Left alone with his nose, Kovalyov is at first ecstatic that it is back, but his joy is moderated by the realization that his nose is still detached and not in its proper place. All of Kovalyov's attempts to attach the nose to his face fail, and not even the local doctor can succeed in making the nose stick to its place between Kovalyov's cheeks.

Instead the doctor offers to buy the nose as a curiosity if it is first pickled in a vinegar jar and if the price is right.

At this point, Kovalyov still believes that the widow Podtochin had something to do with what has happened, and he decides to write her a letter, accusing her of witchcraft and threatening legal action. Mrs. Podtochin answers with her own letter, the wording of which convinces Kovalyov of her innocence in any plot against him or his nose, and so the affair remains as mysterious as ever.

Meanwhile, all sorts of rumors circulate in St. Petersburg about Kovalyov's nose. Claims are made that Kovalyov's nose has been seen taking a stroll on Nevsky Prospect every day at three o'clock in the afternoon. Thousands of curious people come out to see it. Tickets are sold to obtain the best places from which to observe this rare phenomenon. One rich aristocratic lady offers to establish an endowment for her children to be given "instructive and edifying explanations" about the vagrant nose. "After that—but here again a thick fog descends on the whole incident."

Suddenly, on the morning of the seventh of April, the nose returns to its proper place on the face of Major Kovalyov. Kovalyov is overjoyed, especially when his manservant Ivan confirms that indeed his nose is back where it belongs. Ivan Yakovlevich, the barber from the first part of the story, arrives to shave Kovalyov as usual; except for his special care in handling Kovalyov's nose while shaving him, the barber does nothing out of the ordinary during the encounter, and neither man mentions the incident with the nose.

Kovalyov dresses and goes out, driving straight to the nearest pastry shop, where he orders a cup of chocolate. On his way home, Kovalyov meets Mrs. Podtochin and her daughter and stops to talk with them at length. Their manner with him more firmly confirms his feeling that they know nothing about what has happened to his nose. Kovalyov increases his social activity out of sheer joy that normalcy has returned to his life.

Themes and Meanings

The first Russian journal to which Nikolai Gogol submitted "The Nose" refused to publish it, labeling it "obscene and trivial." Perhaps the editors noticed the aggressive satire on Russian society, as well as on the government bureaucracy and its stupid, smug, and self-serving officials, and were therefore wary of being associated with antigovernment propaganda.

There also exists the possibility of a biographical interpretation. Gogol was always fascinated by his own elongated, pointed, birdlike nose, a fact that has opened the way to a kind of Freudian reading of "The Nose," in which the story becomes Gogol's symbolic representation of a castration fear.

Knowing Gogol's others works, it is easy to see "The Nose" as a wild comic fantasy with no "meaning" as such. From this viewpoint, the story can be seen as an example of pure creative art, parodying the then popular notion that literature must have some "message" or "point."

Style and Technique

Snuff-taking, smelling, sneezing, and snoring are leitmotifs in all of Gogol's works. The human nose was for Gogol an unlikely organ: so prominent a facial feature yet somehow and at the same time so ridiculous and otiose. So much on his mind was nasal imagery that the main character in one of Gogol's other stories goes mad and insists that the moon is inhabited by noses.

Alogisms abound in the story. For example, the police officer who brings Kovalyov's renegade nose back says that it was lucky that he had on his glasses because otherwise he would not have noticed that the gentleman was really a Nose. He goes on to say that nearsightedness runs in his family—even his mother-in-law is nearsighted. Full of digressions and irrelevant "asides" (for example, the gratuitously detailed description of the young girl whom Kovalyov sees in the cathedral), the story constantly aims at mystification. Nothing about the bizarre incident of the Nose is ever explained, yet the characters in the story take the circumstances of Kovalyov's spontaneously amputated nose in a completely matter-of-fact way, expressing no shock or amazement.

R. E. Richardson

NOT A GOOD GIRL

Author: Perri Klass (1958-   )
Type of plot: Realism
Time of plot: Around 1980
Locale: Boston
First published: 1983

Principal characters:
THE NARRATOR, a young, unnamed woman biochemist
ERIC, a graduate student with whom she has a two-day fling

The Story

The narrator comes to Harvard University from New York City to present two academic seminars in immunology. After her first presentation, she is taken to an Italian restaurant by young faculty members and graduate students. When she leaves, a graduate student named Eric gives her a ride, puts his hand on her knee, and asks her if she wants his company for the night. Stirred by his hand on her leg and his sweet and disarming manner, she accepts the proposal and takes him to her hotel room. Although she neither expects nor wants any real romance, his direct style disappoints her a little. However, after he turns the light off and they make love on the moonlit bed, she concedes that he excels at the enterprise.

Afterward, as they make small talk, the narrator realizes that Eric wants her to see him as a caring, sensitive person—what he believes to be the feminist ideal in men. Her realization that they are jumping so far ahead in their relationship, skipping the customary "first-night trappings," irritates her, but she decides that casual encounters do not warrant much scrutiny. As Eric drives her to the Harvard campus the next morning, they seize on the beautiful day to saunter around the Boston Public Gardens. When they behave a bit passionately in public, three young boys urge them on and the flustered Eric chases them off. His overreaction annoys the narrator, who again senses they are becoming more deeply involved with each other than she wishes.

The narrator's second seminar goes so well—partly because she enjoys playing up to Eric in the audience—that she takes him back to her hotel a second night. They repeat their success in bed, but at 2:30 A.M. her friend Eleanora calls from New York. Left in charge of feeding the narrator's cat, Eleanora has accidentally broken a big blue platter in the narrator's apartment. Maudlin with drink and guilt, Eleanora runs on and on with her apologies. However, after she learns that the narrator is not alone, she giggles and hangs up, feeling much better about the broken platter. The narrator explains Eleanora's phone call to Eric, adding that her cat is named Carmen. She cannot help pondering whether Eric thinks Carmen a ridiculous name, but this banal pillow talk dissolves into more sexual activity, and cats and platters fade into the background of their consciousness.

This brief insight into the narrator's private life alters Eric's perception of her, encouraging him to confide to her that he worries about writing his dissertation. She answers with hackneyed reassurances, concealing her private doubts. This conversation all takes place in his car on the way to the airport, and it concludes with his question, "If we lived near each other, would you have an affair with me?" She hesitates before agreeing that they should give it a try, and is saved further embarrassment by their arrival at the airport. She jumps out of his car with a quick kiss, a good-bye, and a clear sense of relief.

As the narrator flies back to New York, she meditates on her experience, wondering what her two-night stand can teach her. Reflecting on the none-too-pleasant implications that she sensed in her brief relationship with Eric, she decides that Eric had been prepared for complications that would have entangled her too deeply with him. She giggles at the realization that Eric had been leading up to an experiment, something long-running with experimental observation and careful data keeping, but that she had kept the brief affair at the seminar level. She knows that short seminars do not develop major lessons but that they can offer new ideas that shake up one's mind and start one thinking along new lines.

Themes and Meanings

It is a point of natural interest that Perri Klass wrote this story when she was a medical school student at Harvard, where she also taught expository writing. This biographical note does not, however, help explain the title or answer other questions about this straightforward six-page story. Why was the narrator "Not a Good Girl," as the title reveals? Certainly not because she goes to bed with an agreeable young man whom she has just met. Nothing that she says suggests that she feels any guilt about the matters to which she alludes quite matter-of-factly. In the first paragraph she explains that going to bed with men she has just met is not something that she does "ferociously often." In fact, in the last six months or so, she has not even slept with anyone. Her celibacy, however, has had nothing to do with principle, only with being hard at work.

One possible clue to the story's title may relate to the fact that Eric is four or five years younger than the narrator. The narrator's realization that he is a student still in his "callow youth" contributes to her feeling that their sexual relations are leading too rapidly into an emotional involvement that she has no wish to develop. Eric's pursuit of the tormenting urchins embarrasses her, making her think that they are deep into "maybe someone else's relationship, certainly not mine."

The narrator's suspicion that Eric is "someone else's man" intensifies with his confession that he worries about his dissertation, followed immediately by his tentative query about the possibility of their having a long-term affair. None of this suits her, and she clearly feels that her sexual interest has almost tied her to an insecure young man looking for a mother. She is thus greatly relieved to limit what might have developed into an exhausting experiment to a two-day seminar.

So she perhaps believes that she is "Not a Good Girl," in that out of physical need she "uses" Eric, uses him in the way that traditionally is associated with a man's exploitation of a woman's body for sexual pleasure. The narrator thus becomes a "bad" girl following in the footsteps of countless roués, reveling in her orgasms and then discarding her coconspirator. The title, then, reveals an ironic backward look at a long tradition, but it conceals a double irony in that the narrator shows no remorse about using Eric. The reversal of traditional sexual roles is stressed by her opening remark about men being "very strange" nowadays, a judgment that Eric repeats exactly about women.

Although this analysis seems neat, it may not be the last word. The story ends with a comment about seminars—on both immunology and sex: "And if, in addition, you enjoy them while they last, then you have to consider them successful, I suppose." What lies behind that "I suppose"? Is her heart, if not laden, at least tinged, with regret? This line is spoken by a young woman, the stereotype of the hardworking young career woman who lives alone with her cat. She is, by her own admission, a woman too busy for sex, that is, too busy for close human companionship—and is that not a bad thing for a girl?

Style and Technique

Language is one of the brightest attractions of this story. The narrator immediately declares language to be important when she explains that the phrase "going to bed" with someone is so "cute" and "euphemistic" that it demands a "schoolgirlish and ungrammatical" phrasing instead of anything so proper as "with whom I went to bed." This concern carries throughout the story. The narrator chirps on in the idioms of her class and rank—Ivy League seminar-givers—and the language flows. When Eric first puts his hand on her leg and propositions her, she describes her "okay" as "appropriately nonchalant." This observation about her own behavior typifies the narrator's cool self-awareness throughout her relationship with Eric. She tosses off easy inventions such as "give-a-seminar outfit," and she knows just how to catch a nuanced word with quotation marks.

The narrator has a sharp eye. Details of dress both reveal their social levels and emphasize their professional rank: Eric's ragged cuffs would mean one thing at a construction site but they signify something else in a Harvard seminar room. In her accounts of the bedroom interludes, she offers no salacious details of their lovemaking, but she speaks unselfconsciously of their desire and their pleasure. She says at one point that "he could indeed get it up," and when he turns out to be slow at the finish line she remarks with characteristic dry wit: "But I kept my eye wide open; it is very bad manners to fall asleep in such a situation." This sophisticated voice well suits a parable of the sexual revolution.

Frank Day

NOW THAT APRIL'S HERE

Author: Morley Callaghan (1903-1990)
Type of plot: Psychological
Time of plot: The 1920's
Locale: France
First published: 1929

> *Principal characters:*
> CHARLES MILFORD, a young American would-be writer
> JOHNNY HILL, his intimate friend

The Story

Charles Milford and his close friend Johnny Hill, who receives a monthly allowance of $100 from his father, leave their Midwestern hometown because they believe the United States has nothing to offer them, even though they have never visited New York or any other American metropolitan area. One autumn, they buy two large black hats and decide to go to Paris and live there permanently. Reading George Moore's *Confessions of a Young Man* (1888) has inspired Charles to start writing about his adventures with Johnny. Johnny supports Charles, types his manuscripts, and calls him the most perceptive and delicate author since Henry James. The two friends love Montparnasse, peer into the windows of art galleries, avoid the Louvre and the museum at the Luxembourg Garden as merely attractions for tourists, and instead frequent various cafés, where fellow drinkers label them "the two boys." Fanny Lee, an American woman now too shapeless to be an entertainer any longer, follows them from bar to bar, has nine or ten drinks an evening on them, and occasions their snickering criticism as they lie in their bed later.

One night at an English-style bar, the two eavesdrop on others and snicker so loudly at what they overhear that Stan Mason, up from Nice and drinking heavily, calls them two little goats. They bow so seriously in response that he is mollified, buys them drinks, and discusses architecture rather learnedly, until Charles suggests that his comments are really not very important. That night, the boys sit on the edge of their bed, talk about Mason, and for half the night snicker some more.

At a bar in November, the pair are listening to a jazz pianist from the United States when rich Milton Simpson and his wife enter. He has come to Paris to start life over again by writing, painting, and composing piano pieces simultaneously. He happens to brush past Charles, who without sufficient provocation pushes him away. They squabble until the pianist lays hold of Charles and drags him away. When the sensitive fellow begins to tremble and cry, Johnny leads him outside. Simpson follows apologetically, buys them brandies, and lectures them on new trends in psychology. He admires their patient, serious attentiveness. Later, after undressing together and while sitting naked on the edge of their bed, the boys agree that Simpson was boring but the brandies he bought them were excellent. Their witty sallies to each other tire them, and they soon fall asleep.

After two full weeks of writing and typing, the boys scrape some money together and go to Nice for the winter. They manage to stay with Mason, who generously lets them use his spare room, and they meet plump Constance Foy. One night Mason overhears their snickering bedtime criticism of him through the thin wall, so he tells them tactfully that he needs the spare room and suggests that they leave. The boys get a hotel room and remain in Nice until April, at which time they toss their bags out the window at two o'clock one morning to avoid paying their large bill.

At last, they are in Paris in April, but their fun is spoiled by cold, damp weather. Johnny pays a one-week visit to his father, now in England and angry with him. People do not notice Charles when he sits alone in the café because he seems so insignificant. On encountering Mason, he discusses casual flings that he and Johnny have had with girls but expresses the hope that Johnny will not get serious in England. Johnny returns, and the patrons of the local cafés are pleased by the boys' reappearance. Johnny says that when his father told him to get a job, he commented that the old man had inherited unearned money himself, whereupon his father slapped him and he punched his father. Johnny also reveals that he picked up some cheap women in London. Nothing serious, Charles concludes to himself.

Toward the end of April, with the air now warm and clear and moonlight on the river, Constance comes to Paris and moves in with the boys. The trio frequent bars at Johnny's expense and at night make love—impartially at first. One evening Constance tells Mason that although they are having a good enough time, strange things are happening. Charles, very much in love with Johnny, criticizes him for getting too serious with Constance. The two boys drink one evening at the English bar; afterward, Charles, growing tearful on the street, tells Johnny not to let a tart ruin their relationship. In a sudden rage, Johnny slaps Charles. Both weep, shake their heads, and will not go home together. Mason happens by on his way to the bar and lets Charles stay with him, drinking and not eating. A week later, Mason suddenly informs Charles that Johnny is returning to the United States with Constance. Charles, not really knowing how he can earn money for drinks, goes to the café one cold, wet evening, sits alone at a table, and for the first time in Paris puts on his big black hat.

Themes and Meanings

The central theme of "Now That April's Here" is the social dangers inherent in becoming involved in relationships that encourage one to waste time and opportunities, with a subsidiary motif of disloyalty. Writing in the 1920's, Morley Callaghan could not openly present the intimate sexual activities of Charles and Johnny, but he hints at them sufficiently. In his classic autobiographical book, *That Summer in Paris: Memories of Tangled Friendships with Hemingway, Fitzgerald, and Some Others* (1963), he revealed that in 1929, when he and his wife were in Paris, he had promised an editor that he would write a story about a pair of bright, bowing, snickering homosexuals whom they both observed in a Parisian café. One of the gay pair was a writer named

John Glassco, whose own memoirs support the conclusion that he and his friend Graeme Taylor were the models for Callaghan's characters.

Charles, who may have some real creative talent, sponges on Johnny, who pays for their room, board, and drinks, types his meager manuscripts for him, and evidently loves him with considerable tenderness. Then three destabilizing things happen: Johnny's father upbraids him and challenges him to get a job; Johnny dabbles again in heterosexuality while in London; and Constance seduces him into decamping for the United States. Charles, although never brave, is somewhat more aggressive than Johnny; it is Charles who pushes Simpson, a total stranger, and who also invites getting slapped by daring to call Johnny's new love a tart. Neither young man is depicted as attractive. Charles has too large a head, "that ought to have belonged to a Presbyterian minister," while Johnny has "a rather chinless faun's head." Constance manages to see more in the latter, undoubtedly because of his money. She willingly participates in a bisexual *ménage à trois* until she can succeed in separating the two men by making Charles jealous.

Style and Technique

"Now That April's Here" falls smoothly into thirds, like a simple sonata: Paris in the autumn, Nice for winter, and Paris again in April. Callaghan adopts a tonally flat, understated, ironic style throughout. His very title is an ironic adaptation of the famous lines that open Robert Browning's "Home-Thoughts from Abroad": "Oh, to be in England/ Now that April's there." Charles and Johnny wait months for their April in Paris, which begins with disagreeable rain and ends with their rupture. Charles, who professes to be an aspiring writer, writes for only a couple of weeks. Johnny calls Charles perceptive and delicate, but they both ignore the great museums of Paris, waste their time barhopping, are manipulated by a woman, and skip out without paying a large hotel bill. Finally, a second grasping female ends their supposedly strong homosexual friendship.

Callaghan caricatures the two boys with their synchronized tiptoeing, angular bowing, distinct finger mannerisms, and contrapuntal witty snickering and out-of-control weeping sessions. The subordinate male figures are lightly sketched, while both females are made unattractively fat and aging. No one seems truly happy, despite the romantic Parisian setting. That magnetic city of the Roaring Twenties is not presented in the round here, because the boys are almost totally lacking in perceptiveness. Their conversation seems to be amusing to others, but certainly not for reasons they ever fathom. Instead of jibing at others, these wastrels have cause to be ashamed of their conduct at every turn.

Robert L. Gale

THE NUN
Story of a Woman Who Never Loved

Author: Pedro Antonio de Alarcón (1833-1891)
Type of plot: Domestic realism
Time of plot: 1768
Locale: Granada, Spain
First published: "La comendadora: Historia de una mujer que no tuvo amores," 1868
   (English translation, 1962)

> *Principal characters:*
> SISTER ISABEL DE LOS ANGELES, a member of the Order of Saint
>   James
> DOWAGER COUNTESS DE SANTOS, her mother
> CARLOS, COUNT DE SANTOS, the six-year-old nephew of Sister
>   Isabel

The Story

The story begins with a description of three people in a sitting room of a manorial house in Granada in March of 1768. A mature woman of noble bearing sits near one of the balconies, watching a pale, sickly child playing on the floor. The little boy is dressed as an elegant little gentleman. In one corner near a window, a beautiful nun of about thirty sits staring toward the sky. Next, the narrator identifies the characters and reveals their family history. The widowed Dowager Countess de Santos had not obeyed the spirit of her father-in-law's will, which stipulated that the family fortune be divided between the two oldest grandchildren in order to ensure the survival of the family name. Instead, the countess, who idolized her oldest child, a male, placed her second child, Isabel de Santos, in a convent when the girl was only eight years old.

When Sister Isabel de los Angeles later renounced all worldly property, her brother Alfonso inherited the entire estate. On the early death of both the brother and his wife, his three-year-old son, Carlos, the only remaining heir to the title, came to live at the family estate. Meanwhile, the ailing Sister Isabel, now a beautiful young woman, has been sent home to recuperate. She has received permission to live at home, as if it were a convent, in order to help rear her nephew. The spoiled young Carlos now tyrannizes the entire household.

When the story resumes, he busily destroys a book on heraldry until going in search of more stimulating activity. A few minutes later the boy bursts into the room, exclaiming that he overheard the sculptor who has been restoring the family emblem on the staircase) say that he would like to see the nun nude. The child then repeatedly demands and finally screams hysterically that he also wants to see his aunt naked. Sister Isabel believes that he is being used by Satan. As the nun is leaving the room, Carlos, seeing that he will be denied his wish, flies into such a rage that he lapses into a catatonic state. His grandmother calls him angel and cradles him in her arms. As the young count begins to recover and repeats the request, his grandmother orders her daughter to comply, stating that it is God's will. One-half hour later, Carlos declares his aunt to be fat and goes off in search of the sculptor. He discovers that the man will be tried for blasphemy by the Inquisition. When Dowager Countess de Santos goes to her daughter's room to comfort her, she finds, instead, a letter left by her daughter. In it Sister Isabel explains that she has made the only decision of her life in which her mother was not consulted: She has returned to the convent. The final brief section informs the reader of Sister Isabel's death four years later, her mother's demise shortly thereafter, and Count Carlos's death approximately fifteen years later during the siege of Menorca. With him the noble title vanishes as well.

Themes and Meanings

Two major themes emerge in the story. One is the Spanish obsession with the preservation of noble titles and estates by primogeniture. The countess's slavish adherence to the custom leads to the extinction of the family name. The pretensions of this custom are further debunked through two actions of the young count: First, he destroys a book of heraldry, the symbol of the importance of noble families; second, his demand, which ultimately leads to the tragic outcome for his aunt, is associated with the sculptor, whose action was that of restoring the family's coat of arms. Ironically, the heritage is not preserved or restored; instead, with the count's death, it is forever destroyed.

A second theme is that of the misuse of both power and love. Sister Isabel's mother withheld maternal affection as well as half of the family fortune, for her daughter was sent to a convent when she was only eight years old. The life of a nun was the only one available to Isabel. The vows that should have been made by free choice were, instead, perceived to be inevitable. Pedro Antonio de Alarcón's story should not be construed as antireligious; rather, it criticizes the manipulative use of religion for selfish ends.

Count Carlos embodies abuse of power, for he knows that the two women will deny him nothing. The narrator implicitly associates the child with the Devil, for he mentions that the child "writhed like a snake on the floor" and "shook like one possessed." Nevertheless, the coercive and coerced grandmother refuses to recognize any fault in the child, calling him an angel and equating Carlos's wishes with God's will.

Style and Technique

"The Nun," written during the period of transition from Romanticism to realism, has some characteristics of both movements. The somber tone, the setting in the distant past, and the tragic lives portrayed are characteristic of Romanticism. Realist elements in the story include detailed descriptions; background information about the characters; an emphasis on daily, domestic life; and the conversational, confidential style used by the narrator. For example, he addresses himself to his readers, inviting them to imagine the scene, and he refers to "our great-grandchildren," meaning his own offspring and those of his readers.

The narration of a slice of life is an important part of the style. The three characters are presented each in turn, as if a camera were panning over the room. Each is carefully described in the same order: first, the face and personality, then the dress, and finally the activity in which each is engaged. Only then are they identified. This is accomplished by a return to the past, in which the events leading up to the day in March, 1768, are explained.

One technique of characterization used by Alarcón is the comparison of his characters to famous artistic portraits, thus making the picture more vivid in the reader's imagination. The child is compared to Diego Rodriguez de Silva Velazquez's paintings of Philip IV's children, Isabel to Greek statues or the statues at the entrance to the Vatican's sculpture galleries, and her hands to those of the statues of Pompeii. Sister Isabel is also compared to many biblical women and saints. In this way, she is shown to be a combination of both worldly beauty and emotions, and otherworldly attributes.

The portrait of the title character is aided by the comparison of this beautiful, isolated creature to the caged birds hanging outside the balcony. The description of those birds, which long for freedom, have no opportunity for love, and try to communicate with birds that are free, is juxtaposed with her hearing the sounds of people going about their daily tasks, singing or telling of love adventures, and her viewing the Alhambra from her window. The Alhambra is the ultimate symbol of the voluptuous Arabic presence in southern Spain.

The tragedy of this story is two-fold, for not only does the family disappear but also, more important for the reader, Sister Isabel dies without ever having experienced life. She has had no childhood, no free will, no love. She is a victim of the manipulation of power.

Eunice Myers

THE NUN'S MOTHER

Author: Mary Lavin (1912-1996)
Type of plot: Domestic realism
Time of plot: The 1940's
Locale: Ireland
First published: 1944

> *Principal characters:*
> MAUD LATIMER, the narrator and protagonist, the nun's mother
> LUKE LATIMER, her husband
> ANGELA LATIMER, their daughter, the nun

The Story

"The Nun's Mother" begins with a sense of finality, of something already completed. Maud and Luke Latimer are seated in a taxi moving away from the convent where their daughter, and only child, now resides. The narrator of the story is Maud Latimer; her interior monologue traces how and why this event occurred and what the consequences will be for the major characters in the story.

The first response to this new situation by Maud is an unexpected one. In contrast to the visible grief of her husband, Luke, she feels some "relief" that it is over. Maud suspects that Luke is brooding about some imagined medieval horrors of the nunnery. In contrast, she is comfortable with such an institution and the "curious streak of chastity" in women. Once the unfamiliarity and strangeness of this event have been overcome, Maud begins to probe the consequences more deeply. First of all, it will close certain options for her. It will mean "no more fun out shopping" for her after her daughter has gone, no need to make plans, no need to collect such things as silver for a future bride, no need "to remain young."

She also wonders what problems her new title, a nun's mother, will bring her. Will she have to change her manner of dress, will she have to "smoke only in a cupboard," will she have to play an unfamiliar and uncomfortable role? In contrast to this disturbing prospect, she imagines that Luke will become accustomed to his role, even like it. He will "quite like going up to Mount St. Joseph and walking around with his cool, stately daughter . . . with a high, firm virgin bust."

After brooding on the effects of their new position, she begins to think once more about why her daughter chose to become a nun. She recalls Luke's sudden response, "Angela?" and his insistent question, "Are you sure she knows her own mind?" In fact, Maud is not at all sure that her daughter knows her own mind. Maud tells Luke, however, that "her mind is quite made up." The reason for this misrepresentation is that she has been unable to communicate with her daughter about what she is giving up by entering the convent. Maud cannot bring herself to address the subject of "the bodies of men and women." She contrasts the frankness with which men speak of such matters to the difficulties women have. Furthermore, Angela seems to resist any conversation about her life or choices. Thus, the question that Luke and Maud want, above all, to ask and be reassured about is never asked. Therefore, Angela's reasons for entering the convent and her knowledge, or lack of knowledge, about the world remain mysteries.

Maud returns to the subject of sex and love later and defines more fully the difficulty in speaking to Angela. She reveals her own closeness to Luke and broods about what Angela will miss. She seems to know love thoroughly, yet she suddenly realizes that the words to describe it are inadequate.

> What would she have said love was? Not generous. Not kind. Not gentle. Not dignified. Not humble. Not to be described, in short, by any adjective that would appeal to a young girl straight from school. There were no words to describe it.

Maud then begins to speculate on some of the other results of becoming a nun's mother. The first thought is an unusual feeling of freedom, freedom from the questioning and demanding generations that would result from Angela's marriage: "Angela had freed her from the future." She wonders if she had been secretly happy about Angela's choice during the early and difficult period of preparing to enter the convent.

Maud returns to the problem of Angela near the end of the story. She is skeptical of Angela's piety and troubled by the regrets that Angela may harbor. She contrasts her own initiation into the world of men and love with Angela's lack of any initiation, not even a kiss. However, some of her doubts are assuaged when she thinks of what Angela looks like: "What flower did she always remind you of? Not a summer one, but some spring chalice flower." This suggests that Angela is in an environment that is proper for her; she is an eternal spring flower and need not pass into summer and shed her blossoms. This is reinforced by Maud's dream of a pervert trying to pluck the folded up petals of a water lily; she wakes before the dream is completed and, once more, Angela seems to be rooted in her proper and inviolable place.

The story ends as the taxi reaches home. Luke is going to call the police about a man he has seen lurking about; he has an outlet in action. Maud, however, still ponders her place and role. She thinks about how difficult it is to be a mother and not know at the end "whether you had failed or triumphed." She may remain in doubt, but the world seems to have made its own judgment. Her maid treats her with an unusual delicacy and kindness. Suddenly, she sees herself being treated with deference and respect by everyone she meets. "For she had proven herself. She was the mother of a nun."

Themes and Meanings

The most important theme of the story is the manner in which people are defined, and thereby restricted, by the roles society gives them. Such roles affect the way people speak to one, treat one, act before one; any individual qualities one may have are lost. To be a "nun's mother" is to be trapped in a role that is inappropriate or confining. Maud Latimer is a warm, loving, acerbic woman, but at the end of the story all these qualities are dwarfed by her unearned title, a nun's mother.

A secondary theme is the inability of the people in the story to communicate with one another. The words or the right tone are lacking to define certain experiences. This is especially true for women in Ireland; as Maud suggests, women cannot talk about sex or love because the society will not allow the words to be spoken. She thinks about how "those who had tried were exiled and their books were burned on the quayside." This can refer only to James Joyce's *Ulysses* (1922), especially the long monologue of Molly Bloom. Mary Lavin is speaking of a problem that, although not restricted to Ireland, seems to be exacerbated there. What Lavin does without the possibility of using certain words or tones is to maintain the mystery of why Angela chooses the convent. She also contrasts the nearly wordless but real communication between Maud and Luke with the barriers that are between Maud and Angela.

Style and Technique

The first element of style to notice is the use of interior monologue. The story is told within the mind of Maud Latimer on the trip home from the convent. She shifts from the monologue only to recall a scene between herself and Angela or herself and Luke. The result is a kaleidoscope of feelings about Angela's choice and its consequences. The reader then must sift the various and conflicting attitudes for the most important ones. One clue is the echo of the title in the last paragraph; the finality of Maud's position as a "nun's mother" is clear.

Another important aspect of style is Lavin's use of metaphor at the end of the story. There has been no hint of literary devices in the commonsense, middle-class mind of Maud Latimer until then. The comparison of Angela to a cool flower with unopened petals defines Angela and reassures the reader of the appropriateness of her choice in a way that the more conscious questions and thoughts of Maud could not.

James Sullivan

AN OCCASION OF SIN

Author: John Montague (1929-   )
Type of plot: Realism
Time of plot: The 1950's
Locale: Seacove, a bathing place ten miles south of Dublin, Ireland
First published: 1964

> *Principal characters:*
> FRANÇOISE O'MEARA, a young French woman
> KIERAN O'MEARA, her Irish husband
> A GROUP OF YOUNG MALE CLERICAL STUDENTS

The Story

Françoise O'Meara is a young French woman recently married to an Irish man. The couple lives in Dublin, where the husband, Kieran, works. Françoise explores Dublin and its environs in the first six months of their marriage; around Easter, she discovers a bathing place on the coast about ten miles south of Dublin near the suburb of Blackrock. Although her husband tells her no one in Ireland goes swimming so early in the spring, Françoise is an independent woman, at ease with herself, and tells him it does not matter what other people do.

In mid-May, others begin to come to the bathing place. Françoise is particularly amused at the excessively modest way the Irish men change into their bathing suits on the beach. She is also somewhat troubled by the way the men look at her when she changes, not with curiosity or admiration, but with something she does not really understand, something almost like anger. When she tells her husband about her concern, he says it is just modesty. When she says the Irish men are as lecherous as troopers but just will not admit it, he says, "You don't understand."

In mid-June, a group of clerical students start coming to the beach where Françoise swims. After a while, the young men begin talking with her, obviously fascinated with her openness and with the fact that she is French. When she tells them about worker-priests she has known in France, one of whom fell in love with a prostitute and had to struggle to save his vocation, they react in stony silence. A world of passion in which people do not go to Mass does not exist for them except as a textbook vision of evil.

When one of the older men on the beach tells her that many people are talking about her friendship with the clerical students and that she is setting a bad example, he is shocked to find out that she is married. When Françoise tells her husband what the man has said, he tells her that in certain circumstances she might be classified as "an occasion of sin."

The next time she talks with the clerical students on the beach, they ask her what it is like to be married. When she tells them the freedom of marriage is the freedom of having committed oneself and then inquires why they ask such a question, they reply that is it well known that French women think about nothing but love. She goes home furious that they have gotten so fresh with her and dreams that one of the other men on the beach grabs her leg and pulls her under the water. She tells the clerical students what the older man has said to her, but they know all about it, informing her that someone has already complained to their dean. When she asks them if they are upset about it, they dismiss it with "Some people would see bad in anything." However, she knows that she will not come to Seacove the next spring.

Themes and Meanings

Different cultural attitudes about sexuality provide the central theme of this story. A key point in the story occurs when Françoise tells her husband about the self-conscious way the Irish men change into their bathing suits under a towel and how they look at her almost angrily, and he responds, "You don't understand." Indeed the key issue of the story is what there is to understand about the male Irish attitude toward sexuality. Part of what there is to understand is the fact that the Irish men—a friendly, fatherly man and a clerk with goggles—do not really welcome a woman on the beach. The reference to the Forty Foot, a bathing place "for men only" where men bath in the nude at all times of the year, suggests this gender difference. The Forty Foot has become a point of contention about Irish attitudes toward sexuality, and women have tried to crash the area and swim there in spite of male protests.

The other central point in the story occurs when Françoise's husband tells her she is an "occasion for sin." She recalls an occasion a few nights earlier when one of her husband's friends solemnly told her that sex was the worst sin because it was the most pleasant. Another of his friends had gripped her arm once while crossing the street and told her to be careful. When she says he was also in danger, he says he is not worried about himself, for he is in the state of sanctifying grace. She encounters the same sort of self-righteousness when the older man on the beach tells her she is a bad example.

Françoise is further reminded of the Irish repressive attitude toward sexuality when she sees a young couple kissing in the rain along the banks of the Grand Canal and wonders why the instinct is to seek darkness and discomfort rather than the friendly light of day. She thinks of her husband as being a nest of superstition and stubbornness, saluting every church he passes, blessing himself during a thunderstorm, and thinking he hears a banshee that portends the death of a relative. The cultural differences between her and her husband make Françoise think her marriage is like living with a Zulu tribesman.

Although at the end of the story it seems clear that the clerical students have only affection rather than lust for her and that they do not take seriously the gossip that has arisen about their friendship, this does not negate the radical difference between her French attitude toward sexuality and their Irish attitude. In spite of their innocent intentions, she will never again feel quite comfortable on the beach.

Style and Technique

"An Occasion of Sin" is a clear example of a story written primarily to illustrate a cultural characteristic rather than to explore a universal human trait. As a result, while interesting and suggestive, the story is not profoundly complex but relatively simple. Indeed, there would be no story at all without the somewhat stereotypical cultural difference between the relatively open attitude toward sexuality of the French and the more reserved and repressed attitude of the Irish, deriving from the influence of the Catholic Church.

John Montague is a well-known Irish poet, but the style of "An Occasion of Sin" is not lyrical and poetic but rather straightforwardly realistic. Although the heart of the story is what Françoise at one point calls the basic difference between men and women, the story does not explore any complex psychological basis for this difference.

The point of view of the story is third person, but it stays with the perspective of Françoise, who is both amused and puzzled at the Irish attitude toward sexuality. One result of this point of view is that whereas Françoise is often angered at what she perceives as a stereotype about the French attitude toward sex, she is never quite aware that she is forming a stereotype about the Irish attitude. Moreover, her basing her knowledge of the Irish male on young clerical students creates a completely asexual atmosphere when she meets with them on the beach, reminding her of when she used to play with her younger brothers.

Although Françoise's relationship with the young clerical students is completely innocent of sexuality or seduction, she is characterized as a possible "occasion of sin" by her husband for no other reason than that she is not ashamed of her body and because, from the point of view of the Catholic Church, to desire a woman purely in the imagination is to be guilty of the sin of adultery; thus, she poses a danger to the students.

The central metaphor for the monster of repressed sexuality in Irish culture in the story is the clerk with the flippers and goggles who comes to swim at Seacove. Françoise dreams that she swims across to the Lighthouse Point without any clothes when she sees the man with the goggles beneath her. His eyes rove over her body, and he reaches for her and tries to pull her under, but she kicks and breaks his goggles and swims to the surface. This image is repeated at the end of the story. When lying on the beach, she sees the man with the goggles, emerging from the water like a sea monster. Remembering her dream, she laughs so much the clerical students look at her inquiringly. However, no matter how silly the grotesque monster is, she knows she will not return to Seacove the following year.

Charles E. May

AN OCCURRENCE AT OWL CREEK BRIDGE

Author: Ambrose Bierce (1842-1914?)
Type of plot: Gothic
Time of plot: About 1863
Locale: Northern Alabama
First published: 1891

> *Principal characters:*
> PEYTON FARQUHAR, the protagonist, a southern plantation owner
> and a patriot
> ASSORTED MEMBERS OF THE NORTHERN ARMY

The Story

"An Occurrence at Owl Creek Bridge" contains three distinct sections: a matter-of-fact opening scene, a flashback to provide some necessary history, and a fast-paced conclusion. The story begins with clear, simple, declarative sentences:

> A man stood upon a railroad bridge in Northern Alabama, looking down into the swift waters twenty feet below. The man's hands were behind his back, the wrists bound with a cord. A rope loosely encircled his neck. It was attached to a stout cross-timber above his head.

In the next sentence, it becomes apparent that this man is about to be executed by a unit of the Union army. The preparations for the execution are described in clinical detail. The narrator seems to be a dispassionate spectator who is unfamiliar with any of the participants in this grim event. The physical setting and movements of the Union company are rendered with such calm accuracy that the scene comes to life clearly and vividly. The condemned man is judged to be "about thirty-five years of age" and is "evidently" a southern "gentleman."

"The preparations being complete," the focus narrows to the condemned planter; the objective description yields subtly to a more subjective point of view, which allows the reader insight into the Southerner's thoughts. The man is calm but, as might be expected, somewhat disoriented; he imagines that the "swift waters" are "sluggish." He is disturbed by "a sharp, distinct, metallic precussion like the stroke of a blacksmith's hammer upon the anvil. . . . [W]hat he heard was the ticking of his watch." As he stands alone awaiting his death, he imagines throwing off his noose, diving into the water, and escaping to his beloved home and family. As these thoughts pass through his brain, the sergeant steps off of the back of a board on which the man is balanced over the water, and the condemned planter falls toward the stream, the noose tight around his neck.

The second section discloses who the man is and what events lead him to his desperate plight. His name is Peyton Farquhar, and he is a member of "an old and highly respected Alabama family." Peyton, who was "ardently devoted to the Southern cause," was prevented from joining the army by circumstance and was eager to serve the South in any way possible. One evening, while he was sitting with his wife, a grey-clad soldier rode up, asked for water, and told them that the Northern army was preparing to advance once the bridge over Owl Creek had been repaired. The soldier indicated that the bridge was poorly guarded and that a brave man could easily burn it down. Farquhar undertook the challenge of destroying the bridge and was captured. The last sentence of section two reveals that the planter never had a chance, because the grey-clad soldier was, in fact, a "Federal scout."

The third section returns abruptly to the present: "As Peyton Farquhar fell straight downward through the bridge, he lost consciousness and was as one already dead." His agony as the rope snaps tight is briefly described; "then all at once, with terrible suddenness, the light about him shot upward with the noise of a loud splash; a frightful roaring was in his ears, and all was cold and dark. . . . [H]e knew that the rope had broken and he had fallen into the stream." He struggles desperately to free his hands and rises to the surface, frantic for air; his miraculous escape fills him with such intensity that he can see "the individual trees, the leaves and the veining of each leaf"; he can hear "the beating of the dragon flies' wings, the strokes of the water spiders' legs." The joy of his resurrection is short-lived, however, for the Union troops immediately open fire on him, and Farquhar is forced to dive deeply and swim furiously in order to escape the ignominy of being shot after having avoided death by hanging and drowning. The troops fire at will and even artillery is brought to bear on the fleeing prisoner; but with the help of the current, the man evades cannon and rifle shot and plunges into the forest.

He drives himself relentlessly through the rest of that day and all through the night toward his home. He apparently falls asleep while walking, for when he awakens "he stands at the gate of his own home. All is as he left it, and all is bright and beautiful in the morning sunshine." His wife "stands waiting, with a smile of ineffable joy. . . . As he is about to clasp her, he feels a stunning blow upon the back of his neck." The story ends brutally with this final sentence: "Peyton Farquhar was dead; his body, with a broken neck, swung gently from side to side beneath the timbers of the Owl Creek bridge."

Themes and Meanings

"An Occurrence at Owl Creek Bridge" is typical of Ambrose Bierce's fiction in that it deals with the outré, the unusual, here violent death and a heightened psychological state; it contains sardonic humor; and it ends with a cynical, ironic twist. This story is one of several that he wrote about the Civil War. (Bierce fought in the Civil War; he was a member of the Indiana volunteers and was apparently a brave and skillful soldier.) The grotesque reality, the horror, of war was one of his persistent themes. There is nothing glorious in Bierce's depiction of the war; the Union army is cold, efficient, and deceitful; the Southern planter is "a slave owner, . . . a politician" who was, there-fore, "naturally an original secessionist." Furthermore, Farquhar suffers from the illu-sion that war provides opportunities for glory, "distinction," and "adventure." The trap is set, and the execution of this rather pathetic quarry is concluded with ruthless effi-ciency. Farquhar's dreams of "service with the gallant army," his "longing for the re-lease of his energies" lead him directly to a sudden and decidedly unremarkable death—a final, brutal release of his "energies."

Another of Bierce's concerns in this, and in various other stories, is the portrayal of intense psychological states. The withholding of information is not mere trickery; rather it is a logical, calculated effort to force the reader into the realization that the mind makes its own reality, that Peyton Farquhar, in fact, experiences an escape, that time and truth are not so simple as one likes to think. If there is a deceiver, it is the hu-man mind, or perhaps the life force, which offers the possibility of escape up to the fi-nal instant when it becomes clear to the reader, at least, that there is no escape. Bierce's rendering of Farquhar's thoughts in the instant before death is quite convinc-ing and compelling.

One other distinctive quality of this story, and of Bierce's fiction in general, is the cynicism. The grim representation of military affairs and the sardonic use of the ad-verb "gently" to describe the movement of Farquhar's dead body in the final sentence are clear indications of Bierce's cynicism. However, an even sharper and more bitter indication of his pessimism is evident in his assumption that the reader will be shocked by the ending, having resolutely ignored all the indications that Farquhar is merely imagining the escape. The third section is filled with "superhuman," improba-ble, or patently impossible acts: seeing the "very insects" in the forest, "the prismatic colors in all the dewdrops upon a million blades of grass." Farquhar is caught in a "vortex" and "flung" on the southern bank "concealed from his enemies." There he finds "giant garden plants; he noted a definite order in this arrangement. . . . A strange, roseate light shone . . . the music of aeolian harps." The forest through which he trav-els is "interminable," "the path wide and straight . . . yet untravelled." The astute reader will perceive the distinct differences between the prose in this section and the realistic prose of the first section and deduce that the third section represents imagined events. Bierce, however, does not expect his readers to be astute; he assumes that they prefer fantasy to reality and will accept whatever preposterous occurrences are neces-sary to provide a happy ending for Peyton and, by extension, for themselves. Far-quhar's fate, he suggests, is the only possible fate: unromantic and untimely death.

Style and Technique

Bierce's mastery of technique is the source of the success of this story. He carefully and skillfully builds a convincing set of realistic circumstances and establishes an at-mosphere of grim intensity; then he subtly begins to introduce the subjectivity and un-reality on which the plot hinges. The opening section is basically objective and natu-ralistic. The language is clear and unemotional; the sentences are straightforward. The reader has no reason to question the authenticity or veracity of the story. In the third paragraph, Bierce very deftly begins to interweave a subjective point of view with the heretofore exclusively objective one. The first insight into the condemned man's mind indicates that he is himself objective and reasonable; he finds the plan for his execution to be "simple and effective." The gulf between physical reality and the prisoner's perception of reality is presented with such calm detachment that the reader believes that he or she is simply being given access to Farquhar's mind by an unemotional, omniscient narrator. In the final paragraph of the first section, the prose returns to the objectivity and precision of the opening lines: "the captain nodded to the sergeant. The sergeant stepped aside."

In section 2, the impassive narrator reports the events that lead up to Peyton Farquhar's execution. He knows how the planter felt about war as well as the true intentions of the "grey-clad soldier." Again the reader has no reason whatsoever to doubt the accuracy of the story. As surely as the Union scout deceived Peyton Farquhar, Bierce has led the unwary reader into a trap that he springs almost immediately in the third section. The reader has come to expect a faithful account of the facts from this narrator and consequently has little reason to question the genuineness of the tale of Farquhar's escape.

Bierce has very carefully prepared the reader to trust him and consequently to ignore all the indications in the final section that Farquhar's escape is imaginary. Numerous technical differences exist between section 3 and sections 1 and 2, each of which suggests that the events are phantasmal. The verbs, "seemed" and "appeared" are used in four of the first five sentences, signaling the story's movement into fantasy. Exclamation marks begin to appear with regularity (two in the first paragraph and seven in the second), calling attention to the improbability of the events being described. Only two exclamation marks were used prior to the third section; they are in section 1 and serve to point up the condemned man's distortion of reality: "What a sluggish stream!" he says of water "racing madly beneath his feet." The explicit, journalistic prose of the first two sections yields to language characterized by abstraction, vagueness, or exaggeration: "inconceivably," "unthinkable," "unaccessible," "magnificent," "superhuman," "preternaturally," "interminably," "ineffable." Farquhar's supposed actions are obviously beyond the realm of human possibility, but Bierce presents them with such authority and conviction that readers, having been conditioned to expect the truth, are cleverly lured into believing in Farquhar's fantasy. Bierce's skillful manipulation of language and point of view makes "An Occurrence at Owl Creek Bridge" a minor masterpiece.

Hal Holladay

ODOUR OF CHRYSANTHEMUMS

Author: D. H. Lawrence (1885-1930)
Type of plot: Realism
Time of plot: The early 1900's
Locale: Nottinghamshire, England
First published: 1911, revised 1914

>*Principal characters:*
>ELIZABETH BATES, the protagonist, a housewife
>JOHN, her five-year-old son
>ANNIE, her young school-age daughter
>MRS. BATES, her elderly mother-in-law

The Story

Set in a rural coal-mining village, this dynamic portrayal of family life among laborers revolves around an able young housewife, Elizabeth Bates. A strong, handsome woman, she has been disappointed in her husband's recent inclination to go drinking regularly, depleting her meager household finances. The time frame of the story is from late afternoon, when the miners are walking home from their shift, until just before midnight.

Elizabeth and her husband, Walter, are both natives of the region; the story opens with a visit by Elizabeth's father, a widower who operates one of the locomotives that carry coal from the Brinsley Colliery. He announces to Elizabeth that he intends to marry again, and she questions whether it has been long enough since her mother's death. The subject of marriage is a sore point for Elizabeth because of her own experience: She is a woman who has been disillusioned, and she is bitter over Walter's behavior. However, she prepares bread and butter for her father, in addition to the cup of tea he requests, and after he leaves, she prepares supper, listening for Walter's footsteps among the miners passing on the lane outside the kitchen on their way home from work.

When Walter does not come, she assumes that he has sneaked past to the local pub, and she fears that his usual Saturday night drinking spree is to become a twice-a-week routine. As she feeds the children, John and Annie, the deep emotional bonds between mother and children are presented in the rich simplicity of a typical domestic scene. This simplicity is complicated by their mutual concern for the father's absence. However, Elizabeth refuses to allow the children to become upset; she banters with them over lighting the lamp and over a sprig of chrysanthemums, which Annie discovers Elizabeth had placed in her apron strings earlier in the afternoon. The children are delighted that their mother has decorated herself with the flowers, and they remark on their beautiful smell. Elizabeth declares, however, that the chrysanthemums do not smell beautiful to her: She says, with a short laugh, that these were the flowers of her wedding, the flowers of the children's births, and the flowers her husband wore the first time he came home drunk.

After supper, the children play while Elizabeth sews, and a balance is struck in Elizabeth between her satisfaction with family life and the anger she feels toward Walter. The first section of the story closes with Elizabeth putting the children to bed, with them hiding their faces in her skirts for comfort from the distress that the father's absence has caused.

The second section of this two-section story begins a short while later with Elizabeth deciding to go look for Walter. She believes that he is at the pub, but her anger has now assumed a tinge of fear for him. Not wishing actually to seek Walter in the pub herself, she goes to the home of one of his coworkers, where she learns that Walter has not been to the pub; the coworker, alarmed at Walter's absence, tells her that he will look for Walter.

Elizabeth returns home to wait, and in the silence of the night, she hears the winding-engine at the pit as the cage descends, and her fear increases. Within the hour, her mother-in-law appears with the news that something, indeed, has happened to Walter in the pit, but that she does not know exactly what. The men had sent her to wait at Elizabeth's home.

During the wait, Walter's mother tells of Walter's life as a child, of his happiness and his high spirits, and she apologizes to Elizabeth for the trouble that Walter has caused Elizabeth with his drinking. Within the hour, the miners carry in Walter's body: He had been trapped by a cave-in at quitting time, and his fellow workers had not known that he had never come up to the surface.

The scene in which the body is carried into the house is one of gripping realism. The pit men, deeply moved and emotionally upset by the accident, are awkward in the presence of the women, Elizabeth and Walter's mother. When the young daughter, Annie, awakes upstairs, and Elizabeth goes up to keep her from coming downstairs and discovering Walter's body, the men quietly, discreetly, leave.

As Elizabeth and her mother-in-law lay out the body, washing the pit dust from it and dressing it, Elizabeth has a deep emotional experience whereby she is able to evaluate her life with Walter with a new clarity. She suddenly realizes how separate Walter and she were in life: "Each time he had taken her, they had been two isolated beings, far apart as now." Their marriage had not been the spiritual joining of a true marriage, and she now knows how wrong she had been never to see him for himself, rather than in terms of him being her husband. As a mother Elizabeth is secure in herself, but "how awful she knew it now to have been a wife. And he, dead now, how awful he must have felt it to be a husband." Their marriage has been a failure. However, now, for Elizabeth, the bitterness is gone, and she is "grateful to death, which restored the truth."

Themes and Meanings

D. H. Lawrence's achievement in this story, his first major short story published, is to view the laboring class from the inside. Previous great English writers—Charles Dickens, George Eliot, Thomas Hardy—had written of laboring people, but always from the framed viewpoint of the middle class, which made up the reading public in England. Lawrence was the first great writer from the working class who wrote of working-class people in their own terms, using their own dialect; he did not "translate" the characters and their situations for a middle-class audience.

In addition to the brilliant portrait of working people, this story develops the classic Lawrentian theme of the nature of the sexual relationship between men and women. Lawrence explores that relationship on a spiritual level; he views as profound the failure of Elizabeth and Walter to achieve the deeper life that marriage can offer. Walter's death leaves Elizabeth unreconciled to the larger spiritual forces of life, for "she knew she submitted to life, which was her immediate master. But from death, her ultimate master, she winced with fear and shame." Her fear and shame reside in her sense of failure in her life with Walter.

To some readers, placing such value in the relationship between man and woman has seemed an imbalance, but to others, Lawrence's genius in presenting that relationship is one of the highest achievements in modern letters.

Style and Technique

Lawrence is known for his use of impassioned language, which is entirely appropriate to his exploration of the strong emotional nature of his characters. He successfully holds his authorial comments to a minimum in this story, presenting the experiences from Elizabeth Bates's perspective. The story is realistic in approach, but like all great realistic stories, it goes beyond surface particulars to suggest the spiritual lives of its characters.

In going beyond the surface details, Lawrence employs the symbol of the chrysanthemums to suggest the complex life that Elizabeth has lived with Walter. The pungent odor of the flowers has accompanied the significant events in Elizabeth's life, as she tells her children: her marriage, the birth of her children, and her disillusionment with Walter—he wears them the first time he comes home drunk. Now the chrysanthemums, which are a common funeral flower, will be present for Walter's funeral, another significant event in Elizabeth's life.

One of Lawrence's most effective strategies in this story is his use of time: After the miners carry in Walter's body, the reader realizes that while the domestic events of the evening were unfolding for Elizabeth, Walter was suffocating in the pit. Time thus operates in a dual framework, which suggests the dual nature of the marriage. Time merges into one focus in the final laying-out scene, which enables Lawrence to create much of the power of the final paragraphs wherein Elizabeth achieves her clarity of vision.

Some readers view Lawrence's style in his novels as flawed because of his use of repetition and abstract terms in exploring the inner, emotional lives of his characters. However, the demanding limitations of the short-story form forced Lawrence to keep such repetition and abstract language to a minimum; consequently, he is viewed as one of the most powerful and accomplished writers in the history of short fiction.

Ronald L. Johnson

OF THIS TIME, OF THAT PLACE

Author: Lionel Trilling (1905-1975)
Type of plot: Psychological
Time of plot: The early 1940's
Locale: "Dwight College," probably in the northeastern United States
First published: 1943

> *Principal characters:*
> JOSEPH HOWE, a poet and English instructor at Dwight College
> FERDINAND TERTAN, a brilliant but mentally disturbed student
> THEODORE BLACKBURN, a pretentious student of Howe's

The Story

"Of This Time, of That Place" opens with Joseph Howe, an English instructor at Dwight College, preparing for the first class of his course in modern drama. After his opening remarks, he sets his students to work on a theme, and as they are writing, a tall, awkward boy enters and announces, "I am Tertan, Ferdinand R., reporting at the direction of Head of Department Vincent." Tertan's essay on the assigned topic, "Who I am and why I came to Dwight College," is remarkable for the breadth of its learning but dismaying for its wild rhetoric. In answer to his own rhetorical question, "Who am I?" Tertan exclaims, "Tertan I am, but what is Tertan? Of this time, of that place, of some parentage, what does it matter?"

That same evening, Howe, who is also a poet, reads in the journal *Life and Letters* a sharp attack on the "precious subjectivism" of his poetry. The author of the essay, Frederick Woolley, practices a criticism informed by "humanitarian politics," and he dismisses as trivial the "well-nigh inhuman" poets who ignore the "millions facing penury and want" while they scribble away in their ivory towers. Woolley identifies Howe as representative of these poets of irresponsibility.

Stung by Woolley's denigration of his poetry, Howe is nonplussed a week later when Tertan appears in his office to announce that he has read Woolley's essay, that he, Tertan, is an aspiring man of letters, and that he is on Howe's side against Woolley. This confession of faith makes Howe uneasy as it reveals Tertan's sense of a complicity between him and Howe against the Philistines of letters.

Howe is still absorbing the import of Tertan's visit when Theodore Blackburn, vice president of the Student Council, presents himself in a flurry of servile yet self-important "sirs." Blackburn expresses his admiration for "Shakespeare who is so dear to us of the Anglo-Saxon tradition," and asks permission to audit Howe's course in the Romantic prose writers. As they enter the classroom, Blackburn takes Howe's arm to guide him in, but "Howe felt a surge of temper rise in him and almost violently he disengaged his arm and walked to the desk, while Blackburn found a seat in the front row and smiled at him."

As the year wears on, Howe ponders the problems represented by Woolley's broadside, Tertan's growing disengagement from reality, and Blackburn's resentment at the low grades Howe awards him. Howe finally presents the case of Tertan to the academic dean, who already has a sense of Tertan's confusion as a result of a letter Tertan sent the dean praising Howe as a "Paraclete," or one who is called to help. Eventually, at the dean's suggestion, a physician examines Tertan and confides to the dean that Tertan is going mad. When Tertan approaches Howe to request a recommendation to the Quill and Scroll Society, Howe writes a brief, noncommittal testimony to Tertan's "intense devotion to letters." Several days later, Blackburn approaches Howe to complain of his grade, threatening to blackmail Howe into giving him a better mark. Blackburn refers to Woolley's essay (which he does not know the dean has already read) and implies that not only will he expose Howe to the dean as an incompetent poet, but also he will charge Howe with recommending to the college literary society a student with an unbalanced mind. Howe's quiet answer is, "Blackburn, you're mad." Howe then strikes out the C-minus on Blackburn's essay and replaces it with an F.

In the conclusion, Howe passes Blackburn in his course simply to be rid of him, and Blackburn becomes the first man in his graduating class to get a job. On commencement day, Tertan appears attired in a suit of raw silk, wearing a broad-brimmed Panama hat and carrying a bamboo cane. As Howe stands reluctantly with Blackburn and the dean, Tertan walks by on his way to nowhere, eliciting a pang of deep sympathy from Howe. Tertan then vanishes in "the last sudden flux of visitors."

Themes and Meanings

Irony dominates "Of This Time, of That Place." That the generous and brilliant Tertan should be mad is inexplicable, especially in a world in which the Blackburns get the first jobs. Although Tertan's paranoia entails an offensive arrogance directed at those he judges less sensitive and perceptive than he and Howe, his intelligence and idealism shine through his oddly inspired but undisciplined rhetoric. His letter to the dean is virtually a declaration of love for Howe, who has become his model of the intellectual and poet. He sees himself and Howe allied in a devotion to art that sets them apart from nonworshiping social critics such as Woolley. Ironically, however, it is Howe who in a sense betrays Tertan by taking the case of his behavior to the dean.

Howe's charge, "Blackburn, you're mad," underscores Howe's grasp of the unfairness of this world. The point is made again at the end when Howe aches with a "general and indiscriminate" pity prompted by the appearance of Tertan. "Of This Time, of That Place" dramatizes no theodicy, no explanation of why the world is the way it is. The unfortunate Tertan, if he could get enough perspective on his plight, would be the first to appreciate the irony of it. Howe and the dean are helpless. They can only watch events take their course. Although Howe is castigated as an ivory-tower poet by Woolley, his compassion for Tertan reveals that he is intimately aware of the sufferings of real people.

The scenes in which Howe conducts discussions in class are convincing and often amusing as the students interact. The discussion of Henrik Ibsen's play *Ghosts* (1881) brings out the differences among the students. De Witt is relentlessly rational as he analyzes the behavior of Captain and Mrs. Alving. His references to contraception elicit from the sturdy football player Stettenhover groans of contempt for his perception that "intellect was always ending up by talking dirty." When Tertan embarks on a florid monologue on free will, Stettenhover can only slump resignedly in his seat, "exasperated not only with Tertan but with Howe, with the class, with the whole system designed to encourage this sort of thing." These scenes of classroom discussions add weight to the narrative by developing the academic setting realistically.

Style and Technique

Lionel Trilling's narrative method is realistic and conventional. He divides his story into four sections told from a third-person omniscient point of view that always looks over Howe's shoulder and maintains Howe's perspective on events. The story is framed skillfully by two scenes in which Howe's landlord's young daughter, Hilda, is taking pictures of Howe. She is a pleasant and attractive girl of whom Howe is obviously fond, and her congenial presence at the story's beginning and at its end, fussing with her camera to get things right, helps to ground the story in the everyday world and to keep Tertan's grand delusions in perspective.

Trilling uses weather and season for conventional mood effects and to help establish a chronology. The story opens on a "fine September day" in "true autumn with a touch of chill in the air." A peach tree "still in fruit" contributes to the setting. The final scene, on commencement day, is "wonderfully bright, the air so transparent, the wind so brisk that no one could resist talking about it." At the end of registration day, Howe notices "a bright chill in the September twilight"; section 2 opens with the sentence "All night the snow had fallen heavily and only now was abating in sparse little flurries." Later in section 2, after Howe makes his important decision to report Tertan's state of mental confusion to the dean, the sun comes out. The symbolic function of the sunlight is evident in Howe's realization that "it made all the commonplace objects of efficiency shine with a sudden sad and noble significance. And the light, now that he noticed it, made the utterance of his perverse and unwanted request even more momentous." These meteorological grace notes help advance the narrative smoothly and contribute to the overall realism of the story.

Finally, "Of This Time, of That Place" is a story about academics, with much talk of literature and ideas. The hapless Blackburn calls William Wordsworth "Wadsworth" and Prometheus "Prothemeus." Tertan alludes to Saint Augustine, Empedocles, Rene Descartes, and many others. At one point, Howe is reminded of Plato's allegory of the cave. This allusiveness gives the story a rich texture and builds up a suitable backdrop for a drama of a youth going mad in a tangle of ideas that he cannot control.

Frank Day

AN OFFICIAL POSITION

Author: W. Somerset Maugham (1874-1965)
Type of plot: Psychological
Time of plot: The nineteenth or the early twentieth century
Locale: French Guiana
First published: 1937

Principal character:
LOUIS REMIRE, a prison executioner

The Story

Louis Remire, convicted of killing his wife, is serving a twelve-year sentence in the remote penal colony of Saint Laurent de Maroni in French Guiana. His is not, however, the miserable existence endured by less fortunate prisoners, for Louis Remire occupies an official position: He is the colony's executioner, a privileged station accorded him not only because of his exemplary behavior toward prison officials but also because of his experience as a police officer in his native Lyons, France. Remire's position brings with it any number of perquisites: He has his own small house on the prison grounds; he is able to wear his own clothes, rather than a prison uniform; he is allowed to grow the mustache of which he is inordinately vain. As if these liberties were not enough, he also receives one hundred francs for every execution, and has been able, he thinks, to save up enough money to establish himself in the outside world on his release. The job is not, however, without its drawbacks. The rest of the convicts hate the executioner and would gladly kill him if given the chance. Louis Remire's predecessor was found stabbed, then hanged, in the jungle.

Still, despite the potential danger of his position, Louis Remire remains undaunted. His experience as a police officer has taught him to protect himself, and two vicious dogs patrol the grounds of his hut. He thinks of himself as quite above his fellow inmates, and is glad to be separated from them. Unlike them, he is an official of the state, a powerful agent of law and order, and he always feels a sense of accomplishment when, after an execution, he hoists the severed head and pronounces, "*Au nom du peuple francais justice est faite*" (In the name of the French people, justice is done). He takes pride in every aspect of his work. He keeps his guillotine in perfect working order, its brass fittings shined to perfection, its blade razor sharp.

As the story opens, Louis Remire is preparing for an especially busy day: Six convicts are to be executed the following morning, besides which his assistant has taken ill and has been confined to the hospital. A multiple execution seems a poor time to break in a new apprentice, for everything must go rapidly and without a hitch. The new man seems suitable, however, and Louis Remire takes considerable pride in explaining the complex workings of the guillotine. Satisfied that the assistant knows how to prepare and clean the machine, Louis Remire dismisses him until midnight, at which time they must move the guillotine into the prison yard.

It is now early evening. On his way home, Louis Remire notices that, as usual before an execution, the convicts are restless. He reminds himself to exercise extra caution.

With several hours to fill before midnight, Louis Remire decides to catch some fish for his supper and tomorrow's breakfast. He is a good fisherman; the sport relaxes him, and this evening it sets him to reminiscing about his marriage and about the wife he killed. He was already a police officer, she a dressmaker, when they met in Lyons. He was impressed by her intelligence, her sexual prowess, and her frugality, and their relationship was at first a happy one. As soon as they married, however, things went sour. She became a shrewish wife, nagging him about the pastimes of which he was most fond. She took exception to his going to cafés after work with his colleagues; she complained of his going fishing instead of spending his weekends with her. She accused him of lavishing money on other women, and Louis Remire was too honest to contradict her.

Matters grew worse until one day, after a particularly grueling day at work, he came home to change clothes before going to a café with his friends. An argument about money ensued, during the course of which she grabbed his gun and threatened him with it. When he grabbed it away from her, she hit him in the jaw, where he had earlier in the day been struck by a striking worker. Enraged, he shot her, then quietly went to police headquarters to turn himself in.

Still, Louis Remire thinks, prison life has treated him well. Since coming to Saint Laurent de Maroni, he has stayed in the favor of the authorities and has finally been rewarded with the comfortable position he now occupies. He wants for nothing, he decides, and is truly happy for the first time in his life. With this soothing thought, he goes home, cooks the fish he has caught, and settles down for a nap.

Everything is strangely quiet when he awakens. After he has washed and dressed, he whistles for his dogs, but they do not come. Perplexed, he sets out toward the prison. In the midst of the coconut grove that surrounds his house, he stumbles against something in the dark and, looking down, discovers one of his dogs lying dead. His situation suddenly becomes terrifyingly clear to him: The convicts have poisoned his dogs, and are now waiting in the dark to kill him. Near panic and at a loss for what to do, he draws his knife and proceeds toward the prison, certain of his impending death. He hears voices, then a cough, but it is too dark for him to see anything. Suddenly he sees a flashlight, and realizes that he is surrounded. He is prepared to fight to the death but is not given the opportunity to do so. Somewhere out of the darkness, a knife is thrown; as it strikes him and bounces off, someone grabs it and rips into his belly. In the next moment, someone else takes the knife and cuts Louis Remire's throat. As he finished off his victim, the murderer utters the line that has so frequently been spoken by Louis Remire: "*Au nom du peuple francais justice est faite.*"

Themes and Meanings

"An Official Position" is about the inescapability of justice. Louis Remire, though a common criminal like the rest of the inmates of Saint Laurent de Maroni, has set himself above his fellow prisoners and above the law. He considers the rest of the prison community lawless rabble, and has nothing but contempt for them. He takes excessive and almost fetishistic pride in the guillotine that he uses to bring them to justice, and feels unnaturally contented after a successful execution. Since coming to the penal colony, he has disdained his own kind and fawned over the authorities, and his sycophancy has, he thinks, paid off. Louis Remire is complacently—and prematurely— counting his blessings as the story opens.

Though he considers himself an agent of justice, however, a sort of police officer on special assignment, Louis Remire is really nothing more than a common criminal himself. He has in a fit of passion killed a woman whose grievances against him were fully justified; worse, he has never felt the slightest twinge of guilt over his crime. Through a complex process of rationalization, Louis Remire has come to accept and even revel in the way his life has turned out. However, the story insists that justice will prevail, no matter how circuitous its methods. Louis Remire is in the end punished not only for murder but also for pride, and it is fitting that one of his fellow prisoners has the last word on the case of Louis Remire, declaring that finally, with the executioner's execution, justice has been done.

Style and Technique

The urbane style and carefully controlled point of view for which W. Somerset Maugham's prose is famous is expertly subverted for maximum psychological effect in "An Official Position." "Rain," for example, makes use of the viewpoint of a relatively objective secondary character; "The Outstation," although sympathetic to one of the main characters, relies mostly on a third-person omniscient narrator. "An Official Position," however, is told almost completely from the point of view of Louis Remire. The reader hears Louis Remire's story via a third-person narrator almost totally sympathetic to the executioner, and is thus forced to share in the protagonist's complacency and self-satisfaction.

Both the complacency and the sense of narratorial control break down, however, when the protagonist senses his own impending death. In the darkness of the coconut grove, Louis Remire's thoughts run amok, and Maugham expertly renders this tortured stream-of-consciousness in one semicoherent two-page paragraph. Only at the end of the story, with Louis Remire's death, is order restored to the narrative; it is also at this point that Louis Remire's past catches up with him, as the nameless convict pronounces that justice has finally been done.

J. D. Daubs

OH, THE WONDER!

Author: Jeremy Larner (1937-   )
Type of plot: Psychological
Time of plot: The 1960's
Locale: New York City and Philadelphia
First published: 1965

> *Principal characters:*
> WILLIE McBAIN, a young graduate student in philosophy at
>   Columbia University
> SARAH, his fiancé, a college student in Philadelphia
> LICKENS, his best friend, another graduate student
> ROGER STENNIS, a graduate student whom Willie envies and
>   dislikes

The Story

Willie McBain is experiencing the psychological turmoil that typically afflicts college students at one time or another to some degree. He is feeling panicky because he finds himself unable to study. Like William Shakespeare's Hamlet, he feels that he is reading nothing but "words, words, words," and sometimes finds himself staring for hours at a single page. It is a psychological phenomenon so familiar to college students that it has been humorously labeled "senior psychosis."

Willie now has only one week to write two overdue term papers and three weeks to write his master's degree paper and study for language examinations that will qualify him for the Ph.D. program. He is also engaged to marry a woman named Sarah, but he is not sure that he really loves her. He phones his friend Lickens and tells him he thinks his problem is that he feels afraid of everything. At one point he says, "Oh, the wonder of it all. Life is unbearable." Later he calls his fiancé and starts a pointless argument.

Although Willie is a difficult person to get along with, he manages to keep the affection of Lickens and Sarah, who appreciate his intelligence and honesty. His studies of the world's major philosophical systems have contributed to his confusion. He is fascinated and terrified by life's unanswerable questions: Who am I? Why am I here? Where am I going?

Willie engages in loveless sex with a promiscuous young secretary nicknamed Luscious Louise. Afterward he storms out of her apartment and borrows Lickens's car without permission. On his way to Philadelphia, he stops for coffee and nearly gets into a fight with five teenage boys. Because he has no money, he siphons gas out of another car, which turns out to belong to the teenagers. They follow but run out of gas.

Willie is driving to Philadelphia partly out of jealousy. He suspects Sarah of having an affair with Roger Stennis, an insufferable young graduate student who obviously has a brilliant career ahead of him. He hopes to catch them in bed together so that he will have an excuse for breaking off his engagement. When he reaches Sarah's apartment at 6:00 A.M., he is both pleased and disappointed to find her alone. Sarah makes it obvious that she wants nothing more than to be Willie's wife and the mother of his children. He feels suffocated by her love, afraid of a lifelong commitment and the responsibilities of fatherhood.

That evening they go out to dinner and run into Roger Stennis on the street. Without provocation, Willie hits Roger in the mouth and bloodies his shirt. Afterward, this confrontation leads to a bitter quarrel with Sarah, who calls Willie immature, self-centered, and self-destructive. He in turn accuses her of being obsequious, conventional, and unimaginative. Their argument escalates until Willie knocks Sarah down, then lands several more blows on her head and ribs. She locks herself in the bathroom, screaming that she never wants to see him again.

At the height of their quarrel, with both screaming and cursing at each other through the door, Willie realizes that they are really and truly in love and will be together for the rest of their lives, hopelessly locked in a complex love-hate relationship that is part of the mystery and the "wonder" of life.

Themes and Meanings

"Oh, the Wonder!" was first published in 1965, in the middle of the now-legendary 1960's, when young Americans were questioning everything in which their elders believed. The seemingly endless war in Vietnam was one of the contributing factors. Many understood, however, that this dirty little war was only a skirmish in the global Cold War that pitted the United States against the Soviet Union for nearly half a century.

Many young people—especially sensitive, intelligent, well-educated people—were finding it difficult to plan for the future because everything that was happening seemed to point to universal doom. Both the United States and the Soviet Union were accumulating so many atomic weapons that they could destroy the earth and everybody on it many times over—a phenomenon dispassionately described by military experts as "overkill." China had the hydrogen bomb and, because of its enormous population, seemed to present a potentially greater threat to the free world than the Soviet Union. It was hard for young people to take such things as career, marriage, and family seriously when time seemed to be running out for the human race. It seemed especially wrong to bring children into a world that was spinning out of control. The Irish poet William Butler Yeats aptly expressed this type of mood in his prophetic poem "The Second Coming" (1921) with the lines, "The best lack all conviction, while the worst/ Are full of passionate intensity."

There is a significant bit of fatalistic dialogue during Willie's telephone conversation with his fiancé when he says: "I'm going to flunk out of school. I'll be drafted and you'll never see me again." Young male college students were given draft deferments if they maintained acceptable grades. Some felt guilty for not sharing the dangers of men being used as cannon fodder in a senseless, unwinnable war. Many young intellectuals were torn by the dilemma of having to choose between killing innocent civil-ians, going to jail for draft evasion, fleeing the country, or staying in school and study-ing subjects that no longer seemed meaningful in view of the impending destruction of civilization or annihilation of humanity. College students were largely responsible for the antiwar protests of the period, and they eventually played a role in forcing the U.S. government to find a way to disengage American troops from the war. The anti-war movement helped fuel the flames of the civil rights and women's liberation move-ments. Young Americans were going to set an example of grassroots democratic ac-tion that the whole world would eventually follow.

The "macho" behavior exhibited by Willie and the teenage boys in the coffee shop was typical of the period in which the story is set. Young men were testing themselves, wondering whether they had the courage to enter military service, if they were drafted, and fight a nearly invisible enemy in the bug-, snake-, and disease-infested jungles of an alien land.

The malaise of the 1960's is reflected in "Oh, the Wonder!" That is one of the rea-sons it is an important story. Editors look for fiction with the quality often described as "timeliness," "social significance," or "contemporaneousness." "Oh, the Wonder!" has been anthologized in several collections because it conveys not only the feelings of an individual but the feelings of a generation. The story's title is intentionally am-biguous and ironic. The 1960's were in many respects "the best of times and the worst of times, the spring of hope and the winter of despair"—especially for the young. They changed America forever.

Style and Technique

Jeremy Larner is writing about a particular young man's inner turmoil but manages to objectify his story, to dramatize it, to put it "on stage" by projecting his protago-nist's internal conflict onto characters in the outer world. Every scene in the story con-tains externalized conflict, either physical or verbal. The story resembles William Shakespeare's *Hamlet, Prince of Denmark* (1600) in dramatizing an internal conflict through the protagonist's interactions with a variety of others. Like Prince Hamlet, Willie is struggling with himself. Willie is an idealist who, on arriving at maturity, is coming up against the contradictions of reality. His quarrel with his fiancé is reminis-cent of Hamlet's quarrel with his beloved Ophelia during which he advises her: "Get thee to a nunnery. Why wouldst thou be a breeder of sinners?" It is because Larner successfully externalizes his protagonist's internal conflict that his story is critically acclaimed.

Larner uses tempo to communicate the feeling of internal conflict. He crams many incidents into a short tale. The typical short story contains only one or two scenes and a small cast of characters. Larner crowds his canvas. He even has his protagonist drive from New York to Philadelphia, pausing to engage in a gratuitous confrontation with five teenagers.

Larner flouts all of Aristotle's hoary unities of time, place, and action. This has the effect of making the reader feel that Willie's world is likely to fall to pieces and, by inference, that civilization itself teeters on the brink. That was the feeling many people had in the 1960's. Never before in history had people felt that the earth itself was in danger of obliteration or that the human race might perish in one spectacular Armageddon.

"Oh, the Wonder!" feels unresolved. It leaves the reader feeling confused, frustrated, perplexed, and agitated. This is the author's intention. He has succeeded in communicating his own mixed feelings. He uses a broad canvas with many minor characters, a great deal of action, a montage of inconclusive scenes full of conflict and acrimonious dialogue, and descriptions of aberrant behavior on the part of his protagonist to invoke the jumbled emotions characteristic of the self-destructive revolutionary, exhilarating 1960's.

Bill Delaney

"OH, WHISTLE, AND I'LL COME TO YOU, MY LAD"

Author: M. R. James (1862-1936)
Type of plot: Horror
Time of plot: The nineteenth century
Locale: The east coast of Great Britain
First published: 1904

Principal characters:
PARKINS, a professor of biology, a disbeliever in the supernatural
ROGERS, another Cambridge professor
COLONEL WILSON, a fellow golfer and retired Indian army officer

The Story

The title is a line of an old folk song, but a horror, not a lover, comes to the whistle in this story. The introduction occurs in the dining hall of St. James College in Cambridge, where the dons discuss their plans for the coming short vacation. Parkins, a serious young professor of biology, who plans a golfing holiday in Burnstow, is offended when Rogers offers to share his room and "keep the ghosts off." Parkins, on principle, believes only in the scientifically explicable. However, he agrees to check the remains of a monastery of the Knights Templars for the antiquarian, Professor Disney.

The story proper occupies the three days and two nights after Parkins has been installed in a room with two beds at the Globe Inn. His first day's golf with Colonel Wilson is trying, and Parkins chooses to walk home alone along the seashore. Near it, he stumbles into a circle of mounds that are the remains of the monastery. While making a plan, he finds, near the altar, a space without turf and under it a rectangular cavity, empty except for a bronze whistle. On it, "Who is this who is coming?" is engraved in Latin. Although the shore had been empty, Parkins, walking home with the whistle in his pocket, sees a vague figure following him. At midnight, a shape is still on watch outside the hotel. When Parkins blows the whistle, the window is forced open by a great gust of wind that soughs through the inn. Sleepless, Parkins seems to hear another person tossing and turning nearby; closing his eyes, Parkins envisions a man hunted along the beach by a figure in pale draperies. As the professor lights the candle, something scurries away from his bed. The next morning, the maids note that both beds have been slept in.

At golf, the colonel remarks that the wind of the evening before sounded as though it had been whistled for—a widespread folk belief that Parkins dismisses as superstition. Back at the inn, the bootboy greets them in terror; he has seen a figure in white, "not a right person," waving from Parkins's window. Though the room was locked, the spare bed, made that morning, is a mass of twisted bedclothes.

That night, bright moonlight shows Parkins a figure sitting up in the empty bed. As he rushes to the window, something gets between him and the door, then gropes its way across the room, feels the empty bed, and moves toward the professor, who leans farther and farther out to escape from the sightless face pressing toward him. The colonel breaks in and sees the figures struggling at the window. Suddenly there is only Parkins—and the twisted sheets.

The next day, Rogers arrives; the three agree that the colonel will throw the whistle into the sea. The bedclothes are burned. The power of the evil thing that answered the whistle lay apparently in its ability to inspire fear, suicide, and madness.

After this experience, not only does Professor Parkins admit the possibility of the supernatural; he is also nervous of linen that appears to have a human shape.

Themes and Meanings

The story exists primarily to chill the reader's spine. It does, however, underline the danger of dismissing as impossible everything that is not scientifically explicable, and suggests that dreams and folklore contain truths of a different kind. Perhaps because he was a medievalist, perhaps because he was director of the Fitzwilliam Museum, M. R. James's stories frequently turn on the uncanny power of objects to call back the past, or to call up the dead and the dreadful. A belief in immortality implies the continued life of both good and evil spirits, the existence of powers of both light and darkness. Thus, James equates the scientist who does not believe in ghosts with the biblical Sadducees who did not believe in life after death. It is the bluff and commonplace characters, Rogers and Wilson, admitting the existence of evil, who repel its invasion, while Parkins, armored in scientific ignorance, calls up the foul fiend.

James also makes ironic use of the word "enlightened," and plays with ideas of light and darkness. In his "unenlightened days," Parkins believed in ghosts. His enlightenment, confronted with the experience of darkness, is shown to be false. He is truly enlightened when he admits the possibility that evil and inexplicable things exist in this world.

Style and Technique

Images of light and dark abound in the story: in the physical description of the seashore with its faint light, pale sand, and black groins; in the black pursuer of evening who becomes a white glint outside, then a "something light-coloured" in the dream, and finally a creature of "pale, fluttering draperies" and of "crumpled linen."

The story is tightly constructed. Parkins's dream on the first night welds the happenings of his walk home and the situation of the fugitive who trips to the mysterious pursuer in fluttering drapery yet to come. Thus, the reader understands (though Parkins does not) why the disarranged bed linen is sinister and realizes the danger that lurks in the room.

James's characters tend to be minimal, to exist as vehicles for the plot, as stereotypes, as exemplars of attitudes. Usually the chief character is a leisured scholar or gentleman dilettante whose curiosity produces the events of the tale. Servants are stereotypes; so, often, are other characters. Colonel Wilson, the retired Indian army officer, full of prejudices and common sense, is an example.

Conversation in James's story sounds stilted to the contemporary ear. It is the speech of a formal age and an educated class and employs periodic sentences, lengthy by modern standards, complex and slow-moving.

The author's strength lies in narrative rather than in dialogue or character. Loose sentences and short sentences are often employed, and the story moves well. However, James's most evident talent as a stylist is his ability to suggest. The fading light, "the wind bitter from the North," the "shape of an indistinct personage," above all, the peculiarities of movement, James describes superbly—the appearance of running, for example, while the distance between pursuer and pursued remains the same: the "little flicker of something light-coloured, moving to and fro with great swiftness and irregularity," "it seemed to feel about it with its muffled arms." The descriptions create the kind of uneasiness produced by something strange, indistinct, on the periphery of vision.

The medieval background, the puzzle in Latin, the allusions to John Bunyan, to Charles Dickens, to the Bible, all enrich the story. Perhaps the most significant association is that of the whistle with the Knights Templars. One of the four great crusading orders of warrior monks (known, in full, as the Poor Knights of Christ and of the Temple of Solomon), they were founded in 1119 and abolished in 1312 by Pope Clement V after accusations of heresy and evil practices. Confessions (extorted under torture) involved black magic, homosexuality, and perhaps human sacrifice. (Historians, however, note that the order was a banker to the papacy and creditor of Philip III of France.) Within two years, the order, in deeply suspicious circumstances, vanished from Europe, and its deserted buildings fell into ruin. The whistle therefore calls up a draped figure with "muffled arms," which suggests a monk wearing a habit. It is a predatory spirit or a vengeful one.

The passage from Bunyan's *The Pilgrim's Progress* (1678-1684) that Parkins remembers refers to Apollyon, the foul fiend, advancing to confront Christian. More significant is a brief reference in the last lines of the story to "the smoke of a burning ascending" as the bedclothes that had served as a body are incinerated. This is an allusion to Revelation 18, the burning of Babylon, which—like the Knights Templars—is destroyed because of wickedness, especially black magic.

> Babylon the great is fallen, is fallen, and is become the habitation of devils and the hold of every foul spirit. . . . They shall see the smoke of her burning . . . for by her sorceries were all nations deceived. And in her was found the blood of prophets and saints.

However, although an awareness of these allusions strengthens the effect of the story, its impact is not dependent on them. James's skill as a writer lies in inspiring fear. This story remains one of those not to be read when alone on a dark night.

Jocelyn Creigh Cass

THE OLD BIRD
A Love Story

Author: J. F. Powers (1917-1999)
Type of plot: Social realism
Time of plot: The early 1940's
Locale: An unspecified city in the northern United States
First published: 1944

> *Principal characters:*
> CHARLES NEWMAN, the "old bird"
> MR. HURLEY, his boss
> MR. SHANAHAN, the personnel officer
> MRS. NEWMAN, the old bird's wife

The Story

Charles Newman is an elderly man, a former white-collar worker who was proud of his position but is now unemployed and desperate for work. As he enters the office of the company where he is hoping to be hired, he feels intimidated by his knowledge of his age and his humiliating status as a supplicant who has known better days. His nervousness and forced joviality are met with kindness by the receptionist, and his job application is reviewed favorably by Mr. Shanahan, the personnel officer, who offers him temporary employment wrapping parcels in the firm's shipping room. Mr. Newman chokes back his feelings of hurt pride and accepts.

His new boss is Mr. Hurley, who grimly advises Newman of the great responsibility involved in making sure that packages get to their destinations intact. Hurley cites the horror story of an unfortunate shipment to Fargo, North Dakota, and Mr. Newman can only nod his head in sad acquiescence to the miseries that great companies endure.

Mr. Newman is put to work immediately, struggling to capture with twine a half-dozen sets of poker chips, a box of rag dolls, five thousand small American flags, and a boy's sled going to Waupaca, Wisconsin. Being born again in the work force is not without its minor traumas for Mr. Newman, who cuts his nose on a piece of wrapping paper and bruises a shin on an ice skate. He perseveres through the morning, however, and gets to punch a time clock for the first time when the noon whistle blows.

Not having brought his lunch, as have his coworkers, Mr. Newman wanders on the sidewalk until he finds a ten-cent hamburger to go with a five-cent cup of coffee. He returns to work feeling good about himself but has to explain to the company-proud Mr. Hurley why he did not eat in the employees' lunchroom. The exchange ends with what Mr. Hurley thinks is a satisfying round of hearty good feeling. Mr. Newman's is increased by some idle chat with a fellow worker, and he begins to feel at home.

This cheer is soon deflated by a remark he overhears Mr. Hurley make to Mr. Shanahan at the water cooler. "'Yeah,' Mr. Hurley said, 'When you said the old bird was handy with rope I thought, boy, he's old enough to think about using some on himself.

My God, Shanahan, if this keeps up we'll have to draft them from the old people's home.'" At the end of the day, Mr. Hurley addresses him as "Charley" ("He had never before been 'Charley' to anyone on such short acquaintance"), and Mr. Newman realizes that any show of ambition on his part would be wasted: He is "an old bird."

At the end of his heroic day, Mr. Newman makes the epic journey home in the snow by streetcar, stopping to buy a newspaper as in the old days. His wife meets him anxiously, waiting patiently for him to explain his long day away from home. He hangs back, forgoing his usual end-of-the-day small talk with her. He grumps over petty matters. He postpones the admission that he got a job in the shipping room instead of in the office. The small drama that ensues grows out of years of living together affectionately:

> She appeared amused, and there was about her a determination deeper than his to wait forever. Her being so amused was what struck him as insupportable. He had a dismaying conviction that this was the truest condition of their married life. It ran, more or less, but always present, right through everything they did. She was the audience—that was something like it—and he was always on stage, the actor who was never taken quite seriously by his audience, no matter how heroic the role. The bad actor and his faithful but not foolish audience. Always! As now! It was not a hopeless situation, but only because she loved him.

Mr. Newman's understanding of his wife's love encourages him to make a full confession of his fall to the shipping room, and from then on they enjoy the evening together as she takes part in his glorious adventure. He even makes his newfound handiness with rope a badge of wage-earning manliness, and they conspire in his fiction that he will be kept on in the job after the Christmas season. On this note the drama ends: "He was the bad actor again. His only audience smiled and loved him."

Themes and Meanings

Although no time period is specified, behind the events in the old bird's life looms the menace of the Depression, of three-cent newspapers, five-cent cups of coffee, and ten-cent hamburgers. Thus, the Newmans' story has a special poignancy that comes from not knowing what will become of these two old people after the Christmas season ends and Mr. Newman's job is finished. The main theme of "The Old Bird: A Love Story" is the humiliation suffered by proud people when their working lives are effectively used up. The Newmans apparently have scant savings, if any, and there is no hint of children whose loving ministrations might ease their passage to the grave. Their future is bleak. After the inevitable Christmas layoff, Mr. Newman will take to haunting the employment offices again, but the result will be rejections and disappointment.

J. F. Powers depicts convincingly the gauntlet that job applicants have to run between the receptionist and the boss. It is a grueling psychological ordeal that saps Mr. Newman's spirit and has ended in defeat and despair for thousands like him. For this reason, "The Old Bird: A Love Story," despite its tender portrayal of love, is a grim piece of social realism that evokes the hardship of economic realities.

However, the story is also and finally another dramatization of the conviction that love conquers all. Mr. Newman is an aging Ulysses who, after a trial of hardships, finally makes his way home to his faithful Penelope. Their love story antedates feminist construals of male-female marital relationships. It is clearly the "old bird" who has always occupied center stage in the Newmans' marital drama, and Mrs. Newman has accepted the supporting role with pleasure. Theirs is a model of an old-fashioned marriage. Mr. Newman's annoying reticence when he arrives home, his sulky behavior as he braces himself to admit to his wife that he is now a mere shipping-room lackey, are received with fond patience as Mrs. Newman amusedly abides his little prima donna performance.

The love story closes with a tableau of two people who have lived together long enough to generate a mutually supporting symbiosis that appears to be the only resource they have against an uncertain future. The ending dodges the difficult question of what is going to happen to them, and it develops a perhaps hackneyed view of marital love with a slick infusion, a la O. Henry, of spurious warmth and comfort, but at the same time it ingratiates itself with a vision of the possibilities of love and devotion.

Style and Technique

Powers strives for no high effects in style and technique. He tells his love story from the conventional viewpoint of the omniscient third-person narrator and divides events into essentially three scenes: the reception room, the shipping room, and the Newmans' home. He has a sure touch with his minor characters: The receptionist takes on exactly the right role with Mr. Newman, putting on a genuine smile and conspiring with him in his feeble witticisms. Mr. Shanahan displays a convincing insolence of office, restrained but unmistakable. Mr. Hurley's pompous worrying about deliveries to Fargo, North Dakota, stamp him as exactly the man for his job, and even Mr. Newman's surly coworker is the quintessential disgruntled employee.

Powers achieves verisimilitude with minor details. Mr. Newman's application form instructs him "DO NOT WRITE BELOW THIS LINE" and occupies him for a moment deciphering personnel codes such as CLN for "clean" and DSPN for "disposition." His company displays a motto boasting that it is "a modern house over 100 years young." The "vaultlike solemnity of the washroom" is presented in detail. All these touches are reassuring for their homeliness and banality.

Descriptions of weather are infallible devices to create mood. When Mr. Newman goes home after his hard day's work, snow is falling as a proper complement to the Christmastime setting. He enters his home to the comfort of the "familiar rug" and the warming radiator. He is now back in his snug lair with his longtime mate, secure from the menaces of the workplace and the hazards of the elements. The creature comforts of the archetypal setting invite hope, optimism, and a simple faith in the inevitable rightness of things. Such careful attention to texture combines with Powers's development of his appealing main characters to produce the story's special poignancy.

Frank Day

THE OLD FOREST

Author: Peter Taylor (1917-1994)
Type of plot: Social realism
Time of plot: 1937
Locale: Memphis, Tennessee
First published: 1979

> *Principal characters:*
> NAT RAMSEY, the narrator, a college professor
> CAROLINE BRAXLEY, his fiancé, later his wife
> LEE ANN DEEHART, his sometime female companion, a "career
> girl"

The Story

Recounted after more than forty years by the aging Nat Ramsey, a former Memphis cotton broker and socialite who has since enjoyed a successful career in college teaching, "The Old Forest" recalls one harrowing week in December, 1937, when Nat, about to marry the debutante Caroline Braxley, found both his engagement and his future jeopardized by the aftermath of a freak auto accident and by the unaccountable behavior of the young woman who happened to be riding with him at the time.

Steeped in nostalgia tinged with irony, Nat's recollections evoke in detail a long-vanished way of life, of a self-styled, self-appointed southern aristocracy that had somehow managed to stave off not only the effects of social change but also those of the Great Depression. Nat's parents and their friends live in large houses and drive expensive cars, both fully staffed by faithful black "retainers" who minister to their employers' every need. Nat and his young male friends, just beginning their business careers under the supervision of their fathers, are expected to marry within their own "class," choosing one of the debutantes prepared for them by years of dancing lessons and finishing school. In the meantime, however, Nat and the other young men-about-town have begun to go out with women of a different sort—the adventurous, assertive "career girls" who staff offices. By Nat's own wry admission, the career girls are almost invariably better educated, hence better conversationalists, than their sheltered debutante counterparts, with serious interests in books, art, and music. To a woman, however, they are less concerned with where they came from than with where they might be going; to them, the country-club snobbery of Nat and his fellows appears quaint, even laughable. The young men, in turn, "know" that they can never marry such girls, much as they might enjoy their company, and have come to refer to them by the French pejorative "demimondaines," inevitably corrupted to "demimondames."

Nat's crisis is precipitated only one week before his planned marriage to Caroline, when, motoring through Overton Park with Lee Ann Deehart, perhaps his favorite among the "demimondames," he fails to avoid an approaching pickup truck that has skidded on the ice and snow. Ignoring Lee Ann's advice to change lanes, Nat stays where he is and sustains minor head injuries when the vehicles inevitably crash. Lee Ann, unaccountably, bolts from the car and disappears into the ancient, wooded portion of the park, the "old forest" of the story's title. Amid speculation that she has been severely injured, or has since fallen victim to unsavory characters known to be lurking in the deep recesses of the park, or perhaps has even committed suicide for unknown reasons, Lee Ann remains missing and unaccounted for. Unless and until she can be found, Nat's marriage plans will remain in limbo; neither his parents nor Caroline's will allow the wedding to proceed under the possible threat of scandal.

Over the next several days, Nat cooperates fully both with the police and with the local press, whose editors are as determined to discover the facts as they are to suppress them: Although friendly with the parents of the prospective bride and groom, the journalists seek also to protect Lee Ann's reputation from contamination through association with the "idle rich"; working girls read the papers too, and are equally deserving of protection. In time, Nat begins receiving telephone calls from other "demimondames," who urge him to stop pursuing Lee Ann, who simply does not want to be found. To his consternation, Nat decides that he has been outwitted by a conspiracy of career girls, a "breed" that he continues to regard with some disdain.

In the end, it is Caroline Braxley who takes charge of the situation, asserting the same measure and kind of control that, by Nat's rueful admission, she has continued to exercise throughout the forty-two years of marriage that have followed. Urging Nat to take her on the same round of interviews on which he had previously accompanied the police, she speaks to one of Lee Ann's female friends after the other as Nat obediently remains in his car. As a woman, Caroline encounters far less resistance than did Nat; once she has located Lee Ann's rooming house, she soon proceeds to find the young woman in her final sanctuary, where she has fled since Nat has rendered her earlier hiding places insecure. In one of the story's more intriguing plot twists, it is revealed that Lee Ann's ailing grandmother, her closest living relative, is the proprietress of The Cellar, a seedy but popular night spot to which Nat has often taken Caroline but to which, inexplicably until now, Lee Ann has refused to accompany him. Exacting from Nat a solemn promise never to set eyes on Lee Ann again, even now, Caroline proceeds to resolve the situation to everyone's satisfaction, not least of all her own. As of the present writing, Nat and Caroline have endured many violent deaths in their family during the long years of their marriage, yet no memory, even from World War II, looms so large in Nat's recollections as that of the accident in Overton Park, and of his wife's solution to the ensuing problem. In a brief concluding section, Nat even credits Caroline with giving him the courage of his convictions when he prepared to switch careers as he approached the age of forty and could at last afford to do so.

Themes and Meanings

Offering an authoritative glimpse at an Old South that appeared, unaccountably, to have survived well into the first half of the twentieth century, and possibly beyond the midpoint, "The Old Forest" also offers valuable, though often conflicting, insights into the problematic civil and social status of women during the years preceding World War II, perhaps outside the Old South as well. Reminiscent in theme and tone of John P. Marquand's novel *H. M. Pulham, Esquire* (1941), which treated similar problems of ethics and manners among "proper" Bostonians of the next previous generation, "The Old Forest" delineates the contrast between self-supporting, resourceful "working girls" and the comfortably reared daughters of the "old order," no doubt equally resourceful yet denied any reasonable outlet for their talents save through the manipulation of those men who, according to custom, maintain them in a state of submission.

In "The Old Forest," both the young socialites and their parents appear to hold such people as Lee Ann in a state of respect mixed with awe, even as they decline to accept or meet them socially. The mothers, it appears, are oddly envious, yet the daughters, exemplified by Caroline, feel just enough empathetic "sisterhood" as to perceive no real threat from the "independent" women of their own generation. The young men such as Nat, meanwhile, remain quite oblivious to the currents of change swirling about, aware of no anomaly in the fact that women whom they "cannot" marry are frequently better company, for good reason, than the women apparently "destined" for their marriage beds. The boys' fathers, meanwhile, are quick to note among the ambitious young career women the same drive and quickness that they value among themselves. Nat Ramsey, even at sixty-five, finds himself caught between what he "knows" and what he might have learned, unable to make up his mind.

Style and Technique

Like Marquand's Harry Pulham, Nat Ramsey proves to be a most unreliable narrator, incapable of evaluating, or learning from, the experiences that he describes with authority and authenticity. Even at sixty-five, Nat has learned nothing about women, or about himself, except what he chooses to remember. Quite in keeping with the generation and perceived social stratum that he represents, Nat has lived "through" recent history without, in fact, living it; he has aged without growth or development. Nowhere in his long, even overlong narrative does Nat begin to perceive either the inaccuracy or the consequences of his odd, incurious double perspective toward women: Crucially, he continues to regard such women as Lee Ann with condescension, even as he accepts, and even encourages, the willful manipulations of his "gently-bred" wife.

As befits a former professor, and quite probably an ineffective one, Nat first resumes his story, complete with his own conclusions, and then proceeds to tell it in a fact-filled, verbose, and often rambling manner: In its length, to be sure, "The Old Forest" pushes close against the limits of short fiction, even as the subject matter remains too slight to justify expansion into a short novel. Like Marquand in much of his later fiction, Peter Taylor here practices irony at a level that risks, and even invites, misinterpretation; his narrator is so well drawn and so "convincing" as to risk confusion with the author on the part of unsuspecting readers. Should such a misidentification be made, the tale would lose the dimension of irony and "double vision" that makes it truly memorable.

David B. Parsell

OLD LIGHT

Author: Barry Targan (1932-   )
Type of plot: Psychological
Time of plot: 1944-1945
Locale: Atlantic City, New Jersey
First published: 1979

Principal characters:
THE NARRATOR'S GRANDMOTHER, a world-famous painter
JOHN PALMER, a U.S. Army corporal stationed in Atlantic City

The Story

The story is told by the unnamed grandson of a famous portrait painter many years after its events take place.

An unnamed woman is a young art student who earns extra money working in an art studio where tourists pay small fees to have their portraits drawn in charcoal, sepia pencil, or full pastels. Young Corporal John Palmer, who admires her craftsmanship, often hangs around the studio to talk to her and have her do his portrait as an excuse for monopolizing her time. By the time that their affair ends, she will have drawn 174 portraits of him. These character studies will have a decisive effect on her future career as an artist. In them she discovers the magic in herself: her ability to find in a charcoal line a man's humor—his wit, compassion, strength, courage, and fear.

A visionary, Palmer regards the world war as only a minor setback to his career. He has grandiose plans for the future. Although just twenty-five years old, he already has a reputation as one of the best boat builders in his home state of Rhode Island. As he shares his vision of a glowing future with the young artist, she feels herself gradually being incorporated into his lifetime plans.

They begin going out together, walking on the beach, sailing in small boats, sometimes staying up all night. Their relationship seems entirely platonic. The woman does not realize that she has fallen in love until after Palmer goes overseas. His exuberance, confidence, and energy radiate through her, inspiring her to continue with her art despite her misgivings about her talent and choice of vocation.

After receiving a bundle of letters that Palmer has sent to her Atlantic City studio, the woman returns to Atlantic City to live in the hope that he will return there and find her. She does not learn until after the European war has ended, however, that Palmer has died in battle.

Eventually she marries another man—the narrator's grandfather—and leads an exceptionally active life, acquiring international fame as a portrait painter. At the end of her own narrative—which her grandchildren have heard numerous times—she confesses that she has never forgotten Palmer but has somehow managed to reconcile her love for him with her love for her husband. The reader is left with the impression that Palmer was a guiding light in her life, who inspired her to achieve greatness.

Themes and Meanings

The story suggests that Palmer's enthusiastic personality, along with the inspiration of first love, had an indelible effect on the grandmother's character and that his accidental encounter with her shaped the future course of her life. It was while she was drawing portrait after portrait of Palmer in the boardwalk studio, and falling in love with him at the same time, that she learned to become a real artist, rather than merely competent at her craft. Without Palmer she might have remained a mediocre artist or have given up art completely. The most important words in Barry Targan's story are the grandmother's final assessment of her wartime romance: "We all need—*must have*—someone like that, or else nothing will ever make enough sense."

One of the many feelings that Targan tries to communicate is how World War II affected individual lives. In a small way, the short story "Old Light" does something similar to what Leo Tolstoy attempts in his enormous novel *Voyna i mir* (1865-1869; *War and Peace*, 1886). After Japan bombed Pearl Harbor in 1941, the United States became involved in wartime arenas covering thousands of square miles of the Pacific Ocean and Europe, North Africa, and the Atlantic Ocean. Millions of men drafted into the armed services had to be converted from civilians to warriors practically overnight. Atlantic City was one of the places the government chose as a training area because it had numerous hotels in which to house trainees and sufficient open space for drilling, and it was near ports of embarkation for the European war zone. Targan (who was born in Atlantic City) uses it as a microcosm to represent the nation at war.

Targan is interested in portraying the accidental quality of life. His narrator's grandmother would never have met Palmer if the war had not thrown them together. She was in Atlantic City only because the presence of so many men created local job opportunities. Palmer himself was there only because the government had sent him to Atlantic City for training. Further, the woman would not have lost Palmer had it not been for the war, so she married another man. Had Palmer lived, she would probably have married him and had different children and different grandchildren. The narrator thus has the uncanny feeling that his own existence is accidental.

A complex story, "Old Light" contains many other themes: What the wartime domestic scene was really like, how war makes casualties of civilians, how a large-scale war makes soldiers out of unlikely types, how lives can be altered by accidental encounters, how one's existence is itself an accidental encounter of two reproductive cells joining out of an infinitude of possible combinations, how anyone might never have been conceived at all, how old people were once young and young people will inevitably become old, and how an intensely dramatic episode can be at the same time a microscopic incident in a great epic.

Style and Technique

Targan uses a complex and sophisticated technique: "Old Light" is a story within a story and a memory within a memory. The narrator—evidently not Targan himself— is remembering a story that his grandmother used to tell him and his sisters about her wartime love affair. His own story is nothing more than a framing device; her story is contained within his story, but his story has no other purpose than to present her story.

Born in 1932, Targan was twelve years old in 1944—when the story takes place. He thus was far too old to have a grandmother who was a young woman during World War II. He adopts a fictitious persona as narrator of "Old Light" partly to get the effect of distance in time. By choosing to present his material as a story within a story, he gets an odd effect resulting from using two different points of view: that of the grandmother talking about the past and that of the narrator talking about the past from the point of view of the present.

"Old Light" contrasts with another Targan story set in wartime Atlantic City: "Caveat Emptor" (1983), in which he employs a more conventional and straightforward narrative technique. Because the narrator of "Caveat Emptor" is a twelve-year-old boy telling about his own experiences, the reader is probably safe in assuming that this story is autobiographical. These two wartime stories—both of which are reprinted in Targan's collection *Falling Free* (1989)—demonstrate Targan's technical versatility. He adapts the literary form to his artistic need, following the excellent and broadly applicable principle that "form follows function."

In "Old Light" Targan tries to convey the feeling that many years had passed since the central events of the story. Time itself thus figures as a character in the story. The "light" illuminating the grandmother's old love story seems "old" because it is pushed so far into the distance by the story-within-a-story format; the light is like the light of a star that has traveled across a vast distance to reach the viewer's eye.

What Targan achieves in this technically sophisticated work is an effect similar to what filmmakers call a "flashback." In a flashback, the scene representing the present on the screen "fades out" or "dissolves" and is replaced by another scene still being viewed in the "present tense" but understood to be occurring in someone's memory and to have taken place in the past. A time dimension has been added. Viewers understand that they are looking through a "window" in time. In this regard, "Old Light" is an example of the cross-fertilization that has taken place between the film and print media since the development of motion pictures in the 1920's. By using this "flashback" technique in a short story, Targan achieves special poignancy by emphasizing that there was a time when the past was the present, when an old woman was a girl, when a global conflict was not a subject in textbooks but a heartbreaking turmoil transforming millions of lives.

Bill Delaney

THE OLD MAN SLAVE AND THE MASTIFF

Author: Patrick Chamoiseau (1953-   )
Type of plot: Impressionistic
Time of plot: The early nineteenth century
Locale: Martinique, West Indies
First published: "L'Esclave vieil homme et le molosse," 1997 (English translation, 1998)

> *Principal characters:*
> THE MASTER, the owner of a plantation on Martinique
> THE OLD MAN SLAVE, a longtime slave
> THE MASTIFF, a huge dog

The Story

The characters in this story do not have names but are referred to as the Master, the mastiff, and the old man slave. The story begins when the Master imports the huge mastiff from overseas to quell the slaves on his sugarcane plantation. The emaciated mastiff arrives in port with a shipload of slaves, having endured the middle passage with them. The old man slave, as he always does, accompanies the Master to pick up the large, powerful dog. The old man slave has been a slave for so long that he moves like an automaton, without personality. He is an invisible man whose presence is taken for granted.

As the Master and old man slave arrive back at the Martinique plantation, six or seven Creole dogs begin to howl but suddenly grow deathly quiet at the sight of the mastiff. The mastiff's effect on the slaves is much the same. The large dog instills instant fear in both the other dogs and the slaves. Slave children approach the mastiff out of curiosity but soon run, afraid the mastiff will "mark" their scent.

They have reason to fear. After a few weeks on a diet of raw, bloody meat, fed to it by the Master, the mastiff regains its strength and is ready for action. The mastiff never growls, barks, or howls but simply eyes the slaves with a malignant look. However, the mastiff demonstrates its might when the next slave, a young man, gets the "surge" (an urge to escape or attack the commanders), snaps, and bolts into the woods. The Master and the mastiff soon run him down and drag him back, so torn apart that from then on the slave walked like an old man. This scene is repeated several times with other runaways, until finally at the story's end the old man slave runs away. Under his zombielike surface, the old man slave is a master of self-control: He has bottled up the "surge" in himself every day of his life, becoming a cauldron of energy like the island's seething volcano, Mount Pelée. The other slaves feel this pent-up energy in the old man and psychologically respond to it as does the mastiff. The old man slave silently cultivates the mastiff's response to him, and at the story's end, the mastiff lets out a tremendous howl as the old man slave escapes one early dawn.

Themes and Meanings

On the surface, "The Old Man Slave and the Mastiff" is a realistic depiction of the horrors and cruelties of slavery as practiced in the Americas, specifically on Caribbean plantations. The story briefly describes conditions on slave ships and shows the daily life on a sugar plantation, particularly the fear and intimidation by which the Master and his commanders rule. They control the slaves by such techniques as using dogs, making examples of runaways, throwing hot pepper sauce into inflicted wounds, and allowing the slaves to vent their resentments and other feelings harmlessly via dancing, drumming, and storytelling in the evening.

However, another level of meaning exists in the psychological warfare going on between the slaves and the master and his commanders. The evening's dancing, drumming, and storytelling reveal a hidden substratum of slave life, an undercurrent of raw emotional energy that sometimes breaks out in individual surges and could erupt in mass rebellion. At any moment, the balance of power could shift. The Master and his commanders recognize this and try to prevent a revolt by maintaining tight control, although their harsh control just fuels the slaves' repressed feelings.

It is this psychological current of energy that the old man slave controls. As a result of his long experience as a slave, he has gained power over this current and maintains control almost instinctively, without being fully conscious of it. However, while hiding his power over this energy from the Master and his commanders, the old man slave commands the respect of the other slaves and even the mastiff, who can sense the old man slave's power, much as he can sense the approach of a hurricane or earthquake before humans can. At the height of the old man slave's power, he even exercises mind over matter: He falls against a red-hot boiler used in distilling cane sugar, feels the intense pain, and hears his skin sizzle, but the "skin emerges intact." This event occurs as the built-up energies in him explode.

Although set in the past, the story has contemporary relevance. The story can be read as a commentary on the psychological makeup behind the historical development of Martinique and other Caribbean islands, where slave rebellions were frequent, former slaves eventually gained power, and the current population is largely descended from slaves. The islands' histories are unfortunately marked by cruelty, fear, and repression that have in some instances (such as in Haiti and the Dominican Republic) extended into the modern period. Faith in the occult survives on many of these islands in the belief and practices of voodoo.

Symbolically, the psychology depicted in the story might have relevance to everyone. Just as the slaves and the Master are involved in a deadly game—the slaves plot their escapes, and the Master smiles as he prepares to chase them—the Master, the mastiff, and the old man slave are clearly involved in an ongoing relationship. Somewhat disturbingly, the threesome symbolically suggest three aspects of any relationship, three roles that anyone might play, or three sides of anyone's personality.

Style and Technique

The symbolic meanings of the story are suggested by the generic names of the characters and the ways the characters relate to each other. For example, the mastiff clearly expresses the cruelty of the Master; however, more subtly, the mastiff is also related to the slaves and specifically the old man slave. The mastiff also is a captive: It shares the slaves' experience of the middle passage, is kept penned in its cage except when it does the Master's bidding, and communicates on an instinctive level with the slaves, especially the old man slave. The mastiff is also linked to the fury of the surge, notably that of the old man slave. In some ways, the mastiff is identified more closely with the slaves than with the Master, and therefore the mastiff produces a forlorn howl at the end when the old man slave escapes.

The reader's identification with each of these generic characters in turn is encouraged by the way the story is told. The narrator, who occasionally sounds like another character in the story, speaks from a limited omniscient point of view, going only partway into the mind of each character. Even the old man slave's consciousness, which predominates toward the story's end, is not fully explained but left a mystery. The old man slave himself does not fully understand what is happening to him, as though he is in the grip of forces beyond rationality.

In keeping with this mystifying point of view, the story is left hanging at the end. The old man slave escapes, but is his escape successful? Apparently it is because he is said to have defied the mastiff. The old man slave disappears into the deep woods to join the zombies that, according to the Master, live there. However, the old man's escape into the woods could symbolize his death, which is another way the slaves have of defying their masters—on the slave ships, they leapt overboard into the shark-infested waters, swallowed their tongues, or impaled themselves on bayonets. From slavery, death is an escape. In any event, the old man's escape at the end, after a long life of slavery, represents a triumph of his spirit.

The author's style, a scaled-down version of Magical Realism, also fits the mystifying effect of the story. For the most part, the author's realism is mixed with impressionistic description rather than casual assertion of fantastic events. The only fantastic event is the old man slave's fall against the red-hot boiler without apparently being burned. The reader's ability to believe this event is perhaps a test to see how well the story's effect has worked. Whether the event is credible or not, the story immerses the reader in a Caribbean sensibility that acknowledges hidden powers undreamt of in most people's philosophy.

Harold Branam

OLD MORTALITY

Author: Katherine Anne Porter (1890-1980)
Type of plot: Psychological
Time of plot: 1885 (in retrospect), 1902, 1904, and 1912
Locale: Western Texas and New Orleans
First published: 1938

> *Principal characters:*
> MIRANDA GAY, the protagonist
> MARIA, her sister
> AMY BREAUX, the girls' late aunt
> ISABEL RHEA, their cousin
> EVA PARRINGTON, another of their cousins
> GABRIEL BREAUX, the girls' uncle
> HARRY GAY, the girls' father
> SALLY RHEA, Amy's great-aunt
> MISS HONEY, Gabriel's second wife
> YOUNG GABRIEL, the son of Gabriel Breaux

The Story

When Miranda Gay is eight years old, she becomes aware, quite in passing, of a formal photograph showing her dead Aunt Amy. Miranda yearns to be beautiful when she grows up, as her aunt was in her wedding pictures. Her cousin, Isabel Rhea, is told that she rides horses almost as well as Amy did; her sister, Maria, is almost as fine a dancer. During her early years, the presence of the past enters Miranda's conscious mind in a number of other ways. The girls are shown Amy's wedding dress; another cousin, Eva Parrington, a Latin teacher, calls back celebrated events from southern history. Amy's widower, Uncle Gabriel, sends letters from New Orleans, Kentucky, and other parts of the country as he pursues his calling of training racehorses.

The impressionable young Miranda thus is exposed from several sides to others' recollections, and family history is assimilated piecemeal along with more remote visions of literary and historical figures from the past. The romantic aura surrounding death is evoked particularly by Uncle Gabriel's verses, printed in gold on a mourning card, which commemorate Aunt Amy's passing: "She lives again who suffered life,/ Then suffered death, and now set free/ A singing angel, she forgets/ The griefs of old mortality."

Packets of letters discovered in a trunk lend credence to other rumors the girls have heard. Once during their courtship Amy returned from a masked ball, her dress disheveled and undone, without Gabriel; there were scandalous hints that she had been seen with another man. Gabriel was on the verge of challenging the interloper to a duel when Harry Gay, Miranda's father, shot at his brother's rival and then fled to

Mexico for a time. Amy quarreled spiritedly with her great-aunt, Sally Rhea, a funda-
mentalist Baptist who feared for her soul. During Mardi Gras, Amy danced all night
three times in one week and suffered an internal hemorrhage. In her last letter, dated
ten days after she married Gabriel, Amy described herself as a "staid old married
woman."

In keeping with her father's religious beliefs, at the age of ten Miranda is enrolled,
with her sister, in a Catholic girls' school in New Orleans. This cloistered existence—
she feels "immured" in a confined world—is interrupted when they are invited to a
horse show near their home in Texas. There Miranda meets Uncle Gabriel, and she is
taken aback at his slovenly appearance, marked particularly by fleshy, overgrown features and bleary, bloodshot eyes. He introduces the others to his second wife, ironically named Miss Honey; she is a stern, upright, big-boned woman with pale features,
who seems to be the epitome of painstaking grooming and manners. Even when
Miranda's father has won one hundred dollars for the girls, she denounces horse racing as immoral. Miranda senses vividly the tension between Gabriel and Miss Honey;
her rigid bearing contrasts uncomfortably with her husband's dissipated demeanor.

Eight years later, Miranda boards the sleeping car of a train on her way home. An
unpleasant old lady rebukes her for bumping against her hat. Miranda is astonished
when the woman introduces herself as Cousin Eva: She seems prematurely aged, and
her protruding teeth and receding chin seem more pronounced than ever. She is coming back to Texas for Gabriel's funeral: Miranda has not heard that her uncle died
from an illness probably brought on by excessive drinking. He will be buried next to
Amy as he wished; Miss Honey has died already and lies buried in Kentucky.

Cousin Eva holds forth on two of her consuming concerns, her work with the
women's suffrage movement and her conviction that Gabriel never recovered from
Amy's death. She implies that Miss Honey also fell in Amy's wake. Eva maintains
that Amy "was a bad, wild girl, but I was fond of her to the last," although Amy invariably seemed to burden others with the consequences of her impulsive, romantic
flings. According to Eva, Amy had a single tragic flaw—"she was simply sex-ridden,
like the rest."

Miranda informs Eva that she has eloped from school. She feels awkwardly torn
between family allegiances and the imperatives of her own situation. She carries on an
internal dialogue, like that of an adult with a wayward child. At the station, after she
has greeted her father and young Gabriel, her uncle's son, she is struck by the thought
that "it is I who have no place," and she asks herself, "where are my own people and
my own time?" Her childlike, romantic view of the past is receding, and she is moving
away from received doctrines of good and evil, and love and hatred.

Themes and Meanings

Contrasting images of life and death form an essential background to Miranda's
early years. Some impressions are grasped directly and others are gathered only at
second hand, as visible artifacts or in others' recollections. Taken together, her views
of the people around her suggest separate and distinct ways of life, which appear to

the young girl fleetingly and in fragments. These types are presented unobtrusively, and nowhere are they disjoined from the people who embody them.

Aunt Amy, who died nine years before Miranda was born, left enduring memories that are revealed in parts to the young girl. The now almost legendary glory and sorrow of her short life are the more poignant for the coincidental, slightly garbled manner by which Miranda learns about the events of Amy's brief existence. Her aunt was high-spirited and effervescent; she flouted convention and heedlessly sacrificed her health and well-being for a few nights' dancing. Unconstrained, and given at times to wild abandon, she must have been coquettish, and probably indeed was capable of touching off deadly rivalries between her suitors. Perhaps settled married life was more than she could endure. No doubt she brought on her own tragic and premature demise, but then death claims other, more conventional types early as well. The reader senses that the force of Amy's personality was felt the more after her passing, and that in retrospect she is cast larger than life.

The development of other characters suggests variant concerns in life. Great-aunt Sally, who is known only from her letters to Amy, was steadfastly committed to saving others' souls. Uncle Gabriel, whom Miranda encounters early in her life, resembles Amy in his romantic fascination with horses and racing; yet where Amy spent herself in exorbitant demands on her substance, Gabriel gives way to weakness and self-indulgence and dies probably from his own bibulous excesses.

Miss Honey, who is very much his opposite, endeavors to restrain Gabriel but dies somehow well before her time. Miss Eva, Miranda's plain cousin, appears at intervals ten years apart; though not devoutly religious, she is frankly disapproving of Amy's youthful ebullience. Eva's proselytism for women's suffrage approaches the devotion of the faithful. It is from these conflicting examples, some tinged with a mythic aura and some distressingly mundane, that Miranda believes that she must find her own way of life.

Style and Technique

"Old Mortality" derives much of its impact from Katherine Anne Porter's use of telling details and from her indirect, insinuating means of introducing essential facts about characters. The crowded events of Aunt Amy's brief life, which are known only from others' recollections and from sundry material objects, are vividly recaptured nevertheless. In her formal photograph, she has clear gray eyes, short oval features, and wide, inviting lips: later the girls are shown her fine, silvery gray wedding dress, and a lock of her dark, cropped, curly hair is discovered in an envelope. Bygone courtships and intrigues are evoked in old letters describing the costume ball where Amy wore a ribboned hat, a black half-mask, and silk skirts. On that occasion Gabriel wore a blond curled wig and carried a shepherd's crook; he challenged a man who had come dressed as the pirate Jean Lafitte.

When Miranda herself finally encounters Gabriel, she is struck by the tired swollen eyes and "big melancholy laugh like a groan" that suggest his degeneration during the years since Amy's death. On each appearance, Cousin Eva's personality is suggested by her lean, sharp rodentlike features, traits that seem to become more obtrusive as time passes.

Many of the circumstances surrounding Miranda's immediate family come to light only after more distant relations have appeared, in one guise or another. Several aunts and cousins are shown before her father is introduced. Some important plot developments enter the narrative stealthily. During the final section of the story, it is after some pause that Miranda recognizes her fellow passenger as Cousin Eva; they converse for some time before it is made known that Gabriel has died. Even later Miranda discloses that she has eloped and left school. Much of what Miranda learns about her family's past is gathered obliquely, and other important revelations later are made indirectly and subtly reinforce the themes of change and mortality that are presaged by the girl's own experiences.

J. R. Broadus

OLD RED

Author: Caroline Gordon (1895-1981)
Type of plot: Character study
Time of plot: The late nineteenth century
Locale: Rural Kentucky
First published: 1933

> *Principal characters:*
> MISTER ALEXANDER MAURY, the protagonist, a sixty-year-old
> fisherman
> SARAH, his daughter
> STEPHEN (STEVE), his son-in-law
> LAURA, his sister-in-law
> HIS MOTHER-IN-LAW

The Story

Mister Alexander Maury, temporarily returned home after only a few years in Florida, leaves his fishing gear piled in the middle of the bedroom, ready for escape on a moment's notice, while he goes down to eat his mother-in-law's batter bread. He carefully reminds himself that his new son-in-law's name is Stephen. He regales his family with the story of how he learned to smell out fish in the water from an old black woman. He proudly displays his best fly, called Devil Bug, an exclusive design by a friend he met in Florida.

While his academically oriented son-in-law works on his essay on John Skelton, Mister Maury goes fishing. The old man was once a professor himself, but he reformed and sought the good life by field and stream. When a leg gave way under him once with some kind of cramp (just like Uncle James, who fell flat getting off his horse after a hard day's hunting), Maury knew he had to stick to fishing. A man could fish even if he was half-crippled.

Maury has a moment of keen elation when he remembers his first sighting of a particularly clever old fox that regularly showed himself on the crest of a hill when Maury was a child. He was so familiar as to have a name, Old Red, and he led them all on a merry chase but always escaped into some secret den in the bowels of the earth.

Steve, the son-in-law, joins him, and they fish together for some time. Maury pities the young man with his serious, abstracted face. Steve is not getting many fish and seems unable to give himself up to the peace and pleasure of the moment. Maury silently judges him "dead to the world"—like most people, actually.

That night, lying in the same bedroom in which they had put him after his wife Mary died, downstairs, Maury meditates on his relationship with Mary. She had never given up trying to change him, to make him over into the man she thought he should be. In fact, she had almost succeeded when the paralysis came on her, and then for a year and a half it was he trying to reconstruct the Mary he had known, his old adversary. However, she had given up, spent with the chase, losing all interest in what he did, merely waiting to die.

The next day, there is talk of Aunt Sally Crenfew's funeral tomorrow. Without thinking, Maury blurts out, "But that's the day Steve and I were going to Barker's Mill." Then the predictable avalanche ensues, his daughter spluttering about the scandal it will cause if he, Professor Maury, known by everyone to be in town, could not spare one afternoon from fishing to attend his cousin's funeral. Maury feels a gust of fear—time to move on.

The next morning, he pretends that his old kidney trouble is acting up. He simply has to go take the chalybeate waters of Estill Springs; they did so much good last year. He will have to leave on the morning train. He will be there by one o'clock, he calculates, and in thirty minutes after he gets off the train, he will have a fly in that water.

Themes and Meanings

"Old Red" is a story about a man whose avocation has become his vocation. This conscious choice carries with it a number of social implications, from the point of view of Mister Maury: In this society, the work ethic dictates that a publicly endorsed career is paramount to a man's identity, and worth cannot be measured by individual development; personal satisfaction is an end in itself, superior to commercial success and public recognition of service; people who neglect interacting with nature become alienated from the roots of their being; people who pursue too ardently some kind of interaction with nature tend to become outcasts from the mainstream of American life.

These are, perhaps, variations on the same theme. One might even add the implication that the rural poor, at least in the South, have more opportunities for a truly satisfying life than do urban well-to-do whites. Despite the implied racism, Mister Maury observes that blacks often live in the best places (by good fishing streams), and Maury's daughter accurately observes that he prefers the company of blacks (as fishing companions) to any social contact with his own relatives.

These ideas are part of an attitude often expressed in southern literature suggesting that mainstream America, with its emphasis on progress and commercial success and its rejection of tradition, has warped many personalities, discarding human values that were carefully nurtured in the past. However, there is another side to this issue: Mister Maury's radical rejection of the social rat race has also created, not a "whole person," but a distorted one apparently incapable of responding to the bonds of family, perhaps the foremost southern tradition. The implication might be, nevertheless, that an older pattern of living in the South allowed the individual to develop in all ways simultaneously: as a family man, as an outdoor sportsman, and as a useful contributor to the world's work.

In any case, the hunter has become the hunted, like Old Red, the clever fox who ran for cover whenever men approached. Unlike the fox, however, a man knows about old age and death. Maury must hedge his bets. He concentrates on fishing because he knows his body is becoming too decrepit for active hunting. He knows also that death is the final hunter, who will hunt him into the ground one day.

From one perspective, Mister Maury's obsession with fishing may seem simply a technique for avoiding responsibility. From another, it may have a certain integrity, like Henry David Thoreau's retreat to Walden Pond to see what was really vital to human life. Thoreau left Walden after two years because he said that he had other lives to live. Maury never intends to leave; he will never be "dead to the world" he has chosen until he is really dead.

Style and Technique

Precisely at the center of the story, at the center of the second of three numbered sections, is the remembrance, with its attendant thrill of elation, of the sighting of Old Red, the fox who always got away. The pursuit of Old Red was a repeated ritual—analogous, perhaps, to William Faulkner's famous hunting rituals in his short story "The Bear"—only Old Red was never caught.

In the remainder of the story, the apparent position of the old man shifts from that of the successful pursuer of wild game to that of the hunted in constant jeopardy of entrapment. While pitying young Steve for his alienation from nature, Maury realizes that his own rapport with nature involves an alienation from humankind. This is the price of the freedom he has gained:

> Poor boy, dead to the world and probably be that way the rest of his life. A pang of pity shot through Mister Maury and on the heels of it a gust of that black fear that occasionally shook him. It was he, not Steve, that was the queer one. The world was full of people like this boy, all of them going around with their heads so full of this and that they hardly knew what they were doing. They were all like that. There was hardly anybody—there was *nobody* really in the whole world like him.

The last section quickly develops and intensifies the impression of Maury as the hunted animal. As he lies in bed, his imagination plays tricks on him as it used to do in this room. The moonlight streams in the window making ominous shadows on the patterned wallpaper:

> It hung there, wavering, bitten by the shadows into a semblance of a human figure, a man striding with bent head and swinging arms. All the shadows in the room seemed to be moving towards him. The protruding corner of the washstand was an arrow aimed at his heart, the clumsy old-fashioned dresser was a giant towering above him.

This gothic touch is followed by his remembrance of his wife, from whom he always managed to escape until she gave up the chase and died.

Close to the end of the story, before Mister Maury coolly removes himself from the bosom of the family with his complaint about the old trouble with his kidneys, his identification with Old Red becomes complete. He is remembering again the pursuit of Old Red when he was a child. He had got off his horse and was running now almost beside the fox, coursing through the trees and turning up the mountain trail. The boy as pursuer seems to dissolve, however, and there is only the panting fox, finding the secret shelter where only a fox can go.

> He ran slowly, past the big boulder, past the blasted pine to where the shadow of the Pinnacle Rock was black across the path. He ran on and the shadow swayed and rose to meet him. Its cool touch was on his hot tongue, his heaving flanks. He had slipped in under it. He was sinking down, panting, in black dark, on moist earth while the hounds' baying filled the valley and reverberated from the mountainside.

That the black shadow of Pinnacle Rock echoes the shadow of the imagined giant in the old man's bedroom, and the sanctuary in the earth also suggests the grave is, perhaps, well understood by Mister Maury. Wild animals, however, do not need funerals.

Katherine Snipes

OLD VEMISH

Author: Barry Targan (1932-)
Type of plot: Social realism
Time of plot: 1969
Locale: The Atlantic Ocean and the Caribbean Sea
First published: 1973

> *Principal characters:*
> MARTIN VEMISH, the protagonist, a store owner
> SARA, his wife
> HERBERT, his son
> CLIFTON BOOTH, the antagonist, a cruise-ship tour director
> BRADFORD BATES, a tourist
> CHARLOTTE, his wife

The Story

For forty years, Martin Vemish has maintained his paint and wallpaper store on Long Island, New York, surviving the Depression and the postwar attempt by an outlet of Macy's Department Store to put him out of business. He is a simple man, a fighter, and he has never taken a vacation. Eventually, his son Herbert, an unsuccessful entrepreneur, becomes his partner and prevails on him and Martin's wife, Sara, to take a Caribbean cruise.

The ship on which they sail is the SS *Solar,* and its tour director is Clifton Booth, who is dedicated to managing the daily routine of the elderly passengers on board the ship.

The trouble starts shortly after the ship sails from New York, when Booth assembles the passengers to tell them what his schedule for them is, as well as to warn them against deviating from it. When Booth finds out from one of his assistants that the Vemishes have not attended the meeting, he confronts them. The Vemishes are sunning themselves on deck, and Martin Vemish, who is always smoking a cigar, and who did not like going on the cruise in the first place, tells Booth to leave him and his wife alone, that they will try to enjoy themselves on their own terms, not Booth's.

From this point on, Booth finds himself at war with the Vemishes, and as the story progresses, his composure and power wither. Booth's opinion is that the passengers in his care are not able to fend for themselves, that they should take it easy. He treats them, in effect, like children. Martin Vemish, however, will have none of it. He swims loudly in the pool while the other passengers lounge around it like convalescents, a bit unnerved by Vemish's antics—all except Bradford Bates, an elderly passenger, a retired accountant, who is excited by what Vemish is doing and by the appearance of Puerto Rico, the ship's first landfall. Bates's wife, Charlotte, gaunt and domineering, opposes this excitement in her husband and complains about Vemish's presence in the pool to him. It is clear that she has taken a violent dislike to Vemish.

The Vemishes are the last to return from the passengers' jaunt in Puerto Rico. They have gone off on their own, and Martin Vemish brings back a box of Cuban cigars, which Booth informs him he will not be allowed to take home after the cruise. When the ship docks in St. Thomas, the Vemishes are so late in returning that the ship's departure is delayed. Captain Harley, an abrupt man, is angry at Booth for this, and when Vemish explains to Booth that his delay was caused by his having saved a boy from drowning on the island, Booth is furious and frustrated.

Later that night, Bradford Bates escapes from his wife and introduces himself to the Vemishes in one of the ship's lounges. He is delighted to be treated to Vemish's tirade, with many of the passengers listening in, against the orgy of junk-buying in which the tourists have indulged, paying more than they would have paid for the same items in a New York department store. Charlotte Bates takes her husband in tow, and Clifton Booth tells Vemish that he is not allowed to smoke in the lounge, at which point Sara Vemish forces Booth to leave.

The next morning, the battle continues and Booth's power is further eroded. The sweepstakes deck games that Booth has organized turn into a shambles from his point of view when Vemish not only enters them but also plays with a vigor and determination that exhaust but galvanize the passengers and horrify Booth. Once again Bradford Bates is delighted, and at the moment when Booth goes after Vemish to tell him he must leave the ship, Bates claps and cheers for Vemish, and Booth vomits over the side.

Vemish is beginning to have an effect on the other passengers, too, despite Booth's carefully planned manipulation of them. The ship docks in Barbados, but the passengers will not be herded onshore as a group. They go in small groups and, as a representative of the Visitors Trade Commission complains to Booth that evening, spend almost no money. Also, they return to the ship when they want, with the result that the ship's arrival in St. Croix is three hours off schedule. Many of the passengers are sick, and the rest are upset, by turns feeling rebellious and that they have done something wrong. Booth believes that everyone is against him, including the captain, who decides to skip Guadeloupe and return to New York. The passengers are not disappointed but begin to welcome this changed state of affairs.

With one of the passengers who had a heart condition dead, and more passengers falling ill, the ship encounters a storm. It releases the anger simmering in the passengers. The cruise has not been what they had expected, and underneath this anger is the sense that the whole idea of such a project is an intrusion into their lives. They gather in one of the lounges, then drift into the bar where Vemish and Bates are drinking. Vemish, slightly drunk by now, and accompanied by Bates, manages to get the dance band to return. Vemish dances with his wife, and soon the other passengers are getting drunk and dancing. The revelry gets so out of hand that members of the crew are stationed at the exits to prevent the passengers from leaving. The passengers raise a cacophony of songs that meant something to them in their lives. Booth struggles through the heaving ship, and when he tries to stop the party, the revelers throw glasses at him and whatever else they can get hold of, driving him out. As the sea begins to calm down, Vemish tells Booth, who has run into him and Sara outside, that he, not Vemish, is responsible for what has happened, that he is in effect the manager of a useless illusion.

When the passengers disembark in New York, they are in a wretched state, though Bradford Bates is happy as he meets his waiting son-in-law. As he goes away with him to relay what had occurred, Vemish tells his own son that there is not much to tell about the cruise, and his wife agrees.

Themes and Meanings

The central theme of this story is time. Who is in charge of it when it comes to an individual's life—the individual himself or the managers of this world? The elderly provide Barry Targan with an especially poignant example of this question. Time is precious for them because they do not have much of it left. The assumption of the children of the elderly is that fun for their parents consists in spending their time doing as little as possible and nothing strenuous. Martin Vemish represents a different view of time. To him, time is equal to an individual's life, and as an individual is in charge of his own life, he should be in charge of deciding what to do with his own time. This is why Vemish rebels against Booth's itinerary on the SS *Solar*. Vemish, for his son's sake, may have taken a vacation he does not want. His son Herbert, after having suffered a string of business failures, needs to feel successful, and to do this he must be allowed to handle his father's business alone. Vemish had made the store a success and had made his own choices on how he would spend his personal time or life, so how can he deny this to his own son? However, Vemish will never allow someone such as Clifton Booth to take charge of his time. He has paid (if reluctantly) for this setting, but not for Booth's tyranny over his time.

Indeed, the significance of "Old Vemish" goes beyond the plight of the elderly, for at bottom it addresses itself to the tyranny of modern management itself, to corporate control of individual lives. Vemish is the hero who takes a stand against this kind of control—first against the corporation (Macy's Department Store) that tries to run him out of business, then against the one (the Lootens Line) that tries, in the form of Clifton Booth, to take over his vacation. Corporate management is the villain in this story, and part of the story's attraction is the triumph of personal time and value over those who would steal them in their own interest.

Style and Technique

Targan uses time itself to frame the episodes of "Old Vemish"—namely, the schedule of the cruise ship. This schedule provides the conflict that rages through the plot. Vemish upsets Booth's and the captain's schedule. He (and subsequently many of the other passengers) does not return to the ship when he is supposed to return. Even in following Booth's schedule, Vemish injects chaos into it—turning the deck games into an intense competition and the leisure hours after dinner near the end into a drunken bash. In fact, the ship's sailing schedule is finally thrown off completely because of Vemish. This use of time as an organizing factor in the plot is meant to dramatize the issue of time itself.

Another technique in the story is the use of the ship and the sea as symbols, and yet another is the use of the motif of illness. The ship represents human life, and the sea, the unpredictable and chaotic forces that inform life in general. Human life is controlled in the end by these larger forces, and to be in league with them in the form of independence and passion is the lesson that Vemish portrays. There is a good and a bad kind of illness in the story. The good kind is natural: It is, like old age, the result of living itself, especially of passionate living. The bad kind is spiritual, in that it inclines the old to take their frailty seriously, so that they become overcautious and allow others to push them around. In Clifton Booth's case, this kind of illness is defined by his greed for power over others' time, and it is dramatized by his increasing physical illness as he loses his running battle with Vemish, for his insomnia and nausea underscore his weakness in the face of such an opponent.

Finally, there are two kinds of rage that the story uses to help illuminate the conflict. Clifton Booth's rage and that of Charlotte Bates and even Captain Harley arise from their commitment to the rational, to schedule—that is, from the failure of their control over others. Sara Vemish's rage and that of many of the passengers on the cruise arise from their commitment to the lives they have led and possess on their own, from the bullying of those such as Clifton Booth who would control them, who would deny them their instincts in the name of reason.

Mark McCloskey

OLD WEST

Author: Richard Bausch (1945-   )
Type of plot: Psychological
Time of plot: 1950
Locale: Somewhere in the United States, probably the West
First published: 1989

> *Principal characters:*
> JOEY STARRETT, an octogenarian storyteller
> SHANE, a gunfighter in a film
> THE RIGHT REVEREND BAGLEY, the drunken preacher-gunfighter
>   whom Shane kills

The Story

Joey Starrett is more than eighty years old, and has been telling a version of the story of Shane for many years. The film *Shane* came out in 1953, three years after Joey narrates his story. Joey's version is a correction of the well-known story. What follows is the real story of Shane, told by the only living witness of the famous gunfight dramatized by Alan Ladd and Jack Palance. It did not happen that way, Joey reveals in Richard Bausch's "Old West." First of all, Shane came back to the valley twelve years after he rode out of it, wounded, with little Joey shouting, "Come back, Shane." When Shane comes back, Joey's father is already dead of cholera, and his mother is living with Joey in their now-broken-down homestead. Joey is twenty-one; his mother is crazy and a bit deaf.

A preacher has recently arrived—the Reverend Bagley—who mesmerizes the folk who hang around Grafton's saloon with his sermons about damnation and salvation. Joey's mother is fascinated by Bagley and cherishes a gift from him, significantly, a six-shot Colt. Then Shane rides into town, his buckskin clothes transformed by the years into stinking rags. Shane is fat and bald. He has become a bounty hunter and is looking for a phony preacher who might be Bagley. Shane admits to Joey that since he rode out of the valley he has been living all these years in the next town, only a few hours away. He has been married as well, unsuccessfully. Joey's disillusion is complete.

Joey rides into town and sees Bagley preaching in Grafton's. Bagley is a gifted talker, a role model for Joey, who already is telling people the story of the heroic, younger Shane of the time when Joey was a child. Bagley's sermon warns of evils to come that sound surprisingly like ones that have already come: "Miseries and diseases we ain't even named!" preaches Bagley, half-drunk. "Pornography and vulgar worship of possessions, belief in the self above everything else, abortion, religious fraud, fanatic violence, mass murder, and killing boredom, it's all coming, hold on!" Bagley suggests that Joey's tale of Shane is an exaggeration, that Wilson, the gunfighter whom Shane had fought years earlier, did not have two guns, but only one stuck out of sight in his pants. Bagley throws doubt on the details of the gunfight Shane won when Joey was seven, and seems to know something of gunplay himself. He certainly knows something of wordplay.

Later, Joey drives his mother in to see Bagley, with Shane riding his decrepit horse alongside the buckboard. They ask for Bagley at Grafton's, and the saloon-keeper obligingly directs them to the barn where Bagley is sleeping off another drunk. As they arrive at the barn, Bagley opens fire on everyone, missing Joey and his mother and killing Grafton and Shane, but is killed by Shane. Joey and his mother are un-harmed, but Joey, crouching in the wagon, has seen a terrified Shane, ducking bullets like anyone else. The random shots and meaningless violence have made Joey see that his earlier tale of Shane was a lie. It did not happen as it was shown in the film *Shane*: The hired Wilson did not have two guns, but only one, and he wore it in his pants, as Bagley had said. There was no glory or heroism after all in Shane's fight with Wilson. It was no more heroic than this second gunfight—fatal for Shane—which the disillu-sioned elderly Joey admits was nothing more than a "stupid, fumbling blur of gun-fighting."

Joey survives the gunfight but not his disillusionment, which he has kept at bay through all these years of telling a false version. He now realizes that while he was in the wagon with all of those bullets flying around and thinking he was about to die any second, a small truth came to him: "The story I'd been telling all my life was in fact not true enough—was little more than a boy's exaggeration." Had he told it truer or at least true enough, he would have dispensed with the heroic overlay to Shane's killing of Wilson and concentrated on the terrible cost of such violence. Now, for once, Joey can tell the truth.

Themes and Meanings

Bausch's story is about the nature of storytelling. The narrator is a professional sto-ryteller who has been telling the story of Shane for most of his eighty years, and now decides to confess that his story was not true. He tells the real story, which is one of the disillusionment not only of love—his mother and Shane have declined into grotesque versions of their former selves—but also of Joey's love for the romance of the Old West, where men like the noble Shane ride alone, righting wrongs through violence. The narrator's true story demythologizes Shane's heroics and replaces them with the sordidness of human motive and the truth of violence.

Bausch's story gains its power from playing the reader's familiarity with the film *Shane* against these belated but damning details: Joey is a twenty-one-year-old drunk-ard; his mother is senile, deaf, and convinced that entropy and decline are everywhere. Even the land for which the heroic settlers fought turns out to be unsuited for farming, good only for cattle grazing. The bad guys in the film, the cattlemen, were right. Shane has devolved into an impoverished bounty hunter. Only Bagley, the seedy preacher, is marked by energy, and his talent is words. Joey says that Bagley's sen-tences line up "one after the other, perfectly symmetrical and organized as any written speech." Bagley is also a corrector of prior texts: He hears Joey's tale of Shane in the saloon that was seen in the film but tells Joey he is exaggerating. When the shots of the final gunfight outside the barn are finally silent, Joey sees that Bagley was right, that his childhood memory of Shane was really false: "The clearest memory of my life was a thing I made up in my head." "Old West" probes the nature of tale-telling while it also tells a powerful tale. If it deflates the myth of Shane as well as other versions of the cult of male violence in the Old West, it builds a new version of Shane that is as symmetrical and organized as any written speech, to end with Bagley's words, which seem more lasting than Shane's gun skills.

Style and Technique

The story is a confession, a belated attempt to clear the record of past stories about Shane, so the speaker's voice is conversational, direct, confiding in the listener ("And this is what I have come to tell you"). The speaker urges the reader to believe that this telling, told in his final years as a storyteller, is the true story. Joey's language is marked by simple diction and colloquial turns of phrases: "I've read all the books and tried all the counsels of the flesh, too." He knows the reader knows a certain story about Shane; readers know that he does not know that this story became a famous film three years after he tells his true story in 1950. So Bausch's "Old West" relies on a number of allusions and recognitions that create amusing ironies, such as when one recalls Alan Ladd in his handsome buckskin outfit and then sees him through the eyes of a disgusted Joey: "His buckskins were frayed and torn, besmirched with little maplike continents of salt stains and sweat."

"Besmirched" is an apt word not only for Shane's buckskins but also for his reputation, and reveals something of Bausch's skillful use of diction—even in a conversational, improvising voice, certain phrases suggest deeper meanings. The style has a playful element as well. Bausch must have enjoyed creating the rantings of Bagley, which are sometimes comic in the tradition of Mark Twain—another debunker of the romance of violence—such as when Bagley shouts in his sermon, "Plagues and wars and bunched towns clenched on empty pleasures and fear, it's on its way, just hold on!" The overall tone, however, is sobering: Joey's description of Shane lying dead does not use his name but focuses instead on the thing he had carried: "The man who had brought his gun back into the valley lay at the back wheel of the wagon, face up to the light, looking almost serene."

Paul R. Lilly, Jr.

OLD WOMAN MAGOUN

Author: Mary E. Wilkins Freeman (1852-1930)
Type of plot: Regional
Time of plot: About 1900
Locale: A New England hamlet called Barry's Ford
First published: 1909

> *Principal characters:*
> OLD WOMAN MAGOUN, the protagonist
> LILY BARRY, her young granddaughter
> SALLY JINKS, her friend
> NELSON BARRY, Lily's father, the last and worst of a good old family
> ISABEL, Nelson's half-witted sister
> JIM WILLIS, Nelson's friend
> LAWYER MASON, who is consulted by Magoun
> MRS. MASON, the lawyer's wife

The Story

Old Woman Magoun is a poor but powerful citizen of the small hamlet of Barry's Ford, as can be seen when she influences the men of the village to build a bridge across the Barry River. A hard worker herself, she has little respect for men or for their dependence on alcohol and tobacco. As she explains to her friend Sally Jinks, "I've worked all my life and never done nuther."

Old Woman Magoun has lived alone with her granddaughter Lily Barry since the death of Lily's mother a week after Lily was born, nearly fourteen years ago. Lily's father is Nelson Barry, who lives with his half-witted sister, Isabel, but spends most of his time at the village store leading the "shiftless" element of the village. He has taken no interest in his daughter in the past, and local rumor has questioned whether Lily is legitimately his daughter, as Old Woman Magoun claims.

As the story opens, Old Woman Magoun and Sally Jinks are preparing roast pig for the men building the bridge. Because she is tired, Old Woman Magoun sends Lily to the store for some salt. Lily is youthful for her age, still carrying a rag doll wherever she goes, and her grandmother has kept her from the store whenever possible in the past. On this trip, Lily is joined by a handsome man who takes her hand and asks her about her family. At first Lily likes the attention, but when he asks her age she becomes wary and pulls her hand away.

At the store, Lily sees her father, who uncharacteristically talks to her and buys her candy. He clearly knows the handsome man, who is Jim Willis. When she returns home with the candy, Lily is questioned closely by her grandmother, who is very upset by what she learns and sends Lily to her room. "When be you goin' to let that girl grow up?" Sally asks her before the workmen come in for their dinner.

After Lily and the men have been fed and Lily is sleeping, Old Woman Magoun is interrupted by a visit from Nelson Barry. He announces that he is ready to claim Lily and to take her to live with him and Isabel. When he mentions the name of Jim Willis, Old Woman Magoun guesses that he has lost to Jim at cards and is claiming Lily to pay the debt. Barry's embarrassed reaction to her explanation convinces her, but he reminds her that he can take what he wants. He promises to return in a week for Lily.

The next morning, Old Woman Magoun and Lily walk to Greenham, three miles across the bridge, so that the grandmother can speak to Lawyer Mason. Along the way Lily admires some berries, part of which are blackberries and part of which are poisonous nightshade. "You can't have any now," Old Woman Magoun explains as they go on.

While her grandmother speaks with the lawyer, his wife entertains Lily with sour apples and milk. Old Woman Magoun admonishes her for upsetting Lily's stomach. After they leave, Lawyer Mason reveals that the grandmother offered Lily for adoption, but though his wife is grieving for a lost daughter he is not willing to adopt Nelson Barry's child.

As they walk home, Lily once more admires the berries, and her grandmother stops long enough for Lily to eat some of them. Before they reach home Lily feels the effects of the poison and sickens steadily. When Sally Jinks visits, however, Lily blames the sour apples and milk, and the rumor spreads even to Barry and Willis. As Lily worsens, her grandmother describes for her the beauties of her future with her mother in Heaven, and by the time Barry comes to take her away, Lily is beyond help. After Lily's death, Old Woman Magoun continues to work hard but begins to carry Lily's rag doll whenever she crosses the bridge to sell her goods in Greenham.

Themes and Meanings

Hester Prynne in Nathaniel Hawthorne's *The Scarlet Letter* (1850) becomes very melancholy when she thinks about the social position of women in her New England; it even occurs to her that the greatest kindness that she could perform for her daughter Pearl might be to send her immediately to heaven to avoid woman's plight. Old Widow Magoun in this story makes precisely that choice, offering her granddaughter Lily a pure and happy afterlife to save her from being awarded to Jim Willis as payment of a gambling debt.

Mary E. Wilkins Freeman seldom delivered a feminist message as directly as she did in this story. In Freeman's turn-of-the-century New England, patriarchy still defined relationships even though the men themselves had degenerated. Certainly the story reflects the realities of Freeman's own life, as her father's business failed and her mother became the support of the family. However, Freeman's life was not unique; rural New England is accurately represented in this story in many ways. A father's rights could not be challenged by a mere grandmother, and a daughter could be legally married off when she was even younger than thirteen-year-old Lily.

Old Woman Magoun has the strength of her Puritan work ethic and of her religious faith to sustain her, but neither gives her power if a man, even a "fairly dangerous degenerate of a good family" such as Nelson Barry, decides to challenge her. Freeman shows the influence Old Woman Magoun has on the "weakness of the masculine element" of Barry's Ford when she pushes them into building the bridge, but this action does not include Nelson Barry.

Nor can Old Woman Magoun expect support from the law, despite her desperate willingness to let Lawyer Mason adopt Lily. Mason's own wife, who yearns for a new daughter, has no say in his rejection of Lily. Wherever they turn, women find the walls of patriarchal power enclosing them in Freeman's story; giving in is as inevitable as growing up. Although Freeman wrote more than half a century after Hawthorne, and although Old Woman Magoun has a "mighty sense of reliance upon herself as being on the right track in the midst of a maze of evil," the story suggests that death is the only alternative for Lily. So too does Edna Pontellier choose to walk into the ocean in Kate Chopin's *The Awakening* (1899) in a southern version of Freeman's New England dilemma; the difference is that Edna makes her own choices.

If the theme of maternal responsibility is given harsh expression in this story, the question of individual choice is implicitly raised as well. At great cost, Old Woman Magoun does what she feels is right for Lily. The reader is also told, however, that she has overprotected her granddaughter, has tried to keep her a child, and has tried to avoid any contact between Lily and her father. Lily, Freeman demonstrates, responds to the handsome Jim Willis, and "instincts and nature itself" draw her to her father. Old Woman Magoun makes a difficult choice, but is the choice really hers to make? Is Lily's fate inevitable, or the outcome as much of her grandmother's overprotectiveness as of her father's degeneracy? Freeman does not resolve the ambiguities implicit in such an imbalanced social reality.

Style and Technique

Writing this story after she herself had left New England for marriage and New Jersey, Freeman nevertheless lost none of her ability to capture the realities of the region of her birth. The flavor of late nineteenth century New England is captured in the subtle dialect as accurately as its social realities are reflected in the tensions between the sexes. "It seems queer to me," Old Woman Magoun tells Sally Jinks, "that men can't do nothin' without havin' to drink and chew to keep their sperits up." Idiomatic terms such as "sperits" and "ary" for "a single" define the region; the description of the new bridge as "a primitive structure built of logs in a slovenly fashion" reflects the declining products of patriarchy in both the human and material heritage of New England.

The bridge frames this tragic tale, appearing in both the opening and closing paragraphs. Built under the influence of Old Woman Magoun, it is yet a "rude" structure and leads her only to Greenham, where the inevitability of the fate she sees in Barry's Ford is simply confirmed for her by the lawyer. Nor are women happier across the bridge, if the grieving Mrs. Mason is any example.

Another symbol Freeman employs in this regionalistic tale is Lily's old rag doll. A symbol of Lily's youth and innocence, the doll is a matter of concern to both her father and Jim Willis. Lily wraps both arms around it to free her hand from Willis; when her father tries to make her throw it away to take some candy, she "hugged the doll tightly, and there was all at once in the child's expression something mature. It became the reproach of a woman."

However, Lily is never to become the woman whose reproach turned her father's threat away in the store; her grandmother will choose instead to send Lily to "a little white bed" with the young mother who had died at sixteen giving Lily life. The final image of Old Woman Magoun is double-edged, as she is described as "a trifle touched" because she carries Lily's doll across the bridge "as one might have carried an infant." Even the beautiful images of heaven that her grandmother offers Lily near the end cannot erase the pain Lily suffers or still the "terrible sobs" of Old Woman Magoun when death becomes the new inevitability of Lily's life.

Thelma J. Shinn

OLD-WORLD LANDOWNERS

Author: Nikolai Gogol (1809-1852)
Type of plot: Pastoral
Time of plot: The early nineteenth century
Locale: Rural Ukraine
First published: "Starosvetskiye pomeshchiki," 1835 (English translation, 1886)

> *Principal characters:*
> AFANASIY IVANOVICH TOVSTOGUB, a small provincial landowner in Ukraine
> PUL'KHERIYA IVANOVNA TOVSTOGUBIKHA, his wife
> THE NARRATOR, a former resident of the region and occasional visitor from the outside world

The Story

The narrator begins "Old-World Landowners" with praise of the rural landowners of an earlier time in Ukraine, people who live "an extraordinarily secluded life, in which not a single desire strays beyond the palisade surrounding the small courtyard, beyond the wattle fence of the orchard, full of plum and apple trees, beyond the lopsided peasant cottages spaced round it under the shade of willows, elders and pear-trees." He quickly moves, however, to a particular couple, who are not only old-fashioned but also old: Afanasiy Ivanovich Tovstogub and his wife Pul'kheriya Ivanovna Tovstogubikha. (The usual feminine form of the family name is here made diminutive and affectionate.)

The narrator then lovingly presents this pair in homely detail, moving from a physical description of each, with brief biography, to mood-setting analogies of their present quiet life. He describes the house where they live, with a famous passage on the "singing doors" in the house, whose various voices comment on the regular pattern of life in this isolated country setting.

The description proceeds to the activities of the old man and his wife; the old woman is the real overseer of any work done by the peasants and servants, all of whom steal most brazenly from the estate, which nevertheless provides, like Eden, God's plenty for the loving pair. The old man teases his wife occasionally with imaginary catastrophes: "What if our house suddenly caught fire?" Such games offer her only excitement.

The main activity of their lives is, however, eating, or overeating, and the ceremony of their daily meals and snacks is meticulously given. Specific dishes that the old lady and her servants provide—pickled mushrooms, poppy-seed patties, fruit dumplings—are set temptingly before the old man all through the day and even in the middle of the night. Bellyaches are common among all members of the house. Even their conversation is mainly about food.

Visitors are most hospitably entertained. The old wife cannot press enough dainties on the visitor. She tells the narrator the secrets of her delicious preserves and flavored vodkas. The old man listens with pleased incomprehension to the visitor's tales of life in the outside world.

In this rich presentation of the idyllic life of two good-hearted and loving nonentities, two-thirds of the story is over before an "event" occurs: Pul'kheriya's little gray cat disappears, wooed away by wild tomcats from the woods, "as a company of soldiers entice a silly country girl." Pul'kheriya looks for the cat but forgets about her when she does not come home. Some time later, however, the cat does return, emaciated and half wild herself. Pul'kheriya feeds her; the cat eats ravenously but again departs, forever. Pul'kheriya interprets this reappearance of the cat, for no apparent reason, as her own "death," and promptly sets about making plans for the old man's care after her demise. Her only concern is that he must be fed and attended to. That matter arranged, she takes to her bed, refuses to eat, and dies within a few days.

The old man's grief is childlike and enormous. The narrator shows him stunned at the funeral and then skips to a return visit five years later. He first interrupts the narrative, though, with his thoughts about the way people respond to grief by telling a story within this story about a man in the great world whose beloved dies suddenly, leaving him to a paroxysm of grief and several attempts at suicide. Nevertheless, the man recovers and marries a year later, plays cards, and enjoys life as before.

It is not so for Afanasiy. At the narrator's return after five years, both the estate and the old man are in great decay, all suffering from the absence of his wife. The widower weeps, misses his mouth when he carries food to it, and spills his dinner. A man who has "never been troubled by any strong emotions," one who has spent his life "eating dried fish and pears," has been destroyed by grief. The narrator questions whether the reaction demonstrates that passion is less powerful over human beings than habit.

The old man dies not long after that visit. He walks out in the garden one day and hears someone behind him distinctly call his name. As Pul'kheriya interpreted the cat's return as her death come for her, so Afanasiy interprets the call as Pul'kheriya's voice from the grave, telling him to join her. He obediently does so.

Before Afanasiy dies, however, the narrator inserts another story within the story: his own hearing of such a voice calling his name, repeatedly, when he was young. He experiences terror at the call and flees in panic to find another human being, whose presence alone can dispel "the terrible feeling of emptiness" in his heart.

The thieving steward, the housekeeper, and the elder carry off much of what is left in the house and grounds, and a distant relative who inherits the estate arrives, makes a few superficial "reforms," and then lets it fall into receivership. The house, like the old people, falls over completely, the serfs run away, and the owner, impoverished, rarely appears and does not stay long.

Themes and Meanings

A richly ambiguous story, "Old-World Landowners" seems an idyll of an old-fashioned way of life in early nineteenth century rural Ukraine. Nikolai Gogol himself defined the idyll as a "vivid representation of a quiet, peaceful way of life, a scene having no dramatic movement"; he calls it "a picture, in the true sense, and by virtue of the objects it chooses, which are always simple ones, a picture of the Flemish school." In this object-filled depiction of the small landowner's way of life, however, the idyllic pattern is interrupted at several points by the first-person narrator, whose shaping of the story allows to surface social criticism of this empty country life, fear of sexuality and of human isolation, the contemplation of death, and reflection on the relative force of habit and passion in people's lives.

The loving picture of an Edenic country life, of this Ukrainian Philemon and Baucis, provides delight in the passive regular years, the days of which move solely by mealtimes. The old man is gentle, the old woman a charming representation of a country wife, an old-time nourisher. The reader laughs gently at their simplicity and weeps at their grief. However, this is an idyll with a difference. From the time of the story's first publication, critics have uncomfortably realized that the pair are vacuous, unable to respond to anything other than food and eating. Furthermore, the estate is already in decay at the beginning of the story and in complete ruin at the end. Is the tale an attack on the fecklessness of such landowners, or on the waste and thievery of estate managers, or of the laziness and moral laxness of the peasants? No idyll should raise such questions. Gogol's reputation as a critical realist arises from such evidence.

Thus it is that the emphasis shifts from the almost mindless couple to the troubled narrator, who sees their life as an escape, a dream of an idealized past. Ambitious, he has left this world for the great world of active achievement, and the unchanging world of the old folks is set against the great world's whirl. (Gogol's letters to his mother emphasize his drive to achieve, to avoid the stasis that this provincial life meant to him.) The world of activity is nevertheless not Eden, either. The ugly image of lawsuits, merciless capitalism, brutal passions, and dreadful loneliness offers no comfort to counter the "death-in-life" of the old-world landowners.

Furthermore, through passivity and orality the pair clearly avoid the challenge of sexuality, an aspect of living that persistently alarms Gogol. The cat leaves her somnolent Eden for an exciting life with the wild cats from the woods, even though she may starve with them. The childless Pul'kheriya's distress at this evidence and her uncomprehending reaction to the serf girls' frequent pregnancies may account for her seeing the cat's visit as a harbinger of her death. Failing to accept sexuality, the means by which life continues, implies ultimate death.

The passivity enables the changeless routine of the old couple's days to continue uninterrupted until the death of Pul'kheriya, and it is this "habit" that the narrator sees as perhaps stronger than passion in shaping human lives. The ambiguity of the author's point persists here as well in his perception that habit links with death, as passion, however terrifying, links with life.

Finally, the form of the old man's death suggests further ambiguity. Afanasiy welcomes the "call" from his wife as his way to regain his connection with her. However, the narrator recalls similar voices with panic as the very death-in-life, the inability to connect with other human beings, which the idyll represents. In the end, one can neither retire from life nor escape its claims. The major theme of the story may be fear both of life and of death, an unnerving subtext of anxiety for what seems at first an image of common everyday bliss.

Style and Technique

The theme emerges not from the content, a little from the structure, but mainly from the style. Two styles, the one intense and lofty, the other colloquial and low, intertwine to express the shifting mind of the teller. The sound of the story communicates the ambiguity of the meaning. Shifts in the oral quality of the narrator's voice, what the Russians call *skaz*, put the writer's duality up front.

Emphasizing lyrical description, with hyperbolic catalogs of real details from Ukrainian domestic life, the story first establishes a nostalgic tone, with exclamations and interruptions in the sentimental style. The gentle humor of the old man's teasing and his wife's chattiness about recipe secrets catch the simple diction of these simpleminded characters. Breaking into these stylistic patterns with digressions comes the brooding narrative voice of the storyteller, with his rhythmic, rhetorical questioning, longing, and reflection. The tonal shift from the patronizing nostalgia of the first part to the pathos of the end defines the structure of the piece and constitutes the formula "laughter through tears" that characterizes much of Gogol's work. Gogol, in the seemingly innocent story, both castigates banality and celebrates an unattainable beauty in styles to match oppositions in all of his writing.

Martha Manheim

ON ACCOUNT OF A HAT

Author: Sholom Aleichem (Sholom Rabinowitz, 1859-1916)
Type of plot: Wit and humor
Time of plot: The late 1800's
Locale: Kasrilevke and Zlodievka
First published: "Iber a Hitl," 1913 (English translation, 1953)

Principal characters:
THE NARRATOR, a nameless scrap-paper merchant of Kasrilevke
SHOLOM SHACHNAH RATTLEBRAIN, a Kasrilevke real-estate
broker and the story's protagonist
SHOLOM ALEICHEM, the listener-recorder of the narrator's story
and the primary narrator, an author

The Story

The story's opening introduces its multilayered narrative structure and the principal characters, particularly Sholom Shachnah Rattlebrain, about whom the (secondary) narrator weaves his fantastic and amusing tale regarding absentmindedness, all the while interrupting himself with amusing observations and comical asides. Prior to unfolding this narrator's yarn, Sholom Aleichem expresses his own doubts about its veracity, thus implicitly shifting to that merchant-narrator any blame for telling a tall tale and expecting the reader to accept it as real.

The merchant-narrator chooses to illustrate the notion of absentmindedness (raised in some unexplained context in his conversation with Sholom Aleichem) by recounting what befell Sholom Shachnah, Kasrilevke's rattlebrain, some time ago before the Passover festival. (The narrator and Sholom Aleichem are in a hurry themselves as they, too, prepare for the upcoming Passover.)

This Sholom Shachnah, a poor Jew and something of a real-estate broker, likes to brag about the company he keeps with wealthy landowners, but he can barely eke out a living for himself and his family. Finally, with God's help, he takes part in an actual real-estate transaction. As soon becomes apparent, though, his share of the profits is jeopardized by some wealthy Jewish brokers of another province who have managed the transaction and are now threatening to cut him out of the commission. Standing up bravely against his adversaries, he finally receives his share, sending most of it back home (the deal is apparently conducted outside Kasrilevke) to defray expenses for the upcoming Passover celebration, pay off some debts, and provide for the children's needs. Sholom Shachnah also keeps some money for his expenses and for gifts for the family.

Just before the onset of Passover, Sholom Shachnah telegraphs home that he will be "arriving home Passover without fail." The only obstacle blocking his journey home turns out to be the time-consuming train ride, whose greatest difficulty is the critical transfer to the Kasrilevke train at the Zlodievka stop, where one must arrive before the Kasrilevke train's departure and spend many late-night hours awaiting its arrival.

Arriving at the Zlodievka stop on the night before Passover, Sholom Shachnah prepares to spend those hours resting (he has not slept for the past two nights). Noticing the dirty floor and walls, he finds that the only possible place to take a rest is on a small spot on a bench left empty by a stretched-out, sleeping Gentile official bedecked with an important-looking hat and button-emblazoned uniform.

Convinced that the sleeping stranger must be an important officer, Sholom Shachnah nevertheless bravely occupies the narrow vacant spot on the bench. Being afraid of falling asleep and missing the sole Kasrilevke train before the Passover, he pays the Gentile peasant porter Yeremei to awaken him on time. Now, assured of not missing his train, Sholom Shachnah sits down and promptly falls asleep, his hat rolling off his head.

In his sleep, Sholom Shachnah dreams of riding home in a slow, horse-drawn wagon. Being in a hurry to arrive before the Passover, he urges—to no avail—the peasant driver Ivan to speed up. When, suddenly, the driver hurries his horses, Sholom Shachnah loses his hat and begins to worry about entering town bareheaded. When the wagon stops suddenly, Ivan asks Sholom Shachnah to get up, his voice mingling with that of Yeremei, the peasant porter, who is trying to awaken the sleeping broker.

Finally awake, Sholom Shachnah hurries to pick up his fallen hat, inadvertently putting on the fallen officer's hat instead. Now he runs to purchase his ticket and notices how the great crowd at the ticket window parts before him as if by magic and the agent—respectful of the hat—most politely serves his customer. Sholom Shachnah suspects that the agent is mocking him but decides that, as a Jew in the Diaspora, he had better not make an issue of such behavior.

Sholom Shachnah is again irritated as the crowds part and people give way as he searches for the third-class car. The conductor, explaining that the car is too full, politely escorts him (and his red-banded, visored hat) to a seat in the first-class compartment.

Still confused, Sholom Shachnah thinks the honors may be because of the recent closing of that real-estate deal he managed. Glancing into a nearby mirror, however, he notices the official hat and, angry with the peasant porter, concludes that the latter did not awaken him (Sholom Shachnah, that is) but the officer. Therefore he (Sholom Shachnah, that is) must be still asleep on the bench, doomed to spend the Passover away from home. Deciding to avert such a mishap, Sholom Shachnah leaps out of the car and runs to wake himself up, as the train pulls out of the station.

Sholom Shachnah's Passover, continues the merchant-narrator, was less than pleasant, spent at a Jewish home in Zlodievka. His wife, on his return, gives him "a royal welcome," angry, it turns out, not at his having to celebrate the Passover away from home, nor for the unusual hat on his head, but, amazingly, at the excessively long telegram he sent her, and particularly at the words "without fail," as if trying to make the telegraph company richer or, as though he were God, presuming to know the future by such a certain promise. The folks in Kasrilevke, too, have their say as they—men, women, and children—endlessly taunt him about his hat, his "official" status, and his absentmindedness.

Themes and Meanings

Ironically, and as if to spite its comical language, situations, and mood, Sholom Aleichem uses this monologue as a vehicle to make some poignant observations concerning the image and self-image of the Eastern European Jew in the late nineteenth century (and also of human nature in general).

The surreal confusion that prevents Sholom Shachnah from taking the train—his inability to recognize himself in the officer's hat—is not merely a measure of the protagonist's nature as an absentminded scatterbrain; it is also an indication of the Jew's grotesque, unnatural mind-set, growing out of his Eastern European way of life and surroundings wherein his (and his Gentile neighbors') preconceptions about Jews stem from internal (Jewish) and external (Gentile) pressures: social, political, economic, and religious. These have given rise to a monolithic self-concept, also reinforced by a clearly defined set of features attributable to a Jew.

Though comical, this episode is also a sad commentary on the hero's narrow self-esteem; following a long and unfortunate "tradition," he has learned to identify himself as a Jew in a confined and limited way, particularly as being less than equal to his non-Jewish countrymen. Such a character is especially prone to humble himself and submit unquestioningly to those whose mere appearance implies authority.

The monologue also mocks the myth of the *Yiddisher kop* (Jewish head) as Sholom Aleichem presents Sholom Shachnah the Every-Jew as a numskull, an absentminded antihero who foolishly assumes that he is more intelligent than others. Adding insult to injury, however, he is portrayed as being ridiculously stupid, particularly when surmising that Yeremei the porter, the one with the *goyisher kop* (Gentile head), failed to awaken him.

The Passover setting of the narrative possesses strong causal links with the pre-Passover preparations of the merchant-narrator and Sholom Aleichem, his patient listener. The author, however, may have chosen this special occasion—marking the exodus and liberation of the Israelites from the house of bondage—to illustrate the sorrowful state and shortcomings reached by one of the heirs of that people. In so doing, Sholom Aleichem calls for a new exodus, whether a personal one (out of a constrained mind-set) or one on a national scale.

Style and Technique

This comic monologue, as do others in Sholom Aleichem's repertoire, features a talkative and amusing narrator who is fully absorbed with the events and problems associated with the story he presents to his listener. Aside from recounting the intricacies of his comical and unbelievable tale, often ending with a punch line or twist of the plot, such a monologuist invariably focuses the reader's attention on the personality of the narrator. What the reader sees, then, are the author's "brushstrokes" whereby the character and personal peculiarities of the narrator are assembled.

This narrative-within-a-narrative, as one notices, is the story of Sholom Shachnah, collected and told by a nameless Kasrilevke merchant to his listener, Sholom Aleichem, the familiar, though fictitious, persona of the author Sholom Rabinowitz (alias Sholom Aleichem). It is this persona-narrator who addresses the reader directly and through whose senses and final reaction the reader partakes of the comic adventure.

Such a multilayeredness is what allows for a dual characterization to take place, depicting (almost simultaneously) the story's protagonist and the narrator's personality. This talkative merchant-narrator ceaselessly turns the reader's attention to him as the significant (second) player in the monologue by means of a number of attention-getting phrases such as "[Do] you hear what I say?" "Are you listening?" and "Now listen to this." Other intrusive comments, evaluative remarks, opinions, and asides further contribute to a fuller rounding-out of the narrator's personality.

The misuse of biblical allusions is a comic technique employed by Aleichem in many of his stories. Although this device is not prominent in "On Account of a Hat," one such reference is particularly obvious in that the complete Hebrew verse is retained in the Yiddish text (and transliterated in the English version). When the narrator quotes a verse from Ecclesiastes to make the point that "We were better off without the train" service (recently instituted to Kasrilevke), he fails to make use of the scriptural source in a meaningful, constructive way.

A pivotal means for delivering the concluding punch of the monologue—namely, the reason for the wife's anger—is a system of devices to mislead the reader throughout the story. Similarly, capitalizing on the reader's desire to know whether, and especially how, Sholom Shachnah will miss his train, Aleichem relies on anxiety-producing situations; he opens up a number of plausible possibilities, each of which may result in the desired effect (of missing the train): the possibility of missing the transfer if the Kasrilevke train pulls out before the hero's arrival; Sholom Shachnah may sleep too soundly to be awakened on time; the porter may indeed be negligent and not awaken him on time; the crowded line by the ticket window may cause him to be delayed and miss the train; and he may not be allowed into the overcrowded third-class compartments and be forced to get off the train.

None of these mishaps befalls the traveler; all seems to work perfectly. They may, however, be compared to a boxer's leading fist, distracting the opponent from the surprising punch coming from the other hand: in this case, the outrageously unbelievable cause preventing Sholom Shachnah from leaving on the train.

Similarly, the "lead and punch line" of the conclusion is couched in the convoluted maze of a humorous narrative and plot; in the latter, the reader is the unsuspecting victim of the comical twist that Sholom Aleichem has in store for Sholom Shachnah's less-than-joyous reception at home. Here, too, it is the surprising ingredient that realizes the author's purpose of bringing a smile to every reader of this comic monologue.

Stephen Katz

ON DISCOVERY

Author: Maxine Hong Kingston (1940-   )
Type of plot: Fable
Time of plot: The distant past
Locale: The Land of Women
First published: 1980

Principal characters:
TANG AO, a warrior who stumbles into the Land of Women
SEVERAL WOMEN, who capture and attend to Tang Ao

The Story

"On Discovery," the first story in Maxine Hong Kingston's collection entitled *China Men* (1980), is a fairy tale that begins as most fairy tales do with "Once upon a time." Tang Ao, a warrior who is looking for the Gold Mountain, the traditional Chinese name for America, crosses an ocean and happens on a kind of utopia called the Land of Women, in which there are neither taxes nor wars. Consistent with the fairy-tale atmosphere is the narrator's comment that scholars cannot agree on the exact time and place for the narrative. Some argue that the Tang Ao incident took place during the reign of Empress Wu, beginning in 694 C.E.; others argue that it was in 441 C.E. Another theory is that the fantasy land existed not in China but in North America.

The action begins when Tang Ao, who cannot imagine a woman with a warlike spirit, is easily captured by the women. Even under guard, he assumes that he has been singled out for some special feminine favor. What follows is not the night of love that Tang Ao might have expected, but many months of physical pain, humiliation, and ultimately emasculation as the women prepare him to serve at the queen's court.

First, they usher him into a woman's ornate room, take off his armor and boots, and shackle his wrists and ankles. Next, they pull his earlobes taut and jab needles through each lobe. The most painful of the preparations involves the foot-binding process. The old women crack Tang Ao's arch, break many bones, plait his toes together, and bind his feet with tight bandages.

Each time that Tang Ao protests, he is dealt a new humiliation. When an old woman's dry fingers scratch his ear and neck, he wants to know what she is doing, but her incomprehensible reply is that she is sewing his lips together. When the women first begin the foot-binding process, Tang Ao weeps with pain. Their response is to wind the bandages even tighter and to distract him by singing foot-binding songs. When he eventually begs to have his feet rewrapped because of the pain from his shrunken veins, the women compel him to wash his dirty bandages. Continuing the feminization process, the captors serve Tang Ao white chrysanthemum tea in order to stir "the cool female winds inside his body" and vinegar soup to improve his womb.

Finally, it is decided that he is ready to serve the queen. For the occasion, jade studs are placed in his ears, curved shoes are strapped to his feet, his facial hair is plucked out, and his eyebrows, cheeks, and lips are painted. In short, he is made up to look like a proper Chinese woman. As he appears before the queen, he sways just as traditional, foot-bound Chinese women did. The makeover is a success as the diners at the queen's court, presumably all women, agree that Tang Ao is pretty and even refer to the former warrior as "she."

Themes and Meanings

The role reversal in which Tang Ao, the male warrior, becomes womanized involves a three-part discovery. First, Kingston protests against the ancient Chinese custom of foot-binding, the products of which were considered marks of beauty, although they rendered women virtually helpless. If the protagonist in "On Discovery" had been a woman, the impassioned description of the horrors and humiliations of the ritual would not be a story at all but merely a history lesson. By making the subject a man, and a warrior at that, Kingston forces the reader to participate imaginatively in each painful step of the hobbling procedure and thereby elevates the event to mythic stature.

The second discovery involves the role reversals that actually took place among the Chinese American immigrants about whom Kingston writes. Chinese men typically left their homeland and traveled to the New World alone until they earned enough money to send for their wives and children. This process often took decades, emptying whole villages of men so that the women left behind were forced to assume governance of both family and town. Thus, a strong matriarchal society arose in certain Cantonese villages. This historical situation becomes the impetus for the imaginary Land of Women society in which the empress Wu allows her subjects alternately to shackle, make fun of, torture, and soothe the hapless Tang Ao.

The third discovery illustrates the intense loneliness of the Chinese male immigrant, or wandering sojourner. Tang Ao, searching alone for the Gold Mountain, a reference to the California gold mines, is further isolated by the strange, unpredictable land in which he is held captive. The isolation of Tang Ao, then, symbolizes the suffering of tens of thousands of Chinese sojourners who came to the alien land of North America. Their survival, like the survival of Tang Ao, depended on their ability to accept both physical and psychological torture at the hands of alien captors.

Style and Technique

"On Discovery," like many other Kingston stories, utilizes the style of "talk-story," the Chinese phrase for storytelling. Based on the oral tradition of passing on both family history and Chinese legend to younger generations, talk-story, as developed by Kingston, becomes a complex fusion of many genres—part myth, part history, part memory—all of which combine to form a search for identity, both personal and racial.

In Western culture, the storyteller, revered as the memory and voice of the tribe, recounts tales of bravery, tales that enable the tribe to preserve and perpetuate itself.

This important function is, in a patriarchal society, almost exclusively a male role. In Kingston's immigrant Cantonese society, it is the women who talk-story while the men, isolated by separation from family and culture and oppressed by New World masters who often forbade them to talk, lose their voices and eventually descend into an eerie silence. Kingston encapsules this point masterfully in Tang Ao's only directly recorded speech when he asks, "What are you doing?" and the old woman replies, "Sewing your lips together." She is joking, of course, but her answer emphasizes the power and importance of words. To be totally silent is to be truly powerless.

Kingston also underscores the silence of the sojourner heroes by both the choice of title and the structure of *China Men*, the autobiographical novel in which "On Discovery" appears. Although separated into two words in Kingston's title, "Chinamen" is a common pejorative term used by prejudiced Westerners. Tang Ao's feminization reminds one of the term "china doll," a phrase commonly used by Westerners to describe exotic but fragile Oriental women.

Structurally, as Kingston herself has pointed out, the *China Men* stories are arranged in pairs, in each case first a myth and then a family history. The mythic tale of Tang Ao, a Chinese Everyman, is paired with "On Fathers," the introduction to Kingston's own father, BaBa. Tang Ao is surrounded by, but also isolated from, his women captors. BaBa is likewise surrounded by and isolated from his children, because they lack the power to distinguish him from another man who dresses similarly. BaBa, like Tang Ao, is noticeably silent: He greets his enthusiastic children with a formal salute but no words.

Kingston originally intended to include "On Discovery" in one lengthy collection of talk-stories. Although she eventually separated the stories into two books, *The Woman Warrior: Memoirs of a Girlhood* (1977) and *China Men*, "On Discovery," in its position as the first story in the second book, stands as the pivotal tale that synthesizes the major motifs in the two books. In *The Woman Warrior*, the female protagonists are strong, articulate women of action. In the women's land of "On Discovery," the women capture Tang Ao, lock him up, and shackle him, all warlike deeds. Furthermore, the women are quite verbal as they explain every step of the process that transforms Tang Ao from exploring warrior to serving maiden. In *China Men*, Kingston's search for the identities of her father and other male relatives, the male protagonists are more complex because the usual concepts of strength and weakness become inverted. It is the ability of the "china men" to suffer repeated tortures and humiliations silently that enables them to survive in an alien nation. One of the old women tells Tang Ao, "The less you struggle, the less it'll hurt." Tang Ao's strength lies in his ability to learn this lesson.

Sandra Hanby Harris

ON HOPE

Author: Spencer Holst
Type of plot: Fable
Time of plot: Anytime
Locale: Gibraltar
First published: 1971

Principal characters:
A GYPSY
A MONKEY
A SHARK

The Story

A gypsy has trained a monkey to sneak into the bedrooms of rich women and steal their jewelry. Without being instructed to do so by the gypsy, however, this "demon monkey" steals the "Diamond of Hope" necklace that was brought to Gibraltar for the princess of England to wear at a state function. The gypsy knows that the fabulous diamond is valueless to him because it is much too famous to be sold. He also knows that there is a curse on the necklace and that misfortune befalls whoever owns it, so he mails it back to the princess, warning her to take better care of it. However, the monkey steals the diamond two more times; the third time the animal is shot by a guard and dies at the gypsy's feet.

When the gypsy receives the diamond the third time, it no longer seems like an accident. Fate is at work. Because he is a gypsy, he fully believes the curse, so he is pleased that fate has chosen him to remove the cursed necklace from the princess and the English throne. Being a good swimmer, he goes down to the shore of the Mediterranean, takes off his clothes, puts the necklace around his neck, and swims out one mile and drops it. As he begins to swim back, the necklace starts to drop a mile down. The necklace falls faster than the gypsy can swim; when it gets to within a hundred feet of the bottom, it alights on the dorsal fin of a shark.

The necklace awakens the shark, who swims up to investigate and begins to follow the gypsy. Proud of himself for extinguishing the power of the curse forever, the gypsy turns and sees the necklace glide past him, as if it is floating in the air. He decides that one of two things is true: Either he is witnessing a miracle—and the whole thing does indeed smack of the miraculous—or he is having a hallucination. Deciding to find out which is true, he swims after the necklace—which turns and begins swimming toward him. The story ends here, but the narrator adds a final comment. Although it appears at first glance that the shark will eat the gypsy, the narrator believes that there are three reasons for hope: First, no shark has ever been approached by a man wondering whether it is a miracle or a hallucination; such a man would smell different. Second, the man is a gypsy and an animal trainer. Third, the shark now possesses the necklace, so it is cursed.

Themes and Meanings

Spencer Holst's impish little story about the nature of hope, probability, and fiction has the classically clean plot line of a fable. Its characters are two-dimensional, existing only for the sake of furthering the suggestive and symbolic plot, and the plot itself is mathematically precise and formal. The story exploits several fictional conventions and puts them in the foreground. The first is the intentional, and therefore meaningful, nature of events in fictions. The gypsy believes that although the first two times that the monkey brings him the necklace may be weird accidents, the third time plunges the whole thing "into meaning." His belief that fate is at work is equivalent to a fictional character realizing that he is a character in a fiction rather than a real person in a real world. Nothing happens by accident in fiction; everything is fated because fictions are closed forms in which all events have already occurred.

This concept of closure is the second convention that Holst exploits, for, like Frank Stockton's famous 1882 story, "The Lady or the Tiger," Holst leaves the ending open, violating the reader's expectation that there will be a meaningful closure, thus creating the illusion that an appropriate final event has not yet occurred. The curse enforces this idea thematically in the story, for a curse is a guarantee that, given certain prerequisites, certain subsequent events will inevitably occur. This sense of inevitability is further emphasized by the geometric equidistance of the shark and the gypsy, who drops the necklace one mile out and one mile down.

The third fictional convention that Holst uses is the ambiguity that the gypsy faces as he sees what seems to be the necklace floating through the air past him. He thinks that one of two things must be true: Either he is witnessing a miracle, or he is having a hallucination. This ambiguity is a familiar fictional device, which structuralist critic Tzvetan Todorov has cogently described. A story in which a miracle takes place is in the generic category of the "marvelous," whereas a story in which one is having a hallucination is in the category of the "uncanny." Although the reader knows that neither is the case here (for there is a realistic explanation for the floating necklace), the gypsy is not sure in what kind of story he is. Edgar Allan Poe was the first short-story writer to make this ambiguity the center of his art; in many of his stories, the reader is never sure whether something supernatural is occurring or the main character is hallucinating. The most famous story in American literature to exploit this ambiguity is Henry James's *The Turn of the Screw* (1898), in which it is impossible to determine whether the ghosts are real or the governess is mad.

Style and Technique

Writers are often concerned with the problem of hope in their stories, for although they are aware of the inevitability of plot, they also want to convey a sense of freedom in their characters. In one of her best-known stories, "Conversation with My Father" (1971), for example, Grace Paley rebels against the inevitability of plot because it vanquishes hope. A basic difference between real life and fiction, Paley suggests, is that real life is open and full of possibility, but a story must move relentlessly toward a predetermined end. Consequently, as much as writers might want their fiction to be "like life," it can never quite be a similitude of life. The closest that a writer can approach to feeling this sense of similitude is when fictional characters are so fully realized that they seem to take on lives of their own and somehow "get away" from their author. "On Hope" is a self-reflexive fable that, like many of the stories of John Barth and Robert Coover, uses the traditional fable form to explore and lay bare the fictional conventions and techniques that writers always use and readers often take for granted. Holst makes no attempt to interest the reader in the character of the gypsy. The gypsy's motivation is determined by the stereotyped conventions of "gypsyness," not by any values particular to himself. The gypsy's belief in the curse, as well as his conclusion that the monkey's theft of the diamond three times is determined by fate, reflects the traditional fabulous nature of the story, as well as its self-reflexive character. For, even as the gypsy believes in cosmic fate, the reader is aware that all fictional characters are fated because their actions are determined by the story's generic conventions.

Given the convention of the curse, the narrator admits that it seems inevitable that the shark will devour the man. However, he also notes that there are three reasons—all of which are in themselves fictional conventions—that may cause the story to end in another way. The first depends on the marvelous/uncanny ambiguity; for if the gypsy is not sure whether the shark is a miraculous manifestation or his own hallucination, then he is in a sort of limbo state in which time stands still and the story is unresolvable at that point. The second depends on the irony of this gypsy's being an animal trainer, and thus possibly capable of diverting the shark. Because irony is a frequently used convention of short fiction, Holst emphasizes it here to suggest that such a reversal of what seems inevitable is a possible appropriate ending. The third reason suggests the ultimate irony: Given the existence of the curse—which determines everything in this story (as in all such stories because curses establish the certainty of a future event)—the shark will die instead of the man. The "hope" that gives both the story and the diamond their names thus refers to the only hope possible in a story: Which fictional convention will dominate its closure? The gypsy's best hope is that the convention of the curse compels the story's closure.

Charles E. May

ON THE GOLDEN PORCH

Author: Tatyana Tolstaya (1951-   )
Type of plot: Magical Realism
Time of plot: The late 1940's
Locale: A small town in Russia, near Leningrad
First published: "Na zolotom kryl'tse sideli," 1987 (English translation, 1989)

> *Principal characters:*
> A YOUNG WOMAN, the narrator
> VERONIKA VIKENTIEVNA, a strong-willed housewife
> UNCLE PASHA, her henpecked husband
> MARGARITA, her younger sister

The Story

"On the Golden Porch" is told in the first person by an unnamed young woman who is attempting to recall her childhood experiences in a small Russian town near Leningrad (now St. Petersburg). The story opens with a detailed description of an enchanted garden, in and around which most of the action takes place. In this garden, several girls experience for the first time some of the secrets of life, including accidentally seeing a naked man. The two main characters, Veronika Vikentievna and her husband, Pasha, become the focus of the reminiscences. Veronika, a strong woman who bragged of killing a calf and possesses "a luxurious, golden, applelike" beauty, is a domineering wife and rules over her husband as well as over the stock and barrel of the household. Even when she does something good, such as selling an egg from her prized hen to the narrator's mother, she does it under the condition that it be eaten right away and not be used surreptitiously for breeding a superior chicken. When she discovers that the narrator's mother has given the egg to someone else, Veronika can never forgive her. For all these reasons, the narrator calls her Tsaritsa.

Veronika's husband, Pasha, whom the children call "Uncle Pasha," is exactly the opposite of his wife. Even though he obeys duly and meekly, he leads a rich life of his own, almost slyly. He walks for hours to and from his job without complaint, and he does his work well. Most important, he plays piano skillfully and sensitively; the piece the narrator remembers best is, fittingly, Ludwig van Beethoven's *Moonlight Sonata*. However, Pasha not only provides a badly needed antipode and balance to his tyrannical wife but also convinces the young children who observe him that life is full of rich and mysterious offerings. Needless to say, their sympathies lie with Uncle Pasha.

Veronika is contrasted also by her younger sister, Margarita, who is just as pale, large, and beautiful as her sister but is of a much more pleasant nature. She laughs a lot and is almost silly. She has sometimes "a Mona Lisa smile" on her "golden face" as she holds open "the sacred door to Aladdin's cave," the room in which Pasha plays the piano. Thus, she and Pasha provide the happiest memories of childhood for the narrator, enticing her to come back to reminiscences time and again and to forget the unpleasant, though all too human, character of Veronika.

Not much of the plot is built into the story, just reminiscences, most of which serve to portray the main characters and, more important, to lend the reminiscences the gossamer of a happy childhood despite the unpleasantries. At the end of the story, the young narrator learns the basic secret of life—the autumn arrives, the leaves fall, and the days grow dark. On revisiting the village and "the enchanted house," she realizes that Margarita has grown stooped, Uncle Pasha has gotten much older, Veronika's white chickens have died, and the north wind howls at night. Inexplicably, Pasha freezes to death on the porch, on which they all often sat (hence the meaning of the title in Russian, "they sat on the golden porch"). The new owner, Margarita's elderly daughter, find it too much trouble to bury him: Instead, she pours his ashes into a metal can and sets it on a shelf in the empty chicken house. The narrator realizes that she too is getting older. Her wonderful memories are overshadowed by the inexorable advance of the golden lady of time, who will strike a final midnight for Uncle Pasha and for all of them.

Themes and Meanings

One of the main themes of the story "On the Golden Porch" is an attempt to bring back the delightful, sometimes odd, sometimes frightening, but always highly influential experiences of childhood, in this case, in a small Russian town. Reminiscences of childhood, however, serve to throw light on other basic themes of human existence, mainly love and death. Even though Veronika seems to be incapable of love, Pasha's affair with her sister Margarita demonstrates the opposite. Also, the children's affection for Uncle Pasha shows a different, nonphysical kind of love.

Tatyana Tolstaya wants to show that life is full of mystery, as epitomized by the "enchanted garden," which the narrator remembers most vividly from her childhood. Another characteristic of life is its constant changeability seen in the mutation of appearances of all living things, especially of the people of the village, the world that the young woman remembers from her childhood and revisits. The most important aspect of this world, as of any other worlds, is death, with which the story abounds. Veronika departs early, despite her robustness, and Pasha succumbs to the inevitable, despite his cheerful disposition. The deaths of birds and animals also are prominent in the story, epitomized by Veronika's boasting of killing a calf. Thus, the transience of all life accompanies the beauty of the village and the garden. The narrator realizes this truth only after she revisits the village and finds it greatly changed.

Childhood is seen in the story as a natural, uncorrupted world of innocence but also of ignorance. Through the myth of Eden and the applicable examples from folklore, Tolstaya enhances her notion of beauty and its inevitable corruption.

Style and Technique

The plot of Tolstaya's story is scant. Dialogue is just as scarce, used on only three occasions. The action is carried on through the narrator's random memories. Thus, the author appears primarily interested in forwarding her views on the matters involved, as seen through the eyes and felt through the emotions of the narrator—life and death, beauty and the lack of it, and the luxurious variety of human behavior personified through Veronika, Pasha, and Margarita. Tolstaya frequently uses citations from poems and other poetic statements to bolster her arguments at particular junctions. For example, she uses an extract from Guillaume Apollinaire's poem "La Chanson du mal-aimé" ("The Song of the Poorly Loved"), in which the poet refers to the Milky Way to which bodies of lovers fly. The extract is used to emphasize the love between Margarita and Pasha, which is forbidden and doomed to end. Thus, two of the main themes of the story, love and death, are illuminated in a surprising manner.

The style is a mixture of realistic descriptions and lyrical prose. Tolstaya creates several highly lyrical prolonged descriptions, resembling the lyrical descriptions of the masterful Russian stylist from the first quarter of the twentieth century, Ivan Bunin. The story opens and ends with such long descriptions. In the opening paragraph, for example, Tolstaya describes the garden as without end, borders, or fences, full of noises and rustling, golden in the sun but pale green in the shade, with the well full of toads, with white roses and mushrooms, with raspberry and huckleberry patches, and with bridges. Such abundance of color and texture makes Tolstaya's prose vibrant and sensuous.

Tolstaya employs symbolism in several instances. Veronika's large stature reflects her tendency and need to dominate people. Other images, borrowed from folklore, magnify the symbolism, such as her yellow guard dog and the magical egg. Pasha's affair with Veronika's sister Margarita symbolizes his youthful rebirth, after having spent most of his life under Veronika's yoke. The nuptial glass-legged bed bespeaks the fragility of Veronika's and Pasha's marriage, yet it is on this bed that Margarita kisses Pasha, as if awakening a sleeping prince (in a reversal of the folklore). The abundance of the color red, derived mostly from blood, symbolizes the inseparability of life and death.

Vasa D. Mihailovich

ON THE ROAD

Author: Langston Hughes (1902-1967)
Type of plot: Satire
Time of plot: 1934
Locale: Reno, Nevada
First published: 1935

> *Principal characters:*
> SARGEANT, an African American vagrant
> MR. DORSET, a white minister
> TWO WHITE POLICE OFFICERS
> CHRIST

The Story

Sargeant, an African American vagrant, seeking food and shelter, arrives in Reno, Nevada, in late 1934 in the midst of a dangerous snowstorm. It is bitterly cold but his overwhelming concern is to find food. To him, the snow falls almost undetected; he is too hungry, sleepy, and tired to notice the storm. The first potential refuge that Sargeant encounters is a parsonage. Its occupant, the Reverend Mr. Dorset, opens the parsonage door and sees Sargeant as "a human piece of night with snow on his face" standing on his porch. Before Sargeant can open his mouth, Dorset directs him to the local relief shelter, emphatically stating that he cannot stay at the parsonage.

The parsonage door shuts in Sargeant's face before he can say that he has already been to the relief shelter and that it is not open to his kind. Sargeant recalls his vast experience with similar relief shelters, which are usually out of beds, out of food, and out of bounds for him.

As Sargeant stands outside the forbidden parsonage, he connects it to the large church next door—one with two large doors. Dazed by hunger and cold, he stands before the church steps observing its high, arched doors, with pillars on each side, balanced higher up by a window displaying a crucifix with a stone Christ hanging from it. As he gazes at the crucifix, Sargeant notices the snow again and feels the cold and hunger more than before. He climbs the church steps and knocks at the doors, but no one comes. He then pushes with all of his strength against the doors, which begin to give, but not before calling attention to his actions. Several white people are alarmed by his actions, but he explains that he simply needs a place to sleep.

Just as the doors give way, two white police officers pull up to the church and attempt to stop Sargeant. As he resists, he grabs an armhold on one of the church pillars. The police beat him over the head and the church falls down.

Sargeant dreams: The whole church falls down in the snow, bystanders, police, and all. He picks up a stone pillar and throws it six blocks up the street and continues walking, the crunch of his shoes loud on the snow. Sargeant discovers that Christ is walking beside him. He is startled but realizes that this is the first time he has ever seen Christ off the cross, apparently a consequence of the church's falling down. They both laugh.

The conversation between Christ and Sargeant continues as they walk toward a hobo jungle, an apparently safe place for Sargeant, but Christ has other plans. He is going on to Kansas City. Sargeant enters the hobo jungle, sleeps, and at 6:00 A.M. hears a train, wakes up, and pulls himself aboard a slow-moving coal car. He climbs into the coal car but discovers it is full of police.

Sargeant wakes up and discovers that he is tightly gripping bars in a jail cell. One of the police officers tells Sargeant, "You ain't in no jungle now, this ain't no train. You in jail." Sargeant has been incarcerated since the incident in front of the church and has been unconscious the entire time. He sits on a wooden bench in the cell, nursing his swollen fingers and various bruises from the beating he has received from the police. As Sargeant vows to break down the cell door, he wonders if Christ is really on his way to Kansas City.

Themes and Meanings

Langston Hughes wrote "On the Road" after visiting Reno, Nevada, in September, 1934, when he was nearly out of funds. After observing the treatment offered to several African American victims of the harsh economic times, he wrote the story in one sitting. Years later in a lecture he gave regarding "On the Road," Hughes recalled that everyone was in desperate search of work and many got stranded in Reno. Many of these people were African Americans, who had even less opportunity for work, shelter, and meals. It was a depression in many more ways than one.

"On the Road" probes the consequences of the Great Depression on one vagrant African American at a low point, perhaps the lowest point in Sargeant's life. Here the reader observes the transformation of an apparently docile, law-abiding man into a militant and assertive person demanding the basic human necessities of food, clothing, and shelter that are denied to him because of his color.

Hughes treads a narrow thematic line here by placing the concept of Christianity as Christ would have it practiced against the harsh reality of how it actually is practiced by the Reverend Mr. Dorset, the observers at the church, and the police. Instead of practicing the Christian concept of being one's brother's keeper, they deny Sargeant basic Christian charity.

The patient, long-suffering Sargeant will never receive equal treatment by white Christians until he asserts himself more clearly and demands such equal treatment. The only figure in the story who treats him as a man and an equal is Christ, the primary focus of the dream sequence.

In this same dream sequence another Christian parallel is developed. As Sargeant attempts to pull down the church's pillars, the scene parallels the biblical story of Samson's pulling down the pagan temple around him. As the church begins to fall in Sargeant's dream, the stone Christ becomes an animate figure walking beside him. Hughes thereby notes that the validity of Christ and Christianity is not in question here. It is the concept of Christianity that is practiced by other characters that is called into question.

As satire, "On the Road" skewers Christians who fail to assist their fellow human beings, especially in times of great economic and physical suffering. The rejection, humiliation, beating, and racism that Sargeant endures pushes him to take actions that are almost heroic. Although Sargeant is technically guilty of attempted breaking and entering, the Reverend Mr. Dorset is fully guilty of prejudice, racism, and hypocrisy.

Style and Technique

Narrated in the third person, "On the Road" first appeared in *Esquire* in 1935. Technically sound and smoothly organized, "On the Road" is a classic in the canon of Hughes. The chief stylistic obstacle Hughes confronted was melding the story's realism with the supernatural elements introduced when the figure of Christ becomes animate. It is accomplished with a deft touch. One believes that Sargeant is a man of great inner strength who becomes capable of acting on a level beyond simple accommodation. His development as a man to be reckoned with sets the stage for his surreal meeting with Christ.

The more Sargeant is denied the basic necessities the more aggressive he becomes. When he is clubbed, he moves into a state of dreaming. When Christ appears to him, he treats him as an equal, and bids him a fond farewell as he has to go to Kansas City. Clearly the symbolic element here is in reference to being one's brother's keeper. Other examples of symbolism include juxtaposing the white snow everywhere against the authority of the brutal white police officers, and contrasting the unyielding material of the church doors against the true spirit of Christian brotherhood and sisterhood.

Joe Benson

ON THE SHORE OF CHAD CREEK

Author: Jack Matthews (1925-   )
Type of plot: Domestic realism
Time of plot: The 1960's
Locale: An unspecified rural area
First published: 1971

> *Principal characters:*
> MELVIN COMBS, an eighty-three-year-old man
> MAUDE COMBS, his eighty-one-year-old wife
> WILKIE THOMAS, the undertaker

The Story

One spring morning, eighty-three-year-old Melvin Combs awakes to find that his eighty-one-year-old wife, Maude, has crossed her arms, turned her head to the wall, and died during the night. Because the couple live in a rural area, on a hill above Chad Creek where cars cannot drive, Melvin knows that he must take the body into town to the undertaker by himself. The most difficult part of his task is carrying the body down the hill and across the footbridge to reach the highway beyond the woods. Telling himself that his wife is not all that heavy and that it will be easy to carry her body down the hill and across the bridge, Melvin first pours himself a drink of corn whiskey and looks at the body on the bed, the feet curled around like a baby's and the head half-buried in the pillow.

He considers going for help but decides against it because his wife did not like anyone coming to the house unless she was expecting them. Repeating to himself that he is strong and that it will be no trouble, Melvin wraps Maude in a blanket and starts down the hill. Halfway down, he slips and goes sprawling; his wife's body bounces several times and rolls out of the blanket, and Melvin hurts his shoulder. He goes back to the house to get another drink and once again considers going for help but continues to repeat his determination that he can get the body to town alone.

After managing to carry his wife down the hill and across the footbridge, he drops her again and she rolls out of the blanket; her arms are still across her chest, her mouth is open, and her eyes show a little crack, as if she is peeking at him now and then to see how he is making out. After setting her in the back seat of his car, he drives into town to the undertaker. There, Wilkie Thomas and his assistant, Paul, take Maude into a back room. The conversation between Melvin and Wilkie seems inconsequential, mainly concerned with getting the doctor over to make out a death certificate.

Melvin talks briefly about having married Maude fifty-two years ago when she was the widow of a man named Chambers, who was killed in a mine accident. Melvin says he had been whoring around, carousing, and drinking before he settled down with Maude. He also talks about having known Maude when they were children, and tells of playfully pushing her into the creek once. After the doctor pronounces Maude dead and leaves, Melvin says, "Hit just don't seem like enough, some how."

He then drives back to his home on Chad Creek and lies down on the bed where his wife died. He thinks that he forgot to tell the undertaker that Maude had pigtails seventy-five years ago; he remembers pulling them, making Maude yell so loudly that the teacher made him stand in a corner. The story ends with the line, "It had all started way back then. Maybe even before."

Themes and Meanings

Jack Matthews's simple story of an old man's efforts to get his wife's body to the undertaker and have her officially declared dead does not appear to have any real conflict or thematic significance. It seems to move along matter-of-factly with the sole purpose of describing how Melvin takes care of things when his wife dies. Because the story is told in such a flat, unfeeling way, the reader may think that the story has no real point, but its purpose is to explore how grief goes beyond language's ability to express it.

"On the Shore of Chad Creek" is about facing death. This is the underlying relevance of the undertaker's seemingly irrelevant remark when Melvin tells him that his wife said that she felt funny before she went to sleep last night: "'They say that a lot before they go,' Wilkie said. "Yes sir, they say they feel funny and brother that's it!" The fact that Melvin's only encounters in the story are with the undertaker and the doctor, who deal with death matter-of-factly every day, further emphasizes this theme, especially when Melvin plaintively says after the doctor leaves, "Hit just don't seem like enough some how," and the undertaker replies, "Oh, it's enough, all right."

Melvin's sense of loss is not communicated by his sorrow at his wife's death, but by his memory of her when he first married her and earlier, when she was a little girl with pigtails. When Melvin says that when he came back from his years of carousing, Maude, recently widowed, was there waiting for him, the undertaker replies, "Things certainly do work out funny. . . . Yes sir, they work out funny. You put that in a story book, and no body in the whole blessed world would believe it." Indeed, the basic theme of the story is that the crucial events of life and death are so beyond human control that ultimately all people can say is, "Things certainly do work out funny."

The story ends with a dual image of Maude in Melvin's mind: at death, her head sunk in the pillow, her legs curled up and her feet tucked back like a child, her eyes slightly open as if she were taking a peek at him, as "stiff as a side of beef"; and as the little girl with pigtails whom he once pushed into Chad Creek. The striking contrast between these two images is so overwhelming that they go beyond any effort to account for them. Melvin is right to think that when someone you have spent your life with dies, "Hit just don't seem like enough, some how."

Style and Technique

Although the narrator is never identified, the story is told from the point of view of someone who is of the same education level as Melvin Combs himself. The opening of the story is typical of the language of the teller: "Melvin Combs, his wife she died. . . . The 2 of them live alone up there. . . . Everybody know them 2 for a long time. Melvin and Maude Combs." Because of the relatively inarticulate nature of the narrator, most of the sentences are quite short; many begin with the pronoun "He," simply and straightforwardly describing Melvin's efforts to get his wife's body down the hill to the car.

The most important effect of this flat and inarticulate narration is its implication that Melvin is little affected by the death of his wife. Showing no strong reaction of sorrow or sadness, he is seemingly concerned only with the practical matter of getting the body to town. In fact, there is little overt difference between the way that Maude's death seems to affect Melvin and the way that it affects the undertaker, who is conditioned by his job to thinking only of the practical matters that surround death. The image of Maude, "stiff as a side of beef," her arms crossed and her eyes slightly open as if watching to see how Melvin is bearing up under it, is a silent comment on his practical and commonsensical efforts. Even the grotesque image of Melvin's falling on the hill, and the body rolling out of the blanket and left to lie there while he goes back up to the house to get another drink, seems to suggest that he is little affected by the death of his wife.

In truth, this is a story about grief that exceeds language's ability to express it directly. It belongs to the tradition that can be seen most clearly in one of Anton Chekhov's best-known stories, "Toska"—the title of which has been translated both as "Misery" and "Lament"—in which an old cabdriver tries to find a way to express his grief at the death of his son. It is the central theme also in Katherine Mansfield's story "The Fly," in which a man's grief about the death of his son seems to be deflected by something so trivial as a fly. "On the Shore of Chad Creek" is a clear example of a story that follows Chekhov's advice to writers: "In short stories it is better to say not enough than to say too much, because—because—I don't know why."

Charles E. May

ONE HOLY NIGHT

Author: Sandra Cisneros (1954-   )
Type of plot: Social realism
Time of plot: The twentieth century
Locale: Somewhere in the United States and Mexico
First published: 1991

> *Principal characters:*
> THE UNNAMED NARRATOR, a young Mexican girl
> CHATO, her lover, also known as Chaq
> ABUELITA, her grandmother

The Story

The narrator has been sent to a dusty town in Mexico to live with her cousins. She describes her lover, Chaq Uxmal Paloquin, who claims to be descended from Mayan kings, and explains that her grandmother, Abuelita, has burned her pushcart and chased Chaq away with a broom. The narrator met Chaq while selling cucumbers and other produce from a pushcart in front of a food store in the United States. She explains that she was not the first to go bad in this way; her mother also "took the crooked walk." She struggles to describe her feelings for Chaq, seeing him as boy, baby, and man simultaneously. She says that she did not want her first sexual encounter to be like a prostitute's and knew that it would be special with Chaq. Each Saturday, Chaq would come to buy fruit from her cart, and at night he would take her to his small room in back of Esparza & Sons Auto Repair. There he brushes her hair, tells the history of his people, and shows her his guns. He tells her how the stars foretell the birth of the boy-child who will restore the Mayan civilization. One night on his dirty cot, with the moon shining through the pink plastic curtains, Chaq initiates her after admonishing her not to tell; she feels that she is his queen and a part of that mainstream that all women wait to enter. On the way home, she wonders if any of the people on the street can tell that she is different.

Unfortunately, the narrator forgets to take the pushcart home with her that night. She lies to Abuelita and her uncle, saying that some children have stolen the cart, but the truth gradually comes out. Neighbor women tell of the dark Indian who pushes the cart behind Esparza & Sons on Saturday nights, and Abuelita finds the pushcart there. Esparza reports that Chaq has packed his things and left, and Abuelita forces the entire truth from her granddaughter. After learning that the girl is pregnant, Abuelita burns the pushcart, sprinkles her granddaughter with holy water, and goes early each morning to Esparza & Sons, hoping to find mail for Chaq. Finally a letter arrives from a convent in Tampico, and Abuelita sends an inquiry.

A reply is long in coming. In the meantime, Abuelita removes her granddaughter from the school, at which she is in the eighth grade. When the letter from the convent does arrive, it brings the truth: Chaq's real name is Chato, and Mayan blood does not run in his veins.

In Mexico, the girl learns from Abuelita's letters that Chaq had returned but was chased away. A later letter contains an article revealing a terrible truth about Chaq: He was arrested for the murder of eleven women. The narrator still loves him and cannot bear to look at the picture.

As the story ends, the narrator is waiting in Mexico for her baby to be born. When her cousins want to know what it is like to be with a perfect man she tells them they will be sorry when they find out. They discuss the meaning of love; the narrator compares it to a mute man she once saw, who kept a harmonica in his mouth all day and walked around wheezing in and out. She says she will have five children, and she will name this first baby Alegre, which means happy, because she knows that life will be hard.

Themes and Meanings

"One Holy Night" presents the traditional tale of seduction, a theme similar to that in Charles Perrault's "Little Red Riding Hood," first published in 1697. Chaq, the charming wolf, is not what he seems. He appeals to the narrator's romantic sensibilities with his stories of Mayan kings; he claims to be one of the people of the sun, of the temples; he tells her his name means boy-child, and as such he would be the savior of the ancient Mayan culture. He promises to love her "like a revolution, like a religion." He is all mystery, refusing to tell his age, saying he is of the past and the future, which are all one. He brings her a drink in a plastic cup and brushes her hair.

The narrator is clearly smitten by this man. Chaq's attentions come from a different and mysterious world. The remainder of the story is familiar. She succumbs, avoids the truth as long as she can, and eventually is forced to face the consequences of her actions. The uncle and grandmother attempt to fix blame and then to find the villain, who has disappeared. Sandra Cisneros's version of the seduction tale is intensified by the age of the victim and the psychopathic nature of the villain. Although the narrator says she is not just a girl, it is revealed that she is only thirteen or fourteen years of age. It is easier to understand, then, her willingness to believe the romantic line of this long-haired revolutionary with broken thumbs and greasy nails. Learning that this "Mayan king" is not only a fraudulent child molester but also a serial killer, the reader wonders how the narrator escapes. The man truly does consume little girls. The moral of this seduction tale remains the same as that of Perrault's: Girls should always beware!

Because of her choice of narrator, Cisneros's story is also the story of sexual awakening and the female rite of passage into womanhood. As the narrator shares her intimate secrets with the reader, she reveals that sex is important to young girls. She thinks about it and knows about the prostitutes in her neighborhood; her cousins ask her questions about being with a man. The narrator has very definite ideas about how she wants her first experience to be, a "coming undone," and she believes that Chaq can make that happen for her. Quickly Chaq weaves his magic spell of temples and

Mayan kings, of revolutions and a boy-child. Although the narrator knows after the initiation that she is changed forever, feels wise, and wonders if others can tell, she also discounts the experience, telling her cousins that they will be sorry. She is, however, awakened and continues to think about how good it is to lie with a man.

While the male rite of passage is an aggressive one in stories, this female initiation is a matter of waiting, and then waiting again for the baby. Instead of the triumphant victory in battle or the hunt that marks a young boy as a man, the young girl becomes a woman by waiting, by acquiescing and accepting, and the moment itself holds no great meaning for her. She must accept the fact that, from her grandmother's perspective, her life is ruined by her rite of passage. Finally, the narrator knows that the man whom she still loves and whom she will never see again is a murderer.

Style and Technique

Although Cisneros's style is direct, using sparse prose and often withholding as much information as she supplies, her writing is richly textured. Irony plays an important role in this story, for the truth lies in the contrast between what the reader knows to be true about this seduction and what the narrator feels about her sexual awakening. There are other ironies: The mother had a similar initiation and was sent from Mexico to the United States; Chaq, who was to bring change, brought only more of the same, as the entire story confirms traditional human behavior.

Cisneros also uses an ironic blending of Christian and pagan imagery and allusion to provide depth and to demonstrate the sense of continuity felt by the narrator. On the "holy night" of her initiation, the little Catholic girl becomes Ixchel, the moon goddess, to Chaq, the rain god.

Finally, Cisneros uses extended metaphors to reveal the attitude of the narrator, who has no sense of exploitation or shame. In the narrator's comparison of love to a crazy man with a harmonica wheezing in and out, she demonstrates an innocence, as well as a wisdom beyond her years. She knows that life will be hard.

Karen A. Pinter

THE £1,000,000 BANK-NOTE

Author: Mark Twain (Samuel Langhorne Clemens, 1835-1910)
Type of plot: Adventure
Time of plot: The 1870's
Locale: San Francisco, California, and London, England
First published: 1893

Principal characters:
HENRY "HAL" ADAMS, a twenty-seven-year-old American
TWO ENGLISH GENTLEMEN, wealthy brothers, owners of the
£1,000,000 note
PORTIA LANGHAM, Henry's twenty-two-year-old fiancé
LLOYD HASTINGS, a former colleague of Henry

The Story

The first-person narrator of the story, Henry Adams, age twenty-seven, is a mining-broker's clerk in San Francisco. He says at the outset that he intends to make a fortune, although he has nothing but his "wits and a clean reputation." While sailing one afternoon, he is carried out to sea and eventually rescued by a small brig bound for London. When he arrives in London, he has only a dollar to his name and is soon without shelter and food. Walking around Portland Place, Henry yearns for a pear that a child has tossed into the gutter. He walks back and forth by the pear, waiting for other people to be out of sight.

Suddenly, a window of a nearby house opens and Henry is summoned into the presence of two wealthy old brothers, who have made a bet. Henry does not learn about the bet or its details until later. The bet centers on a one-million-pound bank note that one of the brothers acquires. The other brother, Abel, bets twenty thousand pounds that "a perfectly honest and intelligent stranger, turned adrift in London without a friend and with no money except the note and no way to account for his being in possession of it," could not live on it. The second brother maintains that "the man would live thirty days, anyway, on that million, and keep out of jail, too."

The brothers select Henry because he has an honest, intelligent face and because he is obviously a stranger to England. Giving him an envelope with instructions and telling him to open it in his lodgings, they dismiss him. Henry, who is hungry, hurries outside and peers quickly inside the envelope. Seeing that it contains money, he rushes to the nearest restaurant, owned by Harris, a place Henry is to make famous. After eating, Henry tries to pay with the money but discovers that he has a million-pound note that no one could possibly cash. Harris extends credit to Henry, who quickly returns to the house of the brothers. They have left the area for one month, leaving behind an explanatory note saying that they are lending Henry the money for one month without interest and that if the second brother wins his bet, Henry "shall have any situation that is in my gift."

Henry quickly considers his situation. He knows that he cannot turn the note over to a bank or to the authorities because he cannot prove that he came into possession of it legally, and he reasons that he may well land in jail. Therefore he will do the best he can with what he thinks is a useless note. Because he is wearing rags, Henry decides to enter a nearby tailor's establishment to purchase a cheap suit. After he flashes his bank note, he is instantly given credit and as many clothes as he could possibly want. Realizing that he has discovered a wonderful situation, he buys everything he needs at all sorts of shops, and he finds himself an expensive private hotel for lodging. Henry soon becomes celebrated as the "vest-pocket million-pounder" and is even written about in *Punch* magazine.

After about ten days, Henry visits the American minister in London. Invited to a dinner party by the minister, Henry meets and falls in love with a twenty-two-year-old English woman named Portia Langham. When he tells Portia about his situation, she breaks into uncontrollable laughter, which surprises Henry. Readers later learn that Portia is the stepdaughter of one of the wealthy gentlemen and knows about the bet.

At the same dinner party, Henry encounters his former colleague from San Francisco, Lloyd Hastings, who has run into a dead end trying to sell Gould and Curry Extension, a California mining stock. Having an option to sell the stock, Hastings can keep anything he earns over a million dollars. However, Hastings has sold nothing whatsoever. After some discussion, Henry agrees to serve as a reference for Hastings and to vouch for the reliability and profitability of the stock. In turn, Hastings is to split his profit with Henry. Within two weeks, Henry himself has cleared one million dollars, which he deposits in a London bank.

At this time, the month required by the bet has expired, and Henry takes Portia to the house in Portland Place to report to the two gentleman. Henry, having looked them up in a directory, calls them by name, which is not given to the readers. Abel has lost his bet, much to the delight of the other brother, Portia's stepfather, who tells Henry that he may have any situation within his gift. Henry surprises everyone by revealing that he now has a million dollars in the bank, but Portia surprises Henry even more by stating her relationship with the bet's winner. Henry immediately applies for a situation with the gentleman: son-in-law.

Henry and Portia wed. Portia's stepfather cashes the million-pound note at the Bank of England, has the bank cancel the note, and gives it to the newlyweds at their wedding. It now hangs in a frame in their home. Realizing that were it not for the note he never would have met Portia, Henry says of the note: "It never made but one purchase in its life, and then got the article for only about a tenth part of its value."

Themes and Meanings

In addition to the enjoyment he takes in the series of adventures that Henry encounters, Mark Twain presents the characteristics needed to be successful in America. As he did earlier in *A Connecticut Yankee in King Arthur's Court* (1889), Twain shows that an American needs wit and practical intelligence, a sense of fairness and honesty, a clean reputation, patience, and self-discipline. Henry has all these qualities and more. His wit and intelligence allow him to seize the opportunities that come his way. Furthermore, his self-discipline allows him to keep his desires in check. Henry does not spend wildly when he uses the bank note for credit. Instead, he keeps careful watch over his expenses, allowing himself to owe no more than what he can repay within two years on the salary that he expects to make in his new job.

Henry also has a sense of responsibility and a concern for the well-being of others. He honestly would like to help Lloyd Hastings out of his predicament; indeed, it is his desire to help Lloyd that gives him the idea that makes both of them millionaires. In addition, Henry repays Harris for being the first to honor his credit by making Harris's restaurant famous throughout London. Finally, Henry is capable of love and even of gallantry for Portia Langham. Twain demonstrates that people such as Henry make their own breaks, and because of their strong character perhaps they deserve these breaks.

Style and Technique

Twain's style is realistic. In this story as in his others, he makes use of the language of everyday working Americans. The colloquial speech adds to the sense of reality that pervades even his most comic tales. His presentation of detail is kept to only what is necessary to advance the story or to present his characters clearly. What one finds, then, is a story that focuses on the bank note from the very opening, right up to the concluding sentence. The story's development and action are direct and to the point, enhancing the reader's sense of the story's organization.

Twain makes use of many of the techniques of humor in this tale of adventure. He surprises the reader in several instances, as, for example, when he reveals that Portia is stepdaughter to one of the old gentlemen. Twain indulges in bold farce when, time after time, Henry delights in pulling out the bank note to disconcert some smart-mouthed clerk or businessman who is not treating Henry well because he seems to have little money. One such detailed scene takes place in the tailor shop when Henry puts the snobbish clerk in his place.

Twain also delights in revealing the eccentric parts of human nature. He pokes fun at English aristocrats who can never manage to dine out with others because they cannot agree on the proper order of precedence in their seating arrangements; thus, all aristocrats have to eat at home before they go out to dinner.

Twain skillfully uses revelations and withholdings to keep the reader's interest. He reveals Portia's relationship to the old English gentlemen only in the final scene, just as he makes Henry a rich man only just prior to the final, climactic scene. The reader of "The £1,000,000 Bank-Note" recognizes that he has been treated well at the hands of a master storyteller as Henry Adams concludes his story.

A. Bruce Dean

ONE OF A KIND

Author: Julian Barnes (1946-   )
Type of plot: Social realism, frame story
Time of plot: The 1970's
Locale: England and Bucharest, Romania
First published: 1982

> *Principal characters:*
> THE NARRATOR, an English writer
> MARIAN TIRIAC, an exiled Romanian dissident
> NICOLAI PETRESCU, a Romanian novelist

The Story

"One of a Kind" is a story told by a first-person narrator, a young English writer, who meets an exiled Romanian dissident, Marian Tiriac, at a literary party. Through the course of their conversation, a subsequent and coincidental trip to Romania, and another chance meeting with Tiriac, the narrator learns the story of Nicolai Petrescu.

At the initial meeting between the narrator and Tiriac, the narrator shares an observation of his regarding Romanian artists: Romania has produced one great artist in each of several disciplines, but only one. He lists several artists and their respective disciplines. Tiriac adds a couple of names and disciplines to the list offered by the narrator, apparently corroborating the theory. However, between the two of them, they cannot name a great Romanian novelist. Tiriac concludes by stating that Romania has no novelists.

Roughly one year later, the narrator travels to a writer's conference in Bucharest, Romania. While touring the city, he and a companion from the conference happen on a prominently located bookstore. An entire display window is given over to a single book. Its author is a man named Nicolai Petrescu, and the narrator concludes that he must be a major Romanian writer to have so much attention from a bookstore that appears to be one of the major ones in the country.

Sometime after returning to England, the narrator meets Marian Tiriac again and asks him about Nicolai Petrescu, the novelist whose book was so prominently displayed. Tiriac tells him the story of Petrescu. It turns out that Tiriac and Petrescu had been close during their young adulthood as writers working within a literary scene dominated and censored by the Communist Party. Tiriac chafed under the restrictions and would eventually go into exile. Petrescu, also frustrated with the oppression, hatched a scheme to write an epic novel that, through deft irony, would ridicule and expose the Communist Party, all the while holding it up for admiration. Also, if the ruse was a success, Petrescu vowed, he would never write another word, so as not to detract from the essential point of his singular gesture. Tiriac left Romania before Petrescu completed his epic, and the two never have contact again. Years later, Tiriac learns in a letter from his mother that Petrescu's novel has been published to great success. The title of the novel is *The Wedding Cake*, an allusion to large public buildings of a particularly vulgar and sentimental style, derisively called "wedding-cake architecture," forced on the large cities of Eastern Europe by the Soviets. Tiriac assumes this is the book that the narrator had seen so prominently displayed in the bookstore in Bucharest.

At the conclusion of the story of Nicolai Petrescu, the narrator tells Tiriac that the novel in the display window was not called *The Wedding Cake*; it was called something different. Neither of them acknowledges the apparent betrayal of Petrescu's vow to never write another word after *The Wedding Cake*. Rather, Tiriac tells the narrator that he now has another piece of evidence to support his theory of great Romanian artists; one great ironist—Petrescu.

Themes and Meanings

The position and function of art in the social and cultural environment is, as in much of Julian Barnes's work, a central concern in "One of a Kind." Petrescu's plan is to manipulate the social and cultural climate of Romania. If the plan is successful, the Communist Party will champion his novel as a great work of socialist art, and as a sanctioned edifice in the prescribed culture, it would, over time, insinuate its subversive irony into the national consciousness.

While writing *The Wedding Cake*, Petrescu, according to Tiriac's tale, consulted frequently with other writers at regular meetings sanctioned and monitored by the party committee. During the consultations, he feigned befuddlement as he attempted to portray certain aspects of Soviet-dominated life, seeking advice and, in effect, making the party and its stable of writers complicit in his creation. The prescribed culture informs the very work of art designed to stealthily ridicule it. Culture and art inform and create each other in a messy partnership.

However, there is another thematic thread in the story that is also a recurring topic in Barnes's work: the intermixing and unreliability of social, national, and personal history and the blurry distinction between fiction and fact when looking backward from the present. Petrescu's book, as he conceives it, is to be, among other things, an epic history of Romania with all the required nods to its inevitable and glorious conversion to communism after World War II. However, more than a simple revision of what went before, it is an insertion of Petrescu's personal vision, a fiction, into the collective understanding of the history of the nation and Romanian culture. His intention is to alter the history of the place and the people by providing a fictive lens through which to view it. By changing the perception of history, he aims to change the unconscious perception of the present.

On a smaller scale, Tiriac's perception of himself is based to some degree on his belief that Petrescu's plan and his book have been hugely successful in Romania; whereas he, Tiriac, has been relegated to the relatively ineffective position of exiled dissident. Perhaps there is some resentment and regret, perhaps there is not—the story is silent on the issue. Regardless, his feelings about himself, his homeland, his old friend, and the relationship between them all are certainly changed after hearing that Petrescu's apparent success is not because of *The Wedding Cake*. This new information fundamentally changes the nature of his personal history.

Style and Technique

The structure of "One of a Kind" is fairly complex for such a short story. A first-person narrator relates to the reader two stories: the story of his own meetings and conversations with Marian Tiriac and the story of Nicolai Petrescu as told to him by Tiriac—essentially a frame within a frame. The effect is that the story of Petrescu is removed from the reader by two layers of representation—a structural reminder that history is not fact; rather, it is a compendium of representations and perceptions filtered through multiple and successive lenses.

The narrator establishes a conversational tone with the reader by framing the story as a recollection and using the second person in the first paragraph. By giving the story the feel of a spoken narrative, the author further undermines the factualness of history, suggesting that this story, the printed story, is just as unreliable and mutable as the oral narrative of Marian Tiriac. Through multiple oral reiterations, historical actuality becomes a fictive history.

The conversational tone of the story is reinforced by long sections of uninterrupted, one-sided dialogue. A third of the text consists of Tiriac's monologue as he relates to the narrator the story of Nicolai Petrescu. Tiriac's telling is not presented as paraphrase; rather, it is enclosed in quotation marks. The language of the text is straightforward, eschewing the use of metaphoric or symbolic language. Again, this places the story in the conversational rather than literary realm.

Interestingly, as the story ends, Barnes does not resolve several contradictory elements: Tiriac's tale of Petrescu and his vow to never write another word, what Tiriac heard from his mother about the great success of *The Wedding Cake*, what the narrator sees in the shop window in Bucharest, and the six or seven other titles by Petrescu that the narrator told Tiriac he had seen in the shop window, which are not mentioned when the narrator is actually standing at the shop window (he in fact makes a point of saying that only a single book is displayed). These conflicting stories are left for the reader to ponder and to wonder where the truth is in all of this and whether there are multiple truths and multiple histories.

Darryl Erlandson

ONE OF CLEOPATRA'S NIGHTS

Author: Théophile Gautier (1811-1872)
Type of plot: Fantasy
Time of plot: About 35 B.C.E.
Locale: Egypt
First published: "Une nuit de Cléopâtre," 1838 (English translation, 1882)

Principal characters:
CLEOPATRA, the queen of Egypt
CHARMION, her favorite slave
MARK ANTONY, her husband, a Roman aristocrat
MEÏAMOUN, an Egyptian of Greek descent

The Story

A barge carries Cleopatra down the Nile River, impelled by fifty oarsmen. She is returning from the celebration of a religious rite at a shrine at Hermonthis, a city above Thebes, and she is suffering from desperately acute boredom. She describes her state of mind in great detail to her slave Charmion, explaining how the deserts, temples, and religion of Egypt combine to produce it. She laments, too, that a queen can never know if she is loved for herself, rather than for her crown.

Meïamoun, an extraordinarily handsome youth, has been following the queen's barge for some time. Like the queen, who is a descendant of the Ptolemys, he is of Greek descent. His love for the queen is every bit as desperate as her ennui.

Cleopatra later catches a glimpse of the swimming Meïamoun from her palace but has no inkling of his purpose, which is to fire an arrow into her room, around which is wrapped a scroll bearing an unsigned declaration of his love. He hides in the palace grounds in the hope of catching a glimpse of her as she bathes. He succeeds, but she catches sight of him and has him seized by her attending eunuchs. When he identifies himself as the person who shot the scroll-bearing arrow into her palace, Cleopatra tells him that she will make his dreams of love come true for a single night, after which he must die. He readily consents.

Cleopatra and Meïamoun share a munificent banquet and watch voluptuous dances, which reach their climax when Cleopatra herself takes to the floor. When daybreak eventually arrives, Meïamoun moves to take the cup of poison that he has agreed to swallow. For a moment, the queen reaches out to prevent his drinking it, but then the sound of trumpets announces the approach of Mark Antony, and she allows him to complete the act.

Cleopatra condescends to shed a single tear on the body of her dead lover—the only one she has ever let fall—but is ready immediately thereafter to meet her Roman consort with a smile and a casual explanation of the presence of the corpse.

Themes and Meanings

The sixth and final chapter of "One of Cleopatra's Nights" begins with the observation that the banquets, orgies, and other assorted delights of the modern world are meager by comparison with the world of antiquity. This is probably untrue, but it is an essential element in the gaudy image of antiquity that Frenchmen of Théophile Gautier's generation had. It was fashionable for them to lament the "decadence" of their own world and to contrast the drab materialism of modern civilization with the supposed color and virility of more primitive ways of life. To the French Romantics it seemed that the world of antiquity must have been infinitely brighter, grander, and more lavishly decorated than their own—at least for the likes of Cleopatra—and that was the way they saw it in their mind's eye.

The reader of this story is expected to know what happened afterward, at least in outline. Mark Antony is also destined to die, ostensibly for love of Cleopatra. History suggests, however, that in spite of the fact that his marriage to her caused him a great deal of trouble in Rome, he married her in 37 B.C.E. as much for her money—which financed his Parthian campaign—as for her beauty. Antony's defeat by Octavian (later the Emperor Augustus, the brother of the Roman woman Antony was pledged to marry) at the battle of Actium in 31 B.C.E. formed a prelude to the peak of the Roman Empire's achievements, which were soon superseded by decadence and decline.

Given all this, it is understandable that Gautier can assure the reader that Cleopatra will not be shedding any tears for Mark Antony. He feels fully entitled to take the view that Cleopatra's single night with Meïamoun—which takes place when she is in her early thirties—provides a climax for her rich and varied career as a lover, just as it provides a climax for Meïamoun's far narrower erotic experience.

It is significant that Meïamoun, like Cleopatra herself and the city of Alexandria, is a relic of the empire of Alexander the Great, on whose ruins the Romans built their own empire. Cleopatra and he are "made for one another" in a way that she and Mark Antony are not. It is much more significant, however, that this most perfect of imaginable loves lasts but a single night, leaving no space at all for the deflating erosion of excitement that is conventionally dignified by its French term: post-coital *triste*.

Gautier, who adored the ballerina Carlotta Grisi but actually lived with her sister Ernesta, wrote many other stories describing fabulous liaisons whose perfection is ensured as much by their brevity as by their feverish lushness. The entire collection to which Lafcadio Hearn's translation of "One of Cleopatra's Nights" gave its name consists of stories of this type, ranging from the blithely comedic "Omphale" (1834) to the devoutly masochistic "Clarimonde" (1836). "One of Cleopatra's Nights" is the most intensely focused and most elaborately gorgeous of them because of the lengths to which the author goes to design a fitting environment for the ultimate sexual encounter. Not a word is said, of course, about the vulgar mechanics of Cleopatra's and Meïamoun's love making; for Gautier authentic sexual intercourse belongs entirely to the world of the imagination.

The ennui that plagues Gautier's Cleopatra was to become a central theme of nineteenth century French literature, along with its more wrathful partner spleen. Both states of mind were elaborately explored by Charles Baudelaire and then extrapolated to extremes by the poets and short-story writers of the Decadent Movement. Cleopatra's account of it is particularly interesting in the way it extends a chain of metaphors likening her mental state to the physical and cultural state of Egypt. Her inability to reach the state of emotional arousal that would permit her to shed tears is likened to the aridity of the desert. The oppression of her spirit is symbolized by the colossal temples and tombs, and by the haunting omnipresence of animal-headed gods and guardian sphinxes.

The awareness of mortality, which threatens to make all human experience seem worthless, is accentuated in her case by Cleopatra's sense of being surrounded by the innumerable mummies of past generations, uncannily preserved. How, she wonders, can a creature like her—a devotee of laughter and merriment—possibly overcome such sinister influences? She has ample cause to be grateful to Meïamoun, who enlivens her soul for an instant, but the episode ends in the only way it can end. She is, after all, the queen of Egypt, a helpless prisoner of history.

For Meïamoun, of course, the ending is truly happy. He attains his one and only desire, in the fullest possible measure, and is triumphantly saved from the ravages of post-climactic disappointment. Gautier was not always as generous to his protagonists; the timeshifting lover of the eponymous Pompeiian courtesan in "Arria Marcella" (1852), for example, is forced to wake from his glorious dream and live to a ripe old age, knowing that he can never recover even the merest emotional echo of his great adventure. However, Gautier was still young when he wrote "One of Cleopatra's Nights," and age had not tainted his fierce Romanticism.

Style and Technique

Modern literary criticism tends to be suspicious of the stylistic excesses of such stories as "One of Cleopatra's Nights," which are faithfully rendered into English in Lafcadio Hearn's translation. It is the kind of writing that is often dismissed as "purple prose." It is, however, the only style that could possibly be employed to create and sustain the mood of the story. The modern erotic fantasies that still insist on representing love as if it were a kind of supernatural force, whose experience is the greatest possible exaltation of human feeling, rarely dress their rhetoric as vividly as this, but they are less powerful in consequence. It would be a mistake to think of Gautier's ornate prose as something garish and false. This Egypt and this Cleopatra never existed outside the literary imagination, but they are authentic in their fashion—perhaps more authentic, in terms of encapsulating a particular view of the world, than the reality of Cleopatra's nights could ever have been.

Brian Stableford

ONE OF THE MISSING

Author: Ambrose Bierce (1842-1914?)
Type of plot: Horror
Time of plot: 1864
Locale: Georgia, near Kennesaw Mountain
First published: 1891

Principal characters:
PRIVATE JEROME SEARING, a soldier in General Sherman's army
LIEUTENANT ADRIAN SEARING, his brother, in the same company

The Story

Although a private, Jerome Searing is no commonplace member of the rank and file of the Union Army, moving slowly closer to Atlanta. He is characterized as extraordinary: an incomparable marksman, a fearless woodsman, a remarkably strong and intelligent young man. Searing has repeatedly refused promotion because he prefers service as an orderly in the perilous role of scout. His mission this day is to get as near the enemy lines as possible and gather information on the Confederates' movements. Searing pushes stealthily through the forest to an abandoned plantation, where he discovers the enemy in retreat. Crouched in the debris of a ruined outbuilding, he cocks his rifle, intending to pick off one of the rear guard before returning from his reconnaissance. Coincidentally, a departing Confederate captain idly discharges a field piece in Searing's direction.

The private regains consciousness and finds himself pinned flat on his back beneath collapsed timbers, unable to move, "caught like a rat in a trap." More horrifying is his discovery that his rifle, a moment ago set to fire, now points directly at his forehead. Looking squarely at death, the man of action is now a man of consciousness. The battle of Searing's life begins; his enemy is his own fear.

To face a loaded gun is not unusual for a soldier, yet Private Searing is uneasy. Eyes averted from the barrel of his rifle, he explores his military past briefly, remembering a time when he brutally clubbed a man to death with his rifle. Each time he looks at the rifle, it seems nearer. Each time he closes his eyes, an initially dull ache grows into an ever sharper pain in his forehead. Memories of innocent childhood play, toying with the idea of death at Ghost Rock and Dead Man's Cave, drift through his mind, then blur. The mouth of that haunted cavern abruptly becomes the menacing barrel of the rifle before his eyes. Fear rises in him: Anticipation of the bullet aimed at his forehead increases. At least, he determines, he will await this death, this lonely and unheroic death, with dignity. Aghast, he realizes that the rats scampering over the debris, inches from the trigger of his gun, may soon be gnawing on his body. Transfixed by the gun barrel before him, he is overwhelmed by the intensifying pain in his head. His entire being contracts into experience of his own danger until both time and world cease to exist and his consciousness erupts in a single scream of pure terror. In a last, desperate act of self-defense, Searing pushes a board toward the trigger of the rifle and presses with all of his remaining strength. The rifle does not explode. It had discharged earlier.

The concluding portion of the story flashes back in space and time to the outer edge of Sherman's camp, where Lieutenant Adrian Searing, the private's brother, sits on the picket line. The lieutenant hears the sound of something like a building falling and notes that the time is 6:18 A.M. A few moments later, the lieutenant leads a troop of skirmishers out along the same path his brother had earlier taken. At 6:40, Adrian moves past the collapsed building on the plantation. He notices a dead body among the timbers, gray with dust, face yellow and contorted, teeth rigidly clenched. Adrian concludes that the body is that of a Confederate soldier, dead a week, and walks on. The reader, however, knows that Lieutenant Searing has just seen the body of his brother, who, only moments before, under the barrel of his own gun, died of fear.

Themes and Meanings

Three interdependent parts make up this story: Jerome Searing's military mission, his entrapment, and his brother's military mission. Like so many of Ambrose Bierce's stories, "One of the Missing" centers on the individual human body and mind in crisis. Juxtaposed to everyday experience, such crises disclose most vividly the fascinating paradoxes inherent in every man's life. In those few moments trapped beneath the timbers, Searing experiences the convergence of the polarities of his existence. His public and private selves face each other. His rational and irrational beings are at war. His life and his death meet.

The polarity between Searing's public military role as fearless slayer of men and his private and very human desire to go on living is symbolically dramatized in his plight as he looks directly into his own murder weapon. The callous killer is ironically reduced to the state of a captive, trembling animal. Dual impulses of the human mind toward control and toward anarchy meet. The man so competent, so disciplined, so daring, becomes the helpless victim of his own emotions. He is literally murdered by his own rampant fear of the death that he imagines awaits him, for in each life is borne the seed of its own death. The hardened maker of widows and orphans loses all control in the face of his own destruction. The vital young warrior dies an unheroic, unsung, and ignominious death.

Bierce explores both the limitations and the amazing powers of the human mind. Searing's acute senses and his self-control allow him to be an efficient military machine. He deals with danger calmly and goes about the business of killing with a cool detachment. Under the gun himself, in contrast, he assumes that his plight is far more hopeless than it is. In truth, he is only moments away from potential rescuers, and the gun pointed at his head is no longer loaded. His false assumptions blind him to reason. The power of the mind to create its own reality is vividly demonstrated when not the unloaded weapon but his own fear kills him.

The Civil War in which he fought became Bierce's most powerful metaphor for man's inhumanity to man. It is also his central metaphor for the human condition: man born but to die, frequently existing in a hell of his own creation. Within the panorama of horror and death that is war occurs a personal experience of horror and death, a private war with fear even more appalling than the surrounding one. The hellish terrain of the march through Georgia through which the scout moves so fearlessly, so gamely, seems prosaic when juxtaposed to the landscape of fear he traverses while helplessly trapped and awaiting a humiliating death.

Style and Technique

The irony so central to Bierce's style is established immediately in "One of the Missing." The major source of his irony is the gap between what the character knows and what the reader knows. In the first line of the story, Searing disappears into the forest, the realm of the unknown. His competence and expertise are emphasized, yet one of the pickets announces, "That's the last of him." Though the reader does not yet know Searing's fate, it is apparent that he is already one of the missing. This tension between what Searing knows and what the reader knows climaxes in the concluding section of the story when the reader knows what Searing did not, what his brother Adrian did not: that the gun had not been loaded, that Searing died not in action but in fear, and that the body in the timbers is not that of a Confederate soldier. In this knowledge resides the horror of the story.

Kinds of knowing are also represented in the shifts in style employed by Bierce. The stark, flat, reportorial style of the opening and closing portions of the story depicts the activities of the brothers as they know them to be, rather routine and emotionally void. These unemotional narratives envelop the dense, shifting, complex account of Jerome Searing's personal terror. In this portion of the story, the escalation of Searing's terror and his loss of emotional control are depicted in the subjectification of time and space. In a few chronological moments, Searing's perceptions of time enlarge greatly. Time accelerates with fear, then slows with pain. Space expands immeasurably, then contracts into a private universe, a prison of timbers. Finally, both time and space disappear for Searing entirely in his unmitigated terror. Only the reader knows the "truth" of Searing's death; only the reader understands where this missing piece fits in the mosaic of history.

Virginia M. Crane

ONE ORDINARY DAY, WITH PEANUTS

Author: Shirley Jackson (1919-1965)
Type of plot: Fantasy
Time of plot: The 1950's
Locale: New York City
First published: 1955

> *Principal characters:*
> MR. JOHN PHILIP JOHNSON, a man who seems too good to be true
> MRS. JOHNSON, his wife
> A CHILD
> THE CHILD'S MOTHER, who is moving to Vermont
> MILDRED KENT, a chance acquaintance of Mr. Johnson
> ARTHUR ADAMS, a chance acquaintance of Mr. Johnson

The Story

John Philip Johnson comes down the steps from his house on a bright morning. His shoes have just been resoled, and his feet feel good. He smiles at everyone and greets the other customers at the newsstand where he stops to buy his newspaper. He has filled his pockets with candy and peanuts and, before he sets out for his walk uptown, he goes into a flower shop and buys a carnation for his buttonhole, but he immediately gives it to a child in a carriage.

Mr. Johnson seldom follows the same route twice. On this fine day, he walks several blocks uptown, then cuts across a side street. Halfway along it, a van is parked. A woman and her child are moving out of their apartment. The woman looks bedraggled, and Mr. Johnson offers to watch her child while she attends to the moving. He and the child get along well, sharing the peanuts in Mr. Johnson's pocket. Mr. Johnson learns that the two are moving to Greenwich, Vermont, and he gives them the name of a friend who lives there, telling the woman that the man will help her in any way he can when she arrives in Greenwich. She is grateful.

Continuing his walk, he meets a young woman, Mildred Kent. He talks with her and, when he realizes that he is making her late for work, insists on compensating her for her lost time. As she waits, he walks out onto the sidewalk and engages in conversation with a young man, Arthur Adams. He then introduces the two and gives them enough money to cover their day's wages. He encourages them to spend the day together doing something they want to do, such as going to Coney Island. He gives them money to cover their expenses.

Leaving them, he continues his walk. He gives a peanut to a man who is begging for money, wrapping the peanut in a dollar bill. He gives another peanut to a bus driver who is leaning out the window of his bus. The driver asks him whether he wants a transfer.

When he sees a young couple searching the classified advertisements looking for an apartment for rent, he tells them of the one that the woman and her child have just vacated. Then he lunches in a pleasant restaurant, eating two desserts, drinking three cups of coffee, and tipping the waiter generously. When he leaves the restaurant, he gives a beggar enough to buy himself a veal cutlet for lunch and to pay the tip.

He goes to the park, doing more good deeds and feeding what is left of his peanuts to the pigeons. When he starts for home, he misses his opportunity to engage the first two or three taxis that stop because he allows people who look as though they need a cab more than he does to take them. Finally, a cab that is not really looking for a fare picks him up, and the driver takes his picking up someone when he did not plan to do so as an omen that he should not bet ten dollars on a horse race. Mr. Johnson gives the man advice about the races and gives him ten more dollars so that he can bet on a sure thing later in the week.

When he finally gets home, Mr. Johnson announces his arrival and asks his wife about her day. She tells him that it was "here and there." She accused a woman in a department store of shoplifting and called the store detective. Then she got on a bus and asked the driver for a transfer, but he helped someone else first, so she took his number and reported him. She speculates that he will likely lose his job.

Mr. Johnson listens to her account and responds, "Fine. But you do look tired. Want to change over tomorrow?" She says she would like to do so, that she could do with a change. He asks what they are having for dinner. She responds that they are having veal cutlet, and he tells her, "Had it for lunch."

Themes and Meanings

Shirley Jackson's stories often deal with the interplay of good and evil, as this story does. Mr. and Mrs. Johnson are Dr. Jekyll and Mr. Hyde types. They are each other's alter egos, and they must alternate their personalities on occasion. As Jackson presents him, Mr. Johnson is tiresomely good. However, one can find clues in the story to suggest that he is not always this way.

Jackson makes a point of saying that Mr. Johnson "did not follow the same route every morning, but preferred to pursue his eventful way in wide detours, more like a puppy than a man intent on business." Mr. Johnson reminds one of Robert Browning's Pippa, in that he does not see the realities that surround him. It is likely that the woman and her child who are moving to Vermont to live with Grandpa are doing so because of a divorce or legal separation, but this information is never presented overtly.

Mr. Johnson's bringing Mildred Kent and Arthur Adams together, keeping them from their jobs in the process, is like playing God, but Mr. Johnson enjoys playing God. It is also notable that his solution to most problems is to provide material assistance. However, Mr. Johnson does not really give of himself, even when his contribution is to watch a child for its mother, as he does twice in this story. Mr. Johnson does not really listen to people. Rather, he reaches his own conclusions about them and imposes his own remedies on them.

Mrs. Johnson causes as many people to frown as Mr. Johnson causes them to smile. Probably the bus driver whom Mrs. Johnson reports is the very bus driver who was asking Mr. Johnson if he wanted a transfer just as Mrs. Johnson was demanding one. The implication here is that if one imposes something on another person gratuitously, even something that seems positive, the imposition might upset a delicate balance of which the giver is not aware.

When Mr. Johnson tells his wife that he had veal cutlet for lunch, he is beginning on the other phase of his personality. Mr. Hyde is about to take over, and Mrs. Johnson, presumably, is about to assume the Dr. Jekyll role. By isolating the good and evil in the nature of her two main characters, Jackson allows her readers to examine the question of good and evil in a context somewhat removed from what most of them have previously considered.

Interestingly, Jackson presents a picture of relative marital harmony and understanding in the small interaction one sees between husband and wife. The harmony and understanding, however, are conventional and somewhat superficial. Probably the most telling comment about their marriage is Mr. Johnson's revelation that he had veal cutlet for lunch. Ironically, the story does not specifically say what Mr. Johnson actually did have for lunch. Aside from telling what his dessert was and how many cups of coffee he drank, the story provides no more information other than to say that Mr. Johnson gives the beggar enough money for him to pay for a veal cutlet luncheon and tip.

Style and Technique

Jackson's technique in many of her stories consists of slowly building up a somewhat commonplace tale about quite commonplace people, then suddenly introducing at the end of the story an ironic shift that will leave readers pondering. Certainly this is her technique in "One Ordinary Day, with Peanuts," just as it was in her most anthologized short story, "The Lottery," a story designed to tweak quite painfully the consciences of its readers.

In this story, as in many of her others, Jackson uses unexceptional language and simple, direct sentence structure, both of which heighten the sense of the ordinary that pervades the story. If Mr. Johnson seems slightly unbelievable, he is not totally so. The world is full of unusual people, and this paragon of goodness, although he has a kind of Daddy Warbucks quality about him, might reasonably be expected to exist in a city as large as New York.

The ironic surprise ending of the story is a Jackson trademark. The title of the story, with its play on the word "ordinary," is appropriate. The title, except for the word "day," sounds like an order one would give to a waiter in a restaurant, and just as one does not eat the same restaurant meal every day, so Mr. Johnson does not lead the same kind of life every day.

One normally expects a degree of consistency in human behavior, but Jackson vetoes that notion. Mr. Johnson is the man who does not go uptown by the same route every day, so why should he be expected to be consistent in other things? Perhaps Jackson is intimating in this story that Mr. Johnson's only consistency is his inconsistency.

R. Baird Shuman

THE ONES WHO WALK AWAY FROM OMELAS

Author: Ursula K. Le Guin (1929-   )
Type of plot: Fantasy
Time of plot: Unspecified
Locale: The city of Omelas
First published: 1973

> *Principal characters:*
> THE NARRATOR
> THE CHILD IN THE CLOSET

The Story

Omelas is a utopian city where the people lead lives that are happy, in the best sense of the word. On the day on which the narrator is focusing, the city's people are celebrating the summer festival. The children ride willing horses in races and race about the fields in their bare feet. The day is bright and clear, music of all kinds fills the air, bells ring, and the air itself is sweet.

The narrator is conscious of the fact that the idea of happiness, and in particular the happiness of an entire city, may be a suspect concept to others. Happiness implies a kind of innocence and foolishness and lacks the complexities that are most often attributed to pain and evil impulses. However, the narrator insists that the people of Omelas lead complex lives.

The people may lack certain things that others have, but they do not feel that lack as a deprivation. These people have come to an understanding of what is necessary, what is destructive, and what is both or neither. Those things that are necessary, they have. Those luxuries that are neither necessary nor destructive, they also have. Omelas is a joyful city inhabited by mature, intelligent, passionate adults. Their lives are not wretched, nor are they puritanical.

This picture of Omelas is not the whole story. There is something that makes the city special in another way. The city has a guarantee of happiness; it has struck a bargain, although how and with whom it is not clear. The bargain is this: In a room under the city is a stunted, frightened, half-starved child, and everyone over adolescence in Omelas knows that the child is there. The child is locked in a closet and shown off to those who wish to see it. It is fed half a bowl of cornmeal mush a day and is left to sit, naked, in dirt and its own excrement. The child barely talks, except for a bit of whining gibberish and a plea, heard less and less often, to be let out. No one is allowed to speak even a kind word to the child, and no one stays with it long.

If the child were rescued from its cell-like closet, the whole of the city of Omelas would falter. The city's great happiness, its splendors and health, its architecture, music, and science, all are dependent on the misery of this one child. The Omelas people know that if the child were released, then the possible happiness of the degraded child—and it is only possible, not probable—would be set against the sure failure of the happiness of the many. Thus, the people have been taught compassion and the terrible reality of justice, and on this they base their lives.

Inexplicably, there are some young people, and sometimes even an adult, who, shortly after viewing the child, leave Omelas through its gates and head into the mountains. They do not return.

Themes and Meanings

Ursula K. Le Guin has given this story a parenthetical subtitle, "Variations on a Theme by William James," referring to the philosopher and psychologist who wrote that "some people could not accept even universal prosperity and happiness if it depended on the deliberate subjugation of an idiot child to abuse it could barely understand." Le Guin's story also has ties to Fyodor Dostoevski's *Bratya Karamazovy* (1879-1880; *The Brothers Karamazov*, 1912), in which Ivan, the realistic brother, asks Alyosha, the religious brother, about God's goodness in a world in which children suffer. Ivan asks Alyosha if he would be willing to be the creator of a world in which every being was happy, if that happiness were based on the suffering of a five-year-old girl. Alyosha is forced to concede that he would not.

These issues are related to the concept of theodicy, which attempts to answer the question of the problem of evil that is summed up by three statements: God is good, God is omnipotent and omniscient, and there is evil. The existence of evil is usually accepted as a given. If God is good, but not omnipotent, he wants to stop evil but cannot. If God is omnipotent, but not good, he could stop evil but would not. In the Judeo-Christian system, however, God is understood to be both good and omnipotent, so some other answer for the existence of evil is necessary.

The concept of human free will has often been used to explain the evil in the world. Theologians use the story of the expulsion from Eden as an example of how human free will, uncoerced choice, may cause evil to occur. The people of Omelas knowingly allow the child to suffer so that they may be happy. Someone in Omelas gave the child up to its incarceration; it remembers its mother. Someone in Omelas may have the child in the cellar of his or her lovely home. Someone is responsible for its poor food. Someone kicks at it to make it stand when it is to be shown to a new group of children. The great majority of Omelas citizens are able to accept their lives at the expense of this helpless other and have rationalized that it could not really be made happy anyway. Even the ones who walk away make no attempt to take the child away with them. They choose to leave it to its suffering, fear, and pleading.

Style and Technique

"The Ones Who Walk Away from Omelas" won the Hugo Award for best short story in 1974. Although the Hugo is an award for science fiction, this story may more accurately be called a fantasy: Science fiction discusses the improbable; fantasy examines the impossible. First published in *New Dimensions 3*, the story has been widely anthologized since then, notably in Le Guin's own *The Wind's Twelve Quar-*

ters (1975). Le Guin's work often has sociological or anthropological elements; this can easily be seen in her novels, including *The Left Hand of Darkness* (1969) and *The Dispossessed* (1974).

Reliability is a problem for Le Guin's narrator in this story. At times the narrator does not know the truth and therefore guesses what could be, presenting these guesses as often essential detail. The narrator says "I think" and "I think there ought to be," rather than telling the reader what is. Asking if the reader believes what he says about the festival, the city, and the joy, or if the ones who walk away are not more credible, implies that the reader should have doubts. Can the narrator be trusted by a reader who is being asked to approve the details of the story? Such questions raise doubts in the reader's mind about what the narrator is conveying. Only the description of the child itself lacks asides.

The narrator of "The Ones Who Walk Away from Omelas" cannot tell a straightforward tale. The story about the summer festival is diverted into a short treatise on happiness, what happiness truly is and how the Omelas citizens have achieved it. This discussion encompasses not only those at the festival, but also those who choose to leave the city. What is happiness? What should one be willing to sacrifice for happiness?

All of the narrator's questions invite the reader to place himself or herself in the position of the people of Omelas. Do you need this to make you happy? Then you may have it. Once the reader begins to enjoy the city and begins to see its happiness as a good thing, then the reader, like the adolescents in the story, must be shown that on which the happiness depends. Readers must face the question of what they would be willing to sacrifice for happiness, for "the beauty of their city, the tenderness of their friendships, the health of their children, the wisdom of their scholars, the skill of their makers, even the abundance of their harvest and the kindly weathers of their skies."

Susan Jaye Dauer

THE ONLY MAN ON LIBERTY STREET

Author: William Melvin Kelley (1937-   )
Type of plot: Domestic realism
Time of plot: About 1880
Locale: A city on the Gulf coast of Alabama
First published: 1963

> *Principal characters:*
> MAYNARD HERDER, a recent immigrant to the United States from Northern Europe
> JOSEPHINE, his mulatto mistress
> JENNIE, their daughter

The Story

As Jennie is playing in the dirt of the front yard of her home, she sees a man ride up the street, dismount, and come into the yard. Jennie sees this man once or twice each week, when he comes to visit her mother, Josephine. Most of the black women who live in the houses on Liberty Street receive such visitors. Jennie's mother has told her that this white man, Mister Herder, is her father, even though he does not live with them.

On this day, however, Herder is carrying a carpetbag of his clothes, and in the house he promises that he will never return to his wife. He explains that it is only when he is with Jennie and her mother that he feels what it is to be at home. Before long, her mother is calling him Maynard, and Jennie feels convinced that he is her father.

Each day afterward, Jennie sees a mysterious white woman pass by in a carriage, peering at the house with a hard and angry expression on her face. One day the woman's driver delivers a letter to Jennie's mother, and the woman shouts that Maynard has one wife, and Josephine is something different. That night, when Herder reads the letter, he angrily vows that he will give up his life before anyone can make him leave Jennie and her mother and go back to his wife. Josephine knows the power of racists, and she makes Jennie promise that when she is grown she will go to the North.

On the Fourth of July, Herder wins the city shooting match, with six excellent shots. As General Dewey Willson, the town's leading citizen, hands him the winner's medal, he advises him that he can no longer protect him. Herder declares that he will do to men what he did to the target, but Willson points out that it is Jennie who will be attacked. Willson's concern for Jennie stems from the fact that she is his only granddaughter; Josephine is Willson's child by one of his slaves. A short time later, Herder sees a rag-clothed white man make a shockingly obscene and threatening gesture toward Jennie. She does not perceive the meaning of the gesture, but Herder realizes that it is his daughter who will suffer if he does not give in. Telling Jennie to do what she has promised her mother, he sends her home without him.

Themes and Meanings

The major theme of this story is the power of self-centeredness, particularly as it is manifested and reinforced by prejudice in the forms of racism and sexism, to generate such hatred and cruelty that relationships based on tolerance, love, and self-sacrifice are destroyed. The word "different," used crucially at three points in the text, implicitly asks the questions, what difference does it make that people are different in color, and should color make any difference at all, when love is what unites persons? The story then demonstrates the terrible difference that prejudice makes in society and in individual lives, by showing a case in which it brings about the triumph of evil and the suffering of the innocent.

The story shows the confusion that color-prejudice produces in a society: A white man who has become a hero in his society by defending racist slavery has fathered a light-complected daughter with one of his slaves; he now loves, but cannot free from racism, his even more light-complected, blue-eyed granddaughter, whose father is a respected, unprejudiced, white man. On a street in another section of the city, Jennie, with her light complexion and blue eyes, would be seen as a white girl from that neighborhood.

Values that are held by the society to be absolute and objective truths, in actual practice are subjective and relative to self-interest. As interests inevitably change, new situations emerge that produce conflicts of values within and between persons. Values that are truly universal and humane come into conflict with traditional but narrowly selfish patterns of behavior, and individuals caught in the old patterns either adopt new perspectives or react, often violently, in self-defense.

Herder's wife, for example, uses racism to justify and effect her violence, as a way of controlling her husband in order to maintain her social status. The shabby clothing of the anonymous white man who makes the threatening gesture suggests that he has been hired to do this, probably by Mrs. Herder and her allies, who might also be political enemies of General Willson. It also illustrates the element of class prejudice that often has been associated with racism, when poor whites have been manipulated into feeling generalized hatred of the black people with whom they have been kept in direct economic competition. The apparent pleasure that this man takes in acting out the imagined violence that his gesture expresses suggests the extreme irrationality and destructiveness to which prejudice can reduce people.

The situation occurs in a society in which the power brought by money and status is monopolized by white men, who are able to take certain liberties with black women within the local pattern of racism, as long as these women are kept in their place on Liberty Street. If a white man declares his love for one of these black women, and shows his allegiance to her and to their child by going to live with them on that street, he is stepping out of his place, thereby threatening the racist and sexist distribution of power—something that he is not at liberty to do. Herder's actions threaten the status quo of the city, but even more threatening is the fact that a man who is respected for his integrity and skill is also unabashedly not prejudiced.

Herder decides to live permanently with Jennie and her mother when he learns that Jennie has been asking her mother why he does not stay with them at night, although he is her father. The story's title, then, suggests that Herder, by being true to his family on that street, is the only male to be seen there who is truly a man. Thus manhood is defined by this story in terms of courageously loving actions on the part of one who is free of racial prejudice. The story also shows the price that might be exacted for such freedom, and the ability of a prejudiced society to overpower even a true man. Because of the defenselessness of women in a society that allows them power and status only by way of their association with guardian men, Herder must see defeat in the mere gesture of a man who has no integrity but has the backing of powerful racists.

Style and Technique

The story is told in the third person, as if by someone who was not within the action. The story's first word, "she"—which begins five sentences in the opening paragraph and then begins the second paragraph—limits the point of view to what the child, Jennie, could be present to observe; and the meaning of the actions of all of the characters is presented as it would be understood by a child. However, William Melvin Kelley provides sufficient details that adult information is simultaneously communicated to the reader, to build the reader's adult understanding of the characters and the situation in which they find themselves. Kelley thereby focuses the reader's attention, interpretation, and evaluation on this episode in life as it would affect a child, which is to say a person who is entirely innocent, precious, and vulnerable. It is in the context of a threat to a child's well-being, and perhaps life, that the reader, with adult perception of the characters' actions, evaluates human life and the life-threatening actions that are motivated and sanctioned by greed and racism.

Tom Koontz

THE OPEN BOAT

Author: Stephen Crane (1871-1900)
Type of plot: Psychological
Time of plot: The late 1890's
Locale: At sea and off the coast of St. Augustine, Florida
First published: 1898

> *Principal characters:*
> THE CORRESPONDENT, the protagonist,
> THE OILER "BILLY,"
> THE COOK, and
> THE CAPTAIN, four survivors of a shipwreck, adrift at sea

The Story

Four men are adrift in an open boat, their ship having gone down about dawn. Now, in the clear light of day, the men begin to perceive the full gravity of their situation. The captain is lying injured in the bow of the boat, and the January sea is tossing the men about, rising menacingly over the gunwales. The oiler and the correspondent are rowing, trying to reach Mosquito Light Inlet, where, the cook has said, there is a life-saving station.

As the day passes, the men grow silent. The captain encourages them. "We'll get ashore all right," he says. As they row, seabirds hover above them, floating in groups next to them, one even coming close enough to be waved off. The men swear at it, deeming the bird an ill omen.

In time, the captain and the cook spy the lighthouse, a pinpoint at the throat of the horizon, and the crew rig a sail from the captain's overcoat. Soon, the lighthouse appears larger, but the wind quickly dies, and the correspondent and the oiler are obliged to row harder. The land begins to loom, and the men can see the shore and hear the roar of the surf. Expecting now to be seen and rescued, the men are at first puzzled, then angered that no one is on the beach. They do not know that there is no lifesaving station here, and as the afternoon wears on, the men row steadily toward shore until their bodies ache.

Suddenly, they spot a man on the beach. In their excitement, they yell and wave a towel at him and the man waves back. Another man appears, riding a bicycle, and finally onto the beach drives an omnibus from one of the large resort hotels. The men in the boat wave and yell frantically, but the party on the beach, obviously there only for an outing, regard the men in the boat as merely fishermen and ignore them. The wind shifts, and night draws on, sealing up the land and leaving the men adrift in the starry darkness.

During the night, the men sleep as best they can, an occasional wave washing into the boat, chilling them to the bone. The oiler and the correspondent take turns rowing, though the oiler, the stronger of the two, plies the oars even as sleep overpowers him. As the correspondent takes his turn, he grows lonely. All about him is darkness and the exhausted sleep of his shipmates. He hears a swish and peers into the water. The dark fin of an enormous shark cuts the water near him, and the correspondent wishes that someone were awake with him against the thing in the sea. In this crucial scene, the correspondent muses on his fate. What an injustice it would be, he thinks, to drown now, after having endured so much, after having come so far and so close. He remembers a childhood verse about a soldier of the Legion dying in Algiers and feels a kinship with him. Finally, the shark swims away, the oiler awakes and relieves him, and the correspondent sleeps until dawn.

The next morning, the men decide to bring the boat to shore. It is a treacherous undertaking because of rough surf and the perils of capsizing. The waves become ferocious as they approach the beach, but the men jump into the raging sea. As he rises to the surface, the correspondent sees the oiler just ahead, swimming strongly. Passing on his left, the captain and the cook are holding on to the capsized boat. As he makes his way to the boat, the correspondent sees a man onshore rushing into the sea to help them.

Battling to stay afloat, the correspondent feels an undertow dragging at him, but in an instant the man from the shore has reached him and pulls him in. Rescuers now arrive with coffee and blankets. The correspondent and his shipmates have been saved—all but the oiler. He lies face downward in the shallows. As night comes, the men stand on the beach, watching the sea, realizing that they have learned a lesson in survival.

Themes and Meanings

"The Open Boat" is not simply a realistic account of the ordeal of four men on the open sea. The story is, indeed, largely autobiographical, based on the sinking of the USS *Commodore*, on which Stephen Crane was en route to Cuba as a reporter covering the Spanish-American War; the character of the correspondent is an obvious persona for Crane himself. Nevertheless, the story goes beyond mere journalistic accuracy and makes a statement about man's relationship to nature, his place in the universe.

The overwhelming theme of the story is the conflict between the men and the cold indifference of the sea. The sea, in fact, is a character in its own right, an elemental force, unmindful of the human struggle to survive. The sea, as an analogue to nature, is cruel or sportive, taunting, menacing, or easeful, having no other motive but the exercise of its own power.

When, for example, the correspondent remembers the childhood verse about the soldier of the Legion dying in Algiers, he realizes that as a child he had no interest in the soldier. Now, on the verge of death himself, the correspondent understands that nature, the sea, has no interest in him. He and the soldier are thus brothers, sharing in the total apathy of fate. Survival on the sea or in Algiers is a matter of chance, of accident, of complete indifference.

Man's struggles in the face of this elemental indifference are often marked by a grim irony. The oiler, the strongest of the group, drowns, but the sea leaves unclaimed the wounded captain and the cowardly cook.

In the concluding passage, the survivors stand on the beach looking at the sea. They "felt they could be interpreters." What they interpret is the sheer accident of their existence, the arrant tenuousness of life.

Style and Technique

"The Open Boat" is characteristic of Crane's naturalistic style. Naturalism in literature is a point of view that often emphasizes the material, the physical environment as a determinant in human behavior. Crane had already shown the detrimental effect of slum life on the character of Maggie, for example, in his first novel, *Maggie: A Girl of the Streets* (1893), regarded by some critics as America's first naturalistic novel. In that work, Crane had used precise detail and an objective tone to record Maggie's fate. In "The Open Boat," one of the finest short stories in the language, Crane relies on tone and imagery to portray the heartless indifference of nature. The famous opening line, "None of them knew the color of the sky," establishes an immediate bleakness, a world void of the emotional value of color. The sea is described as gray and the only green, suggestive of hope, is that of the land that the men cannot reach.

In support of the theme of indifference, the tone is consistently maintained by the men's having no names. They are merely "the correspondent," "the captain," "the cook"—trades, occupations, things, not persons; they are anonymous, like so much flotsam. Ironically, only the oiler has a name, "Billy," and he alone does not survive, as if having a name has marked him.

Finally, imagery is consistently employed, almost as in a poem, to reinforce meaning. The men are belittled by the sea, their boat compared to "a bathtub," the waves "slate walls" or "snarling" crests. When the correspondent fears drowning, he regrets the injustice of his fate, dying before he could "nibble at the sacred cheese of life"—as if he were a mouse, a puny thing, more of a pest than a noble creature.

Edward Fiorelli

OPEN HOUSE

Author: Nadine Gordimer (1923-   )
Type of plot: Social realism
Time of plot: The late 1960's
Locale: South Africa
First published: 1969

> *Principal characters:*
> FRANCES TAVER, the central character, a white South African
> woman with a long involvement in black causes
> ROBERT GREENMAN CERETTI, an American political columnist
> on his first visit to South Africa
> JASON MADELA, a black businessperson invited by Frances to
> meet Robert
> EDGAR XIXO, a black attorney, another guest
> SPUDS BUTELEZI, a black reporter, another guest
> A BLACK AFRICAN FRIEND OF FRANCES, banned because of his
> membership in the outlawed African National Congress

The Story

Robert Greenman Ceretti has come to South Africa to learn "the truth" about the country. He wants to see more than the officially organized tour for visitors allows. In particular, he wants to talk directly with black Africans about how they experience apartheid. To arrange such a meeting, he telephones Frances Taver, one of the few "right white people" able to do so.

Frances has had a long history of friendship with black Africans. In the 1940's, she worked with them in the labor unions. When such unions were outlawed in the 1950's, she managed a black-and-white theater group. Not too many years before Robert's arrival, she frequently entertained racially mixed groups at her house, parties at which a foreign visitor might, paradoxically, enjoy more open contact with nonwhite people than at home.

South Africa has changed. New laws have made apartheid more repressive and have sent the more politically active black Africans to jail or to life underground. One such friend, a member of the recently outlawed African National Congress (ANC) and therefore fearing arrest, still visits Frances occasionally when she is alone.

Frances first resists Robert's request: "The ones you ought to see," she informs him, "are shut away." However, because she likes Robert and is flattered by his attention, she arranges a luncheon for him to meet three black Africans. The ones she invites are neither close friends nor men she most respects: Madela, a successful promoter of hair straightener and blood purifier, is too "curiously reassuring to white people." Xixo, a cautiously ambitious lawyer, differs markedly from his politically active predecessor who has been arrested. Butelezi is a mediocre reporter and self-promoting playwright of the black African experience.

Despite Frances's reservations, the luncheon is a great success. The Africans describe their conflicts with apartheid. Their complaints, while legitimate, are chiefly personal, and Robert is too delighted by his contact with the three to be critical of them. He believes that Frances has provided him with a privileged insight into South African life and is thrilled that Madela offers to give him a lift back into town.

Frances has been caught up in the role of hostess. Her mood quickly changes after her guests leave. She discovers in her kitchen a note from her ANC friend. While she was entertaining Robert, he had come by to see her but chose not to stay. He writes that he hopes her party went well, and she wonders what he would have made of her open house had he been present.

Frances does not see Robert again, but when she calls him to say goodbye, she worries that she has misled him about the real South African experience. She warns him not to be "taken in" by the blacks he has met at her house. They have been corrupted by their need to survive. Robert only comprehends that "something complicated was wrong" and that he will never discover what that "something" is.

Themes and Meanings

Nadine Gordimer has devoted her career as a writer to exposing what she has called "the great South African lie." In this story, the lie begins in the title, which suggests an image of the country the government seeks to foster—namely, that South Africa is an open house where people are free to come and go as they please. The government does not deny that blacks are not welcome everywhere. However, through tours of "model black townships, universities and beer halls," it seeks to convince foreign visitors that within their own areas, blacks are as free and content as are their white counterparts. Robert's conversation with the three black Africans easily explodes that official claim. Gordimer's title makes a more subtle point: that all South Africans, whites as well as blacks, are victimized by the ruthless separation of races. Frances Taver's interracial luncheon may impress Robert Ceretti, but as the story reveals, even Frances's house is not as open as Ceretti believes it to be.

Frances and her guests act out an unwitting charade of good fellowship. Frances and Madela (the one she knows the best) "both knew they had seen each other only across various rooms perhaps a dozen times in five years, and got into conversation perhaps half as often." They behave toward each other as equals when, in fact, as Frances acknowledges, she is as "culpable" as the rich industrialists Madela envies. Like them, she is "white, and free to go where she please[s]." She expresses her gratitude to Madela for excluding her from his criticism silently, "like a promissory note [passed] beneath the table." The arrest of their friend is also not openly discussed; Frances and Madela express their concern for him and his family only in an aside.

The most dramatic sign that Frances's house is not open appears when Frances discovers the note left by her ANC friend. His absence reminds her how apartheid has compromised her luncheon, for not only was she unable to invite the friend she respected, but also she inadvertently barred his entry to her home. Her thoughts of this uninvited guest frustrates Frances's final conversation with Robert. Because she cannot openly name this friend, she cannot explain to Robert why the blacks he met are "phony."

Style and Technique

"Open House" deliberately underplays its criticism of apartheid by not focusing on sensational outrages—the arrest, imprisonment, and torture of blacks—but by describing a seemingly benign luncheon given by a white South African woman for a foreign visitor. By revealing that ordinary discourse is false in a country where open houses are actually closed, the story suggests that hospitality has no place in South Africa.

The dialogue between Frances and Robert seems increasingly false and sinister. This false note begins when Frances agrees to invite Robert to meet black Africans at her house. As though trying to ignore her misgivings, she sets out "to cook a good lunch, just as good as she had ever cooked." To look her best, she has her hair dyed in a manner she believes to be "pleasingly artificial," a description that foreshadows the tone of the luncheon itself. When she greets Robert like any suburban hostess seeking to put her guest at ease—"mix the Martinis, there's a dear"—the reader further senses that something is amiss.

Robert's response to Frances's hospitality seems to be similarly strained. Throughout the luncheon, he plays the part of the grateful, diffident guest, at one point looking at Frances with "the trusting grin of some intelligent small pet." When he leaves at the end of the afternoon, his effusive thanks—"I certainly enjoyed myself. . . . I hope we haven't put you out"—is altogether too conventional, just as is his gushing farewell— "Everyone's been marvellous . . . really marvellous." South African reality demands something more.

The seemingly commonplace note of Frances's ANC friend—"Hope your party went well"—serves to alert the reader as it does Frances. Like the other expressions of goodwill, the note might simply be taken at face value, expressing in conventional words a friend's good wishes. Unlike the others, however, her friend's words seem to Frances to contain "reproach" or "contempt." She recognizes that even a friendly note resonates with political overtones, and that an open house can also serve to mask oppression. Robert may not grasp this fact at the story's end, but the reader does.

Jerry M. Bernhard

THE OPEN WINDOW

Author: Saki (Hector Hugh Munro, 1870-1916)
Type of plot: Wit and humor
Time of plot: The early twentieth century
Locale: A middle-class country estate in rural England
First published: 1914

> *Principal characters:*
> FRAMTON NUTTEL, an extremely nervous hypochondriac, new to the neighborhood
> MRS. SAPPLETON, a neighbor whom he visits
> MR. SAPPLETON, her husband, who is fond of hunting
> RONNIE, one of her two brothers, both of whom are Mr. Sappleton's hunting companions
> VERA, her niece, "a very self-possessed young lady," who is fifteen years old

The Story

Framton Nuttel, an eccentric hypochondriac, has moved to the country on his doctor's advice to effect a cure for a nervous condition from which he suffers. His sister has lived in the area he visits and has given him letters of introduction to his new neighbors. The story concerns his visit to the home of one of these neighbors, a Mrs. Sappleton.

Mr. Nuttel is first met by Mrs. Sappleton's niece Vera, who entertains him until her aunt is available. Vera, apparently bored with her guest, is graced with an overactive imagination and a sense of mischief. Once she determines that Mr. Nuttel knows nothing about the family and is a very literal-minded fellow, Vera spins a gothic yarn involving her aunt, whom she characterizes as a mentally disturbed widow.

Three years ago, Mr. Sappleton and his two younger brothers-in-law went hunting, leaving the house through a French window, which was left open until their return. However, all three of them were lost in a bog that day, Vera asserts, and their bodies were never recovered. The aunt, driven to distraction by her grief and loss, left the window open thereafter, anticipating that "they will come back some day" with "the little brown spaniel that was lost with them, and walk in that window just as they used to do."

When Mrs. Sappleton finally appears, she explains why the window is open, apparently confirming Vera's story. Mr. Nuttel then tells Mrs. Sappleton about his nervous disorder and his need to avoid any "mental excitement." Mrs. Sappleton is clearly bored, but at that very moment she sees her husband and brothers returning from their hunt. Vera appears to be horrified by the sight of them. The nervous Mr. Nuttel is therefore terrified and beats a hasty retreat from the house.

In the closing paragraphs, the issue is clarified. The men had only that day gone hunting, and Vera's yarn was purely imaginary. Mr. Nuttel has obviously been duped by Vera's story, but Vera, a habitual liar, does not explain his odd behavior to the others. Instead, Vera invents another story that suggests Mr. Nuttel had once been frightened by "a pack of pariah dogs" in a cemetery "on the banks of the Ganges" and apparently had bolted at the sight of the spaniel accompanying the hunters. Thus, Mr. Nuttel is perfectly victimized by the young girl's imagination.

Themes and Meanings

Saki was known for his satiric wit and his adroit dialogue, which perfectly reveals characters typical of the Edwardian social setting of his stories. His characters are very often eccentric bores and colossal liars, types that can be found in his other stories, such as "A Defensive Diamond" and "The Strategist."

The meaning of "The Open Window" depends on the narrator's final statement about Vera: "Romance at short notice was her specialty." The story is little more than a practical joke played by Vera on the susceptible Framton Nuttel, a champion bore and a character-type familiar to readers of Saki. After a very short conversation with him, Mrs. Sappleton quickly reads the character of Mr. Nuttel as a "most extraordinary man" who "could only talk about his illnesses."

The reader, too, is quickly bored with Framton Nuttel, a weakling who thinks only of his health and has no topic of conversation other than his nervous disorder and the opinions of his doctors. Vera, the fifteen-year-old niece who greets him on his arrival at the Sappleton house, is a surprisingly perceptive girl. She is able to read the man's character accurately as that of a gullible hypochondriac and proceeds to fabricate the absurd story of her aunt's "great tragedy" for her own amusement. The deception is almost forgivable because Mr. Nuttel is such a boring person, but the deception is also cruel, and the man's terrified response to what he thinks must be a supernatural visitation is pathetic—there is no sympathy here for the weak. Mr. Nuttel is out of his league when confronted by Vera.

The story, then, centers on an ironic deception that transforms momentarily the ordinary into what seems to be the supernatural, then snaps the circumstances back into reality through the clever use of irony. Vera is a typical Saki character type, related to the tall-tale tellers and liars of his other stories, just as Mr. Nuttel is a deserving dupe.

Style and Technique

The story is told from the third-person point of view, limited in the opening paragraphs to the naïve perception of Mr. Nuttel, who is tricked by Vera's mischievous fantasy. Because the fantasy is so bizarre and inventive and totally unexpected from a fifteen-year-old girl, the reader is also momentarily duped. Vera's practical joke, which borders on being cruel, is perfectly consistent. When Mr. Sappleton and the brothers are seen returning from the hunt, she pretends to be horrified. The reader, like Framton Nuttel himself, can only assume, therefore, that this is a supernatural event.

The narrator stays in the house, however, after Mr. Nuttel's frightened and abrupt departure, so as to reveal the ironic twist and to enjoy Vera's second demonstration of her ability to produce "romance at short notice," when she explains to her aunt and uncle that Mr. Nuttel has "a horror of dogs" because of an imagined incident he had in a cemetery in India. By this time the reader has reason to doubt that Mr. Nuttel would be adventuresome enough to travel to India.

Vera clearly has a talent for ornamenting the ordinary and the commonplace, and she is too quick-witted to tolerate boredom. She first makes Mr. Nuttel think that her aunt is a lunatic, then tricks him into a state of panic and fear, taking advantage of the poor man's nervous disorder. Vera is not only "self-possessed" but also clever. Before setting her trap, she is careful to ascertain that Mr. Nuttel knows "practically nothing" about her aunt or her family.

Saki satirizes Mr. Nuttel's banality in this miniature comedy of manners, lacing his treatment with his typical dry wit and malice and allowing his characters to reveal themselves through meticulously crafted dialogue. Saki has been ranked with O. Henry as a master of the surprise ending, and no less a craftsperson than Noël Coward, in his introduction to *The Complete Works of Saki* (1976), praised "The Open Window" as a masterpiece of high comedy.

James M. Welsh

MASTERPLOTS II

SHORT STORY SERIES
REVISED EDITION

TITLE INDEX

TITLE INDEX

TITLE INDEX

TITLE INDEX